Literary Adaptations in Black American Cinema

Literary Adaptations
in Black American Cinema:

From Micheaux to Morrison

Barbara Tepa Lupack

THE UNIVERSITY OF ROCHESTER PRESS

First published 2002
by the University of Rochester Press

The University of Rochester Press
668 Mount Hope Avenue, Rochester, NY 14620, USA
www.urpress.com
and Boydell & Brewer, Ltd.
P.O. Box 9, Woodbridge, Suffolk 1P12 3DF, UK

Library of Congress Cataloging-in-Publication Data

Lupack, Barbara Tepa
    Literary adaptations in black American cinema: from Micheaux to
    Morrison / Barbara Tepa Lupack
        p. cm.
    Includes bibliographical references and index.
    ISBN 1-58046-103-4 (alk. paper)
        1. African Americans in motion pictures. 2. American fiction--African
    American authors--History and criticism 3. Film adaptations--History and
    criticism I. Title.

    PN1995.9.N4 L87 2002
    791.43'6520396073--dc21

                                                                2002022332

British Library Cataloging-in-Publication Data
A catalogue record for this item is available from the British Library

Designed and typeset by Christine Menendez
Printed in the United States of America
This publication is printed on acid-free paper.

For my husband, Al,

*Who taught me how to lift my soul
and sing of faith and hope.*

Acknowledgments

I am grateful to a number of friends and colleagues who lent their assistance and offered me much support. Barry H. Leeds, Connecticut State University Distinguished Professor of English, gave the manuscript a careful, thoughtful reading; suggested excellent ideas for its improvement; and engaged me in lively discussions of film and culture. Russell A. Peck, John H. Deane Professor of Rhetoric and English Literature at the University of Rochester, shared with me both his expertise and his resources on black film, including his fine filmography, "Framing Blackness." Kevin J. Harty, Professor and Chair of the English Department at La Salle University, kept me apprised of new resources and advised me on various film and research issues.

At Boydell and Brewer/University of Rochester Press, Director Susan Dykstra-Poel encouraged the project from its inception, as did Editorial Director Tim Madigan, who gracefully shepherded the manuscript through editing and production. John Blanpied, whose knowledge of film is exceeded only by his enthusiasm for it, edited the manuscript with great sensitivity and skill. Molly Cort offered her advice and technical expertise in the production phase. Christine Menendez also contributed her skill to the project.

Terry Geeskin, formerly of the Museum of Modern Art Film Stills Archive, was once again gracious and expeditious in locating appropriate silent film stills. Christy Schurmann and Donna Schurmann assisted with other figures and illustrations.

At the Robbins Library of the University of Rochester, Rose Paprocki and Anne Zanzucchi offered much needed help at the eleventh hour. The Rush Rhees Library at the University of Rochester provided me with numerous materials and services. The George Eastman House/International Museum of Photography also facilitated my research: in particular, Becky Simmons, Ed Stratmann, and Rachel Stuhlman lent me valuable assistance.

The work of a number of distinguished film scholars, whom I have long admired and who are listed at greater length in the Preface, influenced my own study and expanded my thinking about black film. I thank especially Thomas R. Cripps, Henry T. Sampson, Daniel J. Leab, and Donald Bogle. I am grateful as well to Phyllis Klotmann, James P. Murray, James Snead, Mark Reid, Clyde Taylor, Manthia Diawara, Gladstone Yearwood, bell hooks, Valerie Smith, Michele Wallace, and Jacqueline Bobo; their studies of black film illuminated and enriched my own. Important recent work by Charles Musser, J. Ronald Green, Charlene Regester, Jane Gaines, Pearl Bowser, and Louise Spence has considerably expanded the study of Oscar Micheaux and his circle of early race film-makers and will surely inspire new interest in this vital area of film study.

Above all, I am grateful to Alan Lupack, whose insights are always keen and whose judgments I value beyond measure.

Barbara Tepa Lupack
April, 2002

Contents

List of Figures   xi

Preface   xiii

1. The Birth of Defamation: *Uncle Tom's Cabin*
and the Beginnings of Black Stereotyping   1

2. "A Credit to the Race": Oscar Micheaux
and Early Race Filmmaking   67

3. "We'll Teach Him Fear": Racial Representation
in Sound Films of the 1930s and 1940s   183

4. Uncle Tom Meets Uncle Sam: Wartime Developments
and Postwar Progress   243

5. From Eisenhower to Black Power:
Radicalizing the Black Hero   299

6. "Tell Them I'm a Man": Popularizing Black History   379

7. History to Herstory: New Voices for a New Century   447

Works Cited   515

General Index   533

Index of Film Titles   551

Illustrations

CHAPTER ONE

1.1   *Uncle Tom's Cabin* Railroad Tent Flyer
1.2   *Uncle Tom's Cabin* (1903)
1.3   *Uncle Tom's Cabin* (1927)
1.4   *Topsy and Eva* Sheet Music
1.5   *Uncle Tom's Cabin* (1987)
1.6   Stepin Fetchit
1.7   Buckwheat, "Little Rascals"
1.8   *Big Momma's House*

CHAPTER TWO

2.1   *The Realization of a Negro's Ambition*
2.2   *The Flying Ace*
2.3   *The Scar of Shame*
2.4   Portrait of Oscar Micheaux
2.5   *The Symbol of the Unconquered*
2.6   *Within Our Gates*
2.7   *The Symbol of the Unconquered*
2.8   *Body and Soul*
2.9   *The Exile*

CHAPTER THREE

3.1   *The Jazz Singer*
3.2   *Hallelujah!*
3.3   *The Little Colonel*
3.4   *Green Pastures*
3.5   *Gone With the Wind*
3.6   *King Kong*
3.7   *Son of Ingagi*
3.8   *The Emperor Jones*

CHAPTER FOUR

4.1   *Imitation of Life* (1934)
4.2   *Imitation of Life* (1959)
4.3   *Pinky*

4.4   *Lost Boundaries*
4.5   *Home of the Brave*
4.6   *Intruder in the Dust*
4.7   *Native Son* (1950)
4.8   *Native Son* (1987)

CHAPTER FIVE

5.1   *No Way Out*
5.2   *The Defiant Ones*
5.3   *In the Heat of the Night*
5.4   *Band of Angels*
5.5   *A Raisin in the Sun* (1961)
5.6   *Take a Giant Step*
5.7   *Bright Road*
5.8   *The Learning Tree*
5.9   *Sounder*
5.10 *If He Hollers, Let Him Go!*
5.11 *Cotton Comes to Harlem*
5.12 *A Rage in Harlem*
5.13 *Sweet Sweetback's Baadasssss Song*
5.14 *The River Niger*

CHAPTER SIX

6.1   *Lethal Weapon*
6.2   *The Autobiography of Miss Jane Pittman*
6.3   *A Gathering of Old Men*
6.4   *Roots*
6.5   *Roots: The Gift*
6.6   *Malcolm X*
6.7   *A Soldier's Story*
6.8   *Devil in a Blue Dress*

CHAPTER SEVEN

7.1   *A Hero Ain't Nothin' But a Sandwich*
7.2   *The Color Purple*
7.3   *Waiting to Exhale*
7.4   *How Stella Got Her Groove Back*
7.5   *Beloved*

Preface

Because my mouth
Is wide with laughter,
You do not hear
My inner cry.
Because my feet
Are gay with dancing,
You do not know
I die.

—*Langston Hughes, "Minstrel Man"*

As film scholar Daniel J. Leab has rightly observed, there is no better evidence of the assimilation of blacks into American society than their depiction in the movies. Until recently, however, that depiction—at least in mainstream Hollywood movies by white producers—has been overwhelmingly negative.

While blacks have appeared on screen almost from the beginnings of film, they have historically been limited to types—more correctly, to stereotypes—popularized in American life and arts, particularly in the nineteenth- and early-twentieth-century minstrel shows and vaudeville stage productions that featured antic performers with cork-blackened faces. Those entertainments burlesqued life in the Old South by re-creating various and often elaborate rituals that had already been established by the time of the Civil War, rituals that emphasized the servile behavior and menial status of blacks. And they succeeded in fixing in the American imagination images of blacks as ludicrous figures who are "prone to frenzied dancing, shiftlessness, garish dress, gin tippling, dice shooting, torturing the language, and, inevitably, addicted to watermelon and chicken, usually stolen" (Leab 8), and who, like helpless children, require the indulgence and the guidance of their white intellectual superiors. Since blacks lacked a strong visual past with which to counter the distortions of their experience, black imagery continued to be shaped by the sentimental racism of the culture and by the literature of the day, which often glorified the plantation tradition, lampooned minorities, and rationalized inequitable treatment, even physical abuse and lynching.

Around the turn of the twentieth century, as movies emerged as the most popular and accessible form of mass entertainment, they reinforced the existing racist stereotypes. "The repeatability of movies," as James Snead observed, while otherwise a virtue of the medium, "offprinted false racial models from celluloid onto mass consciousness again and again; real viewers came to expect unreal blacks on the screen and in the real world" (107-08). Whites in many small communities throughout the United States who had never seen or encountered black people on or off the stage gained their first impressions from viewing film images of blacks portrayed as the composite of qualities that diametrically opposed the values admired by white American society. The popularity of American films in other countries also spread the negative images to the remote corners of the world, everywhere American movies were shown (Sampson 26).

Thomas Cripps, in his numerous groundbreaking studies of Hollywood's treatment of black imagery, and Donald Bogle, in his excellent interpretive black film history, have suggested perhaps the definitive categories for analysis of the cinematic stereotypes, most of which reproduced black images that were drawn from the days of slavery yet continued to dominate black characters throughout much of the twentieth century. Those include the faithful, submissive Uncle Tom, a contented slave willing to sacrifice himself for his kind master (as in Edwin S. Porter's version of *Uncle Tom's Cabin* [1903], *The Confederate Spy* [1910], and *For Massa's Sake* [1911]); the devoted domestic, with variants like the fat cantankerous Mammy (a film role that earned *Gone With the Wind*'s supporting actress Hattie McDaniel the first Oscar awarded to a black performer); the "coon" (from the amusing "pickaninny" and the lazy "darky" in such early films as Edison's *Ten Pickaninnies* [1904] and the slapstick comedies based on the character of crazy Rastus [ca. 1910-11] to the congenial Uncle Remus-type of later films such as *The Green Pastures* [1936] and *Song of the South* [1946]); the tragic mulatto (a favorite subject of filmmakers, beginning with early films like *The Debt, In Humanity's Cause, In Slavery Days,* and *The Octoroon* [all ca. 1911-1913]); and the brutal black "buck" (a racist mythic type introduced by D. W. Griffith and imitated in subsequent films like *Broken Chains* [1916] and *Free and Equal* [1915/released 1924]). Over the years, from pulpits to picket lines, blacks protested these dishonest and demeaning screen depictions; and, as increasingly enlightened social attitudes prevailed (especially after post-Second World War governmental initiatives and after postwar agreements between Hollywood studio heads and the National Association for the Advancement of Colored People to present more balanced racial representations), a few of the more blatant stereotypes disappeared. But, in many cases, the old stereotypes that stressed black inferiority were replaced by other more subtle modern caricatures, like the libidinous welfare mother in *Claudine,* the indestructible moral outlaw in *Superfly,* and the "sex machine" in *Shaft.* By contrast, in the works of black writers from Oscar Micheaux to Toni Morrison, the black experience has been more fully, more accurately, and usually more sympathetically realized; and from the early days of film, select filmmakers have looked to that literature as the basis for their productions.

Unfortunately, even in a contemporary Hollywood that is growing more cognizant of black moviegoers and shifting demographics, adaptation of black literature to the screen remains a relatively rare practice. And, in fact, when black novels are adapted as motion pictures, they are often reworked or popularized for mainstream audiences so that much of their cultural and idiosyncratic importance is lost, as was the case with the downplaying of the tribal solidarity ritual of scarring and the African-American practice of "signifying" in Steven Spielberg's version of *The Color Purple* and with the rewriting of the ending of Donna Deitch's adaptation of *The Women of Brewster Place.* Recently, however, prominent black writers, performers, and celebrities like Oprah Winfrey and Bill and Camille Cosby, concerned about conveying and preserving the integrity of black texts, have gotten involved in film production, while black filmmakers, both commercial and independent, are increasingly helping to challenge and change black cinematic images by turning to black sources for their inspiration. And Hollywood studios are also beginning to take heed both of the growing discontent over negative portrayals and formulaic representations of ethnic and minority cultures and of the commercial prospects of translating popular or enduring black works to the screen.

An historical examination of the practice of such adaptation offers telling insights into the portrayal—and progress—of blacks in American cinema and culture; it reveals that while blacks, on screen and behind the scenes, were often forced to re-create the demeaning film stereotypes, they learned how to subvert and exploit the artificiality of their caricatures. It also reveals the ways that black filmmakers, beginning with Oscar Micheaux and his lesser-known colleagues like William Foster and Emmett J. Scott, worked within the conventions of film and of society yet managed to produce films that were, at their best, unconventional and pioneering. It demonstrates that as far back as the 1920s and 1930s, black writers like Paul Laurence Dunbar and Langston Hughes already recognized the need for involvement with film production in order to create pictures that were more representative of black life. It illustrates the fact that as black voices chronicling the black experience found their way to the screen, among the strongest were the voices of women. And above all it confirms that within the rich tradition of black literature of all genres lie many exciting cinematic possibilities for audiences of all colors.

I am indebted to a number of film and cultural scholars, whose work shaped my own ideas and interpretations and influenced this study. Foremost, perhaps, is the prolific and pioneering work on black film by Thomas Cripps, from his early essays in *Negro Digest* and other journals to his seminal book-length studies, particularly *Slow Fade to Black* and *Making Movies Black;* it is no exaggeration to say that Cripps has helped to define contemporary black film studies. Another invaluable source is *Blacks in Black and White* by Henry T. Sampson. Drawing extensively on articles and reviews from the black press, Sampson's comprehensive, encyclopaedic study offers an excellent overview of Oscar Micheaux, the Johnson brothers, and other race filmmakers, both black and white; and it includes production information and plot synopses of early films, material that is virtually unobtainable elsewhere. Daniel J. Leab's hallmark volume *From Sambo to Superspade* chronicles the development of the black movie image from the beginnings of cinema through the early 1970s, while another classic study, Donald Bogle's *Toms, Coons, Mulattoes, Mammies and Bucks,* establishes useful categories for the historical investigation of black types through the early 1970s as well. (Updated and expanded editions of Bogle's study cover black performers and films of the 1970s and 1980s, as does Bogle's illustrated encyclopedia of *Blacks in American Film and Television.*) Also of significance are two earlier books, Peter Noble's *The Negro in Films* (originally published in 1948 and reprinted in 1970), and Jim Pines's *Blacks in Films,* both of which stimulated interest in black representation and continue to lend vitality to the ongoing debate over what defines black film. And Phyllis R. Klotman, in her extensive filmographies of black cinema, especially *Frame by Frame,* compiles cast lists and other film information that is vital for researchers.

In various of their works, James P. Murray, Edward Mapp, Lindsay Patterson, V. J. Jerome, James Snead, Mark Reid, and Ed Guerrero analyze black images and perspectives in black-oriented films directed and produced by white filmmakers (and in some black independent films as well); Toni Cade Bambara, Clyde Taylor, Anna Everett, Manthia Diawara, and Gladstone Yearwood attempt to define a black aesthetic, largely by demonstrating that black film criticism must be oppositional to Hollywood's regressive representations; and bell hooks, Jacqueline Bobo, Valerie Smith, Michele Wallace, and other black feminists, by arguing for a reinterpretation of black stereotyping and an appreciation of the role of female spectatorship, encourage alternative, innovative approaches to black film.

Among scholars of Micheaux and of other early and silent black filmmakers, groundbreaking work has been published, particularly of late, by Charles Musser (whose earlier study *The Emergence of Cinema: The American Screen to 1907* is indispensable to all students of cinema), J. Ronald Green, Charlene Regester, Jane Gaines, Pearl Bowser, and Louise Spence. Not only do these critics and scholars examine the cultural and social milieux within which Micheaux worked; they also analyze the remarkable ways in which Micheaux explored issues of racial identity, gender, caste, and class in his many productions. And, perhaps most importantly, they reaffirm the significance and singularity of Micheaux and suggest new directions for further study of his cinematic achievements and those of other black filmmakers.

Not many of those films, however, are extant. Silent film, in particular, was a notoriously ephemeral medium: original nitrate prints degraded easily and rapidly, while transfer usually produced copies of low quality. More ephemeral than silent and early films in general were silent and early films produced by black independent filmmakers. Even the prolific Micheaux rarely had more than a handful of original prints of his early films that he could circulate or distribute at any given time; and no copy of his final film, *The Betrayal,* released in 1948, almost three decades after Micheaux began filmmaking, is known to exist. It is no surprise, then, that so few productions by lesser-known race filmmakers survive.

Only three of Micheaux's silent films are extant; of those three, two were rediscovered just within the past decade. (According to the recent "Oscar Micheaux Filmography," compiled by Charles Musser, Corey K. Creekmur, Pearl Bowser, J. Ronald Green, Charlene Regester, and Louise Spence, prints of Micheaux's *Within Our Gates* [1920] can be found at the Library of Congress and at La Filmoteca Española; of *The Symbol of the Unconquered* [1920] at the Museum of Modern Art and Cinématèque Royale; and of *Body and Soul* [1925] at the George Eastman House. Of the films produced by the Colored Players Film Corporation, only *Ten Nights in a Barroom* (1926) and *The Scar of Shame* (1926 [1929]) are extant. (Prints of those films can be located at the Library of Congress. For more information on the films themselves, see Charles Musser's "A Colored Players Film Corporation Filmography.") Of the films produced by the Lincoln Motion Picture Company, none—apart from fragments of *By Right of Birth* (1921)—survives. Of the films produced by the Norman Film Manufacturing Company, extant materials are preserved in the American Film Institute Norman Collection, Library of Congress; the AFI Norman Collection also preserves films distributed by the Norman Company. (See Phyllis R. Klotman's "Norman Film Manufacturing Company: Production and Theatre Release Dates for All-Black-Cast Films.")

One of the most important repositories for silent and early black films, the Library of Congress includes among its general black film holdings (a listing of which is available online) a number of important titles such as *The Birth of a Race* (fragments) (1918), *A Black Sherlock Holmes* (1918), *By Right of Birth* (fragments) (1921),

The Comeback of Barnacle Bill (1918), *The Flying Ace* (1926), and *Spying the Spy* (1918). Also among those holdings are several sound films produced by Oscar Micheaux, including *The Darktown Revue* (1931), *The Exile* (1931), *The Girl From Chicago* (1932), *Lying Lips* (1939), *Ten Minutes to Live* (1932), and *Underworld* (1936). The Library of Congress Black Films: Print Collection includes a number of seminal comedies such as *The Barnstormers, A Kiss in the Dark, A Nigger in the Woodpile,* and *Who Said Chicken?,* as well as important dramas such as *His Trust, His Trust Fulfilled, Uncle Tom's Cabin* (1903), and *The Zulu's Heart* and documentaries/newsreels such as *Colored Troops Disembarking* (Spanish-American War), *A Scrap in Black and White,* and *A Watermelon Contest.* In the Library's Copyright Collection are a large number of more recent black films such as *Cotton Comes to Harlem* and *A Raisin in the Sun;* still other black films are currently being added to the American Film Institute Collection. The extant prints and film fragments as well as contemporary reviews in the black press (and, occasionally, in white newspapers) highlight the racist distortions of some of those films; suggest the extent of the rich black cultural life that was chronicled in other of those films; and confirm the fact that much research, especially on early and silent black film, remains to be done.

Chapter 1

The Birth of Defamation:
Uncle Tom's Cabin and the Beginnings
of Black Stereotyping

> Even today the motion picture has not quite outgrown its
> immaturity. It still uses talented Negro players to fit into
> the old stereotypes of the loving Mammy and the comic
> servant that have both almost disappeared from the the-
> ater.
>
> —*Edith J. R. Isaacs, "Theater Arts" (August 1942)*

D. W. Griffith's venomous and controversial *The Birth of a Nation*
(1915) was the first important full-length film to depict the figure
of the brutal, villainous, sexually aggressive black and to establish
many of the other racist stereotypes that would be imitated by
filmmakers for years to come. But it was another, earlier film,
Edwin S. Porter's *Uncle Tom's Cabin*, that introduced into cinema
culture the character most immediately associated with black servility and subservience. Uncle Tom first appeared in *Uncle Tom's
Cabin*, Harriet Beecher Stowe's novel of protest against the passage
in 1850 of the Fugitive Slave Act that enforced the return of
escaped slaves to their owners. A remarkable and unusually strong
character, Stowe's Tom suffered tremendous hardships but
remained faithful to God as well as to his own principles.
Although it aroused the wrath of the wicked slave trader Simon
Legree, Tom's saintliness inspired the love of Little Eva and the
admiration of Eva's father Augustine St. Clare, of Tom's fellow
slaves, and of Stowe's many readers; and it made his martyrdom,
precipitated by his refusal to betray another slave, as redemptive
as it was tragic.

Yet even before the final serial installment of the novel was
published in 1852, Stowe's eponymous character had become part
of American popular culture.[1] His story—routinely truncated to

eliminate the harsh reality of his suffering and martyrdom—was so frequently dramatized throughout the second half of the nineteenth century and into the early twentieth century that it became known as "the world's greatest hit." Tom's popularity spread quickly to England and to the Continent, where he was featured prominently in British mime shows and European theatrical pieces; but in America, where adaptations of *Uncle Tom's Cabin* abounded, he was simply ubiquitous. In addition to the legitimate American stage versions, there were lucrative Tom spectacles, like the one mounted by renowned showman Phineas T. Barnum; musical extravaganzas, which included festive black musicians, singers, and dancers (and occasionally even fireworks) and which anticipated the "Tom Jubilees" and the Tom operas of the 1870s and 1880s; Tom show circus parades, a notable one of which comprised a "Lady Zouave Drum and Bugle Corps, 18 Real Georgia Plantation Shouters, Mlle. Minerva's New Orleans Creole Fife and Drum Corps, the 'Original Whang-doodle Pickaninny Band,' Eva's $1500 gold chariot, a log cabin, floats, phaetons, carts, ornate banners, dazzling harnesses and uniforms, 3 full concert bands, the drum major, an 8-foot colored boy, 10 Cuban and Russian ferocious, man-eating hounds, 25 ponies, donkeys, oxen, mules, horses, and burros, all trained as entertaining tricksters" (Hughes 301); itinerant road shows known as Tomming troupes or Tommers that varied in size from casts of hundreds of players to family groups of four or five; "Double Mammoth" Tom shows, which "fed the Yankee fetish for bigness" (Birdoff 311) by offering two Topsys and Markses or twin Toms, Elizas, and Legrees; and countless parodies and ethnic take-offs, like the Irish *Uncle Pat's Cabin* and *Uncle Mike's Cabin*. (Fig. 1.1.) Common to all of the Tom productions, however, was a distortion of the title character himself: increasingly, Stowe's dignified and exemplary Uncle Tom was portrayed as a sappy wooly-white-haired plantation slave content to abide by his master's wishes. Such vulgarizing not only carried a message substantially different from the novel's strong condemnation of slavery; it disinclined Americans from taking seriously the pathos of Uncle Tom's plight and encouraged their perception of Tom's acquiescence and obedience as a model of good racial behavior.

Early films were no better. As in the many nineteenth-century theatrical versions, Tom's character was significantly distorted and

Figure 1.1. A railroad flyer announces an upcoming "thrilling, powerfull, gripping" performance of *Uncle Tom's Cabin* by one of the many traveling Tomming troupes.

Tom himself reduced from a touchstone for the national conscience to an object of national amusement, even ridicule. *Uncle Tom's Cabin's Parade*, for instance, a 125-foot-long polyscopic film produced in 1903 by the Selig Polyscope Company, depicted a traveling Uncle Tom's Cabin Company; and while the short featured "Uncle Tom, Little Eva, Marks [the lawyer] . . . together with the blood hounds, donkeys and everything connected with a production of Uncle Tom's Cabin," its purpose was not to edify but simply to entertain by exaggeration. A "picture [that] pleases the children" (*AFI Catalog: Film Beginnings, 1893-1910* 1122), *Uncle Tom's Cabin's Parade*—brief as it was—focused not on Uncle Tom but on the spectacle of "the tallest colored man in the world" who apparently was a part of the parade.

Released in the same year was Edwin S. Porter's *Uncle Tom's Cabin or Slavery Days* (Edison, 1903), the most important of the early Tom films and one of the most remarkable of all early silent films.[2] Comprised of a prologue and fourteen scenes or tableaux modeled after the *tableaux vivant* or living pictures popularized by French film artist Georges Méliès, it ran 1,100 feet and was considered both the longest and most expensive film made up to that time. Porter, who vouched that "the story has been carefully studied and every scene posed in accordance with the famous author's version," explained his approach as "a departure from the old methods of dissolving one scene into another . . . by inserting announcements with brief descriptions" (Birdoff 396).[3] The tableaux, an episodic series of highlights that provided little plot summary, however, assumed the reader's familiarity with both the character and the story.[4]

In the first tableau, "Eliza Pleads with Tom to Run Away," Eliza goes to Uncle Tom's cabin at night, during a heavy snow; Chloe calls her husband Tom to the door; and after Eliza explains that she is planning to escape, Tom shakes her hand and wishes her well in her journey. As "Phenias Outwits the Slave Traders" in the second tableau, Eliza and her child exit through the window in the very room in which the traders are gathered. "The Escape of Eliza" (tableau 3) shows the rapidly moving ice floes on the Ohio River, onto which Eliza leaps to escape the four hounds that are pursuing her. One of the slave traders follows her onto the ice but falls into the water and is rescued by his colleagues. Eliza survives the river's hazards, and the "Reunion of Eliza and George Harris" (tableau 4) occurs at the home of friendly Quakers. The scene then shifts to the "Race Between the Rob't E. Lee and Natchez" (tableau 5), an episode never depicted in Stowe's novel and extraneous to the plot of the film as well, and to the "Rescue of Eva" (tableau 6), which occurs as passengers debark the winning boat. Eva slips off the Lee's platform and is saved by Uncle Tom, who is purchased on the spot by Eva's grateful father. In "The Welcome Home to St. Clair Eva Aunt Ophelia and Uncle Tom [*sic*]" (tableau 7), happy slaves await the return of their master; the centerpiece of the tableau is a very lively Topsy, who dances almost maniacally and waves a long ribbon, causing obvious consternation to Ophelia. Happy slaves appear again in "Tom and Eva in the Garden" (tableau 8), where Eva falls ill and is carried away by Tom, who joins her grieving family at the little girl's bedside as she ascends into heaven in the ninth tableau, the "Death of Eva" (fig. 1.2). A distraught St. Clair, with Tom standing solemnly at his side, then drowns his sorrow at a saloon, where a slave trader strikes Tom in the face. As "St. Clair Defends Uncle Tom" (tableau 10), he is mor-

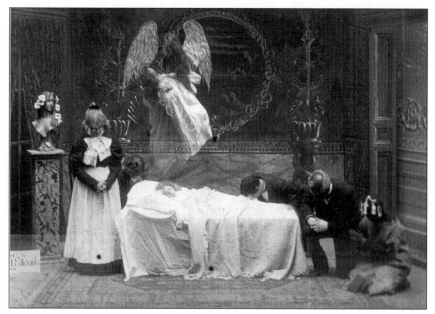

Figure 1.2. With Uncle Tom at her bedside, Little Eva ascends into heaven in Edwin S. Porter's *Uncle Tom's Cabin* (1903). *(Courtesy of Museum of Modern Art/Film Stills Archive)*

tally wounded; the distressed slave can only raise his eyes—and arms—to heaven. At the "Auction Sale of St. Clair's Slaves" (tableau 11), young slave boys and girls dance merrily in front of the auction block as a couple of black men shoot dice and a group of black women dance and sing. After the auction begins, the evil Legree buys two new slaves: a young woman, Emaline [sic], and Tom. As Legree roughly handles his chattel, both slaves fall to their knees, in servitude or prayer—or both. Once at the Legree plantation, "Tom Refuses to Flog Emaline" (tableau 12) and, after being tied to a whipping post, is severely flogged until Emaline grabs the whip and threatens to retaliate against the overseers. In the next scene, Tom is beaten again, this time by Legree himself, but "Marks Avenges Death's [sic] of St. Clair and Uncle Tom" by shooting the evil slaveholder on his own veranda.

The film closes with "Tableau Death of Tom," in which the dying Uncle Tom has a vision that includes images of a heavenly angel, of gallows-bound abolitionist John Brown embracing a black child, of the Civil War dead, of Lee and Grant shaking hands, of Lincoln the Emancipator, and of a society at peace. Yet while Tom, victimized by the plantation system and by the brutal whites who profit so handsomely by it, is very clearly the central character, the film suggests that the real heroes are men like St. Clair, who gives his life for that of his retainer, and Marks, the white lawyer who appears at Legree's home to exact retribution for the deaths of St. Clair and his slave. At the same time, by linking Tom's mistreatment with emancipation and reunification, Porter—as Linda Williams suggests—imposes a kind of "historical happy ending . . . on the now somewhat truncated, sad ending of Tom's death and glory, permitting audiences to feel good about the now corrected horrors of slavery." With the more disturbing aspects of black suffering subsumed by the reassuring notion of national union, whites could not only enjoy Porter's story but also "ease their consciences about the past sins of slavery."[5]

Among the most significant new dimensions that this first filmed version of Uncle Tom's Cabin brought to motion pictures was Uncle Tom himself, the American movies' first major black character. Yet ironically, as Donald Bogle observes, Porter's Tom was not black; in keeping with the old stage traditions, he was "a nameless, slightly overweight white actor made up in blackface"—

a practice that continued for some time in early films, so as not to offend the sensibilities of white audiences, who insisted that even movie "blacks" observe the racial code.[6] And, like the stage Toms of the previous century, he tended to be "white-haired rather than the vigorous, broad-shouldered middle-aged man of Stowe's novel . . . for reasons that have quite a bit to do with the fact that his role called for the frequent handling of Little Eva" (Williams, *Race* 87). Nevertheless, with Porter "the first Negro character had arrived in films, and he had done so at a time when the motion-picture industry itself was virtually non-existent" (Bogle, *Toms* 3)[7]—when the movies were without stars or studios or sound, when there were no great directors or writers, and when the community of Hollywood had not yet come into being.

That "first Negro character," however, quickly metamorphosed into one of the earliest and most enduring black caricatures or stereotypes: Porter's saintly Uncle Tom became "Tom," the first in a long line of "socially acceptable Good Negro[es]" who are chased, harassed, hounded, flogged, enslaved, and insulted but who "keep the faith, n'er turn against their white massas, and remain hearty, submissive, stoic, generous, selfless, and oh-so-very kind. Thus they endear themselves to white audiences and emerge as heroes of sorts" (Bogle, *TCMMB* 4, 6). Such loyal, unctuous Tom types appear in numerous early films such as *The Confederate Spy* (1910), in which dear "Uncle Daniel" defends his owner's home, runs messages through the swamps, and even dies happy before a Northern firing squad knowing that his service was for the sake of "massa and little missi," and *For Massa's Sake* (1911), in which Old Uncle Joe, a devoted retainer of the St. Clairs, sells himself and his family back into slavery to redeem his master Harry's gambling debts. But it is in Porter's film and in the subsequent adaptations of the work from which the stereotype takes its name that the most memorable and vivid depictions of the Tom occur.

The notion of the contented, adoring slave and the genteel, kindly master who provides for him was an integral part of the early cinematic romance—and the cinematic artifice—of the Old South, whose mystique had crept into the national psyche. Before the advent of film, people had only imagined or seen in prints or paintings the magnificent mansions and the romantic steamboats, and most knew or thought little about the blacks whose lives and labors subsidized the illusion. But Porter brought a certain vitality to their vision. His appealing plantation tale, full of splendor, diversion, and local color, was, to be sure, a far cry from Stowe's harrowing abolitionist account and indictment of slavery. In Porter's South, after all, not only do the masters leap heroically to the defense of their loyal slaves; the slave women (Topsy excepted) are well-coiffed and wear long white dresses as they pick cotton in the fields; children lead idyllic existences, attended by loyal family retainers; and even the lawyers act ethically. Early moviegoers, drawn to escapist entertainment rather than serious fare, enjoyed and accepted the sentiment behind such mythology, which was evoked in virtually all of the *Uncle Tom's Cabin* film versions until the late 1980s and which helped to fix the most persistent of the black stereotypes in the minds of the white viewing public.

Only a few months after Porter's *Uncle Tom's Cabin*, Sigmund Lubin released his version of *Uncle Tom's Cabin* (1903).[8] As Porter and the Edison Company had done, the Lubin Company presented an elaborate panorama comprised "of a grand estate graced by comfortable Negroes, singing and dancing," that attempted more to glorify than to examine critically the Old South. In a publicity booklet, Uncle Tom's surprisingly attractive abode was labeled "a typical Southern log cabin," and the tale of his trials was called, amazingly, "one of the prettiest stories ever written" (Campbell, *Celluloid South* 39-40).[9] It is likely that neither the Edison nor the Lubin film intended to hold the South up as a model society. But in effect that was the result: and as long as traditional antebellum legend and contemporary black stereotyping complemented each other and remained acceptable and profitable, the South continued to be portrayed as "a timeless, lost home, a safe imaginary childhood of innocence,"[10] and a graceful agrarian society, which wanted what was best for its black citizens and knew best how to ensure it. In fact, as Edward D. C. Campbell, Jr. observed, "the movies eventually placed the burden of secession and war not on the Southern system, but on the few who abused it, such as [the Northerner] Legree and other radicals" (*CS* 40).

Uncle Tom's Cabin was remade again in 1910, by two different companies: Thanhouser and Vitagraph. Although Donald Bogle writes that these remakes "had little in style or treatment to distinguish them" (*TCMMB* 6), there were indeed some interesting, if minor, differences. The Vitagraph version, directed by J. Stuart Blackton and produced in three parts of one reel each (approximately 1,000 feet to a reel) that corresponded closely to an early dramatic adaptation by George L. Aiken, was advertised by the Vitagraph Company as "The Most Magnificent, Sumptuous and Realistic Production Ever Attempted of *Uncle Tom's Cabin.*" Ironically, while it promised "the real thing in every respect—real ice, real bloodhounds, real Negroes, real actors, real scenes from the real life as it was in the antebellum days," it made little attempt to avoid the clichés of antebellum plots. Although the film is not extant, the promotional lobby cards "hinted at the view to come." One, for instance, shows the wild black Topsy being given to her new white mistress Ophelia for social and moral instruction; the card depicting that scene is bordered by drawings of watermelons. Another portrays Uncle Tom and Aunt Chloe in their "comfortable cabin" on the Shelby estate; the caption is: "His pickaninnies live in happy ignorance of their fate." And on another card, as he is being led away by the slave trader Haley, Tom persuades his compatriots to "Obey the good mas'r—for obedience to Him alone is the first step to the kingdom of Heaven" (Campbell, *CS* 41).

The Thanhouser version, released at virtually the same time as Vitagraph's, was billed as "The Prize Thanhouser Classic"; and it claimed a tremendous triumph over its rival insofar as it was "Not a Tedious Drawn-Out, Continued-in-Our-Next Affair, but COMPLETE IN ONE REEL" (Birdoff 397). Frank Crane starred as Uncle Tom; child star Marie Eline, the extremely popular "Thanhouser Kid," was Little Eva; and the scenes between the two were among the most poignant in the production. As a contemporary reviewer noted in *The Moving Picture World* (30 July 1910), the last act of Eva's life is to present Tom with a little locket containing her picture. "Just before he dies, he presses to his lips the locket with the picture of his beloved mistress, and in a vision sees her in the clouds, holding out her arms to him that he, too, may enter with her the pearly gates, inside of which all souls are equal, and all free." Apparently, at least according to these films, obedience to "the good mas'r"—and the good little mistress, too—truly was "the first step to the kingdom of Heaven" for Tom and other blacks.

Two new productions of *Uncle Tom's Cabin* followed in 1913.[11] Little is known about Kalem's 1913 two-part "Special," which featured Anna Q. Nilsson as Eliza and Hal Clemmons as Legree and which seemed to follow closely the outline of Stowe's novel, from Eliza's flight and Tom's purchase by St. Clare to Eva's death and Uncle Tom's brutal flogging by Legree, "who drowns the humiliation of the blow in drink and dies in a delirium shortly afterward" (*The Moving Picture World* 13 Dec. 1913).[12] But the Universal-Imp (Imperial Company) release, "a four-reel, super-super-special" directed by Otis Turner, "was the most pretentious *Uncle Tom's Cabin* adaptation up to that time" (Birdoff 397). A review in *Variety* (5 Sept. 1913) noted that "the playlet is a veritable scenic and costume panorama of the old ante bellum [*sic*] South . . . [with] vistas of cotton country, stretches of far Southern rivers, kinetic glimpses of old side-wheel steamboats, freighted with passengers of the period, the women in crinolines, the men in quaint frocks and sombrero shaped hats, the children in ruffled pantalettes"; and, for the obligatory humor, there was "the wench [Topsy] skedaddling with the ribbon trailing behind like a flying rein."[13]

A more distinctive film version of *Uncle Tom's Cabin* was the five-reel 1914 production by the World Film Corporation. Directed by William Robert Daly and written by Edward McWade, the film again featured the rising child star Marie Eline (the "Thanhouser Kid") as Little Eva, as well as Sam Lucas, Irving Cummings, Theresa Michelena, Roy Applegate, Paul Scardon, Boots Wall, and Fern Andra. Using "good judgement in his presentation," noted the reviewer for *The Moving Picture World* (15 Aug. 1914), Mr. Daly "has chosen to follow the book rather than the stage version"[14] and has also incorporated a variety of realistic details into his film. "It is no stage ice," for instance, "on which Eliza crosses the river. The real article is present in abundance." But the main reason that the production company could claim greater authenticity than any of the earlier movie versions was its casting of seventy-two-year-old actor Sam Lucas, described by the *New York Age* as the "dean of the colored theatrical profession" (Leab 13), in the title role. Lucas became both the first black man to play a leading role in a movie and the first black man to be cast in a prominent black role (although, significantly, in the film Topsy and Eliza were still played by whites in blackface). Considered the "Grand Old Man of the Negro Stage," he lent what authority and skill he could to the *Uncle Tom's Cabin* production. Yet, while the casting of Lucas as Uncle Tom was almost universally applauded, a subtle racism was directed against the other black actors, as is evident in the tone of at least one of the reviews, in which Daly was praised for "his fine discrimination in depicting pathos so that it never verges on bathos—and this all the more notable by reason of the fact that of necessity he was using many colored players" (*The Moving Picture World* 15 Aug. 1914).

Perhaps the most memorable feature of Daly's film was its unprecedented depiction of violence perpetrated by blacks against whites. After Legree indicates a sexual interest in the newly-purchased slave Emmeline, his housekeeper (actually his reluctant mistress) Cassy steals his gun in order to prevent him from raping the girl and holds the weapon to the sleeping Legree's head. Unable to shoot, she instead devises an escape plan for herself and Emmeline. Later, when Tom is beaten almost to death in punishment for that escape, the young black male slave whom he has befriended finds the gun that Cassy has abandoned and uses it to stalk and kill Legree. "These two moments in which black hands hold guns to white human targets," Linda Williams argues, "are unprecedented in the Tom tradition, and perhaps in all American film. Until this moment, interracial violence has been pictured exclusively as that of the white masters abusing black slaves." In Stowe's novel, Legree's guilty conscience and his "haunting" by Cassy and Emmeline had seemed revenge enough; even in the stage versions in which Tom's death was avenged, the retribution was always at the hands of a white man, George Shelby, Jr., the son of Tom's original kindly owner. The surprise demonstration in Daly's film of wronged slaves who not only foil their masters by plotting escape but also redress the violence committed upon them must have contributed to the sense of white terror at interracial and sexual violence that D. W. Griffith exploited in *The Birth of a Nation* the following year.[15]

Uncle Tom's Cabin was soon remade again, in 1918, this time by Famous Players-Lasky Corporation (which later became Paramount), as a five-reeler, directed by J. Searle Dawley and starring Marguerite Clark, a white actress in the dual roles of Little Eva and Topsy (a trick accomplished by the use of double exposures), and Frank Losee, long identified in Tom shows with Simon Legree, as the pious Uncle Tom. Yet while the production was notable for its geographic scope, especially its reproduction of the Underground Railroad, "there was so much left out it appeared more like a series of episodes than a running story" (*Variety* 9 Aug. 1918).

Figure 1.3. The movie poster from the lavish Carl Laemmle production of *Uncle Tom's Cabin* announces all of the key players, including celebrated black actor James Lowe as Tom and Margarita Fischer, wife of director Harry A. Pollard, as Eliza. *(Universal Pictures, 1927)*

Almost a decade passed before the next remake, *Uncle Tom's Cabin* (Universal Pictures, 1927), directed by Harry A. Pollard, a version that had some interesting connections to earlier Tom films and to Tom typing. Pollard, by then a distinguished director, had starred as Uncle Tom in the 1913 Universal "super-super-special four-reeler"; his wife Margarita Fischer had appeared as Topsy. Weather and budget had limited the earlier production, and, as Harry Birdoff writes, "for fourteen long years Pollard cherished the hope of doing the movie realistically" (398).

His opportunity came when Carl Laemmle decided to film the classic story. (Fig. 1.3.) The two million dollar budget allocated for the project broke all records. (By contrast, the 1913 film had cost only fifteen thousand dollars.) Technicians were dispatched to the many towns and places described in Stowe's novel; they spent eight months traveling throughout the South and researching archives and other data to ensure that even the most minute props employed in the film (e.g., the slaves' drinking cups hollowed out of gourds, the twisted papers used as tapers to light the fireplaces in the mornings) would be accurate. Later, replicas of buildings were erected. The St. Clare home was constructed at a cost of $70,000, the Shelby home at $62,000, and the Legree plantation, in its run-down condition, at $40,000; all were furnished with period furniture. The Shelby estate even had a "slave street," complete with parallel rows of squalid cabins, authentic down to the cobwebs and the quaint utensils inside the huts. Over one quarter of a million feet of lumber was used; more than one hundred tons of plaster went into the walls. Instead of the grass matting usually employed for exteriors, one thousand full-grown trees were hauled in from the mountains of southern California, and fifty bales of Spanish moss were transported from Mississippi. Artificial magnolias, oleanders, and other varieties were intermingled with tens of thousands of jasmines, Spanish dagger, and all the flowers native to the Old South. Even the dogs received special attention. Unhappy with the usual mastiffs or Great Danes, Pollard insisted on "real bloodhounds" and paid a record price of $20,000 for a team of registered bloodhounds from England, whose bloodlines could be traced back to slave days in Virginia (Birdoff 399). The detail was so great, in fact, that it even involved the refurbishing of a noted side-wheeler, the "Kate Adams" (rechristened "La Belle Riviere," as in the novel), which exploded and burned immediately after the filming.

For further authenticity, Pollard cast a black actor in many ways true to Stowe's original—the handsome, forty-year-old James B. Lowe. Congratulating itself on its liberalism, writes Donald Bogle, Universal sent out press releases about "its good colored star." What made the star so "good" in the eyes of the studio, however, was not only his performance on screen but also his behavior off screen. The releases, which inadvertently reinforced the Tom stereotype, asserted that Lowe "has made history. A history that reflects only credit to the Negro race, not only because he has given the 'Uncle Tom' character a new slant, but because of his exemplary conduct with the Universal company" (*TCMMB* 6).

Lowe, however, was not the first choice for the part; the talented black actor Charles Gilpin, who had created the part of the ambitious Pullman porter-turned-despot Brutus Jones in Eugene O'Neill's landmark play *The Emperor Jones*, was initially cast as

Uncle Tom. But, according to Peter Noble, Gilpin, an intelligent, proud, and sensitive person, had many heated discussions with director Pollard about the manner in which the novel should be filmed and the beloved Negro character portrayed. Finally, either as a protest or as a result of being fired, "Gilpin left the cast and returned to New York, where it is said he went back to his old job as lift-man rather than play a well-paid screen role, the treatment of which, in his opinion, helped to malign his people" (Noble 32). A similar fate was in store for Lowe. Although he waited until considerable footage had already been shot, Lowe protested to the studio about the crude and unrealistic way his character was being presented.[16] But, as Daniel J. Leab notes, those protests "made no difference. [Lowe] never made another movie, and five years later he was found by a correspondent for a black weekly working as a tailor in Paris" (54).

Completed in nineteen months, Pollard's film ran a record-breaking 977,000 feet (twelve reels).[17] The production had employed five thousand players and utilized sixty-five sets, as opposed to the eight or nine required for other big features (Birdoff 400). Yet, as much as Pollard had sought realism in most aspects of the production, he apparently took some great liberties with the story itself, "spinning out three plots and a comic line" in a script that "plodded on for over two hours" (*SFB* 160). Eliza, played by his wife Margarita Fischer, got all of the close-ups in the film; Uncle Tom (filmed in long shot during the first half—and infrequently at that) became a secondary character. Moreover, whereas Stowe wrote her novel in 1851-52, Pollard carried the plot to the end of the Civil War and used the defeat of the Confederacy by the Union forces as a kind of historical act of redemption for the horrors of slavery. Harry Birdoff notes that "some of the new situations—purely cinematic—revealed a brief flash of Lincoln, and Sherman's march to the sea, with Atlanta under shell fire and in flames; then a martial finale, when the General stopped long enough in the internecine strife to rescue Eliza and Cassy from Legree's clutches; startled by the sudden appearance of the Union Army, Legree fell out the window." This postbellum triumph, however, subordinated Tom's tragedy to the exploits of Eliza and the Northern troops, who fought for the emancipation of blacks and gave the familiar story a reassuring, even happy ending.

Yet despite its many flaws, Pollard's Uncle Tom had the distinction of being the best of a bad lot. Even Thomas Cripps concedes that, despite a picaresque plot that winds "through years and miles too improbable with coincidence, too laden with Yankees to effectively indict the Southern 'peculiar institution,'" and other cinematic faults that cutting could not redeem, "the picture spreads wide a vision of blackness that had not been seen in years. Lowe's Tom, while not abandoning the accretion of sentimentality that had crusted like barnacles over Mrs. Stowe's character, restored some of his strength"—enough, at least, to make some white Southerners grumble and Yankees exult. And even blacks felt that "their cause was represented as well as possible" (*SFB* 160-61).[18] Reviewers like Edith Isaacs in *Theater Arts* agreed: "Uncle Tom in this 1927 version," she remarked, "seems to wear his ball and chain with a difference" (qtd. in Noble 33). But when Pollard's *Uncle Tom's Cabin* was re-released by Jules B. Weill and Carroll L. Puciato of Colorama Features, Inc., with a prologue by Raymond Massey and a new soundtrack, in 1958—a time when sit-ins were erupting in the South and other civil rights protests were occurring nationwide—"many wondered if by reissuing this film Universal Studios hoped to remind the restless black masses of an earlier, less turbulent period, when obeying one's master was the answer to every black man's problem" (Bogle, *TCMMB* 7).[19]

At the time of the original release of Pollard's *Uncle Tom's Cabin*, a rival picture was already in production, United Artists' *Topsy and Eva* (1927). Considered by many film historians to be the worst Tom adaptation or spinoff ever, it brimmed with overt racist stereotypes and demonstrated the Hollywood studios' ignorance of—and insensitivity to—black criticism. Starring Rosetta and Vivian Duncan, *Topsy and Eva* (fig. 1.4) was simply a cinematic extension of the popular blonde sisters' blackface minstrel act, which had grossed well over $900,000 a year, an extraordinary amount for the time, and which had played in twenty-three major American cities over a three-and-a-half-year period (Birdoff 401). United Artists eventually acquired the project, but director Lois Weber quit when she learned that she would not be allowed to shape a serious drama from the sisters' vaudeville routine. The studio then hired Del Lord, a director for Mack Sennett's comedies and serials (and eventually for the Three Stooges). When Lord reportedly started making "a mess of it," the producers turned to a director with more experience and reputation, D. W. Griffith, who claimed he had always wanted to do a Tom show. In ten days, Griffith reshot, recut, and patched *Topsy and Eva* into "a pathetic, regressive, burlesque of his racial beliefs" that proved to be a tribute more to Tom shows than to Tom himself; in this way, according to Thomas Cripps, Griffith's legendary racial cant "found its way into yet one more American film" (*SFB* 163, 165). Even as the

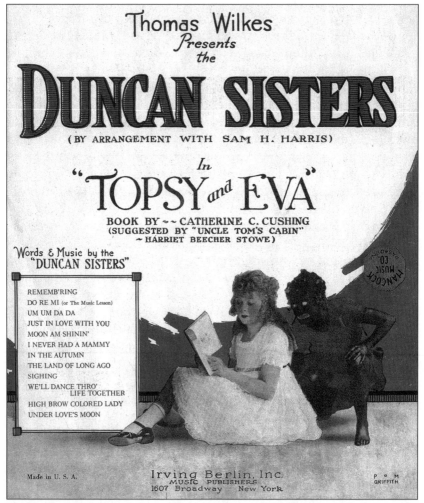

Figure 1.4. Sheet music from *Topsy and Eva*, a 1927 film in which the popular Duncan Sisters re-created their blackface minstrel act.

picture was opening, the studio still hoped to save it by bringing in an experienced cutter who had worked for Mary Pickford; nevertheless, the results were disastrous.

Drawing rather loosely on incidents and details from Stowe's novel, the film opens with several original miniature shots. A white stork races—and beats—the doctor to the St. Clare home to deliver the beautiful Little Eva on St. Valentine's Day. Two months later, a black stork raises havoc by flying through rain and lightning; after being turned away from the crude homes of several "colored folks," the stork simply drops Topsy into a barrel of trash. Above, in the "Colored Department" of Heaven, two black angels roll dice while another registers Topsy's birthdate, April Fool's Day.[20] The remainder of the film follows the two girls' comic—and often intertwined—adventures as Topsy ultimately saves the day by foiling Legree, who is carried over a waterfall to his death; restoring the rightful fortunes of Marietta De Brie, Legree's ward and Shelby's sweetheart; and bringing Eva back to life. ("Oh, Lord, don't take little missy!" reads Topsy's prayer. "Take me instead. You got plenty of white angels. Have a black one!" [Birdoff 402].) Played by the fine black actor and former filmmaker Noble Johnson, who tried unsuccessfully to preserve Tom's dignity, Uncle Tom is an incidental character who is relegated to minor scenes in the film as a kind of aged companion to the brash young Topsy. (Both, for example, are sold at the same auction, and later they are removed together from the St. Clare plantation by Legree.) Reviewers noted only that "he [Johnson] played in the meek fashion of the play and had no big moments to get over" (*Variety* 22 June 1927).

Over the next few decades, new versions of *Uncle Tom's Cabin* were discussed: in the late 1930s, by David O. Selznick, producer of the critically and commercially acclaimed plantation saga *Gone With the Wind* (1939), who proposed a new Uncle Tom film—and even, to that end, filed with the MPPDA (Motion Picture Producers and Directors of America); and in 1944, by Metro-Goldwyn-Mayer, which considered making a new movie version, with Lena Horne suggested for the role of Eliza, Margaret O'Brien for Eva, and Lewis Stone for Augustine St. Clare. But nothing came of either plan, in part because of objections raised by black organizations and liberal groups (Cripps, *Making Movies Black* 11 [cited henceforth as *MMB*]; Gossett 404),[21] which were drawing increased attention to the unrealistic and negative portrayals of blacks in Hollywood films.[22]

Throughout these years, however, Tom continued to be depicted in numerous cartoons and shorts that often employed his character for broad, crude humor: *Uncle Tom's Caboose* (Century/for Universal Films, 1920), a two-reeler directed by Jim Davis; *Alice Gets Stage Struck* (Walt Disney/M. J. Winkler Productions, 1925), a live-action frame story,[23] in which the popular Alice plays Little Eva in an *Uncle Tom's Cabin* show that she has staged; two animated shorts by Walter Lantz, *Colonel Heeza Liar in Uncle Tom's Cabin* (J. R. Bray, 1923; dir. Vernon Stallings) and *Dinky Doodle in Uncle Tom's Cabin* (Bray Studios, 1926; dir. Walter Lantz), featuring the familiar characters Colonel Heeza Liar and Dinky Doodle; *Uncle Tom's Crabbin'* (Educational Films, 1927), in which Felix the Cat outwits Simon Legree; *Topsy Turvey* (Paramount, 1927), whose hero is another feline, Krazy Kat; *Uncle Tom and Little Eva* (alternatively titled *Pickaninny Blues* [1932]); *Uncle Tom's Bungalow* (Warner Brothers, 1937), a Merrie Melodies Cartoon; and *Uncle Tom's Cabaña* (Metro-Goldwyn-Mayer, 1947), which climaxes with Uncle Tom opening a "chicken shack" at the corner of Hollywood and Vine.[24] As Thomas Cripps writes, the patently backward-looking cartoons proved "a particular nettle" to black audiences, especially black activists, who saw in the exaggeration of black style and idiom (e.g., the "mix of jive-talk, hepcat body english, and flashy zoot suits") a return to the Jim Crow tradition and a jarring offense to black sensibilities (*MMB* 197).[25]

The next film version of *Uncle Tom's Cabin* (1965; American distribution, 1968) was produced not by an American company but by a West German one, Melodie-Avala. *Onkle Toms Hütte* (dir. Géza van Radványi)—released in two versions, the original at two hours, the second edited to one hour—was filmed in Yugoslavia and included Eartha Kitt as a player and Ella Fitzgerald as a "dubbing voice." Full of self-righteous indignation that no American producer had wanted to refilm the Stowe classic, Kroger Babb, the distributor of the picture, "exclaimed that his version 'told the story of slavery in the Deep South with amazing accuracy and tremendous spectacle,' and that it also 'explained what no teacher can'" (Campbell, *CS* 183).[26]

In fact, *Onkle Toms Hütte* offered some spectacle but little accuracy. "Full of anachronisms and liberties," the production included Yugoslavian cavalrymen unconvincingly cast as "southern plantation types" and ruddy Serbian farm workers in ludicrous blackface as slaves. The result was unintentionally hilarious, noted a reviewer for *Variety* (19 May 1965), who also commented on the chases and barroom brawls that "come off, at best, as stereotypes from some American Western."

Radványi's alterations to Stowe's novel were as radical as they were silly. Purportedly a guest in the Shelby household, the grossly scarred Lagree [*sic*] is actually there to collect on Shelby's bad investment in a gold mine: ten slaves (including Uncle Tom [John Kitzmiller], who asks to be sold as part of the biblical invocation "to lay down his life for a friend") in trade for the ten notes Lagree holds. After saving the life of Eva, Tom is purchased by her grateful father Saint Claire [*sic*], who by coincidence happens to be Lagree's neighbor. But when Eva dies (her death, in this version, precipitated by her father's affair with his mistress), Saint Claire agrees to grant her dying wish that their slaves be freed. Yet on the very day—Independence Day—that the manumission is to occur, Saint Claire is shot by Lagree and his murder blamed on a young black barman, who is promptly lynched by a mob of slave owners. Finding himself indentured once again, Tom rescues Lagree's reluctant mistress from being trampled by the evil master's team of horses, an act of heroism and defiance for which he is severely flogged. With his dying breath, Tom urges the other slaves to run away. They do—and, after a Western-style shoot-out at the monastery in which they have taken shelter, they escape on a boat chartered for them by Eliza's husband George Harris, a former slave.

Apart from its absurd departures from its source and its own glaring plot inconsistencies, *Onkle Toms Hütte* is memorable only for the gruesomeness of some of the scenes, like the death by alligator of the young slave Napoleon after he jumps ship, and for its recasting of the Old South as the Wild West. Not simply a bad reinterpretation of Stowe's novel, *Onkle Toms Hütte* is a bad film, and one that proves the extent to which the stereotyping of Uncle Tom had permeated film culture not just nationally but internationally as well.

It was not until 1987—in a Showtime/Edgar J. Scherick Associates Production/Taft Entertainment Television version of *Uncle Tom's Cabin*, directed by Stan Lathan and starring Avery Brooks (Uncle Tom), Phylicia Rashad (Eliza), Samuel L. Jackson (George Harris), Edward Woodward (Legree), and Bruce Dern (St. Clare)—that Tom was finally allowed the opportunity to transcend his cinematic stereotype. According to executive producer Scherick, Stowe's novel was "a good yarn," and he felt that it was time to revive it. Scherick was also interested in correcting the misimpressions about the story, which had "changed from an antislavery novel into an anti-Negro play." By restoring the strength and virility of the original character of Tom, Scherick hoped to make people "understand why this novel had the tremendous social and political impact that it did" (Stephen Farber, *NYT* 13 June 1987: I50).

The first American sound version of *Uncle Tom's Cabin*—and the first new American version since Pollard's film sixty years before—Scherick's adaptation for the cable network Showtime was not only contemporary but also occasionally revisionist (e.g., Eliza escapes the slave traders by riding a frail raft across a stream, not by leaping across ice floes on the river); yet in other significant ways, it followed closely the plot of Stowe's novel—more closely, in fact, than previous versions did. As John O'Connor noted in his *New York Times* review, the film attempted to go "back to the original source and to set the record straight." By toning down the stereotyping and paring away the broad theatrical elements, veteran television writer John Gay got "back to the core" of the actual people about whom Stowe wrote and effectively distilled her compassion and moral outrage (*NYT* 12 June 1987: C30). "As a portrait of slave life," concluded another reviewer, *Uncle Tom's Cabin* continues to "show slaves singing to ease their burdens; [but] it also has the strength to show much of that burden" (*Variety* 17 June 1987).

Shot in and around Natchez, Mississippi, the film strove for realism in the depiction of its characters: Uncle Tom is portrayed not as old and long-suffering but as young, dignified, and courageous—a man whose behavior is governed by his religious convictions, a man whose body may be bought but whose soul cannot be touched (O'Connor 30). Edward Woodward's Simon Legree is "poor-white mean and downright stinging" (*Variety* 17 June 1987), a legendary villain who is actually believable. And Cassy (Paula Kelly) and Emmeline (Troy Beyer), both victims of Legree's brutality, convey the urgency of their plight and the precariousness of their plan to escape. (The Cassy and Emmeline episode, so crucial to the book, is downplayed or even eliminated in earlier adaptations.)

Director Stan Lathan admits that he initially had reservations about taking on the movie. Lathan had already directed other literary projects, including an award-winning television adaptation of James Baldwin's *Go Tell It on the Mountain* (1984). Yet friends warned him "to leave [*Uncle Tom's Cabin*] alone." Even the Hollywood chapter of the National Association for the Advancement of Colored People (NAACP) was apprehensive about a new adaptation. But Lathan "liked the challenge this production presented: a black man's interpretation of a white woman's interpretation of black reality—a reverse of *The Color Purple*" (O'Connor 30). And, like Scherick, he felt motivated both by the importance of the book itself, which "pointed out the horrors of slavery [and the fact] that black Americans had strong human qualities," and by the desire to retrieve Stowe's original conception of Uncle Tom, "an admirable figure . . . a man of God with a sense of community and a strong sense of family . . . an inspiration to everyone around him" (Farber 50).

In Avery Brooks, the film found precisely the kind of hero that Scherick and Lathan envisioned. Starring at the time as the formidable Hawk in the television series *Spenser: For Hire*, Brooks based his powerful performance in large part on the life of Josiah Henson, a slave who escaped to Canada and then published an autobiography in 1849. Brooks's Tom is steadfast in his principles and resilient in his spirit; his forceful yet nuanced portrayal contributes to what *Variety* called the innocence of the first part of the film and the momentum "that capture[s] the imagination" in the second.

Just as Stowe's novel did, the film effectively utilized contrasting images: the congenial atmosphere at the St. Clare home vs. the wretched desolation of Legree's house, for instance, and the humane treatment that Eliza and George receive at the hands of the Quakers (fig. 1.5) vs. the brutality that Tom experiences from

Figure 1.5. The Harrises (Samuel L. Jackson and Phylicia Rashad) revel in their newfound freedom in *Uncle Tom's Cabin*, the first American non-silent version of Stowe's enduring story. *(Showtime, 1987)*

Legree. And while the film devotes considerably less attention to some of the novel's particulars—the details of Tom's family life with Aunt Chloe at the Shelby plantation; the developing relationship between Tom and Eva before her illness (which occurs much earlier in the film than in the novel); the way in which Tom rediscovers his religion at Legree's—it nonetheless evokes the essence of the classic story, especially by visually emphasizing Stowe's themes (e.g., the theme of redemption, reinforced by the image of

Tom being strapped to a cross and flogged). A vision not just of its own age but of Stowe's as well, Lathan's film succeeds largely by shattering the traditional cinematic Uncle Tom stereotype.

OTHER TOM STEREOTYPES

To be sure, that particular stereotype was not restricted to remakes or adaptations of Stowe's novel; in hundreds of shorts and feature films, the Tom became a familiar character that white movie audiences came to like and black audiences grew to hate. The Tom's loyalty could reach ridiculous extremes, as in the pair of films that D. W. Griffith produced several years before his divisive *Birth of a Nation* (which, in the character of the Camerons's faithful retainer, also featured a Tom). In Griffith's two-part story of *His Trust* and *His Trust Fulfilled* (Biograph, 1911), the devoted black servant stays with his owners throughout the Civil War, saves their little daughter and his late master Colonel Frazier's sword when Union soldiers burn the house, and—after the war and the death of Mrs. Frazier—sacrifices his meager savings to educate the girl and make it possible for her to marry well (an ironic and particularly disturbing plot twist, as Daniel Bernardi points out, given "that the restriction of African Americans from education was a tool used to maintain slavery and segregation" [116]). After glimpsing the wedding at a distance and watching the newlyweds depart, "Old George" returns to his little cabin, takes down the Colonel's saber, and fondles it happily. Clearly, as Bernardi demonstrates, "the sword is a prominent symbol of George's devotion and loyalty to the values and ideals of both the South and the white patriarch." But, since it confers no power on the domesticated slave, the sword is also an emblem of "George's perpetual servitude"; in fact, "once put in charge of the sword, George loses everything—his shack, his money, and all ties to black culture—making him more a slave after the North's victory than before."[27] Aged, alone, and impoverished, George receives neither recompense nor recognition for his lifetime of unselfishness apart from a handshake from the bridegroom. (Earlier, even the bride had ignored George's proffered hand.) But he is content in the knowledge that he has fulfilled his trust. And that, suggests Griffith, is adequate reward. As Thomas Cripps notes, through George's behavior, which "apart from the veiled and probably unconscious sexuality, [is marked by] his fealty, his ardor in the absence of personal gain, and his treasuring of white expressions of gratitude, all [of which] formed the outline of blacks on screen for years to come," Griffith "gave future moviemakers a model, a cinematic language, and a rich romantic tradition that would define an Afro-American stereotype" (*SFB* 29).[28]

Like Old George, who is willing to give his life not only for his master and his master's family but even for their possessions, Uncle Wash in *Hearts and Flags* (1911) protects Colonel Dabney's daughter from Union foragers; a black family in *The Informer* (1912) saves the master's house from being burned by Federal forces; and faithful slaves in *A Special Messenger, Mammy's Ghost or Between the Lines of Battle* (1911), and *Uncle Pete's Ruse* (1911) conceal wounded Confederate soldiers from Yankee patrols. (Uncle Pete is especially inventive; he paints smallpox on the family to prevent Union soldiers from entering the home and discovering the rebel.) Uncle Mose, "loyal to his savior, but even more loyal to his master" (*SFB* 32), rescues his master from prison in *None Can Do More* and dies in his cause. Jim, the loyal slave in *A Slave's Devotion* (1913), rebels not against the institution of slavery but against his cruel overseer; after becoming a Confederate runner, he even saves his old master, Colonel Trent. Old Mose exhibits a comparable loyalty in *The Old Oak's Secret* (1914): since it contains a manumission clause that would force him to leave his plantation home, Mose hides his master's will in a tree. And like Old Mose, Uncle Dan in *Marse Covington* (1915) refuses to take advantage of his legal right to freedom; instead he shares with his master the years of misfortune that follow the loss of Covington's property and money.[29]

Toms found their way into many later sound films as well, especially into period plantation movies like those starring Shirley Temple and Bill "Bojangles" Robinson. In *The Little Colonel* (1935), for example, a film adapted from the novel by Annie Fellows Johnston, Robinson, as the faithful family retainer Walker, dutifully attends old Colonel Lloyd (Lionel Barrymore) and his granddaughter, Miss Lloyd Shermon (Temple). And in *The Littlest Rebel* (1935), Uncle Billy (Robinson) becomes guardian to Virgie Cary (Temple) after Yankees invade the plantation, her mother dies, and her father is taken to a Northern prison. Billy protects the little girl and helps get her to Washington, where President Lincoln pardons her father; significantly, however, Lincoln does not free Billy, who returns with his master and little mistress to their happy life in the South (although he is noticeably absent in the final scenes).[30] Another fine black actor, Clarence Muse, also portrayed lots of good Toms throughout his career, including Uncle Nappus in *Hearts in Dixie* (1929) and Huck's friend, the kindly slave Jim, in *Huckleberry Finn* (1931); but even after brief forays into directing, screenwriting, and consulting on film productions, Muse—like most black actors of his day—found himself typecast in subservient roles. Even the smart, refined middle-class characters played by Sidney Poitier in the 1950s and 1960s were, as Donald Bogle suggests, reminiscent in many respects of "the old [unselfish, mild-mannered Tom] type that America had always cherished." As militant student Gregory Miller in *The Blackboard Jungle* (1955), for instance, Poitier comes to the assistance of the white teacher (Glenn Ford) who represents the oppressive system that Miller so vehemently opposes; as the kind, hardworking Tommy Tyler in *Edge of the City* (1957), he befriends—and ultimately sacrifices his life for—a white army deserter (John Cassavetes); and, as Noah Cullen in *The Defiant Ones* (1958), he gives up his own freedom to rescue a white man, a fellow convict played by Tony Curtis. When insulted or badgered, the Poitier character (who, additionally, was denied opportunities for sexual expression) generally stood by and took it—although, unlike earlier "good Negroes" in the movies such as Bill Robinson who accepted their Tommish treatment, at times he "screamed out in rage at the injustices of a white racist society" (*TCMMB* 176). Still, Poitier's articulate yet ultimately acquiescent characters, like earlier Toms, usually posed little actual threat to the white establishment.

THE BIRTH OF A NATION

Whereas the submissive black character of Uncle Tom was introduced in Porter's *Uncle Tom's Cabin*, it was another film, D. W. Griffith's controversial *Birth of a Nation* (1915), that popularized an even uglier image—the brutal black male, or black buck—and reinforced most of the other black stereotypes that had been developing in movies since the 1890s and on stage throughout the last half of the nineteenth century. Griffith's film was based largely on *The Clansman* (1905), the second in a trilogy of novels by former Southern Baptist minister Thomas Dixon and on a dramatization of the novel that was produced the following year.[31] Retrogressive and racist, Dixon was as romantic in his glorification of the Old South as he was vicious in his depiction of black Americans, and he used his works—all of which were notorious for their attacks on liberal ideological movements like integration, feminism, and pacifism—as an attempt to counter the anti-slavery sentiments of Stowe's *Uncle Tom's Cabin*. Reportedly, his inspiration for *The Clansman* came in 1901 at a performance of a Tom play (Williams, *Race* 101). Infuriated by what he saw as the injustice of the play's attitude toward the South, he vowed to tell what he considered to be the "true story" of American history, from the glory of the antebellum South to the evils of miscegenation and postwar reconstruction and finally to the emergence of the Ku Klux Klan, an order of contemporary knights whose holy quest, in Dixon's view, was the restoration of the American way of life (or rather Dixon's idea of the American way of life). At the opening of a stage version of his novel in 1906, Dixon spoke at the intermission about his hopes and intentions:

> My object is to teach the north, the young north, what it has never known—the awful suffering of the white man during the dreadful reconstruction period. I believe that Almighty God anointed the white men of the south by their suffering during that time . . . to demonstrate to the world that the white man must and shall be supreme. (qtd. in Cripps, *SFB* 44)

The panoramic sweep of *The Clansman* certainly appealed to Griffith, whose own vision was as epic and whose perspectives on history were as sentimentalized as Dixon's. Born a child of the Confederacy in Kentucky in 1875, Griffith was steeped in an atmosphere of racial intolerance. Keenly sensitive to the South—its travails, its burden of race, its rural inferiority—and full of reverence for its heroes, among whom were numbered some of Griffith's own forebears (including his father, "Roaring Jake"

Griffith, a Confederate veteran), he displayed a "unique mind-set [that] made him the most credible interpreter of Southern and black experience on film, at least to a generation wanting relief from the clatter of urban change, with the result that the new Negro of the cities was drowned in the martial vision of Griffith's Southland" (*SFB* 26-27).[32] Not only in *His Trust* and *His Trust Fulfilled* but also in the scores of other Civil War melodramas like *In Old Kentucky* and *The Battle* that he produced for Biograph and released between 1909 and 1911, Griffith promoted his racist attitudes about "faithful" and "right-thinking Negroes"—attitudes that most Southerners shared and that many Northerners and Middle Westerners casually accepted. As long as the black stayed loyal to his family and his land, Griffith's films seemed to say, all was right with the world; the black's mistreatment, impoverishment, or other sacrifices were inconsequential.

It was Biograph writer and scenarist Frank Woods who arranged a meeting with Griffith, Dixon, and several possible backers for the film, after which the director and the novelist struck a deal that included not only the purchase of the idea and royalties on the production but also the promise of collaboration in the actual filmmaking. Soon after the Christmas holidays of 1913, Griffith and Dixon left for the West Coast, whose atmosphere, suggests Cripps, reinforced their traditional Southern values. Remote from urban life, the two romanticized the Old South; cast several actual Southerners (like Henry B. Walthall, who played Ben Cameron, and Lillian Gish, Griffith's favorite actress at the time) in key roles; and even replicated Dixie to the extent of segregating the barracks of the black extras, most of whom were Californians so grateful to have work that they did not complain (*SFB* 45). According to Karl Brown, Griffith's assistant camera operator, the director also instructed the carpenters to build the street set in such a way as to re-create the familiar and crucial architecture of the "Tom shows."[33]

As the rising cost of the production forced Griffith to continue raising capital throughout the summer and into the fall of 1914, several adaptations were prepared, including one based on Dixon's unsuccessful dramatization of his novel and written for Dixon by Frank Woods (eventually billed as Griffith's co-scenarist on the project); yet Griffith is said to have worked largely without a written script. Rehearsed for six weeks, filmed in nine weeks, and edited for three months,[34] the film previewed under the title *The Clansman* in California early in 1915 and premiered under its new title *The Birth of a Nation* a few weeks later in New York. In an age during which most films were crude shorts made on small budgets, Griffith's $100,000 spectacle was a polished, well-edited, and well-lit masterwork with an unprecedented running time of two and a half hours (twelve reels). After a private screening of the film in the White House,[35] President Woodrow Wilson, one of Dixon's former classmates at Johns Hopkins, reportedly compared it to "writing history with lightning" and regretted "that it is all so horribly true" (qtd. in Bosley, "Birth" 80, and elsewhere).

Contrary to Wilson's pronouncement (which Wilson later disavowed), *The Birth of a Nation* was not horribly true; but it was remarkable in other ways. Griffith, a bigot in his politics, proved to be a technical genius in his filmmaking. Utilizing numerous innovations in cross-cutting, close-up and fade-out shots, effect lighting, iris shots, and split screens, he was able to create stunning images and sequences like the battle scenes and chases. Most surprising, perhaps, was Griffith's reworking of Dixon's novel into a compelling (although still poisonously racist) story of the Cameron family, who—along with their happy and devoted slaves—lead an idyllic existence in Piedmont, South Carolina. That existence, of course, is shattered by the Civil War. Terrorized by Negro raiders during the war, the Camerons must deal with even more horrors during Reconstruction, as carpetbaggers and Northern blacks move into the area and exploit the Southern former slaves by unleashing their bestial natures and turning them into renegades. Under the new "Negro rulership," blacks begin subverting the whole social order: they push whites off the walkways, steal their property, keep them from the ballot boxes, turn a legislative session into an occasion for chicken-eating and whiskey-chugging rather than goverance, and—worst of all, in the film's view—assault white women and attempt to intermarry. Meanwhile, the Northern Senator Austin Stoneman, patriarch of the Pennsylvania Stonemans whose lives have become intertwined with the Camerons, insists on pushing for the equal rights of blacks.[36] After first dispatching his mulatto protégé Silas Lynch "to aid the carpetbaggers in organizing and wielding the power of the Negro vote" (according to the title card), Stoneman travels to Piedmont and sees for himself the damage that has been wrought. As blacks continue to terrorize whites, even Gus (Walter Long), a former Cameron family slave, becomes "the product of the vicious doctrine spread by carpetbaggers." In a harrowing seven-minute sequence, Gus pursues the Camerons's daughter Flora (Mae Marsh) through the woods until she jumps to her death into a ravine to escape his lecherous advances.[37] Then Lynch (played by white actor George Seigmann in dark theatrical makeup to heighten the effect of his blackness, which Griffith equated with savagery) presumes to marry Elsie Stoneman, portrayed by the light-haired, pale-skinned Lillian Gish.[38] When Elsie refuses, he binds and gags her in order to enact a "forced marriage."

The social chaos created by arrogant and aggressive blacks in *The Birth of a Nation* leads the disenfranchised Southerners to form the Ku Klux Klan, who begin their nights of terror by capturing, castrating (a scene excised from most versions), and murdering Gus and depositing his corpse on the mulatto Lynch's doorstep.[39] After learning of Lynch's intention to marry his daughter, Stoneman finally recognizes the error of his views on racial equality (which the film attributes to the wiles of his mulatta mistress and housekeeper, whom Griffith calls the "weakness that is to blight a nation"). Naturally, Ben Cameron and his fellow Klansmen rescue Elsie in time to thwart Lynch's evil plans and to save Dr. Cameron and his family from the renegade blacks who have surrounded the cabin where they are hiding; and, in a symbolic new union of opposing sides, Ben and Elsie join Phil and Margaret Cameron on a double honeymoon. With the white Southerners again in command and the blacks obediently under control, the world is set aright—a conclusion reinforced by Griffith's final original allegorical shot, of Christ ascending into Heaven after having vanquished the God of War.

If the film was like history written by lightning, then the black response could only be analogized as thunderous. With immediacy and intensity, blacks decried *The Birth of a Nation* as sheer propaganda for the Ku Klux Klan, who actually used it as an organizing and recruiting tool;[40] and they argued—correctly—that the film's sympathetic portrayal of mob violence as a kind of divine retribution would lead to more lynchings.[41] (The Klan itself had been revived and reinvigorated in 1915 by Joseph Simmons, an ex-minister "inspired" by the film. As Terry Ramsaye observed, "The picture . . . and the K.K.K. secret society, which was the afterbirth of a nation, were sprouted from the same root."[42]) The NAACP, formed a few years earlier in 1909, picketed the New York premiere; branches of that organization in other cities led large demonstrations against the film's showings. Some of those demonstrations were minimally effective: in Boston, for example, Mayor James Curley—in an effort to keep black votes—agreed to small cuts before the film was screened. Yet he defended the film and argued that its characterizations were no more grotesque than Shakespeare's. A few black protesters in Boston managed to get by the two hundred police officers stationed outside the Tremont, a segregated theater: inside, they egged the screen and threw a stink bomb into the crowd; outside, brawls erupted.[43]

Religious and civic groups joined the various protests nationwide, and a number of newspaper editorials came out strongly against the picture's racism. White reviewer Jane Addams wrote caustically that the movie misused history and that Griffith gathered "the most vicious and grotesque individuals he could find among the colored people" and then tried to show them "as representatives of the . . . entire race" (*SFB* 58). The black press, even more direct in its attacks, used the film as a vehicle to promote black self-determination and to encourage filmmakers to provide more complimentary and realistic representations of black life in their productions. James Weldon Johnson, for instance, charged in the *New York Age* (15 April 1915), "Not in this whole picture, which is supposed to represent the birth and growth of the nation, is there one single Negro who is both intelligent and decent" (Regester, "Press" 36). Lester Walton, publisher of the *New York Age*, angry that Griffith had managed to create the perception that blacks were not "true" Americans, demanded action. Hinting darkly that the matter would be regarded differently had it been the Jews and the Irish who were so badly maligned, Walton concluded that "the photoplay is vicious, untrue, unjust, and had been primarily produced to cause friction in Northern cities" (*SFB* 58). As *The Crisis* editor W. E. B. Du Bois reported, while the backlash may have failed "to kill *The Birth of a Nation*, [at least] it succeeded in wounding it" (Gaines, *FD* 230).

Griffith professed shock at blacks' resentment of his work and, somewhat disingenuously, pointed to one of the opening titles that explicitly stated the film did not reflect on "any race or people." He added that "[saying I am racist] is like saying I am against children, as they [Negroes] were our children, whom we loved and cared for all our lives."[44] Famously, he offered to contribute $10,000 to charity if Moorfield Storey, the white head of the Boston branch of the NAACP, could find a single example of historical inaccuracy in the film—an offer Storey declined because he refused to view the film. And until his death in the late 1940s, Griffith continued to maintain that *Birth of a Nation* was not a racial attack.[45] Dixon, on the other hand, countered the criticism of his part in the controversial motion picture by saying that he did not hate blacks, just the mixing of black blood with white, and suggested that even Abraham Lincoln would have admired his position.

Despite the controversy, which continued for years with each proposed or scheduled revival of the film, *The Birth of a Nation* was a tremendous commercial success; even at the steep ticket prices that Griffith charged, the film found a large and receptive audience.[46] (By the end of 1915 alone, an estimated six percent of the American population had seen the film [Leab 34].) And precisely for that reason—the enormity of Griffith's audience and the ease with which they accepted his racial cant—Griffith was able to shape the way that blacks would be portrayed in American films for years to come. Of the many stereotypes that *The Birth of a Nation* fixed in the popular mind, probably the ugliest and most damning was that of the brutal black or the black buck; a far cry from the complacent and grateful slave of cinema lore, he was unlike anything ever seen before on screen. Oversexed and barbaric to the point of being subhuman, the buck lacked all sense of conscience: in Griffith's film he expressed his rage through his frequent physical assaults—on white men, even on the Camerons's black slave and other loyal black family retainers. But, for many white viewers, his most frightening characteristic was a lust for white women, which whipped him into a frenzy and led to his most heinous attacks. For those white viewers, Gus's pursuit of Flora, which results in her suicide, and Lynch's coercion and literal bondage of Elsie simply illustrated the hideous extreme of the rapacious buck's behavior. (By comparison, as Michele Wallace notes, in an earlier scene, an ordinary white Union soldier stares longingly at Elsie but does not dare to speak to her. "The inference is that the good man of superior race holds his tongue and settles for unrequited passion whereas the man of inferior race has no control over his passions" ["*Within*" 61].)

It is through these two characters of Gus and Lynch, "one always panting and salivating, the other forever stiffening his body as if the mere presence of a white woman in the same room could bring him to a sexual climax," Donald Bogle writes, that Griffith revealed the tie between sex and racism in America.[47] By playing on "the myth of the Negro's high-powered sexuality" and then articulating the great white fear that every black man longs for a white woman, both because she is desirable and because she symbolizes "white pride, power, and beauty" (*TCMMB* 13-14), Griffith portrayed the black male as innately animalistic and psychopathic. Fear of rampant black sexuality, after all, was—as Bowser and Spence demonstrate—a cornerstone of white supremacist ideology, and the image of the black male as savage brute who wanted only to violate the sanctity of Southern womanhood became a "powerful weapon used by white men to reassert control over Black labor in the post-slavery age" ("*Symbol*" 82). To reinforce that negative perception, Griffith repeatedly used stereotype to emphasize the physical ugliness of his black characters and the repugnant, animalistic features of their bodies: their flat feet, their yellow eyes, their large noses and mouths, their inability to stand up straight.[48] Worst of all, knowing that such a bestial screen type could arouse only hatred, Griffith exploited it at every opportunity in his film.[49]

The image of the hulking and lusting black buck was thus indelibly etched.[50] But, unlike the subservient Tom or the "faithful soul" (the acquiescent black who knew and kept his place in *The Birth of a Nation* and Griffith's other pictures), the buck did not become ubiquitous—largely because that image ran counter to the enduring plantation myth of contented blacks as well as to the Southern thinking that rationalized slavery because it was in the best interests of the blacks who were enslaved. While the buck was occasionally featured in early films like *Broken Chains* (1916), most studios remained mindful of the controversy over Griffith's production and refrained from depicting so hostile and explosive a character. *Free and Equal* (1915), for instance, the only picture of the period to approach Griffith's "in a direct appeal to race hatred" (Reddick 9), was not released until late 1924 because its producer Thomas Ince insisted on waiting until the initial adverse criticism of *The Birth of a Nation* had simmered down. The two films, in fact, portrayed similar characters: like the Northern Senator Stoneman, the liberal Northern Judge Lowell in *Free and Equal* bets that blacks are equal to whites. But after Alexander Marshall (played, in black-face, by white actor Jack Richardson) hotly pursues Lowell's daughter, rapes and strangles the family's maid, and reveals at his trial that he has wed the Judge's daughter (even though he is already married to a Negro woman), the embittered and disillusioned Lowell tears up the lengthy treatise he had been writing in favor of intermarriage, since "the 'perfect' Negro" has been exposed as "the perfect rogue" (Bogle, *TCMMB* 25). With exceptions such as the African jungle movies and the quasi-historical Southern film *So Red the Rose* (1935), based on a novel by Stark Young, in which old Cato (played by Clarence Muse, in a departure from his usual role as the faithful Tom or benign servant) leads his fellow slaves in a short-lived rebellion that is quelled by their young mistress (Margaret Sullavan), it would be more than half a century before overtly aggressive or sexually assertive blacks made their way back to the screen. As Donald Bogle and other film historians have demonstrated, it took the success of Melvin Van Peebles's *Sweet Sweetback's Baadasssss Song* (1971) to signal that the times had changed sufficiently for audiences to accept a radicalized and sexualized black; the screen was then bombarded with an array of heroes descended from the buck in films such as *Shaft* (1971), *Superfly* (1972), *Slaughter* (1972), and *Melinda* (1972).[51] And those films, in turn, opened up an entirely new genre of black action pictures (and arguably a new "type" as well).

THE MULATTO STEREOTYPE

If brutish blacks were to be avoided, mulatto characters were to be embraced—at least by filmmakers, who recognized their box office appeal. On screen, especially in white studio productions, mulattoes were typically portrayed as malicious, duplicitous, and conniving figures whose only concern was to better their status. Their attempts to assimilate and to insinuate themselves into a culture that was not properly their own, moreover, posed a threat to the social order, challenged the racist exclusions of white society, and played into white fears of "mongrelization" of the races. The very presence of mulattoes also raised the ugly specter of interraciality, especially interracial sexuality—although ironically, as Jane Gaines and others have shown, the very mulatto class that white filmmakers sought to discredit was the vestige of slavery days and "the product of the indiscretion of the men of the planter class" (*FD* 188).

In literature, the mulatto had become an effective device for contrasting black and white cultures, and "passing" developed into a literary trope that offered rich possibilities for writers such as Frances E. W. Harper (*Iola Leroy, or, Shadows Uplifted* [1892]), Charles Chesnutt (*The House Behind the Cedars* [1899]), Sutton E. Griggs (*The Hindered Hand* [1905]), James Weldon Johnson (*The Autobiography of an Ex-Colored Man* [1912]), Walter White (*Flight* [1926]), Jessie Fauset (*Plum Bun* [1928]), and Nella Larsen (*Passing* [1929]). Kate Chopin revealed in her bold late-nineteenth-century story "Désirée's Baby" just how great a scourge black blood could be. After the darkness of Désirée's baby raises questions about the orphaned mother's racial purity and about the ways that black blood can surface after generations of whiteness, a crazed Désirée carries the baby into a swamp; but the discovery of a lost letter proves that Désirée's aristocratic white husband Armand is actually the parent with black blood.

For filmmakers, the opportunities were even more dramatic; yet black and white filmmakers took diametrically opposite approaches. Early black filmmakers learned to use the passing theme subversively: to refute silently and stoically white misconceptions about black characteristics and capabilities and to undermine white attempts to create racially pure cultural spaces (Gaines, *FD* 158). Oscar Micheaux turned repeatedly to the passing story as a version of race pride and black community affiliation: presumably "white" characters Agnes Stewart in *The Homesteader* (1919) and George Eldridge Van Paul in *Thirty Years Later* (1928) happily discover their black racial heritage, while the light-skinned mulatta Rena Walden (in the silent *The House Behind the Cedars* [1924/1925] and in the sound remake of that film, *Veiled Aristocrats* [1932], both adapted from Chesnutt's novel) renounces her decision to pass and reclaims her black identity by re-racialization.[52]

White filmmakers, however, employed the character type of the mulatto in a far more stereotypic way: to evoke horror and titillation. Contrary to Micheaux's films, in which racial discovery or affirmation brought acceptance and happiness, the passing or mixed-blood story in white productions inevitably led to rejection, death, or other disastrous results.[53] In *The Birth of a Nation*, Griffith had vilified both Silas Lynch, the mulatto leader of renegade blacks and defiler of white women, and Lydia Brown, Senator Stoneman's mulatta mistress, who blinded him to the evil ends for which some blacks were using him.[54] Yet while Griffith's film helped to popularize the stereotype, mulatto characters had already appeared in quite a few earlier short films. And in almost all instances, their racial taint contributed directly to their treachery and served as the basis for some misfortune or tragic event. As Jim Pines observed, the initial portrayals were of "a thoroughly wicked and villainous character whose destructive anguish provided the plot's principal antagonistic element. . . . In impact certainly, these villainous mulattoes were far more viciously caricatured than their relatively simplistic counterpart, the conventional black character" (67). In *In Slavery Days* (1913), for instance, Carlotta, an octoroon substituted during childhood for the daughter of the Warners, turns into a half-caste monster who, out of jealousy over a suitor, sells the real daughter Tennessee into slavery. (Tennessee, of course, is soon rescued from the slave traders, while the evil Carlotta is burned to death along with her mother, who had originally substituted Carlotta for Tennessee, in a cabin that has been set afire during a quarrel between them.)

Even in slightly more liberal characterizations, the mixed-blood characters' hopes for love or happiness were dashed because of their shameful racial impurity, which white filmmakers used iconically "to reflect (and advocate) a particularly obsessive aspect of American racism, i.e. that culture's tremendous fear of, and profound disgust at, even the mere thought of inter-racial sexuality." According to Pines, "in all these early mulatto/octoroon characterizations the idea of having mixed blood (and therefore, by implication, the idea of miscegenation) was superlatively degrading, fundamentally evil, and necessarily unforgivable" (67); consequently, it resulted in some form of literal or symbolic self-destruction or both. For example, in *The Nigger* (later cut and retitled *The New Governor*), a film made by Fox in 1915 and based on the popular play of the same name by Edward Sheldon, Philip Morrow (William Farnum), a newly-elected governor, learns from his rival Cliff Noyes that he has black blood. The discovery compels Morrow to resign his office, give up his life of public service, and sacrifice his relationship with a white woman, Georgiana Byrd, who loves him and wants to stay with him. In *In Humanity's Cause* (1911), the outcome is even more devastating, as a wounded Confederate officer is saved by a transfusion of blood that comes from a black man. The title card reads "Blood Will Tell," and soon—according to the film's logic—it does just that: the officer, now a man of "mixed blood," is changed from a pleasant and loving fellow into a brute so disgusting that he repulses even his sweetheart. The horror of his racial situation so overwhelms any possible sense of gratitude that he hunts down his black donor and grapples with him at the edge of a cliff; locked arm-in-arm, they fall to their deaths below. Like Flora in *The Birth of a Nation*, who chooses death over the thought of sexual relations with a black man, the officer prefers death to the knowledge that he is racially impure. In *The Octoroon* (ca. 1911), which was based on the successful play by Dion Boucicault, Zoe, the octoroon of the title, brings sorrow to all who are associated with her: by the end of the film, Mrs. Peyton, Zoe's former mistress, is impoverished; her son George Peyton is brokenhearted over Zoe's loss; a little boy is murdered; and Zoe herself is dead from poison, which she prefers to life as a slave of the evil McCloskey, her new master. And in *The Debt* (1912), a young man fathers children by both his wife and his octoroon mistress; the children grow up, meet, and fall in love, only to find out melodramatically, on the eve of their marriage, that they are brother and sister. According to the film, far worse than the ruined relationships and the disrupted lives is the mere presence of black blood. The only happy outcome in these types of films is the revelation that the suspicion of mixed raciality turns out to be a mistake: in *The Bar Sinister* (1917), for instance, Annabelle Stilliter, who is convinced that a drop of black blood has made her "a Negress!," is overjoyed to learn that she is pure white after all. (Her "whiteness" is proven by a "mark on her arm made by her father when he threw a glass over the railing of the porch of their old house in a fit of rage at a negro" [*Variety* 20 April 1917].)

Perhaps the most popular and recognizable "tragic mulatto"-type in white-produced films was the light-skinned Peola in *Imitation of Life* (1934), a film based on Fannie Hurst's best-selling novel. After repudiating her dark-skinned mother Delilah (Louise Beavers) and her own black heritage, Peola (Fredi Washington) runs away from home; but her rebellious actions only hasten Delilah's death and force her own return in order to weep belatedly at Delilah's casket. Although, as black viewers were quick to realize, Peola does not so much want to be white as to have "white opportunities" (Bogle, *TCMMB* 60), her mixed blood nonetheless consigns her to a typically tragic cinematic fate. *Imitation of Life*, which broke new ground by the casting of a black actress in the mulatto part and by the realistic treatment of her situation, proved to be one of the most lucrative and important films of the 1930s. Its box-office success convinced Hollywood to put more black-themed and even black-cast films into production and led to both a revival in the 1940s and a remake in 1959. But the remake was as retrogressive as it was formulaic: the Delilah character, renamed Annie (Juanita Moore), subordinates herself to her white employer (Lana Turner) as much by choice as by necessity, while the Peola character, renamed Sarah Jane (Susan Kohner), is almost pathological in her self-hatred and race denial. When her secret is discovered, Sarah Jane endures a brutal beating by her white boyfriend (Troy Donahue), after which she demeans herself further by running off to California to become a chorus girl. And like Peola, she returns only to throw herself on her mother's coffin and mourn the death that her selfish actions have caused.

The early depictions of the mulatto or mulatta, like those of Peola and Sarah Jane, evoked many of the emotive elements of moral guilt and retribution.[55] The denigrating perspective, however, changed somewhat in the late 1940s and into the 1950s, particularly with the 1949 cycle of black-oriented "problem" films, in which the mulatto/octoroon evolved from a "tragic" to an "unfortunate" type whose plight as a half-caste was viewed with sentimentality, occasionally even sympathy—and ultimately, as an ideological (if flawed) appeal for civil rights. Of those "problem" films, among the best was *Lost Boundaries* (1949), which was based on a true account of a black New England family who lived for more than two decades as whites. But when the small-town doctor, patriotic Scott Carter (Mel Ferrer), decides to enlist as an officer in the still-segregated Navy, his racial identity is revealed. The once-supportive community turns against him and his family until, in true Hollywood fashion, the white minister restores the peace by preaching a sermon on tolerance. Yet the would-be sins of the parents are visited upon the children: troubled son Howie embarks on a frightening odyssey of self-discovery through Harlem, and daughter Shelley feels so ostracized that she is unable to face even her fellow parishioners.

Similarly, in *Pinky* (1949), based on the novel *Quality* by Cid Ricketts Sumner, a fair-skinned nurse (Jeanne Crain) who has been passing for white in the North returns home to the South, where her grandmother Dicey (Ethel Waters) and an old white woman, Miss Em (Ethel Barrymore), teach her important lessons about self-respect. Ultimately, Pinky breaks up with her white fiancé, who initially is unaware of her black heritage; decides to stay in the South, where she successfully fights to keep the property that Miss Em has bequeathed to her; and turns it into a black nursing clinic. Although Waters brought great dignity to Dicey, her role was still circumscribed by cinematic tradition; and the film itself was typical of *Lost Boundaries* and of earlier tragic mulatto films (with the notable exception of the original *Imitation of Life*) in its casting of Jeanne Crain, a white actress, in the lead role and in its easy resolution of racial issues—Pinky's realization, for example, that she can be happy only by knowing her proper place.

The mulatto continued to fascinate Hollywood's white directors even into the late 1950s and 1960s—and the mulatta character continued to be played by white actresses like Ava Gardner, who appeared in *Show Boat* (1951), based on Edna Ferber's novel, as Julie, a woman whose doomed interracial love for Steve is expressed in the pathos of "Bill" and the other torch songs that she sings as well as in the film's narrative.[56] (As James Snead observed in his study of *White Screens, Black Images*, casting of whites as mulattoes made "sure that a visual ambiguity [did] not compound an already difficult conceptual leap" [5].) *Band of Angels* (1957) turned Robert Penn Warren's novel into a Civil War costume drama and love story between Amantha Starr (Yvonne De Carlo), a proud Southern belle who discovers that she has black blood, and Hamish Bond (Clark Gable), the ex-slave trader turned planter who "purchases" her, falls in love with her, and ultimately looks to her to secure his escape from Union soldiers. In *Kings Go Forth* (United Artists, 1958), a lovely Franco-American girl Monique Blair (Natalie Wood) is pursued by two American solders, Sam (Frank Sinatra) and Britt (Tony Curtis), who desert her at the hint of her mixed parentage. Like Pinky, she decides to turn her sorrow into good and opens her home to war orphans, who share her sense of social and cultural displacement. In the end, Sam returns to beg her forgiveness. Since both, however, are changed and injured people—he, by the recent loss of his arm; she, by her racial circumstance—the film retrogressively suggests that only a maimed white man could love a tainted woman (a resolution reminiscent of *Home of the Brave*, another of the "problem" films of 1949, in which a maimed white man, the amputee Mingo, befriends a fellow soldier, the psychologically scarred black Moss). Similarly, Susannah (Elizabeth Taylor), the white Civil War belle in *Raintree County* (1959), a film based on Ross Lockridge, Jr.'s novel, is doomed by the mere suspicion of racial impurity, which causes her mental collapse and death. Such mulatto-themed films, which teased white audiences with suggestions of interracial sexuality and of forbidden erotic desire, eventually started to fade in popularity[57] as Hollywood began exploring the related but decidedly more integrationist themes of interracial romance and marriage in films such as John Cassavetes's *Shadows* (1961), *One Potato, Two Potato* (1964), *A Patch of Blue* (1965), and *Guess Who's Coming to Dinner* (1967),[58] and as a new generation of actors like Sidney Poitier, Harry Belafonte, Dorothy Dandridge, and Lena Horne established themselves as stars in mainstream movies.

SERVANTS, DOMESTICS, AND MAMMIES

Whereas the mulatto was generally an unhappy figure, another black cinematic stereotype, the servant or domestic, was generally a happy one—or so white producers tried to make it seem on screen. Initially a minor role, the servant was limited in early shorts and features to the mumbling of a few words as he or she entered or exited a room. Langston Hughes once described the standard direction for black actors in such parts: "Upon opening the car door for one's white employer in any film, the director would command, 'Jump to ground. . . . Remove cap. . . . Open again. . . . Step back and bow. . . . Come up smiling. . . . Now bow again. . . . Now straighten up and grin!'" (Bogle, *TCMMB* 37).

Sound pictures brought little added depth to the traditional servant roles. By the 1930s, blacks were still being depicted behind brooms or pots and pans and in other stereotypical postures; the only consolation was that at least they were appearing with greater frequency in Hollywood films. Their appearances, Donald Bogle writes, met the demands of their times in several critical ways: their antics, dialects, and other absurdities provided jocularity to a Depression age; their wisecracking and foolishness offered relief from the harsh financial realities of the day; and their joy, zest, and loyalty demonstrated that life was not hopeless. Ready to lend a hand, black servants were always available—and usually indispensable—to their white employers: many down-and-out movie heroes or heroines, from Shirley Temple to Bette Davis, realized that their black servants were their only real friends (*TCMMB* 36).

Servant roles, however, were never leading; they were menial and, at worst, utterly demeaning. The simple-minded valet to Al Jolson in *Go Into Your Dance* (1935), for instance, was called "Snowflake"; playing on an old Southern superstition, Jolson would rub the valet's head for luck. When the same actor, Fred Toones, portrayed similar roles in films like *Twentieth Century* (1934), *Lady by Choice* (1934), and *The Biscuit Eater* (1940), he continued to be billed as Snowflake and not by his given name, a confirmation of the fact that in the Hollywood of that era, all blacks— and certainly all black servants—looked the same. (And unfortunately, given the limited range that blacks were afforded, in most films they *did* look the same.)

Occasionally, though, servant roles provided more than just a way for blacks to work in movies; they allowed a handful of fine actors who were consigned to minor parts an ingenious way to specialize and to exploit or expose the very stereotypes they were inhabiting. As Bill "Bojangles" Robinson did with his urbane style and Eddie "Rochester" Anderson did with his raspy voice, the actors evoked their own unique personalities and created memorable characters and comic worlds in which they often outshone their employers. In films such as *She Done Him Wrong* (1933), *I'm No Angel* (1933), and *Belle of the Nineties* (1934), for instance, wisecracking black maids served as comic foils to Mae West. But even in those pictures, the stereotype prevailed: Robinson was relegated to the usual self-sacrifices in the service of his young mistress, Shirley Temple, while the desexed domestics, typically named Beulah or Pearl, held their own in conversations but clearly posed no challenge to the status or the sexuality of the wicked West.

A favorite servant type in white studio films was the Mammy. Usually middle-aged, she was dowdy, big, and dark (sometimes exaggeratedly so, as in the many early films in which she was played by white actresses in blackface). But whereas most servants were respectful, she could be cantankerous and feisty. With her silent looks and sassy rejoinders, the Mammy often undermined her employer's authority; yet the fact that she did it in a good-natured and familiar way made her behavior seem acceptable, even affectionate. And white audiences loved her irrepressibility. In *Aunt Huldah, Matchmaker* (1911), for example, Mammy Huldah devises a scheme to reconcile Leslie Fairfax and Hawley Caldwell, two lovers who are estranged from each other because of a misunderstanding. Mammy urges Hawley to fake a fall from a runaway horse as a way of testing Leslie's affection; once the pair is happily reunited, she sits chuckling to herself by the kitchen fire.

One of the Mammy's early appearances was in a 1914 comedy called *Coon Town Suffragettes*, a blackface version of *Lysistrata* in which a group of domineering washerwomen led by Mandy Jackson organizes a militant movement to keep their idle husbands out of the saloons and at home. But most film Mammies were less political—and certainly less sexual—than the Suffragettes. Like the faithful female servant who remains with the Cameron family throughout the war and defends them against the Reconstruction Negroes in D. W. Griffith's *Birth of a Nation* or the constant companion played by Hattie McDaniel in early films such as *The Golden West* (1932) and *The Story of Temple Drake* (1933), they tended to be loyal and nonthreatening, especially in their sexuality (in sharp contrast to an opposing stereotype, the sultry, hip-swiveling temptress like Chick in *Hallelujah!* [1929], Georgia Brown in *Cabin in the Sky* [1943], or Carmen in *Carmen Jones* [1954]). Depicted in films like *Rainbow on the River* (1936) and *Saratoga* (1937) as warm and loving surrogate mothers to their charges, Mammies seemed content in their privileged family positions—so content that in the former, the ex-slave Toinette, played by Louise Beavers, intimates that she never really wanted her freedom.[59]

It was precisely in such a role that Hattie McDaniel earned the first Academy Award ever given to a black performer. McDaniel, who had worked her way up from parts in road companies to appearances on radio and ultimately to movies, played many domestics and Mammies on film because, as she famously claimed, it was better to *play* a domestic than to *be* one. Her turn as a maid contemptuous of the employers who hire her to impress their dinner guests in *Alice Adams* (1935) was a highpoint of the film. But it was as the Mammy to Scarlett O'Hara in *Gone With the Wind* (1939) that McDaniel succeeded in defining the role that for years had defined and delimited so many other black actresses. Proud of the fact that she has diapered three generations of O'Hara women, McDaniel's Mammy is privy to all of Scarlett's secrets, from her infatuation with Ashley Wilkes to her enduring love for Rhett Butler. And Mammy is the person to whom Scarlett consistently turns for counsel and protection. Accordingly, when Rhett returns with Scarlett from their honeymoon, he brings a red petticoat as a gift for Mammy because he knows that to keep Scarlett's affection, he must win Mammy's as well.

In adapting *Gone With the Wind* to film, producer David O. Selznick, who purportedly wanted to be sure "that Negroes come out decidely on the right side of the ledger" (Cripps, *SFB* 361), insisted on casting Mammy as a principal, not a supporting role. Once McDaniel was selected, he rewrote portions of the script to accommodate her special brand of humor. And indeed, as Bogle writes, "Mammy has a self-righteous grandeur that glows" and that frees her character from the sense of innate inferiority that is the greatest burden that slavery, on screen and off, inflicted on blacks (*TCMMB* 89). At the same time, Mammy's dedication to and affection for Scarlett and eventually for Scarlett's daughter, Bonnie Blue, lends a certain poignant authenticity to the adaptation. Yet, despite the acclaim for her performance in *Gone With the Wind*,

McDaniel—like other fine black actresses, including Ethel Waters and Louise Beavers—found herself restricted, for the most part, to domestic roles for the remainder of her career.

Typical of McDaniel's character and of all film Mammies was their absolute devotion and their willingness to sacrifice themselves and even their own families for "missy" and "massa." In *Mammy's Ghost or Between the Lines of Battle* (1911), for example, Mammy hides Colonel Berkly and his son from Union soldiers and then cares for the boy throughout the war until his father returns. In *Old Mammy's Secret Code* (ca. 1912), Mammy uses her laundry line to signal in code from inside Grant's headquarters, an act of treason for which she is executed. In *Old Mammy's Charge* (1913), Mammy travels north with her mistress, Beatrice Prentis; after Beatrice and her husband die, she cares for little Beatrice and endures many hardships until Major Prentis, little Beatrice's grandfather, finds them and takes them back home to the South. And in *Mammy's Rose* (1916), the old Mammy dies dreaming of her young charge Frank, who was killed by "Yanks," and of his loving wife Beth; as a reward for her loyalty, her soul flies heavenward to be reunited with the white family she had served.

To be sure, it was not just the plantation-era Mammy who displayed such unconditional devotion. The contemporary "Aunt Delilah" (Louise Beavers) in the high-grossing *Imitation of Life* (1934), for instance, not only tends the household of the widowed Miss Bea (Claudette Colbert) but also ensures Bea's fortune by sharing with her an old family recipe for pancakes. Bea markets the recipe, which brings millions, and in turn offers to share the profits with Delilah, albeit in a grossly inequitable eighty-twenty split. Delilah, however, does not want to be independent. Begging Bea not to send her away, Delilah reiterates her desire to stay on as cook and as caretaker for "Miss Jessie," Bea's daughter. Delilah's desire not to leave Bea's home finds its parallel in the earlier Mammies' desire never to leave the plantation, just as her self-effacing Christian stoicism, again like that of the earlier Toms and Mammies, allows her to accept her fate of inferiority and to resign herself to other social injustices.[60] In these vital respects, Delilah is simply an Old-South Mammy in modern dress (although that dress, which usually consists of a cook's apron and kerchief, is not all that modern). Even the women's names suggest that Delilah is a devoted "auntie" to her darling "missy" Bea, an essential inequality that underlies the status of virtually all black film domestics.

SAMBO, RASTUS, AND COON TYPES

A final important black stereotype, the coon (sometimes called the Sambo), was also—as the very terms suggest—the most demeaning. The historian Stanley Elkins described the figure as "docile but irresponsible, loyal but lazy, humble but chronically given to lying and stealing"; and Daniel J. Leab characterized him as "subhuman, simpleminded, superstitious, and submissive" to whites, frequently childlike in his dependence, with foolishly exaggerated qualities, including an apparently hereditary clumsiness and an addictive craving for fried chicken and watermelon (Leab 1). In early silent films, the coon was best exemplified in the character of crazy Rastus, which, like Sambo, became a generic name for black stooges on screen.[61] The first two of a series of slapstick comedies centering on the adventures of Rastus were Lubin's *How Rastus Got His Pork Chops* (1908) and Pathé's *How Rastus Got His Turkey* (1910), in which Rastus tries to steal Thanksgiving dinner for his wife Eliza and daughter and ends up carrying off a piece of the fence as well.[62] In *Rastus in Zululand* (1910), Rastus falls asleep in the sun (since, as the film suggests, a "darky" likes warmth) and dreams that he is shipwrecked in Zululand, where cannibals capture him and prepare to boil him for their dinner. Although the chief's large and ugly daughter intercedes on his behalf, Rastus prefers the pot to matrimony (a preference the chieftain, another black savage, almost accommodates); but he awakens from his dream just as the pot's water is about to boil. Rastus continued his chicken-thieving and antic behavior in other shorts, including *Rastus and Chicken*, *Pickaninnies and Watermelon*, and *Chicken Thief*, all released around 1910-1911.[63] In Vitagraph's "Sonny Jim" films, produced by Tefft Jonson, Jim and "his little colored friend Lilly" (as studio advertising described her character) have similar comic adventures. In *Cause for Thanksgiving*, for instance, Jim trades his turkey for Lilly's baby brother (also named Rastus) because Lilly's family has no food but plenty of children.

And in *The White and Black Snowball* (1915), after rescuing Lilly from some young rascals who want to steal her mittens, Jim tries to rub her cheeks and forehead white with snow since he knows that his mother will not allow such a "dirty" face in her house. Coon types similar to Rastus and Lilly persisted into the early 1950s: for instance, in cartoons like *Jasper and the Watermelons* and *Jasper and the Haunted House*, part of Paramount's animated *Jasper* "Puppetoon" series, the bug-eyed little black Jasper, accompanied by his protective Mammy, a hustling black scarecrow, and a glib crow who serves as his wisecracking partner in crime, "strode through a trail of venal deacons, ghosts, dialects, grins, and song" and devoted their days "to filching and grifting watermelons and pies" (*SFB* 230).

Lazy and shiftless, the stereotypic coon was always looking to get something for nothing, like the black man who steals a farmer's wood in the 1904 Biograph short, *A Nigger in the Woodpile*; the poultry-thieving blacks in shorts like *The Chicken Thief* (1904),[64] *C-H-I-C-K-E-N Spells Chicken* (1910), *A College Chicken* (1910), *Chased by Bloodhounds* (1912), *A Hen House Hero* (1912), and *Christmas Turkey* (1912); or Parson Johnson in *Black Magic* (1917), who devises a scheme to rob a farmer of the watermelons he is taking to market.[65] The coon, however, was not afraid just of work; he was afraid of everything, including his own shadow. And films exploited his ridiculously fearful posture—eyes wide open, face frozen, hair standing on end (or occasionally turning white)—for comic effect. It was common to see the coon character cowering in fear at his master's side or, alternatively, running in pop-eyed terror from any sign of danger (usually imagined, not real). Ghosts posed an especially big scare for several generations of coon characters on screen, from the unnamed black man in a watermelon field who sees two girls dressed in sheets and thinks they are "two live ghosts" in *Dixie Duo Down South* (1910) to Eddie Anderson in *Topper Returns* (1941); even films as late as the blockbuster *Ghost* (1990)[66] featured superstitious and often terrified blacks.

The most prominent of the early coon type was Stepin Fetchit (fig. 1.6). As a lackey in *In Old Kentucky* (1927), as an easy dupe in *Stand Up and Cheer* (1934), or as an inept handyman to Will Rogers in *Judge Priest* (1934), *Steamboat 'Round the Bend* (1935), and other films, Fetchit perfected the slow-gaited, dim-witted demeanor that

Figure 1.6. Stepin Fetchit quickly became one of film's most recognizable and successful black character actors.

the role demanded and his name ("step" and "fetch" it) suggested. Tall, thin, his head clean-shaven, dressed in clothes so loose-fitting that they always looked passed down, he gave the appearance of being naïve or clownish. Yet in real life Fetchit (born Lincoln Theodore Monroe Andrew Perry) was no fool. Keenly attuned to popular taste, he took the coon caricature of the day and in turn caricatured it, thus creating a character at once comic and ironic— and a character the white public clamored to see. Fetchit became one of the first blacks to be a contract player or to receive feature billing and one of the first black superstars (as well as the first black millionaire actor [Murray 17]), with an extravagant lifestyle that reportedly included six homes, sixteen Chinese servants, a pink Cadillac with his name on the side in neon lights, and eleven other cars.

Despite the fortune they brought him, Fetchit's stammering and shuffling portrayals were belittling. Nevertheless, he continued them for several more decades, until his performances became self-parodic and audiences tired of his blatantly racist clowning. Fetchit's popularity, however, opened up the studio doors to a whole generation of actors who learned to imitate some of his comic techniques. Willie Best, whose nickname Sleep 'n' Eat seemed to sum up all of the coon character's needs, found success alongside Shirley Temple in *The Littlest Rebel* (1935) and Bob Hope in *The Ghost Breakers* (1940), even though his almost somnabulistically slow character was ultimately more degrading than Fetchit's. Mantan Moreland, with his remarkably expressive face, perfected eye-popping looks of surprise and doubletakes; his frequent comedic screen appearances included the recurring role of chauffeur Birmingham Brown in the Charlie Chan films and a wonderful supporting performance late in his career as a counterman in *Watermelon Man* (1970). Even the great jazz musician Louis Armstrong, who made his acting debut in Bing Crosby's *Pennies from Heaven* (1936), amiably mugged his way through stereotypical "coon" casting that belied his great talents over four decades of film.

There were as many variations on the coon character as there were black actors relegated to the demeaning role. A particularly popular version was the pickaninny, a staple of peep show films like *The Pickaninnies Doing a Dance* (1894), of early shorts like Edison's *Ten Pickaninnies* (1904), and of plantation pieces, in which the character was usually featured as part of a group, dancing wildly, in the background. Interestingly, the pickaninny was among the first black film roles actually played by blacks, even when Mammy, Tom, and other black roles were being performed by whites—no doubt because the pickaninny was considered so inconsequential.

Probably film's most recognizable pickaninny—and one of film's most damning early examples of racist portraiture—was Topsy, the wild slave child entrusted to Aunt Ophelia for moral and social instruction in the many versions of *Uncle Tom's Cabin*. Stowe wrote of Topsy in the novel that she just "growed and growed," and so did her cinematic counterpart. Topsy's silly on-screen clowning, which obscured and thereby diminished the suf-

fering of slaves like Tom, gave her a life—and at least one eponymous film—of her own. In *Topsy and Eva* (1927), the vulgar minstrel act that the Duncan Sisters brought to the screen, Topsy (purchased by Little Eva for a nickel at a slave auction in which no one
else bids) turns into an utterly foolish blackface version of the
Keystone Kops as she flies downhill on borrowed skis, lands atop
a snowshoe-wearing horse, and leaps onto cakes of ice. Slave life,
the garish and insipid film implies, is nothing but a series of laugh-
out-loud low adventures to be savored by white audiences.

Other popular pickaninny characters were featured in the Hal
Roach "Our Gang" comedies, which premiered in 1922 and continued throughout the next decade (and for many years beyond, in
reruns, syndication, and a remake in 1994). The Little Rascals

Figure 1.7. Buckwheat, one of the popular Little Rascals in the
"Our Gang" series, has an unexpected encounter with a skeleton.

"Sunshine Sammy," "Pineapple," "Farina," "Stymie," and "Buckwheat" (fig. 1.7) broke new cinematic ground in showing that black children could actually share adventures and misadventures with white children.   Unfortunately, the black Rascals rarely rose above stereotype in their looks, dress, or speech patterns. Frederick Ernest Morrison, who played Sunshine Sammy, was so well-liked that he appeared and sometimes headlined in other comedies; but even in those films, he was often billed by type as "Pickaninny Sammy" or "Sunshine Sammy" and not by his given name.[67] Another kind of racism was evident in salaries: even in the "Our Gang" comedies, Sunshine Sammy was paid considerably less than his white co-stars. In the early 1920s, his salary of $250—considered by at least one newspaper to be the highest salary paid to any "colored actor" steadily employed in film at that time—was a mere fifth of the pay the white Rascals received (Leab 54).

Whereas pickaninnies were most often portrayed by young blacks, the "Uncle Remus," another variation of the coon character, was portrayed by older blacks. Bogle calls the harmless and congenial Remus, who distinguishes himself by his quaint, naïve, and comic philosophizing, to be "a first cousin to the tom," and he notes that "Remus's mirth, like Tom's contentment and the coon's antics, has always been used to indicate the black man's satisfaction with the system and his place in it" (*TCMMB* 8).[68] Although there are foreshadowings of his character or character type in silent films like *Uncle Remus' First Visit to New York* (1914)[69] as well as in later films like *The Green Pastures* (1936), Remus is most closely associated with *Song of the South* (1946), a technically innovative Disney adaptation of Joel Chandler Harris's Uncle Remus tales. Set on a nineteenth-century plantation full of contented slaves and a devoted Mammy named Aunt Tempy (played by the ubiquitous Mammy, Hattie McDaniel), that film intercut the clever animation of Brer Rabbit, Brer Fox, and Brer Bear with live action of the happy old black Remus (James Baskett), who tells uplifting stories to Johnny (Bobby Driscoll), the lonely and troubled white boy who has been sent to live on his grandmother's plantation after his parents' separation. Although Remus himself is a kindly, wise, even patriarchal figure, the picture of joyful life on the plantation is so distorted and hopelessly obsolete that *Song of the South* was roundly condemned by blacks and picketed more heavily than any film since *The Birth of a Nation*. (At the premiere of the Disney film, some protesters shouted that "We fought for Uncle Sam, not Uncle Tom" [Snead 93].) Baskett was posthumously awarded a Special Oscar for his performance, and the film, irrefutably retrogressive though it was, proved to be a commercial success; nonetheless, it forced Hollywood to reconsider the way black characters were being depicted, especially following the agreements that had been struck a few years earlier between the Hollywood studios and the NAACP and in light of the increased emphasis on racial tolerance in the postwar period.

Yet even in films as recent as *Big Momma's House* (2000), many of the old stereotypes survive and persist. (Fig. 1.8.) As James Snead observed, "the roles of 'mammy' (the urban or Southern domestic maid), Uncle Tom (the household retainer and quiet collaborator), the black buck (unregenerate, sexy, violent), as well as the agrarian or rural peasant worker still hover over . . . mass cultural depiction[s] of blacks like unquiet ghosts" (127). And while some of the most blatant racist stereotypes may have disappeared, others have either evolved or been replaced over the years by more subtle but still demeaning caricatures: the libidinous welfare mother in *Claudine* (1974), the sexy superwoman in *Coffy* (1973) and *Foxy Brown* (1974), the crazy con man in *Bustin' Loose* (1981), the trusty sidekick in *The Empire Strikes Back* (1980), the nervy hustler in *Trading Places* (1983), and the sassy housekeeper in *Clara's Heart* (1988). By contrast, in the works of early black filmmakers beginning with William Foster, Emmett J. Scott, and Oscar Micheaux—underappreciated or neglected independents who, against often formidable economic and political odds, offered an alternative cinematic expression of black experience— Hollywood's imagery was, for the first time, seriously and significantly challenged. Those black filmmakers took it upon themselves, as Jane Gaines (*FD* 254) writes, "to 'image back,' to return the image of themselves given by whites, to 'face off' against white-produced 'blackface,'" and to bring about change "by means of an imaginative incorporation, not a simple assimilation." On the surface, their films seemed much like inexpensive versions of Hollywood films; but thematically, they were worlds apart—the same genres, perhaps, but "emptied and filled with different issues and outcomes" (*FD* 254, 270). Topical and frank, they portrayed uplift achieved through education, exposed and punished race betrayal, and revealed black aspiration—usually by redefining white notions of black community and by inverting or exploiting the familiar white stereotypes of black life and culture.

Figure 1.8. FBI Agent Malcolm Tucker (Martin Lawrence) goes undercover as a modern-day Mammy in *Big Momma's House*. *(Twentieth Century-Fox/Regency Enterprises, 2000)*

NOTES TO CHAPTER 1

1. For a fuller discussion of the various incarnations of *Uncle Tom's Cabin* as nineteenth-century theater hit and as twentieth-century film, see Barbara Tepa Lupack, "*Uncle Tom* and American Popular Culture: Adapting Stowe's Novel to Film," in Barbara Tepa Lupack, ed., *Nineteenth-Century Women at the Movies: Adapting Classic Women's Fiction to Film* (1999), 207-56.

2. Uncle Tom also appeared in another Edison production, a 1909 Edison short, *Uncle Tom Wins. The Moving Picture World* (8 May 1909) describes him as "an old colored man" who is rewarded for his persistent pursuit of the Goddess Fortune by a $20,000 lottery win. Although Tom rejoices over his new wealth, two men follow him and try to discover its hiding place. Tom has to keep moving the money, from a trunk to a carpetbag to an old chair in the garret. Ultimately, as the wily Tom removes the money and leaves, the men are chagrined to learn that they had been sitting on his stash.

3. In fact, the film was based as much on George Aiken's popular stage version, then the most frequently performed play in the history of the American theater (Hansen 45), as on Stowe's classic novel.

4. The "tableaux," writes Linda Williams in *Playing the Race Card* (cited henceforth as *Race*), are "inherited from the melodramatic stage. Tableaux are dramatic moments of a play in which the actors freeze their positions in order to heighten and prolong emotional or pictorial effects." Stage tableaux also "generally served to introduce abstract interpretive frameworks that put the audience at one remove from the immediate plot. A tableau might summarize a plot point (as when in the play Eliza prays on one bank of the river and Haley curses on the other), offer an allegorical comment on the action (as when Eva is seen in heaven on the back of a snow-white dove), or portray a moment of dramatic impasse (as when Cassy and Legree stand opposed to one another over the fate of Uncle Tom)" (88).

5. Williams makes a correlation between the "historical happy ending" of Porter's film and those of many of the late nineteenth-century stage versions of *Uncle Tom's Cabin.* In both versions, history often "becomes the *deus ex machina* whose subsequent events serve to soften the blow from Legree's whip" (*Race* 90). In Porter's film, Tom and Eva die, but not in vain, since John Brown's martyrdom, the conflagration of war, emancipation, and reunification soon follow.

6. Daniel J. Leab writes: "At least one social scientist has contended that 'the white man in blackface serves the psychological function of reducing audience anxieties that might occur if real Negroes were used,

especially in scenes of overt or covert sexual nature or when the Negro gets the upper hand over the white man.' But it is more likely that white actors were used because the filmmakers of the time, a crude and pragmatic lot on the whole, accepted the prevailing beliefs about the limited abilities of the black and proceeded accordingly" (11). Even early productions of a work such as *Othello* often featured white actors in the role of the black Moor.

7. The full title is *Toms, Coons, Mulattoes, Mammies, & Bucks*, to be cited henceforth as *TCMMB*.

8. According to Charles Musser in *The Emergence of Cinema: The American Screen to 1907* (361), in the "Auction of St. Clair's Slaves" scene, Lubin himself played the role of the auctioneer.

9. Cited henceforth as *CS*.

10. Linda Williams (*Race* 71) suggests that such a construction of the antebellum South occurred through minstrelsy, particularly through the popular "sad home" songs of Stephen Foster and others. The South, "America's rural everyhome," she writes, "the melodramatic 'space of innocence,' became fixed, through this music, as stereotypically southern and, for subsequent generations, as eternally antebellum."

11. Edward D. C. Campbell, Jr. writes that, in 1913, "the American studio" produced a new version of *Uncle Tom's Cabin*. Campbell's, however, appears to be the only reference to this production (*CS* 41). At one time, Powers, an independent film company whose features were distributed by Universal, had planned a version of *Uncle Tom's Cabin* as well. That version, billed as a "Three Reel Powers" and listed as "Almost Ready for Release" in several issues of *The Moving Picture World* (2 Aug. 1913 and 16 Aug. 1913), was produced by Otis Turner. The brief summary of the film, published in *The Moving Picture World* (3 May 1913) while the film was still in production, suggested that it would be "a special three-part feature offering" and that "producer Otis Turner deserves credit for what is, on the whole, an artistic picture." The summary also praised the film's good "character drawing" and its "marked Southern atmosphere in the home of the St. Clairs and in the steamboat scene." There is no record, however, of the actual release of the Powers's film version. In fact, the reviews of the 1913 three-reel Imp version "directed" by Otis Turner suggest that the "Three Reel Powers" was released not by Powers but by Imp-Universal. (At the time, Universal served as the distributor for a number of smaller independent film companies, including Powers and Imp.)

12. After the death of Uncle Tom and of Legree, "[young master] Shelby reverently takes Uncle Tom's body back to the old plantation, where it is laid away near the old slave's cabin" (*The Moving Picture World* 13 Dec. 1913).

13. Prominent players in this production included Robert Z. Leonard (Legree), Eddie Lyons (Marks), Gertrude Short (Eva), Harry Pollard (Tom), and Margarita Fischer (Topsy). As Linda Williams (*Race* 91) notes, reviewers of the film, like reviewers of a number of other post-Porter productions, were increasingly given to praising the authentic locales more than the excitement and feeling of the familiar story.

14. Hannah Page Wheeler Andrews disputes this point. She writes that "the World Film version varied considerably in its plot from the earlier films because it was based on a novel written by Edward Wade which drew upon, but did not copy Stowe's story, rather than upon the Aiken playscript" (133). The review from *Variety* (4 Sept. 1914), however, includes a summary of the film; and it seems clear that the film is indeed based very much on Stowe's novel. "The story," writes *Variety* reviewer "Sime.," is fully described "in the programed [*sic*] synopsis," which follows:

> Geo. Shelby is forced to sell his faithful old slave Tom and the infant son of Eliza Harris in order to save his property from Haley, the slave trader and holder of the mortgage. Eliza, hearing she is to be separated from her baby, makes her escape to join her husband, George Harris, who, with Vance [Jim Vance, his would-be servant], were well on their way to freedom. Learning of the departure, Haley immediately puts the hounds on her trail. The searching party arrives on the river bank in time to see Eliza leaping over the broken ice, upon which the dogs and men feared to tread. A second party is organized by Lawyer Marks, but fails to capture the fugitive, who has been befriended by a kindly Quaker and has in the meantime joined her husband. During the sail to Haley's plantation Tom's attention from his Bible, is attracted by the cry of 'Overboard.' Making a bold rush, this wonderful old man leaps into the water and brings little Eva St. Clair [*sic*], who had wandered from her Aunt and fallen overboard, to safety. This noble deed caused his purchase by St. Clair, who treated him with every kindness, making him a companion for his small daughter Eva, who joyed in Uncle Tom's explanation of the Bible. Sadness finally came, when little Eva dies, and a second calamity when her father is killed while separating two roughs in a quarrel. This necessitates the sale of his slaves and property. Uncle Tom falls into the hands of Simon Legree, the most brutal slave owner of the South. His life here is simply a matter of how long it can last under the terrible strain and treatment he receives. The final blow came when Legree's housekeeper, Casey [*sic*], and his favorite slave, Emmeline, escaped during one of his debauches. Going to Tom, he demands to know their whereabouts. Being unable to give this information, Tom is flogged and cast into a corner to die. Young Shelby, now a man, searched the South to fulfill his youthful promise to buy Tom. He reaches the little hut just in time to cheer the dying hour of his old slave, who has just enough life left to show his gratitude.

There are, however, variations from the text. Some are small: Emmeline, for the sake of propriety, is introduced as Legree's new "housekeeper" rather than as his mistress. Other variations are more significant: at Legree's plantation, Tom is forced to whip an unnamed young black male slave, not Casey. Later, that young man, moved by Tom's earlier protectiveness of him and upset by the older slave's subsequent punishment, takes a gun and shoots Legree to death. Before dying, Tom has a vision of Little Eva. And, in the film's final scene, Abraham Lincoln is depicted freeing the slaves.

15. Had Daly's film "been as powerful in its action sequences as it was in its authentic locales and in this one shocking image of black-on-white revenge," concludes Williams (*Race* 93-94), "it might have lent a new lease on life to the Tom material, spurring it to develop these deep-seated issues of interracial violence with black actors at their center. It might even have represented a counterforce to the violent, negrophobic, 'anti-Tom' tradition that emerged the following year in Dixon and Griffith's *The Birth of a Nation* . . . . In all other ways, however, this version of Uncle Tom is singularly ungripping."

16. Peter Noble writes that Lowe's "Tom still came off as a genial darky, furnished with new color but no new sentiments. Yet to Lowe's credit, he did his tomming with such an arresting effectiveness that he was sent to England on a promotional tour to ballyhoo the picture, thus becoming the first black actor to be publicized by his studio" (6).

17. Thomas Cripps disagrees on this point: in *Slow Fade to Black*, he writes that the final film came in at fourteen reels—"less than half its intended length" (159). Subsequent references to this work will be cited as *SFB.*

18. Compared to previous interpretations, the story, according to Edward D. C. Campbell, Jr., "did expose certain plantation evils. In one shot a brutally beaten Uncle Tom appears in a crucifixion pose, after which a likeness of Christ is visible. Legree is grotesque, stumbling about with food drooling from his mouth and blood trickling from his forehead. In a revised conclusion Legree gets his just retribution at the hands of William Sherman's troops. However, when contrasted to the rest of the picture these scenes did little to counteract what had become a standard view of the plantation" (*CS* 67).

19. The "narration by Raymond Massey, in front of an old barn at Mrs. Stowe's birthplace in Litchfield, Connecticut," wrote William L. Slout, "prepared modern viewers for the antique picture" (149). But in fact it was intended to do much more—e.g., to remind viewers of happy times in plantation society when everyone knew his place.

20. The publicity for the film, notes Campbell, "was as disrespectful as the plot. One publicity release revealed that 'the money paid for the huge amounts of burned cork bought for the use of Rosetta Duncan . . . would buy four dozen pairs of ladies' silk stockings of a very fair grade'" (*CS* 71).

21. Although no new adaptations of *Uncle Tom's Cabin* were made during the thirties and forties, Uncle Tom—a cinematic standard, by virtue of both legitimate and parodic presentations—continued to be a familiar motif in American films. In *Dimples* (1936), for example, Twentieth Century-Fox Pictures recast the early history of *Uncle Tom's Cabin* into an entertaining film starring a young Shirley Temple. *Dimples* related the story of a broken-down old rapscallion actor (Frank Morgan), whose little granddaughter attracted the attention of a young producer who was launching the memorable play at the National Theatre. As Eva, Temple has numerous opportunities to shine: in the sequences with Topsy in the attic room; in a later scene, in which she and Tom engage in the famous discussion of the New Jerusalem; and in the deathbed scene, where she is conveniently propped up to deliver Eva's final words: "I can see those great gates made of pearl, and they're opening wide—and there are the angels—they're calling me! I'm coming! I'm coming!" There is also some backstage humor, reminiscent of the Double Mammoth days, when the grandfather, after palming off a fake watch on his hostess (Helen Westley), tries to evade the police "by blacking up as Uncle Tom, and the audience at the National Theatre was regaled by two Uncle Toms entering the stage from opposite wings!" (Birdoff 407). In *Everybody Sing* (1938; dir. Edwin L. Marin), Judy Garland stars as Judy Bellaire, a precocious youngster of thirteen who is kicked out of the Colvin School for Girls. She returns home to her nutty theatrical family, which is trying, unsuccessfully, to mount a new show. Without her parents' knowledge, she auditions for the producer; dressed as a blackfaced Topsy, she sings a swing version of "Swing Low, Sweet Chariot" ("Uncle Tom's got a new routine; Eliza crossed the ice in a limousine, while Simon Legree shakes a mean tambourine. . ."). Of course, her talent ultimately saves the show (though not this otherwise awful movie). In *Can This Be Dixie?* (Twentieth Century-Fox, 1936), another child star Jane Withers, as Eva, belts out "Uncle Tom's Cabin Is a Cabaret Now," while the same treatment is given to the double Topsys—Betty Grable and June Haver—in *The Dolly Sisters* (Twentieth Century-Fox, 1945) (Birdoff 407). And in *The Naughty Nineties* (1945; dir. Jean Yarbrough), a film memorable mostly for its classic "Who's On First?" baseball routine, Abbott and Costello outwit the villains who want to steal a showboat from its kindly and honest owner. The film ends with a showboat-style production of *Uncle Tom's Cabin*, in which Abbott and Costello, as Simon Legree and Eva, suffer the typical theatrical mishap of the broken rope during Eva's ascension to heaven.

22. Interestingly, as Cripps (*SFB* 72-73) writes, one of the film projects that early race filmmaker Emmett J. Scott and Booker T. Washington considered, around 1915 or 1916, was an update of *Uncle Tom's Cabin*. The two were looking for a black film project that would serve as a "counter-

force to *The Birth of a Nation*," and Amy Vorhaus, an author with connections at Vitagraph, proposed "an updated *Uncle Tom's Cabin* that would use the medium to teach men that 'prejudice is a conservative reaction and an ill-founded habit.'"

23. *Alice [Gets] Stage Struck* was one of Disney's many popular "Alice" productions. According to Russell Merritt and J. B. Kaufman in *Disney in Wonderland: The Silent Films of Walt Disney*, in this silent short, which premiered on 23 June 1925 at the Rivoli Theater in New York City with *The Light of Western Stars* (Paramount), "Alice and the gang stage an Our-Gang style *Uncle Tom's Cabin* show. Playing the part of Little Eva, Alice is accidentally knocked out, and dreams herself in snowland with Julius [her cat], who is building a snowman. They run afoul of Pete the Bear who chases them into a winter cabin and across ice floes" (138). The silent film was later reissued with sound, and the main title of the sound version reads *Alice Gets Stage Struck*; but studio records for 1925 give the title simply as *Alice Stage Struck*.

24. Thomas Cripps, in *Making Movies Black*, notes that the climax of *Uncle Tom's Cabaña*, the opening of Tom's chicken shack, "had already been a bit in the liberal revue *Jump for Joy*," and blacks wondered "how it would play Azuza [a pejorative term for squares]" (197). In *Slow Fade to Black*, Cripps discusses at greater length *Jump for Joy*, "a liberal romp that ran for three months" and was attended by "Hollywood celebrities, 'middle-class ofays,' 'dicty Negroes,' and just plain folk." In the satire, "Uncle Tom's deathbed is surrounded by his children singing 'He lived to a ripe old age. Let him go, God Bless him!' as a brace of producers struggle to keep him alive by pumping adrenalin into his arms. The first act finale was a comic song in which Uncle Tom's Cabin becomes a drive-in 'chicken shack' at Hollywood and Vine. In case anyone might miss the point, the program helped the 'square' to become temporarily 'groovy' by providing a handy glossary of black urbane idiom" (374-75).

25. *Uncle Tom's Cabin* reached other media as well. With the inception of radio, serious treatments (e.g., *The Gray Spirit*, by Ohio State University, over the Blue network, NBC, in February, 1937) as well as travesties (e.g., *Uncle Tom's Cabaña*, by Al Barrie's "Mellerdrammers," over WNYC in September, 1937) found their way to the air waves. Even Al Jolson performed the venerable old Tom ("Star Spangled Theatre," on NBC-Blue [WJZ], 10 August 1941) (Birdoff 439).

26. Babb also alleged that his important effort was "equally as entertaining and informative" for children as for adults, black and white. Yet the poster for *Uncle Tom's Cabin* seemed neither entertaining nor informative: it was "dominated by a very scantily clad slave girl in the eager clutches of Simon Legree" (Campbell, *CS* 185).

27. Bernardi continues: "[The Colonel's sword] is a phallic icon with

a particularly white and patriarchal charge. In the possession of George, however, the sword is not a phallus: It does not, in other words, confer power on the domesticated slave. . . . Instead, the long and shiny sword empowers the myth of an honorable and romantic South where 'good' slaves sacrificed their freedom and any sexual desire for the honor and virtue of Southern whiteness" ("The Voice of Whiteness" 116-17).

28. That model was reinforced by the scores of subservient blacks that Griffith featured in many of the more than 450 films that he directed or directly supervised, particularly in those shorts that were set during or after the Civil War.

29. Cripps (*SFB* 23) observes that even in films like *The Kaffir's Gratitude* (1915), in which the title character has no investment in the outcome, he nonetheless "saves a white fortune in diamonds from a 'social parasite' with the zeal of a slave defending the master's plantation."

30. Robinson responded to charges of "Tomism" in a *Courier* article (13 Jan. 1937) entitled "Morris Interviews 'Bojangles': Learns He Is Real Race Man." Robinson told the interviewer: "This is not true. I am a race man" (qtd. in Everett 213).

31. The play also incorporated aspects of Dixon's first novel about the Reconstruction period, *The Leopard's Spots: A Romance of the White Man's Burden 1865-1900.*

32. According to Bosley Crowther, "he believed that the white population had been abused and exploited by Northern carpetbaggers and Southern scalawags who had incited the emancipated Negroes, and he wanted to make a film on this theme" ("The Birth of *Birth of a Nation*" 77).

33. As Brown explained in his memoirs: "I doubt if there was a man on that work crew who hadn't been out with a 'Tom' show, as the *Uncle Tom's Cabin* shows were called. There were Tom shows scattered all over the country by tens and dozens. It was not so much a show as an institution, a part of the American scene for the past sixty-odd years" (qtd. in Williams, *Race* 97).

34. Bogle, *TCMMB* 10; other critics offer slightly varying times for filming and editing.

35. Lawrence Reddick, in "Of Motion Pictures" (6), notes that *The Birth of a Nation* was the first film ever to be honored by a White House showing.

36. Stoneman was modeled on Congressman Thaddeus Stevens, leader of the Radical Republicans in the United States Congress (Taylor, "Re-Birth" 21).

37. The "extreme 'better dead than raped' implications" of Flora's tragic suicide, writes Jane Gaines (*Fire and Desire* 239, cited henceforth as *FD*), reinforce Griffith's portrait of "the Negro as nothing more nor less than a sexual monster." Gus's chase of Flora is, in fact, prefigured in other

Griffith films such as *The Girls and Daddy* (1909), in which a "lowdown Negro" burglar and sexual predator preys on two angelic white girls (Bernardi, "Whiteness" 122).

38. According to Clyde Taylor, "the later sequence in which Lynch, the upstart mulatto carpetbagger politican, salaciously entraps Elsie Stoneman, serves to communalize the threat that by Gus's action alone might be taken as individual aberration" ("Re-Birth" 22).

39. Gaines (*FD* 242-43) comments on the symbolism of Lynch's name. Griffith and Dixon avoid "the imagery of hanging" in *The Birth of a Nation*, she writes, "even trying to lay the blame for the practice of lynching on Negroes by the curious device of naming the mulatto villain Sylas [*sic*] Lynch." In *Playing the Race Card* (107), Linda Williams cites Michael Rogin, who also remarks on Lynch's name, which he suggests "turns black victims of lynching into aggressors." Williams also raises questions about the "missing scene" of Gus's castration—that is, about whether it ever actually existed or whether it is simply a misremembering of the film's plot by Seymour Stern; see pp. 124-27.

40. Chester L. Quarles, in *The Ku Klux Klan and Related American Racialist and Antisemitic Organizations: A History and Analysis* (54), notes that "In Atlanta, *The Birth of a Nation* ran for three weeks. William Simmons, a Ku Klux Klan organizer, placed a newspaper ad [for the Klan] which ran right beside the newspaper movie listing. Simmons, like Dixon, had romanticized the Klan and wanted a revival of this reconstruction movement." Wyn Craig Wade, in *The Fiery Cross: The Ku Klux Klan in America* (143), writes that "Colonel Joe 'Doc' Simmons's hopes for a revived Ku Klux Klan were realized by the Atlanta premiere of *The Birth of a Nation* and the Frank murder case." In an illustration in *From Sambo to Superspade* (35), Daniel J. Leab reproduces two advertisements—presumably the two to which Quarles refers—that appeared on facing pages of the Atlanta *Constitution* (8 Dec. 1915). One is for Griffith's film *The Birth of a Nation*; the other announces the chartering, on 6 December 1915, of the "Knights of the Ku Klux Klan . . . a High Class Order for Men of Intelligence and Character . . . The World's Greatest Secret, Social, Patriotic, Fraternal, Beneficiary Order," and offers a contact person and local address.

41. Among the incidents cited by the NAACP was the shooting and killing of a young black boy by a white man in Lafayette, Indiana, who had just left a screening of *The Birth of a Nation*. That incident clearly raised speculation about "effects," as did reports of white patrons leaving the film and remarking that they "wanted to kill niggers." W. E. B. Du Bois, in a memo to NAACP head Walter White, concluded that the campaign against *The Birth of a Nation* was a "special case that was justified by an unprecedented emergency situation." He cited statistics to support

his argument. Among them: "In 1914, 60 Negroes were lynched; in 1915, 99; in 1916, 65, and the number of lynchings per year kept on at the rate of at least one per week from 1915 until 1922. More Negroes were lynched in 1915 than in any other year since the beginning of the century" (Gaines, *FD* 227, 232-33).

42. Ralph Ellison, "The Shadow and the Act," in *Shadow and Act* 275. Ellison concluded that "in subsequent years they reacted upon each other to the large profit of both. The film presented predigested dramatic experience and thrills. The society made the customers all actors in costume."

43. This incident is reported by Cripps (*SFB* 59-60). Jane Gaines records other instances of egging (*FD* 219-20).

44. Cited by Cripps (*SFB* 56-58) and Leab (33). Clyde Taylor notes that Griffith subscribed "to a traditional Southern view of African Americans as 'Pre-moral children' of whom moral understanding was not to be expected" ("Re-Birth" 31).

45. Clyde Taylor reviews a number of the apologist views of *The Birth of a Nation*. According to Taylor, some film scholars "simply accept Griffith's denial of racist intent. Some specify the 'unconsciousness' of his racism. Others argue that Griffith's portrait of the Reconstruction era and the role of Black people in it is essentially accurate." Still others contend "that Griffith's posture towards Blacks, and its easy acceptance by mass audiences, attests to the conventional racist thought of his time." For a fuller discussion of such views, see Taylor's "The Re-Birth of the Aesthetic," especially pp. 17-20. See also Anna Everett's *Returning the Gaze: A Genealogy of Black Film Criticism, 1909-1949*, particularly the chapter on "*The Birth of a Nation* and Interventionist Criticism," pp. 59-106.

46. Viewer interest was further sustained by various effective stunts like "having a troop of horsemen dressed in the white sheets of the Ku Klux Klan ride through towns in advance of showings of the film" (Crowther, "Birth" 82).

47. "In *all* Hollywood film portrayals of blacks," according to James Snead (8), "the political is never far from the sexual, for it is both as a political and as a sexual threat that the black skin appears on screen." Snead makes this particular argument at length in his discussion of the film *King Kong*, as treated more fully in chapter 3 of this study.

48. Michele Wallace, "Oscar Micheaux's *Within Our Gates*" 60. Wallace adds that "one thing is for sure: in Dixon and Griffith's world, blacks are neither the harmless children of *Uncle Tom's Cabin* nor the shrewd survivors found in *Uncle Remus*; rather, they are dangerous if not kept under control."

49. "Only in wartime," observed Pauline Kael, have Hollywood movies had such "primitive power to encourage hatred of a race or a national group" ("Notes" 263).

50. Despite the negative sentiments he evoked, the buck was a strong on-screen presence. As Leab writes, "If Griffith had emphasized the black as wrongdoer, at least he had presented him as a prominent one. For the remainder of the silent period the black on screen was presented not as a human being but as a cliché representing the lowest form of behavior, aspiration, motivation, and performance" (39).

51. Wallace believes that Gus may be considered "a forebear of Richard Wright's *Native Son*," but she takes exception to the notion that the buck influenced later black characters like Sweetback, Superfly, or Shaft. In "Oscar Micheaux's *Within Our Gates*" (61), she writes: "Indeed, either 'brutal buck' is a misnomer or the figure needs to be divided into at least two or three versions which evolved over time. Sweetback, Superfly, and Shaft are all presented as cool, fearless, daring, first-rate fighters, good-looking and sexually proficient. And they never get caught. Gus has none of these qualities. Gus is not a heroic figure, nor can he be made into one, while the protagonists of blaxploitation films are obviously intended to be heroic, whatever one may think of their antics."

52. Micheaux, according to Wallace, "was intent upon correcting the false impression that Griffith had tried to give that mulattos were malicious and scheming by portraying them with as much dignity and humanity as possible." He also "makes it clear that this is a serious-minded class of people who are more concerned about education, thrift, virtue, and decency than they are about trivial matters such as caste or social status within the race" (*"Within"* 63).

53. Valerie Smith, in *Not Just Race, Not Just Gender* (39), notes that "the logic of these texts [passing films] for the most part condemns passing as a strategy for resisting racism." Yet "in fact, several actually use this racialized politic specifically to restrain the options and behavior of black women. Passing male characters can either be re-educated and returned to the bosom of home and community to uplift the race, or they can remain in the white world and be constructed with some measure of condescension, ambivalence, or even approval. Passing women characters, on the other hand, are either re-educated and returned to the bosom of home and community, or they receive some extreme form of punishment such as death or the sacrifice of a loved one."

54. Historian Patricia Morton points out that "in turn of the century literature, the mulatto woman emerged as a figure as menacing as the stereotypical black male threat to white 'purity'" (cited in Wallace, *"Within"* 61).

55. Pines (37, 67) writes that, with few exceptions, "none of the early octoroon characters managed to avoid some form of self-destructive fate. This, by the way, also includes the racial sub-plot of *Imitation of Life* (both 1934 and 1959 versions), in which the 'tragic octoroon' wallows in pathetic self-hatred to the point of 'killing' her black mother."

56. *Show Boat* was actually filmed three times: in 1929, as a Universal silent film to which sound sequences and some music were added and from which the miscegenation subplot was deleted; in 1936 (dir. James Whale), with Helen Morgan as Julie, Paul Robeson as Joe, and Hattie McDaniel as Queenie; and in 1951 (dir. George Sidney), with Ava Gardner and Kathryn Grayson in the lead roles. For an excellent discussion of *Show Boat* as popular melodrama, see Williams, *Playing the Race Card*, especially pp. 158-86.

57. Consequently, as Michele Wallace suggests, the mulatto has evolved more than any of the other black filmic stereotypes: "there really is no contemporary counterpart to this figure in our current lives, nor is [the mulatto] generally reinvoked as a stereotype in portrayals of mixed-race people in contemporary films" ("*Within*" 58).

58. *Shadows* "attempted to show the world of Negroes as closed and esoteric by juxtaposing it with the world of whites through the medium of the anxieties of a young girl who has been passing," writes Thomas Cripps ("Death" 63). "This is not the cheap, sexually charged situation of the earlier films [such as *Pinky*, *Saratoga Trunk*, *Band of Angels*], but only the contrast of two worlds and the need, in American society, to choose one or the other." *One Potato, Two Potato* was a sensitive treatment of a love affair and marriage between Frank (Bernie Hamilton), a black man, and a white divorcée, Julie (Barbara Barrie). As Albert Johnson writes, "the screenplay, by Rafael Hayes, is honest in its dialogue and emotional understatement" ("The Negro in American Films: Some Recent Works" 177). *A Patch of Blue* and *Guess Who's Coming to Dinner* were both Poitier films (discussed further in chapter 5). In the former, Poitier befriends a blind white girl (Elizabeth Hartmann) and rescues her from her slum home and her hectoring, whorish mother (Shelley Winters) and drunken grandfather; in the latter, he plays a Nobel Prize-aspiring doctor who must overcome both the prejudices of his family and the family of his white fiancée (Katharine Houghton).

59. The editors of the *Dispatch* were critical of Beavers's performance in the film: "the role she plays is certainly not appreciated by our modern, high school colored girls and boys. We understand that she pleads in the picture that she wants to remain a slave, and that she shows every solicitation for the education of a little white boy, while she lets a little colored boy grow up in ignorance" (qtd. in Everett 211).

60. The notion of undying devotion to the master goes back to early films. In *Selling Old Master* (1911), for example, the master dies suddenly and his daughter is left in the hands of two faithful family retainers. After she matures, she moves north and marries well; the servants later move north as well. One day, at an auction, they find a portrait of their "Old

Master." The girl sees them with the portrait and brings them to her home, where they again become her faithful servants. According to *The Moving Picture World* (18 Jan. 1911), this was "a picture filled with the pathos of humanity and depicting graphically the loyalty of the Southern darkey to his master and the family."

61. In addition to the Sambo series, the Sambo character appeared in numerous films, including *The Haunted Bachelor* (1912), in which a rich bachelor strikes his black valet Sambo and believes that he has killed him; but Sambo revives and frightens his employer, who thinks he has seen a ghost. The antics attract the attention of the police, and the pair ends up in the station house. And in *Darktown Wooing* (1914), Sambo almost loses his girlfriend Verbena to his rival Rastus; on the day of Rastus's wedding, however, Sambo steals a suit, which Rastus in turn steals from him. With the aid of the clothing dealer and a policeman, Sambo gets Rastus arrested and is reunited with Verbena. And, of course, there was also the *Little Black Sambo* book by Helen Bannerman, now considered a racist classic, and the popular cartoon film based on it (Ub Iwerks, 1935).

62. The original Rastus series was produced by Lubin. But the Rastus character was such an audience favorite that other companies produced Rastus shorts as well. In Lubin's *Rastus Knew It Wasn't* (1914), for instance, police station porter Rastus Remington leaves his scrub pail in the path of the chief. The chief throws the pail at Rastus but hits the Sicilian Luigi instead. Luigi vows to be avenged and places a bomb in the station. Rastus, assuming that the bomb is just an alarm clock, tries to dismantle it but it explodes. In Pathé's *Rastus' Riotous Ride* (1914), Rastus, now an old man, steals a turkey for his daughter's wedding in Coontown. He attempts to have himself and the bird mailed by parcel post, knowing that the sheriff must keep his "hands off the mail." In *A Barnyard Mix-Up* (1915), Farmer Corntossel pursues the chicken-thieving Rastus through the haystacks; eventually, however, the former enemies join forces against a ferocious goat. And in *Rastus' Rabid Rabbit Hunt* (1915), an animated cartoon produced by Electric, Mrs. Rastus Lazybones sends her husband out to stock the larder for Christmas; Rastus and his dog, old Caesar, encounter a hornets' nest and experience other misadventures before a lucky shot loads him down with game for the holidays. The Rastus type also appears in numerous other early shorts and films, including *Darktown Duel* (1912), *Darktown Wooing* (1914), *The Elite Ball* (1913), and the cartoon *A Hot Time in Punkville* (1915).

63. Chicken-snatching was a common plot device in early comic shorts. As Leab writes, "A 1910 advertisement for *C-H-I-C-K-E-N Spells Chicken*, an Essanay production, began 'Ah love mah wattah melon but Oh, You-OO Chicken.' The black man, usually dubbed Rastus in the title

or in advertising blurbs, generally was shown in these movies to be child-like, foolishly pretentious, shiftless (except where gambling or chickens were concerned), clumsy and vulgar" (14).

Some films even managed to incorporate several stereotypes simultaneously into the plot. *The Ranch Chicken* (1911), for example, combined chicken-stealing with the fear of ghosts. According to *The Moving Picture World* (22 Jan. 1911): "Here is a lively Western comedy, containing an illustration of the so-called darkey's desire for chicken. They [the cowboys of the Circle C Ranch] scare the pair of darkey chicken-stealers with ghosts, and the way Rastus departs [the chicken coop] leaving [his wife] Dinah to her fate, is funny. The last scene, with the chicken suspended down their chimney [by the ranch boss, who is rewarding them for the entertainment being had at their expense] and their devoted belief that it is a gift of the gods is as funny as the rest."

64. *The Chicken Thief*, released by the American Mutoscope and Biograph Company in 1904, was the first multi-reel film produced in the United States with black actors in the title role (Sampson 32).

65. It was not uncommon for blacks to protest such depictions, usually to no avail. In the *Chicago Defender* (4 May 1918), for example, Lester Walton wrote bitterly about a scene in a Universal Screen Magazine film playing in a Harlem theater that showed "colored men who were so lacking in self respect as to pose as chicken thieves for a few paltry dollars" (Bowser and Spence, *Writing* 93).

66. Judith Mayne, in *Cinema and Spectatorship* (142), notes that, in the years between 1939, when Hattie McDaniel won an Academy Award as Best Supporting Actress for playing the Mammy to Scarlett in *Gone With the Wind* (the first Academy Award won by a black performer), and 1991, when Whoopi Goldberg won an Academy Award as Best Supporting Actress for playing the "handmaiden to the interrupted romance of two yuppies" in *Ghost* (1990), film parts for black women remained unfortunately consistent. "As far as black actresses and the roles they enact in Hollywood cinema are concerned," she writes, "little has changed."

67. "Sunshine" became a favored nickname for blacks on screen, even in later films. Nick Romano's black friend Jim (uncredited, but played by Davis Roberts) in the 1949 film adaptation of Willard Motley's *Knock on Any Door*, for instance, is pejoratively referred to as Sunshine rather than by his given name, even when he is called to the stand to testify.

68. Wallace (*"Within"* 58) notes that he is also a "trickster figure" and a "cunning survivor."

69. A contemporary critic in *The Indianapolis Freeman* (26 Nov. 1914) observed that in *Uncle Remus' First Visit to New York*, produced by the Hunter Haynes Photoplay Company, "the modern and the ante-bellum

Negro are shown in sharp differentiation, imparting a lesson that cannot fail to inspire, as well as interest and amuse" (qtd. in Sampson 275). The cast of the film included Wesley Jones (Uncle Remus), Maude Jones (Remus's wife), Tom Brown (Rastus), Abbie Mitchell (Rastus's wife), Allie Gilliam, and Billy Harper.

Chapter 2

"A Credit to the Race": Oscar Micheaux and Early Race Filmmaking

Nothing has done so much to awaken race consciousness
of the colored man in the United States as the motion picture. It has made him hungry to see himself as he has
come to be. Rather unconsciously it has brought to him a
spirit of resentment against the traditional portrayal presented everywhere of the Negro.

—*William Foster*

The Hollywood film industry, beginning its quick rise to prominence in the early decades of the twentieth century, saw the opportunity to gain an economic foothold in American society by
exploiting the tremendous mythmaking potential of motion pictures. Implicit in that mythmaking, however, was an acceptance of
anti-black images, which—as Chester Fontenot suggests—"can
probably be explained by the willingness of white Americans to
see confirmed in visual images their belief that black people were
subhuman" (111). Like their Hollywood counterparts, early black
independent filmmakers also understood cinema's mythmaking
potential; but rather than promote the old pejorative types in their
films, many of them tried to present more realistic portraits of
black Americans by creating an alternate set of cultural referents
and establishing new black character types and situations. While
these black-produced and black-cast movies (often called "race
movies" or "race pictures," because they were intended primarily
for black audiences[1]) did not, by any means, shatter the worst of
the stereotypes of blacks that had been introduced by filmmakers
from Edwin S. Porter to D. W. Griffith or halt the negative racial
imagery that dominated American film, they did offer a response
to those troubling depictions and a challenge to other movie pro-

ducers to strive for more balanced racial and ethnic portrayals in their pictures. And they took up the call to "duty" that publisher Lester Walton issued in the *New York Age* (18 Sept. 1920): "to present the Negro in a complimentary light, . . . to gladden our hearts and inspire us by presenting characters typifying the better element of Negroes" (Regester, "Press" 44).

An expression of group consciousness, race movies essentially imagined into existence a separate community, one that white filmmakers simply did not see and could not understand; and they became a source of pride for black filmmakers as well as for black viewers, who identified them as products that were created by and for the community.[2] According to Pearl Bowser and Louise Spence, "race consciousness and identification were cohesive and binding forces and these movies were an articulation of self that challenged the dominant culture's ordering of reality" (*Writing* 14).[3] Of particular significance, as Jane Gaines suggests, was "the way in which they would be counterhegemonic without symmetrically 'countering' white culture on every point; for their oppositionality, if it could be called that, was in the circumvention, in the way they produced images that didn't go *through* white culture. Seen by blacks, unseen by whites, race movies featured an all-black world, a utopian vision of 'all-black everything'" (*FD* 13). Although almost all were underfinanced, technically inferior to the Hollywood product, and poorly distributed, the early black independent films were thus, in themselves, remarkable achievements.

EARLY RACE FILMMAKERS

Oscar Micheaux, now widely regarded as America's first important black filmmaker, was not the first black American to try his hand at independent filmmaking. Born in 1884, the same year as Micheaux, was William Foster, a former newspaper man, vaudeville booking agent, and theatrical manager who recognized the incredible economic promise of the developing motion picture industry. As Henry T. Sampson writes, "Foster also saw an opportunity to make films that countered the objectionable racial stereotypes so prevalent in motion pictures being made by white film companies and being shown in the black theaters located along a five-block section of South State Street near 29th Street in Chicago known as 'The Stroll'" (2-3).

Foster had been living and working in New York City as a paddock man, a clocker, and eventually a commissions man for Jack McDonald, one of the nation's premier horsemen in the late 1800s. While still on the job for McDonald, he became interested in show business and took on the role of publicist for Cole and Johnson's "A Trip to Coontown" Company and later for the musical shows "In Dahomey" and "Abyssinia," starring the legendary comedy team of Bert Williams and George Walker. Attracted by the opening of Robert Motts's Pekin Theatre in 1904, Foster moved to Chicago, where he became the Pekin Theatre's business representative, a position that allowed him to view and book numerous black vaudeville acts. Under the pen name of "Juli Jones," Foster also began writing articles on black show business for various black weeklies,[4] including the *Chicago Defender*; and by 1913, he decided to enter the movie profession himself. After scraping together enough money to found the Foster Photoplay Company, he produced his first short, a two-reel comedy called *The Railroad Porter* (also released under the title *The Pullman Porter*), starring Lottie Grady and Howard Kelly, both former members of Pekin's stock company.[5] The short opened strongly at a few theaters in Chicago and later was shown in the East; often it would be featured on the same bill as Foster's footage of a YMCA parade, now considered to be the first black-produced newsreel.

Described by a contemporary journal as "one of the best informed men in theatricals hereabouts," Foster had great hopes for black filmmakers. In an article in the *Chicago Defender* (9 Sept. 1915), he observed that "in a moving picture the Negro would offset so many insults of the race—could tell their side of the birth of this great race . . . . It is the Negro businessman's only international chance to make money and put his race right with the world" (qtd. in Bowser and Spence, *Writing* 97). And in an earlier article published in the black weekly *Indianapolis Freeman* (20 Dec. 1913), he noted happily that the "colored man" was already establishing for himself a place in the film world and "that he is commencing to weigh the import and to calculate the value of the motion picture as a medium for portraying the finer and stronger features of his particular life. . . . Our brother white is born blind and unwill-

ing to see the finer aspects and qualities of American Negro life. . . .
We must be up and doing for ourselves in our own best way and
for our own best good." Asserting "that the business among
Negroes is bound to become the basis of a great and profitable
industry," with the profits accruing "to the Negro himself," Foster
predicted "phenomenal success for those among us who have the
bravery and foresight to wrestle with the problems of production
and presentation." With the motion picture "here to stay, the
Negro is sure to do his part of the work and certain to reap his portion of the reward" (qtd. in Sampson 174-75).

To demonstrate his own foresight, Foster headed to Florida,
where Lubin, Pathé, Kalem, and other licensed film manufacturers
were making films, to evaluate the feasibility of building a studio
there. But his optimism soon turned to frustration. Like his contemporary Hunter Haynes, a black producer of film shorts whose
Afro-American Film Company was partially financed by whites in
New York City, Foster discovered that the major motion picture
rental and distribution companies simply did not book black independent films into the widening market of white theaters; yet
those same companies regularly booked white-produced films
into the smaller number of exclusively black theaters. Moreover,
the same white theaters that booked black vaudeville acts and
black-cast motion pictures by white companies refused even to
rent movies by black producers; and though the major theatrical
publications like *Billboard*, *Variety*, and *The Moving Picture World*
regularly advertised and reviewed black-cast films by white companies, they did not carry ads or run reviews of the films produced
by Foster, Haynes, and other early black-owned companies.
According to Henry T. Sampson, it was "this de facto economic
boycott of the first black film producers that gave birth to a separate black film industry in the United States," which "during the
next forty years produced over 500 films featuring blacks which
were shown in theaters catering to blacks with little distribution
anywhere else" (3). But Foster would not be among those black
filmmakers for whom he had earlier predicted such "phenomenal
success." Although he went on to produce a few more shorts,
including *The Fall Guy*, *The Barber*, *The Butler*, and *The Grafter and
the Maid* (also released under the title *The Grafter and the Girl*), he
quit the motion picture industry in 1917 to become circulation

manager of the *Chicago Defender*, which he helped to make one of the most widely circulated newspapers among blacks. In 1928, hoping to resurrect his film career, Foster moved to Los Angeles,[6] where he directed for the Pathé Studios a series of black musical shorts featuring such legendary performers as Clarence Muse, Stepin Fetchit, and the song-dance-and-comedy team of Buck and Bubbles. He also began selling stock subscriptions to revive and finance his Foster Photoplay Company and struggled bitterly "trying to get somewhere in this Business as a Producer" of "Pictures That Talk-Sing-Dance Reflect Credit" because, as he said, "if a colored producing co dont make the Grade now it will be useless later on after all the Big Co.s get merged up—they will set about controlling the Equipment then the door wil be closed [*sic*]" (qtd. in *SFB* 221).[7] Foster's morose estimate was ultimately correct, and his production company released no new films.

The shorts that Foster managed to produce before his company folded were generally crude efforts that followed the established comedy formulas of the day.[8] *The Railroad Porter* (1912), for instance, told the story of a young wife who, thinking her husband is out on his run, invites to dinner a well-dressed man who turns out to be a waiter. Returning home, the husband pulls out his gun; the waiter, according to the *New York Age* (25 Sept. 1913), "gets his revolver and returns the compliment . . . no one is hurt . . . and all ends happily" (Reid 8). And in *The Barber* (1916), a barber posing as a Spanish music teacher engages in a series of Keystone Kops-type of chases as he tries to evade an angry husband, the local police, and even an old woman, whose boat he overturns when he jumps in a lake to avoid capture. Foster's shorts, however, were rarely distributed outside of the Midwest, and his players, despite their strengths as stage actors, failed to attract national recognition as film stars, even in the black press. Nevertheless, Foster's efforts marked an important beginning for blacks in film. As Mark A. Reid writes, Foster "broke with the 'coon' tradition established by Thomas Alva Edison's *Ten Pickaninnies* (1904) and *The Wooing and Wedding of a Coon* (1905) as well as Sigmund Lubin's Sambo and Rastus series (1909, 1910, and 1911)" and tried to create comedy that "would appeal to the widest segment of his [black] audience" (9). William Foster therefore remains a significant—if largely neglected—figure in black cinema history.

Around the time that the Foster Photoplay Company was producing its early shorts, Emmett J. Scott, the personal secretary to black leader and Tuskegee Institute president Booker T. Washington, determined to make a major black film that would counter the racist portrayals in *The Birth of a Nation*, which had recently been released. But he was not alone in his ambition.[9] The National Association for the Advancement of Colored People (NAACP), formed only a few years earlier in 1909, was already planning a film in response to Griffith's cant and had even begun negotiations with Carl Laemmle of Universal. Within the NAACP, however, there was division about the direction that film should take and the message that it should convey to whites. As Thomas Cripps writes in "The Making of *The Birth of a Race*," the NAACP wished to reach beyond Washington's personal rise from slavery but "could agree on no clear-cut means of breaking with its Horatio Alger line of argument." Elaine Sterne, a scriptwriter at Universal who was working with the NAACP's scenario committee to shape the project, liked the idea of engaging white attention through a film to be called *Lincoln's Dream*, which would define black aspiration and celebrate black progress. Harvard historian Albert Bushnell Hart, a member of the NAACP's Boston branch, opened his private library to Sterne for her research, but eventually he decided to write his own rough-draft scenario. Mary White Ovington, a social worker and one of the NAACP's liberal urban founders, argued for a tale of "'black sufferings and strivings' that would meet with favor from conservative and radical alike.'" W. E. B. Du Bois, the NAACP's ranking black intellectual and editor of its in-house publication *The Crisis*, soon withdrew entirely his support of the NAACP project in favor of his own, a "pageant of Negro history and some plays of my own and in moving pictures based on them" ("Making" 44; *SFB* 71-72). To complicate matters further, Laemmle insisted that the NAACP raise $50,000 towards the production costs, to offset the $60,000 investment by Universal; but the organization, even after appealing to its liberal white allies, was unable to come up with the funds. When the NAACP finally dropped the project, choosing instead to fight the Griffith picture through the courts and the picket lines, Emmett J. Scott stepped in.[10]

Together with Booker T. Washington, Scott had been seeking a way to get involved in a black-controlled film production. Both men already knew something about movies from negotiations over the rights to shoot motion pictures on the Tuskegee campus. (D. W. Griffith, in fact, had at one point expressed interest in rights to old campus footage that he intended to use in a conciliatory prologue that he proposed to add to *The Birth of a Nation*.) After discussions with the NAACP over *Lincoln's Dream* broke down, Elaine Sterne came to Scott, hoping that he could revive the NAACP's interest and thereby salvage the project. But Scott was unsuccessful. Laemmle withdrew, as did several other producers that Scott had courted; and the dream of *Lincoln's Dream* faded.

Undaunted, Scott shifted his attention back to the project that he had originally hoped to promote, the filming of Washington's autobiographical *Up From Slavery*. Initiating correspondence with the Advance Motion Picture Company of Chicago, Scott promised a "package" of incentives that included motion picture rights to the book; the offer of himself as writer-consultant on the film, the services of Tuskegee and the use of its campus, and a tie-in with Washington's publisher, all of which would afford "*the colored man's viewpoint*"; and an alliance with six hundred National Negro Business League chapters and connections to over one hundred black newspapers that would "be harnessed to the publicity" in the interest of the photoplay (*SFB* 73-74). When Washington's death brought that particular project to a halt, Scott hastily signed a new contract to produce a different film, to be called *The Birth of a Race*. According to its prospectus, that film—"the true story of the Negro—his life in Africa, his transportation to America, his enslavement, his freedom, his achievements, together with his past, present and future relations to his white neighbor and to the world in which both live and labor"—would be an inspirational plea for mutual respect between the races and would draw on numerous black talents. But financial mismanagement (including the fraudulent promotion and sale of stocks) and confused leadership created numerous and ultimately insurmountable problems. William Selig, the original producer, and his associates pulled out halfway through production, and Daniel Frohman, a New York veteran vaudeville producer, took over. Frohman, however, had a different concept of the film, and he immediately began shooting vast amounts of biblical footage in Tampa, where he had located a public park with mock Egyptian architecture—footage that had no relation to what the Selig Company had already shot. After Frohman dropped out, the film passed through the hands of several other white independent filmmakers before being completed at the Rothacker Film Manufacturing Company plant in Chicago. Scott and the other blacks involved saw themselves losing virtually all control of the venture; and eventually both Scott and all vestiges of *Up From Slavery* were "dumped" (Cripps, "Making" 45-46).

In 1918, almost three years after it was first conceived, *The Birth of a Race* finally premiered at Chicago's Blackstone Theater. Promoted as "The Greatest and Most Daring of Photoplays . . . A Master Picture Conceived in the Spirit of Truth and Dedicated to All of the Races of the World" (Bogle, *TCMMB* 103), the film was actually a complete flop. As released, it moved from the creation of the world to numerous other scenes from sacred history, all of which were re-created employing mammoth sets—and all to no artistic purpose. Instead of hailing black achievement within the context of the development of civilization, *The Birth of a Race* emphasized such decidedly anti-black images as the victimization of the Jews by the black army of the Pharaoh and the invasion of a white tribe by a black one, an incident that leads Noah to suggest that the "prejudice" that results from "living apart" is somehow tied to black failings; and instead of synthesizing the Gospels, the film carried forth the notion of racial separation in the person of a very white Jesus before cutting abruptly to the voyage of Columbus, the ride of Paul Revere, and (curiously skirting any visual depiction of slavery itself) the proclamation of emancipation by Lincoln (Cripps, "Making" 48-49). Finally, according to *The Moving Picture World* (10 May 1919), in keeping with contemporary anti-German propaganda, "a disconnected war story [was thrown in] for good measure," but it rendered the film both formless and essentially structureless and made it "a striking example of what a photoplay should not be" (qtd. in Sampson 208-09). That subplot, about Oscar and George Schmidt, two brothers in a German-American household divided against the war, tried to rouse patriotic fervor and celebrate America's entry into World War I; but it may also have been meant to parallel the internecine North/South division in *The Birth of a Nation*. Like the Stonemans and the Camerons, who initially hold opposing beliefs about the principle of Southern sovereignty, the two Schmidt brothers respond in different ways to the world events: Oscar, the elder, decides to return to fight for the Kaiser; George, "a true blue American," marries a girl employed in the munitions factory run by his father, goes overseas only after the United States enters the war, and successfully holds back several assaults by the vicious "Hun" (including an attack on a hospital by German forces led by his brother, whom he kills).[11] As its garbled plot suggests, the film was indeed "the most grotesque cinematic chimera in the history of the picture business" (*Variety* 25 April 1919).

Especially since only a portion of the film is extant, "we cannot know," Cripps writes, "the details of the internal struggle over control of *The Birth of a Race* nor can we know the extent to which the surviving film represents the conscious intentions of its makers" ("Making" 53). But this much is certain: as *Variety* (6 Dec. 1918) noted, the film was started "on the premise of a nationwide defence of the Negro race"; a lot of stock was sold, largely to black investors who had been hustled into believing the film would have a legitimate race angle; "everything went along swimmingly" until America got into World War I and "the character of the picture was altered"; more stock was sold and "another scenario was written"; and ultimately the film shifted completely away from the aspirations, advancement, and achievement of blacks that were its original focus (Sampson 209). Moreover, a disillusioned Emmett J. Scott left filmmaking—although he continued to be prominent in the black community as the Army's Assistant Secretary for Negro Affairs, a position in which he was able to help other filmmakers, and in various other leadership roles.[12]

The bungled *Birth of a Race* marked a lost opportunity for achievement in black film. Yet even before that film had been completed, the noted black actor Noble M. Johnson, with the support of his brother George P. (Perry) Johnson, formed the Lincoln Motion Picture Company, a black movie company based in Los Angeles and incorporated in 1916. Inspired by the efforts of those blacks originally involved in the *Birth of a Race* project but cognizant of the reasons for their frustrations and failures, Johnson determined to produce race films designed to speak to black audiences unmediated by Hollywood stereotypes. Lincoln's first release was *The Realization of A Negro's Ambition* (1916), a two-reel feature film that starred Johnson and featured black actors

Clarence Brooks (one of the company's founders), Dudley Brooks, Beulah Hall, and Lottie Boles, all of whom played nonstereotyped, middle-class roles. In the film, which was a black recasting of the Horatio Alger story, a young Negro civil engineering graduate of Tuskegee Institute named James Burton leaves his parents' farm and his sweetheart Mary Hayden to seek his fortune in the West. After being rejected for a job at an oil field in California because of his race, he rescues the owner's daughter and is offered employment as the head of an exploration team. Eventually he realizes that the same kind of geological conditions that he is studying exist on his father's farm; with a subsidy from the owner, he returns home and starts drilling for oil. Meanwhile, Doris and George Babbit, the children of wealthy gentleman Sam Babbit,

Figure 2.1. The Realization of A Negro's Ambition, Lincoln's first release, offered a view of black middle class aspiration and achievement. (Lincoln Motion Picture Company, 1916)

who owns land adjacent to the Burton farm, try to discredit Mary. But James, who strikes oil and becomes rich, proposes to Mary anyway; and together they realize all of their ambitions: family, friends, and home. (Fig. 2.1.) Significantly, as Jane Gaines notes, given the means and opportunity, James goes "directly back to his 'own people,' a recurring narrative device in race movies, which restrict action to an all-black world within which everything is won or lost—a circumscribed miniature of the white world" (*FD* 107).

Not only was *The Realization of A Negro's Ambition* well received; Henry T. Sampson writes that it "set the standard for future films produced by the Lincoln and other companies and was the first successful classy Negro feature film produced without burlesque comedy" (130). A black reviewer described it as a reflection of "the business and social life of the Negro as it really is and not as our jealous contemporaries would have us appear" (Bowser and Spence, *Writing* 110). Shown in churches and schools as well as in movie houses, the picture created great demand for a new Lincoln feature, which the company met with *Trooper of Troop K* (1916), also known as *Trooper of Company K*, a fictional story about the massacre of the Negro troops of the "famous fighting Tenth Cavalry" during the battle of Carrizal in Mexico.[13] Starring Noble Johnson as "Shiftless Joe," a goodhearted but careless fellow who eventually proves his heroism, Beulah Hall as Clara Holmes, the young woman who takes an interest in his welfare, and Jimmy Smith as Jimmy Warner, who competes with Joe for Clara's affection, the film was another story of racial achievement: through Clara's faith in him, Joe improves himself and becomes a good race man. In fact, as Jane Gaines (*FD* 109) writes, the implication is that every "Shiftless Joe" can be reformed and can better himself personally and socially, particularly if he adopts the values of the black middle class. The film played to capacity houses from Chicago to the West Coast. And in 1917, after both films were shown at the Tuskegee Institute, the *Tuskegee Student* raved that "such pictures as these are not only elevating and inspiring in themselves, but they are also calculated to instill principles of race pride and loyalty in the minds of colored people" (qtd. in Bowser and Spence, *Writing* 90).

Another Lincoln film, *The Law of Nature* (1917), quickly followed. In that film, which again starred Noble Johnson and included

Albertine Pickens, Clarence Brooks, Estelle Everett, Stebeno Clements, Frank White, Elsworth Saunders, and Sallie Richardson in the cast, a woman leaves her rancher husband and children to revisit the glamorous East of her former days; but she soon finds herself humiliated, alone, and ill. Realizing her folly and the inevitable consequences of her violation of "Nature's Law," she returns west to rejoin her family. Like the company's earlier productions, *The Law of Nature* proved to be "a fine story," "an artistic and well portrayed success," and a "good box-office attraction" (Sampson 132). An ad for the Omaha run described it as a "classy" and uplifting picture with "a wholesome moral" (Bowser and Spence, *Writing* 90). The manager of the Palace, a black-owned, black-managed theater in Louisville, Kentucky, wrote to George Johnson that *The Law of Nature* "took on like wild fire"; and even the white-owned, white-managed Alamo Theater in Washington, D.C., listed the film as the "biggest drawing card" of all of Lincoln's productions (Gaines, *FD* 102).[14]

Lincoln's fortunes changed, however, with the resignation of Noble Johnson in 1918. The Universal Picture Company of Hollywood, which employed Johnson as a featured player, had exerted pressure on him to step down from his responsibilities at Lincoln: it was in fact a condition of Johnson's contract with Universal that he sever his ties with the company he founded and that Lincoln be prohibited from using Johnson's name or likeness in new advertising; similarly, Lincoln could not utilize existing advertising in new ways, including "any part of the negative or positive films, slides, stills, plates, cuts, heralds, or lithographs" (Gaines, *FD* 99). The minutes of the September 3 company meeting record that Johnson tendered his resignation because he could no longer devote the necessary attention to company business and requested, as Universal insisted, that the company no longer use his name in association with new productions or products (Sampson 135-36). Such a repressive and cutthroat demand was no doubt precipitated by Johnson's immense popularity as an actor: the multi-talented Johnson, who had appeared in thirty-four films between 1915 and 1918, was such a box-office draw in the black community that black audiences would readily turn out for the white studio pictures in which he was featured. Ironically, therefore, Johnson's very popularity spelled doom for his own fledgling black company, which Universal perceived as potentially serious competition for their productions.[15]

After Noble Johnson's departure, the company turned for leadership to his brother, former newspaper and real-estate man George P. Johnson. George accepted the position of Lincoln's General Booking Manager but insisted that he be allowed to work from Omaha, Nebraska, so that he could keep his job as the first Negro clerk in the Post Office. George soon forged a number of strong alliances for Lincoln, most notably with Tony Langston, the influential theatrical editor of the *Chicago Defender*, which publicized the company's films, and Romeo Daugherty, an editor at the *New York Amsterdam News*; opened several branch offices; employed advance men to promote Lincoln's features at smaller theaters; and, perhaps most importantly, established the first black-operated national booking organization to increase and facilitate the distribution of its race films (Sampson 138, 140). During George's tenure, the company released *A Man's Duty* (1919), a story of conflict between a man's moral obligation and his new-found happiness, with Clarence Brooks in the lead role that was originally meant to be Noble Johnson's, and *By Right of Birth* (1921), another picture of race achievement in which slavery is reversed and negated by a legacy of wealth for succeeding generations, with Clarence Brooks and Anita Thompson starring in a screenplay written by George Johnson himself. (Interestingly, in an early example of a movie tie-in, with the help of Robert L. Vann, the publisher of the *Pittsburgh Courier*, Johnson published a novelization of *A Man's Duty* in Vann's magazine, *The Competitor* [Gaines, *FD* 103].[16]) Plans for a new production, *The Heart of a Negro*, featuring Clarence Brooks, Edna Morton, and Lawrence Chenault, were announced in 1923; but the film was never produced.

Shortly afterwards the Lincoln Motion Picture Company, the first black independent to enjoy national distribution of its race pictures, discontinued operation. Renowned for the quality of its features and its serious treatments of middle-class black life, the company—beset by various financial difficulties that were exacerbated by the increased competition from white studios—apparently felt unable to compete successfully in the developing market of longer feature-length films. Yet even after the demise of Lincoln,

George Johnson continued to be interested in the movie industry: he started a new venture, the National News Service, which he operated part-time out of his garage. And "until the end of his life he made a business and eventually a hobby of collecting and disseminating information about the status and progress of African Americans in the entertainment industry" (Gaines, *FD* 103).[17]

Founded around the same time as Lincoln was another important black company, the Frederick Douglass Film Company of New Jersey, whose officers included some of the most prominent black citizens of Jersey City and whose purpose was "to give the public motion pictures which do not degrade the race" (Sampson 5). Douglass's first production, *The Colored American Winning His Suit* (1917), aimed—according to the press book—"to offset the evil effects of certain photo plays that have libeled the Negro and criticized his friends; to bring about a better and more friendly understanding between the white and colored races; to inspire in the Negro a desire to climb higher in good citizenship, business, education and religion" (Sampson 181). The film, whose screenplay was written by Reverend Dr. W. S. Smith, was a kind of modern morality play: young Bob Winall (Thomas M. Mosley), a humbly born black who graduates from Howard University and becomes a lawyer, must fight various obstacles to win the hand of Alma Elton (Ida Askins), the woman he loves. In court, he is forced to go up against a white man, Mr. Hinderus (F. King), in order to defend Alma's father against a charge of theft; and with the help of Colonel Goodwill (Fred Leighton), he prevails. The white man's attempt to "hinderus" having failed, Winall—through "goodwill"—indeed wins all. The *New York Age* (20 July 1916) hailed the film as "the first five-reel Film Drama written, directed, acted and produced by Negroes" (Bowser and Spence, *Writing* 73) and praised the company, which was "owned and operated by Negroes" and "whose aim is to present the better side of Negro life, and to use the screen as a means of bringing about better feeling between races" (Gaines, *FD* 98).

The company's second film, also released in 1917, was *The Scapegoat*, an adaptation of "The Scapegoat" by the distinguished black writer Paul Laurence Dunbar. In Dunbar's story, which is told in two parts, Robinson Asbury is an ambitious young black man who goes from bootblack to barbershop owner and eventually to lawyer. "The big Negro of the district and, of necessity, of the town [of Cadgers]" (5), Asbury gains the patronage of local politicians, who believe that he will be useful to them in mustering black votes. But when the "fevers of reform" threaten the politicians' authority, they offer up Asbury as a scapegoat, and he is sent to jail for ten months. Upon his release, he returns to town, where he rebuilds his business and works quietly to bring down all of those who plotted his ruin. Though he repeatedly professes "I am not a politican," he proves that he is just that—and a very effective one—by winning the support of the town's black citizens, ousting his former rivals, and exercising greater power than he ever wielded before.

The film version of *The Scapegoat*, according to a reviewer for the *New York Age* (17 May 1917), was noteworthy if less impressive than the story; told in three parts, the film lacked "a certain cohesiveness of sequence" and the characters at times were "thrust into new environments and new conditions with startling abruptness." Moreover, the doctors, ministers, and other "race representatives [who] are supposed to be classed among the 'intellectuals' of the race" were forced to speak in the dialect that "seems to be the rage among writers of dramas and photoplays" (qtd. in Sampson 269). Nevertheless, the film appealed to its audiences in both the "white and colored motion picture houses" in which it was booked.[18] Like so many other black film companies, however, the Douglass Company struggled to develop appropriate outlets for the distribution of its films, while lack of capital stalled plans for new projects. The company released its final production, *Heroic Negro Soldiers of the World War*, in March, 1919. A pictorial demonstration of the bravery of black soldiers, including the "Black Devils," the "Hell Fighters," the "Buffaloes," and the "Red Devils," in action under fire in France, it was considered the best black documentary film yet produced.

Emerging after World War I was another film company that quickly distinguished itself in several significant ways. Reol Productions of New York City, headed by Robert Levy, the white former manager of the Quality Amusement Company that sponsored the Lafayette Players Dramatic Stock Company, aggressively promoted its black performers to black audiences—Edna Morton, one of the first black movie stars, was billed as "the colored Mary Pickford"—and established large circuits of theaters throughout many sections of the South and in a number of northern cities where the company distributed its films. But perhaps Reol's most important achievement was its recognition of the culture of the market that it served by the production of films that were adapted from classic black literature.[19] According to Pearl Bowser and Louise Spence, Reol "promoted its films to theaters by emphasizing that they were based on the stories and plays of Negro authors"; the company even announced to the press that it was seeking talented Negro writers on college campuses to provide material for its films (*Writing* 102).[20]

Reol's first film, in fact, was *The Sport of the Gods* (1921), based on a novel—and a screenplay—by Paul Laurence Dunbar. Berry (Leon Williams), a faithful, loyal, and innocent black man, is thrown in jail after being convicted of theft against his employer, Maurice Oakley (Lindsay J. Hall). Disgraced, humiliated, and unable to find work, Hamilton's family moves from their home in Virginia to New York, where son Joe (G. Edward Brown) takes up with evil companions; daughter Kitty (Elizabeth Boyer) is placed in jeopardy as an underworld singer; and mother Fannie (Lucille Brown), believing that a penitentiary sentence is the same as a divorce, is persuaded to marry a man who wants only her money. After being cleared of the crime and released from jail by the ingenuity of his daughter's lover, who reveals that Maurice's brother Frank was actually the thief, Hamilton travels to New York, where he rescues his family members, who have fallen "into the hands of vice traffickers" and found themselves "on their way to the depth." He takes them away from the urban depravity and returns them to Virginia, "where they take up the life that leads to true happiness" (Sampson 339). The film's ending is thus more upbeat than the novel's, in which Berry and Fannie—having nowhere else to go—return to their cottage on the Oakley property. "It was not a happy life," Dunbar writes in the novel, "but it was all that was left to them, and they took it up without complaint, for they knew they were powerless against some Will infinitely stronger than their own" (404). As the reviewer for the *California Eagle* (30 July 1921) noted, "the thrilling movie taken from Paul Laurence Dunbar's beautiful Folk Poetry . . . depicts the highest type of Negro life [in the opening scenes], and very cleverly points out the fine points of the relationship between the two Races from a Southern viewpoint."

Another early Reol film was *The Call of His People* (1922), which was advertised as an adaptation of "The Man Who Would Be White," the "famous story" by black writer Aubrey Bowser about a black who is light enough to pass for white. Passing, or racial duplicity, was a popular theme among black writers and filmmakers, who employed it as a way to explore the meaning of race pride and sometimes, more subversively, to refute white misconceptions about black characteristics and capabilities as well as white attempts to create racially pure cultural spaces (Gaines, *FD* 158). According to Donald Bogle, like other passing films, *The Call of His People* "seemed to be the wish-fulfillment yearnings" of its producers, and it "revealed the preoccupation of black America at the time: how to come as close as possible to the great White American Norm" (*TCMMB* 105). The film ran six reels and included in its cast Lawrence Chenault, the popular actor who also starred in several of Oscar Micheaux's films, as well as Edna Morton, George Brown, Mae Kemp, James Stevens, Mercedes Gilbert, and Percy Verwayen.

In *The Call of His People*, Nelson Holmes, a black man who is posing as white, advances from office boy to General Manager of the Brazilian-American Coffee Syndicate; his responsibilities include the enforcing of contracts with the rival Santos Company. Holmes's new position stirs up jealousies within the Syndicate, particularly on the part of a fellow employee, Beauregard Stuart, who feels that Holmes's job should have been his. Meanwhile, James Graves, an old childhood friend who is the brother of Holmes's first love Elinor, arrives seeking employment. Fearful that his secret will be revealed, Holmes offers Graves a position as his personal secretary but encourages his old friend to pose as a Spaniard. Graves, who refuses to deny his race, does agree to keep Holmes's secret, even though he despises his hypocrisy.

On the verge of ruin by the Syndicate, the Santos Company sends a representative to tempt Holmes with a big bribe if he destroys the contracts. Holmes throws the man out of his office, but Stuart assaults Graves, escapes with what he believes to be the contracts, and decides to frame Holmes in their theft. The next morning, as Stuart confronts Holmes in front of their boss, Elinor arrives with the missing papers, entrusted to her by her brother, who could not come forward himself because of the injury he suffered in the attack. Cleared of wrongdoing and overwhelmed by Graves's loyalty, Holmes confesses the secret of his identity to the boss, who assures him that it is the man, not the color, that counts. The brave deeds of James and Elinor give Holmes, who had felt caught in the paradox of assimilation—that is, trying so hard to act white that he loses his black cultural identity—a new appreciation of race; proud to be one of Elinor's people, he visits her to beg forgiveness and propose marriage. *Billboard* (16 July 1921) reviewer J. A. Jackson noted that the "natural story [is] based on a condition that is quite familiar to all of us" and that it "depicts in a dramatic manner the conflict of sentiments that assail the lighter complected among us who 'pass,' and the ever present anxiety that is associated with the practice that has become so prevalent" (qtd. in Sampson 293). Moreover, according to a writer in the *Chicago Defender* (6 Aug. 1921), *The Call of His People* was "without a doubt the finest picture ever made with an all-Colored cast, the story being a gripping one, the directing being perfect and the photography the best that could possibly be made. . . . [T]he resultant production places the Reol Corporation in a class far in advance of any producing companies making pictures in which our people are featured" (Regester, "Press" 38, 40).

Although Reol Productions occasionally made comedies like the two-reeler *The Jazz Hounds*, the company specialized in dramatic features such as *The Burden of Race* (1921), a film about the risks of interracial romance, and *Secret Sorrow* (1921), about the two Morgan brothers who take very different paths in life. The latter was based on a work by "the celebrated Race author, J. C. Brown" (Bowser and Spence, *Writing* 102). In the film version, Arthur Morgan, having been given up for adoption by his widowed and impoverished mother Anne, grows up as the son of a prominent black doctor, graduates law school, and becomes Assistant District Attorney in New York; Joe Morgan, on the other hand, drifts into a world of crime as a henchman for the corrupt politician Sam Dugan. After Joe is accused of a murder that he did not commit, Arthur—unaware of his brother's identity—prosecutes him; but Grace Dugan, Sam's daughter, uncovers the real murderer. Reunited with his mother and his now-reformed brother, Arthur marries Grace; and they all become part of a happy family. Environment, the film suggests, dictates racial success: Arthur distinguishes himself as a young man because he had enjoyed many advantages as a child; but given the opportunity, even Joe can better himself.

In addition to the films it adapted from works by Dunbar, Bowser, and Brown, Reol planned to bring to the screen Charles W. Chesnutt's *The Marrow of Tradition*, although there is no record that the film was ever completed or released (Cripps, *Black Film as Genre* 29).[21] Before going out of business in 1924, however, Reol produced at least ten feature films that were notable both for their high quality and for the lack of stereotyping of the black characters. Yet, despite Reol's success in black theaters, Levy was disappointed that he did not get more support and encouragement from the black community—a sentiment shared by many black filmmakers. An article in the *Baltimore Afro-American* (2 May 1924) quoted Levy as saying: "Negro amusement buyers are fickle and possessed of a peculiar psychic complex, and they prefer to patronize the galleries of white theatres than theirs." Levy's sentiments seemed only to confirm William Foster's earlier fears that whites would inevitably "step in and grab off another rich commercial plum from what should be one of our own particular trees of desirable profit" (qtd. in Sampson 215, 174-75).

By the 1920s, other film companies were springing up throughout the country to produce Negro films for the proliferating race movie theaters (sometimes called ghetto theaters). Among the black independents were the Unique Film Company of Chicago, whose first and only production was *Shadowed by the Devil*, a three-reeler based on an original story by Mrs. Miles M. Webb, the wife of the director of the company; the Seminole Film Producing Company of New York, formed by Peter P. Jones (formerly of the Peter P. Jones Photoplay Company), whose uncompleted first production *Shadows and Sunshine* was adapted from an original story by Jessie Shipp, a distinguished black stage director who had been associated with the Williams and Walker musical comedies of the early 1900s; the Leigh Whipper Film Company, headed by actor Leigh Whipper, who had already released several newsreels for black theaters through his Whipper Reel Negro News; the Booker T. Film Company of Los Angeles, founded by actor Sidney P.

Dones, who starred in the company's only production, a Western entitled *The $10,000 Trail*; the Maurice Film Company of Detroit, whose three releases carried strong moral messages and starred the company's founder, Richard Maurice; Colored Feature Photoplay, Incorporated, headquartered in Harlem, which included several whites on its board of directors and whose stated objectives were "to carry a message to the hearts of those who patronize motion pictures in every land" and "to feature colored people and the beautiful home life and achievements of the Negro" (Sampson 189); the Paragon Pictures Corporation of Jamaica, Long Island, and later of Harlem, which owned its own studio and film-developing laboratory; and the Rosebud Film Corporation of Hollywood, which convinced Clarence Brooks to come out of retirement to star in its only release, *Absent* (1928).[22] As Thomas Cripps writes, most of the emerging black companies "floated on a wave of good intentions, but only a few struggled into production" (*SFB* 177), while others survived long enough to release only one or two pictures. Their ambition often outstripped their capacity and their potential so that in the end "they did not fail so much as they were overwhelmed by the impossible"(170).

Already battling problems of underfinancing, production quality, and unheralded releases, black independents also had to compete with white and white-backed independent filmmakers, who had begun to recognize the profit potential in race films. The efforts of these white companies had decidedly mixed results. Many persisted in re-creating old formulas like the "funny Negro picture," which Dr. A. W. Smith, one of the founders of the Frederick Douglass Film Company, described dismissively as "Negroes in some hen roost, shooting craps, eating watermelons or [engaging in] razor fights" (Sampson 5, 7). The white-run Ebony Film Corporation of Chicago, for example, which owned both indoor and outdoor production studios and employed its own company of black actors, drew on racist caricatures and stereotyped plot lines in more than twenty one- and two-reel comedies such as *The Busted Romance* (1917), about "a stray 'coon' living by his wits, a town gambler, and a parson whose conscience can be made retroactive when money is shown" (*Exhibition Herald*, 22 Feb. 1917 [qtd. in Sampson 244]); *The Bully* (1918), about a bully in a bakery who is subdued by a loaf of bread that contains a horseshoe; and *The Comeback of Barnacle Bill* (1918), in which a depressed loser named Sam tries to kill himself, accidentally shoots a thief instead, and then steals the thief's money in order to win the hand of his girlfriend Skeeter. Another Ebony short, *A Black Sherlock Holmes* (1918), a vulgar parody of the adventures of Arthur Conan Doyle's detective, included characters named I Wanta Sneeze, Sheeza Sneeze, and Reuma Tism, while *Spying the Spy* (1918) featured "Sambo Sam," who finds the initiation paraphernalia used by members of a black lodge and believes that he has uncovered a nest of German spies. In addition to its own films, Ebony re-released under its name a series of racist shorts originally screened around 1915 by Historical Feature Films. Typical of those shorts were *Aladdin Jones*, about a shiftless "darky" named Jonesy who finds a magic lamp but uses it to wish only for liquor and "fo' a shack to sleep in," and *Money Talks in Darktown*, in which the uncultured, dark-skinned Sam tries to win Flossie's affection by lightening the color of his skin before realizing that her only concern is the color of his money.[23]

Although Ebony promoted its offerings in the trade press as "REAL NEGRO COMEDIES WITH REAL NEGRO PLAYERS, Animated with the Matchless Native Humor of the Race," its advertisements clearly seemed aimed at white exhibitors.[24] "Colored people are funny," stated one of the company's full-page advertisements (*The Moving Picture World* 10 Aug. 1918). "If colored people weren't funny, there would be no plantation melodies, no banjoes, no cake walk, no buck and wing dance, no minstrel show and no black-face vaudeville—and they are funny in the studio" (Sampson 199). In response, the black press was harshly critical. Tony Langston, theatrical editor of the *Chicago Defender*, characterized Ebony's degrading and offensive comedies as "what is commonly called 'crap'" (Sampson 207) and advised "members of the race" to save their money and their self-respect by avoiding the productions.[25] Ultimately black theaters began refusing to book Ebony's films, a move that led to the company's demise in 1919. But other filmmakers continued to produce comparably low cinematic fare. In 1921, for instance, the Harris Dickson Film Company released *The Custard Nine*, a film based on Dickson's series of "Colored stories" from the *Saturday Evening Post* in which Virgil Custard leads Vicksburg's black baseball team through various farcical adventures. Notable only for the debut of Clarence Muse, *The Custard Nine* offered naïve and negative portrayals of black life, to which black audiences reacted with great disdain. Lester Walton wrote in the *New York Age* (29 Oct. 1921) that Dickson's stories, which "sought [not only] to make the plantation Negro ridiculous, but the professional Negro as well," were the very reason that he stopped reading the *Post*. "Mr. Dickson has never heard colored physicians use the language of the illiterate and uneducated," wrote Walton, "yet he does not hesitate to poke fun at them with the same vigor and consistency as he does at lower types" (qtd. in Sampson 213-14). Similarly, in the mid- to late-1920s, Octavus Roy Cohen teamed with Al Christie on a series of "all-colored shorts," most of them based on Cohen's stories for the *Saturday Evening Post*. Those shorts, which included *Brown Gravy*, *The Framing of the Shrew*, *The Lady Fare*, *The Melancholy Dame*, *Music Hath Harms*, and *Oft in the Silly Night*, incorporated "Negro dialect" and many of the other familiar stereotypes that black filmmakers both avoided and deplored; typically "made fun of Negro lawyers and doctors by depicting them as familiar coons"; required the actors to appear in blackface; and ultimately "represented the underground movement at its worst" (Bogle, *TCMMB* 105, 107).[26]

Whites, however, were also behind the Norman Film Manufacturing Company, which throughout the 1920s turned out high-quality black-oriented feature films like *The Flying Ace* (1926) and *Black Gold* (1928), which were free of derogatory stereotypes (fig. 2.2), and the Colored Players Film Corporation of Philadelphia, which produced four pictures, two of which are extant and are of special interest and significance.[27]

Ten Nights in a Barroom (1926), starring Charles Gilpin and Lawrence Chenault, was a black version of a familiar temperance novel, *Ten Nights in a Bar-Room, And What I Saw There* (1854) by Timothy Shay Arthur (later adapted as a melodrama for the stage, *Ten Nights in the Bar Room* [1858], by William W. Pratt, and as a white film version, *Ten Nights in a Bar Room* [Oscar Apfel, 1921]), in which Joe Morgan's drinking causes him to lose his money, his business, and even his daughter, who dies an accidental death when she is struck by a glass aimed at her father. Consequently, Morgan reforms his wicked ways (as an earlier Joe Morgan, in

Reol's *Secret Sorrow*, had); a changed man, he is reconciled with his wife and elected mayor of his town. Unlike some adaptations, however, *Ten Nights* was "more than just a rehash." As Thomas Cripps writes, "the brief film used its all-black cast to achieve a certain poignancy, as though the actors themselves were making a special plea to urban blacks, warning them against urban vices in a manner reminiscent of Micheaux" (*BFG* 29).

Figure 2.2. A poster advertising *The Flying Ace*, one of the Norman Film Manufacturing Company's race productions. *(Norman Studios, 1926)*

The second and even more remarkable film produced by the Colored Players was *The Scar of Shame* (1926 [1929]), which not only presented black audiences "with sharply etched messages of advocacy, aspiration, group unity, and slogans against racism" but also "laid the blame for black misfortune at the door of poor environment."[28] The story of an ill-fated marriage between Alvin Hillyard (Harry Henderson), a promising black composer, and Louise Howard (Lucia Lynn Moses), a former washwoman now employed at Mrs. Lucretia Green's "select boarding house," the film revealed the caste divisions that existed even among black Americans. A decent man, the educated and comfortably middle-class Alvin marries Louise out of pity, to protect her from her drunken and abusive stepfather Spike Howard (William E. Pettus) and from the racketeer Eddie Blake (Norman Johnstone), who covets her and wants to make her the star attraction at his nightclub. But like Joe Morgan in Reol's *Secret Sorrow*, Louise is "a child of environment" who lacks "proper training . . . [in] the finer things of life, the higher aims, the higher hopes." Swayed by the promises of stardom, she rips up her marriage license to Alvin (thereby, according to Jane Gaines, destroying her marriage by her own hand ["*Scar*" 69]) and decides to leave town with the brash Eddie. But the two men engage in a confrontation during which Louise is wounded by a bullet and her beauty marred by the resulting large and disfiguring scar on her neck. Convicted of the crime on the basis of Louise's testimony, the innocent Alvin is jailed but escapes after a few years and assumes a new identity as "Mr. Arthur Jones, Professor of Music, Piano and Voice," in a distant city. There, he meets and falls in love with Alice Hathaway, a woman of his class; and through a series of coincidences, he again encounters Louise, who still wants him and who threatens to expose him if he does not do as she says. (Fig. 2.3.) But, writes Cripps, while Alvin has already "won the game of life by wanting it badly, Louise has lost because she sold herself cheaply" ("Race Movies" 56). After admitting that it was actually Eddie who shot her, Louise—burdened by her shame—kills herself, leaving Alvin free to marry Alice. The message of the film is synthesized in the final titles, as Alice's father, a corrupt lawyer, ironically observes that "our people have much to learn," particularly about the kind of class strife that is behind the picture's various tragedies.

Figure 2.3. Unable to overcome the limitations of her environment, Louise Howard (Lucia Lynn Moses) commits suicide in *The Scar of Shame*. *(Courtesy of Museum of Modern Art/Film Stills Archive)*

The Scar of Shame effectively incorporated a variety of techniques, such as the intercutting of scenes that contrast the two very different women and their social worlds (the debauched Louise at the noisy Club Lido and the proper Alice alone at home with her piano) and the recurring use of music, which serves not just as a leitmotif but also as a way of defining and identifying the principal characters. Also noteworthy is the use of symbols like the black baby doll puppet that Louise is first seen holding after her marriage to Alvin. When Alvin confesses that his family is unaware of their relationship and then leaves to attend to his sick mother, he inadvertently strikes the doll with his suitcase. The doll falls to the floor; in his haste he steps on it, crushing its face and destroying its beauty (just as Louise's hopes are dashed and her beauty soon destroyed—albeit inadvertently—by Alvin's actions). Although Louise cradles the doll and tries to make it whole again, it is as irreparably damaged as her marriage and her prospects for a better life.[29] In ways such as these—ways both subtle and sophisticated—*The Scar of Shame* makes a powerful statement on race relations among dark-skinned and light-skinned and among middle and working class blacks (motifs that recur in Micheaux's productions); and the film itself remains one of the best black or white independent productions of the silent era.[30]

The growth of the new black audience in that era, which spanned the early decades of the twentieth century, was truly rapid. By 1921, there were hundreds of movie houses in the United States—in different issues, the trade paper *Billboard* estimated the number to be 178, 600, even 800[31]—that catered primarily to blacks;[32] and by the late 1920s, there were at least a dozen independent black companies operating across the United States, producing full-length features and newsreels and plugging them into black cinemas, the black vaudeville circuits, and matinées or midnight rambles for blacks in white theaters.[33] But the burgeoning black film industry, which had enjoyed a kind of golden age in the early 1920s with the support of the black press and the availability of fine theatrically trained black actors, was soon halted by a series of unfortunate events. A flu epidemic in 1923 had an immediate and devastating effect by forcing the closing of many ghetto theaters and amplifying the problem of distribution. White businesses, meanwhile, began buying up black theaters or building new ones in black neighborhoods; and by the late 1920s, they became increasingly unwilling to pay the costs of booking race films. As D. Ireland Thomas observed in a column in the *Chicago Defender* at the beginning of 1925, white theater owners "want it as cheap as a regular production of a white corporation and they know that this is impossible, as the producer of Race pictures is forced to get his profit out of a few Race theaters, while the white productions encircle the globe. Mary Pickford is just as popular in China as she is in America, etc. All Race movies make money regardless of their merit, yet the manager of a theater will try to tell you that his patrons do not like Race pictures" (qtd. in Sampson 9).

Even the black press started turning its attention away from the achievements of black filmmakers and toward the gains being made by blacks in Hollywood and in mainstream theater. Perhaps, as Pearl Bowser and Louise Spence suggest, black filmmakers received less coverage in the black weeklies because they invested less in advertising; "or perhaps the press was deserting Race pictures for the more costly, better-made Hollywood films where Blacks were beginning to find roles" (*Writing* 210). Whatever the reason, the same papers that had proclaimed that "no picture draws like a good Race production" and had urged theater managers to "all start booking colored pictures" and black patrons "to bear with men like Oscar Micheaux and other pioneers" by seeing their pictures even "if it hurts" (Regester, "Press" 41-42) became more direct in their criticism of the shortcomings of race movies. The intention of the black press, Charlene Regester suggests, may have been to encourage black filmmakers to strive for higher quality productions; but the timing proved to be especially inopportune, since "African-American filmmakers were engaged in a desperate struggle for survival." And although that press "never really abandoned its role of attacking white racism and encouraging the promotion of racial self-determination, its harsh words for African-American filmmakers may have unwittingly harmed this dimension of the industry, at least to the extent that press reviews affected the box office" ("Press" 49).

Similarly, black audiences, even though they craved black images on screen, increasingly patronized only the highest quality race pictures, which often were not those produced by black film companies. Furthermore, the release in 1929 of the black-oriented big studio productions *Hearts in Dixie* and *Hallelujah!* spelled disaster for many small black independents, who lacked the capital to keep up production and to acquire the sound equipment the new era of "talkies" demanded. By the end of the decade, the Depression had finished off all but the sturdiest (Bogle, *TCMMB* 107).

THE EMERGENCE OF OSCAR MICHEAUX

One filmmaker, however, survived the various adversities. Oscar Micheaux, founder of the Micheaux Film and Book Company (later the Micheaux Film Corporation), the most successful of all of the black film production companies, was not only a shrewd businessman and self-promoter; he was also one of the most colorful characters in the history of American film.[34] In a career that spanned almost thirty years, Micheaux produced over forty films, which he distributed both nationally and internationally. Most significantly perhaps, as Henry T. Sampson notes, Micheaux's was the only company "which released one or more black films yearly between 1918 and 1940" (142), a stunning accomplishment considering the low survival rate of black independent production companies, many of which folded before they completed or released even one picture.[35] Moreover, Micheaux, who premiered his first short feature *The Homesteader* in early 1919, made a successful transition to sound pictures with *The Exile* (1931), the first all-talking motion picture by a black company, even though "talkies" forced many independent filmmakers, white as well as black, to close; and he persisted into the 1940s, long after Hollywood began regularly marketing films for black audiences and drove most producers of race movies out of business. Micheaux's final film, *The Betrayal*, released in 1948 and premiered at a white theater in New York, was touted as the "Greatest Negro photoplay of all time." It is only recently, however, that Micheaux's tremendous achievements have gained some of the critical appreciation by film scholars and historians and the recognition by the motion picture industry that they so richly deserve.[36]

Unfortunately, many of Micheaux's films, both silent and sound, have been lost. Only three of his silents—*Within Our Gates*, *Body and Soul*, and *The Symbol of the Unconquered*—survive, two of them having been rediscovered within the past decade; and the sound version of *Birthright* exists merely as a fragment. But those works alone justify Micheaux's reputation as the first great black filmmaker in America (Moon 245) and the "first African-American film *auteur*" (Green, *Straight Lick*[37] xi), and they confirm his seminal role both in race cinema and in American film history.

Micheaux's films were not technically brilliant.[38] Often forced to work on a very tight budget, Micheaux would shoot in empty and outdated studios in Chicago, Fort Lee, and the Bronx or in the houses and offices of his acquaintances. Sets, of necessity, were usually small in scale; many of the important scenes in *God's Step Children* (1938), for example, take place at the foot of a staircase in a friend's home, a spot that provided the best lighting angles.

Especially in the beginning, Micheaux would rent equipment by the day. Retakes were a luxury he could not afford, and editing was minimal: consequently, dialogue flubs and other mistakes such as misspellings of words on title cards and even of actors' names in the credits are evident in a number of the films (e.g., in *Lying Lips*, Juano Hernandez appears as Jauno Hernandez). Micheaux's crews were usually comprised of unemployed or underemployed cameramen who had been left behind as the dominant white film industry moved westward to Hollywood; his casts, which tended to be uneven in their talent, ranged from fine veteran actresses like Micheaux's second wife Alice B. Russell and his sister-in-law Julia Theresa Russell to family friends and local citizens, whom he drafted in lieu of professional actors to keep down his costs.[39] Always trying to maneuver within restricted circumstances, Micheaux was known to shoot footage whenever the opportunity arose and to compile those pieces of film for future use. Actress Shingzie Howard recalled that one morning, when no one was home, Micheaux took her to a white neighborhood and shot her in front of an elegant house; another time, when a woman in a fur coat arrived for an appointment, Micheaux escorted her to an interior office and then quickly returned to shoot Howard wearing the fur (Bowser and Spence, *Writing* 40).

Unlike white filmmakers, Micheaux was in charge of virtually all aspects of the production of his films, from the writing of the scenarios and the supervising of the shooting to the handling of the books. Charles Fontenot notes that his early pictures "took an average of ten days to shoot and usually cost ten to twelve thousand dollars" (122); even his later films rarely ran more than $20,000 in production costs.[40] (By comparison, D. W. Griffith produced *The Birth of a Nation* in 1915 for $100,000; and the 1927 Carl Laemmle major studio production of *Uncle Tom's Cabin*, directed by Harry A. Pollard, was budgeted at $2,000,000.) Nevertheless, Micheaux's production style gave texture to his black genre films even if his work was not noted for its technical excellence. His black and white crews, according to Thomas Cripps, "exhibited a fellowship that blended the ideals of African tribal communities"; and by sharing poverty, late paychecks, and shabby working conditions, somehow they managed to give a generic texture to the films (*BFG* 26).[41] In fact, as J. Ronald Green provocatively suggests, in a vital way, the very flaws in Micheaux's medium became part of his message. His "constant purpose," writes Green, "was to show, through art and through business, the capacity of African Americans to overcome American adversity"; consequently, "the inexpensive production values that inform his difficult predicament and difficult style reflect, and also *represent*, adversity." Micheaux's technical hardships, which resulted in his film's low production values, can thus be seen as "an apparatus inseparable from a complex, conscious discourse of class" (*SL* 68-69)

Still, in most cases, the Micheaux feature was far superior to that of other black independents; and, although technically inferior to the Hollywood product, in other respects it "resembled the best B movies of the time" (Bogle, *TCMMB* 115). What particularly distinguished Micheaux's work, however, was its angle: just as the Negro newspapers and magazines of the day took major news stories and reported on them from a black perspective, Micheaux took the familiar Hollywood script and gave it a distinctly racial slant.[42] *Underworld* (1937), for example, was on one level an ordinary gangster film and *A Daughter of the Congo* (1930) a typical African adventure story; but, atypically, the former featured black gangsters and a black gun moll,[43] the latter a rich black girl lost as a baby in the jungle, imprisoned by slave hunters, and rescued by a black officer. Yet even as Micheaux "translated standard Western, gangster, and melodrama fare to a black context," he always, according to Richard Gehr, added "something unique, if only in the form of his rough-hewn, self-taught technique" (36). And in his challenge of conventional portrayals and his addressing of black concerns from a black perspective (a method Jane Gaines called "transforming without changing"), Micheaux originated a form of the protest film upon which later filmmakers, from Richard Wright to Spike Lee, would build.

Early on in his production career, Micheaux established a cadre of performers, many of them gathered from prestigious black acting companies such as the Lafayette Players in New York,[44] whom he would cast by type, model after white Hollywood performers in order to boost their box office appeal, and promote accordingly. The handsome Lorenzo Tucker was first referred to as the "black Valentino"; later, after "talkies" became popular, he was the "colored William Powell." Sexy and insolent Bea Freeman was the "sepia Mae West." The character actor Alfred "Slick" Chester, who often played gangster roles, was the "colored Cagney." And the lovely light-skinned actress Ethel Moses was sometimes publicized as the "Negro Harlow" (Bogle, *TCMMB* 114). Evelyn Preer, who first appeared on screen in *The Homesteader* (1919), went on to play key roles in numerous other Micheaux films and became the most famous black female star of the 1920s before her untimely death in 1932. Lawrence Chenault, who was the first leading man with the then newly formed Lafayette Players Stock Company, became one of Micheaux's favorite actors after he appeared in *The Brute* (1920), the third film released by the Micheaux Film Corporation; eventually he played more leading roles than any other performer in black pictures during the silent film era. Paul Robeson, a young football player, singer, and budding actor, made his film debut in *Body and Soul* (1924) in the dual roles of the greedy and licentious preacher Reverend Isiaah Jenkins and his conscientious, responsible brother Sylvester.[45] Among the other notable players whom Micheaux sought out were the boxer and celebrity Sam Langford, whom he starred in the fight scene of *The Brute*; the fine character actor Juano Hernandez, who appeared in *Lying Lips* and *The Notorious Elinor Lee* and who later received an Academy Award nomination for his sensitive portrayal of Lucas Beauchamp in a non-Micheaux film, *Intruder in the Dust*; and Oscar Polk, who was featured in *Underworld* but is best remembered for his role as Scarlett O'Hara's servant in *Gone With the Wind* and in other major Hollywood films such as *The Green Pastures* and *Cabin in the Sky*.

Even more than the technical aspects of filmmaking, most of which he learned on his own, Micheaux understood the art of self-promotion. He had acquired that skill from marketing his own novels, usually door to door, among the white farmers of the prairie where he had lived as a young black pioneer and in the black communities of the South that he would visit. And he applied that same skill to the underwriting, promotion, and distribution of his films. To finance his productions, he would personally call upon theater managers to offer them first rights to his works; often he would bring along several cast members to act out scenes that he was planning to shoot. Once a film was completed, Micheaux would carry stills to the theaters where his features were scheduled to play and try to get advance bookings for his next film. To increase box office receipts, he scheduled promotional junkets and encouraged his stars to make personal appearances in the cities where his films were opening—a gimmick that many of the actors appreciated, since the extra publicity enhanced the stage careers that often constituted their principal livelihood. And the provocative, teasing one-sheet lithographs and theater lobby cards that Micheaux designed himself were among the most colorful and artistic in the business (Sampson 487).[46]

Micheaux also traveled widely on behalf of his company, adapting his approach to the particular audience he happened to be addressing. At black church meetings and community functions, he would extol the merits of his race films and highlight the ways that they managed to uplift the Negro. With Southern whites, he would speak of the untapped black market and suggest that there were huge profits to be made by subsidizing his productions. To attract crowds of all colors to his movies, he would schedule special matinées or late-night showings; and he even hand-delivered the prints to the theaters himself.

In person, Micheaux had a distinctly theatrical flair. (Fig. 2.4.) Actor Lorenzo Tucker recalls that Micheaux "was so impressive and so charming that he could talk the shirt off your back" (Woodland 223). Tall and solidly built at "over 300 pounds," Micheaux often appeared in public in long Russian fur coats and wide-brimmed hats. Later in his career, when he was living in New York, he would drive "in a 16-cylinder car with a white chauffeur" to Chicago, where—as a colleague reported in 1940— "two-thirds of the movie houses in the Negro district of Chicago continuously show 'Oscar Micheaux production [*sic*]'" (Hebert 65). His success at creating an image and his mastery of other similar kinds of tricks of the trade were, in fact, essential to his longevity. Like so many other black independents, Micheaux's film corporation was perpetually underfinanced, and it was by the sheer force of Micheaux's personality and his tireless and aggressive self-promotion that he was able to survive through almost three decades of filmmaking. Although he experienced a variety of financial setbacks, reorganizations, and even bankruptcies, most notably a voluntary bankruptcy in early 1928 precipitated by the mismanagement of the company by his brother Swan, Micheaux endured. Even in the 1930s, when he was increasingly forced to seek back-

Figure 2.4. The frontispiece portrait of Oscar Micheaux, as it appeared in Micheaux's novel, *The Conquest.*

ing from white theater owners and white financiers (sometimes called white "angels") like Frank Schiffman and Jack Goldberg, he continued to exercise strict control over his projects.[47]

Above all, Micheaux seemed to understand his audience. Unlike many of the black companies that produced simple race films, Micheaux felt that moviegoers were more interested in good story lines than in blatant racial propaganda. "The first thing to be considered in the production of a photo-play," he wrote, "is the story. Unfortunately, in so far as the race efforts along this line have

Figure 2.5. The Klan tries to scare a black rancher off his land in Micheaux's *The Symbol of the Unconquered* (1920).

been concerned, this appears to have been regarded as a negligible part" (qtd. in Everett 134). So Micheaux offered his viewers engaging characters with whom they could identify[48] and popular plots that incorporated elements generally ignored by other filmmakers: lynching, race purity, prostitution, underworld crime. Intertwined in—and underlying—all of Micheaux's films was a definite racial, even politically activist, theme, usually drawn from topical and often controversial events. In *The Symbol of the Unconquered* (1920), for instance, one of several films that Micheaux produced as a black response to Griffith's *Birth of a Nation*, the Ku Klux Klan, at the instigation of white racist ex-Southerner Tom Cutschawl (Edward E. King) and Jefferson Driscoll (Lawrence Chenault), a light-skinned black man who hates his own race and is passing for white, attack black rancher Hugh Van Allen (Walker Thompson) and attempt to drive him off his oil-rich property. (Fig. 2.5) And in *Birthright* (1924/1925), restrictive racial covenants prevent Harvard graduate Peter Siner (J. Homer Tutt) from building a school that might ameliorate the conditions of impoverished and undereducated blacks in his community. As Thomas Cripps observes, movies gave Micheaux the power to say, however ama-

teurishly, "what no other Negro filmmakers even thought of saying. He filmed the unnameable, arcane, disturbing things that set
black against black. When others sought only uplifting and positive images, Micheaux searched for ironies" (*BFG* 27). Black novelist and cultural critic bell hooks offered a similar analysis: calling
Micheaux's screen images disruptive, she suggested that they challenged conventional racist representations of blackness. According
to hooks, by being less concerned with the creation of "positive"
images than with the creation of images that would convey complexity of experience and feeling, Micheaux delineated "a politics
of pleasure and danger" (hooks, *Black Looks* 135).

Micheaux was also one of the first black filmmakers truly to
understand the cultural and political significance of adapting
black literature to film. Whereas adaptation of plays, novels, even
poems was a fairly common practice among white filmmakers,
who found in classic literature both a good story line and a way to
deflect or defeat the objections of censors, few black filmmakers
seemed to appreciate as fully as he did the potential that literature
offered them. Micheaux initially turned to adaptation as a means
of filming his own work; but he soon branched out—not only to
the works of established black authors like Charles W. Chesnutt,
whose novels *The House Behind the Cedars* and *The Conjure Woman*
he filmed, but also to popular fiction and stories that focused on
subjects like the music and culture of Harlem. ("Before we expect
to see ourselves featured on the silver screen as we live, hope, act
and think today," he contended, "men and women must write
original stories of Negro life" [qtd. in Everett 136].) Micheaux usually sought out literature by writers whose views were compatible
with his own; he never, for example, filmed the works of the
emerging Harlem Renaissance writers, from whom he differed in
background, outlook, and artistic results and whose fiction and
poetry tended to be more intellectual, more radical, and more
scornful of popular melodrama than his.[49] But by bringing both
high- and low-cultural black works to the screen, Micheaux found
an unparalleled way to give power and resonance to the black
voice.

Yet while he was as much a pioneer in the film industry as he
had been in real life, Micheaux was not without his detractors.
Some were critical of Micheaux for using light-skinned blacks,

especially light-skinned women (called "light-brights" or "high-yellows" ["high yallers"]), a practice that seemed to promote a caste system that discriminated between light and dark blacks. Black critic Theophilus Lewis, for instance, in the *New York Amsterdam News*, decried Micheaux's "intraracial color fetishism" and argued that he made "artificial associations of nobility with lightness and villainy with blackness" (Sampson 161); and in 1938, the Communist Party, which picketed the showing of *God's Step Children* at Harlem's RKO theater, objected that the film "slandered Negroes" by suggesting that "all light Negroes hate their darker brethren" (Gehr 39).[50] Others charged that Micheaux's characters were not typical of black society, that they were simply darker versions of white society. Micheaux's depiction of a black bourgeoisie, they claimed, ignored the interests and outlooks of ghettoized blacks, whose lives were replete with racial misery and decay, in favor of almost unrealistic black professionals. Conversely, still others criticized Micheaux for his grimly realistic and unflattering portraits of the black underclass, which included gamblers, alcoholics, loose women, hustlers, and other unsavory types; and they suggested that by portraying black characters in such a poor light, he was guilty of race hatred and of reinforcing the stereotypes perpetuated by whites.[51] "What excuse can a man of our Race make when he paints us as rapists of our own women? Must we sit and look at a production that refers to us as niggers?" wondered William Henry, a reviewer for the *Chicago Defender* (22 Jan. 1927) (qtd. in Regester, "Press" 46). And a theatergoer writing to the *Baltimore Afro-American* (5 May 1928) blasted Micheaux's productions for being so "suggestive of immoral and degraded habits" and for featuring "only the wors[t] conditions of our race and the worst language" with "no attempt whatever to portray the higher Negro as he really is" (Regester, "Press" 46).

While it is true that Micheaux employed a large number of light-skinned actors (as other black filmmakers did), he also used dark-skinned blacks in his many productions. And, in fact, as J. Ronald Green writes, Micheaux's light-skinned beautiful people "are not always his 'good' people" (*FQ* 21): the same qualities of beauty and goodness are found as well in his darker people,[52] like the industrious Jimmy Saunders in *God's Step Children* and the faithful, striving Frank Fowler in *The House Behind the Cedars* and

Veiled Aristocrats. Light-skinned actor Lorenzo Tucker, who appeared frequently in Micheaux's sound films, confirmed Micheaux's willingness to cast against type and stereotype; and he recalled that Micheaux employed "all the shades of the black race" (*The Black Valentino* 71).[53] Moreover, Micheaux himself criticized the color-caste system within the community as destructive social behavior (Bowser and Spence, "Legend" 71).

As for the focus in Micheaux's films on the difficulties facing black "professional people," Donald Bogle suggests that Micheaux was simply attempting to reverse common black film stereotypes by "moving as far away as possible from Hollywood's jesters and servants" and by giving his audience something "to further the race, not hinder it" (*TCMMB* 115). Micheaux's distinctive, if sometimes controversial depictions of middle-class blacks derived from his commitment to racial uplift, or class advancement despite racism; and he viewed elevation as being consistent with exposing the social ills that all too often kept blacks politically and economically exiled from the lifestyles that whites enjoyed.[54] His intention, however, was not to urge blacks to emulate aspects of white behavior but rather to demonstrate that blacks had the potential to be just as affluent, educated, and cultured as whites were.[55] And indeed the remarkable diversity of his character types—Secret Service agents, teachers, Broadway producers, explorers, men of fortune, oil men, farmers—serves only to illustrate that belief. "It makes sense," Jane Gaines observes, "that a man who would want to homestead the vast plains of South Dakota would also want to fill the screen with the largest and most deeply felt images of black life" (*FD* 9).

Over the years, Micheaux also had numerous problems with the censors, usually because of the explicitness of his films. *Within Our Gates* (1920) was originally rejected (and ultimately censured) by the Chicago Board of Censors, who feared that its graphic rape/incest scene would shock viewers' sensibilities and its explosive lynching scenes might provoke race riots, particularly after the racial uprisings during the summer of 1919, which James Weldon Johnson termed the "Red Summer of 1919." (Fig. 2.6.) Even on the day that *Within Our Gates* opened (to a packed house), a committee of whites and blacks from Chicago's Methodist Episcopal Ministers' Alliance was putting pressure on the Mayor

Figure 2.6. Eph (E. G. Tatum), a notorious black tattletale, fears retribution from the white community in *Within Our Gates* (1920).

and the Chief of Police to prevent the showing. White theaters in the South that catered to black patrons on a segregated basis refused to book the film because of its "nasty" story (Sampson 153); several white managers of black theaters in Louisiana also banned the film. The controversy, however, did not deter Micheaux from subsequently restoring the footage that censors insisted on cutting or from including a lynching scene in another picture, *The Gunsaulus Mystery* (1921), that he based on a 1915 Georgia murder case in which a white Jew named Leo M. Frank was convicted of killing Mary Phagan, a young white Irish woman, and later lynched. As Henry T. Sampson writes, "Micheaux hoped that the large coverage this case was given in the white and black press would guarantee good business at the box office. The black press also made the point that a newsreel film showing Frank's body had been barred because it would have been objectionable to the Jewish community, but *Birth of a Nation* was still being shown, over protests by the black community" (156).[56]

Micheaux's problems with censors, as recent scholarship has revealed, continued throughout his career.[57] *The Dungeon* (1922), for instance, was disapproved for exhibition in New York State "on the basis that it was inhuman, immoral, and would tend to incite crime"; in particular, the censors seemed disturbed by the portrayals of a woman being exploited by a man and enticed by a drug fiend (Regester, *SPC* 63). (Those same censors, however, failed to remark on the film's important subplot involving political hypocrisy, in which a corrupt black politician works against the interest of his people in order to be elected to Congress.) *Body and Soul* required rather radical editing before it received approval in New York: Micheaux ultimately reduced the film from nine reels to five, added new title cards, and altered the theme by deflecting some of the villainy from the minister to other characters. White censors in New York, in fact, insisted on changes in many of the early films, including *The Virgin of the Seminole* (1923), *Birthright* (1924/1925), *A Son of Satan* (1924), *The Spider's Web* (1926), and *The Millionaire* (1927); and, ironically, they initially withheld approval of *Deceit* (1921), a film based on the problems that Micheaux had experienced with film censor boards over his first production, *The Homesteader* (1919). *A Son of Satan* (1924), whose plot involved an overnight stay in a haunted house, included an inflammatory protest scene of a race riot, which Virginia censors insisted be cut because they feared that the film would incite "ill-feeling" among black audience members; *Wages of Sin* (1928), a tragic story of two brothers, one of whom cheats and steals from the other, was temporarily banned by the Chicago Board of Censors. As late as 1938, members of the Young Communist League and the National Negro Congress halted a showing of *God's Step Children* (1938) at the RKO Regent Theatre in New York City: the picketers objected to the "false" division of blacks into light and dark groups and argued that the film was slanderous in "holding them [Negroes] up to ridicule" (Cripps, *BFG* 42). Even though Micheaux believed that the criticism of that film was unwarranted, especially since he was trying to expose rather than condone color prejudice, he ultimately deleted a scene that caused particular tension, in which an actor playing the role of a white man knocks down and spits upon Naomie, the girl who is passing for white, when she reveals that she has "colored blood" in her veins.

In truth, Micheaux enjoyed and even cultivated his reputation as a controversial filmmaker; and he often exploited the objections of the censors by incorporating them in his own promotions. In Omaha, for example, the ad for *Within Our Gates* announced that this was the "Race film production that created a sensation in Chicago, [and] required two solid months to get by the censor board." To encourage viewers in Chicago to see the picture again, Micheaux guaranteed that the 1200 feet of film that had to be eliminated during the first engagement of *Within Our Gates* "have been restored and the film will positively be shown from now on as originally produced and released—no cut-outs" (Bowser and Spence, *Writing* 17-18).

Explicitness was not the only way that Micheaux's films were ahead of their time; the prominent and largely positive portrayal of black women was another. A genuine advocate of rights for women, Micheaux "created a space in cinema where black women could be portrayed as desiring subjects. He portrayed them as plump, thin, light, dark (though they were never too dark), sensual. In so doing, he countered the demeaning images of black women in Hollywood films" (hooks, *Black Looks* 139). While even the less reputable ones like underworld figures "The Catbird" in *Murder in Harlem* (1935), Dinah in *Underworld* (1937), and Elinor Lee in *The Notorious Elinor Lee* (1940)[58] commanded a certain authority, most of Micheaux's women were middle-class, well-educated, and sensible—in short, modern race women. In *Within Our Gates*, for example, Sylvia Landry is—as J. Ronald Green suggests—"the agent of much of the dramatic action in the film." The intellectual Sylvia encourages her foster father to confront the abuses of the tenant system and motivates his progressive confrontation with "the white aristocracy"; rescues a white child from the wheels of a rich woman's automobile; argues persistently and successfully with that woman, a Northern philanthropist, to support her struggle against institutional racism by raising money for a poor black school in the South; and finds love with a hardworking Bostonian black man, Dr. Vivian, through a relationship that will "unite the *African*-American North and South after the northward migrations, and will yield a new narrative understanding of the black middle-class couple" ("Micheaux v. Griffith" 43).[59] In *The Dungeon*, Myrtle Downing, a woman engaged to a young lawyer, Stephen Cameron, awakens one morning to find herself married to Cameron's enemy, "Gyp" Lassiter, a bigamist who has murdered his former wives and a notorious crook who is plotting to permit residential segregation in exchange for a Congressional seat. Myrtle manages not only to escape the house where Gyp has confined her but also to warn her people of his evil intentions, thus destroying his political ambition.[60] And in *The Symbol of the Unconquered*, Evon Mason, a beautiful young quadroon, helps to rescue the black oil-man Hugh Van Allen by jumping on a spirited horse and riding off to sound the alarm against the "Knights of the Black Crow" who are threatening him. (Fig. 2.7.) Jane Gaines remarks on the wonderful reversal of custom and expectation in this scene, which plays up the anomaly: "a black woman in buckskin riding against the Klan on her thundering steed!" (*FD* 213). Naturally, after thwarting the Klan, Evon marries her good man.[61] Micheaux thus transforms Sylvia, Myrtle, and Evon, each of whom survives great personal danger, into iconic representations of the dilemma and situation of all black people (Taylor, "Black Silence" 9).

Figure 2.7. Evon Mason (Iris Hall), in chaps and cowboy hat, prepares to ride off to warn Hugh Van Allen (Walker Thompson) of danger in *The Symbol of the Unconquered* (1920).

MICHEAUX'S LIFE AS THE SUBJECT OF HIS EARLY NOVELS AND FILMS

The typical Micheaux film not only offered an important vision of contemporary black life—of intrafamilial and race relations, and of race ambition (both admirable and wrong-headed); it also served as a reflection of Micheaux's life and ideologies. Richard Gehr (36), in fact, goes so far as to suggest that "Micheaux appears to have only one story to tell—his own—and he tells it repeatedly"—an observation with which many other scholars and critics would concur.[62] Yet originally Micheaux did not aspire to be a filmmaker. Born near Murphysboro in southern Illinois in 1884, Micheaux was the fifth of thirteen children.[63] His father Calvin S. Micheaux (or, by some accounts "Michaux," which is how a number of family members spelled the name), a farmer who was a former slave, had migrated north from Kentucky after the Civil War; his mother Bell (Willingham) Micheaux, a schoolteacher and a "shouting Methodist," persuaded her husband to move the family to the city of Metropolis so their children could get a better education. While still in his teens, Micheaux left home to make his way in the world; by nineteen, after working various jobs in factories and on farms, he secured a position with the Pullman Company on a seasonal train that carried vacationers to summer resorts in Wisconsin. Over the next two years, he assumed new routes that took him from coast to coast and provided him with knowledge that he would eventually put to good use as a novelist and as a filmmaker.

Micheaux began saving his money; but porters—who were not yet unionized—made low wages, relied on tips to increase their salaries, and often resorted to the practice of "knocking down," that is, illegally pocketing fares to supplement their pay. (In *The Conquest*, Micheaux describes his protagonist's reluctant collusion with an alcoholic conductor to skim and split fares.) In time Micheaux's account grew to several thousand dollars, with which he purchased a relinquishment of government land and established a homestead near the Rosebud Reservation in South Dakota, to which he moved in the summer of 1905.[64] Despite his limited experience of farming, Micheaux learned quickly how to till the soil, plant seed, and harvest crops; and he even built himself a sod house in which to live and a barn for his livestock. His hard work paid off: within a year of his arrival, he had cultivated one hundred and twenty acres of land and established himself as a successful farmer and as the only black homesteader in the area. As he wrote in an article for the *Chicago Defender* (19 March 1910), the solution to the "Negro problem . . . depends first on individual achievement." Micheaux was obviously already practicing the kind of self-determination that he was preaching to others.

After a few more hard and lonely years on the prairie, he began corresponding with several women and eventually proposed to a young schoolteacher, Orlean McCracken, daughter of the Reverend N. J. McCracken, who had been the pastor of the black Methodist church in Metropolis when Micheaux was a young boy. Orlean accepted, and they were married in 1910—but not before Micheaux had convinced her to file on one of three relinquishments that he had purchased by mortgaging his own land. (For the remaining two relinquishments, Micheaux had gotten his younger sister Olive and his grandmother Melverna to file claims.) Unfortunately, Orlean did not adapt well to life in South Dakota: she found life on the prairie to be uncomfortable, the farm work to be extremely hard, and the distance from her family to be upsetting. The strain on the couple's relationship was exacerbated by Reverend McCracken's dislike for and distrust of his son-in-law, whom he believed had used his daughter simply as a way of acquiring more land for himself, and by financial difficulties caused by money Micheaux had lent to his sister to help with her claim. After Orlean's pregnancy ended in a stillbirth (with Micheaux absent from home at the time), Reverend McCracken and Orlean's sister arrived from Chicago, accused Micheaux of neglect, and persuaded Orlean to travel home with them. Despite Micheaux's efforts to visit her in Chicago and to plead his case for reconciliation, Orlean refused to return with him to the homestead. In fact, she never saw him again. (She died just a few years later, in 1917, in Chicago.)

Back in South Dakota, Micheaux was facing new worries: prairie fires and drought, which damaged his crops; more financial problems, which rendered him unable to meet his mortgage payments and led to the foreclosure of some of his properties; and the loss of Orlean's relinquishment, which his wife signed over to a white banker who then filed his own claim on the land. In his final months of homesteading, Micheaux, bitter over the failure of his marriage and the loss of much of his original land, decided to write a book about his experiences. That book, *The Conquest: The Story of a Negro Pioneer*, published in 1913 by the Woodruff Press in Lincoln, Nebraska, used fictitious names for some of the cities in Illinois and South Dakota and for some of the people; but it was essentially Micheaux's autobiography of his first twenty-nine years.

The novel's main character, Oscar Devereaux,[65] an enterprising young man, determines to prove that black people have a host of possibilities in life. After leaving home at seventeen, he assumes a series of jobs that offer low wages and few opportunities—in a car-manufacturing company; in the Chicago stockyards; at the steel mills in Joliet; in a barbershop and on a farm in Eaton (the fictionalized Wheaton of Micheaux's youth)—before finding more secure employment as a porter with the P—n Company. With his savings, Devereaux travels west and purchases a homestead in Oristown, a small town on the edge of the Little Crow Reservation (the fictionalized Rosebud Reservation) in South Dakota. As M. K. Johnson notes, the purchase of the homestead has special significance: "Devereaux's acquisition of land marks his difference from his ancestors who as slaves *were* property rather than property-owners. The frontier offers him the opportunity as well to own his own labor, to employ the actions of his body in order to increase *his* wealth and status" (234-35). Overcoming his ignorance of farm life, Devereaux successfully cultivates much of his acreage and wins the respect of his white neighbors, who no longer regard him as a "free-go-easy coon" (99).

After falling in love with a Scottish girl whom he knows he cannot marry,[66] he proposes to Orlean McCraline, the daughter of a black minister. The marriage is more of a business proposition than a love match (he buys a relinquishment so that she can file on it); and, although Devereaux and Orlean are happy for a time, the marriage is quickly ruined by the hardships that Orlean experiences on the frontier, by the stillbirth of her baby, by her father's divisive influence and intrusions, and by the drought and other uncontrollable circumstances that occur.[67] Orlean leaves him and returns with her father to Chicago, where she refuses Oscar's pleas to reunite. The broken marriage is not Devereaux's only disappointment: his capital depleted, he finds himself in debt and unable to sustain his dream of property ownership.

The Conquest is not a skillful novel: the style is flat and dry, and there is little wit or symbolic imagery in the writing. It is, however, a fascinating chronicle of life on the frontier as well as an important expression of Micheaux's view that, despite the obstacles they face, blacks can succeed if they take the initiative—a view of racial achievement that Micheaux promoted not only in his novels but also in his films.[68] Devereaux, whom Micheaux tries to cast as a kind of epic hero, accepts one demeaning job after another because each brings him closer to his goal, which, according to Jayne Brown, is the ultimate articulation of attained freedom: the transformation of himself from "property" to "propertied." "It was," Brown writes, "a black man's success at economic enterprise that ultimately decided his national status. As he tamed and sowed the virgin soil of the West, a black man claimed his place in the American territory" ("Black Patriarch" 145).

To achieve his goal, Devereaux deprives himself of luxuries, even of love. His personal situation is both mirrored in and foreshadowed by Madam X, a play that he and Orlean attend while they are courting.[69] In that play, a businessman is unable to give his immature young wife the attention she craves, so she leaves him; after a few years she returns but he rejects her, and she is left to live out her pathetic life as a wanton and an inebriate. Devereaux dislikes the play for its simplicity and melodrama and is disappointed by the weakness of the wife, who fails to realize that her husband "had not been a bad man" (229). By contrast, Orlean and her friends find the play immensely enjoyable, and they believe that the husband should have forgiven the wife and taken her back, even though "she [did] not remain good" (229). As Joseph A. Young writes, "The pathetic nature of those who respond favorably to the play, or at least to its protagonist, suggests to Devereaux a flaw in the black personality. He sees their kind of immaturity as one example of that which prevents Blacks from aspiring to certain standards or ideals that would encourage them to be hard working, courageous, forthcoming, and virtuous" (21).

Like Micheaux, who dedicated his first novel to Booker T. Washington,[70] the leader who urged his fellow blacks to work for economic and social betterment in their own communities, Devereaux is a proponent of Washington's views. In *The Conquest*, Devereaux describes the "two distinct factions of the negro race" as split between progressives and reactionaries. "The Progressives," he writes, "led by Booker T. Washington and with industrial education as the material goal, are good, active citizens; while the other class distinctly reactionary in every way, contend for more equal rights, privileges, and protection, which is all very logical, indeed, but they do not substantiate their demands with any concrete policy, and are too much given to the condemnation of the entire white race for the depredations of a few" (*Conquest* 251). While Devereaux appreciates that the black man is the object of discrimination, he refuses to identify with those of his race who blame the whites for keeping them "down" and who choose not to pursue any of the white ideals of success; such blacks, Devereaux asserts, "can not very well feel the thrill of modern progress" because they are "ignorant as to public opinion . . . and unable to cope with the trend of conditions." They become "condensed" in the idea that the race has no opportunity (145).

Arlene Elder notes that as Devereaux's own story progresses, "it becomes increasingly apparent that despite his desire to inspire and lead other Blacks into the glories of the plains" (299), Devereaux actually defines himself in contrast to them in order to demonstrate his pioneering, entrepreneurial spirit. As Devereaux recalls, even his first bank account "led me into channels which carried me away from my race" (33). When he arrives in South Dakota, he is "the only colored homesteader on the reservation" (81); and when he succeeds in breaking one hundred and twenty of his acres within the first year, he not only challenges his neighbors' opinions "regarding the Negro" but also begins "to be regarded in a different light" (98-99). Yet his acceptance by the white farmers is offset by his rejection among the blacks he knows in Chicago, whom he can neither convince "that a colored man can be anything" (145) nor persuade to follow him to the great West. Thus, as Elder demonstrates, the contrast between "the City," where Devereaux is unable to achieve his hope of becoming a leader of and model for his people, and "the Wilderness," where Devereaux's intense frontier individualism allows him to fulfill his personal ambition, serves as the organizing principle of the novel's discussion of race. The city/wilderness contrast even carries over to the two women with whom Devereaux becomes romantically involved: Orlean, his black wife, "is rooted in the sterile soil of Chicago's ethnic mentality" and trapped by the backwardness, improvidence, and ignorance so rampant in the city (Elder 304). "The Scotch girl," on the other hand, is artistic, ambitious, appreciative, and hardworking—all traits associated with the plains. Unfortunately, the Scotch girl is also white, so Devereaux—a good race man, like Micheaux himself—is unable to wed her (a problem that Micheaux resolves in later novels and films by giving the seemingly white woman enough black blood to make her an acceptable partner).

Micheaux's success with *The Conquest* marked the start of his career as a writer. He soon completed a second novel, *The Forged Note: A Romance of the Darker Races* (1915), the story of Sidney Wyeth, an independent and prosperous ex-homesteader who goes on tour throughout the South to promote his book, *The Tempest*, and Mildred Latham, a proponent of black literacy and betterment who loves Wyeth and shares his world view. Wyeth, who reappears in later novels, is one of Micheaux's favorite fictional personae: an educated, assimilated man, he "speak[s] standard English and uphold[s] middle class values and morality while retaining a strong race pride" (VanEpps-Taylor 80). And Wyeth's novel, *The Tempest*, in terms of plot, essentially retells *The Conquest*: "It concerns a young man, restless and discontented, who regarded the world as a great opportunity. So he set forth to seek his fortune. . . . Thus it began, but shortly it led through a maze of adventures, to a land in the west. It is perhaps, the land of the future; a land in which opportunity awaits for courageous youths, strong men, and good women. . . . This land is called *The Rosebud Indian Reservation*" (61; ellipses and italics original). There, the hero of Wyeth's narrative "came into a share, a creditable share, and, although far removed from the haunts of his own, and surrounded on all sides by a white race, he was duly inoculated with that spirit which makes men successful." After rejecting a white woman whom he loved, he married "one of his own blood," with whom he lived happily "until that other"—her father—came between them and caused them to disagree upon all points (61). Wyeth, however, fares more satisfactorily in his personal relationships than the hero of *The Tempest* does: after misjudging and twice rejecting Mildred, he learns the secret of her past—that, to protect her father, a minister who had embezzled church money in order to be made a bishop, she had agreed to become the mistress of a white man. The revelation of her blamelessness restores her to virtue in Wyeth's eyes and allows him to "forge" a union with her. After their marriage, they go west together to embark on a new life.

The Forged Note was written in Sioux City, Iowa, where Micheaux had settled after launching his career as a writer, businessman, and entrepreneur with *The Conquest* and after traveling around the country, from the small towns of the prairie to the large cities of the South, selling his books and vigorously promoting himself. And in Sioux City, with the money that he had earned from his first novel, Micheaux founded the Western Book Company, through which he published not only *The Forged Note* but also his third novel, *The Homesteader* (1917).

Whereas *The Forged Note* featured a more urbane version of the entrepreneurial hero than *The Conquest* had and offered a criticism of the destructiveness of black urban life, *The Homesteader* revisited directly the situations and characters of Micheaux's first novel, particularly the self-styled black pioneer who sets out to create a new frontier society free of decadence and disruption in the utopian environment of the West. In reworking *The Conquest*, however, Micheaux made an important change: he recast the original story of that pioneer's failed American dream into a tale of his triumph. As Joseph A. Young writes, "Micheaux reshapes his protagonist's qualities so that they more squarely reflect the tradition of the pioneering white settler by providing this new hero with a spiritual, intellectual, and superhuman dimension. . . . By making the antagonist more powerful, more sinister, and more awesome, Micheaux ennobles his hero and transforms the original tragedy of *The Conquest* into a success story" (63).

In *The Homesteader*, Oscar Devereaux becomes Jean Baptiste, a man of the wilderness whose voice, like that of his namesake, the martyred prophet John the Baptist, is often misunderstood and unappreciated; the formerly unnamed Scottish girl is called Agnes Stewart; and Orlean McCraline is Orlean McCarthy, daughter of the Reverend Newton Justine McCarthy. (Micheaux describes Orlean in his list of "Leading Characters" as being "Without the

Courage of Her Convictions"; the semi-autobiographical Sidney Wyeth of Micheaux's earlier novel *The Forged Note*, by contrast, was "An Obsever [*sic*], Who Had The Courage of His Convictions.") Told in four "epochs" of approximately 130 pages each, *The Homesteader* opens with the meeting of Baptiste, who is called "The Homesteader," and Agnes, a "sweet" and "beautiful" twenty-year-old with an "unusually white" (14) complexion. They fall in love, but Baptiste, mindful of the *"custom of the country and its law"* (40)[71] and of the "example" of the black man who had married a white woman and afterward felt compelled to reject his race, realizes that they have no future together. "The Great fact," Micheaux writes, was apparent: *"The fact that between him and his dream girl was a chasm so deep socially that bridging it was impossible"* (40, italics original). Baptiste's act of resisting Agnes, Jayna Brown observes, is key to his positioning himself as a race leader, "for it is out of race loyalty that he sacrifices marriage to the woman he loves. His noble sacrifice to the race is the sublimation of his passion. In so doing, Baptiste proves his manliness" and, through his self-denial, "establishes the particular criteria by which a black man affirms his masculinity" ("Black Patriarch" 140).

In Chicago, Baptiste, determined to "court one in his own race" (147), meets and proposes to another woman, Orlean, whose hypocritical and promiscuous preacher father persistently plots to keep them apart. After bringing Orlean to South Dakota so that she can stake a claim on a nearby homestead, Baptiste detects a certain reluctance on her part; but later the two are married in Chicago. Problems arise as Orlean's claim is contested by the banker Eugene Crook and his cronies, yet the newlyweds seem to be happy until Baptiste travels away from home; Orlean delivers a dead son (symbolic of her inability to mother a new generation);[72] and Reverend McCarthy spirits her back to Chicago.

Baptiste tries to reconcile with his wife, but McCarthy and his other daughter Ethel effectively poison Orlean's mind against her husband. After a year of separation, Baptiste—"breaking down under the strain," "his manhood . . . gone," and feeling "alone in the world" (347)—travels to Chicago, where he and Orlean reunite briefly. But when he gets into another argument with the Reverend, Orlean takes her father's side and lashes out "as if gone insane" at her husband. "With a strength born of excitement, she scratched him, she abused him so furiously until gradually he began to sink [to the floor]. . . . She struck him then with all the force in her body," punctuating her blows with harsh words; and "suddenly she raised her foot and kicked him viciously full in the face" (383). Jayna Brown likens her attack on Baptiste to a "symbolic castration, the denial of his sexual right as husband" (143). Orlean, the timid but caring wife of *The Conquest*, is here transformed into Orlean, the hysterical, hateful, and violent harpy.

Returning to his homestead, Baptiste faces drought and financial problems, which result in the loss of most of his properties; only one parcel, registered in his sister's name and therefore not subject to foreclosure, remains in his possession. Determined to regain his lost land, he farms his sister's homestead and decides to write about his own unfortunate situation, "his life of hell, the work of an evil power!" (401). Once his book is published, Baptiste relies upon his "great personality" to sell it through solicitation; eventually he engages the assistance of an old friend, Irene Grey, whom he had thought about marrying before meeting Orlean. (Irene and her father Junius, the successful "Negro Potato King," are sensible and practical people who advocate black literacy and encourage education; Micheaux presents them in sharp contrast to the hypocritical and dishonest Orlean and Reverend McCarthy, who bring no credit to their race.)

After Orlean, at her father's instigation, sells her relinquishment for a fraction of its actual cost to the banker Crook, Baptiste decides to sue the Reverend for alienating his wife's affection. Public sympathy is on Baptiste's side, but Orlean lies in court to give her father an alibi, and he is found not guilty. Yet the Reverend's victory is short-lived: his reputation is ruined; and even Orlean is forced to admit his moral weakness. In despair because of her misdirected loyalty to him over her loving husband, Orlean stabs the Reverend to death and kills herself. Since the text implies that Orlean's relationship with her father is sexual, her ultimate act of retribution also assumes a perversely erotic dimension.[73]

Accused of the crime, Baptiste is eventually cleared. Agnes Stewart, now the star of a musical revue (her signature song is "O, My Homesteader"), reappears in time to support him during his troubles. Their reunion is joyful. And when Agnes discovers that she is actually a mulatto, Baptiste—who has gained prominence as an author and has regained his prosperity as a farmer—is finally able to marry his dream girl.

The Homesteader not only provided a more detailed portrait of pioneer life on the prairie than *The Conquest* but also expressed more fully Micheaux's racial ideology. Although Baptiste had great "confidence in education lifting people," he (like Micheaux himself) "was very critical when it came to morals. He had studied his race along this line, and he was very exacting; because, unfortunately as a whole their standard of morals was not as high as it should be." He felt that blacks, not having been "brought up to a regard of morality in the higher sense," were generally "possessed with certain weaknesses," from stealing and lying to lax "physical morality." While Baptiste recognized that these weaknesses dated back to the days of slavery, when a certain moral laxity was necessary for survival, he believed that even "with freedom his race had not gotten away from these loose practices. They were still given to lustful, undependable habits, which he at times became very impatient with. His version was that a race could not rise higher than their morals" (160).

To Baptiste, among the most immoral of his race were the preachers and ministers like Reverend McCarthy. Based on Micheaux's real-life father-in-law, Reverend N. J. McCracken (who in turn is thinly fictionalized as Reverend N. J. McCraline in *The Conquest*), McCarthy typifies those inept, even corrupt black leaders who use their positions for personal gain and not for the best interests of their communities.[74] (Hypocritical preachers and ministers consistently fare poorly in Micheaux's works: in *The Forged Note*, for example, Mildred's father Bishop Latham betrays those who believe in him by buying himself a church title and forcing his daughter into a compromising relationship with the white man who has evidence of his crime. And in a later novel, *The Story of Dorothy Stanfield*, the incompetent Reverend Simms aspires to become a bank president, even though his only training is "in the art of selling religion."[75] Such clerical greed and self-absorption also carries over to a number of Micheaux's films, including *Within Our Gates*, in which the preacher Old Ned [Leigh Whipper] is complicit with the white man in depriving blacks of opportunity; *Body and Soul*, in which the licentious Reverend Isiaah Jenkins robs his

poor faithful follower Martha Jane of the money she has been saving in her Bible and then rapes her daughter Isabella, whom he
considers simply an "Offering" (fig. 2.8); *Deceit*, in which a group
of preachers tries to ban the hero's first film, ironically titled *The
Hypocrite*; and *The Symbol of the Unconquered*, in which August Barr,
one of the Klansmen who tries to drive the decent Hugh Van Allen
off his own land, turns out to be a former minister.)

Figure 2.8. Hypocritical Reverend Jenkins (Paul Robeson, in his film
debut) betrays the trust of his followers in *Body and Soul* (1925). *(Courtesy
of Museum of Modern Art/Film Stills Archive)*

Although Reverend McCarthy acts like "the most pious saint
you ever saw" and demands absolute subservience from his family, he is in fact a philanderer and a cheat, "the very embodiment of
rascalism, deceit and hypocrisy," perhaps even "the worst old rascal in the state of Illinois" (162-63). Guilty of "lordlyism" (333), the
ignorant, opinionated McCarthy refuses to acknowledge that education, especially integrated schools, could provide important
social and cultural opportunities ("to develop thought, and the
habit of observation" [430]) for blacks. "It seemed," Micheaux

writes, "that the church contained so many of the same kind—from reports,—until it was a common expectation that a preacher was permitted to do the very worst things—things that nobody else would have the conscience to do" (311).

As a five-year-old boy, Baptiste had been severely—and unfairly—beaten as punishment that the Reverend McCarthy invoked; Baptiste's only crime had been hunger. The poor child had simply gazed with "anxious eyes" at a plate of quail that McCarthy and his fellow preachers were greedily consuming. "'Didn't your mother say that you were to wait,' growled the preacher [McCarthy], and his face was darker by the anger that was in it. . . . 'You're an impudent, ill mannered boy, and you need a spanking!'" (167).[76] Consequently, the boy is whipped into unconsciousness and almost killed. Twenty years later, Baptiste receives another terrible and equally undeserved beating, this time from his wife Orlean, who is enraged by his "abuse" of the Reverend and his refusal to accommodate the Reverend's stubbornness—even though it is the Reverend who has acted inappropriately by spiriting Orlean away from her South Dakota homestead and back to his home in Chicago and who has turned her against Baptiste, the one man who genuinely loves her. The melodramatic resolution of the marital conflict in *The Homesteader*, in which a hysterical Orlean redirects her violent and unprovoked attack on her husband Baptiste towards her hypocritical father, killing him and then stabbing herself, thus affords Micheaux a fictional way by which he can avenge the betrayals and the other wrongs that the Reverend (and, by implication, other blacks of his ilk) have perpetrated against him for his self-reliant philosophies. The reward for Baptiste's travails is the happiness that he finds afterwards with Agnes, who possesses "just a least bit of Negro blood" and who is right-thinking and appreciative of Baptiste's generous and pioneering spirit.

The Reverend McCarthy also serves another important purpose in Micheaux's novel, as dishonest, lazy, and philandering preachers do in other of Micheaux's early works: he represents the chief antagonist of the striving young man who is the new secular example of the black working class. As Jayna Brown argues, the old patriarch, the preacher-father figure, must be de-crowned in order for the son, the new, enterprising capitalist, to be transformed. "The preacher represents the old, or traditional, African-American way of life, while the rugged, individualistic, hard-working young black man symbolizes the possibilities for a prosperous future." The de-crowning of the father and the mantling of the son are thus "key elements in the construction of Micheaux's self-made American man" ("Black Patriarch" 145); and the exposure of McCarthy's corruption and hypocrisy acknowledges and reaffirms Baptiste's individual achievement.

ADAPTING MICHEAUX'S NOVELS TO FILM

In 1918, *The Homesteader* came to the attention of George Johnson, who was then the booking manager of the Lincoln Motion Picture Company in Los Angeles. Johnson, whose company had already released three films, initiated a correspondence with Micheaux and invited him to Lincoln's regional office in Omaha, Nebraska, to discuss the purchase of film rights to the novel.[77] By most accounts, negotiations between the two occurred, and contract papers were drawn up. At the last moment, however, Micheaux insisted on new demands: to have the film made in six or eight reels, not as the three-reeler that Johnson had proposed; and to be allowed to travel to Los Angeles to oversee the filming himself.[78] The conditions proved unacceptable to Lincoln, causing the deal to fall through. According to Jane Gaines, however, neither their mutual correspondence nor George Johnson's "memoirs" of Micheaux support such a version. Instead, she proposes, the correspondence indicates that a cordial meeting took place between Johnson and Micheaux in Omaha in late May, 1918, after which the two continued to exchange letters and ideas. In one of those letters, Micheaux suggests that he could assist in the production and even play the part of the villainous minister; but even in that letter, Gaines contends, his main concern seems to be with details of book royalties. Although in his various "memoirs" about Micheaux, Johnson never explicitly stated who terminated discussions, he does write that "As he [Micheaux] knew nothing of film production, had no Los Angeles connections or any money either, we could not come to any agreement. We offered to let him come to Los Angeles and act as an advisor." As Johnson recollects, the negotiations were more important to Micheaux for the ideas they gave him than for anything else. The film bug, he concludes, was already in Micheaux's ear, and "he decided that he didn't need Lincoln" (*FD* 118-19).

Whatever the particulars of their discussions and negotiations, the experience with Johnson convinced Micheaux that he wanted to be personally and directly involved in filmmaking, and in that same year he founded the Micheaux Film and Book Company of Sioux City and Chicago, whose first project would be the production of a film version of *The Homesteader*. With the same efficiency with which he had solicited orders for his novels, Micheaux embarked on an ambitious campaign to underwrite the film production by selling stock in his company for $75 to $100 per share, starting with the white farmers and businessmen he knew in the Midwest. His stock prospectus stated that "aside from the general public, who themselves have never seen a picture in which the Negro race and a Negro hero is so portrayed, . . . twelve million Negro people will have their first opportunity to see their race in stellar role [*sic*]. Their patronage, which can be expected in immense numbers, will mean in itself alone a fortune" (Bowser and Spence, *Writing* 11).

Once he secured sufficient capital to proceed, Micheaux drafted actors from the renowned Lafayette Players in New York. Charles Lucas was cast as Jean Baptiste, "The Homesteader," whom the *Chicago Defender* (22 Feb. 1919) described as "the embodiment of strength, courage and conviction"; Vernon S. Duncan played Reverend McCarthy, "the embodiment of vanity, deceit and hypocrisy" (Sampson 252). Evelyn Preer appeared as Baptiste's wife, Orlean; Iris Hall as his first and true love, Agnes; Inez Smith as Orlean's sister, Ethel; and Trevy Wood as Ethel's spineless husband, Glavis. The screenplay was written by Micheaux, who managed to keep some of the production costs down by shooting farm scenes on location in and around Sioux City.

Apparently, according to the *Chicago Defender*, "Mr. Micheaux had a world of trouble in landing permits for his picture" before "favorable action was taken by the local board of censors" (Sampson 150-51). But the film—advertised as "Oscar Micheaux's Mammoth Photoplay"—eventually opened, to great acclaim, in Chicago in February of 1919. Ever the showman and entrepreneur,

Micheaux opportunistically promoted the film as "Passed by the Censor Board despite the protests of three Chicago ministers who claimed that it was based upon the supposed hypocritical actions of a prominent colored preacher of the city!" (Bowser and Spence, "Legend" 61). Moreover, he arranged to have the premiere at the Eighth Regiment Armory, a site symbolic of racial valor and accomplishment, just as the city of Chicago was celebrating the return of the troops from the war. So, although the film in no way treated the war, Micheaux succeeded in connecting himself with an enormously patriotic event that could only bring increased visibility to himself and to his work (Bowser and Spence, *Writing* 123, 113).

The *Chicago Defender*, to which he kept news releases and paid advertising flowing from his new Chicago offices of the Micheaux Book and Film Company (VanEpps-Taylor 98), called *The Homesteader* "the greatest of all Race productions" and described it as a "remarkable picture both as a story and photography. . . . It takes eight splendid reels of gripping interest to tell it all, and those who are able to witness the running of it should take full advantage." Another *Defender* (22 Feb. 1919) reviewer hailed *The Homesteader* as "a creditable, dignified achievement . . . on the part of the Negro in the silent art" and concluded that "it is obvious this should be a [photo]play worth the watching," since "every detail of the production has been given the most minute care [and] the characters for their particular parts have been chosen and conform to the description in the book so fully that it is marvelous" (Sampson 151-52, 252, 254).[79] The *Half-Century Magazine*, in a 1919 article on Negro life in Chicago, praised *The Homesteader* as "the best motion picture yet written, acted and staged by a Colored Man" and pointed out that, contrary to the "know-alls" who predicted that the film had run its course after the big crowds at the Armory, "it has filled fourteen other engagements on the South Side and the show houses are clamoring for its return."[80] Micheaux's own publicity materials described interest in the film as being "of such intensity that it holds one in that particular thralldom from which there is no escape until the word 'finis'" (Gaines, *FD* 121).

As his first film and first literary screen adaptation, *The Homesteader* had a special import for Micheaux. No doubt that is why he returned to the largely autobiographical story in two subsequent films. The first retelling was *The Exile* (1931), which—as the first all-black-cast independently produced talking film—proved to be a milestone in American film history and helped Micheaux and his film company to make the leap from the era of silent to sound film.[81] Produced at the Metropolitan Studios in Fort Lee, New Jersey, *The Exile* followed the adventures of Jean Baptiste, a "decent colored man" of high moral values, as he seeks to fulfill his ambition and to find love.

But whereas the novel explored at length Baptiste's disastrous first marriage to Orlean and the machinations of her hypocritical preacher father, the more condensed plot of the film eliminated both characters. Instead, *The Exile* opens in Chicago, where Baptiste's fiancée, a new character named Edith Duval (Eunice Brooks), has inherited a mansion on South Parkway that she plans to turn into a cabaret and house of ill repute. Although Edith tries to solicit Baptiste's help, he refuses to have anything to do with such "a shady operation," and he criticizes her for her low-minded desire to run "a joint, a dive" and to be "mixed up in the rackets completely." Edith responds by accusing Baptiste (Stanley Morrell) of being "too nice" to live in Chicago. "You're not like other men," she tells him; "you don't drink, you don't stay out late at night." Realizing that they have little in common, Baptiste leaves Chicago for the plains of South Dakota.

Five years later, Baptiste meets and falls in love with one of his new neighbors, a beautiful young white woman named Agnes Stewart (Nora Newsome). Like her father Jack Stewart (Charles Moore), Agnes is enlightened enough to judge Baptiste by his abilities and not by his race; and she speaks openly to him of her affection. But Baptiste writes her a letter informing her that he loves her too much to pursue an untenable relationship that can only hurt and humiliate her. After Jack Stewart reads the letter, he makes his own confession to Agnes: her mother, it turns out, was "of Ethiopian extraction" and so Agnes is actually a Negro. Together, the Stewarts try to track down Baptiste to tell him the news, but he has already left for Chicago, where—as the title card notes—"drawn like a moth to a flame, Baptiste returns to the scene of his former haunts."

Almost immediately, Baptiste encounters Edith, who regrets that her "unwise and insane ambition" had driven him out of her life and who admits that she is still in love with him. They plan to wed the following day. But that evening, "Jango" (Carl Mahon), one of Edith's former lovers, sneaks into her room seeking "an understanding." Apparently, Jango had left his native Abyssinia to complete his education in America, after which he intended to return to help and teach his fellow Africans. Edith, however, caused him "to quit school, to smoke those filthy reefers, to drink, to gamble, to do the many evil things" that have ruined him. With his "hopes, dreams, and ambitions" shattered, Jango wishes he could commit suicide. After taunting him and calling him a coward, Edith offers him a pistol, which he then uses not on himself but on her so that she can "never ruin another man." When Baptiste shows up the following morning and discovers Edith's corpse, he is taken into custody for her murder. Agnes, having read about the case, departs for Chicago to help her beloved, who is cleared by the testimony of one of the cabaret's employees. In the final scene, the reunited lovers Agnes and Baptiste are seen cuddling on the train back to South Dakota. (Fig. 2.9.)

As is typical of Micheaux's films, there is a dramatic contrast between the two women in Baptiste's life. The virtuous, long-haired Agnes is as plain and simple as the prairie from which she hails; the fashionable but loose-moraled Edith is as disreputable as

Figure 2.9. Happily reunited, Agnes Stewart (Nora Newsome) and Jean Baptiste (Stanley Morrell) return by train to their home on the plains in *The Exile* (1931).

the cabaret she runs. The latter's iniquitous profession, however, affords Micheaux an excellent opportunity to make a statement about the laziness, materialism, and depravity of black urban life. In an establishing shot, he captures the noise and bustle of the overcrowded city, which contrasts dramatically with a later establishing shot—of the South Dakota homesteads, where cows graze lazily, wheat blows in the wind, and hardworking farmers harvest their crops.

Although they imply a certain moral laxity that he otherwise condemned, the elaborate cabaret scenes that Micheaux worked into the film offered him the chance to highlight the kind of musical and dance action that he knew audiences wanted to see. In an ad that Micheaux placed in a major motion picture trade publication, he underscored that his corporation, the "only consistent producers of All-Talking Negro Photoplays," gave moviegoers who are "crying for 'something different'" films that are "modern in theme" and that "please your flapper patrons—each picture has a bevy of Creole beauties—with bits of the floor shows from the great night clubs of New York, with singing and dancing as only Broadway Negro entertainers know how to deliver" (qtd. in Sampson 163). Having observed the crowds of whites who regularly filled Harlem nightspots, Micheaux reasoned that nightclub scenes on film would appeal not only to white audiences but also to blacks in the South who had never seen such entertainments. Thus, beginning with *The Exile*, club scenes "including jazz music, a dancing chorus, and a comedy routine, which sometimes featured blackfaced comedians" (Sampson 162) or other stereotypical black entertainments like the "coon" character and the "shouting" preacher in *The Darktown Revue* (1931) or the "cooning" boy dancer in *Swing!* (1938) that Micheaux knew whites craved,[82] became a characteristic feature of his pictures. J. Ronald Green notes that Micheaux was more interested in the entrepreneurial business aspects of such material than in its artistic value (*SL* 140); nonetheless, Micheaux used the music and dance sequences in ways that were often both entertaining and formally radical in the way that they disrupted the narrative flow.[83]

Micheaux had already begun to introduce dance sequences into a few of his silent films: *The Millionaire* (1922), for example, included a cabaret scene filmed at the Plantation Club in Chicago. But sound ensured far better possibilities for showcasing black performers. And, while Micheaux could not pay top black stars like Ethel Waters, Duke Ellington, or Bill "Bojangles" Robinson to appear in his films, he was able to draw on other excellent but lesser-known talents who often worked for free, as well as on the beautiful chorus girls of the Cotton Club and other clubs in Harlem and Chicago, who were usually bused to his sets for late-night shoots. In this and in other ways, Micheaux astutely recognized that through "talkies" he could exploit black music and dance to convince distributors to book his films in white theaters.[84] So while other black production companies bemoaned the introduction of sound because it added to a picture's production time and costs, Micheaux embraced the new technologies and incorporated them as fully as he could.

Whereas the band and dance sequences in *The Exile* were well-conceived and executed,[85] other scenes were considerably less sophisticated. As in Micheaux's earlier films, many of the sets were small and crude: when Agnes encounters Baptiste in Chicago, for example, their meeting is shot in front of a single exterior door with no defining background. Similarly, when Baptiste originally leaves Chicago for the South Dakota heartland, one of the few clues to the western locale is an almost incongruously large cowboy hat sported by the local Bill Prescott, a boorish, lecherous, lazy man who is Baptiste's rival for Agnes's affection.[86] Baptiste's cabin is itself almost as incongruous as Prescott's hat: spare to the point of being spartan, the cabin contains a small table, two chairs, and a window with no view. Yet Baptiste is said to be one of the wealthiest landowners in the area—so wealthy, in fact, that he can afford to take Jack Stewart's son into his employ. By contrast, another interior shot reveals that the newly arrived but impoverished Stewarts enjoy a well-furnished and considerably more lavish home than Baptiste's; and their clothing is comparable, if not superior, in quality and fashion to Baptiste's modest garb. Such inconsistencies, however, do not distract from the melodramatic momentum of the homesteader's tale or from its message of racial striving and achievement.

Reviews of the film were generally favorable.[87] The *Baltimore Afro-American* (14 March 1931) remarked on the "good acting done in the picture," on the "nice register" of the actors' voices, and on "the magnificent tapping of Roland Holder, the cootch of Jota Cook," and the "fine rendering" of Donald Heywood's orchestra, which "played a prominent part all through the picture" (Sampson 371). The entire New York run of *The Exile*, in fact, proved to be quite successful. But in Pittsburgh, the first showing of the film was halted by two members of the Pennsylvania Board of Censors, both white women, ostensibly because the film did not carry the seal of the State Censor Board. More likely, the women objected to a scene of the black Baptiste passionately kissing the white Agnes (although she is later revealed to have "Negro" blood) and to another scene (eventually cut) in which a black man thrashes a white man who is trying to take advantage of a woman. The *Pittsburgh Courier* wrote that the refusal to run *The Exile* recalled the fury over *The Birth of a Nation*, which the *Courier* called "a race-hating and mob-inciting film," and noted that "it's all right for a picture to arouse hatred, apparently, if the victims of the mob's spirit are Negroes" (Sampson 162). But despite the various controversies, *The Exile* gave great hope to other race filmmakers that black films could compete in the new market of sound movies.[88]

The Exile and *The Homesteader* were not the only films that Micheaux adapted from his own books. *The Gunsaulus Mystery* (1921), based on the actual 1915 murder case of Leo M. Frank in Georgia, was not strictly an adaptation of *The Forged Note*, but it had interesting connections to Micheaux's second novel. In the Frank case, Mary Phagan, a young Irish factory worker who had come to collect her pay, was found strangled, her body half-burned, in the factory basement. Frank, the building foreman, was accused of forcing himself on her and, with the help of a black janitor whom he threatened into aiding him, of carrying the body to the cellar. Frank, who tried to blame the crime on the janitor, was convicted and sentenced to death. A few years later, after the Governor commuted the sentence to life imprisonment, Frank was removed by a band of men from the prison farm hospital where he was recovering from an assault by another inmate, carried to the town where Mary had lived, and lynched (one of the few whites to suffer such a fate).

In Micheaux's silent film version, the young woman found mysteriously murdered in the basement of a factory is Myrtle Gunsaulus; the black night watchman who discovers her body, Arthur Gilpin, is charged with the crime. To defend her brother Arthur, Ida Mae Gilpin (Evelyn Preer) enlists the counsel of a young black lawyer who had once been in love with her but who had rejected her because he mistakenly believed that she was immoral. That lawyer, Sidney Wyeth (Edward Abrams), eventually untangles the very complicated circumstances of the crime. He gets Arthur Gilpin to confess—not to the murder, but to his knowledge of the double life and the sexual perversity of general manager Anthony Brisbane (Lawrence Chenault), who killed Myrtle to cover up his other heinous crime. Once the trial is over and Gilpin is cleared, Wyeth publishes another book, in which he reveals a secret about his own life. Ida Mae reads the book, realizes how Sidney came to misjudge her, and clears up the misunderstanding in a letter to him.

In *The Gunsaulus Mystery*, Micheaux not only retold the story of the Frank murder case but also integrated plot details of *The Forged Note*. The black lawyer in the film is named Sidney Wyeth, after the protagonist in *The Forged Note*. Like the novel's Wyeth, who writes a book about his experience homesteading on the Great Plains and then begins promoting it by knocking on doors, the film's Wyeth is "a West Indian young man, who comes to America with his literary abilities, writes a book and starts out to sell them door to door." Like the novel's Wyeth, who initially believes that Mildred Latham (the young woman who devotes herself to promoting Wyeth's book) is guilty of immorality, the film's Wyeth misjudges Ida Mae and believes her to be immoral. And like the novel's Wyeth, who realizes his error and his love for Mildred, the film's Wyeth recognizes his mistake in judgment and is reconciled with Ida Mae. While it lends both topical interest and excitement to the production, the murder trial in *The Gunsaulus Mystery* thus becomes a kind of cinematic device, a frame within which Wyeth and Ida Mae, like the lovers in *The Forged Note*, are able to become reacquainted and to establish a new relationship that leads to a happy ending.

As he had done with *The Homesteader* and *The Exile*, Micheaux reworked *The Gunsaulus Mystery* and refilmed it as a 1935 sound feature film that was released as *Murder in Harlem* (and also shown under several different names, including *Lem Hawkins' Confession* and *The Brand of Cain*). The plot of the sound version basically followed that of the silent: a black janitor at National Chemical Laboratories, here named Arthur Vance, discovers the body of a beautiful white girl, Myrtle Stanfield, and runs upstairs to call his supervisor Anthony Brisbane, who is curiously absent from his home. Vance then calls the police, who do not believe his story and who charge him with the crime. Meanwhile, Claudia Vance (Dorothy Van Engle), Arthur's sister, contacts Henry W. Glory (Clarence Brooks), a lawyer and an author whom she had met and fallen in love with three years earlier, when he was still a law student selling his book door to door. Glory, however, had mistakenly come to believe that Claudia was part of a house of ill repute and that she had betrayed him by helping "The Catbird" (Bea Freeman) to plot a crime in which he was blackjacked and robbed; he has not seen her since. Thrown together again, Glory and Claudia work to solve the murder and save her brother. The resolution of the murder mystery, however, is even more convoluted than in the earlier version. An infatuated Brisbane had in fact made advances to Myrtle when she came to his office to pick up her pay. He had watched as she fell and was knocked unconscious; and he had threatened and schemed with another employee, the gullible black Lem Hawkins, to dispose of Myrtle's dead body. But it turns out that Brisbane, despite his self-presumption of guilt, was not the killer. Myrtle's jealous boyfriend George Epps had followed her to the factory, where—from a fire escape—he glimpsed her in the arms of Brisbane and believed that she was cheating on him. After Brisbane ran out of the room to get help moving the unconscious woman, Epps entered and strangled Myrtle. Revealed to be the "Baby Face Killer," Epps is then killed in a prison raid while trying to spring two of his incarcerated friends. Once the crime is solved, Henry returns to his law practice; after his new book, *A Fool's Errand* (incidentally, the title of a lost Micheaux silent film from 1922),[89] is published, Claudia reads it and learns that he had mistaken her for an accomplice of "The Catbird." She contacts him to clarify the error; he admits both his mistake and his love for her; and the two decide to marry.

Although not a great film, *Murder in Harlem* is interesting in many respects, particularly in its portrayal of some of the supporting characters. While "The Catbird" is a black female underworld figure who consorts with other unsavory black gangsters, the film's biggest villains are not blacks but whites. As if to counter the ingrained stereotype of the black man as sexual predator (and to reverse racist stereotypes, as he had done in *Within Our Gates* by making the white Arnold Girdlestone an attempted rapist and Sylvia his innocent black victim), Micheaux depicts the two white males as predatory. The first, Anthony Brisbane, forces his attention on the young woman Myrtle; rapes her; then, fearing that his actions have caused her death, conspires to frame the innocent black Arthur Vance for the crime. Brisbane is convinced that his accusation, compounded by the two forged notes he arranged to be found on the victim's body (one of which reads "he tell me lay down like night witch"; the other, "that tall Negro did this; he will try to lay it on the night . . ."), will be sufficient not just to convict Vance if he is tried but to get him lynched before the case gets to court. Should the original frame-up fail, however, Brisbane is ready to sacrifice Hawkins, whom he threatens and browbeats into serving as his accomplice. The real killer, George "Baby Face Killer" Epps, is likewise a psychopath who hurts women: he breaks the heart of his adopted mother, Mrs. Epps, and even fires a bullet into her home to keep her from discussing the nature of his crimes with Glory; and he strangles his girlfriend Myrtle for imagined indiscretions, victimizing further the poor girl whom Brisbane has already victimized and violated.

Perhaps the film's most intriguing and complex portrayal is that of Lem Hawkins. At first glance, Hawkins comes off as a simple caricature of the "coon" who shuffles happily when he is thrown a coin[90] and who becomes pop-eyed in fear when frightened. The moment he has any real cash in hand, Hawkins looks to get drunk, either at a local bar or at the more upscale buffet flat run by the Catbird, where he is clearly out of his element. Once drunk, he oversleeps and fails to return to the office to clean up the mess that Brisbane has left. Gullible and susceptible to flattery, he spills the "secret" about Myrtle's death to Claudia. Terrified by Glory's badgering, he turns his interrogation into a scene of self-ridicule that causes the courtroom audience to erupt into laughter. But Micheaux inverts the stereotype that Hawkins assumes: he makes clear that any weakness in Hawkins's character is due not to his race but to his willingness to betray his race (as did the traitorous Eph in *Within Our Gates*, the self-loathing Driscoll in *The Symbol of the Unconquered*, and the snitching Persimmon in *Birthright*).[91] Hawkins knows that Vance is innocent of the crime; as he confesses to Claudia, the "poor jig is just being railroaded. . . . he don't know nothing." Nevertheless, Hawkins does nothing to help exonerate Vance. He tells the truth only after Glory confronts him on the stand with his own drunken confession.

Yet Hawkins's complicity is mitigated by his fear of the authority of the white man Brisbane, who threatens his life, and of white justice itself, which rarely allows even innocent blacks to prevail. The scenes in which Brisbane plays on Hawkins's fear of arrest and punishment are just as disquieting to modern viewers as they were to contemporary black audiences because they confirm the extreme societal and racial inequities of the era. Brisbane is correct in assuring Hawkins that his word, especially if given against a respected white man, will not be trusted. Thus Hawkins, like Vance, is turned into a victim of white intrigues. But whereas Vance, who appears articulate and well dressed on screen, is afforded a tragic dignity in his suffering, Hawkins, given to stammering dialect and rube-like attire, is also the victim of class discrimination within his own race. Not only does the educated, middle-class Henry Glory berate him on the witness stand; the elegant guests at the Catbird's club look down on him for his cheap clothing and his awkward dance movements; and even the club's black waiter treats him with condescension, if not outright contempt. Yet Hawkins is not without what J. Ronald Green calls a certain "proletarian intelligence" of his own: he understands perfectly how Brisbane hopes to implicate him, and he realizes that he is entitled to some compensation from Brisbane for the risk he is being forced to take. Ultimately, as Green concludes, "Micheaux's treatment of caricature in lower class figures is less cruel than it may seem, because Micheaux's interrogation leads to a pay-off: freedom. In the case of Hawkins, Glory's interrogation leads to Hawkins's release from white manipulation, and possibly from prison, execution, or lynching" (FQ 29).

Murder in Harlem, by focusing on the murder and its complicated solution, deemphasizes the love relationship that was central to *The Gunsaulus Mystery*. Nonetheless, as in the earlier film, many of the plot details of *Murder in Harlem* recall the plot points of Micheaux's second novel, *The Forged Note*. In *Murder in Harlem*, even though the protagonist has a different name (Henry Glory, not Sidney Wyeth), he too is an author who is selling his books "anonymously" door to door. And he too becomes estranged from the woman he loves because of an erroneous impression of her morality that is eventually corrected; but—as in the novel and in *The Gunsaulus Mystery*—all turns out well for the couple in the end.

MICHEAUX'S ADAPTATIONS OF WORKS BY OTHER AUTHORS

Apart from his own novels, Micheaux also adapted to the silent screen the works of other writers, both white and black. *Birthright* (1924) was a ten-reel adaptation of a novel by T. S. Stribling, the most important work by a white author to treat a black character since Harriet Beecher Stowe's *Uncle Tom's Cabin*. The story dealt with the idealistic Peter Siner, a black Harvard graduate who returns to Tennessee with the intention of reforming people's attitudes but who encounters instead the brutality and bigotry of both races. According to contemporary reviews, the plot of the film generally paralleled that of the book. Siner, heading south, is kicked off the Pullman car in Cairo, Illinois, and told to board the Jim Crow car for the remainder of the journey. On the railroad platform he meets Tump Pack, a rough, loud-spoken, but decorated black veteran who is returning from overseas. On arrival home, Tump is given a huge welcome, which is interrupted by the constable Dawson Bobbs, who arrests the veteran on a four-year-old charge of crapshooting. A few days later, Bobbs shows up at the house of Siner and his mother; claiming to be in search of missing poultry, he ransacks the place.

After meeting and falling in love with Cissie Dildine, Siner learns that she is Tump's girlfriend. Meanwhile, with $100 in local lodge funding, Siner signs a purchase agreement for a piece of property on which to build his school for black children; the deed, however, contains a clause known as a "negro stopper" that prohibits all "colored people" from using the land. He is ridiculed by everyone except Cissie, who comes to his defense, an act that enrages Tump. After encountering Siner with Cissie on the street, Tump starts a fight; but, when he returns to shoot Siner, Tump is arrested and sent to a chain gang.

After his mother dies suddenly, Siner is visited by a strange old wealthy white man, Captain Renfrew, a fellow Harvard graduate who decides to act as Siner's benefactor (and who, it is suggested, is actually Siner's father); yet, while he is supportive of Siner, Renfrew only confirms many of the white prejudices against blacks. Renfrew, for example, advises Siner to stay away from Cissie: "You don't want to marry a negress" or watch your children "grow up under a brown veil" [of race], he warns (*Birthright* 214). Nonetheless, Cissie and Siner become engaged. But on the night before their wedding, she tells him that she is unfit to be his wife. Soon afterwards, Cissie is arrested for grand larceny, although her only crime turns out to be her refusal to give herself to Sam Arkwright, the white man who has brought the larceny charges against her. Tump proves his heroism when he dies trying to free Cissie from jail; Arkwright's family drops the charges; and Siner and Cissie are married. Together, they travel north to Chicago, where they hope to escape the provincialism of "Niggertown."

The film, an effective story of race achievement through education and perseverance and an indictment of discriminatory practices like restrictive racial covenants, was a great success. It starred J. Homer Tutt as Siner, Salem Tutt Whitney as Tump,[92] and Evelyn Preer as Cissie. As the *New York Age* (19 Jan. 1924) noted, "in adapting the story for the screen, Mr. Micheaux followed the book very closely, even using in the headlines the identical language contained therein"; a sort of "colored Main Street," complete with all of a small town's ignorance, prejudice, and crimes, the two-hour-long film "is the best colored moving picture that has so far been produced" (Sampson 284). *Billboard* (26 Jan. 1924) concurred both that "Micheaux has made a really great picture" and that "the film man [Micheaux] has presented an only too true story of conditions that have handicapped the harmony between the Races." Calling the film a "modern Uncle Tom's Cabin," *Billboard* concluded that it may not be popular in some quarters, but that very fact "will but confirm its value. It was apparently not intended for colored audiences alone. Its brutal frankness hurts, and some of the titles put a sting into the evening's entertainment, and just because it has been so well done every one should see it" (Sampson 285). The *Baltimore Afro-American* (25 Jan. 1924) agreed that "Every school teacher, every Negro who has purchased property in the south, all who have ever had a contact with the police and sheriffs or constables in the southern states, every returned soldier, and every pretty colored woman who has or does live in a southern state will find some big truth that a personal experience or observation can confirm." The *Philadelphia Tribune* reviewer also praised the film's truthfulness: "Conditions as presented in this picture are not at all overdrawn," wrote Wally Peele, "and exist at this very moment in places too numerous to mention in the Southland. If we are to help our own to a higher place, then we must know the truth; the best way to make the truth impressive is to have it reflected upon the mind through sight" (qtd. in Bowser and Spence, *Writing* 205-06). Not surprisingly, Southern censors objected to scenes and intertitles in most of the reels and were particularly offended by the suggestions of miscegenation, the questioning of white authority, and the depiction of racist attitudes in everyday transactions; the Virginia Censor Board released letters saying that *Birthright* "touches most offensively on the relations" between blacks and whites (Bowser and Spence, "*Symbol*" 87).

In an article for the *Pittsburgh Courier* (13 Dec. 1924), Micheaux acknowledged that *Birthright* had occasioned some adverse criticism and that "newspapermen have denounced me as a colored Judas, merely because they were either unaware of my aims, or were not in sympathy with them." His aims, he wrote, were simple: to "present the truth, to lay before the race a cross section of its own life, to view the colored heart from close range" (qtd. in Sampson 169). Stribling's story was apparently so consistent with those aims that Micheaux chose to refilm it as a sound picture in 1939, with Carmen Newsome as Peter Siner, Ethel Moses, Alec Lovejoy, J. A. Jackson, Laura Bowman, and George Vessey. Although the plot was presumably the same as that of the silent version, the sound movie (subtitled "A Story of the Negro and the South") gave greater prominence to Renfrew and his racial attitudes; and it depicted in more detail the tribulations of Siner, a man beset by the opposition of the white community.

But the ending of the sound version (which is extant only in a fragment), and probably of the silent version, differed radically from the ending of the novel. Instead of returning north with Cissie, Siner receives a telegram that informs him that he has inherited money from Renfrew. The implication is that he will finally be able to build his school of higher education for Negroes through which blacks in the community can learn to challenge the caste system that represses and oppresses them. Thus the ending, as Pearl Bowser and Louise Spence conclude, is "more typical of Micheaux's narrative resolutions" (*Writing* 140) and of his commitment to race uplift, as achieved through education and hard work. Furthermore, according to Donald Bogle, in its own "sly way" the 1939 version of *Birthright* made "a definite plea for black unity while seriously satirizing the old-style toms" (*TCMMB* 115).

In adapting literary works to film, Micheaux looked especially to black writers.[93] *The House Behind the Cedars* (1924/1925) was based on the novel of the same name written by the well-known black author Charles W. Chesnutt.[94] In the novel, which takes place in the post-Civil War South, Rena (Rowena) Walden, a beautiful light-skinned mulatto woman, is convinced by her ambitious brother John to leave their mother's home in North Carolina; move with him to his mansion in South Carolina, where he lives as a "white" widower with his young son; and pass for white herself. Rena soon meets George Tryon, one of John's wealthy white colleagues; and the two make plans to wed. But a recurring dream about her ailing mother prompts Rena to return to her hometown, where she accidentally encounters George, who discovers her secret and breaks off their engagement. Refusing to deny her race again, Rena chooses not to return to John's home; instead, she accepts a teaching position in Sampson County, South Carolina, where she is pursued by a duplicitous black farmer, Jeff Wain, and where she unexpectedly crosses paths with George, whose family lives nearby. One afternoon, to escape the advances of both men, she tries to hide in a swamp but becomes lost and trapped. After being rescued, she is sick and delusional; in that sorry state, she starts walking the many miles to her mother's home. Frank Fowler, the dark-skinned black man who has adored her from afar for years and who knows and keeps the family's secrets, finds her on the road and brings her back in his mule cart. With her dying breath, Rena recognizes that Frank "loved me best of them all." But it is too late even for Frank's love to save her. Just as Tryon arrives to beg Rena to marry him, "in front of the house behind the cedars, a woman was tying a piece of crape upon the door-knob" (195).

The themes of Chesnutt's novel—the desire of the light-skinned black to pass for white, the problems that arise from such

attempted repudiation of race, and the potential for black achievement that Frank demonstrates[95]—were familiar and favorite
themes in Micheaux's novels and films as well.[96] In the silent film
version of *The House Behind the Cedars*, which like so many of
Micheaux's films is no longer extant, Rena (Shingzie Howard), the
mulatta, goes away from home, where she passes for white and
becomes engaged to an "Aristocratic Gentleman" (Lawrence
Chenault). In the meantime, Rena's former boyfriend Frank
Fowler (Douglass Griffin) has managed to rise to power, despite
his color. In the end, a "miserable" but apparently still hale Rena
returns to her mother's house and to Frank, admitting that,
although she fooled others into believing she was white, she could
not fool herself. Micheaux's treatment of the theme of passing
drew immediate fire from censors, who criticized the film for presenting "the grievances of the negro in very unpleasant terms and
even touching on dangerous ground, inter-marriage between the
races," and for depicting the white suitor's lust for the young
mulatta: "Even after the woman has severed her relations with the
man he is pictured as still seeking her society; nor does his quest
end until she has become the wife of a dark-skinned suitor" (qtd.
in Bowser and Spence, "*Symbol*" 87).

Micheaux's 1932 remake, a sound film entitled *Veiled
Aristocrats*,[97] virtually retells the plot of the silent version: John
Warwick (Lorenzo Tucker), formerly John Walden, returns for the
first time to his mother's home (known as "The House Behind the
Cedars") on Front Street in Fayetteville, North Carolina, and is
shocked to learn that his beautiful, pale-skinned twenty-two-year-
old sister Rena (Lucille Lewis) is engaged to a dark-complected
black man named Frank Fowler (Carl Mahon). John convinces his
mother to allow Rena to move with him to the city, where he plans
to introduce her into his white society. According to the title card,
"it was silently understood that she, as had he, was to forget that
she had a mother—or had ever belonged to the Negro Race at all."
One of John's acquaintances, the white and wealthy George Tryon,
falls in love with Rena and proposes, but she rejects him and goes
back home. "I am not a white girl but a Negress," she tells John,
and she is "happy and sorry" to partake of the various happiness-
es and sorrows that blacks experience. No longer "miserable" over
having to act as "a liar and a cheat," Rena is welcomed back by

Frank, now a successful builder and contractor, who is waiting with a car to take her to her sick mother—and then to a preacher, where they will be married.

In both of his film versions, Micheaux simplified Chesnutt's plot by eliminating most of the second half of the story (Rena's desire to be of service to her race by becoming a teacher, her unwelcome relationship with Jeff Wain, her encounters with George at his ancestral estate near Sampson County). And he allowed Rena, who even in Chesnutt's novel is a reluctant participant in John's ambitious passing schemes, to be redeemed after rejecting her racial heritage. Jane Gaines suggests that Rena's redemption is possible because "all passing is not equal and all passing is not necessarily masquerade." Arguing that Micheaux makes distinctions between the inadvertent passing of a character like Agnes Stewart in *The Exile* and the malfeasance of intentional passing exemplified by the villainous Driscoll in *The Symbol of the Unconquered*, Gaines concludes that Rena offers a variant of the race pride allegory: "she is surreptitiously 'passed off' as white against her will—a story of *coerced* passing" (*FD* 156). Whatever the degree of her complicity in the decision to pass, in both film versions Rena repudiates the white aspirations of her brother, who has rejected his blackness (an inauthentic form of uplift available only to light-skinned blacks); and she reclaims her black identity, through which she is able to find happiness with Frank Fowler, the man who loves her for what she truly is and who exemplifies Micheaux's vision of genuine black uplift. So whereas Chesnutt's Rena dies, sadder and wiser for her travails, Micheaux's Rena survives, happier and wiser for her experiences. Significantly, contrary to Hollywood's version of the passing film in which the offending black or mulatto had to be humiliated for daring to affect whiteness, Micheaux rewards Rena for reasserting her black heritage.

Micheaux's *The Conjure Woman* (1926), based on another of Chesnutt's works, was released not long after the silent version of *The House Behind the Cedars*. Apart from the fact that the cast included Evelyn Preer and Percy Verwayen, little information about the precise nature of this film, assumed to be of feature length, has been discovered. An interesting and remarkably evocative collection of seven related tales, Chesnutt's *The Conjure Woman*

(1899) certainly offered Micheaux a wonderful vehicle by which to introduce modern viewers to the rich nineteenth-century folkloric culture of the South—although Micheaux may have reworked Chesnutt's story to incorporate more of the contemporary characters and topical themes that were consistent with his other films. Chesnutt's tales are told by old Uncle Julius, to amuse and edify John and his sickly wife Annie, the affluent Northern couple who have purchased the plantation on which the former slave was once indentured. Underlying each story is an element of "goopher," or conjure, which serves as a source of hope, power, and even survival for the slave characters. In "Sis' Becky's Pickaninny," the slave woman Becky is sold to a new master and separated from her beloved son. But the conjure woman Aunt Peggy turns the boy into a bird who is able to fly to his mother and raise her spirits with his songs until they are reunited. "Po' Sandy," who is forced by his master to work other peoples' properties, is transformed into a tree so that he will never again have to leave his new wife, Tenie. And Henry, a slave whose fortunes are tied to the land, is magically rejuvenated with each year's new crop in "The Goophered Grapevine." Julius's storytelling, however, casts its own conjure— not only by restoring the spirits of the ailing Annie but also by affording the slave a way to get the best of his new white employers. For example, by telling them a tale about a mule possessed by a human spirit, Julius persuades them to buy a horse instead—a horse, it turns out, in which he has a financial stake. And through his folk parable about the white master who is punished for demanding too much of his slaves, he convinces Annie and John to give his lazy grandson a second chance in their employ.

Micheaux apparently proposed to Chesnutt that he could "develop a good synopsis" from the first story of *The Conjure Woman*. "Write the case of the man and woman into a good love story," Micheaux urged Chesnutt; "let there, if possible, be a haunted house, the haunts being intriguers to be found out near the end, the heroine to have run off there and in hiding—anything that will thrill or suspend, but will have a delightful ending and give opportunity for a strong male and female lead" (Letter to Chesnutt [30 Oct. 1921], qtd. in Musser et al., "An Oscar Micheaux Filmography" 260-61). Whether Chesnutt followed Micheaux's suggestions or whether Micheaux implemented his story ideas over Chesnutt's objections is uncertain. Chesnutt early on had voiced his reservations about Micheaux's methods: expressing fear that his work would be "chop[ped] up" and "the emphasis of certain characters" changed, he "only hope[d] that it will be done with reasonable taste" (Cripps, "Race Movies" 53). In a symposium in *The Crisis* on "The Negro in Art: How Shall He Be Portrayed" (Nov. 1926) several years later, Chesnutt articulated even more strongly his displeasure over Micheaux's tendency to "distort" and "mangle" Chesnutt's plots to "appeal to a Negro race prejudice" (Creekmur, "Telling" 148).

At first Micheaux, himself a "primitive writer" compared to the more accomplished Chesnutt, could not appreciate fully the nuances of Chesnutt's fiction: he believed that Chesnutt's work "could not very well be filmed" except as "two reel comedies" (Cripps, "Race Movies" 53). But he soon grew to admire Chesnutt and corresponded extensively with him; and he even asked the author to consider writing original stories that Micheaux could adapt directly to film. Yet, as Thomas Cripps writes, Micheaux's admiration did not prevent him from "reveal[ing] his most unabashed nerve" in the way that he persuaded Chesnutt to sell the movie rights to *The Conjure Woman* and *The House Behind the Cedars* (a negotiation that Charlene Regester has described in great detail) and managed to get Chesnutt to tolerate his own "heavy-handed rewriting" (Cripps, *BFG* 28) and his insistence on happy endings. After Chesnutt's death, Micheaux exercised an even more heavy-handed "rewriting" by literally lifting the entire plot of Chesnutt's *The House Behind the Cedars* and retelling it, using all of Chesnutt's characters (even their original names), in his own seventh and final novel, *The Masquerade* (1947), which he may also have hoped to adapt to film.

OTHER FILM ADAPTATIONS BY MICHEAUX

Among the other silent films that Micheaux adapted from literature were several based on his own stories. In *The Symbol of the Unconquered* (1920), Micheaux had incorporated chapters and events from his novel, *The Homesteader*; *A Son of Satan* (1924) was supposedly based on an original story by Micheaux, "The Ghost of

Tolston's Manor" (though the film is not extant, and the story appears to be unpublished). More is known, however, about *The Spider's Web* (1926), a "Mighty Melodrama of New York's Harlem" that was adapted from "The Policy Players," another original story by Micheaux (date of publication, if any, unknown).[98] After moving to New York with her niece Norma Shepard, Mary Austin (Evelyn Preer) begins playing policy. But when her number finally comes in, she finds herself implicated in the death of the "banker" (Edward Thompson). It is left to Norma and her boyfriend, Elmer Harris, a black Secret Service agent, to unravel the mystery and free her.

In *The Girl From Chicago* (1932), a sound picture that reworked *The Spider's Web*, Alonzo White (Carl Mahon), a young black Secret Service agent fresh from an assignment with Scotland Yard, is sent to Batesburg, Mississippi, to work on a new case. After arresting Jeff Ballinger, the object of his criminal investigation, he falls in love with a young teacher, Norma Shepard (Star Calloway). Together, they decide to go "home to Harlem," where they save Mary, the former landlady of their boarding house in Batesburg, from a sentence of execution in the electric chair for the murder of policy "banker" Gomez (Juano Hernandez). Alonzo reveals that the real killer is Liza, Gomez's girl (formerly Jeff Ballinger's girl in Batesburg), from whom he has elicited a drunken confession. The crime solved, Norma and Alonzo—emblems of the well-educated, striving new black middle class—depart on their honeymoon to Bermuda.

Although the silent film *The Spider's Web* and the sound film *The Girl From Chicago* were based on the same popular short story,[99] both were also reworkings of a portion of one of Micheaux's earliest films, *Within Our Gates* (1920).[100] In that film, Jasper Landry (William Starks) has picked, ginned, baled, and delivered his cotton crop; according to his adopted, intelligent daughter Sylvia (Evelyn Preer), who does her father's accounts, he should clear almost $700. Eph (E. G. Tatum), "an incorrigible 'tattletale'" whom blacks consider a traitor and call "the white man's friend," goes to his employer, the wealthy planter Philip Girdlestone (Ralph Johnson), to warn him that Landry is buying land, educating his family, and keeping track of all of his transactions. In this way Eph, who relies on a charade of obsequious behavior to gain white acceptance, becomes a stereotype that Micheaux appropriates to comment on the aspirations and social behavior of those who kow-tow to whites (Bowser and Spence, "Legend" 63). "Ya won't git ta cheat him no mo," Eph warns. When Landry indeed appears in Girdlestone's office bearing his bill, the two become embroiled in a dispute during which a gun is fired through the window. Girdlestone falls dead to the floor, shot by a "poor white trash" farmer whom he had earlier mistreated; Eph, who has been spying through another window, rushes to accuse the defenseless Landry of the crime. But whereas in *The Spider's Web* and in *The Girl From Chicago*, the innocent Mary Austin is eventually saved from execution by the intervention of the black Secret Service agent who is convinced that she is not guilty of the murder with which she has been charged, the innocent, honest Jasper Landry becomes a vic-tim of the worst kind of mob vengeance imaginable. In a disturb-ing sequence, Landry and his wife (Mattie Edwards) are hunted down by white farmers and community members out to avenge Girdlestone's death; and, without benefit of trial, they are lynched and their bodies incinerated in a bonfire.[101] In the meantime, Sylvia escapes the mob's brutality only to be confronted in her home by another kind of violence, the lascivious advances of Girdlestone's brother, Arnold (Grant Gorman).[102] But when Sylvia's torn dress reveals a scar on her breast, Girdlestone realizes that Sylvia is actu-ally his long-lost daughter by a black woman.[103] The intercut scenes of the graphic, horrific murder of the elder Landrys and of Girdlestone's lecherous abuse of Sylvia, which suggest the histori-cal correlations between these two acts of white brutality (lynching and rape) and call up associations with the whole tumultuous his-tory of sexual relations between blacks and whites in the American South,[104] are among the most sophisticated and disquieting in the film.

A violent attack is also central to the plot of *The Broken Violin* (1928), another lost silent film that Micheaux presumably based on his own original story entitled "House of Mystery" (date of publi-cation, if any, unknown).[105] According to contemporary reviews, Leila Cooper is a beautiful and talented musician. One day, after her drunken father loses his week's pay in a card game, he returns home demanding that Leila's mother, a hardworking wash-woman, give him her earnings. When she refuses, the enraged father struggles with Leila, takes her violin, and bashes it over his wife's head. Leila's younger brother intervenes, but the father tries to steal his money and then beats him too. Another struggle and a long chase ensue, during which the father runs into the path of a truck and is killed. Although it is not clear from the reviews what happens to Leila, it is quite possible that, like Micheaux's other good race women, she is rewarded for her steadfastness with marriage or other personal success.

The Wages of Sin (1928), a silent film that tells the story of two brothers, was another adaptation based on an original unpublished Micheaux story, "Alias Jefferson Lee." When the older brother, Winston Le Jaune, goes home to bury his mother, his sister tells him of their mother's dying message: that Winston should look after his younger brother, Jefferson Lee. Winston returns to the city and to his position as a movie producer; soon he sends for J. Lee and offers him a job. But J. Lee, who proved to be a coward as a soldier in France, seems to have learned little from experience: he steals money, spends carelessly on women and parties, and forces his brother to make repeated fund-raising trips to replace the sums he has misspent. Winston eventually fires—and then, remorsefully, reinstates—his younger brother, who manages to wreck the company and betray him in the process. On one of his trips, however, Winston meets and falls in love with a woman, and her affection helps to compensate for his brother's betrayal.

The production must have been a difficult but cathartic one for Micheaux, since the story had many painful and personal reverberations. According to Henry T. Sampson, in 1920, Micheaux had hired his twenty-five-year-old brother Swan Micheaux, Jr., to manage the Chicago office of his Micheaux Film and Book Company; a year later, Swan was promoted to Secretary, Treasurer, and General Booking Manager. That same year, the company was sufficiently prosperous to be able to offer a cash dividend of twenty-five cents per share, and Micheaux decided to open a New York office so that the company could avail itself of better studio facilities and the larger pool of talented actors based in the city. But by March, 1927, Swan resigned his position with the Micheaux Film and Book Company to become the New York manager of imported films for the Agfa Raiv Corporation of Berlin; a year later, he became vice president of the Dunbar Film Corporation in New York. Sampson speculates that Micheaux had "forced his brother to resign from the company because Swan's mismanagement of the company finances had almost brought the company to ruin" (160). After Micheaux married veteran actress Alice B. Russell in 1926,[106] the couple traveled widely in behalf of his film company and had to take other drastic measures, such as reducing operating costs, to salvage what Swan had mismanaged. Together, they were able to move the company into a new era of filmmaking. But it would never be entirely self-sufficient again, and during the 1930s Micheaux would need to rely on the help of white "angels," or sponsors, like race film producer Jack Goldberg.

Two other Micheaux silent films, neither of which is extant, were also adaptations—of works by black author and dramatist Henry Francis Downing (1851-1928). *Thirty Years Later* (1928) was presumably based on Downing's "The Racial Tangle," also known as "The Tangle," a play first performed by the Lafayette Players in 1920. The theme of the film treated "a question of the day, 'should a colored girl marry a white man?'" And, according to the *Philadelphia Tribune* (16 Feb. 1928), "the method in which Mr. Micheaux deals with the issue is unfolded to a surprising and interesting manner" (Musser et al., "Filmography" 265). The wealthy clubman George Eldridge Van Paul falls in love "with a race girl and poses as a man of color to be near her. Later he finds that he is the son of his housekeeper, upon whom he had looked with scorn because of her color" (*Baltimore Afro-American*, 14 April 1928, qtd. in Musser et al., "Filmography" 265). A later Micheaux film, *A Daughter of the Congo* (1930), was also based on a work by Downing, a novel entitled *The American Cavalryman: A Liberian Romance* (1917). In the film, a black army officer, Captain Paul Dale (Lorenzo Tucker), encounters the Arabs who have taken hostage the beautiful mulatto girl Lupelta (Katherine Noisette), who was stolen as a baby and brought up in the jungle; Dale frees Lupelta and takes the slave hunters prisoner. Since the film is not extant, it is difficult to know the extent to which Micheaux altered his source, in which Dale turns out to be Lupelta's cousin. (Dale's black mother is the sister of Lupelta's father, John Calvert, "one of New York's wealthiest and most influential citizens" [*The American Cavalryman* 11], who is passing for white.) But clearly both films reversed Hollywood conventions—*Thirty Years Later*, by making the male lead, not the female, the character who passes in order to marry outside his race (a gender reversal that also reworked Micheaux's familiar formula in films like *The Homesteader* and *The Symbol of the Unconquered* of the race man who loves but cannot marry the white woman who is the object of his affection until it is revealed that she has black blood); *A Daughter of the Congo*, by racially recasting both the hostage and her rescuer as characters of color.

Even after his successful transition from silent to sound films with *The Exile*, Micheaux continued to look to fiction, especially black fiction, for story ideas.[107] *Ten Minutes to Live* (1932), starring Lawrence Chenault and Laura Bowman, was based, according to the film credits, on the short stories "The Faker" and "The Killer" from a collection of short stories entitled *Harlem After Midnight* (author and date of publication unknown). The *Kansas City Call* (15 July 1932) noted that the film was "an all-talking epic of Negro night life in Harlem, showing life behind the scenes of the famous citadels of fun in New York's famous Harlem." Sixty-three minutes of "thrills and excitement," it was considered to be "a worthy successor" to *The Exile* (qtd. in Sampson 432). In "The Faker," the first part of the film, a black con man who keeps "luring girls to their ruin" is shot to death in a Harlem nightclub by the confidante of his first wife, whose death he caused. More gunplay occurs in "The Killer," the second part of the film, in which Letha Watkins, a beautiful young woman who is visiting the same Harlem club with her boyfriend Anthony, receives a note informing her that she has only "ten minutes to live." Apparently a shady character named Morvis, who is known as the "Escape King," intends to kill Letha, whom he holds responsible for his imprisonment and hard labor on a chain gang. But when Morvis discovers that it was actually his own girlfriend, Charlotte Evans, who had set him up, he murders her instead. Letha, no longer fearful for her safety, can now live and love happily again.

Although he terrorizes Letha, the film's heroine, Morvis was not, for Micheaux, an entirely unsympathetic character. Described as "deaf and mute," he is, as bell hooks suggests, "a symbolic mirroring of the voicelessness of black masculinity in racist culture during the 1930s." The film reveals that Morvis, like several of Micheaux's cinematic and literary characters and like Micheaux himself, had begun life as a Pullman porter but that he fell into disrepute and ended up on a chain gang, "a site," according to hooks, "where white domination over the black male body is expressed by excessive exploitation of their physical labor." After committing his act of revenge against Charlotte, Morvis writes Letha a note of apology, an expression of regret that "enables him to reconnect within human society. His reputation as 'villain" is mediated by this confession of wrongdoing" (*Black Looks* 137, 142-43). Micheaux thus demonstrates in *Ten Minutes to Live* that things are not always what they may initially seem to be, and he offers a kind of modern, psychosocial explanation for the nature of some black criminals who, though victimizers, are themselves victims of white society—a variation of the "environment is destiny" theme effectively explored by other black filmmakers in *Secret Sorrow* and *The Scar of Shame*.

Micheaux's *Underworld* (1937), another film of gangster life, was also an adaptation, this time of a short story entitled "Chicago After Midnight" by Edna Mae Baker (date and publication unknown). Paul Bronson, an honest but naïve young black graduate of a Southern college, becomes involved with Leroy, a gambler and a murderer who is a fugitive from the police; Leroy's girlfriend, the beautiful but nefarious Dinah Jackson; and Dinah's husband, the gangster Big Sam. After Leroy shoots and kills Sam, Dinah, angry that Paul had scorned her, frames him for the crime, and Paul is convicted. His faithful girlfriend Evelyn Martin, however, remains convinced that his death sentence will be overturned. And indeed Sing Lee, a Chinese man who was hiding in the room where the murder occurred, comes forward to implicate Leroy and clear Paul. (Like the melodramatic revelation of his characters' mixed racial background, the surprise revelation of criminal guilt or innocence is a common device in Micheaux's films: the testimony of a cabaret employee, for instance, clears Baptiste in the murder of Edith in *The Exile*.) In the last shot, Paul and Evelyn are seen arriving by taxi at the railway station, a site that in Micheaux's fiction and film has important symbolic associations. Like the boat that is used as a recurring motif in *The Girl From Chicago*, the train in *Underworld* becomes both the method of Dinah's punishment and the means by which Paul and Evelyn can begin their new life together in Oklahoma. Dinah cannot escape her evil past; she dies on the tracks near Chicago when her car is struck by an oncoming train. By contrast, the lovers (like

Micheaux's familiar mythic hero, the homesteader, and like Agnes Stewart and Jean Baptiste in *The Exile*) leave the city by rail and head west, where new possibilities await them.

Like Dinah in *Underworld*, Naomie Saunders is unable to conceal her true identity in *God's Step Children* (1938), a film based on another story of unknown origin, "Naomi, Negress." A light-skinned girl who has been abandoned by her real mother and left to be raised by her foster mother Mrs. Saunders (Alice B. Russell), Naomie (played as a child by Jacqueline Lewis and as a young woman by Gloria Press) rejects her black heritage. At the Negro school she is forced to attend, she raises havoc by telling vicious lies about her teacher (Ethel Moses) and creates a scandal that shakes the community. After twelve years in a convent, she returns home, where she immediately goes back to her old ways and tries to seduce her foster brother Jimmy (Carmen Newsome), a hard-working former Pullman porter turned farmer, who rejects her. Eventually Naomie marries Jimmy's friend, a dark-skinned black man, but grows to resent him; leaving her baby boy with Mrs. Saunders, she runs away to another city, where she passes for white and marries a white man, who discovers her secret and abandons her. When Naomie finally comes home again, she sees her foster brother happily married and raising a large family of his own; feeling guilt and shame over her conduct and realizing that she has lost the chance for black middle-class respectability (the goal of most of Micheaux's fictional and cinematic heroes and heroines), she commits suicide by jumping into a river.

The film, which featured strong performances, especially by Alice B. Russell and Gloria Press, stirred up quite a bit of controversy. An objectionable scene that showed Naomie being struck and spit upon by her white husband when he learns of the "colored blood in her veins" was deleted by Micheaux after it caused "many of the patrons to get up and walk out of the theatre." Yet protests continued. According to the *Kansas City Call* (28 May 1938), "Other objections raised to the film were that it slandered colored people, holding them up to ridicule, playing light-skinned persons against those of darker complexion, and contained speeches by characters in the film implying that colored people fall for any kind of gambling game" (qtd. in Sampson 378). What some of the reviewers and protesters neglected to note, however, was the film's portrait of strong, loving black families—of Mrs. Saunders and her children, in the first half; of Jimmy and his family in the second—or the criticism implicit in Naomie's choice to quit her community and her race. In particular, the film extolled the virtues of the aspiring Jimmy, who represents Micheaux's familiar type of the ambitious homesteader (and of Micheaux himself).

Another Micheaux film, *Swing!* (1938), adapted from the story "Mandy" (author and publication unknown),[108] explored both the affection that hardworking Mandy Jenkins (Cora Green) feels for her ne'er-do-well husband Cornell (Larry Seymore) and the uplift that she ultimately achieves despite him. After Mandy moves to New York, her friend Lena helps her find work as a wardrobe mistress for a Negro musical show that a black producer, Ted Gregory (Carmen Newsome), is staging. As Mandy begins to re-create herself, new opportunities arise: before the opening night, Cora Smith, the show's unpleasant and inebriated star (Hazel Diaz, who played Cornell's girlfriend in an earlier segment of the film), injures herself by tumbling drunkenly down the stairs, and Mandy is asked to step in. She agrees, if Cornell—who has "hoboed his way up to New York"—can be her piano player. The show promises to be a huge success, and a wealthy white man offers to premiere it in one of his theaters (with only a single request: that the show's name be changed from "Swing!" to "I Lubs Dat Man," which suggests the white producer's—and, by implication, the white society's—tendency to stereotype blacks and limit them to restricted roles). Now a star, Mandy is happy to have her man back, even though he has not yet shed his wicked ways.

Mandy rises to stardom partly because she is not averse to playing the familiar Mammy role upon which the white producer insists: but, as J. Ronald Green (*SL* 121) suggests, like some of Micheaux's other characters, Mandy interrogates the stereotype by "signifying" on it rather than inhabiting it. In fact, it is not Mandy who draws laughter but the producer, "for it is his act of stereotyping that is held up for ridicule, not the stereotyped actors or characters themselves." Moreover, a newly empowered Mandy uses her clout in her own behalf to bring Cornell into the production, in the hope that steady employment will make him a better man.

Yet for Micheaux, the couple are somewhat secondary figures: Micheaux's primary interest is in Ted and Lena, characters who offer a better race model than the traditional pairing of Mandy and Cornell and who exemplify the true entrepreneurial spirit that he so admired and the ideas of racial uplift that he espoused. As he did with many leading characters in his films, Micheaux made Ted, the pioneering black producer and real hero of *Swing!*, a kind of surrogate for himself. Like Ted, who notes that he is the first "Negro [ever to produce a musical] colored show," Micheaux prided himself on the variety shows and Harlem revues that he was able to showcase in his films, shows that lauded black talent and transcended simple minstrelsy. Thus, as J. Ronald Green writes, Gregory (capably assisted by Lena, who becomes his wife) is not just a Doppelgänger for the filmmaker, who "is supposed to represent an appropriate figure of uplift and to be above reproach"; like Micheaux (who was capably assisted by his wife Alice B. Russell), he also creates opportunities "for class advancement" by providing blacks with starring roles and, perhaps most importantly, for "increased control of the entertainment image and thus defeat of ethnic caricature" (*FQ* 25). Even the last scene in *Swing!* advances Micheaux's personal philosophy as it warns that white financing of black musicals (like white financing of race movies), while structurally necessary, "threatens uplift through the possibility that it might insinuate racist stereotyping and caricature into black culture" (*SL* 123).

MICHEAUX'S RETURN TO WRITING

By 1940, financial problems made it impossible for Micheaux to continue his filmmaking, so he returned to the career that had initially brought him such success: the writing of fiction. Between 1944 and 1947, Micheaux completed four new novels that he self-published through a new company he founded, the Book Supply Company of New York. The first three of the four—*The Wind from Nowhere*, *The Case of Mrs. Wingate*, and *The Story of Dorothy Stanfield*—were, according to Micheaux, based on his earlier films; and they demonstrated how intricately interconnected his fictional and cinematic productions actually were. In the "Acknowledgment" with which he opened his seventh and final novel, *The Masquerade*, Micheaux noted that:

> Since retiring from the production of Motion Pictures in
> 1940, and returning to writing, I have written and caused
> to be published, three novels, which plots I was able to
> select very carefully from among the stories I filmed
> while making pictures some years ago. I had merely to
> select and rewrite whatever one of the old stories I liked
> best, which in fact, was not nearly so arduous as creating
> a new theme entirely, and, due to the fact that the story
> had been worked out very carefully when it was filmed,
> I found that it made a better and more convincing novel
> after I had worked it back to story form.

The most significant of those novels was *The Wind from Nowhere*, which again reworked Micheaux's familiar story of the homesteader, his ill-fated first marriage, and his happy reunion with and marriage to his first love. That story, first told in *The Conquest* and retold in *The Homesteader* and adapted to the screen in Micheaux's first silent film *The Homesteader* and again in the first black sound film *The Exile*, takes a few new twists in *The Wind from Nowhere*, in which the backstory is downplayed and the relationships among the principal characters are emphasized. The homesteader, here named Martin Eden,[109] meets and falls in love with a white woman, Deborah Stewart, whom he feels compelled to reject because of "the Customs of Society" (316). Instead, he marries Linda Lee, who—according to the novel's cast of characters—"loved him dearly, but lacked the courage and strength of her convictions." Linda is the daughter of the Rt. Reverend Dr. N. J. Lee, "an hypocritical rascal, who was the cause of all their trouble" and who takes advantage of Martin's absence to lure his daughter back home. In this version, however, the Reverend's crime is all the greater because he succeeds in separating Martin not just from his wife but also from his son. (In the two earlier novels, the baby does not survive.)

At this point, *The Wind from Nowhere* devolves into melodrama of the most improbable but amusing sort. Back in Chicago, the Reverend, unable to support Linda and the child, decides not to oppose Martin's next attempt to reclaim his family. Martin, unaware of the Reverend's change of heart, arrives in Chicago with a gun, with which he plans to force Linda's return. In the excitement of their reunion, Linda shoots and wounds Martin, after which he leaves for South Dakota without her. Shortly thereafter, as Deborah is traveling east by train, she overhears Eugene Crook, the white banker, planning with an accomplice to purchase for a nominal fee Linda's valuable homestead by appealing to her father's greed and vanity. Deborah follows the men to Chicago, where she arrives too late to prevent Crook from getting the Reverend's signature on the relinquishment; but she confronts Linda, berating her for her timidity in turning her heart against her husband and allowing her father to ruin their lives. Recognizing the truth that Deborah has revealed, Linda kills her father and plans to kill herself as well; before doing so, however, she tries to reach the home of her black neighbor Nelson Boudreaux—who, coincidentally, is the grandfather that Deborah has just met—to make arrangements for Deborah to take her child back to South Dakota so Martin can raise him to be "brave and strong, resolute and courageous!" (384). But as Linda is running down the street, a truck strikes and kills her. Fortunately, Deborah is gifted with "second sight" and already knows what Linda had planned to say to her. Deborah then makes a hasty retreat to South Dakota, where she intends to nullify Crook's purchase of Linda's relinquishment by establishing her own prior claim (on behalf of Martin). Crook and his accomplice, who happen to be on the same train, become aware of her plot; and upon arrival, they speed by car to the disputed homestead. Not to be beaten, Deborah rents a horse and races them—during a terrible storm—to the property. With the road flooded, Crook can drive no farther; but Deborah, on horseback, fords the high waters and arrives safely to find Martin waiting for her at the property. The next Monday, after an affidavit concerning Linda Lee's death arrives at the land office, Crook's application is rejected and Deborah's claim is upheld. Martin, having learned of Deborah's racial heritage and of the other events that transpired in Chicago, is free to marry his dream girl. Martin's joy is intensified when he discovers that the homestead that Deborah labored so hard to protect and preserve for him contains a mountain of manganese that is worth a million dollars.

After a honeymoon "to a far country," Martin and Deborah bring Martin Junior back to the Rosebud Country, where "they began their life's work." With the wealth accumulated from the manganese deposit, "they bought more than a hundred thousand acres of Rosebud lands," worked the soil with mighty tractors, and harvested huge yields of crops. "Then Deborah and Martin went East, where unfortunate families of their race had been forced on relief. They selected from them the worthy and industrious ones, brought them hither and permitted each to buy and pay for out of earnings, ten acres of rich, deep plowed land. And with each purchase they supplied a cow, a horse, chickens and pigs. Each family then grew its own food. The women were able to make their pin money from eggs and chickens and milk; the men were given work in huge food product factories and manganese alloy plants that were built, where they were given a few days work each month" (384-85). In twenty-five years, Micheaux concludes, "a great Negro colony will call the Rosebud Country home." Teaching "the philosophy of common sense" to themselves and their children, the Edens build a new Eden, a Utopia for blacks; and they "prospered and lived happily ever afterward" (385). Micheaux, as Jayna Brown writes, "wanted to claim for black people the right to status as the new Adams and Eves of the virgin soil, the right enjoyed by European immigrants to 'shed their repulsive pasts.'" By making his main migratory trope the westward journey, he afforded the Edens (and the protagonists who anticipate them) the opportunity to define themselves by taming the land and proving their own mettle—the opportunity, also, to reiterate a single goal: the act of production.[110]

In this way, Micheaux brought the story of the homesteader, his new mythic hero, full circle: from the industrious Oscar Devereaux of *The Conquest*, who aims admirably high but whose dream fails; to the ambitious Jean Baptiste in *The Homesteader*, whose hard work brings happiness, despite the machinations of those who would have him fail; to the ultimate pioneer Martin Eden in *The Wind from Nowhere*, who succeeds beyond his wildest expectations by establishing his own society, through which he is able to help other aspiring blacks to achieve their dreams.

In his next novel, *The Case of Mrs. Wingate* (1945), Micheaux revisited Sidney Wyeth, another of his favorite fictional and cinematic counterparts. Wyeth, who had made his first appearance in print as a best-selling novelist in Micheaux's *The Forged Note* and on screen as a novelist-turned-lawyer and detective in *The*

Gunsaulus Mystery, is depicted here as a successful novelist and filmmaker. In the course of the novel, he becomes involved with two women, the duplicitous and stage-struck actress Edrina Vinson, whom he rejects, and the beautiful, highly educated Bertha Schultz, a Negro Nazi spy whom he converts to his own beliefs and ultimately marries. A parallel yet often intersecting story line involves Mrs. Florence Wingate, a white woman married to a dysfunctional but wealthy textile manufacturer, and the black Kermit Early, a childhood friend whom Florence had known from her hometown. Years before, Florence had tried unsuccessfully to seduce Kermit. When she meets Kermit again in Atlanta, she sets him up in her house and showers him with the passion she is unable to share with her husband. (Mr. Wingate is "not a normal man" [50], she admits to Kermit; he suffers from the same unspecified perversity that Leo M. Frank did.) In addition to her sexual attentions, Florence gives Kermit the financial means to complete his education, which culminates in a doctorate from Harvard. When she discovers that she is pregnant with Kermit's child (and when her husband conveniently suffers a fatal heart attack, leaving her a very rich widow), the lovers marry and move to Harlem. Despite his education, however, Kermit (whom Micheaux based— rather unflatteringly—on W. E. B. Du Bois) is unable to pursue a meaningful career. The one project at which he persists is a "hate picture, purporting to expose the Jews [*sic*] exploitation of the Negro" (88); and, of course, he tries to get Wyeth—with his "maturity from the standpoint of character," his "long experience," and his "insight into human emotions so essential to the story" (89)— to direct. Wyeth, after all, has been pushed into retirement, in large part because of "the Goddamned Jews" and "Jew sons a bitches" (294) from whom he had to beg "to put up money to make [his] pictures" (90) and to book them in their theaters.[111] "Wyeth, alone [of the makers of 'better' pictures], with no money and trying to get along, was forced out," after which "the entire making of colored pictures, due to their [the Jewish producers'] interference, collapsed, and Wyeth had to quit and turn back to writing novels to make a living" (71). Nonetheless, Wyeth refuses Kermit's offer, thereby illuminating the contrast between himself, as a man of character and high principle who seeks to uplift his race by his positive depictions of blacks, and Kermit, a divisive hatemonger anxious to establish his own reputation and to "find his star" (473) by diminishing others.

Even more blatant than the novel's anti-Semitic portrait of Hollywood is Micheaux's self-adulation, which he conveys through the laurels that are heaped upon Wyeth.[112] As a novelist, Wyeth created "a splendid story" (307); but, writes Micheaux, his books never "featured any mammies or uncles or any colored people who would be speaking in dialect," and "white people in general were not interested in the modern, intelligent and aggressive type of Negro" (306). As a filmmaker, Wyeth also avoided "Dinah and old Sambo" stereotypes. "The only Negro in America that has ever made a motion picture" (71) and the "pioneer Negro Motion Picture producer," he had filmed "the first full length all colored cast one, and many of the ones that had been produced since until it was considered his line and nobody had sought to interfere seriously" (73). His "uncanny insight into Negro life" (71), into "what pleased them only as a Negro could understand" (70), allowed him to make movies that were "as good as the best picture ever made" (91), even if his audience was limited to those "500 theatres catering almost exclusively to Negroes" (90). Yet despite Wyeth's mastery of print and film, he is not as well-reviewed as his contemporaries, including the Southern white woman who wrote *Passion*, who "has been invited to speak to endless groups of Negroes . . . [who] are falling over each other to hear her" (212), and Frank Knight, author of *Nature's Child*, who looks at blacks "with distorted eyes" (92). Wyeth, in this instance, is without doubt a barely fictionalized persona for Micheaux, who in real life wondered why his own works were not reviewed as well as Lillian Smith's *Strange Fruit* (*Passion*) or Richard Wright's *Black Boy* and *Native Son* (Frank Knight's *Black Narcissus* and *Nature's Child*).[113] Micheaux was particularly confounded by the critical and commercial success that had eluded him but that Wright had attained with his more radical racial protest fiction.

Wyeth appears again, albeit in a lesser role as a friend of several of the principal characters, in Micheaux's next novel, *The Story of Dorothy Stanfield* (1946).[114] That novel begins with a foreword ostensibly by "The Publishers" (Micheaux himself being the sole publisher) about the state of the Negro in American film and literature. "The Publishers" write that over the past few years—precisely the same time period that Micheaux has been retired from filmmaking—"except for a menial role now and then, in which he is required to roll his eyes, say all his lines in dialect, and in short, be stupid and funny," the Negro "has been practically barred from the screen! . . . As regards literature, it would seem that he enjoys a wider range of thought and activity. Except in the novels by Oscar Micheaux, however, he is never shown as a contemporary American citizen, talking as most colored people have long been speaking, in plain and simple English. In the matter of romance, he seems presumed not to have any whatever." Yet curiously, "every book by or about Negroes" is widely reviewed "in all publications, many at great length, and most times very favorably—*except those by Mr. Micheaux* [italics original], which have outsold all other books by Negro authors during the past five years with two single exceptions." The explanation offered for the critical neglect of Micheaux is that he breaks "the 'pattern' as designed for Negroes and writers" in his plots, themes, and characters.

The Story of Dorothy Stanfield indeed offers some unusual characters and plot twists. Walter Le Baron, a black ace detective from New York City (similar to Elmer Harris in *The Spider's Web* and Alonzo White in *The Girl from Chicago*), encounters a beautiful black woman, Dorothy Stanfield, at a gas station in Memphis; within twenty-four hours, they are madly in love and ready to commit to marriage. Dorothy, however, is still married to Dr. N. D. Stanfield, who is incarcerated for mail fraud related to an insurance scam. Stanfield, whom Dorothy wed upon her graduation from Vassar College, has had—it would seem—a rather checkered career. After performing an abortion that caused the death of a young black woman, Stanfield lost most of his patients and became allied with Junius Brown, the local undertaker, in a scheme to retrieve and recycle coffins. From there, he and Brown concocted an even bigger scam: to assume the life insurance premiums for blacks who have let their policies lapse, then to record and report the deaths of the policy holders and collect the insurance money themselves. Although Stanfield beats the charges of swindling, he is convicted of using the mails to defraud and sent to jail. Like Mrs. Wingate's husband, however, who suffers a fatal accident just before his wife plans to tell him of her pregnancy by Kermit and her intention to seek a divorce, Stanfield conveniently suffers a fatal heart attack just as Dorothy and Walter decide to marry.

In the meantime, Le Baron pursues and captures Cleo "Scarface" Johnson, who is wanted for killing "a Jewish rent collector by the name of [Isadore] Zacarrio" (142) and for the subsequent murders of Johnson's black girlfriend Lizzie O'Neal and her wealthy white "sugar daddy" Lawrence Van Revel in Memphis. With thirty thousand dollars of reward money in hand, Le Baron returns to take Dorothy on a six-month-long honeymoon cruise around the world. "And thus ends this story of a brave, resolute and courageous man, and a kind, tender, affectionate and beautiful woman" (416).

Dorothy and Le Baron, like Sidney Wyeth and his wife Bertha (who also appears briefly), are Micheaux's models of good racial behavior. Educated, ambitious, successful, they marry within their race and attempt to uplift it by their high moral conduct. By contrast, Lizzie O'Neal, Van Revel's "Negress concubine," demonstrates few scruples about accepting material favors from either her black boyfriend, Cleo, or her white lover; she plays the two men against each other, and ultimately pays the highest price for her illicit affairs. Even in death, she is deprived of dignity: the white press identifies her only as Van Revel's "housekeeper." Florence Wingate-Early, the wealthy white widow who married her black lover Kermit Early (both of whom reappear in *The Story of Mrs. Dorothy Stanfield*), also cannot seem to find social acceptance of their union. Unwelcome in the South, she and her new husband have moved north to Harlem; but even there, blacks, especially black women, judge them harshly and assume the worst about her. ("And she wasn't no—whore when he married her?" wonders one acquaintance. Replies another: "She *had* to have satisfaction—and it took a Negro to see that she got it" [131-32].) "The Publishers" of the novel (that is, Micheaux himself) observe in the foreword that it is precisely Micheaux's courage in writing about such forbidden themes—of "race-mixing" and of reversing "the old order"—that predisposes reviewers to overlook his work and penalizes the author for exhibiting "democracy and 'free speech.'" According to "The Publishers":

> It so happens that during the past few years, and particularly since the rise of Communism in America, there has been an increased amount of race-mixing, mostly

between white women and colored men—so much so, in fact, that it has become alarming to the better class of Negroes, who are wondering how far it is likely to go. This is a fact—and the practice is increasing *right here in our own America!* The fact that the press, in the matter of reviewing books, chooses to ignore it, because, no doubt, they do not like the idea, and by their silence with regard to Mr. Micheaux's books, tacitly condemn them just because the author dares touch upon the subject, has not lessened or decreased the practice. [Italics original]

Indeed, Micheaux was progressive in his focus on issues that "were the subject of conversation and debate among Negroes the country over"—even if he continued to be retrogressive in his condemnation and stereotyping of other ethnic groups like Jews. (It is, he writes pejoratively, "the smart, Jewish lawyer, Leo Bernstein" [413] who managed to get Dr. Stanfield acquitted of murder charges after his patient died following an abortion, while another lawyer, Max Goldstein, offered a summation that "stupefied" the court and "paralyzed the jury's imagination" during Stanfield's subsequent trial for insurance fraud—although everybody knew Stanfield *"was as guilty as hell!"* [413-14].) And while neither *The Case of Mrs. Wingate* nor *The Story of Dorothy Stanfield* is a particularly artful or well-crafted novel, both demonstrate Micheaux's abilities to integrate black characters into all aspects of American society, to exploit topical events, and to "write [the colored woman] into romance and beauty and other things along the lines white writers shower on their women" (*Case* 112)—talents that were confirmed by *The Girl From Chicago*, which contains many of the themes of the two novels, and by a number of his other popular films, especially those that featured detectives and underworld figures.

Following the familiar pattern of his first six novels, in his seventh and final book Micheaux depicts another ambitious black man who overcomes obstacles to win the woman he loves. Based on "a scenario from a novel by Chas. W. Chesnutt, published almost fifty years ago," which Micheaux had filmed twice, "first, as a silent picture in the twenties, and as a talking picture early in the thirties," *The Masquerade* retells *The House Behind the Cedars*, a story of a free Negro family during the years just before and after the Civil War. Chesnutt's novel "made no mention, however, of Abraham Lincoln, the Dred Scott Decision, John Brown, or the Civil War, all among the most turbulent, grave and exciting events in our history." But, as Micheaux admits, "the story provided a splendid background to work in these characters and events as I saw fit, and I desired to do" (7-8).

Unfortunately, the historical embellishments that Micheaux saw fit to add are among the dullest and most extraneous parts of *The Masquerade*. Much of the first half of the book, in fact, is overladen with summaries of or references to various developments in black and American history; included are excerpts of the Lincoln-Douglas debates and other of Douglas's arguments, newspaper accounts of Lincoln's rise to the presidency, Horace Greeley's open letter to Lincoln denouncing slavery, even the text of Lincoln's Emancipation Proclamation. Yet the connections between those historical events and the characters in the novel are, at best, tenuous: on a visit to the white Judge Straight, for example, young Johnny embarks on a lengthy and highly improbable analysis of the implications of the Dred Scott case for the black race.

The central story of *The Masquerade*—of John Walden's passing, of Rena's brief romance with George Tryon, of Jeff Wain's relentless pursuit of her, and of Frank Fowler's devotion—derives almost entirely from Chesnutt's novel, even down to the characters' names. But as Micheaux had done with his earlier filmed versions of Chesnutt's novel,[115] he gave his novel a happy ending in which he redeems Rena for her attempt to repudiate her race by blaming her actions on John and rewards Frank for his years of loyalty to Rena's family by giving him her hand in marriage. Micheaux writes that, having suffered the hatred of the white race as well as of the light and dark members of their own race, the newlywed Fowlers plan to move to Chicago, where "color discrimination and the caste system among Negroes" (400) do not exist. Yet Chesnutt's more realistic and complicated scenario suggested that caste and class divisions such as those that separated the "yellow," relatively prosperous Waldens and the dark-skinned, working class Fowlers (who had originally been slaves assigned by their master to attend Molly, his black mistress, and who now lived more equally as her neighbors) were not so easily resolved. Chesnutt's Rena loves Frank as a "good friend" but is herself too close to white in the white-mulatto-Negro racial and social hierarchy ever to consider marrying him.

MICHEAUX'S FINAL FILM

Although he claimed to be retired from motion pictures, it is possible that, had he been able to muster the resources, Micheaux would have tried to film *The Masquerade*. During the war years, after he had returned to the writing of his books, Micheaux had offered his experience as a filmmaker to the federal Office of War Information (OWI): if Hollywood was determined to present more positive racial images on screen, then Micheaux asserted he was the one who could get blacks "in the war spirit." Although OWI declined his offer, Micheaux did return to film production long enough to work on one final picture, *The Betrayal*, based on his novel *The Wind from Nowhere*. Having adapted to film both earlier versions of the tale of his semi-autobiographical mythic hero (*The Conquest* as his first silent film *The Homesteader*, and *The Homesteader* as his first sound film *The Exile*), Micheaux must have thought it both natural and fitting to bring his latest retelling of that story to the screen. But *The Betrayal* was not the career-reviving success that Micheaux hoped it would be; outdated in its themes and conventions, it was, in fact, quite possibly his biggest failure.

Directed by Micheaux, *The Betrayal* was the only one of his films to be released by a film company other than his own, the white-owned Astor Pictures. *The Betrayal* premiered at the Mansfield Theater, a white theater in New York, and was promoted as the "Greatest Negro photoplay of all time." But, as the reviewer for the *New York Amsterdam News* (3 July 1948) observed, everything about it was substandard: "[T]he film should never have been shown. This reviewer was so embarrassed in watching the film . . . that she wanted to run and hide in a corner. The film from the beginning to end is bad; the acting is worse than amateurish; the dialogue ridiculous; the story down right stupid" (qtd. in Sampson 166, 168). The *Chicago Defender* (10 July 1948) was even more pointed in its criticism: describing the film as boring, unprofessional, and plotless, it concluded that "from the viewpoint of

competent critics, *The Betrayal* is a betrayal and is pretty awful"
(Regester, *FH* 429). Leroy Collins starred as Martin Eden; Myra
Stanton played Deborah Stewart; and featured performers included Verlie Cowan, Harris Gaines, and Yvonne Machen; but, as
Thomas Cripps writes, the cast was "an uneven mix of school-
teachers, a radio actor, a dancer, and an understudy in *Anna
Lucasta*, . . . an ensemble so varied in talents as to jangle against
rather then complement each others' work."[116] With a running time
of three hours and fifteen minutes, Micheaux's film was among the
longest ever produced to date, second only to *Gone With the Wind*.
Production costs exceeded $100,000, a significant portion of which
comprised Micheaux's own investment. After failing completely at
the box office, *The Betrayal* was withdrawn after just a few showings. (No copy of it survives.) Micheaux reportedly suffered so
severe a financial loss from his involvement in the production that
he never fully recovered. Despite his arthritis and his immobility
that necessitated the use of a wheelchair, he was forced to get back
on the road to sell his books; and, in 1951, on one of those trips—
to Charlotte, North Carolina—he fell ill and died.

Almost three decades earlier, in an article for the *Pittsburgh
Courier* (13 Dec. 1924), Micheaux had assessed the concerns that
the black independent filmmaker faced. "The colored producer,"
he wrote,

> has dared to step into a world that has hitherto remained
> closed to him. His entrance into this unexplored field, is
> for him, trebly difficult. He is united [*sic*] in his themes,
> in obtaining casts that present genuine ability, and in his
> financial resources. He requires encouragement and
> assistance. He is the new-born babe who must be fon-
> dled until he can stand on his own feet, and if the race
> has any pride in presenting its own achievements in this
> field, it behooves it to interest itself, and morally encour-
> age such efforts.

Micheaux's own aims in filmmaking were to make photoplays
that were truthful to the heart and to the race. "My results," he
observed, "might have been narrow at times, due perhaps to certain limited situations, which I endeavored to portray, but in those
limited situations, the truth was the predominate [*sic*] characteris-

tic. It is only by presenting those portions of the race portrayed in my pictures, in the light and background of their true state, that we can raise our people to greater heights. I am too imbued with the spirit of Booker T. Washington to engraft false virtues upon ourselves, to make ourselves that which we are not" (qtd. in Sampson 169).

In his productions, Micheaux did indeed endeavor to portray black experience in the light and background of its true state. He removed his black characters from the proverbial hen roosts and away from the watermelon contests and razor fights that the white public expected of blacks on screen, and placed them instead in middle-class living rooms and on frontier ranches that signaled the unlimited opportunities he felt were within reach of those aspiring blacks who were willing to work hard to achieve their ambitions.[117] And while Micheaux's pictures, like those of many black independent filmmakers of his time, may not have fulfilled his hope of being "on a par with those of the white producer," they nonetheless were, as Micheaux had intended them to be, "a credit to the race" and a remarkable and worthy achievement in American cinema.

NOTES TO CHAPTER 2

1. Blacks were not, by any means, the only producers of race films. White-run and white-backed independent filmmakers quickly realized the profit potential in black-cast films. In fact, as demonstrated in this chapter and the next, it was the white producers—and ultimately the major Hollywood studios—that helped to run the black producers of race films out of business.

2. "The chain of historical events that produced this short-lived cinema," writes Jane Gaines in *Fire and Desire*, "were not self-evident or inevitable but contingent and unexpected. The race pioneers carved something significant out of nothing—race movies were an audacious invention that helped to make an audience that most white entrepreneurs did not see, that helped to imagine a separate community into existence" (17).

3. In his "Foreword" to Pearl Bowser and Louise Spence's *Writing Himself into History*, Thulani Davis writes that race films indeed validated blacks' self-perceptions and counterbalanced notions of inferiority within the black communities. Davis quotes the authors, who conclude that "by bringing Black voices and visibility to popular culture, by portraying identities more diverse and more complex than had previously been expressed in mainstream commercial culture, by declaring their own identity, they [black race filmmakers] were writing their world into existence" (xiv).

4. "Jones" was one of the first and harshest critics of Griffith's *Birth of a Nation*. In an article for the *Chicago Defender* (15 May 1915), he not only voiced his anger at a picture that "has caused more trouble than all the moving pictures made in ten years" and whose "every scene is made up with subjects of race hatred"; but he also argued in support of films like those Micheaux would make, films that offered the "true facts" of black life, including some "spicey [*sic*] scenes." The Negro, he concluded, "is trying to forget the days of lash and cruelty and to appreciate his white friend, but if the truth must be told nothing can beat a moving picture to tell it. . . . If the people of the north [want] to see the Birth of a Nation so bad, let's deal fair: let's see the Negro side of it" (qtd. in Green, *Straight Lick* 2-3).

5. In keeping with some of vaudeville's traditions, when the Foster Photoplay Company toured, Lottie Grady would sing while the projectionist changed reels.

6. As the white film industry initially moved west, black filmmakers—for the most part—remained behind in the Midwest and the East.

7. As Thomas Cripps (*SFB* 220) writes, Foster claimed that "tests proved one great outstanding fact—the low mellow voice of the Negro

was ideally suited for the pictures." Foster therefore tried to promote "the peculiar ability of the Negro" that allowed him to fit "right into the new age." Apparently, in this regard, the black press from Mississippi to New York encouraged him and agreed that "'TALKIES' OPEN UP NEW AVENUES FOR PROFESSIONAL ACTORS.'"

According to Daniel J. Leab, when Foster had a renewed burst of enthusiasm and tried to organize another Foster Photoplay Company to produce all-black films to be underwritten by the sale of stocks, the prospectus read that "white companies defiantly say 'if you want better pictures of your race, make them yourself,' and the reply of the Foster Photoplay Company is 'we will'" (189).

8. Leab, in fact, writes that *The Railroad Porter* "was a comedy that does not seem to have been very different in style and content from the films depicting blacks that were turned out by the industry" (59).

9. Scott was not the only filmmaker interested in countering Griffith's racist portrayal. As Bowser and Spence demonstrate, the Peter P. Jones Company of Chicago produced, among other films, "a three-reel compilation, *The Dawn of Truth,* billed both as the 'Progress of the Negro: Facts from Farm, Factory and Fireside' and as 'The Re-birth of a Nation.'" In a review (1 April 1916) of the program, "the *Freeman* praised it for showing 'the victories' of the Race, 'an answer to that orgy of contempt . . . *Birth of a Nation*'" (*Writing* 104). And, according to Henry T. Sampson, *Injustice* (later retitled *Loyal Hearts* for distribution in the East), a film released in 1919 by the white-owned Democracy Film Corporation, was "billed as an answer to the racist book *The Clansman.* It was well-received by most of the black community; however, it was not well-received by the white press." An article in the *Leader,* a white Los Angeles daily, for example, called the film "a frank appeal to the emotions of colored folk to revolt against the social handicaps which have been imposed upon them. Surely no good purpose can be served by such an appeal at the present time" (qtd. in Sampson 210-11).

10. For the best discussion of Scott's disastrous involvement with *The Birth of a Race* film project, see Cripps, "The Making of *The Birth of a Race*"; see also Cripps, *Slow Fade to Black,* 72-75.

11. For a full plot synopsis of *The Birth of a Race,* see the film review in *Variety* (25 Apr. 1919).

12. In late 1918, Emmett J. Scott, who was then Army Assistant Secretary for Negro Affairs, met with George P. Johnson of the Lincoln Motion Picture Company. As a result of the meeting, Johnson was able to purchase a copy of a war film of black troops in action in France during the First World War. As Henry T. Sampson writes, "The film was distributed by the Lincoln Motion Picture Company to black theaters all over the United States" (140-41).

13. A later Lincoln Motion Picture Company production revisited the Tenth Cavalry. *A Day with the Tenth Cavalry at Fort Huachuca* (1921) featured newsreel-type footage of the black cavalry in training at Fort Huachuca, Arizona.

14. Similarly, Chester Paul, manager of the Washington Theater, is quoted in the *Chicago Defender* (17 July 1917) as saying: "I will always be glad to use the Lincoln company's productions, as they are uniformly excellent and I consider them good box office attractions" (qtd. in Sampson 258-59).

15. Jane Gaines, *Fire and Desire* 99. Gaines notes that Noble Johnson went on to costar in such Universal films as *The Lure of the Circus* (1919) and *The Adventures of Robinson Crusoe* (1922) as well as in the popular serial, *The Bull's Eye* (1918). In later years, after the advent of sound films and until 1950, he appeared in about 150 film productions (304).

Clyde R. Taylor, in "Black Silence and the Politics of Representation," also comments on the way that Johnson's resignation "from Lincoln Pictures, the most adventuresome and promising Black movie company of its day," altered the course of race movies. "Universal," he writes, "was exercising the power of monopoly against weaker competitors, in this case monopolizing talent the way the industry did through contractual development of superstars. By all accounts, Noble Johnson had the potential to become a very large star in race movies, a phenomenon they had never produced. So his departure was also a kind of brain drain" (6).

16. For a discussion of the "novelized" version of *A Man's Duty* by George Johnson and Rose Atwood, see Anna Everett, 148-49.

17. Johnson's collected papers, now housed at the University of California at Los Angeles, have been an invaluable resource for scholars interested in black American cinema, particularly the history of race filmmaking.

18. According to Bowser and Spence, the *New York Age* (14 July 1916) "suggested motion picture houses should book the company's second release, *The Scapegoat*, for two reasons: 'First because it possesses undeniable merit; and secondly, because it is a racial business venture which ought to be encouraged by all managers who make their money off Negro patrons'" (*Writing* 73).

19. A few other race film companies also looked to literature. *When True Love Wins* (1915), a Southern Motion Picture Company movie, was adapted from a work by Tuskegee Institute essayist Isaac Fisher, who also wrote the screenplay. And *The Green-Eyed Monster* (1921), a film released by the white-owned Norman Film Manufacturing Company, was also based on an original story, "The Man Who Could Turn White" (Sampson 276, 311).

20. White independent producer Ted Toddy, founder of Dixie National Pictures, Inc., announced a similar intention. Sampson (225-26)

quotes comments made by Wendell Hatch, president of the Film Acceptance Corporation, a subsidiary of Dixie National, to the *New York Amsterdam News* (25 Oct. 1941): "The quest for story material and Negro writers was started by Dixie National Pictures. If the colored writers will send in their scripts, we'll use them and pay if they are possible for film production. Everyone tells us that no Negro epic will be written until a Negro writes it. We are willing to believe that and we're ready to receive the epic, the comedy or the drama that bears out that idea. Dixie National Pictures extends this challenge to Negro writers!" But, as Sampson notes, there is no record that the company actually used scripts submitted by black writers.

21. Hereafter cited as *BFG*. Chesnutt's *The Marrow of Tradition*, as Corey K. Creekmur discusses in his essay "Telling White Lies: Oscar Micheaux and Charles W. Chesnutt," shared some basic thematic and descriptive correspondences with Micheaux's film *Within Our Gates*.

22. For more information on these and other black and black-oriented film companies, see Henry T. Sampson's indispensable study, *Blacks in Black and White*, especially the chapter on "Other Black Independents."

23. Sampson provides excellent summaries of these and other shorts and features in *Blacks in Black and White*.

24. Unlike the black press, the white press believed that Ebony's films were completely innocuous. In reviewing Ebony's *Wrong All Around* (1917), for instance, *Exhibition Herald* (22 Dec. 1917) suggested that "the comedies depict without affectation the happy-go-lucky characteristics of the colored race." And *The Moving Picture World* (8 Dec. 1917) wrote of the same film that it "might be booked in almost any theatre as a lighter of the program. It isn't likely to offend" (qtd. in Sampson 280).

25. In response to criticism of some of Ebony's films from black readers, Tony Langston replied in the *Chicago Defender* that "it would hardly be good policy for any theatre in this district to book pictures from a company whose photoplays carry 'comedy' that causes respectable ladies and gentlemen to blush with humiliation." Furthermore, he urged black moviegoers to avoid the "so-called 'all-colored comedies.'" Some day, Langston concluded, "we will have race dramas which will uplift, instead of rotten stuff which degrades" (Bowser and Spence, *Writing* 92-93).

26. As with the Ebony comedies, the white press generally found Cohen's shorts to be amusing and full of good humor. For instance, according to reviewer George Kent Shutter in *The Moving Picture World* (20 April 1929), *The Melancholy Dame* "is not only funny, it is harmless. Which means that it can offend neither the white or colored race. Its characters are drawn entirely from the negro population so there is no clash

in interest or prejudice" (qtd. in Sampson 324). For a fuller discussion of some of the shorts (*The Melancholy Dame, Music Hath Charms, Oft in the Silly Night, Brown Gravy*) based on Cohen's stories, see Thomas Cripps, *Slow Fade to Black*, 222-24.

27. David Starkman, sometimes called the "Oscar Micheaux" of the white independent producers of black films, was the driving force behind the Colored Players Film Corporation. Thomas Cripps, who in "'Race Movies' as Voices of the Black Bourgeoisie: *The Scar of Shame*" (54) called Starkman a "little Napoleon," and others have commented on Starkman's methods of raising capital (from his wife's inheritance, from local lawyers and merchants) and of filmmaking (from writing the scripts to delivering the prints personally).

Lenora Starkman recalled that her father decided to make all-black-cast films because he "was a crusader. Nobody played the black people as heroes and heroines. This fit in with his ethic. He felt the black people shouldn't be stepped on, that at the same time he was making money he could glorify their position" (Sampson 218). After the release of *The Scar of Shame*, Starkman found himself in severe financial difficulties. In a last desperate move, he tried to merge his company with that of black vaude-villian Sherman H. ("Uncle Dud") Dudley, but the new company never got off the ground, and Starkman's short career as a black film producer ended.

In "Colored Players Film Corporation: An Alternative to Micheaux," Charles Musser discusses the company's history and points out that while the CPFC "was launched by European-American Jews," admitted-ly fragmentary evidence suggests that the company "was the site of sub-stantive interracial collaboration" (178) as well as "interethnic collabora-tions" (180).

28. Thomas Cripps, "'Race Movies' as Voices of the Black Bourgeoisie: *The Scar of Shame*" 47. Cripps also suggests that the film is "one of the best examples of a movie intended to convey black middle-class social values to a black urban audience" (47). As with many early films, which generally did not list a date on the print itself, there is some question about the actual release date of *The Scar of Shame*. For many years, film scholars have assumed that date to be 1926. But Charles Musser, in "A Colored Players Film Corporation Filmography" (278-85), Appendix C in *Oscar Micheaux and His Circle*, uncovers new evidence that indicates the film may have been several years in production and that its first screening may actually have been as late as April, 1929, in New York City.

29. Another good use of imagery occurs in a scene near the end of the film, when Louise poisons herself. As she dies, the candle that has been lighting her chamber is extinguished, and the room is thrown momen-

tarily into darkness. By contrast to the single candle, there is a brightly shining candelabra in the Hathaways's home.

30. For an interesting discussion of "the case for the culpability of the upper as well as the lower classes," as supported by the structure of *The Scar of Shame*, see Gaines's *Fire and Desire*, 109-112.

31. The estimates vary widely. Richard J. Norman of the Norman Film Manufacturing Company wrote in 1922 that in 1921-1922 there were 354 "Negro theatres" in the United States scattered over twenty-eight states but that, by 1922, some of those were already closed. Henry T. Sampson suggests a similar number: around 300. Bowser and Spence write that the broad discrepancies in the numbers of black movie houses would seem to indicate that "some of the counts may have included theaters that reserved the balcony or another section for Blacks or had special days or hours set aside for Colored audiences. Some may even have been vaudeville houses that played films only occasionally" (*Writing* 114-15).

32. By comparison, as Daniel J. Leab writes, "by 1922 there were over 16,000 movie theaters in the United States, many of them new and luxurious" (41). As with estimates of black theaters, however, the numbers vary. Filmmaker Richard Norman in 1921, for example, estimated there to be 22,000 white theaters throughout the country; yet there were only 121 theaters he considered to be outlets for his films (Gaines, *FD* 105). And filmmaker Hunter Haynes, in an article for the *Indianapolis Freeman* (14 March 1914), put the numbers at "238 colored houses in the United States as against 32,000 white houses" (Sampson 178).

33. Jim Pines (33) also notes the cultural impetus of the Harlem Renaissance and the "1920s concept of 'race' records, i.e. black music produced strictly for the black market," in enhancing the market for race entertainment.

34. George Johnson called him precisely that: "one of the most colorful characters in the history of the Negro in motion pictures" (Gaines, *FD* 116). Johnson, who maintained a lengthy and longtime correspondence with Micheaux, wrote several biographical accounts of Micheaux throughout his lifetime. According to Richard Gehr (34), Micheaux was also "cinema's most mysterious and prolific African-American *auteur*"; a "naïve genius of a control freak"; "a combination of Samuel Goldwyn and Samuel Glick who embraced the self-determination philosophies of W. E. B. Du Bois, Booker T. Washington, and Marcus Garvey"; and "a bona fide artistic pioneer."

35. Micheaux's volume of production, Bowser and Spence concur, "was not typical. Reol, when organizing, announced its intention to put out a photoplay each month, and did produce seven or eight features but

stayed in business less than four years. Richard Norman produced six features in nine years before discontinuing production. The first six years George P. Johnson was working for the Lincoln Motion Picture Company, he could not afford to leave his job at the Omaha Post Office and his brother Noble did not draw a salary from his two and a half years of presidency and three starring roles" (*Writing* 116-17).

36. In 1986, in a special ceremony in Hollywood, Micheaux was posthumously awarded a Lifetime Achievement Award by the Directors Guild of America; he was the first black filmmaker to receive the honor. Soon afterwards, a prestigious award given to black artists and filmmakers by the Black Filmmakers Hall of Fame was named for Micheaux, and he was also given a star on Hollywood's Walk of Fame. In recent years, with the rediscovery of several early Micheaux films, Micheaux and his work have become the focus of increasing scholarly attention, as evidenced by the numerous conferences, symposiums, and film festivals convened and critical books issued of late. Several important new studies were published in 2000 and 2001 alone: Pearl Bowser and Louise Spence's *Writing Himself into History: Oscar Micheaux, His Silent Films, and His Audiences*; Jane M. Gaines's *Fire and Desire: Mixed-Race Movies in the Silent Era*; J. Ronald Green's *Straight Lick: The Cinema of Oscar Micheaux*; and *Oscar Micheaux and His Circle: African-American Filmmaking and Race Cinema of the Silent Era*, edited by Pearl Bowser, Jane Gaines, and Charles Musser.

37. Cited henceforth as *SL*.

38. James Hoberman (*Film Comment* 12) writes: "His camera ground relentlessly on while the key light wandered, traffic noise obliterated the dialogue, or a soundman's arm intruded upon the frame. Actors blew their cues, recovered, and continued. Wasting nothing, he re-used footage with impunity, carried the post-dubbing of his soundtracks to the outer limits of possibility, saved up his out-takes and fashioned them into second films." J. Ronald Green agrees that Micheaux's production values were often low, but Green argues, significantly, that Micheaux's stylistic values were high (Green, "The Micheaux Style," *Black Film Review* 7.4 [1992]: 32-33, qtd. in Regester, *Film History* 442).

39. Robert Earl Jones, the father of actor James Earl Jones, reportedly was discovered by Micheaux in the front of a Young Communist League picket line that was protesting the director's film, *God's Step Children*. Jones, who appeared as a naïve boxer in *The Notorious Elinor Lee* and as a detective in *Lying Lips,* recalls that "Micheaux always knew what he was doing, and he really knew how to cut corners. He paid me $100 for each movie, which was a lot of money then. There was always the joke that he'd only give the extras carfare because they were getting experience" (qtd. in Gehr 37).

40. Micheaux followed a certain pattern in his filmmaking. Gehr (37) writes that, for almost thirty years, Micheaux would "shoot a film in the spring and summer, edit it in the fall, then travel with a driver through-out the Northeast, South and East, where he would show stills of his stars to ghetto theater owners."

41. "By merely finishing a film," writes Thomas Cripps (*BFG* 26), "Micheaux's film company was like the legendary tricksters of black folk-lore, who win the game against the system. Thus the low pay, borrowed equipment, and nagging debtors helped define the character of the com-pleted movie."

42. Micheaux also used events from the black and white press to promote his films. Charlene Regester, in "Headline to Headlights: Oscar Micheaux's Exploitation of the Rhinelander Case," demonstrates how Micheaux used the 1924 media frenzy that "erupted surrounding the annulment of a marriage between an African American, Alice Jones, and white millionaire Kip Rhinelander" to garner additional publicity for his movies. Micheaux, writes Regester, "strategically capitalized on the attention this case received, utilizing the coverage to promote his own works," including *The House Behind the Cedars* (1924/25) and *Thirty Years Later* (1928/also titled *Thirty Years After*). (In reality, the situations were much different: in the Rhinelander case, the white millionaire married his black lover; in *The House Behind the Cedars,* based on Chesnutt's novel, the white admirer is unaware that his lover is black. Both, however, end with the white males pursuing and demonstrating their love for the black women.) Regester also writes that "interracial marriage apparently intrigued Micheaux, and that interest combined with public appeal, caused him to frequently integrate the theme into his writings and films" (195, 201, 196).

Jane Gaines (*FD* 157) demonstrates that Micheaux incorporated cur-rent events even into his own advertising. She cites one of Micheaux's ads from the *Baltimore Afro-American,* in which he "hawked the passing story: '*The House Behind the Cedars* is a remarkable parallel to the famous Rhinelander Case. . . . It tells the story of a beautiful mulatto girl who poses as white, and is wooed and won by a young millionaire. Although worried, she does not betray her secret. Then comes the discovery as in the Rhinelander case.'" Micheaux also exploited other events from the press, such as the 1915 Leo Frank murder case. As discussed in this chap-ter, *The Gunsaulus Mystery* (1921) and *Murder in Harlem* (1935), a sound remake of *The Gunsaulus Mystery,* incorporated a number of plot events that were reminiscent of the Frank case.

43. As Henry T. Sampson shows, a number of white-owned compa-nies also tried to capitalize on the gangster film craze. For example, the

brother team of producers, Harry M. Popkin and Leo Popkin, founded Million Dollar Productions in 1937 "and up until 1940 turned out several of the most stylish black films produced during the period." The company "specialized in gangster films that fell well within this popular Hollywood genre of the late 1930's. They made no attempt to deal with the unique experiences of blacks in America, but their films were black versions of the type of films that were made by James Cagney and Humphrey Bogart which dominated the industry in the early thirties" (222-23).

44. For a good history of the Lafayette Players, see Sister Francesca Thompson's "From Shadows 'n Shufflin' to Spotlights and Cinema: The Lafayette Players, 1915-1932."

45. *Roseanne*, "a play of Negro life in the South, having to do with a transgressing preacher and his, finally, avenging congregation," by Nan Bagby Stephens, a white woman from Georgia, was likely—according to Bowser and Spence—an uncredited source for *Body and Soul*. That play, never published but first produced at the end of 1923 at the Greenwich Village Theatre in New York with a white cast in blackface, depicted Roseanne, a middle-aged woman bringing up her younger sister Leola, and Cicero Brown, her pastor. In the play, the two sisters compete for his attention. The play "doesn't suggest the same incestuous conflict of Micheaux's mother-daughter relationship [in *Body and Soul*], nor is there the complication of the immorality of his [the minister's] drinking and gambling." But there are indeed interesting similarities between the two works. *Roseanne* moved from the Greenwich Village Theatre to Broadway for a short run; and then, for a week, it was performed with an "all-star colored cast," including Rose McClendon and Charles S. Gilpin, at the Schubert-Riviera Theatre at 97th Street. The production then moved even more uptown, to the Lafayette Theater in Harlem; at that time, Paul Robeson replaced Gilpin in the role of the preacher (Bowser and Spence, *Writing* 192, 206). Jane Gaines, in *Fire and Desire* (276), attributes the discovery of *Body and Soul* as an adaptation of *Roseanne*—that discovery being "a significant contribution to Micheaux scholarship"—to Hazel Carby. (See Carby, *Race Men: The Body and Soul of Race, Nation and Manhood*, 67-70.) Charles Musser also explores the correspondences between *Body and Soul* and *Roseanne* in "To Redream the Dreams of White Playwrights." In that essay, Musser suggests links as well to other white-authored works, especially Eugene O'Neill's "two race plays," *The Emperor Jones* and *All God's Chillun' Got Wings*.

46. Some of the publicity materials that Micheaux produced were quite graphic. As Gary Null notes in *Black Hollywood: The Negro in Motion Pictures* (11), Micheaux's "exploitationary gimmick[s]" included the dis-

play of "large photos of rape scenes and semi-nude figures" in the posters that promoted his films. Null adds that Micheaux would also "insert sequences quite unrelated to the story into his films," such as a Harlem dance troupe in a Western movie. "The audiences," Null concludes, "loved the nudity and voiced their approval to the theater managers."

47. The extent to which Micheaux relied on white sponsorship is not absolutely clear. Richard Gehr writes that after the 1928 bankruptcy, Micheaux "was forced to rely on ever-greater infusions of white capital" (39). Charlene Regester (*FH* 428) concurs that "during the second period of his filmmaking career (1930-48) . . . [Micheaux] had to rely on financial support provided by whites if he was to continue cultivating his film-making craft." Thomas Cripps also notes that "especially after depression-induced bankruptcy, [Micheaux] accepted 'white' financing" (*BFG* 3) and, by the late 1930s, "affiliated with white 'angels,' . . . first with Frank Schiffman, then with Jack Goldberg" (38). Mark A. Reid, in his essay on "African-American Filmmakers" (5) in *The Political Companion to American Film,* suggests that Micheaux secured an "uneven partnership with Leo Brecher and Frank Shiffman [*sic*], who owned several theaters in the black communities of New York, Philadelphia, Washington, D.C., Baltimore, and Norfolk." That partnership, Reid argues, made Micheaux "the first African-American to successfully make the transition from black independent cinema to a corporate partnership with white financiers of African-American theaters in the 'chitlin' circuit' (comparable to Jewish theaters in the 'borscht belt')." Pearl Bowser and Louise Spence write that, after his voluntary bankruptcy, Micheaux reincorporated again in 1931 with "new capital provided by Frank Schiffman" in order to make *The Exile*. Micheaux was president of the new corporation; Schiffman was vice president and secretary; and Leo Brecher, a white theater owner and an associate of Schiffman, was treasurer (*Writing* 212).

48. According to Chester Fontenot (110), Micheaux's characters were not "subhuman creatures incapable of carrying out the most ordinary human functions" but rather "dignified people whose problems are much like those of white Americans."

49. Green writes that "Micheaux hated much of the literary work of the Harlem Renaissance and found some of it trivial" (*SL* 222). Charles Musser ("To Redream the Dreams of White Playwrights" 127-28) shows that the feeling was mutual: "In background, outlook, and artistic results, Micheaux was at odds with the shapers of this emerging movement." Micheaux was "too plebeian, too crude, even too propagandistic. The Harlem Renaissance celebrated its Phi Beta Kappa scholars from prestigious schools. Micheaux was an autodidact. His working methods and the audiences he addressed differed as well. The Harlem Renaissance Inc. was based on black-white collaboration. Micheaux's approach as a pro-

ducer-director-writer ensured that he would be in full control behind the camera while the actors in the film were almost exclusively black. His sympathies in this respect were with the politics of Booker T. Washington rather than the NAACP and Urban League integrationists. W. E. B. Du Bois supported Eugene O'Neill; Micheaux attacked him."

50. Moreover, fights between light- and dark-skinned audience members reportedly broke out in the theater during the showings of *God's Step Children* (Gehr 39).

51. Regarding Micheaux's allegedly negative portrayals, Richard Grupenhoff has suggested that, while some of Micheaux's characters exhibit negative behavior, Micheaux never depicted blacks negatively. On the same issue, Jane Gaines writes that: "It is really no wonder that the cultural products of an aspiring Black intellectual in this period gave us black men as scoundrels, religious hypocrites, gamblers and sluggards, and black women as madames, seductresses, and cheats. For he [Micheaux] was seeing this Black culture through the eyes of the White culture, for which this vision of an irredeemable Black underclass was flattering and entirely functional." And Eileen Landay argues that, while some of Micheaux's films "dealt with the problems of being black, this was never from the point of view of the ghetto dweller or the sharecropper; his subjects were the black bourgeoisie. By presenting them, Micheaux hoped to instill race pride in all who saw them." See Regester, "The Misreading and Rereading of African American Filmmaker Oscar Micheaux: A Critical Review of Micheaux Scholarship," 439, 446, and 431.

In her biography of Micheaux, VanEpps-Taylor offers a slightly different perspective. Micheaux, she writes, "drew criticism for calling attention to embarrassing flaws within black society, flaws typical of any large and diverse group emerging from oppression, and for examining and perhaps supporting the color, ethnic, and class prejudices in African American circles. Micheaux believed that his films and books portrayed an accurate cross-section of black America with both positive and negative dimensions, and that this broad portrayal was central and essential to the integrity of his work" (7).

52. In that same essay, Green also writes: "As Pearl Bowser had pointed out, Micheaux had to work within the conventions of skin tone in race-entertainment, conventions that explicitly favored light skin; consequently it is difficult to generalize today about the ultimate meaning of Micheaux's choices of skin tone." In *Straight Lick*, Green again takes up the issue of the use of light and dark skin tone to represent a system of racist values. He writes that "the deployment of skin color in Micheaux's films does not, however, constitute a scheme or template. A cursory survey of important characters in the films viewed shows that about 75 percent are light and 25 percent are dark. Of the dark-skinned actors, about half of them are good (constructed to evoke sympathy and identification),

and half of them are bad. Of the light-skinned actors, about two-thirds are good, and one-third of them are bad" (61). Similarly, Green points out that, while many of Micheaux's white characters are bad (the white lynchers in *Within Our Gates;* the bank teller, sheriff, and some towns-people in *Birthright*), some—like the philanthropist in *Within Our Gates,* the schoolboard chairman who defends the schoolteacher in *God's Step Children,* and the foolish but benevolent white producer in *Swing!*—play a positive role.

53. For further discussion of skin tone in Micheaux's work, see "Light Skin in Black Films," in Richard Grupenhoff's *The Black Valentino,* 66-74.

54. Charlene Regester ("Press" 46) demonstrates that Micheaux frequently challenged the position of those of his critics who faulted his use of negative representations and wanted only the "positive aspects of African-American life to be unveiled on the screen."

55. As J. Ronald Green (*SL* 31) writes, many of the middle-class traits that he urged blacks to cultivate—"upright carriage; articulate, grammatical speech; broad literacy; clean, well-tailored clothes in the British and Northern European tradition or clean, homespun clothes for individuals living in rural environments; urban sophistication; thoughtfulness, even intellectuality; culture; education; sexual morality; self-reliance; entrepreneurial ambition; economic conservatism; political liberalism; patriotism; racial and ethnic loyalty; ethnic tolerance; broad travel and perspective; respect for privacy; the work ethic; fair play; collegial confidence and trust; candor; and romantic love"—were similar to those to which middle-class whites aspired.

56. "What suggests comparison between *Within Our Gates* and *The Birth of a Nation*," according to Jane Gaines ("Fire and Desire" 50), is "primarily the caldron of protest around racial imagery into which both films were flung. However, in almost every other way, Micheaux's film is the antithesis of *Birth*, especially in its middle-class, Black-centered view of American society. Also, in contrast to the NAACP protest around *The Birth of a Nation* (centered upon a notion of falsehood in representation), the *Within Our Gates* controversy implicitly focussed on the fear of 'too much truth.'" Consequently, the attempt to ban screenings of Micheaux's film "was an attempt to silence the protest against lynching, but also a law-and-order move to suppress active protest against worsening housing and employment conditions in the North. *Within Our Gates* was thus historically linked to fear of cataclysmic social change, a linkage obfuscated by the smoke screen of 'race riot.'"

57. As Charlene Regester writes in "Oscar Micheaux on the Cutting Edge: Films Rejected by the New York State Motion Picture Commission," "Micheaux had difficulty in obtaining censor approval for his works in many states" (62). Regester's study focuses on New York, since it is one of the few states where censor activities of that period are

available. Jane Gaines, in *Fire and Desire* (234), writes that "the list of titles we know to have been either banned or cut by censor boards" includes *The Homesteader, Within Our Gates, The Brute, The Symbol of the Unconquered, Deceit, The Gunsaulus Mystery, The Dungeon, The Virgin of the Seminole, Birthright, Body and Soul, The House Behind the Cedars, A Son of Satan, The Spider's Web,* and *The Millionaire.*

58. Elinor Lee buys up the contract of prizefighter Benny Blue (Robert Earl Jones) and plans to build him up, have him win a series of fights to get him into the heavyweight championship, and then to have him throw the fight. But her gigantic swindle is upset when a German fighter beats Blue. But Blue, unaware of the swindlers' schemes, fights back, winning the championship and the opportunity to fight the German in a rematch.

59. Moreover, according to Green, "The crucial action of *Within Our Gates* occurs in a narrative triangle of women. Sylvia (the black heroine of uplift) is pitted specifically against Mrs. Stratton (the reactionary white supremacist) in a debate that is adjudicated by Mrs. Warrick (a northern feminist)" ("Micheaux v. Griffith" 43, 45).

60. After Myrtle frustrates his political ambitions, an enraged Gyp sets out to murder her and locks her in a dungeon, from which Cameron rescues her by killing Gyp, her torturer.

61. Micheaux liked to reverse formulas. As J. Ronald Green shows, "the formula of sexual transgression by the female and her redemption by a male is an inversion of the Griffith formula of the last-minute rescue of the sexually threatened woman" (*SL* 14). Micheaux even reversed his own formula; for instance, whereas in several of his films and novels, the woman becomes aware of her black identity and is successfully re-racialized, in *Thirty Years Later* (1928), it is a male character who discovers that he is of mixed blood.

62. While Micheaux tells that story repeatedly, he does not—according to Jane Gaines (*FD* 189)—tell it finally. There is "no 'real' story, no final version," she writes, because he was so adept at writing the same narrative a multitude of ways.

63. Apart from his autobiographical novels *The Conquest* and *The Homesteader,* Micheaux did not write an actual autobiography; moreover, there are few printed biographical materials about him. Reconstructing his background is therefore difficult. This difficulty helps to explain the discrepancies in various accounts of his life. Learthen Dorsey, for example, writes that Micheaux was born in 1884 to Calvin and Bell Willingham Michaux [*sic*] and that he was the fifth of thirteen children; Henry T. Sampson, on the other hand, writes that Micheaux's parents were Swan and Belle [*sic*] Micheaux, and that Oscar—born in January 1883—was one of eleven children.

64. Janis Hebert, relying on testimony from Don Coonen, one of Micheaux's fellow pioneers, suggests that Micheaux originally acquired

his properties for purposes of speculation, not farming. "Micheaux's game," according to Coonen, "was trying to outfox the railroad [that would soon pass through a small town in a section adjoining Micheaux's land], and his farming efforts merely a front." But the railroad "put out decoy plans and surveys to throw the land speculators a curve. From Bonesteel they first said they were going northwest and then said to the southwest. After they got everyone touted off, they put her right down the middle. Micheaux got sucked in on the southwest route" (Hebert 63).

65. In "One-Man Show" (34), Richard Gehr writes that Micheaux's middle name was Devereaux.

66. The black church and black popular culture, notes Betti Carol VanEpps-Taylor (5), reflected the pressure that black Americans of Micheaux's generation had "to raise their sights, achieve academic credentials, and 'become a credit to their race.'" There was also "strong community disapproval of marrying or 'consorting' outside the race"—a pressure that was "soon to include undertones of color prejudice that discriminated against those of darker complexion."

67. M. K. Johnson suggests that the death of Devereaux's son anticipates Devereaux's failure in the novel. "Devereaux's own attempt at self-making, at being reborn on the frontier," Johnson writes, "is figured in the end of the narrative in the form of his dead son—a failed attempt at both birth and rebirth. If in the 'story of a man's life' that story is completed through the 'change in status' indicated by assuming 'patriarchal responsibility for families and kin,' by fathering and supporting a family, the child's death prevents Devereaux from assuming that desired masculine identity—and from achieving the symbolic position of race leader, of an exemplary figure whose success demands imitation" ("Stranger" 245).

68. Green finds that some of the homesteading stories from *The Conquest* recur later in Micheaux's films. "A version of the chapter entitled 'The Oklahoma Grafter,' for example—in which Micheaux's surrogate, Devereaux, is bilked by a crooked horse trader—appears in the film *The Symbol of the Unconquered*" (*SL* xii).

69. Devereaux prefers another play, *The Fourth Estate*, which "instead of weakness and an unhappy ending," was one of "strength of character and a happy finale" (229). In that play, a newspaperman falls in love with the daughter of a corrupt judge whom he is investigating; eventually the daughter becomes aware of the nature of her father's dishonesty and turns her affections from him to the newspaperman, whom she marries. The parallels to Devereaux, his wife, and her duplicitious father are obvious; but Devereaux's situation lacks the play's "happy finale." Both J. Ronald Green and Joseph A. Young have noted that the fictional *Madam X* was in fact based on Bisson's *Le Femmin X* (1909).

70. VanEpps-Taylor (4) writes that "Oscar Micheaux was an early and ardent follower of the Alabama educator's [Booker T. Washington] prin-

ciples of entrepreneurship, ambition, and self-help, but he could not accept Washington's belief that the South offered black Americans their best hope. Over the years, Micheaux's political and social beliefs steadily changed as he matured as a filmmaker and writer, although he continued to believe that African Americans' best hope lay in an expanded middle class. That middle class, he believed, could best prosper if individuals would establish businesses or seize the unlimited opportunities for successful farming ventures in the 'Great Northwest.'"

Micheaux's admiration of Washington is evident also in his films: for example, Washington's image hangs on the walls of Sister Martha's home in *Body and Soul* and of the cabin in *The Symbol of the Unconquered.*

71. Micheaux repeats this phrase, almost as a choric refrain, numerous times throughout the novel. See, for example, pp. 57, 68, 138, 145, 147, 432, 526, and 529.

72. As Baptiste learns upon his return, "his wife had given birth to a baby which had come into the world dead." Apparently, it was "a big, fine kid. [But] She couldn't give it birth, so they had to kill it in order to save her life" (257-58).

73. Brown writes that "as Orlean lacks the strength to willingly transfer her loyalties from father to husband, she can only act out her desire to do so in a destructive manner. In a dreamlike swoon, Orlean performs the ultimate act of retribution, as if acting out Baptiste's most heartfelt desire" ("Black Patriarch" 143).

74. Micheaux apparently had other reasons to dislike clergymen. J. Ronald Green (*SL* 16) writes that "all his life he obsessively blamed black ministers for absorbing the attention of his mother while he was growing up, [and] for holding back the economic and cultural uplifting of his ethnic group with their preaching."

75. In *The Story of Dorothy Stanfield* (216), Micheaux writes that "In banking, the matter of delivery of goods is a most important factor. About the only thing Reverend Simms has ever delivered was a sermon, and as the president of a bank he'd perhaps make a good head-waiter in a livery barn."

76. McCarthy resents Jean for another cause: McCarthy—a notorious womanizer—is trying to press his attentions upon the young teacher; but the teacher is more concerned about the hungry little boy than she is about McCarthy. The beating upon which McCarthy insists is ostensibly for Jean's having spoiled his meal; yet in fact, it is for Jean's having foiled his seduction attempt.

77. The correspondence between the Lincoln Motion Picture Company and Micheaux's company from 1918 to 1923 about the prospects of doing business together is, Bowser and Spence suggest, a "rich area of archival research. The letter writers debated such issues as the relative profitability of shorts versus features, adaptations of novels

versus original screenplays, war movies versus domestic fiction, and, importantly, representations of racial progress versus more combative racial themes" (13).

78. VanEpps-Taylor (96-97) suggests that Noble Johnson "objected to certain themes in . . . [*The Homesteader*] (perhaps the suggestion of inter-racial romance), but company officials assured the author that they could make a first-class feature film from the book." But Micheaux, "always sensitive to criticism of his work, . . . decided to make the film himself." VanEpps-Taylor concludes that "the Johnsons never forgot his slight, and forever disapproved of his business methods, style, and continual spats with censor boards, remaining nervous enough about him to maintain a spy in his office."

79. In an interview with the *Pittsburgh Courier*, Evelyn Preer, who made her screen debut in the film, remembered the shooting of the principal scenes in Chicago and Iowa and especially "the terrible long time it took the cameraman to film the scene of my spirit coming back to haunt the people who had mistreated me" (Sampson 556).

80. The magazine concluded that *The Homesteader* "deserves all the loyal support the race has given it" (Bowser and Spence, *Writing* 13).

81. While the plot of the film suggests that it was derived from Micheaux's second homesteader novel (*The Homesteader*) and not from the first (*The Conquest*), one of the ads promoting *The Exile* announced that the "mighty modern ALL TALKING epic of Negro life" was "adapted from *The Conquest*."

82. Micheaux used this kind of negative stereotyping in other films as well, as Green (*SL* 58) illustrates. The character of the "dirty old Negro" who is Ballinger's henchman in *The Girl from Chicago* is simply a racial slur: he has a shuffling walk and exaggerated facial features, including bugged eyes and a hanging lower lip. Another character in that film, Cornbread, a numbers runner for Gomez, also walks with a shuffle; responds to complicated situations by scratching his head and "contorting his face" like a buffoon; and even tap dances as he waits for his next assignment. These instances of negative stereotyping, which are rare, differ from Micheaux's use of stereotypes in an ironic or parodic way.

As Henry T. Sampson (230, 232) has demonstrated, it was not uncommon for producers of the 1930s musical shorts to incorporate many of the derogatory racial stereotypes into these films in order to play them in white theaters. "In *St. Louis Blues* (1929), the first and only screen appearance of Bessie Smith, the opening scene shows black men shooting craps and one of them lets his 'yallar' girlfriend rub the dice for luck. The opening of *Black and Tan* (1929), featuring Duke Ellington and his band, along with Fredi Washington, shows two black men who can neither read nor tell time, and who are bribed by a bottle of gin when they come to repossess Ellington's piano. The young Nicholas Brothers, who do a superb tap dance routine in *The Black Network* (1936), portray two young policy run-ners. In *Rufus Jones for President,* brilliant performances by Ethel Waters and Sammy Davis, Jr. (his first screen appearance) are marred by scenes showing blacks, in roles as U.S. Senators, checking razors, shooting craps in the halls of Congress, and passing laws to make chicken- and water-melon-stealing legal."

83. Filmmaker Arthur Jafa says of Micheaux's song and dance squences that "they're totally jagged and they completely disrupt the nar-rative flow. It's certainly pretty different from anything I've found in Hollywood films of the same period" (Jafa, "An Interview" 13).

84. The club routines were certainly appropriate to films such as *Swing!,* which revolved around a theatrical musical production. But, as Bowser and Spence have shown, Micheaux at times incorporated song and dance in unusual ways; for instance, "in *Veiled Aristocrats,* the maids in the wealthy brother's home wear tap shoes!" (213).

85. Anna Everett notes that Micheaux's interracial alliance with Schiffman was double-edged in that "it saved the mercurial company from bankruptcy, but that salvation had a Faustian dimension." For the first time, "there was placed at his disposal an up-to-date modern studio with crews of trained cameramen, electricians, stagehands, scenic artists, lighting experts, make-up artist, assistant director, etc. Donald Heywood and a little staff of music writers wrote a special musical score: Leonard Harper organized a complete revue for the cabaret scenes" (187).

86. Prescott, "lazy, crude, and sexually lascivious, [is] everything Baptiste is not. In the middle of the workday, when Jack [Stewart] is at work in the field, Prescott rudely presents himself with his intentions for Agnes" (Brown, "Black Patriarch" 141).

87. Thomas Cripps (*SFB* 323), however, called the film a "disaster" and noted that *Variety* was moved to advise Micheaux "to abandon drama in favor of more easily controlled and marketable comedy."

88. Charlene Regester (*Film History* 430) notes, however, that in "reviewing" the film, Thomas Cripps stated that *The Exile* "revealed both the virtues and the needs of black filmmaking. Even though no white man appeared on the screen, the plot still moved on white terms."

89. Spencer Moon (*Reel Black Talk* 251) writes that "this [film] story may have been suggested by or based on Eulalie Spence's one-act play by the same title from 1927." That seems unlikely, since the film was pro-duced and released in 1922, not in 1928, as Moon writes. Rather, Micheaux may have drawn on *A Fool's Errand,* the best-selling novel by Albion W. Tourgee.

90 When Brisbane throws Hawkins the coin outside the factory door and Hawkins goes into a shuffle, "that 'insert coin, get shuffle' trope," writes J. Ronald Green (*FQ* 28), "turns Hawkins into a white man's living juke box."

91. "Eph in trying to secure his own 'privileged' position among the Whites in the big house," write Bowser and Spence ("Legend" 64) "separates himself and betrays a fellow Negro. Driscoll, by internalizing negative perceptions of blackness, isolates himself and betrays the Race. Micheaux criticized the social behavior of both characters and both get their just desserts."

92. At the time, Tutt and Whitney were "well-known show producers and head of the Smart Set Company" (Sampson 159).

93. *Dark Princess,* based on W. E. B. Du Bois's novel *Dark Princess: A Romance* (1928), is listed as a completed Micheaux film in some filmographies but was almost certainly a film that Micheaux never actually produced, although he may at one time have intended to do so.

94. In "Oscar Micheaux the Entrepreneur: Financing *The House Behind the Cedars,*" Charlene Regester chronicles in great detail how Micheaux negotiated the film rights to Chesnutt's *The House Behind the Cedars.* Micheaux first approached Chesnutt in July, 1920. In January, 1921, the actual negotiations began; Micheaux offered Chesnutt $500, an offer that Chesnutt had to have approved by his publisher, Houghton Mifflin & Company. But soon after Chesnutt and his publisher agreed, Micheaux restructured the payment from a full $500 at the signing of the contract to a two-step schedule. The payment schedule was then further restructured, so that Micheaux would make a payment of $100 at the time of signing, with $100 to follow each month until the full contract was paid. But Micheaux was often late in making payments or made payments from accounts that had insufficient funds; consequently, Chesnutt was occasionally charged "protest fees" by his bank. At one point, Micheaux offered to make payment in "gold notes" rather than in cash, an offer that Chesnutt declined. "As late as January 1923," writes Regester, "Chesnutt still had only $400 of the $500 owed for the screen rights to his novel. Micheaux, it can be speculated, actually had to wait for returns on his picture before he could make that final payment. Chesnutt was remarkably understanding and patient with Micheaux's delinquency. Perhaps this was because Chesnutt, a writer who himself must have experienced difficulties as he attempted to have his works published, was aware of the struggles that African American filmmakers or writers often confronted" (23).

95. As Bowser and Spence point out, "in a telling note to C. W. Chesnutt, Micheaux suggested that the screenplay for his adaptation of *The House Behind the Cedars* make the blacksmith Frank more striving—in order to make Rena's affection for him more believable! 'I would make the man Frank more intelligent at least towards the end of the story permitting him to study and improve himself, for using the language as he does in the story, he would not in anyway be obvious as a lover or that

the girl could have more than a passing respect for him.'" Micheaux also worried about how audiences might respond to the ending of *The House Behind the Cedars*. He wrote Chesnutt: "You have created a wonderful heroine in Rena—but for her to die in the end of the story as therein detailed, I have grave doubts as to the outcome." A happy ending, he believed, would ensure a stronger box office (*Writing* 21, 141).

96. Micheaux's most significant inheritance from black writers like Chesnutt, according to Corey K. Creekmur in "Telling White Lies: Oscar Micheaux and Charles W. Chesnutt" (158), may have been more "in form" than in actual content.

97. Larry Richards (179) suggests that the title of the film may have come from a novel, *The Veiled Aristocrats*, published by Colored Publishers of Washington, D.C., and written by a white woman, Miss Gertrude Sanborn of Chicago, Illinois.

98. A number of the stories and novels that (according to the films' credits) Micheaux adapted are not listed in any of the standard bibliographies or reference works. According to Micheaux's own statements and references, it is possible that some of the literary works in question were in fact written by Micheaux himself. See, for instance, the "Acknowledgment" that opens *The Masquerade,* in which Micheaux writes that three of his last four novels were based on "stories" he had filmed years before. He adds that he simply rewrote "whatever of the old stories I liked best."

99. *The Girl From Chicago* was a remake of *The Spider's Web,* which was based on Micheaux's story, "The Policy Players." Creekmur (150), however, writes that *The Girl From Chicago* was based on Micheaux's story, "Jeff Ballinger's Woman."

100. Micheaux took the title *Within Our Gates* from an epigraph to D. W. Griffith's *The Romance of Happy Valley* (1919): "Harm not the stranger / Within your gates, / Lest you yourself be hurt." Green (*SL* 8) also notes that Micheaux duplicated in *Within Our Gates* certain scenes (such as the final shot of Sylvia and Dr. Vivian as a married middle-class couple) from *The Birth of a Nation* (in which the two marriageable women, Margaret Cameron and Elsie Stoneman, together with their new husbands, typify the new white nation that is being born).

101. The *Nebraska Daily* noted of *Within Our Gates* that "this is the picture that required two solid months to get by the censor board and it is the claim of the author and producer that while it is a bit radical it is also the biggest protest against race prejudice, lynching and 'concubinage' that was ever written or filmed and that there are more thrills and gripping, holding moments than ever seen in any individual production." The review concludes that "the author has not minced words in present-

ing the facts as they really exist." The *Chicago Defender* concurred, agreeing that, despite the "outrages perpetrated in the south" over the opening of the film, "there is nothing in the picture but what is true and truly legitimate" (Sampson 279).

102. The only surviving print of the film was found in Spain and preserved in 1993 by the Library of Congress. That version of the film, retitled *La Negra,* used slightly different names on the title cards: Gridlestone rather than Girdlestone, Armand rather than Arnold.

103. Jane Gaines writes in "*The Birth of a Nation* and *Within Our Gates:* Two Tales of the American South" (186) that "Sylvia calls up associations with other similarly scarred light-skinned black women in film history." Like the neck wound Louise hides in *The Scar of Shame* and the breast wound borne by Susannah in *Raintree County,* Sylvia's scar is a clue, a metaphor to express the "twin terrors—sexual and racial difference—[conflated] into the same bodily sign: a wound." Pearl Bowser and Louise Spence also associate the linking of rape and lynching, two "instruments of terror" that are part of the "systematic dehumanization of Black Americans and a direct attack on the African American family." They comment further on the intercutting as "an indictment of white perfidy and hypocrisy" (*Writing* 134).

104. According to Gaines (*FD* 187), by the intercutting between the scenes of lynching and burning and of sexual assault: "Simultaneously, Micheaux is also able to represent Sylvia's sexual torture as an ordeal by fire, for the agonies she suffers are likened to the experience of being burned alive." And in "*Within Our Gates:* From Race Melodrama to Opportunity Narrative" (74), Gaines observes further that the assault scene, crosscut with the lynching scene, evokes "the imagined crimes of black men against white women of the Reconstruction era to the real and ordinary sexual attacks of the plantation masters on slave women. . . . the scene cries out against the master's sexual encounters with his own slave women, even representing the incestuousness of every one of those acts."

105. Charles Musser et al., in "An Oscar Micheaux Filmography," suggest that "House of Mystery" was a short story; Henry T. Sampson writes that it was a novel. Either way, it appears to have been unpublished. Furthermore, Musser et al. list the date of release for the film version, *The Broken Violin,* as 1928; both Sampson and Richards, however, list the title as *Broken Violin* and the release date as 1926.

106. There is some dispute about the date of Micheaux's marriage to Alice B. (Bertrand) Russell: some critics/biographers suggest that it may have occurred as late as 1929. The 1928-29 issue of *Who's Who in Colored America* gives the date as March 20, 1926. Betti Carol VanEpps-Taylor suggests that Russell may not have been Micheaux's second wife; she points out that in the 1918 *Polk City Directory,* there is a listing for two per-

sons living at Micheaux's Sioux City address: Oscar Micheaux, a "colored author," and "Sarah." VanEpps-Taylor writes that Sarah may have been a woman who "only helped him out in his business," or "perhaps they were married and the marriage did not endure" (88-89). Bowser and Spence also imply that Micheaux was "involved in another marriage after Orlean McCracken Micheaux died" and before he married Alice B. Russell.

107. *Easy Street* (1930), a film in which city slickers try to swindle an old man of his honestly earned money, was presumably based on an original story, "Caspar Olden's Will." It is possible that the story may have been one of Micheaux's; but, to date, the story's authorship is uncertain and its publication, if any, is unknown. (The film itself is not extant.)

108. Corey K. Creekmur ("Telling White Lies" 150), writes that while the title cards and posters for Micheaux's films often clearly identify them as adaptations, the exact identity "of these 'original' sources often remains vague at the next level. For example, Micheaux's musical *Swing!* (1938) is identified as an adaptation of 'Mandy' but so far as I know, no one has actually determined what 'Mandy' is—is it a short story, or novel, or perhaps a play? And whatever it is, who wrote it and was it in fact published?"

109. Joseph A. Young links Martin Eden's name to Jack London's novel, *Martin Eden,* in which a self-educated protagonist—much like Micheaux's Martin Eden—learns "to see through the artificial conventionality and the narrow-mindedness of middle-class hypocrisy" (79). See Young, *Black Novelist,* 77-84, for a fuller discussion of the correspondences between Micheaux's characters and London's.

110. Jayna Brown ("Black Patriarch" 145-46) notes that "the central protagonists of his earlier novels and films are aspiring and/or prosperous agriculturalists, while the heroes of his later works are writers and stage directors." But all "are linked in their reiteration of one goal, which was neither aesthetic nor technical virtuosity, but the act of production itself."

111. It is not just Wyeth who felt such anti-Semitic sentiments; apparently, Micheaux shared them as well. VanEpps-Taylor suggests that Micheaux disliked Robert Levy, the Jewish owner of Reol Pictures, whom he saw as a serious rival. In a letter to George Johnson in 1920, Micheaux complains about "Levy and many other Jews who are making negro pictures, going under negro producers, which they can afford to do." Micheaux's "resentment of these companies with their large Jewish components would continue, to the extent that some of his public remarks and some of the language in his later novels reflect a bitter anti-Semitism that he always denied" (115-16).

112. Green argues that while Micheaux "had an attitude toward the Jews, . . . virtually everyone did." But that attitude "*resisted* bigotry when

bigotry would have helped excuse Micheaux's own recent failure in the film industry." Green adds that "Wyeth (and Micheaux) treated Jews as he treated himself and his own ethnic group. He felt that, like African Americans, some Jews were good, some were bad, and those Jews who were competent, honest, and trying to advance themselves (in the movie industry, for example) need not apologize to anyone, including Aryans and blacks, for their success or power" (*SL* 219, 222). Ultimately, however, Green's argument for Micheaux, which certainly has some merit, is not wholly convincing.

113. Micheaux also makes reference to Zora Neale Hurston and her work. In the novel, she appears as Ora Thurston, the much-married journalist-turned-adventuress "who calls herself an anthropologist" (303). But the "girl . . . let herself develop temperament, and was on the way to a controlled insanity," a kind of "temperamentalism on the part of Negroes" (305). Eventually she "wrote five books, all within a few years, and one of the biggest publishers brought them out." After that, however, "she went into the business of acquiring scholarships, awards and into so many ways of getting money to live on from white people that her life and career and entire existence has become a mystery" (307). Interestingly, in the mid-1920s, Micheaux had announced plans to film one of Hurston's stories; but apparently nothing came of that plan and the film was never made.

Hurston herself was involved in early film production, with ethnographic footage that she shot herself: "ten rolls of motion pictures in the southern United States in 1927-29 to document logging, children's games and dances, a baptism, a baseball crowd, a barbeque, and Kossula, last of the Takkoi slaves." See Gloria Gibson, "Cinematic Foremothers: Zora Neale Hurston and Eloyce King Patrick Gist," especially pp. 204-09.

114. Micheaux had used the name Stanfield before. In his film *Murder in Harlem*, the white victim was called Myrtle Stanfield. There is nothing in the novel, however, that explicitly connects Myrtle to Dorothy.

115. Unlike Micheaux's two filmed versions, which truncate the second half of Chesnutt's novel, Micheaux's novel includes that portion of the story (Rena's decision to teach, Jeff Wain's pursuit of her, etc.).

116. *Making Movies Black* 146. Cripps also makes the point that "only two years beyond a war that had transformed movies, he [Micheaux] reached back to one of his familiar dramatic devices, a mistaken racial identity." Furthermore, his uneven cast ensured "that the movie would wear a caste mark peculiar to the genre."

117. As D. Ireland Thomas wrote in the *Chicago Defender* (31 Jan. 1925), "I do not want to see my Race in saloons or at crap tables. But it is what the public clamors for that makes the coin jingle" (qtd. in Sampson 159).

Chapter 3

"We'll Teach Him Fear":
Racial Representation in Sound Films
of the 1930s and 1940s

I always leave a picture show disgusted—Holy Smokes!
Don't they know colored people are just like other folks?
Why do they always think that all we know is sin and strife,
Tho' we have many of our race in every walk of life?

Are Hollywood producers mindful of their harmful acts,
Or are they just plain ignorant and do not know the facts?
They show us all as comics, gangsters, and slowpokes,
Don't they know colored people are just like other folks?
—*Songwriter Andy Razaf (1940)*

Throughout the silent era, the black independent filmmakers like Oscar Micheaux and the Johnson Brothers and the white-owned race film companies like Reol Productions and the Norman Film Manufacturing Company constituted a kind of black underground that had grown outside the major motion picture studios and attempted to reach the black audience that was, at least initially, virtually ignored by Hollywood. Despite problems with poor distribution channels, small budgets, amateurish actors, untrained crews, and other technical failings, those production companies were somehow able to release films that went beyond mere representation of blacks on the screen to depict blacks as a presence in American life (Cripps, *BFG* 23-24). In *The Realization of a Negro's Ambition* (Lincoln Motion Picture Company, 1916), for example, Tuskegee Institute engineering graduate James Burton, a representative of the burgeoning black middle class, achieved racial uplift through his tenaciousness and industry; in *Trooper of Troop K* (Lincoln, 1916), "Shiftless Joe" proved his heroism with the "famous fighting Tenth Cavalry" during the battle of Carrizal in Mexico; while in *The Flying Ace* (Norman Film Manufacturing Company, 1926), the bravery of Captain William Stokes (Lawrence Criner) recalled the significant contributions of America's Fighting Colored Regiments in the First World War. Micheaux's films, which racialized and at times radicalized many of Hollywood's genre films, from Westerns to gangster tales and adventure stories, incorporated the broadest possible range of both male and female black protagonists, from homesteading pioneers and cavalry officers to Broadway producers and Secret Service agents.

The end of the 1920s, however, brought many changes. For black Americans in general, as Thomas Cripps notes, the Great Depression proved a shattering experience that hit sooner and more severely than it did for whites. Migrations from the South into urban centers like Harlem and Chicago's South Side had already left many blacks only marginally employed and living in segregated warrens that further removed them from white contact and culture. Even the Republican party at Herbert Hoover's so-called "lily white" convention of 1928 cast blacks aside and gave rise to a kind of laissez-faire apathy in the face of economic decline that reinforced the racial discrimination, residential covenants, closed ballot boxes, and Jim Crow accommodations that the Wilson years seemed to celebrate almost a decade earlier (*SFB* 150-51, 263, 43).

For black filmmakers in particular, the changes were even more revolutionary. The new technology of sound, which had evolved in the 1920s, marked both the end of the silent film era and the beginning of the modern Hollywood film industry. As a handful of established oligopolistic producers and distributors gained prominence and consolidated power, many individual filmmaking companies were forced to close. This was especially true of black producers, most of whom had struggled mightily to compete in the silent market and therefore had neither the resources nor the technical expertise to make the transition to "talkies." Moreover, the major studios, stumbling over each other as they tried to exploit the new medium through the use of "Negro themes and motifs" (*BFG* 30) and to tap the growing minority market, were so successful that their work instigated the turning away of black audiences (and, to a lesser extent, of the influential black press) from race movies and toward Hollywood features. And over the next few decades, the practice of adapting black literature—with few exceptions—came to a halt. Hollywood's images of blacks again derived almost exclusively from the visions of white authors, directors, and producers, whose depiction of blacks and the black experience tended to differ radically from the portrayal of blacks in black fiction and in the films of Micheaux and the other early race film producers.

Nonetheless, at least initially, hopes for blacks in sound films were high. As early as 1913, pioneering black filmmaker William Foster had predicted "unquestionable ultimate success" and a "rapid growth in this industry among Negroes"; and, in an article for the *New York Amsterdam News* (31 July 1929), Romeo L. Daugherty suggested that sound films could fulfill Foster's prediction. "The greatest factor in favor of the Negro in talking pictures," Daugherty wrote, "is the song and dance, a sphere in which he is predominate [*sic*]. He can sing anything from jazz to grand opera, assemble any orchestra and write his own songs and music. . . . The possibilities [in performance as well as in production and distribution] appear to be unlimited." Daugherty even ventured that "the all-talking, singing and dancing movie will lead the picture industry in the future" and that "Negro actors and entertainers will be easily 25 percent of it" (qtd. in Sampson 10-11). Similarly, as James Weldon Johnson wrote to Foster in 1929, "I do not see how they are going to keep the Negro from achieving a permanent place in the movie world so long as they have talkies" (Cripps, *SFB* 218). Robert Benchley, in a 1929 issue of *Opportunity*, went even further: it "may be that the talking movies must be participated in exclusively by Negroes," he observed, because of "a quality in the Negro voice, an ease in its delivery, and a sense of timing in reading the lines that makes it the ideal medium for the talking picture" (Benchley, "*Hearts*" 84-85).

Indeed, for its pioneering first synchronous sound and spoken film, Hollywood looked not so much to black actors and entertainers but to an enduring, if antiquated, aspect of black and popular American culture. Warner Brothers' *The Jazz Singer* (1927), based on "The Day of Atonement," a short story by Samson Raphaelson published in 1922 and adapted to Broadway in 1925 as *The Jazz Singer*, starred white singer Al Jolson as Jakie Rabinowitz, a cantor's son. Torn between an assimilative desire to be part of

America and a more melancholy pull toward the traditional song and religion of his fathers, Jakie ultimately chooses assimilation.[1] Transforming himself into "Jack Robin," he rejects the Orthodox Judaism of his parents, falls in love with a gentile girl named Mary Dale (May McAvoy), and prepares for his big premiere on Broadway as a so-called Mammy singer who performs a vulgarized minstrel-type blackface act. On the very day that the show is to open, however, Jakie's father falls gravely ill; and Jakie's mother appears at the theater to implore him to come home and sing "Kol Nidre," the prayer for the Day of Atonement, in place of his ailing father. Feeling confused and culpable, a blackfaced Jakie goes on stage for the dress rehearsal, where he turns his performance into both a prayer and a reflection of his moral dilemma; his song "Mother of Mine," in particular, sentimentalizes his guilt. As Jim Pines writes, "through the emotive visual content of the tragic minstrel image, through the suggestive emotive content" of the song, and finally through the "pseudo-blues pathos" (17) with which it is rendered, the song is actually for the protagonist's parents and about his own sense of familial loss; and the performance as a whole, with its racial and emotional overtones, serves essentially as a vehicle of moral retribution, after which Jakie gives up his opening night and returns home—and to orthodoxy—to sing "Kol Nidre" instead. Hearing Jakie's fervent song of devotion through an open window, the elder Rabinowitz proclaims "Mamma, we have our son again," and dies happy. The film's final number, which occurs some time later, shows "Jack" on the Broadway stage performing "My Mammy" (Jolson's signature song), as Sara Rabinowitz gazes adoringly from the front row and Mary watches from the wings. (Fig. 3.1.) Jake thus succeeds, as Michael Rogin (87) notes, in achieving it all: assimilation to a whiteness that includes access to the gentile woman and the continued adulation of his mother after his father's death.[2]

"The narrative device of showcasing music within the context of a 'backstage' or 'show musical' plot was," according to Linda Williams, "a natural for movies, permitting a maximum of singing with a minimum of narrative justification" (*Race* 139). Films like *The Barnstormers* (1905), *The Open Road* (1913), *The Death of Simon La Gree* (1915), *Little Eva Ascends* (1922), *Uncle Tom's Gal* (1925), *Show Boat* (1929; remade 1936 and 1951), *Dimples* (1936), *Everybody Sing* (1938), and *The Naughty Nineties* (1945), whose plots involved the

Figure 3.1. "Jack Robin" (Al Jolson) performs as a blackfaced "Mammy singer" in *The Jazz Singer. (Warner Brothers, 1927)*

staging of Toms shows and similar entertainments, quickly became a cinematic tradition. But while *The Jazz Singer* capitalized on the pathos and nostalgia of a cross-racial performance reminiscent of the popular Tom-type shows, it managed to eradicate the particularism of black history by emptying Jolson's "pathetic figure in blackface" of its iconic black suffering and investing it instead with the Jewish dilemma of integration and intermarriage (Williams, *Race* 158). The following year, Jolson reprised his blackface role from *The Jazz Singer* in another hit film, *The Singing Fool* (1928). And the blackface minstrelsy tradition—the absurdity of which was already apparent, even on stage—was further ritualized in a corrupted form and carried into the decade of the 1930s with films such as *Big Boy* (1930) and *Wonder Bar* (1933), both based on Jolson's Broadway performances,[3] and with similarly naïve and sentimental films such as *Mammy* (1930) and *Swanee River* (1940).

THE ADVENT OF BLACK-CAST MUSICALS

As Warner Brothers had done with *The Jazz Singer*, other studios began looking to black life for the subject of some of their feature films; in fact, within a year of the release of *The Jazz Singer*, both Fox and Metro-Goldwyn-Mayer had all-black-cast productions in the works. Hollywood's interest, however, derived neither from liberal nor humanist tendencies; rather it reflected a newly acquired recognition of the viability of exploiting blacks on the sound movie screen and in the movie houses. But unlike the intense and genuine fascination with black folk drama that was occurring concurrently in literature, in films "Negro themes" remained an awkward concern and enjoyed at best modest though cautious commercial consideration, largely due to the stage popularity of vernacular entertainments (Pines 22), including the black-face masquerades by Jolson that blacks found so pernicious.[4]

Fox's film, generally acknowledged to be both Hollywood's first all-black "talkie" and all-black musical, reached theaters before MGM's did. *Hearts in Dixie* (1929) was originally conceived as a two-reel musical entertainment that would showcase minstrelsy, spiritual, and dancing by the sixty members of the Billbrew Chorus, the forty Fanchon Steppers, and the Four Emperors of Harmony; but, writes Edward D. C. Campbell, Jr. (*CS* 86-87), the rough cuts were so impressive that Walter Weems, a Southern minstrel man known as "The Boy From Dixie," was hired to write a connecting story. The resulting feature-length film of plantation life, although actually set in the first years of the New South, fully captured the familiar mythology of the Old South by rehashing many of the standard and stereotypical elements of earlier silent productions: Toms dutifully served their masters; contented blacks worked the fields; happy pickaninnies ran playfully about; and steamboats traveled down the river to the melodious strains of old Negro spirituals.[5] So convincing to white audiences were these sentimentalized images that even the reviewer for the *New York Times* (28 Feb. 1929) praised the film for cleverly capturing "the spirit of the Southern negro." That reviewer also found "something that is restful" in "a talking and singing production that is gentle in its mood and truthful in its reflection of black men of those days down yonder." *Billboard* (9 March 1929) similarly lauded the "great human appeal" of the story: "Negro life in the raw, so to speak, showing the happier and more sorrowful moments in the quaint existence that is theirs, gives the picture a background of sentimental beauty and realism that enraptures the onlooker." And the British *Bioscope* (3 April 1929), which raved about the "unfathomable charm" of the whole picture," wondered "Is it the

novelty appeal? Is it the colorful mysticism of the cotton plantation? Is it the delightful childlike simplicity of great-hearted nig-
gers? Is it the vivacity of the younger negroes who, with the sun-
down, charge the levees with laughter and melody?" (qtd. in
Sampson 317). Even the black press sought to find recuperative
elements in the film. In an accommodationist essay entitled "Folk
Values in a New Medium," Sterling A. Brown, a professor at
Howard University, and Alain Locke, a founding father of the
Harlem Renaissance literary movement, praised "the first all-
Negro talkie" for expressing the "vibrancy of the race" through
acting and singing. And while they agreed that "the usual types
are there—the Daddy, Uncle, the Mammy, and the inevitable pickaninnies"—Brown and Locke suggested that "in this group they
are real flesh and blood Negroes evoking a spontaneous and
human interest"; and they concluded that although "the story is
sketchy," *Hearts in Dixie* is nevertheless "the truest pictorialization
of Negro life to date" (26-27).[6]

Advertised by Fox as an "all-talking, all-singing, all-comedy
feature" and "a triumph of comedy and music," *Hearts in Dixie*
depicted events that in fact were far more tragic than comedic.[7]
Nappus (Clarence Muse), an old black former slave, toils in the
cotton fields to support his extended family, which includes his
daughter Chloe (Bernice Pilot), her husband Gummy (Stepin
Fetchit), their young son Chinquapin (Eugene Jackson), and their
baby Trailia. When Chloe falls ill with fever, Nappus must decide
whether to rely on the allegedly infallible "Voodoo Woman" (A. C.
Billbrew) whom the other blacks trust. Overcoming his own superstition, he persuades the white doctor—the sole white character in
the film—to come to his cabin only to find the conjure woman
whom Gummy has summoned performing a voodoo rite over the
dying family. Upon the deaths of Chloe and Trailia, Gummy
mourns deeply but briefly and soon finds himself a new wife, who
turns out to have little patience for his lazy ways. Nappus, however, realizing that much of the suffering that his race endures is
the result of their ignorance, expresses his grief in a different way.
He sells his farm and his few possessions and, against the advice
of his friends, determines to send his young grandson north to
study medicine; his hope is that Chinquapin will avoid the kind of
ruination that seems to befall Southern black men like Gummy

and that he will ultimately return to help others overcome similar obstacles. The film ends as the tearful but happy old man watches the boy's boat sail away.

As the patriarchal Nappus, Clarence Muse—despite the occasional Tommish submissiveness of his character—offered a performance that was both disciplined and sincere. Undercutting Muse's dignity, however, was the low comedy of Stepin Fetchit.[8] As a slow-witted, slow-talking, and slow-walking plantation slave who, according to a reviewer, was among "the most typical Negroes that could have been found," Fetchit—in one of his first important film roles—virtually stole the show. With the buffoonish mannerisms and irrefutably racist behavior that quickly became his Hollywood trademark, he managed to excite and delight white movie audiences, who roared as the shiftless Gummy complained that the "misery" in his feet prevented him from working—but never deterred him from dancing or finding food to satisfy his voracious appetite.[9] Donald Bogle, calling Fetchit "the strongest performer in the picture," writes that *Hearts in Dixie* was actually expanded "because Fetchit's work in the first half [of the film] had proved so good" (*TCMMB* 28). Fetchit's unrestrained antics were matched only by the enthusiasm and vitality of the choir and of the dancers, who provided a measure of balance by bringing a significant, legitimate element of black African-American culture to the Hollywood screen.[10]

Ultimately, though, the film's infatuation with sound never got far beyond depicting blacks in the context of endless plantation song-and-dance sequences. According to Jim Pines, *Hearts in Dixie* "did not (or could not) develop, nor reassert in a dynamic way, racial image conventions through the new technology" and thus was "a trite inception into the sound era, both cinematically as well as racially" (22). Donald Bogle went even further, suggesting that the actors, most of them recruited from the New York stage, overplayed their parts and unconsciously "came across as a group of black-faced jesters rather than as valid representations of black folk culture." Their "blackface fixation" would haunt black performers for the next half century. "Directed by whites in scripts authored by whites and then photographed, dressed, and made up by whites, the Negro actor, like the slaves he portrayed, aimed (and still does aim) always to please the master figure"; consequently, Bogle concludes, he gives a performance that is not his own and that does not interpret black life but rather is one in which "he presents for mass consumption black life as seen through the eyes of white artists" (*TCMMB* 27), a spectacle duplicated in numerous later major studio films from *The Green Pastures* to *Porgy and Bess* and beyond.

Hallelujah!, the second and more memorable of Hollywood's pioneering black musicals, was also released in 1929; but it surpassed *Hearts in Dixie* in virtually every way, particularly in the realization of its characters. A modern-day morality tale, *Hallelujah!* told the story of Zeke Johnson (Daniel L. Haynes), a decent young black man who is tempted and seduced by various pleasures of the flesh. As the film opens, Zeke lives simply but happily on a small farm with his family of honest, hardworking, God-fearing folk: Mammy and Pappy Johnson (played by Fannie Belle DeKnight and Harry Gray, reportedly a ninety-year-old former slave[11]); their adopted daughter, Missy Rose (Victoria Spivey); and his four younger brothers. But after he and his brother Spunk (Everett McGarrity) take the family's cotton harvest to town for sale, Zeke becomes distracted by the flashy, busty, and lusty Chick (Nina Mae McKinney), who conspires with her gambler boyfriend "Hot Shot" (William Fountaine) to cheat him out of his earnings. When Zeke tries to reclaim his losses, he ends up in a barroom fight during which Spunk is accidentally killed.

To atone for his actions, Zeke becomes a traveling preacher whose powerful voice stirs the souls of the community. Yet his own faith is tested when he encounters Chick again, and he deserts his congregation to follow her. Although Chick professes to be reborn, her religious "conversion" turns out to be short-lived, and she starts two-timing Zeke with her former lover. In a jealous rage, Zeke pursues the pair as they try to run away. But when Hot Shot's horse-drawn wagon loses a wheel, Chick is thrown to the ground and dies in Zeke's arms. (Fig. 3.2.) Zeke then hunts down and kills Hot Shot, a crime for which he is sentenced to hard labor on a prison chain gang. After serving his time, Zeke returns home to the welcome of his beloved parents and the embrace of the ever-faithful Missy Rose.

Now considered a landmark in sound films, *Hallelujah!* was a project of particular interest to its director, King Vidor, who had long wanted to film a story of "real Negro folk culture" and to "show the Southern Negro as he is" (Bogle, *TCMMB* 28, Pines 26).

Investing his own money in the production even before Metro-Goldwyn-Mayer had finally approved it, Vidor determined to make the film as authentic as possible. In addition to casting members of the spiritual-singing Dixie Jubilee Choir, he chose to shoot a number of scenes on location along the Mississippi and in the

Figure 3.2. Chick (Nina Mae McKinney) dies in the arms of Zeke (Daniel L. Haynes) in the landmark black musical *Hallelujah!* (*Metro-Goldwyn-Mayer, 1929*)

swamps and forests of Tennessee. And, in the film itself, he sought to incorporate not only the traditional aspects of black folk culture but also more recent and innovative styles such as the dance forms popularized on the vaudeville stage in the 1920s (something black filmmaker Oscar Micheaux also endeavored to do). One such innovative dance device was "trucking," or "static motion" (that is, the act of moving without actually gaining ground), which Vidor employed at several critical points in the film. In an early scene, a flush Zeke overhears the sound of men shooting craps and having fun. Tempted to join them, he engages in a trucking motion that slides him slowly backwards and forwards and that expresses his dilemma—to stay or to go—with great visual effectiveness. A more sustained use of trucking occurs during the revival meeting, when Zeke, now a preacher, "trucks" along the stage wearing a conductor's hat and kerchief and urging his followers to debark the "Express [train] to Hell" at any one of three stations: Faith, Obedience, or Repentance.[12] As Jim Pines writes, "Vidor utilized this theatrical vernacular convention [of trucking] in cinematic, plastic terms, exploring its visual expressiveness as a dramatic means of conveying Zeke's psychological and physical state of being." By balancing racial perspectives with aesthetic concerns, Vidor thus achieved "a kind of formal relationship between film art and black racial imagery which few directors have equalled" (Pines 26).

Even though the plot of *Hallelujah!* bordered at times on operatic absurdity, Vidor managed—especially in the film's gospel music and dance sequences—to capture a rich emotional aura and to create one of the finest records of black grief and passion to reach a movie screen. White audiences responded enthusiastically, if with occasional condescension, to the idealized black cinematic world of his creation. The *New York Times* reviewer Mordaunt Hall (21 Aug. 1929), for instance, praised the film for its verisimilitude in conveying what he called the "peculiarly typical religious hysteria of the darkies and their gullibility" as they seek salvation.[13] Black viewers also found much to applaud,[14] from the all-black casting and the vitality of the songs and dances to the rich and loving portrait of the Johnson family, which, as Donald Bogle (*TCMMB* 30) observed, "remains the first of Hollywood's attempts to deal with the black family, and is directly related to subsequent black family dramas such as *The Learning Tree* (1969) and *Sounder* (1972)." Nonetheless, they took umbrage both at the resistance of certain Southern exhibitors to show all-black pictures and at the inherently racist way that MGM marketed the film, premiering it simultaneously at the Lafayette, a black theater in Harlem, for black audiences and at the downtown Embassy, a white theater, for white patrons who wanted to watch—but not necessarily sit next to—"real" blacks.[15]

Some urban blacks and white liberals, moreover, were concerned by what they perceived to be the film's sentimental regressiveness. Pointing to the faithful Mammy, the zoot-suited gambler, the loose-moraled temptress, and the long-suffering good woman at home, they argued that many of the characters in *Hallelujah!* harked back to the old black stereotypes and established the screen models that Hollywood would imitate for many years to come. (Sammy Davis, Jr.'s portrayal of "Sportin' Life" in *Porgy and Bess*, for instance, clearly derived from William Fountaine's flashy, derby-sporting crapshooter "Hot Shot"; and the sensuous Carmen [Dorothy Dandridge] in Otto Preminger's *Carmen Jones* and the sexy Georgia Brown [Lena Horne] in *Cabin in the Sky* were patterned upon McKinney's brassy, hip-swiveling, and whorish Chick.) Perhaps more importantly, these viewers saw evidence of Vidor's racial and cultural paternalism in the very structure of the film, which seemed to suggest that the black is best off on the plantation, where his familial and spiritual values can be fostered and his baser instincts controlled. Indeed, within the plantation community of *Hallelujah!*, the funerals, weddings, baptisms, revivalist meetings, and other religious activities reinforce the more secular, social aspects of black culture; by contrast, in the city, away from the plantation, sin and temptation are rampant. Zeke, who achieves a kind of folk-hero status within his community, suffers only pain and hardship—from the murder of Spunk to the deaths of Chick, to whose charms he succumbs (against Mammy's better instincts), and of her wily, hustling lover Hot Shot—when he leaves; and his redemption is incomplete until he returns home and re-engages with his family and his neighbors. Significantly, the film ends exactly as it began, with the annual harvest. But it is clear that Zeke, restored to his rightful place, has learned his lesson: he will not stray from home again.

Still other critics blasted *Hallelujah!* for its "insulting niggerisms" (Reddick 10), like the misrepresentation of black religion. Noted black actor Paul Robeson, in *Film Weekly* (1 September

1933), spoke for a number of viewers when he decried "the box office insistence that the Negro shall figure always as a clown," a depiction that he believed spoiled *Hallelujah!* just as it had spoiled *Hearts in Dixie.* "In *Hallelujah!,"* wrote Robeson, "they took the Negro and his church services and made them funny. America may have found it amusing," but to others "the burlesquing of religious matters appeared sheer blasphemy" (qtd. in Noble 54).[16]

Yet while *Hallelujah!* drew on admittedly familiar types and situations,[17] the film's depiction of black concerns was often sensitive and sympathetic—and certainly, by Hollywood's standards, unconventional. Without white antagonists to challenge, influence, or limit them, the characters revealed a complexity and a humanity that went beyond the usual racial depictions; and they demonstrated that blacks are subject to the same joys, frustrations, and temptations as whites. Zeke, for example, is neither brutal nor heroic, neither evil nor saintly; he is simply a good man whose actions go horribly wrong. Although he loves his family, his careless behavior with money and his foolish infatuation with Chick almost rip that family apart. Yet even after he causes one death and contributes to two others, he is able to repent and receive forgiveness. Moreover, the moral conflicts that Zeke confronts in the course of the film suggest very real social conflicts in the first half of the twentieth century, including the problems of urban migration (problems also explored in pictures like Micheaux's *Ten Minutes to Live* and Colored Players' *The Scar of Shame*). Thus, Zeke's moral progress not only has social and racial implications; the allegorical nature of his progress makes his plight universal as well. So even if *Hallelujah!* ultimately fell short of Vidor's intention to portray the "real Negro," it was still a noteworthy cinematic accomplishment, even in some ways a "radical racial film, in that racial imagery was built into the formal dynamics of the film" and possibly, according to Jim Pines, "the only film apart from Griffith's *The Birth of a Nation* in which the marriage of film mechanics (the technology) and racial image is graphically interwoven with remarkable and resounding efficiency" (22).

Another distinguishing feature of *Hallelujah!* was its use of black consultants. Whereas Clarence Muse and other less prominent cast members reportedly offered advice on various aspects of Fox's production of *Hearts in Dixie*, MGM formally appointed Harold Garrison, a black employee of the studio, as "assistant director" of *Hallelujah!* and acknowledged him accordingly in the film's credits.[18] And, although Thomas Cripps suggests that the directorial title may have carried less weight in terms of actual production responsibilities than in promotional releases about the film to the black press, Garrison nonetheless worked with the white screenwriter, novelist Wanda Tuchock, to ensure that "even if their lines of observation of Negro life curved from different approaches, they were at least tangential" (*SFB* 243). Early in the planning process, executive secretary of the NAACP James Weldon Johnson, who himself had had some silent film experience, also consulted with Vidor.[19]

Surprisingly, though, despite the vitality of black life that it brought to the screen, *Hallelujah!* did not stimulate other innovative approaches. Instead, it ushered in a slew of films that reverted to old derogatory types and situations, like Stepin Fetchit's racist clowning in *Stand Up and Cheer* (1934), *David Harum* (1934), *Judge Priest* (1934), and *Steamboat 'Round the Bend* (1935), and Bill "Bojangles" Robinson's vaudeville routines in Shirley Temple films (fig. 3.3) such as *The Little Colonel* (1935), *The Littlest Rebel*

Figure 3.3. Bill "Bojangles" Robinson (as Walker) dances with Shirley Temple (as Miss Lloyd Shermon) in *The Little Colonel,* one of several films in which they were paired. *(Twentieth Century-Fox, 1935)*

(1935), and *Rebecca of Sunnybrook Farm* (1938). Even Vidor, the director of *Hallelujah!*, returned to a naïve romanticizing of the Old South in his next racial film, *So Red the Rose* (1935), an adaptation of Stark Young's novel about a Civil War-era belle (played by Margaret Sullavan) who, while nursing her dying father, must quell a slave insurrection on the family plantation.[20] Thomas Cripps relates the persistently reactionary trend in filmmaking to Hollywood's inflexibility and to the motion picture industry's fundamental inability to transcend or deviate, even vaguely, from its own racism. The regressiveness is also attributable in large part to the commercial failure of both *Hearts in Dixie* and *Hallelujah!*, whose disappointing box office grosses seemed to indicate the unwillingness of white audiences to accept blacks in important starring roles. Hollywood columnist Harry Levette, whose work appeared in a number of black newspapers, went so far as to predict that "there will be no more all-colored-cast films made" because the South was "not quite ready for dark stars in the real sense of the word," an assessment with which many industry insiders concurred.[21] The reluctance of the major studios to experiment further with black leads relegated black actors to minor and supporting parts again and helped to account for the long interval before the production of the next big black Hollywood spectacle.

That spectacle was Warner Brothers' *The Green Pastures* (1936), a feature-length musical based on Marc Connelly's long-running, Pulitzer Prize-winning play that was in turn suggested by *Ol' Man Adam an' His Chillun*, a collection of Southern sketches by another white writer, Roark Bradford. Directed by Connelly and William Keighley, *The Green Pastures* told the story of Mr. Deshee (George Reed), a kindly old black Sunday school teacher in Louisiana, who makes the stories of the Bible come alive for his students by transforming the biblical characters into contemporary men and women. "God appears in many forms to those who believe in Him," asserts the "Foreword" of the film. "Thousands of Negroes in the Deep South visualize God and Heaven in terms of people and things they know in their everyday life. *The Green Pastures* is an attempt to portray that humble, reverent conception."

The film's Heaven, as heavily laden with Spanish mosses and wisteria as any nineteenth-century Southern plantation, is indeed a comfortable and happy place where all the inhabitants purportedly look and speak like modern blacks—a place where male angels in straw hats chat with friends or stroll with their favorite female angels; where Mammy angels discipline their mischievous cherubs for riding on clouds; where domestic angels wear checkered aprons and matching dusters on their wings to clean the celestial offices; and where "De Lawd," appearing very much like a distinguished Southern gentleman in his black tie and long-tailed jacket, passes out good ten-cent "seegars," drinks "b'iled custard," and discusses the upcoming fish fry. (Fig. 3.4.) Biblical events on earth assume a similar vernacular quality. The film's Noah is a modern preacher who cannot prevail upon his hard-drinking, crap-shooting, tobacco-chewing, gun-toting, policy-playing townspeople to attend Sunday "meeting"; and when he

Figure 3.4. De Lawd (Rex Ingram) shares a cigar with one of his angels in *The Green Pastures*, based on Marc Connelly's long-running, Pulitzer Prize-winning play. *(Warner Brothers, 1936)*

reviews aloud the lengthy list of cargo for the ark ("buffaloes, bed-bugs, butterflies; guess that winds up the B's"), he is mocked for his craziness. Plaid-shirted Moses is a stuttering "tricker" who must outdo Old King Pharaoh's magic by sleight-of-hand with an old walking stick. A modest old prophet is gunned down by the flashy, trashy King of Babylon, whose court resembles a modern nightclub with hula girls and cootchie dancers. And Adam's descendant Hezdrel, clad in contemporary military gear and armed with a rifle, bayonet, and cannon, contests Herod's control of Jerusalem because he believes that "if they kills us, we leaps out of our skins right into the lap of God."[22]

To be sure, there was much to like in the film, from the wonderfully rich melodies of the Hall Johnson Choir's spirituals to the superb acting by some of the best black actors of the day, including Rex Ingram as the patriarchal Jehovah who could be at times vengeful, at other times merciful; Oscar Polk as Archangel Gabriel, De Lawd's capable but understated assistant; Eddie Anderson as the good Noah, a man who obeys God but who cannot resist a taste of alcohol and tobacco; and Ernest Whitman as the arrogant, trick-loving Pharaoh who devises increasingly sadistic ways to punish the Israelites. Moreover, by playing multiple roles, the actors created a clever continuity within the stories: Ingram was also Adam and Hezdrel; William Cumby appeared as both the Pharaoh's chief wizard and the carousing King of Babylon; and the children in Mr. Deshee's Sunday school class doubled as heavenly cherubs.

But, as Donald Bogle has observed, *The Green Pastures* rested on the cruel assumption that "nothing could be more ludicrous than transporting the lowly language and folkways of the early-twentieth-century Negro back to the high stately world before the Flood." The juxtaposition of high and low, which implied Negro ignorance and inferiority, passed under the guise of a "Negro miracle play"; yet such a cinematic concept, as Bogle writes, based as it was on white perceptions, was as artificial as it was absurd, since "Negroes of the period never pictured historical or biblical events in terms of their own experience. Indeed, the problem was that they always dreamt of a white heaven and a white heavenly host" (*TCMMB* 68). Yet white filmmakers, in their condescending, sentimentalized view of blacks, gave full expression to a wide variety of stereotypes, particularly concerning religion, beginning with a God who decides to "r'ar back and pass a miracle." As the film medium transformed theatrical illusions into cinematic realities, no caricature of the black seemed too grotesque for what Daniel J. Leab called "the Great Fish Fry in the Sky" (97).

Whereas the white press unanimously hailed the film as a sub-lime and heartbreaking masterpiece of American folk drama, black audiences rejected the demeaning portrayals of their group by staying away from the performances.[23] "'Green Pastures' Not Liked by Negroes," headlined a *New York Age* article. Zora Neale Hurston acknowledged that the film was getting "profuse and lav-ish praise" from whites and even from a few "supposed" black leaders, but she blasted it as the work of a "hungry Nordic [who] is suddenly bitten by Negrophobia" and who "sets out to scribble a 'true' picture of his darker brother at so much per word" (qtd. in Everett 184). Similarly, the *Afro-American*'s reviewer condemned the movie's characterization of black faith as caricature. "Let *The Green Pastures* go for what it is," that reviewer wrote: "an interest-ing and entertaining spectacle with a cast of underpaid colored actors portraying Connelly's conception of . . . unlearned earlier-day beliefs of heaven and the Bible" (Bogle, *TCMMB* 68). And Roi Ottley, a major figure among black newspapermen, commented that "'The Green Pastures' will no doubt receive magnificent and glowing accounts," possibly even in some black papers; but that kind of boosterism arises from "a false sense of values" based on the premise that anytime a black appears in a white production, "it should be applauded regardless of its merits." Ottley concluded that "Oscar Micheaux, with his inferior equipment, would have produced a better picture" (Cripps, *SFB* 260-61).

Nonetheless, *The Green Pastures* became one of the most suc-cessful black-cast films of all time. On opening day at Radio City Music Hall in New York, tickets sold at the rate of 6,000 per hour. Its enormous popularity, which led to the film's being held over for an entire year's run at some theaters, also helped to convince Hollywood filmmakers that, in the aftermath of the Depression, the social and racial climate was slowly but certainly changing. The positive response to important films like *The Emperor Jones* (1933), about the despotic Brutus Jones, and *Imitation of Life* (1934), about two widows, one white, one black, who share their tribula-tions and successes, indicated that the same white audiences who had failed to embrace *Hearts in Dixie* and *Hallelujah!* only a few years earlier were finally beginning to appreciate and accept blacks in major character roles. Blacks, too, represented a strong and growing market for Hollywood: they had already demonstrated their interest in black-related stories and black-produced films by their attendance at race theaters. Yet studios continued to proceed with caution in their production of films about black life; and the movies they released were usually a compromise between reviving the old stereotypes and increasing black visibility on screen. Such compromise is evident in a film like RKO's *Rainbow on the River* (1936), produced by Sol Lesser, in which Louise Beavers plays Toinette, an ex-slave who fights for the custody of a small boy (Bobby Breen) whom she has raised throughout the hardships of the Civil War. Although her character was surprisingly well developed—and so tenacious as to raise questions from white reviewers about her plausibility—Beavers's role nevertheless marked her return to the tradition of selfless Mammies that had dominated the portrayal of black women for many years. Even more offensive to some viewers was her intimation that she never really wanted her freedom.

The relationship of the black servant to a white child was explored with slightly more success in another RKO story of antebellum life, *Way Down South* (1939).[24] What distinguished this particular project, however, was its pair of black screenwriters, actor Clarence Muse and noted poet and writer Langston Hughes. For many years Muse, a law school graduate and highly trained performer affiliated with both the Lincoln and the Lafayette Players, had found himself restricted to Tommish, mild-mannered servant roles in films like *Huckleberry Finn* (1931), *Show Boat* (1936), *Follow Your Heart* (1936), and *Spirit of Youth* (1937), or to other stereotypic parts like that of a razor-wielding coonish sidekick in *A Royal Romance* (1930) and a brutish black insurrectionist in Vidor's *So Red the Rose*. After an early experience as director, producer, and star of a silent biographical short titled *Toussaint L'Ouverture* (1921)[25] and especially after being engaged as an advisor and consultant on black themes to the Fox studio during the production of *Hearts in Dixie*, he sought to define better and stronger film roles for black actors and to expand his own involvement in the industry. *Way Down South*, produced by Sol Lesser, seemed to offer precisely the right opportunity. Together with Hughes, one of the most brilliant literary voices of the Harlem Renaissance, Muse was hired to create dialogue and vignettes, to advise the white director Bernard Vorhaus, and even to compose some of the original music, includ-

ing "Louisiana" and "Good Ground," as well as several of the spirituals sung by the Hall Johnson Choir, which had so memorably
serenaded De Lawd in *The Green Pastures* several years earlier.[26]

Largely a vehicle for popular child actor Bobby Breen (the
juvenile male counterpart to Shirley Temple), *Way Down South*
reworked the familiar story of Uncle Tom. After Master Reed, the
kindly owner of the Bayou Lovelle Plantation, is trampled to death
by a team of his own horses, Reed's orphaned son, Timothy
(played by Breen), is too young to assume control of the plantation;
so executorship is awarded to Reed's former lawyer, Mr. Dill, a
greedy, self-serving, Simon Legree type who treats the slaves with
cruelty and contempt. When Dill decides to sell off the slaves and
liquidate the estate so that he can spend more time with his mistress in New Orleans, Timothy realizes that he must take action.
Assisted by his beloved and devoted black house servant Uncle
Caton (Clarence Muse), Timothy entreats the local magistrate
Judge Ravenall to revoke Dill's executorship and to stop the scheduled slave auction. Based on Caton's testimony that Master Reed
would never have sanctioned such a sale ("He *never* want to sell
none of the slaves"), Ravenall relieves Dill of his authority; and a
joyous order is restored to the plantation.

Way Down South was to have been a bold film: Hughes and
Muse had intended to use the plantation tradition as a voice of the
modern temper. Sol Lesser even told his staff that "Messrs. Muse
and Hughes are to be given the utmost liberty in developing the
Second Draft Screenplay, so that it will contain every element of
their conception" (Cripps, "Winds" 149). But the completed film
fell far short of both writers' expectations—to such an extent, in
fact, that even the practice of slavery came across as rather benign.[27]
The mischievous slave boy Gumbo, for instance, walks freely
about the big house, eating leftovers from the master's plate and
drinking from his fine china cup; Gumbo even ignores his chores
without any fear of punishment to join the Reeds in celebrating the
sugar cane harvest. Yet the film managed to depict or allude to
some of the ugly realities of the peculiarly Southern institution,
from flogging as extreme and unfair discipline to the forced separation of slave families; and it created a picture of the strong interrelationships among blacks on the plantation, who alone appreciated and shared each other's experience of bondage, and of the

importance of religion and ethnic custom in sustaining their hopes for a better life.[28] The film also gave Caton a role of considerable significance—although much of it was played for laughs, especially when Timothy disguises the old slave as his matronly, heavily veiled, deaf-mute aunt in order to smuggle him into Papa Doudon's, the renowned New Orleans inn owned by Monsieur Bouton.

Unfortunately, as Thomas Cripps (*SFB* 262) notes, most of the original ideas that the black writing team of Langston Hughes and Clarence Muse brought to the film were offset by the return of Breen, the Hall Johnson Choir, and "a hoary slave who gratefully testifies to his old master's kindness" as well as by other stereotypical characters such as the Stepin Fetchit-like chimney sweeper whom Timothy and Caton encounter on the street in New Orleans. But what saved the film from devolving into another typical Hollywood plantation saga of dutiful Toms and Mammies, happy slave children, and loving white masters was its suggestion of social consciousness. Master Reed believes "in a little happiness for everyone," including all of his slaves; just before his death, in fact, he makes plans to build them new living quarters in appreciation of their hard work at Bayou Lovelle. (The regressive Dill, on the other hand, rejects Reed's plans; and, as executor, he even usurps the existing homes in order to expand the plantation's pantries and storehouses.) And young Timothy, a representative of the next generation of landowners, by his actions on behalf of Caton and the other slaves, seems to question the very justice of the plantation system. In a scene that occurs on the night before the scheduled auction, the orphaned boy commiserates with the slaves, many of whom expect to be separated from their families as a result of the sale, by singing the spiritual that begins, "Sometimes I Feel Like a Motherless Child."[29] Thus, in ways more subtle than revolutionary, *Way Down South* implied that racial inequality was a moral issue not just of regional but of national importance.

Muse's next—and last—co-written screenplay, *Broken Strings* (1940), released by the independent film company L. C. Borden Productions, was also race-oriented; but in many respects, it was more intriguing than *Way Down South*. The film, whose theme concerned the "raising of Negro music to the dignity of European music" (Cripps, *SFB* 336), featured an injured classical violinist

Arthur Williams (played by Muse) who battles with his son Johnny (William Washington), a gifted young musician who wants to perform swing music. At a radio contest that he has entered in order to earn money for his father's operation, Johnny discovers that Dicky Morley, a jealous competitor (and one of his father's pupils), has tampered with his instrument; unable to play the classical piece he had originally selected on the damaged violin, he must perform swing instead. The father, moved by his son's talent, applauds so loudly that he restores movement to his own fingers and is soon able to return to concert performances. The independent film, in which Muse gave perhaps the finest and most sensitive performance of his long career, was also a small triumph for Muse as a screenwriter; the *Pittsburgh Courier* (25 March 1940) called *Broken Strings* "an extraordinary picture because it contains no gun shooting . . . and tells the simple story of an ordinary family." The picture is also "extraordinary because you see Negroes conducting successful business," including, among others, "neat and trim Negro nurses at the hospital" (qtd. in Sampson 359) and a fine black surgeon with whom Williams's daughter Grace consults about his condition.

Like Muse, Langston Hughes maintained a personal interest in the political potential of films. In the Langston Hughes Papers, a part of the James Weldon Johnson Collection housed in Yale University's Beinecke Library, and in collections at Fisk University in Nashville are treatments, drafts, and outlines of Hughes's projected films. They include *The Negro Speaks of Rivers*, based on his evocative poem about the endurance of the black and of his unparalleled contribution to Western culture; *The Chocolate Sailor*; *L'Amitié noire*; a story of Kansas "exodusters"; and an untitled "Paul Robeson Screenplay" (Cripps, "Winds" 152).[30] There is, however, no record that any of Hughes's projects apart from *Way Down South* reached production.[31]

Films about the Old South remained popular throughout the 1930s and into the 1940s; and they continued to promote the sentimental Southern mythology by reworking familiar Hollywood formulas, most of which harked back to early silent films, which in turn were based on nineteenth-century Tom shows and minstrelsy traditions. Heroines were depicted as the fairest "flower[s] of the Old South," to borrow the term that Duncan (Randolph Scott) uses to describe his cousin Vallette (Margaret Sullavan) in *So Red the Rose*—although, like Dixiana (Bebe Daniels) in *Dixiana*, Lucy Rumford (Joan Bennett) in *Mississippi*, and Julie (Bette Davis) in *Jezebel*,[32] those flowers could also be flirtatious, spoiled, and strong-willed; planters were proud and aristocratic gentlemen, dutifully attended by their retainers and kindly to their slaves, like General Rumford, played by Claude Gillingwater in *Mississippi* and Buddy Rogers in *River of Romance* (both films based on Booth Tarkington's *Magnolia*); and children were precocious orphans like Bobby Breen or adorable moppets like Shirley Temple, who irresistibly but absolutely asserted her superiority not only over the black children with whom she played but also over her adult black servants.

THE IMPACT OF *GONE WITH THE WIND*

The most enduring and beloved picture of plantation legend—and arguably the greatest Hollywood film of all time—was *Gone With the Wind* (1939), released in the same year as *Way Down South*.[33] Adapted from the 1936 best-selling novel by Margaret Mitchell, a white woman from Georgia,[34] David O. Selznick's production, which took two years and four million dollars to complete, offered a vision of the South that, quite apart from its material reality, "had a life of its own in American intellectual history" (Pyron 185) and in the popular imagination.[35] The film's box office success was ensured not just by its antebellum period atmosphere (captured in brilliant Technicolor) but also by its epic scope, which surpassed even Griffith's *Birth of a Nation*,[36] and by its elaborate romance involving the rebellious Scarlett O'Hara (Vivien Leigh), the reluctant and anemic object of her affection Ashley Wilkes (Trevor Howard), and Scarlett's dashing, iconoclastic lover Rhett Butler (Clark Gable).

Mitchell, who prided herself on the historical accuracy of her book, reportedly scoffed at what she called the "lavender-and-old-lace-moonlight-on-the-magnolia" tradition, ridiculed the sweet sentimentality of the "gentle Confederate novel" of the "Thomas Nelson Page-type," and scorned professional Southerners; and long before the film's production, she complained about readers who expected an artificial movie-set version of the South that was "all white columns and singing darkies and magnolias" (Pyron 186). In turn, in presenting Mitchell's "patrician world, a land of Cavaliers and cotton fields . . . [now] no more than a dream remembered, a Civilization gone with the wind,"[37] producer Selznick tried to be sensitive to certain racial and social concerns. Insistent that "the picture not emerge as anything offensive to negroes" (Cripps, "Winds" 140), he excised all references in the film to the Ku Klux Klan and to renegade Negroes; banned the use of words like "nigger" in the script; and reconstructed some of the most inflammatory scenes from the novel, like Scarlett's sexual assault by a pair of men, one of whom is black, near Shantytown. In the novel, it is the black attacker who rips Scarlett's dress from bodice to waist as he violates her and the sacred sense of Southern womanhood that she represents. In the film, however, the rape is turned into an attempted robbery of Scarlett's carriage, during which a swooning Scarlett sees only the face of the *white* man leering down at her (an alteration consistent with the racial film codes of the time) before being rescued by a former family slave, Big Sam (Everett Brown).[38] But, as Linda Williams observes, the drawback to the excision of this and many of the overt racial components of the novel was the weakening of the intensity of the racial melodrama of the film compared to the novel. "Ironically," according to Williams, "the more Selznick's good intentions toward Negroes were implemented, the more Scarlett's mixed emotions of rage, impatience, and protectiveness toward Pork, Prissy, Mammy, Uncle Peter, Big Sam, and other blacks were eliminated." The result was "a general whitewashing of the theme of race altogether" and an unintended accompanying idealization of the plantation legend Mitchell had done so much to debunk (*Race* 215).

In his desire to achieve historical accuracy in the film, Selznick hired Wilbur Kurtz, an Atlantan architect and Civil War buff, and Susan Myrick, a white reporter for the *Macon Telegraph* who championed black concerns; but, though Selznick tried, he was unsuccessful in getting Walter White of the NAACP to join his team. Kurtz apparently provided good counsel on manners, dress, and architecture (although he curiously neglected "details such as whips and chains" that characterized the slave experience), while Myrick served as an active liaison between Hollywood and Atlanta by preventing gross errors and misstatements of Southern lore. Thomas Cripps notes that Margaret Mitchell hoped Kurtz and Myrick, as the film's advisors, "would head off both the triteness that rankled white Southerners and the stereotypes that spoiled movies for blacks." To a friend, Mitchell had written, "I feared greatly that three hundred massed Negro singers might be standing on Miss Pittypat's lawn waving their arms and singing 'Swing low, sweet chariot, Comin' for to carry me home' while Rhett drives up with the wagon" ("Winds" 141-42).[39]

Contrary to Mitchell's fears, no Negro singers materialized on Pittypat's lawn; but other equally objectionable Hollywood conventions found their way into the film. The cotton fields of Tara, for example, boasted contented slaves presided over by their cheerful foreman Sam, with no white overseer in sight, while the personal servants, relegated to peripheral and often comic roles (the ever-fearful slave girl, the stammering "house hand," the buffoonish attendant), reflected similar, familiar stereotyping. And Tara itself, with its feminine, maternal, and sentimental associations, became—even more than Dixon's and Griffith's paean to the virtues of the Old South—an unapologetic celebration of the economic system of chattel slavery for which the plantation home stood (Williams, *Race* 188).

But possibly the most conventional aspect of the film was its sense of nostalgia for happier days. Even Mitchell, a staunch Georgian whose sympathies to Southern issues often differed from the national perspective, was ambivalent in her vision of the idealized past. As Gerald Wood writes, she "was aware of the sense of regret that goes with having a secure and beautiful past, but she also respected the courage and resilience that it takes to live for the future"; consequently her novel "values both recognition of the past and strength for the future" (131), particularly in its depiction of Scarlett as a woman conventional in her desire for romantic love but unconventional in her notions of the role of woman in society and in business. Selznick, on the other hand, displayed an unambiguous longing for the chivalric and orderly prewar society of the Old South.[40] In his version of the story, Scarlett's essential problem is how to return to the charm and grace of her past; it is not, as it was for Mitchell, an internal struggle between traditional morality and opportunism. So, as Wood notes, while Scarlett's uncertainty and fickleness are apparent in both the novel and the film,

"Selznick's Scarlett is the more attractive one because the film emphasizes her passion and willfulness without giving attention, as Mitchell does, to the evasion and denial in her personality" (131). Scarlett's now-famous calls in the film for "home" (a home, ironically, she had earlier rejected) and for "tomorrow" are thus attempts to reclaim her losses and revive her family traditions, whereas in the novel those calls signal her recognition of a New South emerging from the ruins of the Old, a New South in which the failure of prewar chivalric codes is symbolized by Ashley's uselessness in postwar society and by Melanie's iconic death.

Nevertheless, on some level, *Gone With the Wind* presented a more realistic portrait of the relationship between whites and blacks, especially between the mistress and her servant, than did any other movie of its time. Scarlett's beloved but contentious Mammy, played by Hattie McDaniel (fig. 3.5), is, on the one hand, so typical of movie Mammies that she possesses no given name apart from that of her generic role and appears to have no life or family of her own apart from the O'Haras. Yet her strength is virtually equal to Scarlett's: it is Mammy who counsels Scarlett on

Figure 3.5. Mammy (Hattie McDaniel) casts a disapproving glance at her beloved charge, Scarlett O'Hara (Vivien Leigh), in *Gone With the Wind*, Hollywood's classic plantation saga. *(Selznick International Pictures, 1939)*

Southern etiquette; who berates Scarlett for her poor judgment of men; who becomes more mother to Scarlett than the actual Mrs. O'Hara; who helps to keep the plantation going throughout the war; who takes pride in diapering three generations of women in the family; who is never reluctant to speak her mind; who appreciates the reasons behind some of Scarlett's seemingly impetuous acts, like marrying Frank Kennedy or visiting Rhett Butler in jail in Atlanta; and who serves as a kind of moral compass for Scarlett throughout the film. In Mitchell's novel, Mammy is described as having "broad, sagging breasts which had held so many heads, black and white. Here was something of stability, thought Scarlett, something of the old life that was unchanging" (*GWTW* 415). And Mammy is just as pivotal and dignified a character in the film. Insisting that she be cast as a principal rather than a supporting role, Selznick even reworked portions of the script to reflect Hattie McDaniel's special brand of warmth and humor. McDaniel returned Selznick's confidence with a defining performance, as rich as it was detailed, for which she became the first black entertainer to win the Academy Award.[41]

While *Gone With the Wind* was justly celebrated for its technical and artistic achievements, not everyone commended its racial content. Dalton Trumbo, speaking at the Hollywood Writers Congress in 1943, called it an "anti-Negro picture" that, along with *The Birth of a Nation*, comprised "the most gigantic milestones of Hollywood's appeal to public patronage." Black dramatist Carlton Moss, in "An Open Letter to Mr. Selznick," complained that whereas *The Birth of a Nation* was "a frontal attack on American history and the Negro people," *Gone With the Wind* was "a rear attack on the same. . . . Sugar-smeared and blurred by a boresome Hollywood love story and under the guise of presenting the South as it is in the 'eyes of the Southerners,' the message of *GWTW* emerges in its final entity as a nostalgic plea for sympathy for a still living cause of Southern reaction." Moss went on to decry the "two-dimensional Negro characters" and the "time-worn stereotype laid down by Hollywood," which included the "shiftless and dull-witted Pork," the "indolent and thoroughly irresponsible" Prissy, Big Sam "with his radiant acceptance of slavery," and Mammy "with her constant haranguing and doting on every wish of Scarlett" (Moss 157, 159).[42] And Walter White, the Secretary of the NAACP whom Selznick had tried to recruit as a technical advisor, complained that "Whatever sentiment there was in the South for federal anti-lynch law evaporated during the 'Gone With the Wind' vogue" (qtd. in Noble 79). But generally even blacks' criticism of the film was muted, especially in light of the national attention paid to McDaniel and the industry's recognition of her work, which they hoped would lead to increased visibility on screen for other black actors.

Although the glorified world of Gone With the Wind—a world that, in Melanie Hamilton's words, "only wants to be graceful and beautiful"—is disrupted by war and changed forever by the adversity that follows, Scarlett and her "folk" not only endure the hardships but also look ahead to the promise of a better "tomorrow."[43] Perhaps that is why contemporary viewers shaken by the Depression and caught between two world wars saw in the film a time that was analogous to their own. But Gone With the Wind caused viewers to look at their own worlds in other more critical ways as well.[44] More than any film since The Birth of a Nation, it released a variety of social forces that foreshadowed a shift in black political and aesthetic attitudes, an alliance of blacks with white liberals who encouraged the expectation that blacks might find their place alongside whites in the American dream of success and self-fulfillment, and even a decline in racism. According to Thomas Cripps, the movie eventually became a template against which to measure social change, the title itself serving as a rhetorical device among black journalists. Opportunity, for example, in its editorial congratulation to Hattie McDaniel for winning the Academy Award, used Gone With the Wind as a reminder of the "limit" put upon black aspiration by old prejudices. When the Cleveland Call & Post attacked journalistic racism, its bannerline was "All Did Not Go With the Wind." And songwriter Andy Razaf's ironic poem in The Crisis used the title to "capture a sense of imprisonment between the past and the future" ("Winds" 148-49):

> What of the black man's liberty?
> Today, he is half slave, half free.
> Denied his rights on every side,
> Jim Crowed, lynched and crucified,
> He's even barred in Washington—.
> Gone with the Wind? You're wrong, my son.

The "muted and ambiguous signals of shifting racial attitudes" sent out by *Gone With the Wind*, Cripps notes, "echoed not only in circles of black critics but in Hollywood itself," as dozens of movies made small gestures in recognition of the trend. For instance, only a few weeks after the first run of *Gone With the Wind*, a story editor at Warner Brothers wrote a memo to Walter Wanger about *Mississippi Belle*, a script that promised a regression to the crudest elements of Old South movies. Reflecting on one of the lessons of *Gone With the Wind*—that by departing from the worst excesses of the plantation tradition, *GWTW* had rendered that genre to be so obsolete as to be unproducible—she wrote: "I confess I am a bit puzzled to know why such a story should be made. I just can't believe that anybody would be interested. . . . It all seems so old-fashioned and remote" ("Winds" 149).

BEYOND *GONE WITH THE WIND*

Still, sentimental plantation films continued to be produced over the next few years, albeit with considerably less frequency than in the previous decade. The unabashedly romantic *Virginia* (1941), for instance, included a scene of an old black returning to die on the plantation, the site of his happy days as a slave; another movie released that year, *The Vanishing Virginian*, incorporated a similar scene (Campbell, *CS* 142).[45] But perhaps the most egregious and regressive film was *Song of the South* (1946), which featured live acting along with some of the most stunning cartoon animation and color techniques ever seen by movie audiences. Based on Joel Chandler Harris's *Uncle Remus* tales, the film fulfilled a private desire of its producer Walt Disney, who admitted in an interview in 1946 that "Ever since I have had anything to do with the making of motion pictures, I have wanted to bring the Uncle Remus tales to the screen. They have been in my mind since childhood" (Snead 81). But only a third of the film consisted of cartoon segments devoted to Harris's tales; the other two-thirds was a framing tale of Johnny (Bobby Driscoll), who is brought to live on his grandmother's plantation after his parents separate, and of Uncle Remus (James Baskett), the family's patriarchal black retainer. After an unhappy Johnny decides to run away, Remus diverts him by telling the story of Brer Babbit and the Fox's Trap. Later, Johnny contends with the bullying brothers of Ginny, his poor little white friend, and saves a puppy that the boys had intended to drown by applying lessons that Remus had taught him through the tale of Brer Rabbit and the Tar Baby. Later still, when Ginny's dress is muddied, she and Johnny feel dejected and decide to skip his birthday party; but Remus cheers up the children with another Brer Rabbit tale, about the "Laughing Place." Rather than being rewarded for his efforts, however, Remus is scolded and accused of interference by Johnny's mother, who forbids him to speak to the boy again. A sad-hearted Remus decides to leave the plantation, but when Johnny tries to follow and is injured by a charging bull, he returns and offers solace at the boy's bedside (a scene common to films like *Jezebel*, *Mississippi*, and *So Red the Rose*), where Johnny's newly reconciled parents have also gathered. Soon Johnny is dancing up hills again with his young friends, leaving Remus behind to try to catch up to them.

While praised for its technical excellence, especially for its innovative animation, *Song of the South* was roundly criticized for its sentimental and retrogressive vision of Southern life. As Donald Bogle writes, "had the film been made in 1929, audiences might have excused it as merely naïve and innocent" (*TCMMB* 135) rather than as corruptive propaganda. But propagandistic it was: and although Southern popular and critical response was overwhelmingly favorable, protesters from New York to Hollywood picketed the film (more heavily, in fact, than any other film since *The Birth of a Nation*); the NAACP condemned its distortions, such as the idyllic relationship between master and slave; and black politicians called for its suppression.

Indeed, as in so many earlier plantation pictures, the blacks in *Song of the South* are portrayed as being an integral part of the white family. "In almost every tableau where significant family events are shown," James Snead writes, "the black appears as a pivot of visual and emotional support"; and Uncle Remus, in particular, resolves every crisis, usually by telling a story drawn from the African traditions on which Harris based his tales. Yet each "instance of assistance meets with criticism from Johnny's elders, as if they realized the instability of their family structure, and resented Uncle Remus's (and the blacks') indispensability to that structure" (97). Remus's plight is further illustrated by the manner in which his narrative—his distinctive black voice—is silenced. By the genius of his storytelling, through which he adapts old folktales to comment on contemporary concerns (as Uncle Julius did in Chesnutt's *The Conjure Woman*), the patriarchal slave emboldens, comforts, and ultimately cures little Johnny—but, unlike Julius, he derives no personal benefit for his efforts. By the film's end, in fact, Remus's stories are usurped and exploited by Johnny, who is now able to conjure the cartoon animals to life on his own; in effect, the devoted and dutiful Remus has made himself redundant. "One must reflect on the white American commercialization of Afro-American blues, rock, and jazz," writes Snead, "to appreciate fully this allegory of cultural plunder" (96-97).

While the film turned a substantial profit for Disney and earned a special posthumous Academy Award for James Baskett, it provoked the industry into a further and even more serious reevaluation of its half-century-long cinematic glorification of the plantation tradition. Already outdated by the 1930s, that tradition was by the late 1940s even more irrefutably archaic: the happy slave singing his master's praises no longer resonated as powerfully in a postwar society in which blacks had proven themselves by going to war, by seeking and getting an education, by exercising votes, and by pressing for more skilled jobs. Moreover, the return of increasingly prosperous times reduced the need for escapist films about the Old South, especially those that failed to reflect realistically the changes in social and racial relationships.[46] As did others, Walter White called Hollywood to task by invoking "the pledges which have been made to broaden the treatment of the Negro in films" and by the need for "picturization of the Negro not as comic and menial figures but as normal human beings" (Cripps, *SFB* 387).

So while the old plantation legends and stereotypes did not disappear fully or instantly from the screen, they did at last begin—as Thomas Cripps suggests—a kind of slow fade. And subsequent film depictions of Southern life tended to be appreciably different from those in *Dixiana* and *Mississippi* or even in *Jezebel* and *Gone With the Wind*. *The Foxes of Harrow* (1947), for instance, based on a work by the acclaimed black writer Frank Yerby, offered a less fanciful picture of the Old South, with a plantation master who was of decidedly ungentlemanly bearing and a slave who was as rebellious as she was desperate. Recognizing that Yerby's "black angle" could transform the stuff of conventional Southern legend into a real black film, Twentieth Century-Fox assigned the movie to "race-conscious people," including Wanda Tuchock, who had written *Hallelujah!*, and John Stahl, who had directed *Imitation of Life*; held open casting calls in Los Angeles, to which both black actors and non-actors responded in large numbers; and gave the project a big budget and massive advertising (*MMB* 209).

In Yerby's bestselling novel *The Foxes of Harrow* (1946), Stephen Fox was a "Dublin guttersnipe," a handsome but dishonest gambler who wins money and land from a quarrelsome German, whom he ultimately kills. With his gambling gains and the backbreaking labor of his many slaves, Fox builds Harrow, the most magnificent plantation in Louisiana; and he marries the proudest and most beautiful Creole woman in New Orleans. But she turns out to be frigid; their life together proves anything but idyllic; and their only son grows to be a cruel, indolent, and unhappy young man whose sense of racial superiority leads him to try to spread the slave system to bordering states. Over the forty-year span of the novel, Fox's fortunes rise and fall: he buries his first wife after she dies trying to give him another heir, finds another Southern belle to wed, and helps the South to lose the Civil War; and in the end, he is forced to turn to one of his former slaves to seek his own release from prison.

The film, which concludes before the Civil War, offers a more upbeat Hollywood-style resolution of events. Born the illegitimate son of an Irish noblewoman on an estate called Harrow and sent away to be raised by peasants, Stephen Fox (Rex Harrison) finds his way to America, where he becomes a gambler. After acquiring both his fortune and the title to his plantation, which he names Harrow, in a riverboat game, Fox seeks social acceptance by marrying the haughty but aristocratic Creole beauty, Odalie Arceneaux (Maureen O'Hara). But an argument on their wedding night over his low-life friends results in Fox's ravishing and then abandoning his bride. As Campbell writes, "From that violent encounter, she gives birth to a son as crippled as was their love" (*CS* 154). For the next few years, Fox turns to other women for affection, while Odalie dotes on her son, Etienne; and only after a series of reverses, including the death of their child (which occurs when he falls down a long staircase during an attempt to stop his parents from quarreling), are the two reconciled. As Phyllis R. Klotman writes, the son is the imperfect child of imperfect parents who are bent on destroying each other; yet "we know that Etienne, the innocent, sacrificial lamb, will eventually bring them together, but not without more travail: financial disaster, emotional pain, and the near loss of Harrow" (218).[47]

Both versions of *The Foxes of Harrow*, however, also tell a second story, about another plantation family: the slave Achille, his "wife" Belle, and their son Inch. Achille, the son of a slave who rebelled against the French in 1795 and was hanged in punishment, proves to be far more loyal to the Fox family than his father was. But Belle—"La Belle Sauvage"—who was "straight out of Africa" at the time of her purchase in New Orleans, persists in her defiance, even after she is brought to Harrow to be "tamed." That defiance reaches its apex when she gives birth to Inch, an event that is coincident with the birth of Etienne. Upon seeing the baby, whom Belle delivered without assistance (in contrast to Odalie and her large retinue of attendants), Fox announces that he intends to make him a body slave to his own boy; but Belle resists and declares that her child will be a warrior for his people, *never* a slave. Holding Inch in her arms, she runs towards the levee with the intention of drowning them both. Although the men manage to save the baby, Belle throws herself into the rising waters of the river and dies, leaving the griefstricken Achille to pronounce "she free now" (and, in the film, to die of sorrow over her loss).

As Phyllis R. Klotman has demonstrated, Belle and Odalie are both proud and beautiful women: "both are pursued by men who inevitably 'win' them; and both produce a coveted manchild" (217). Their sons, however, are markedly different from each other. Yerby's Etienne is a mean-spirited, spiteful child who whips his pony and beats his body slave; and he grows into a brutal man who is both a rake and a drunkard. Inch, on the other hand, is an intelligent and charming child; schooled by his grandmother Caleen, who tells him to be polite, "think fast—think good," he learns to "outwit his enemies. . . . In seeming surrender, he must conquer" (162). Eventually, as a free man, Inch becomes commissioner of police in New Orleans after the fall of the Confederacy, and it is to him that Etienne must appeal for the release of his father from prison. In the film version, however, the crippled

Etienne, who is physically and ethically inferior to Inch, is conveniently dispatched in a fall. And Odalie does not die attempting to produce another heir; rather, improbably, she turns Inch into a kind of surrogate son.

While the film of *The Foxes of Harrow* made appreciable gains over other more regressive Southern sagas in depicting some of the harshness of plantation life, it nonetheless deemphasized the unique strengths of black women that Yerby had highlighted: La Belle Sauvage, who resists white exploitation; Desiree, the mulatto who experiences abuse by white men only to find a black husband—Inch—of far higher morals than his white masters; and Tante Caleen, who sees through white hypocrisies. Yerby's Caleen, in particular, had been a crucial presence in both the white and black worlds of Harrow: it was she who had been with Belle at the levee; she who had named the baby Little Inch (after Achille's father); she who predicted his future as a "man" and a "warrior" who had "in him the blood of his grandfather and of this girl" (157). And it was she who had "divined" or presided over many of the novel's most important events: the unseasonal storm that might have ruined Fox's first crop (but instead makes him wealthy); the ball to celebrate the completion of Harrow; Odalie's attempt to win back Stephen from his mulatto mistress (whom Etienne rapes and Inch later marries); the yellow fever epidemic that almost claims young Etienne's life. Predictably, though, the film reduced Caleen's role to a few peripheral scenes involving voodoo rituals. Had it been bolder in its depiction of black triumphs as well as tragedies, *The Foxes of Harrow*—as Klotman observes—would have been a more authentic portrait of its time and "a [more] harrowing experience indeed" (221).

AFRICA-BASED FILMS

Almost as popular as Hollywood's sentimentalized tales of plantation life in the Old South were jungle or tribal films with African settings. Noting the interrelationships between the two genres, James Snead wrote that the "notorious 'Africa' films" served to reinforce various familiar stereotypes, particularly of the black as primitive and bestial, and that blacks in these movies "behave with the same ineptitude and shiftlessness, even before the three hundred years of slavery and oppression, that they exhibited, according to Hollywood films, years later in America." The only explanation, Snead suggested, can be "an enduring 'black nature' that no historical tragedy or intervention has ever or could ever have been responsible for." Consequently, the history of black film stereotypes is in effect "the history of the denial of history in favor of an artificially constructed mythology about unchanging black 'character' or 'nature'" (3).

As plantation films had, jungle films distorted numerous aspects of black—and black African—culture and portrayed black characters in a decidedly unflattering way. In most Hollywood productions, James R. Nesteby observed, Africa was "used to construct a fantasy world in which film audiences could adventurously play out formulaic rituals and tensions over and over again to reaffirm the Anglo superiority complex." African natives, closely associated with the apes, gorillas, and other wild beasts that surrounded them, typically spoke "a language of mishmash with a few clearly enunciated 'ooga boogas' and 'bwanas' tossed in"; the white man usually prevailed (since white, in these films' racist vocabularies, was equal to "good," while black was equal to "bad"); and white goddesses like Tarzan's Jane existed "in the midst of blackness, literal and symbolic, just as in the film culture's vision of the Old South glorified by D. W. Griffith" (115). It was up to whites to introduce the savage blacks to civilization—and, ultimately, to subservience, even bondage—through religion or science (or some combination of the two); and only "white magic" could successfully counter the evil "black magic," or voodoo, of the natives.

The prevailing image of African blacks as ignoble savages in silent and early sound films was no doubt influenced by the Zulu revolt against the British in 1906-1907, an event portrayed by British filmmakers in *How a British Bulldog Saved the Union Jack* (1906).[48] D. W. Griffith was among the first to depict Zulus for American audiences in his film *The Zulu's Heart* (1908), in which he turned a Zulu chief (played in blackface by an unknown white actor) into an African version of the stereotypically loyal family servant: the chief defies his own people to defend a white widow and her young daughter. Comic versions soon followed. In *Rastus in Zululand* (1910), Rastus finds himself in Zululand, faced with the choice of wedding the chief's repulsive daughter or being boiled as dinner by the cannibalistic tribe; but he is soon relieved to discover that he had dreamed the entire adventure. In *The Zulu King* (1913), the henpecked John Smith runs away, uses a blank pistol to convince the Zulus who capture him that he is bulletproof, and briefly assumes leadership of the tribe before being deposed by Mrs. Smith, who in his absence has become a missionary. And in *In Zululand* (1915), a rare early all-black-cast production, Zebo (John Edwards), a lazy black man looking for an easy life, pursues Queen Cocoa (Mattie Edwards), but their romance is curtailed by the appearance of two "ghosts" (actually the Queen's daughters in disguise).

Zulus, however, were not the only native peoples to be so trivialized and misrepresented on screen; as Nesteby writes, "by the time that *The Birth of a Nation* codified the Afro-American image in film, interest was high in Africa as an alternative to the Old South as a setting for superiority fantasies" (117). That interest, fed by early documentaries like *Tuaregs in Their Country* (1909) and *Life in Senegal* (1910), led to fictional film versions like *Voodoo Vengeance* (1913); *A Night in the Jungle* (1915); *The Lad and the Lion* (1916), the first film based on a work by Edgar Rice Burroughs, the creator of Tarzan; and, of course, *Tarzan of the Apes* (1918), which introduced the legendary character to the screen and spawned a host of sequels (including *The Romance of Tarzan* [1918]; *The Adventures of Tarzan* [1920/serial; 1928/feature]; *The Son of Tarzan* [1920/serial]; *Tarzan and the Golden Lion* [1927]; *Tarzan the Mighty* [1928/serial]; and *Tarzan and the Tiger* [1929/serial])[49] as well as generic Tarzan imitators in films such as *The Jungle Trail* (1919). Burroughs's work, as Thomas Cripps has shown, rested on a firm base of nineteenth-century exploration and curiosity about the new anthropology and remote peoples, leavened by the safaris and hunts of Theodore Roosevelt and other public figures, and booms in conservationism and in western camping; yet unlike earlier silent movies that featured expeditions and wild animals, Burroughs's contribution to American cinema was "a white man lowered as a *deus ex machina* into the jungle, where, in the author's racist scheme, he learns to use its lore with greater effect than the natives" (*SFB* 124-25).

Silent film treatments of the jungle theme varied widely, from serious or melodramatic to comic. In *Missionaries in Darkest Africa*

(1912), a Kalem film produced by Sidney Olcott and the first photoplay actually to be shot in Africa, the chief of the tribe falls in love with—and kidnaps—Reverend Elbert Lawrence's daughter Faith, who kills herself rather than submit to the savage (much as Flora in *The Birth of a Nation* preferred suicide to rape by the ex-slave Gus).[50] In *The Jungle Outcasts* (1916), which harks back to the loyal Tom tradition, the old black warrior Waji is abandoned by his tribe but continues to care for shipwreck victim Margaret Wright and her daughter Louise until she is reunited with her husband.[51] Comic treatments, on the other hand, featured cannibals, stewpots, and love-starved primitive queens, usually of elephantine proportions. In *King of Cannibal Island* (1908), for instance, henpecked Heinie Holtmeyer escapes his wife Lena by taking to the seas, where he weds the cannibal queen, becomes king of the island, and—after Lena finds him—consigns her to the pot as retribution for her earlier behavior. In Edison's *The Missionary and the Maid* (1909), missionary Henry Herbert is saved from the tribal pot by the chieftain's fat daughter Umplika, whom he is forced to wed; but, as in *Rastus in Zululand*, the entire misadventure turns out to be just a dream—real enough, though, for Henry, who chooses to give up the cloth. And in *Wurra Wurra* (1916), the cannibal queen must decide whether to boil or wed the shipwrecked sailors who wash up on her island's shore. (Notably, the black tribal kings and queens in these period pictures—like the early Toms and Mammies—were played by white actors and actresses in blackface.)

With interest in unusual and exotic locales stirred concurrently by novels like Edith M. Hull's *The Sheik* and theatrical productions like *White Cargo*, jungle films remained popular throughout the 1920s; and, by the early era of sound movies, they reached both new heights and new depths. *Trader Horn* (1931), one of the classic African melodramas of the period, was distinguished by the fact that it used actual location footage; but otherwise the tale of a blonde jungle queen dressed in wisps of monkey fur who surrenders her authority to a white invader was standard fare, particularly in its depiction of blacks as ignorant savages. (Interestingly, even in jungle films, blacks—like the few but fearsome brutal buck types of early silent films—could never be *too* savage: Daniel J. Leab [103] cites one of the filmmakers of *Rhodes of Africa* [Gaumont, 1935], who noted that battle scenes between Zulus and whites in the film were cut to a minimum since "it was not thought wise . . . to show in full scale such a realistic battle between black and white.") Realism was also often forsaken for spectacle that emphasized the strangeness of blacks' behavior, such as the wild native dance and the tribal flagellation ceremony in *Dark Rapture* (Universal, 1937).

Tarzan, the Ape Man (1932) revived the Tarzan craze: Jane, an Englishwoman accompanying her father, realizes that she prefers the pure beauty of Africa (depicted in film footage recycled from *Trader Horn*) to the civilized world she has left behind; and, of course, she prefers the noble Tarzan, who rescues her from an angry ape, to the witless fiancé she abandons. The success of this first sound version of Tarzan gave rise to many sequels, portions of which were later pieced together for the *Tarzan* television series, which ran on the NBC network from 1966 until 1968.[52] Significantly, as Thomas Cripps outlines in *Slow Fade to Black*, the direction of the Tarzan movies changed over the years, from films that focused on animals, contrasted the simple pleasures of the jungle to the decadence of civilization, and "appealed to a self-satisfied racial cockiness rather than hyperaggressive racism" to less ambiguously racist depictions of inferior tribesman that cheapened—and ultimately abandoned—Burroughs's original concept. Responding to pressure from the NAACP and from the Hays Office to downplay black heavies and miscegenation subplots,[53] the producers of the Tarzan films started moving their hero out of the jungle and into other exotic locales: Thailand, where he travels to protect a young heir to the throne from his malevolent uncle; the Amazon, where he saves treasures that archeologists attempt to plunder; India, where at the request of a dying maharajah he preserves a herd of elephants imperiled by the construction of a dam; even Manhattan, where—on separate occasions—he rescues Cheetah and Boy. With each successive film, however, Tarzan lost some of his primitive grandeur and eventually became, as Leonard Maltin called him, a kind of jungle James Bond for hire; and in the worst of the pictures, his adventures were overshadowed by chauvinistic and invidious comparisons of whites with other races.[54]

As had the earlier silent *Tarzan of the Apes*, the 1932 sound version of *Tarzan, the Ape Man* led to a host of Tarzan imitators, like the short *Kid 'n Africa* (1932), in which Shirley Temple, playing an

African missionary, is captured by tiny cannibals and rescued from the pot by a small Tarzan named "Diaperzan" and his elephant; *King of the Jungle* (1933), starring black actor Sam Baker and Olympic champion Buster Crabbe, "king of the jungle"; and other African-themed features like the bizarre *Africa Speaks English* (1933), with ventriloquist Edgar Bergen. Yet ironically, in many of these films set in or about "black Africa," blacks were offered parts that were at best peripheral and always stereotypical. Even in major productions like *The African Queen* (1952) and *Mogambo* (1953), the black actors served largely as scenery rather than as characters who are seminal to the plot developments—a trend evident even in films as recent as *Raiders of the Lost Ark* (1981).

Like jungle films in general, jungle animal films had great popular appeal for white audiences. "Elaborate unconscious allegories for the 'black brutes' of white Southern folklore" (Cripps, *SFB* 155), these films usually failed to depict African life authentically or honestly. Silents like *Gorilla Hunt* (1926), *Through Darkest Africa: In Search of the White Rhinoceros* (1927), *The Bushman* (1927), and *Simba* (1927), for example, offered staged bits like pygmy action and tribal dances along with glimpses of wild animals. Even more contrived was another silent, *Ingagi* (1930), which introduced an especially vicious "type": the gorilla—a coded image of the bestial, lustful black—who lusts after a white woman. ("Gorilla," with its obvious racist overtones, was a word that Thomas Dixon had used to describe blacks in *The Clansman*.)

But it was another animal film, *King Kong* (RKO, 1933), that became a classic, both of cinematic folklore and of racist Hollywood filmmaking, and that—according to numerous film critics and historians—is considered an underground allegory for the black experience. Kong, a monster ape who is king of an island that seems lost in time, is captured by Carl Denham (Robert Armstrong), brought in bondage to America, and chained on a New York City stage where he is gawked at and tormented. (Fig. 3.6.) "He has always been king of his world," shouts one of his tormentors, "but we'll teach him fear." As Thomas Cripps writes (*SFB* 278), Kong thus "becomes a tragic figure, colonized, enslaved, cut from bucolic roots, destroyed by the city atop the empty engineering triumph, the Empire State Building, but to the end capable of love, cradling his miniature blonde co-star aloft

Figure 3.6. *King Kong,* the victim of colonization and ridicule, became a coded image of black enslavement. *(RKO, 1933)*

before his fall from the great tower. In the end Kong became an enduring mythic figure, part 'bad nigger' and part universal victim of exploitation." James Snead, who in his essay on "Spectatorship and Capture in *King Kong*: The Guilty Look" examined the film's various images of enslavement—e.g., Kong's journey to America as "an allegory of the slave trade" (17) and his captivity on the stage platform as "an 'auction block'" (18)—concludes that *King Kong* is also the "most blatant [cinematic] linkage of the black with that of the monster" (7). Surprisingly, unlike Snead, many white critics entirely failed—or chose not—to make the black-white connection. For Andrew Bergman, for instance, *King Kong* was a film not about racial relations but about "the nation's ambivalent feelings toward her greatest metropolis and its concern over social and economic chaos and incipient collapse," a "popular culture's reflection of the 'back to the earth' movement" that was full of "sentimental yearnings for a Jeffersonian life on the land" (70).

In the disappointingly weak sequel *Son of Kong* (1930), Denham (Robert Armstrong) ventures back to Skull Island, where he discovers Kong's son and offers an apology of sorts for his earlier actions; but the poor ape, along with all of the natives, ends up dead—although not before he saves Denham and his female companion from the earthquake that drowns the island.[55] A later film, *Mighty Joe Young* (1949), returned to—and tried to reverse—the original King Kong theme, as the eponymous ape is transported to America and exploited by Max O'Hara (Robert Armstrong), the sleazy owner of the African-themed "Golden Safari" club that Joe destroys, before escaping execution and returning to Africa with Jill, the white woman who raised him.[56] Back home in a now-colonized Africa, however, Joe is much less mighty than he was before. Yet while Joe, like Kong's son, is marginally less threatening than the amorous Kong who runs amok in New York City with the white woman he has abducted, all three are—as Snead (36) demonstrates—"coded blacks," whose racial color signifies their primitivism, elementalism, and menace; and the purpose of the films in which they appear is largely "to demonize blackness" by glorifying and mythifying archetypal white male and female types.

BLACK VARIATIONS ON THE AFRICA THEME

A decade after the original *Ingagi* was released, *Son of Ingagi* (1940; dir. Richard C. Kahn) introduced audiences to another "big ape"; but the film also distinguished itself in other more important ways. The first horror film with an all-black cast, *Son of Ingagi* was based on "House of Horror," an original story written by Spencer Williams, Jr., best known for his role as Amos Brown on the old *Amos 'n' Andy* television series that ran from 1951 to 1953 (Moon 367-68). Williams was truly a veteran of the industry: in New York, he had worked as a call boy to Oscar Hammerstein and learned comedy from the legendary performer Bert Williams; in Hollywood, he initially found employment with Al Christie at Paramount Studios, where he moved from technician to continuity writer for the Christie Comedies (a role in which he redrafted material like the comedic and usually racist stories of Octavus Roy Cohen to include more authentic black nuances) and finally to actor at Paramount and other major studios.[57] Eventually, he also became a film director—Mark A. Reid called him "the last important African-American filmmaker before Hollywood began hiring black directors in the Seventies" (Crowdus 5)—and an activist who lobbied for more honesty in black film roles and for other vital changes, like the appointment of "a national Negro censor" in the film industry.

No doubt Williams's acting work in such original films as the first all-black Western musicals *Bronze Buckaroo* (1938), *Harlem on the Prairie* (1938), and *Harlem Rides the Range* (1939)—all filmed on a black dude ranch near Victorville, California—led him to embark on an even more pioneering project: the writing of the screenplay for the first all-black horror film, which incorporated some of the elements of the familiar Kong story. In *Son of Ingagi* (fig. 3.7), a reclusive woman scientist, Dr. Helen Jackson (Laura Bowman), returns from Africa with In'Gina (Zack Williams), the half-ape, half-man son of Ingagi, whom she confines to the basement of her gloomy mansion and uses as the subject of her experiments. After

Figure 3.7. A lobby card from the first all-black-cast horror film, *Son of Ingagi*, written by and starring Spencer Williams, Jr. *(Richard C. Kahn/Hollywood Productions, 1940)*

accidentally killing the doctor, the beast kills her brother, an ex-convict named Zeno (Arthur Ray), and a greedy lawyer (Earl J. Morris), both of whom are in search of the gold that she had brought back from Africa and hidden in her home. In'Gina, wounded in the confrontation with Zeno, finds himself trapped in the basement and left to perish in a fire that he has inadvertently caused. Afterwards, Detective Nelson (Spencer Williams, Jr.) discovers the gold and awards it, as Dr. Jackson had willed, to the newlywed daughter (Daisy Bufford) of a man the doctor once loved.

In an interview with the *Pittsburgh Courier* (28 Dec. 1939), Williams declared that he and the film's other producers "felt that the gangster type of motion picture was played out" and it was his intention to "give the public a different kind of vehicle." In'Gina, the son of Ingagi, he stated, "is in truth symbolic of the baser natures of people. Laura Bowman as a great woman scientist actually represents our better qualities. And the age-old struggle between good and evil is personified in this film production" (qtd. in Sampson 424). In fact, by casting both the "good" and the "bad" in the same "Hollywood sepia," Williams managed to deflate some of the racism underlying the Kong myth. And, like Oscar Micheaux, by choosing to tell a familiar story in an unfamiliar way (with nontraditional black casting), Williams challenged Hollywood's formulas and inverted an old genre to create a new one. Ultimately, though, *Son of Ingagi* is memorable less for its plot than for its place in black cinema history.

Hollywood's African-themed films also featured a lot of voodoo. Occasionally invoked for the benefit of whites, as in the Metro production, *The Voice of Conscience* (1917), voodoo was more often used against them, as in Columbia's *Black Moon* (1934), in which blacks try to kill off white islanders.[58] And voodoo legends, especially those that originated in West Africa about zombies, became a motif in yet another movie cycle that tried "to keep alive the African flavor in films and to emphasize the primitiveness of people who believe in black magic and witchcraft" (Nesteby 126). Zombies appeared in, among others, the Bob Hope-Willie Best comedy, *The Ghost Breakers* (Paramount, 1940); *King of the Zombies* (Monogram, 1941); *Revenge of the Zombies* (Monogram, 1943); and *I Walked with a Zombie* (RKO, 1943); and their appearance served either to underscore the notion of the black as a grotesquely "unhuman" object and a purveyor of fear and evil or to high-light—and ultimately ridicule—the stereotypical black fear of ghosts and similar apparitions by placing iconic emphasis on white racial superiority (Pines 43, 41).

Even *Drums O'Voodoo* (1933), alternatively titled *Voodoo Drums* and *Louisiana* and re-released in 1940 as *She Devil*—one of the few films of the period to be adapted from black literature—hardly managed to rise above the usual Hollywood fare in its depiction of African customs and motifs. The first known feature-length sound movie to be adapted from a dramatic work by a black playwright, *Drums O'Voodoo* was based on the stage play *Louisiana* by J. Augustus Smith. Its plot focused on a small Louisiana community whose citizens are divided among Christians who attend the church run by Elder Amos Berry (played by J. Augustus Smith), voodoo followers who worship at a shrine in the nearby swamps tended by Aunt Hager (Laura Bowman), and the godless sinners who frequent the jook joint run by Thomas "Tom" Catt (Morris McKinney). The story begins with Myrtle Simpson (Edna Barr), Elder Berry's niece, who after many years returns home, where she is pursued by Tom Catt, to whom her uncle is secretly paying hush money. Myrtle, it turns out, is in love with Aunt Hager's grandson Ebenezer, whom she is unable to marry because a voodoo curse has been cast upon her. After Berry refuses to persuade Myrtle to work at the sinful jook joint, Catt exposes him by revealing that the Elder is a murderer and a fugitive from a chain gang. For his evil acts—and in fulfillment of a voodoo curse—Catt is struck by light-ning, blinded, and finally killed by quicksand. Berry then admits that his crime was committed in self-defense, and he receives for-giveness from his congregation. And after Aunt Hager sounds the voodoo drums to remove the curse from the young woman, Myrtle and Ebenezer make plans to wed. According to Cripps, the "'amateurish' support," the "improbable string of brandished razors, heavies blinded by lightning, voodoo drums, a 'snakehips' dance in a brothel, and a rousing revival meeting" all "broke Loew's Harlem house into laughter" (*SFB* 326).

By contrast, a better and more interesting treatment of black religion also rooted in African cultural belief was *Go Down, Death!* (1944), another film adapted from black literature and directed and produced by Spencer Williams, Jr. and his "Harlemwood

Studios."[59] "Go Down Death"—the short poem by James Weldon Johnson upon which the film was based and by which it was "inspired"—is, as its subtitle suggests, "A Funeral Sermon" for Sister Caroline, a good woman called home to rest "in the bosom of Jesus." Seeing Caroline "tossing on her bed of pain," God commands Death to "go down," through "heaven's pearly gates, past sun and moon and stars," and "bring her to me." Death does not frighten Caroline; in fact, "he looked to her like a welcome friend." In his icy arms she is taken to the Great White Throne. "And Jesus took his own hand and wiped away her tears, / And he smoothed the furrows from her face, / And the angels sang a little song."

In Williams's film, Caroline (Myra Hemmings) is the kindly foster mother to Jim (Spencer Williams, Jr.), the owner of a local nightclub. When Reverend Jasper's preaching cuts into Jim's business, he conspires to set up the man of God by photographing him in a compromising situation with three streetwalkers. The high-moraled Caroline tries to convince Jim to return the photos, which are hidden in his safe; and when he refuses, she is led to them by the ghost of her dead husband. After Jim catches her, they argue and she falls unconscious to the ground. Awakening just long enough to announce that "I'm going home," she dies. At her funeral, the Reverend delivers a moving sermon taken almost verbatim from Johnson's poem. Overcome by the voice of his conscience and by the graphic images of hellfire that it connotes, Jim (who lied and said it was a burglar who had assaulted Caroline) is found dead only hours later. The beauty of the film lies not in any technical innovation or sophistication—like many race films, it is relatively crude—but rather in its simple yet stirring evocations of cultural and religious rituals, such as the funeral that is arranged by the women's burial society and attended by all members of the community; of the music, spirituals, and prayers that evoke an African folkloric quality; and of the contrasting visions of Heaven and Hell that illustrate "the Triumph of Good Over Evil."

Although Hollywood's African jungle films were at worst blatantly racist and at best distorted or contrived, they did offer occasional employment to many of the finest black performers of the day, including Clarence Muse, Dorothy Dandridge, Ernest Whitman, Noble Johnson, Daniel Haynes, and Rex Ingram. Yet even as brilliant an actor as Paul Robeson found himself, to some extent, typecast in such limiting and often insulting productions. In *The Emperor Jones* (1933), a critically hailed film based on the Eugene O'Neill play (1920), which was one of the first important attempts by a white writer to deal with black characters in a serious drama, Robeson had successfully re-created his role as anti-hero Brutus Jones, an American ex-Pullman porter, who—by sheer nerve—becomes emperor of a tropical island, assumes a dictatorship, and is finally killed by the uprising natives.[60] (Fig 3.8.) A commanding black character who is the intellectual and social equal of whites, Jones did not fall into the traditional categories of comic servant or naïve folk type; and Robeson's nuanced portrayal of Jones remains among his most memorable performances. Yet while later films returned Robeson to similarly exotic locations, they failed to offer parts with the same substance or sense of majesty. For instance, in the British-made *Sanders of the River* (1935), based on an Edgar Wallace story, Robeson appeared as Bosambo, an African ruler who commands the blacks but acts subserviently to whites. According to his biographer Edwin P. Hoyt, Robeson accepted the role because the project was "described to

Figure 3.8. Brutus Jones (Paul Robeson) is haunted by the spirits of the islanders in *The Emperor Jones. (United Artists, 1933)*

him as an opportunity to show much of the true African culture."
Robeson, inspired by the proposed use of native song and dance
that coincided with his interest in Africa and its culture and with
his artistic curiosity about and theatrical interpretation of racial
folk motifs, realized only when the film was being edited that the
studio had reshaped it from its original description "into blatant
imperialist propaganda" (Pines 31). In *Jericho* (1937), another
British film, Robeson played an American soldier who avoids a
death sentence for a crime he did not commit by becoming
involved with a Tuareg tribe in the Sahara and eventually becoming its chief. In *Song of Freedom* (1937), he starred as Zinga, an
African expatriate who tries to return to help his people; in *King
Solomon's Mines* (1937), based on H. Rider Haggard's 1885 novel,
he was Umbopas, the Mashona chief who leads the whites to the
elusive mines. As James Nesteby (130) observed, though
Robeson's performances were consistently dignified and effused
his strong presence, in his many jungle films he was "always portrayed as being in the service of whites." And Robeson's hopes for
engendering major changes in the industry—like those of other
actors and activists—were for the most part frustrated.

In the early decades of sound film, then, although blacks had
begun increasingly to appear in major studio productions and to
be accepted as a popular and permanent aspect of Hollywood cinema, their onscreen image continued to be patterned on the racial
and ideological influences as well as on the reactionary and paternalistic values of the late silent film era. Racial representation
throughout the 1930s and well into the 1940s remained largely a
matter of black and white—that is, of black inferiority and white
superiority—as racial myths were reinforced and re-created
through "the continuous flow of reactionary Southern drama plas-
tered with Old South Civil War romanticism, Jim Crow Musicals,
a monotonous collection of family retainers and comic relief characters, and the occasional appearance of a black character
endowed with racial dignity" (Pines 44). In addition to glorifying
the Old South by fostering the myth of the kindly master and his
happy slaves, popular films also exploited the African "Dark
Continent" by giving white audiences a taste of the exotic locales
they craved—both in the films actually set in Africa and in the
films that featured African-themed nightclubs or other "tribal"

forms of entertainment—while reaffirming the primitivism of native blacks. These pictures, moreover, promoted a kind of racial segregation by suggesting that blacks belonged among their own kind, whether it be on the plantation or in the jungle, but always under the guiding hand of the superior whites. (After all, as James Nesteby implies, what is Tarzan if not "the fictional overseer of the world's largest plantation" [137].)

Even as the escapist Depression-era urge for nostalgic and sentimentalized visions of the Old South began to fade and as stories with African locales eventually fell into B-movies, serials, comedies, and cartoons (Cripps, *SFB* 277), Hollywood films continued to be marked by vulgar racial images of subservience (e.g., the typecasting of such fine character actresses as Hattie McDaniel, Louise Beavers, Ethel Waters, and Butterfly McQueen as domestics) and of ineptitude and buffoonishness (e.g., the "darky" roles played by Stepin Fetchit, Willie Best, and Mantan Moreland). Only a small number of race film producers were still in business by 1940, a point by which even the tenacious Micheaux had retired from film to return to novel-writing (although he came out of retirement, briefly and unsuccessfully, for *The Betrayal* [1948]). And the few who remained were largely white-financed (as even Micheaux had been in his final decades of filmmaking) and turned out a product that, with a few notable exceptions like Clarence Muse's *Broken Strings* (1940), had "dissolved into a mirror reversal of Hollywood": black gangsters, black molls, black heavies, black cowboys, even stereotyped mimics such as Fetchit and Moreland duplicating their Hollywood roles in race films (*SFB* 330). The infrequent Hollywood film like Mervyn LeRoy's *They Won't Forget* (1937), based on Ward Greene's book *Death in the Deep South*, that marked a liberalization of racial attitudes was more a reflection of the commitment of the individual movie director than of the industry in general.

With the new race problem and social message films of the postwar period, however, would come a modification and liberalization of black racial imagery, both in Hollywood mainstream movies and in the independently produced *Native Son*, based on the best-selling protest novel by Richard Wright, that suggested a new perspective on the black urban experience and signaled an important direction in American cinema.

NOTES TO CHAPTER 3

1. Williams, *Playing the Race Card* 141-42. Williams cites Michael Rogin's argument that blackface was a means of whitewashing the assimilated Jew. Since Jewishness disappeared behind the mask of blackface, posing as black ultimately became a way of passing as white.

2. The film is ultimately a critique of "the reduction of Jewish-American history to a family melodrama . . . in which the generalized woes of slaves speak for the woes of Jews." For Rogin, anti-Semitism is "the film's structuring absence, while blackface performance, reaching back to the origins of American mass entertainment in minstrelsy, disguises this absence through the substitute pathos of mammy songs" (Williams, *Race* 154).

3. *Wonder Bar*, another Warner Brothers' film, contained "one of the most tasteless production sequences that ever caricatured black men and women"; in that sequence, Al Wonder (Jolson), the owner of a Montmartre cabaret, takes the stage in blackface and—joined by a small army of singers and dancers—wends his way to a black heaven, "a place of eternal watermelon feasts, gambling, chicken thieving, and choral syncopation" (Leab 84-85). In *Big Boy*, Jolson took his routine even further: he played not just a blackface minstrel but an actual black character named Gus, a jockey at the Bedford Stables, who knows his humble place and observes Southern custom. Only at the end of the film does Jolson become his white "self." The performance, it turns out, was all part of a sales pitch for a new musical that Jolson is promoting. Thus, as Cripps writes (*SFB* 254), "as he betrayed blacks in the picture, so in the end he betrays the audience by denying everything."

4. Jolson raised the ire of blacks in other ways as well: as the *California New-Age Dispatch* (1 April 1938) reported, Jolson became involved in a restrictive residential covenant designed to discriminate against "non-Caucasians" and bar such individuals from certain neighborhoods. Around the same time, however, Jolson was perceived by some blacks as "an ardent friend of the Negro" for his professional alliance with black featherweight boxing champion Henry Armstrong (qtd. in Everett 214-16).

5. It was precisely the film's postwar setting, writes Edward D. C. Campbell, Jr. (*CS* 86-87), that made the film's idyllic South appear even more appealing. "The picture gave few signs of any significant changes from the antebellum culture, thus implying strongly how persevering the system was. In fact, many reviewers were confused and indeed regarded the movie as a tale of the Old South. The film was thus representative of the fascination with the delights of both the prewar and postwar South and how the two periods in fact blended in the public's imagination."

6. Despite its shortcomings, the full-length production of *Hearts in Dixie* was, as Campbell notes, "unique among major Depression films in showing rural black joys, sorrows, and ambitions without constant white influence" (*CS* 86).

7. Contemporary critic Henry Dobb, writing in *Close Up*, observed that "The tragedy is not the tragedy in the film, but the tragedy of the film; the tragedy of these untainted folk strutting their stuff to the required pattern, playing their parts as the white man likes to believe they do. . . . if 'Hearts in Dixie' is a specimen of colored expression under the aegis of Hollywood let us next time hand the whole process over to the Negroes themselves" (qtd. in Noble 51).

8. Lawrence Reddick acknowledged that Stepin Fetchit was "the star" of the film, but he stated that "his [Fetchit's] great art was used to drive in deeper than ever the stereotype of the lazy Negro good-for-nothing" (11). Contemporary opinion of Fetchit's performance, however, was more favorable. Alain Locke and Sterling A. Brown called Fetchit's acting "incomparable" and concluded that "Fetchit in this picture is as true as instinct itself, . . . a real child of the folk spirit" (26-27). Robert Benchley, in "*Hearts in Dixie* (The First Real Talking Picture)," offered even higher praise. Fetchit, with his "amazing personality," Benchley wrote, "is the best actor that the talking movies have produced. His voice, his manner, his timing, everything that he does, is as near to perfection as one could hope to get" in this new medium. "When Stepin Fetchit speaks, you are there beside him, one of the great comedians of the screen" (85).

9. Surprisingly, while they praised Fetchit's performance in *Hearts in Dixie*, which projected "the folk manner," Locke and Brown criticized "siren and villain" McKinney and Fountaine in *Hallelujah!* for their "obvious type acting," which "furnishes no such folk values as the nuances of the other characters" (28, 26).

10. A certain racism was also evident in the promotion of the film. Many theaters chose to announce their bookings of *Hearts in Dixie* by emphasizing the film's "blend of Southern charm and Negro happiness and gratitude" and by deliberately downplaying the story's black cast. "The practice," writes Campbell (*CS* 89), "also forestalled any adverse reaction to a nearly all-Negro company until the viewer could see for himself how traditional the interpretation actually was. In Richmond and Louisville, posters were accented by a mansion surrounded by trees covered with Spanish moss; the movie included no such scene." Similar advertisements, usually depicting affluent whites who played no part in the film, appeared throughout the North. By contrast, in the South, the film's promotions incorporated the romanticism involved in the picture's view of black workers. Posters bordered with cottonballs depicted dancing blacks and riverboats and promised "shufflin' feet and levee lyrics" that displayed the "loves of mammyland."

11. Thomas Cripps (*SFB* 245) writes that "in the white press the patri-archal Gray was called 'Dad' and reported to have been a North Carolina slave 'discovered' either on the street in New York or preaching in a Chicago church. But to blacks on the *Tatler* he was a fool 'who struts around Harlem in a plug hat and cutaway coat reminiscent of the days when minstrelsy was in flower.'"

12. The train to Hell was a popular device not only in black sermons but also in other early black pictures. Black female filmmaker and "cine-matic foremother" Eloyce King Patrick Gist, for instance, produced *Hell Bound Train* sometime in the late 1920s or early 1930s; and by the mid-1930s, she and her husband toured with that and another of their films, *Verdict Not Guilty*, in and around Washington, D.C. Both films, writes Gloria J. Gibson, advocated "Christian behavior and the importance of family" (200). *Hell Bound Train* was structured as a journey; the various scenarios were personal accounts of struggles between right and wrong, good and evil. "Satan, Lucifer," who is the train's engineer, offers "Free admission to all—just give your life and soul. No round trip tickets—one way only." For a fuller discussion of the film and of Gist herself, see Gibson's "Cinematic Foremothers: Zora Neale Hurston and Eloyce King Patrick Gist," particularly pp. 199-204.

13. Mordaunt Hall also noted that "the humor that issues from *Hallelujah* is natural unto the negro, whether it deals with a hankering after salvation, the dread of water in baptism, the lure of 'come seven, come 'leven,' or the belated marital ceremonies."

14. Although Locke and Brown noted the "obviousness" of the per-formances of Nina Mae McKinney and William Fountaine and the over-ly "determined" utterance of dialect by Zeke (Daniel Haynes), they con-cluded nonetheless that *Hallelujah!* was "important": "Its pioneering, its very faults, promise a great deal" (29).

15. Mainstream films typically were booked in separate and stag-gered premieres at white and black theaters, so the simultaneous pre-mieres of *Hallelujah!* broke with established practices. There was, howev-er, racism motivating the simultaneous premieres in the de facto segre-gated black and white theaters. See Everett, 175-77.

16. Similarly, Leab (93) noted of Vidor that "If his presentation of the black was less crude than those in films such as *Hearts in Dixie*, the dif-ference was one of sophistication rather than content, for he succeeded merely in dressing up the old image rather than in creating black human beings."

17. Locke and Brown called it "the usual claptrap. It is obviously ambitious, attempting to fuse elements as diversified as Cohen's humor and *Porgy*'s rhythmic design, as Berlin's mammy songs and the spiritual. It results in a potpourri, made no more palatable by its great dependence on rather stale ingredients" (27).

18. Harold Garrison may have been the film's assistant director, but, as Cripps (*SFB* 250) notes, "at a white opening," he was "herded to the Jim Crow gallery" of the theater.

19. Johnson had had some earlier experiences with silent film. He recalled that in the 1920s, "I wrote a half-dozen short scenarios and promptly sold three of them. We saw the exhibition of the first picture and were so disappointed in it that we were actually ashamed to see the others" (*That's Black Entertainment*, OnDeck Home Entertainment Video, 1997).

20. According to Arthur Draper in "Uncle Tom Will Never Die!," *So Red the Rose* "deliberately portrays the Negro masses of the South as stupid, sullen rioters. . . . The story is a libelous presentation of Southern Negroes of the Civil War period. It pictures their revolt from the owners as based upon laziness, greed, and hysteria. In the picture, its leaders are opportunists, misleading a simpleminded people" (30-31).

21. Leab writes that, in fact, a movie company executive told a black newspaperman that "it does not suffice that the East, West, and North accept Negro pictures . . . [since] the South refuses to accept pictures wherein Negroes are starred" (95).

22. The "nameless enemy" whom Hezdrel fights, according to Cripps, "can only be racism" (*SFB* 260).

23. "In view of the play's enormous popularity with white audiences," Anna Everett concludes, "which resulted in the production being held over for an entire year's run, the theater owners concluded that black patronage was inconsequential" (206).

24. Cripps (*SFB* 262) writes that there were, in fact, two versions of *Way Down South*, both produced by Sol Lesser and utilizing—albeit minimally—the writing talents of Clarence Muse. The first was a short film directed by Leslie Goodwins and released in 1937, the plot of which involved the marriage of two slaves. Zeke and "Ca'line" are anxious to marry and to celebrate their union; their friends, the other pickers, "are saddened only by the demands of picking that will keep them from raising a house for the lovers—saddened, that is, until the white boss paternally lets off the whole gang." The scene, full of church singing, moves quickly from a fine country barbeque to the wedding feast, a "gran' march," a cakewalk, and finally the houseraising, after which the newlywed couple stand in the doorway of their new place as the chorus sings "My Old Kentucky Home." Two years later, Lesser expanded the film into a feature, at which time Langston Hughes joined Muse to form the writing team of the revised 1939 version of *Way Down South* as a vehicle for child star Bobby Breen.

Larry Richards, however, in *African American Films Through 1959: A Comprehensive Illustrated Filmography*, indicates that the earlier film about the black couple who celebrate their wedding with the other slaves in their plantation community was called *Deep South* (1937), not *Way Down South*; and he makes no links between the two films. Richards also lists Bert Gilroy, not Sol Lesser, as producer of the former and Leslie Goodwins as director.

25. Larry Richards (174) suggests that *Toussaint L'Ouverture* (Blue Ribbon Pictures), in which Muse made his debut as producer and director (and was also the sole cast member), may never have been released. Thomas Cripps (*SFB* 76) notes that some of Muse's work, like that of "other early pioneers, went largely unrecorded."

26. The Hall Johnson Choir became a staple in many of Hollywood's black-oriented films. The Choir appeared in, among other pictures, *The Green Pastures*, *Dimples*, *Lost Horizon*, *Way Down South*, *Swanee River*, *Lady for a Night*, and *Tales of Manhattan*. In "Winds of Change: *Gone With the Wind* and Racism as a National Issue" (143), Cripps states that NAACP member Walter White suggested to David O. Selznick, producer of *Gone With the Wind*, the name of Hall Johnson as a possible advisor on the film. (White himself had earlier been approached by Selznick to serve in that same capacity.) Cripps writes, "For a black adviser on the set he [White] recommended Hall Johnson, a veteran Hollywood choir director whose livelihood depended upon getting along with studio bosses. Indeed, Johnson confessed to Myrick [a white female technical advisor to Selznick] that he was 'unhappy that some of his race failed so miserably to understand' *Gone With the Wind*." There is no record, however, that Johnson went on to serve in any official capacity in the production.

27. As Campbell writes in *The Celluloid South* (115-16), even the advertising for the film was traditional. "Bulletins stressed banjo-strumming, grinning, and dancing slaves. And captions promised 'a loveable, thrilling show of plantation life resplendent with magic and songs,' or 'happiness from ringing Dixie-land' with its 'jungle-born dances.' Studio-supplied publicity articles repeatedly claimed that the picture of the 'land the Lord shakes hands with' was 'realistically held together' by the plot which with its estate of four hundred slaves presented 'all the charms of easy-going life.'"

28. Additionally, some of the dialogue managed to capture the richness of black folk drama. When the slave Luke realizes that he is to be sold off and separated from his beloved Lulu, he prays aloud: "Oh, the foxes, they have holes in the ground; the birds have nests in the air; and everything's got a hiding place. But us poor sinners ain't got nowhere."

29. Interestingly, the same spiritual is sung in *The Littlest Rebel*. When Mrs. Herbert Cary, mother of Virgie Cary (Shirley Temple) dies, she is buried—notably in an almost all-black funeral (Shirley's father being the only other white in attendance); appropriately, the blacks sing

"Sometimes I Feel Like a Motherless Child" for the little girl. Moreover, as James Snead (58) writes, to demonstrate that "blacks are not here [in this film] for themselves, clearly, but mainly for others, and more precisely, *for whites* . . . they—among other things—set up elaborate scouting networks to allow the Confederate Captain Cary to slip past Union lines, preside over the secreting of household items, and organize Mrs. Cary's funeral."

30. According to Cripps in *Slow Fade to Black* (208-09), after cinema made the transition to talking films, Kenneth Macpherson brought together a group in Territet, Switzerland, that hoped to "purge cinema of commercialism, bring it to bear on social problems, and shape it into a universal language." But that group lacked "organization, money, and artistic definition." Nonetheless, Macpherson pressed forward to form Pool Films, which he hoped would "produce 'jagged' visual poems filled with 'tension' and 'vague symbolism.' In 1929 they attempted to enlist the American Negroes Langston Hughes" and others, like Walter White and Elmer Carter of *Opportunity*. Hughes, Cripps notes, "stalled," and Pool Films produced only one film (*Borderline*) before experiencing serious distribution problems and dampened ambition.

Hughes eventually traveled to Russia with the intention of making a film there about the treatment of blacks in the United States. (The film was never made.) After returning to America, Hughes wistfully realized that, with the end of the Jazz Age and the Harlem Renaissance, "Negroes had lost some of their cachet in white intellectual circles." He wrote, "We were no longer in vogue, anyway, we Negroes. Sophisticated New Yorkers turned to Noel Coward. Colored actors began to go hungry, publishers politely rejected new manuscripts, and patrons found other uses for their money. The cycle that had charlestoned into being on the dancing heels of *Shuffle Along* now ended in *Green Pastures* with *De Lawd*" (Cripps, *SFB* 218).

31. One of Hughes's stories was produced in 2000 for public television by Masterpiece Theatre's "American Collection." Directed by Deborah M. Pratt from the screenplay by Ann Peacock, *Cora Unashamed* starred Regina Taylor as Cora Jenkins, the black housekeeper for the white family of Arthur and Lizbeth Stedevent. After silently enduring a lifetime of repression and loss (including the early death of her beloved daughter, Josephine), Cora uses the occasion of the funeral for the Studevents's daughter Jessie (who is the same age as Josephine would have been and of whom Cora was especially fond) to expose the hypocrisy and lies of her employer, Mrs. Studevent (Cherry Jones). Jessie, who had become pregnant by the working class Willie Matsoulis, had (without her father's knowledge) been pushed by her mother into an abortion that led to her death. (The snobbish Mrs. Studevent had also

been instrumental in running the hard-working immigrant Matsoulis family out of business and out of town.) The telefilm offered a particularly sensitive portrait of black family life, especially of the multi-generational household of Jenkins women, including Cora's strong-willed but loving mother (CCH Pounder).

32. Many of these films, significantly, were adaptations of novels. The story line of *Dixiana*, for example, was taken from a book by Anne Caldwell, and of *So Red the Rose* from Stark Young's best-selling novel. *Mississippi*—like *The Fighting Coward* and *River of Romance*—was adapted from Booth Tarkington's *Magnolia*.

33. David O. Selznick, who was the son-in-law of Louis B. Mayer, intended to use the film as a way of establishing himself independently in the movie industry. With the financial support of friends like Irving Thalberg and associates like John Hay Whitney, he formed Selznick-International; and he employed some of the best talent to promote his own vision. (That talent included directors George Cukor, Victor Fleming, and Sam Wood—although only Fleming got billing on the final production—and screenwriters Sidney Howard and F. Scott Fitzgerald, followed by Ben Hecht who, in marathon sessions, wrote in collaboration with Selznick himself.) Selznick also orchestrated one of the most incredible publicity campaigns in Hollywood history for *Gone With the Wind*, beginning with the nationwide search for Scarlett. And he helped to keep the public's interest with suggestions that Mrs. Roosevelt's maid was being considered for the role of Mammy.

34. In "Winds of Change: *Gone With the Wind* and Racism as a National Issue" (139), Cripps writes that "In the novel, Mitchell had wavered between realism and romance, even as her art and politics straddled racial issues. As she told her editor, she would be 'upset and mortified if Left Wingers like the book,' but, on the other hand, 'I sweat blood to keep it from being like Uncle Remus.'"

35. "*GWTW* was, as everyone knows," writes Linda Williams, "the most expensive, longest (3 hours, 46 minutes) 'event' in motion-picture history. It would go on to win eight Academy Awards," gross over three hundred million dollars, and generate more viewers than any other television program in history (a record that would stand until *Roots*). To put its media ubiquity in perspective, Williams notes, "it helps to understand that Selznick's film has been seen by more people than the entire population of the United States" (193)

36. Peter Noble (75) notes many similarities between the two films: "Both were extraordinary from an artistic and technical point of view, both were heralded with almost fantastic publicity, both were remarkably long ('Gone With the Wind' lasted nearly four hours) and both were huge financial successes." For a more detailed discussion of the two films, see

Gerald Wood's "From *The Clansman* and *The Birth of a Nation* to *Gone With the Wind*: The Loss of American Innocence."

37. Interestingly, this description, which appears in the film's prologue, was not taken from Mitchell's novel; rather, it was written directly for the film by Ben Hecht.

38. In fact, Big Sam, a former O'Hara family slave, comes to Scarlett's defense in both the novel and the film. In contrast to the downplaying of the Shantytown episode is the highlighting of the scene of Scarlett's marital rape by Rhett. Whereas an on-screen depiction of sexual assault on Scarlett by a black renegade would have been unthinkable, it appears that her rape by a white Southern "gentleman" was not only cinematically acceptable but also quite agreeable (judging by Rhett's drunken smile and Scarlett's post-coital glow).

39. Edward D. C. Campbell, Jr. notes in "The Old South as National Epic" (178) that both Mitchell and her husband John Marsh "were weary 'at seeing the combined Tuskegee and Fisk Jubilee Choirs bounce out at the most inopportune times and in the most inopportune places. . . ,' as such groups had done from *Hearts in Dixie* in 1929 to *Jezebel* in 1938."

40. Nell Battle Lewis, a reviewer for the *Raleigh News and Observer*, focused on precisely this aspect of the film. "The return to Tara," Lewis wrote, "to dead Ellen and to senile Gerald, was the best part of the picture. There Scarlett was really the heroine, at grips, at death grips with life in the raw. There she rose to something more than herself, the representative, the symbol of hundreds of other Southern heroines and heroes in the flesh who, not celebrated as the heroes in war, rebuilt with immeasurable suffering and self-sacrifice the New South on the ashes of the old" (Lewis 174).

41. A former radio vocalist, McDaniel enjoyed a long film career with little variety; in more than forty movies, she performed numerous variations of the Mammy character. "She was obviously unhappy with this type-casting," writes Daniel J. Leab (99), "but she also recognized if she did not play the role on screen, she would end up playing it in real life."

42. According to Lawrence Reddick, "the New York State Committee of the Communist Party resolved that: '*Gone With the Wind* revives every foul slander against the Negro people, every stock-in-trade lie of the Southern lynchers. While dressed in a slick package of sentimentality for the old "noble" traditions of the South, this movie is a rabid incitement against the Negro people. The historical struggle for democracy in this country which we have come to cherish so dearly is vilified and condemned'" (16).

43. In bringing Mitchell's story to the screen, Selznick successfully "universalized for all white Americans the romance of southern history as the American story of nation-making" at the same time that he con-

structed "an entirely new kind of American hero in selfish-greedy-head-strong Scarlett" (Williams, *Race* 194).

44. *Gone With the Wind* also created important changes behind the cameras. Linda Williams reports that a delegation of blacks on the set threatened to walk off unless racially segregated restrooms were eliminated. And Butterfly McQueen's objection (originally noted by Thomas Cripps) to "one of Vivien Leigh's overly forceful slaps—'I'm no stunt man, I'm an actress'—would cut in half the number of times Scarlett would slap Prissy in the film compared to the novel" (*Race* 218)

45. The former slave coming home to die is also the theme of a more recent film, *Shadrach* (1998), based on the story "Shadrach," one of William Styron's *Tidewater Tales*. The film *Shadrach* was produced by Millennium Films, Inc. and Nu Image and was directed by Styron's daughter, Susanna Styron.

46. See Edward D. C. Campbell, Jr.'s chapter on "Hollywood and the Reinterpretation of the South, 1941-1980" in *The Celluloid South* and Andrew Bergman's *We're in the Money: Depression America and Its Films*.

47. As Phyllis R. Klotman writes in "Frank Yerby's First Novel to Film" (218), "Etienne dies, when hardly more than seven, from a fall down the stairs—that ubiquitous long flight so much a part of Hollywood's Southern *mise-en-scène*. The tragedy is unwittingly of their doing because he falls trying to stop his parents from quarreling. Although it is not clear that he knows their argument is over him, he hears their passionately angry voices raised against each other, loses his footing, and plunges down the stairs."

48. As James R. Nesteby (116-17) demonstrates, however, it was not until 1964, with the release of the British film *Zulu*, directed by Cy Endfield, "that a film at all accurate about the Zulu war with the British was made. Prior to that film, Zulus and other 'natives' of a similar ilk appeared as loyal to whites, as fierce savages or exotic natives, as fantasy symbols for sex couched in comedy, and as a haven in which whites could become dominant when on the run from Anglo society."

49. See Nesteby, especially chapters 9 ("The Tarzan Formula for Racial Stereotyping") and 10 ("The Invisible Genre: Tarzan Jungle Films"), 137-56.

50. Gale Gauntier, in blackface, starred in the film, which reportedly was based on a story by Gauntier.

51. *The Jungle Outcasts* was a Centaur film and starred William Clifford, Margaret Gibson, and Samuel Bigelow (in blackface as Waji).

52. Those sequels included *Tarzan the Fearless* (1933); *Tarzan and His Mate* (1934); *New Adventures of Tarzan* (1935); *Tarzan Escapes* (1936); *Tarzan's Revenge* (1938); *Tarzan and the Green Goddess* (1938); *Tarzan Finds a Son!* (1939); *Tarzan's Secret Treasure* (1941); *Tarzan's New York Adventure*

(1942); *Tarzan Triumphs* (1943); *Tarzan's Desert Mystery* (1943); *Tarzan and the Amazons* (1945); *Tarzan and the Leopard Woman* (1946); *Tarzan and the Huntress* (1947); *Tarzan and the Mermaids* (1948); *Tarzan's Magic Fountain* (1949); *Tarzan and the Slave Girl* (1950); *Tarzan's Peril* (1951); *Tarzan's Savage Fury* (1952); *Tarzan and the She-Devil* (1953); *Tarzan's Hidden Jungle* (1955); *Tarzan and the Lost Safari* (1957); *Tarzan's Fight for Life* (1958); *Tarzan and the Trappers* (1958); *Tarzan's Greatest Adventure* (1959); *Tarzan, the Ape Man* (1959); *Tarzan the Magnificent* (1960); *Tarzan Goes to India* (1962); *Tarzan's Three Challenges* (1963); *Tarzan and the Valley of Gold* (1966); *Tarzan and the Great River* (1967); *Tarzan and the Jungle Boy* (1968); *Tarzan's Jungle Rebellion* (1970); *Tarzan's Deadly Silence* (1970); *Tarzan, the Ape Man* (1981); *Greystoke, the Legend of Tarzan, Lord of the Apes* (1984); and *Tarzan in Manhattan* (1989).

The NBC series, produced by Banner productions, ran from 8 September 1966 until 13 September 1968; it was filmed on location in Brazil and Mexico and starred Ron Ely as Tarzan. Tarzan was also featured in several CBS cartoon shows, including *Tarzan, Lord of the Jungle*, which ran 1976-77 and again from February through September, 1984; *Tarzan and the Super 7* (1978-80); *The Tarzan/Lone Ranger Adventure Hour* (1980-81); and *The Tarzan/Lone Ranger/Zorro Adventure Hour* (1981-82). For more information about these television shows, see Alex McNeil's *Total Television*, 745.

53. "Blacks," writes Cripps, "began to suffer on the screen more from the invisibility imposed by liberal white writers, made timid by their ignorance of Negro life, or embarrassed by their lack of alternatives to old-fashioned Southern lore. Moviemen were helpless to translate the new Negro [e.g., in an urban habitat removed from the locales of Southern literary tradition] into artful or mythic truth" (*SFB* 151).

54. See *Slow Fade to Black*, 125-26. Cripps not only outlines how the Tarzan movies changed but also describes how Burroughs sold the rights to Tarzan and lost control of the films' direction. "Burroughs's success had rested not so much on chauvinistic and invidious comparisons of whites with other races, but more on his faith in the average man's capacity for overcoming adversity with common sense." Yet the movies changed the nature and role of Tarzan to the point that they diminished his heroic stature.

55. Other, later Kong "sequels" followed, including *King Kong vs. Godzilla* (1963), *King Kong Escapes* (1968), and *King Kong Lives* (1986); and *King Kong* itself was remade (as *King Kong*) in 1976.

56. O'Hara's Los Angeles club, the "Golden Safari," features black doormen dressed as "natives" and played by the same actors who portrayed actual natives in the opening sequence, supposedly (according to a superimposed title) set in "AFRICA." The club's stage curtain is modeled after the containing fence on Skull Island. As James Snead writes,

"Here, the overall conceit of the 'Kong' series is made manifest: reintroducing the trappings, and even the representatives, of barbarity into civilization, albeit in a 'defanged' form. Even the Skull Island natives had used King Kong in this way, 'staging' his periodic appearance and propitiation behind their containing fence 'curtain,' regulating his performance by their elaborate rites and human sacrifices. The 'natives' were to King Kong as the 'Golden Safari' audience is to the real Mighty Joe Young as the movie audience is to the movies *King Kong* and *Mighty Joe Young* themselves" (33).

57. It was, writes Cripps (*SFB* 222), "Williams's craft and wit, combined with his ability to squeeze honest black roles into the crevices of white movies, [that] enabled him to build a long career, at first with Christie, then with the majors, punctuated by occasional all-black pictures." Specifically, the combination of Cohen and Williams "introduced a striking amount of Negro lore to the screen. It was as though the two Southerners (Williams came from Louisiana) hammered out a motif based on the tension between their black and white points of view, yet promising white Southerners no threat to segregation of the races" (224).

58. Voodoo as practiced in contemporary Harlem was even part of a documentary series, Louis De Rochemont's *The March of Time* series for Henry Luce. The black press was naturally outraged by the depiction (Cripps, *SFB* 298).

59. An earlier film directed by and starring Spencer Williams, Jr. that treated the same theme of black religious experience was *Blood of Jesus* (1941), in which a pious wife accidentally shot to death by her husband is brought back to life by her faith in Jesus.

60. The commercial response to the film was excellent. Thomas Cripps notes that "the most striking instance of white awakening to the box office power of black themes was *Emperor Jones* . . . which did surprising business and helped persuade Hollywood to re-examine its racial policies. Shot on a low budget in Astoria, Long Island, the picture grossed an amazing $10,000 in one Harlem week. But even more astonishing was the $11,000 it made in Washington, D.C." (*SFB* 216-17). Cripps also notes that "the climax of Jones's death becomes a black social variant of the inevitability of Greek tragedy given new meaning through an artful use of environmentalism" and a marvelous score that divides the picture into four movements and motifs—African, to Gullah, to Harlem jazz, to Voodoo—that attempt "to symbolize a long race-memory." Cripps concludes that "when Jones dies in a revolt, he is not a Pullman toady or a high-roller under the stairwell; he is a black king dying in pain and rage at his demeaning fall."

Chapter 4

Uncle Tom Meets Uncle Sam:
Wartime Developments and Postwar Progress

> Hollywood can only visualize the plantation type of
> Negro—the Negro of "Poor Old Joe" and "Swanee
> Ribber." It is absurd to use that type to express the mod-
> ern Negro as it would be to express modern England in
> the terms of an Elizabethan ballad.
> —*Paul Robeson, Film Weekly (1 September 1933)*

American rhetoric directed against the racist theories of Nazi
Germany during the Second World War in turn brought about a
reaction against racism at home. As Thomas Cripps writes, the
war years "became a seedtime for a heightened racial consciousness" among blacks, whose membership in the National
Association for the Advancement of Colored People (NAACP)
increased tenfold, as well as among whites; and pressure developed within American society to provide racial equality (*SFB* 349).
Although some complained, as novelist and screenwriter Dalton
Trumbo did at a Writers Congress in the early 1940s, that the
movie industry continued to demean blacks by making "tarts of
the Negro's daughters, crap shooters of his sons, obsequious
Uncle Toms of his fathers, superstitious and grotesque crones of
his mothers, strutting peacocks of his successful men, psalm-
singing mountebanks of his priests, and Barnum and Bailey side-
shows of his religion" (Leab 120), the stirrings of change were in
fact being reflected by Hollywood, although at least initially with
timidity and tentativeness.

One of the first hints of real change for blacks in the business
was the front-page headline in *Variety* in the spring of 1942
announcing "BETTER BREAKS FOR NEGROES IN H'WOOD."
That promise was the result of a long series of discussions and

meetings held in Los Angeles in 1942 between studio heads and officials of the NAACP, including Walter White, a ranking figure in that organization as well as a syndicated columnist who had become a hero among blacks for his reportage of lynching, and Wendell Willkie, the defeated Republican Presidential candidate and counsel for the NAACP, whose negotiations marked a new beginning for Hollywood by pressing for the elimination of many of the old racial stereotypes on screen.[1] White pointed out to the studio heads that the NAACP was not asking "that Negroes be pictured as superhuman heroes" but rather that Hollywood "have courage enough to shake off . . . fears and taboos and . . . depict the Negro in films as a normal human being and an integral part" of American life. Willkie took a tougher stand, castigating Hollywood for fostering anti-Americanism abroad through its caricaturing of nonwhites and declaring that the industry needed to give the black "a better break."[2] Industry executives responded by giving assurances that blacks would receive fairer treatment on screen. Darryl Zanuck, then a vice-president of Twentieth Century-Fox, publicly urged that "the program of casting colored persons in more normal roles be put into effect at an early date," a suggestion with which Will Hays, head of the industry's trade organization, and producers Sam Goldwyn and Sol Lesser concurred; MGM vice-president Al Lichtman promised to do his "utmost in whatever way" to help the cause; and Jack Warner affirmed that his studio had already scheduled for production several films that portrayed the "colored" in the same way "as any other human being" (Leab 129-30).

Some film executives, however, worried about the implications of such change, especially with relation to the Southern censorship boards that objected to depictions of non-servile or non-comic black characters and that often required cuts or even blocked films from being exhibited in their regions. Blacks within the industry expressed their concerns as well: fearing that the campaign to upgrade film roles might result in fewer parts and less work for them, a number of black actors and actresses seemed reluctant to accept the NAACP effort and even grew to resent supporters of it, like Lena Horne. At first, the Hollywood bargain appeared to have little impact; but, as Cripps observes, gradually it gave thrust and direction to the liberal drift and gave pause to the purveyors of the

old Southern attitudes. Yet even as the old submissive and secondary roles for blacks continued, positive changes seemed afoot:
talented black actors were being recruited for major Hollywood
productions like *Cabin in the Sky* and *Porgy and Bess*; some of the
familiar character types and themes slipped into the category of B
movies; *Tarzan* shut down at MGM and went independent;
Southern exhibitors discussed ways of entertaining black troops;
and the black press expressed increasing displeasure at black
stereotyping and mourned the dead end to which Hattie
McDaniel's Oscar seemed to point (*SFB* 376). Moreover, individual
artists, notably Hazel Scott, Ethel Waters, Katherine Dunham, and
Lena Horne, began refusing to appear in films that they considered
to be derogatory.[3]

Yet the change that was being felt in Hollywood was hardly
revolutionary. Black theater throughout the 1930s had already
begun bringing black themes to American audiences in works like
Paul Green's *In Abraham's Bosom*, Frank Dazey and Jim Tully's
Black Boy, Hall Johnson's *Run Little Chillun*, and Langston
Hughes's *Mulatto*; at the same time, that theater was training a
new generation of black actors who would be ready to take advantage of the opportunities wartime Hollywood would offer. As R.
Dana Skinner observed in the liberal Catholic weekly *Commonweal*,
the black penetration of the theater at the end of the Harlem
Renaissance was "progressing apace" and quickening the hopes of
those who "feel the inner poignancy of the Negro's handicap in the
American environment"; and by the 1930s, drama was actually "a
weapon" that liberals were using "to state the Negro's case for
equal treatment" (Cripps, *SFB* 349-50). In the early 1940s, while
Hollywood was still drawing on stereotypical images of blacks
that harked back to the nineteenth- and early-twentieth-century
minstrelsy traditions, *Jump for Joy*, a socially progressive satire,
opened on stage in Los Angeles. Showcasing such fine young
black performers as Dorothy Dandridge and Herb Jeffries and
composers such as Duke Ellington, Billy Strayhorn, and Langston
Hughes, *Jump for Joy* featured Uncle Tom in a crucial scene that
expressed blacks' frustration with the old derogatory theatrical
and cinematic typing. Lying on his deathbed, Tom is surrounded
by children singing, "He lived to a ripe old age. Let him go, God
Bless him!" (*SFB* 375); but a crowd of movie producers struggles to

keep him alive by pumping adrenaline into his arms. In the first act finale, which exemplifies how fully the familiar symbol of protest had been absorbed, even vulgarized, by the popular culture, Uncle Tom's Cabin becomes a drive-in "chicken shack" on the corner of Hollywood and Vine.

Nonetheless, the New Deal in Washington seemed to be having reverberations for a new deal in Hollywood as well. An article in the *New York Times* in February, 1943, reported that the Administration, which "felt that its program for increased employment of Negro citizens in certain heretofore restricted fields of industry would be helped by a general distribution of important pictures in which Negroes played a major part," was providing the impetus for a number of black-cast and black-themed movies that were being discussed or that were already in production. That official support, coupled with the social spirit of the day, was giving rise to a "New Negro" on screen (Bogle, *TCMMB* 136-37).[4]

The "New Negro," however, was not altogether new to film. As Donald Bogle (137-38) points out, audiences had glimpsed him in a few sympathetic black roles before the war: the confident and heroic Dr. Marchand (Clarence Brooks)—one of the first of Hollywood's screen portrayals of professional blacks—who fights the plague that is raging through the West Indies in John Ford's *Arrowsmith* (1931); the massive inmate (played by an uncredited Everett Brown) who helps James Allen (Paul Muni) escape from the inhumane chain gang in Mervyn LeRoy's *I Am a Fugitive from a Chain Gang* (1932); the innocent janitor Tump Redwine (Clinton Rosamond) who discovers the body of a murdered white girl and is accused and brutally interrogated by the small-town racist police in LeRoy's *They Won't Forget* (1937); the crippled and battered old Crooks (Leigh Whipper) who helps out the derelict heroes George and Lennie in Lewis Milestone's *Of Mice and Men* (1939); the somber preacher Sparks (Leigh Whipper) who stands up to an angry mob and urges them to show mercy to three wrongfully accused men in William Wellman's *The Ox-Bow Incident* (1943); and, of course, the many faces of Paul Robeson, in roles ranging from the confident and powerful Brutus Jones in *The Emperor Jones* (1933) to the sensitive Joe who resents white privilege in *Show Boat* (1936) and the self-sacrificing miner David Goliath in *The Proud Valley* (1941).

Perhaps the best example of the New Negro on the screen—and of the balanced portrayals that Hollywood studios could indeed achieve—was *In This Our Life* (1942), a John Huston film that attempted to interweave the tragedies and triumphs of white and black Southerners. Based on Ellen Glasgow's Pulitzer Prize-winning novel about changing times and values, *In This Our Life* focused on the destructive selfishness of the contemporary Southern belle Stanley Timberlake (Bette Davis), who cheats on her fiancé Craig, steals her sister's husband, pits family members against each other, and then tries to blame Parry Clay, a young black man in her father's employ, for a car accident that she caused in which a child is killed and a woman seriously injured. The very antithesis of the spoiled and self-absorbed Stanley, Parry is a decent, hardworking young man who aspires to a better life for himself and his family by becoming a lawyer. Law, he believes, is the only profession in which an American can be black and still do his work without interference or persecution: "A colored boy can keep a job or lose a job," he says, "but he can't get any higher up, so he's got to figure out something he can do that no one can take away." Humiliated by his wrongful imprisonment for Stanley's crime, Parry is eventually cleared with the help of Stanley's former fiancé Craig Fleming (George Brent) and her sister Roy Timberlake (Olivia de Havilland), who believe in his innocence and who force Stanley to confess.

Although *In This Our Life* included some of the predictable details of life in the cinematic South, such as the casting of Hattie McDaniel as the Timberlakes's domestic Minerva, the film, as Daniel J. Leab observed, "made some very frank references to the kind of injustice that often was legally meted out to blacks" (125). That injustice is highlighted in the scene in which Stanley confronts Parry in his cell and tells him that he may as well admit to the hit-and-run accident since no one will accept his word over that of a white woman (a scene reminiscent of the treatment and forced confession of Lem Hawkins in Micheaux's *Murder in Harlem*). Even after her guilt is exposed, the contemptuous Stanley still hopes to use Parry as a scapegoat by promising to negotiate a reduced sentence for him and to give him a fresh start after his release. Despite his poor treatment, the intelligent young man—an excellent representative of the New Negro emerging in American film and society—maintains his dignity and refuses to let his people down by lying, even if his refusal exacerbates his own grave situation.[5] "Miss Stanley, she knows," Parry insists. "Miss Stanley, you know that ain't so. I remember every word you said." No doubt, it was Parry's resolve that prompted black soldiers on a segregated post to stop the film with their shouts and applause so that the jail scene could be rerun (Cripps, *MMB* 32, *SFB* 370). Bette Davis recalled the import of Anderson's performance, which she admits ultimately served to enhance her own. "There was a first in this film," she wrote in her memoirs. "The Negro boy played by Ernest Anderson was written and performed as an educated person. This caused a great deal of joy among Negroes. They were tired of the Stepin Fetchit version of their people" (*MMB* 32).

After the guilty Stanley tearfully attempts to enlist the help of her Uncle William Fitzroy, she soon meets a fiery death in a second car crash. Roy and Craig are free to live and love happily ever after; yet Parry, who presumably has been exonerated and allowed to return to his mother Minerva, is never seen again. Still, "the brief but frank allusion to racial discrimination" through Parry's wrongful incarceration, according to contemporary critic Bosley Crowther, is quite significant; and it "is presented in a realistic manner uncommon to Hollywood by the depiction of the Negro as an educated and comprehending character" (qtd. in Bogle 138-39).[6] Consequently, as Lawrence Reddick notes, "this picture won a place on the Honor Roll of Race Relations for 1942" (19).

It was not exclusively the agreement between the studios and the NAACP, however, that prompted Hollywood's changing view of blacks and the changing portrayal of blacks in Hollywood pictures; an important contributing factor was the government, which continued its involvement with the film industry throughout the war years. The Office of War Information (OWI), for example, assumed an increasingly larger role as arbiter and censor of racial themes: it ran an inspirational column in *Variety* and issued guidebooks to the industry on matters of racial content. One such Army manual noted that "When the Negro is portrayed in the movies, or elsewhere, as a lazy, shiftless, no-good, slew-footed, happy-go-lucky, razor-toting, tap-dancing vagrant, a step has been taken in the direction of fixing this mental picture in the minds of whites" (*MMB* 104). Moreover, acccording to Thomas Cripps, an OWI man nearly always sat through rough cuts of films, recommended deletions and modulations, and occasionally even commissioned movies. "*The New York Times*," in fact, "gave OWI the bulk of credit for the wartime cycle of Negro films" (*SFB* 379).

The New Negro at War

One significant film that resulted from the wartime collaboration between government and the movie industry was *The Negro Soldier* (1944), "a forty-five minute tribute to Negro hope and aspiration—an intricate mixture of stock footage, thin historical narrative, and fictive binder couched in the form of a Negro preacher's sermon" (*SFB* 380), with Carlton Moss, the film's young black writer, in the pulpit.[7] The film, which the Army planned to use in troop training, proved to be possibly the single most notable cinematic marriage of art and politics. It drew on the efforts of various people, including John Houseman, formerly of the Federal Theatre, and William Hastie of Franklin Delano Roosevelt's "black cabinet," both of whom put political pressure upon the Army; Truman Gibson, Hastie's successor and a black adviser to the War Department on matters of race, who shared his dossier of discriminatory acts against black troops in the South; Frank Capra, the renowned filmmaker who had already produced a series of *Why We Fight* training films for the Army; and Carlton Moss, who reworked the Army's approved script into a hit film that eventually ran in hundreds of movie houses and received wide praise from black journalists.[8]

The War Department had been keenly aware of the need to respond publicly to the issue of black war participation, particularly since race moviemakers were already taking up the subject in their films. Oscar Micheaux, the greatest and most enduring producer of race movies, had complained to Elmer Davis in OWI that only a "tiny fraction of wartime film shows the Negro from any standpoint," and he offered himself as one who had "learned how and what to do to get [blacks] into the war spirit" (Cripps, *MMB* 104). Ted Toddy, president of Toddy Pictures, hinted that he had Paul Robeson ready to make a movie about the 99th Pursuit Squadron. Meanwhile, Alfred Sack and his black director and actor

Spencer Williams, Jr. had completed *Marching On*, a grainy film about life on a black post where the troops silence a clandestine Japanese radio station; and the team of Jack Goldberg, another white race filmmaker, and Elder Solomon Lightfoot Michaux (no relation to Oscar Micheaux) were finishing a documentary using much of the Signal Corps's own footage, *We've Come a Long, Long Way*. Only when the latter film came in, coincident with the completion of *The Negro Soldier*, did the War Department realize that the ideology of the race movies differed from that of the Pentagon.[9]

Previous Army training films had demonstrated little sensitivity to racial concerns. For instance, in *Know for Sure*, a squad of black soldiers on a pass follows a white squad to the local black brothel; but afterwards, back on base, only the blacks contract venereal disease from their libidinous escapades (thus giving credence to the NAACP complaint that, according to the film, "all Negroes have syphilis") (Cripps, *MMB* 118). Racism was equally obvious in *Easy to Get*, another sexual cautionary tale, in which disease is rampant among blacks, who require the services of the exceptional white doctors for a cure.

By contrast, *The Negro Soldier* was determined to portray a more genuine vision of blacks in the military and in American life. As the film opens, the unnamed preacher played by Moss decides to put aside his prepared sermon and speak instead about the contributions of blacks in the current war effort. After recognizing several soldiers, including the female "Private Parks, First Class," among his audience, he recalls Joe Louis's defeat of his German opponent Max Schmeling in the ring and reminds the congregation that Louis—a national hero who represents all black soldiers—is in an even greater fight now, a metaphorical fight for the championship of the world. The preacher then reads a passage from *Mein Kampf*, in which Hitler claims that "from time to time the illustrated papers show how a Negro has become a lawyer, a teacher, perhaps even a minister. [Yet] it never dawns on the degenerate middle-class America that this is truly a sin against all reason, that it is criminal madness to train a born half-ape until one believes one has made a lawyer of him."

A chronology of black war participation follows, beginning with the Revolutionary War (the Negro Minutemen at Lexington and Concord, Peter Salem at Bunker Hill, Prince Whipple at Valley

Forge); continuing with the War of 1812 (black soldiers with Admiral Perry at Lake Erie, black troops with Andrew Jackson at the Battle of New Orleans), the Civil War (the famous Massachusetts 54th Regiment of volunteers), and the Spanish-American War (Ninth and Tenth Cavalry and 34th Infantry at San Juan Hill); and culminating in action near Marseilles, near Verdun, at the Argonne, and elsewhere during the great battles of the First World War (with black soldiers being among the first troops to receive the Croix de Guerre for heroism), and at Pearl Harbor, which "was at once a central metaphor of the army's wished-for black dedication to the war and a repudiation of Japanese racial propaganda" (Cripps, *MMB* 110). Although jack-booted Nazis representative of German racism are depicted destroying "our monument" (a tribute by the French to the bravery of black soldiers), the preacher exhorts his listeners to honor the "monuments" that can never be erased—that is, the monumental achievements of Booker T. Washington; George Washington Carver; and the many other blacks who have made invaluable contributions to American culture through law, medicine, education, sports, music, and the arts—and to take up the fight for freedom's cause. At this point Mrs. Bronson, a well-dressed and well-spoken black woman portrayed in diametrical opposition to the rag-headed, dialect-speaking Mammies, rises from the congregation to read a letter from her son, Lt. Robert A. Bronson, in which he describes in blissful terms his basic training as an army inductee, his preparation for Officers' Candidate School, and his pride in being an American soldier. The film ends with a montage of American military men and women, who embody the nation's strength and hopes, marching across the screen to the sound of the church choir's spirited rendition of "Onward Christian Soldiers."

Originally shown only to black recruits, "OF-51"—the Army's code name for *The Negro Soldier*—was soon mandatory viewing for all troops at continental American replacement centers. And when the film was released for exhibition to civilian audiences, many found in its appeal to take up the "good fight" an inspiration for the struggle for civil rights as well. In fact, as Thomas Cripps writes, "Clearly, by the end of 1944 *The Negro Soldier* had become a monster unintended by the army, a black-driven message of 'racial tolerance' that conscience-liberals came to regard as a weapon for mounting a postwar assault on American racism" and that blacks and their allies effectively used "to breach two redoubts of white privilege, Hollywood and the Pentagon, and turned them to African American purposes" (*MMB* 114-15).[10] Yet, as effective as the film was in its respectful presentation of black characters like the intelligent black recruit, his proud and articulate mother, and the many dedicated black troops fighting overseas, there was much that it neglected. Daniel J. Leab observes that "for all its merits, *The Negro Soldier* was, as one critic said, 'painfully, pitifully mild.' It was a Jim Crow film, reflecting the segregation practiced by the Army. None of the real problems faced by blacks in military service were touched on. Relations between the races, whether in the armed forced or in civilian life, received no real examination" (128).[11] Nevertheless, the film marked a significant, symbolic beginning and served as a harbinger of postwar social change.

"Army Shows Hollywood the Way," announced the black paper *Negro*; and Hollywood indeed began reflecting the more liberal wartime ideology in some of its productions. Several of the major studios released films such as *Crash Dive* (Twentieth Century-Fox, 1943), with Benny Carter as Oliver Cromwell Jones, a role inspired by the heroism of black sailor Dorie Miller at Pearl Harbor; *Sahara* (Columbia, 1943), with Rex Ingram as Tambul, a French officer who is part of a group of Allied soldiers in the Sahara Desert during the North African campaign; and *Bataan* (MGM, 1943), with Kenneth Spencer as American GI Wesley Epps, who is among the last of a brave patrol besieged by the enemy at Bataan. At the heart of all of these films was a depiction of the New Negro at war that mirrored the increased liberal outlook of the period. In *Sahara*, for example, the sympathetic and gallant Tambul is equal in every respect to his intrepid fellow soldiers and unaffected by racial barriers; in fact, he is attended by a white man, a captured Italian soldier who serves as his personal servant, and becomes the confidant of a white boy from Texas (Bruce Bennett), with whom he shares many common concerns.[12] As Peter Noble (198) writes, "in one scene he [Tambul] uses his hands as a cup for the dripping water which quenches the thirst of the other men. Each of the whites drinks out of the water in the hands of the Negro, and none of them appears to find this extraordinary; a small point but none the less subtle, and certainly effective."

Similarly, in *Bataan*, demolitions expert Epps lives, laughs, and courageously meets death along with his comrades and is included in all of their plans and discussions. The balanced portrayal of characters, in fact, won the film a special award from the NAACP as well as high praise from OWI reviewers. Even in *Lifeboat* (Twentieth Century-Fox, 1944; dir. Alfred Hitchcock), about a group of Americans forced onto a battered lifeboat after their passenger freighter has been torpedoed by Germans, the steward and sole black Joe (Canada Lee), who is initially the object of ridicule, assumes a heroic status after it is revealed that he has saved the life of a drowning woman and her child.[13] The armed services' propaganda films and documentaries also stimulated a number of all-black-cast Hollywood movies, such as the musicals *Cabin in the Sky* (1943), in which the Lord's General and his white-clad soldiers of Heaven fight Lucifer, Jr. and the black-uniformed forces of Hell for the soul of Little Joe Jackson, and *Stormy Weather* (1943), based in part on the life of Bill Robinson and on a variety of Negro revues, including Jim Europe's Jazz Band, which played to Allied troops in France during the First World War. Unlike the integrated war dramas, however, the segregated musicals had an unintended effect: they "brought into play the tension between integration and cultural uniqueness and produced in the minds of black activists no end of anxiety over the implied retreat from integration."[14] And they stirred equally strong reactions from the black press, which found the plots of the musicals (particularly *Cabin in the Sky*) "insulting," a "disservice to race relations," "vulgar," and reminiscent of false folksy fables like *The Green Pastures* (*MMB* 83).

THE POSTWAR "PROBLEM FILMS"

The years immediately following the war continued the impetus for integration and ushered in other social changes, including real development of a black middle class and a dramatic increase in the number of black workers, especially professionals. The civil rights movement also gained strength; by 1948, in fact, the Democratic platform included a civil rights plank (though it ultimately split the party in a presidential election year), and the Supreme Court struck down racially restricted covenants as a violation of the fourteenth amendment to the Constitution. Hollywood responded to the public's growing cultural and racial awareness by launching an era of "problem" or "message" movies often based on literary works, which featured sensitive themes such as anti-Semitism, juvenile delinquency, mental health, and race relations—the last of which proved to be a particularly controversial and lucrative screen topic. "The 'Negro problem' film," writes Jim Pines (63), quickly "emerged as an all-embracing social film vehicle which derived its effectiveness ('meaning') from the genre's modification of racial image conventions. . . . [and marked] probably the first time when cinematic racial developments more or less coincided with social racial developments." In some of the more traditional or conventional of these films, such as the remake of *Imitation of Life*, the results were often disastrous; the more liberal and innovative treatments such as *Pinky*, however, offered idealistic and optimistic resolutions consistent with the new postwar spirit of social tolerance and inclusion.

The original version of *Imitation of Life* (1934) had been the first important film of the 1930s about blacks; an editorial in the *Pittsburgh Courier* had in fact hailed it as a "daring moving picture" and "A New Departure in Movies" (Everett 219). An outgrowth of the conscious prewar liberal sentiment and the new social order that was starting to discard some of the old racial proprieties, *Imitation of Life*, according to Donald Bogle, "prided itself on its portrait of the modern black woman, still a servant but now imbued with dignity and a character that were an integral part of life" (*TCMMB* 57). Based on a best-selling novel by Fanny Hurst, it told the story of two poor young widows, the white Beatrice Pullman (Claudette Colbert) and the black Delilah (Louise Beavers), both of whom are hard hit by the Depression; after meeting by accident, they decide to live and raise their daughters together. At first, Delilah stays at home cooking and caring for the children while Bea tries to earn money by selling maple syrup. But Delilah's culinary skills, particularly the pancakes that she makes from a secret old family recipe, turn the women into restauranteurs and ultimately into entrepreneurs who successfully market "Aunt Delilah's Pancake Flour." Their newfound wealth allows them to move from the back rooms of their boardwalk restaurant in Atlantic City to an elegant townhouse in Manhattan, yet it fails to ensure their happiness. Bea's daughter, Jessie (Rochelle Hudson), falls in love with Steve Archer (Warren William), her mother's beau, which causes Bea to postpone and perhaps abandon her plans for marriage (although, in keeping with romantic cinematic conventions, Steve promises to wait for Bea, no matter how long it takes). Delilah's daughter, Peola (Fredi Washington), on the other hand, defies the racial standards that restrict her, rejects her dark-skinned mother, and runs away to live as white. Only after the stoic and Christian Delilah dies, her heart broken by her only child's betrayal, does Peola return to make amends.

As played by black actress Fredi Washington—the casting of a black woman to play a mulatto being itself a significant departure from period studio films—Peola was perhaps the film's most interesting and most complex character. "Her drama is the most poignant," according to Lawrence Reddick, "but the producers not only confine her to a minor and carefully handled subplot, but appear to regard her with a bit of distaste" (12). Having been raised alongside the white Jessie, Peola longs for the same opportunities that Jessie enjoys. And when she is denied those opportunities solely on the basis of race, Peola—a "New Negro demanding a real New Deal"—rebels. Yet, as Donald Bogle points out, she is unjustly punished for her rebellion: "Her weeping by her mother's casket was Hollywood's slick way of finally humiliating her, its way of finally making the character who had run away with herself conform to the remorseful mulatto type" (*TCMMB* 60). Nevertheless Peola's very desire for freedom and equal justice struck a particularly responsive note with the film's black viewers, who saw her as "the true symbol of the American Negro struggling against . . . the bars of race prejudice in this country" (Everett 221).

The inequities that Peola perceives, experiences, and reacts so strongly against are readily apparent in the relationship between her mother and Bea, a relationship that reveals much about the real state of racial relations in the 1930s. Delilah (who, like the generic Mammy of early films, lacks a surname) is content to work as Bea's "girl" simply for room and board.[15] Even after she shares with Bea the very profitable secret for pancake flour that quite literally changes their fortunes, Delilah receives not the half of the business that she rightly deserves but instead a mere 20% portion—enough,

Figure 4.1. Two widows, Bea (Claudette Colbert) and Delilah (Louise Beavers), form an unequal partnership in *Imitation of Life*. *(Universal, 1934)*

however, to allow her to buy a car and a home. (Fig. 4.1.) Yet Delilah cannot conceive of such independence: "My own house? You gonna send me away?" she asks Bea. "Oh, honey chile, please don't send me away. . . . How I gonna take care of you and Miss Jessie if I ain't here? . . . I'se your cook, and I wants to stay your cook." To that end, Delilah makes "a present" of the recipe to Bea—an act of submissiveness that, as Bogle and others have argued, helps to justify Bea's exploitation of her.[16]

Moreover, like the self-effacing, stoically Christian Toms and Mammies of earlier films, Delilah not only accepts her inferior fate but also tries to teach Peola the same resignation: "You gotta learn to take it." A loyal "auntie" to her darling "missy" Bea, Delilah remains as deferential as she is subservient. She always addresses Bea as "miss" or "ma'am"; rubs Bea's feet, even though it is she herself who spends long hours cooking and keeping house; and lives with Peola in the basement rooms of the townhouse while Bea and Jessie occupy the more elegant quarters upstairs. Unlike the fashionable and sexy Bea, who is the object of Archer's affection and of other men's admiration, the typically apron-clad Delilah—at a self-confessed "240 pounds"—is portrayed as utterly sexless. Yet it is Delilah and not her own mother in whom Jessie Pullman confides; it is Delilah who, by her example, teaches the importance of loyalty and of other timeless family values;[17] and it is Delilah whose selflessness is honored and whose generosity is recognized by a funeral consisting of a "long procession" with "plenty of bands playing," a hearse with a white velvet interior, and white horses that is the largest ever seen in Harlem.

With its pleasingly conventional rags-to-riches plot and its unconventionally strong lead characters, *Imitation of Life* became an immediate hit with white audiences. But black audiences, too, appreciated its innovative, at times subversive approach to critical contemporary concerns. As the *Pittsburgh Courier* noted, never before had "the question of the proper relations between a white and colored person in a business partnership been propounded" or had "colored people appeared as dignified, intelligent, well-dressed human beings and not as jovial cretins on the silver screen." Unlike other moving pictures with black actors, there was "no hoofing, no blues singing, no vociferous horselaughs, no razor wielding, no barnyard amours!" And even though there was "much in *Imitation of Life* which is dreadfully superficial and needlessly sentimental and far-fetched, . . . it will really set America to thinking furiously" (Everett 220).[18]

The film's strong box helped convince other major Hollywood studios, which had been disappointed by the poor gross of earlier films such as *Hearts in Dixie* and *Hallelujah!*, to put more black-themed and black-cast films into production. The increasing popularity of problem films, moreover, led to a successful revival of the film in the 1940s. A remake of *Imitation of Life* in 1959, however, was far less effective. In that version, produced by Ross Hunter for Universal-International, Lora Meredith (Lana Turner), an aspiring model and actress, and Annie Johnson (Juanita Moore), a congenial but homeless black woman, meet on the beach in Atlantic City. After Lora invites Annie and her daughter, Sarah Jane, back to her apartment, Annie quickly makes herself indispensable; by taking in shirts, cleaning the staircases of their building to defray rent costs, and addressing envelopes, she helps to keep the strug-

Figure 4.2. In the remake of *Imitation of Life*, Annie Johnson (Juanita Moore) devotedly serves her employer, Lora Meredith (Lana Turner). *(Universal-International, 1959)*

gling household afloat. Eventually, Lora achieves celebrity by starring in the Broadway plays produced by her companion David Edwards; Annie remains devotedly at Lora's side, assisting with all of her personal needs, managing the large new home they share, and raising Lora's daughter, Susie (Sandra Dee), along with her own. (Fig. 4.2.) But Sarah Jane (Susan Kohner), an angry and rebellious child who refuses to accept that she is black and who lies about her parentage to teachers and friends, grows into an even angrier and more rebellious young woman: she passes for white with a rich boy from town, who physically abuses her when he learns that her mother is "a nigger"; tells Annie that she is working in her college library when she is actually dancing in a New York nightclub; and ultimately runs away to become a chorus girl at the Moulin Rouge in Hollywood. "Don't try to find me," she warns her mother. "This is my life, and I am going to live it my way." Blaming Annie for all of her own troubles, Sarah Jane makes her mother promise that "if by accident we should ever meet on the street, please don't recognize me," a promise that breaks

Annie's heart. Meanwhile, Lora flies to Europe to make a film, and in her absence Susie becomes infatuated with Steve Archer (John Gavin), a photographer-turned-executive who has loved Lora for years. Lora returns home to great turmoil—to an embittered daughter, who tells her that "Annie's always been more like a real mother to me," and to a dying Annie, whose only regret is that she loved her own daughter too much. Soon a repentant Sarah Jane returns as well—too late to take back her harsh words, but in time to see her mother's coffin loaded onto the hearse and to be welcomed back into the family by Lora, Susie, and Steve. (Jim Pines calls this ending a masterly piece of racial image manipulation disguised by the emotive diversion of soap opera: with Annie dead, there is no one left to remind Sarah Jane of her blackness, and so "we find Sarah Jane and all the other self-assured *white* characters neatly framed together like a happy family—as if nothing really happened" [69].)

Almost cheaply melodramatic at times, the 1959 *Imitation of Life* eliminated many of the elements that made the original version so effective.[19] Unlike Bea, who relied on Delilah for support as well as for the secret to her success, Lora achieves everything from her brilliant career to her impending marriage on her own (or through the men in her life—a conventional and socially acceptable alternative to female ambition in the Eisenhower era). Annie, on the other hand, is even more unfortunate than her counterpart Delilah; she lacks even an old family recipe to call her own. Director Douglas Sirk tried to rationalize the plot changes. "Nowadays," he explained, "a Negro woman who got rich *could* buy a house, and wouldn't be dependent to such a degree on the white woman . . . . So I had to change the axis of the film and make the Negro woman just the typical Negro, a servant, without much she could call her own but the friendship, love, and charity of a white mistress" (Leab 213). Yet it is precisely this notion of "the Negro woman [as] *just the typical Negro, a servant,*" wholly reliant upon the kindness of her "white mistress," that underscores the regressiveness of the remake. So does the abusiveness of Sarah Jane's white boyfriend (Troy Donahue), who beats her up to the sounds of cacophonous jazz that is supposed to evoke their clash of cultures. Worse yet, the film seems to suggest that the dissembling Sarah Jane deserves such punishment.

Even the film's imagery is heavy-handed. On her first day in the Merediths's apartment, for instance, Sarah Jane refuses to accept the black doll that Susie gives her; instead she insists on playing with the white doll. And when Lora shows Annie the spare room just beyond the kitchen, Sarah Jane petulantly exclaims, "Why do we always have to live in the back?" Yet when Sarah Jane eventually runs away, she assumes the most demeaning sort of "back room" identity possible: as a cheap chorus girl who dates clients from the club. In fact, Sarah Jane's distorted self-image and neurotic obsession to prove that she is white ally her more closely to Lora, who is so driven by a selfish need to be a star that she is willing to forsake her daughter and the other people who love her, than to any of the other characters—black or white—in the film. Furthermore, since Sarah Jane lacks even the liberal conscience of the mulatto characters in the popular postwar films, she never gains any deeper sense of her own black identity; instead, like the self-hating "tragic mulatto" of earlier films, she causes only pain (and, in this case, even death) to those closest to her.

A more liberal, if ultimately still problematic, resolution occurs in *Pinky* (Twentieth Century-Fox, 1949; dir. Elia Kazan), another problem film about "passing"[20] and one of an important cycle of black-themed films produced or released during the late 1940s. In *Pinky*, which was based on the novel *Quality* by white novelist Cid Ricketts Sumner, a fair-skinned nurse (Jeanne Crain) who has been passing for white in the North returns home to the Deep South, where her grandmother Dicey Johnson (Ethel Waters) and an old white woman named Miss Em (Ethel Barrymore) teach her vital lessons about self-respect. A hardworking and honorable Christian whose meager wages as a laundress have paid for her grand-daughter's education, "Aunt Dicey" is ashamed of Pinky for "denying [her]self like Peter denied the good Lord Jesus" and for "pretend[ing] you is what you ain't." Pinky gets similar advice and a similar reprimand from Miss Em, a once-powerful gentle-woman who now is sick, impoverished, and forgotten by everyone except the loyal Dicey. "Be yourself," Miss Em tells Pinky, because "nobody deserves respect as long as she pretends to be something she isn't." At first Pinky, who has reluctantly been pressed into the old woman's service, despises Miss Em's outmoded and arrogant notions of aristocracy because they underlie—and often justify—

Southern racism; and she balks at the thought of "living on the scraps" that white people give her, as Dicey does. But soon she and Miss Em develop a real understanding of and affection for each other. After Miss Em dies, willing her home and all of its belongings to Pinky "with confidence in the use to which she will put the property," she decides to stay in the South, where she successfully fights to retain the place and turn it into a black nursing clinic and nursery school named for Miss Em. (As Thomas Cripps notes, by making Pinky's struggle to bring the clinic into being the "core-conflict," the film offered a plot "in which something *black* was at stake"; and it called attention—long before the NAACP's *Brown vs. Topeka* case—to the courtroom as a civil rights arena [*MMB* 236]). Pinky also finds the courage to break up with Tom, her white fiancé who is willing to accept her "secret" but who insists that they move far away, both from her family and his, in order to erase her past and ensure that there will "be no [more] Pinky Johnson" after their marriage. (Fig. 4.3.) But Pinky is unwilling to renounce her identity. "I'm a Negro," she tells Tom. "I can't forget it and I

Figure 4.3. Pinky (Jeanne Crain), surrounded by her white fiancé and her black grandmother Dicey (Ethel Waters), goes to court for the property that has been bequeathed to her in *Pinky*. *(Twentieth Century-Fox, 1949)*

can't deny it. I can't pretend to be anything else and I don't want to be anything else." She realizes, as Em and Dicey did, that "You can't live without pride." So the film ends with Pinky standing proudly, but alone, in front of her clinic.

Although characterizations of minor characters like the shiftless, double-dealing Jake Waters (Frederick O'Neil) and his whorish, razor-toting girlfriend Rozelia (Nina Mae McKinney) resurrected and reinforced negative black typing, *Pinky* did endeavor to offer a more realistic depiction of contemporary race relations. For instance, when Pinky visits Jake's home to insist that he repay Dicey's money, two police officers pull up alongside the curb. Suspecting trouble, the deputy frisks Jake and orders Rozelia to "pull your dress up, girl," so he can search her garter for a concealed weapon, which he finds; moments later, he slaps Rozelia in the face. By contrast, assuming Pinky to be a white woman, the captain calls her "ma'am," expresses concern that Jake may have "molested" her, and threatens to punish Rozelia for any "impudence" she may have shown. But when he realizes that Pinky is not white but "colored," the captain changes his tone; forcing her into the police car, he takes her to the station, where he crassly searches under her skirt and tries to arrest her, even though she has broken no law. A few days later, Pinky has a similar experience. Walking home, she is followed by two inebriated young white men who nobly declare that they "can't let a white girl walk through this section" of town. Once they become aware of her race, their solicitousness ends: calling her a "swamp rabbit" and "the whitest dinge" they have ever seen, they assault and fondle her and rip her dress before she makes good her escape. And after Miss Em's death, when Pinky stops at Goolby's Dry Goods store to buy a mourning veil, she again becomes the victim of racial discrimination. The salesclerk, Miss Viola, shows Pinky the store's best quality merchandise, a veil that costs $2.98. But after a white woman complains that the clerk is waiting on a "Negro before white folks," Mr. Goolby questions the "honesty" of Pinky's money, charges her $4.98 for the same veil, and then refuses to place the change in her hand. Instead, he throws the two pennies onto the counter.

Yet, despite the realism of such scenes, the film makes numerous compromises. In addition to its optimistic, almost syrupy

Hollywood ending—a significant departure from the book, in which Pinky wins her claim in court, only to have the house that formerly belonged to Miss Em burned to the ground by the Ku Klux Klan—there is the casting of a white actress, Jeanne Crain, to play the mulatto role. Such cinematic concessions were common, even expected; as V. J. Jerome noted: "clearly, it would be going 'too far' to let an *actual* Negro woman, even in a film pretending to have a Negro heroine, defy, in a white man's court, the white supremacist code of robbery of the Negro's right to inherit; or to let an *actual* Negro woman be seen in a white lover's embrace, even though that love remains, by the taboo of the Hollywood racist code, unconsummated." After all, as Jerome concluded, "if a degree of concession must be made in a Negro character, let it at least be made to a white player, says Hollywood. The logic is plain. The logic is cruel" (27). But the use of Crain did more than just cede to Hollywood's tradition of "white" mulattos; it blunted the movie's impact. "The casting of someone like Lena Horne," Daniel J. Leab observes, "would obviously have elicited a different audience response, especially with the romantic attraction of Pinky and the doctor" (155), just as the casting of black actress Fredi Washington lent an authenticity to her role in the original *Imitation of Life* that the remake, featuring a white actress, could not recapture.

Another compromise was the film's easy and somewhat regressive solution to its "problem": that only by knowing—and keeping—her place can Pinky be happy. *The Daily Worker* went so far as to suggest that since Pinky "finds herself" through Miss Em, the film itself is a deception that insists that the answer to black concerns must come "not by organization or political struggle" but by individual reward from "the white ruling class" (Bogle, *TCMMB* 151). Yet it is true, even from a less Marxist perspective, that Pinky's realization of place and self results not so much from any significant experience of her own blackness or even the example of her black granny but from the generosity of the white woman she has—at first reluctantly—served. Pinky, after all, is not anxious to accept or embrace her racial heritage: she despises the ethnic life in which she has been raised, the baseness of which inclines her to pack her bags and head north in the first place. She returns to the South not to reimmerse herself in black culture but rather to escape the need to reveal her past to her white fiancé; and she allies herself more closely with Miss Em (to whom she asserts, "I am as white as you are!") than with her dutiful grandmother Dicey or with the neighboring black children whom she walks by without acknowledging. Even when Pinky does decide to stay, her actions derive less from any genuine group identification (though that is the film's high-toned suggestion) than from what Jim Pines called "an emphatic sacrifice based on the liberal conception that *anyone* committing themselves to (what the films portray as) such a lowly and deathly existence is highly commendable indeed" (67). The final scene, in which Pinky goes out on the lawn of her property, and—in close-up—gazes heavenward, "lips parted in an expression of benign acceptance of her mission and her prospective celibate existence," implies that even God is drawn into the film "to prevent miscegenation" (Leab 155).

Furthermore, Pinky's commitment to establish a segregated school seems to endorse the separatist—and ultimately racist—principles that she earlier tried to repudiate and that the film's liberal idealism purports to redress.[21] As V. J. Jerome writes, Pinky "moves 'forward' into a segregated existence in which she administers a segregated school—a nice, well-mannered, trim Negro woman who 'knows her place'—and is liked and helped by the 'best' white folk." That "reformist, segregationist, paternalistic solution" to racial concerns is a "'solution' which, as in all past Hollywood films, builds on acceptance of the 'superiority' of the whites and ends in endorsement of Jim Crow—in this case, 'liberal,' 'benevolent,' Social-Democratic Jim Crow" (28).

Nevertheless, despite its compromises, *Pinky* remains noteworthy for its ambition in attempting to depict the nature and extent of racial inequality and especially for the brilliant performance of Ethel Waters as the illiterate old laundress who maintains her dignity, be it under cross-examination in court or in discussion of her feelings of gratitude for the dead Miss Em, who bequeaths to her for her years of faithful service only used shoes and clothing. In the original Philip Dunne-Dudley Nichols screenplay, the character of Aunt Dicey was, according to Donald Bogle (*TCMMB* 152), "a combination tom and mammy, a further elaboration on Aunt Delilah of *Imitation of Life*." But unlike previous screen Mammies, Waters—who earned an Academy Award nomination as Best Supporting Actress in 1949 for her performance (only the second black performer to receive an Oscar nomination)—was "neither all Christian resignation (like Louise Beavers) nor all rage and indignation (like Hattie McDaniel)," and her portrayal helped to bring an end to the one-sided Mammy figures in film—even if the film did, albeit subtly, create new stereotypes in addition to the older ones it reinforced.[22]

Another Hollywood problem film, *Lost Boundaries* (RD-DR Productions, 1949; dir. Alfred L. Werker), released in the same year as *Pinky*, also focused on what Jim Pines called "that much over-rated and highly emotive racial theme, the Negro 'passing' for white"; and, like *Pinky*, it exploited "the sentimentality of the 'trag-ic mulatto' image to the full, while simultaneously overstating some banality about social responsibility (the mulatto's towards his/her Negro people) being more worthy than personal happi-ness in 'passing' for white" (Pines 66). Still, as in *Pinky*, it was this attempt to create some sense of ethnic group identity that distin-guished the film from earlier cinematic stories with "mixed blood" themes. An immediate critical hit, *Lost Boundaries* was hailed even by the black press, which had originally been critical of producer Louis De Rochemont for casting white actors in the black roles; an assistant managing editor of the *Afro-American*, in fact, described the finished film as "one of the best treatments of a racial story I have ever seen out of Hollywood" (Leab 152).

The film was based on journalist William L. White's nonfic-tional book about a black Midwestern doctor, Albert H. Johnston, who moved first to Maine, then Massachusetts, and finally to Keene, New Hampshire, where he settled with his black wife and family and for almost two decades passed for white in order to avoid the discrimination endured even by blacks in the profes-sional class. Only when Dr. Johnston volunteered for Navy service just before Pearl Harbor was the secret of his race exposed. In the film version *Lost Boundaries*, the white actor Mel Ferrer stars as Scott Carter, a black doctor unable to find work: understaffed and underfunded "Negro hospitals" improbably consider him to be too light-skinned, while white hospitals reject him because he is black.[23] After Scott saves the life of another physician, he is recom-mended for a practice in a small New England town. Deciding to say nothing at all about their race, Carter and his wife (played by Beatrice Pearson, a white actress) are accepted by the townspeople, with whom they form good friendships, and raise a son and daughter. After the patriotic Carter enlists and his "Negro blood" is revealed, however, the community turns against the family (fig. 4.4)—until, in true Hollywood fashion, the white minister gives a sermon on tolerance and harmony is restored. Yet the sins of the parents are visited upon the children, particularly upon the troubled son Howie (Richard Hylton), who embarks on a frightening odyssey of self-discovery through Harlem, a descent-into-hell sequence that—as Thomas Cripps observes—"visually echoes the red-light district in the Army's VD film *Easy to Get*" (*MMB* 229). (In real life, Johnston's two younger children were able to cope with the revelation, but the oldest dropped out of college and traveled not in Harlem but throughout the country looking up black relatives and learning to cope with his new identity.)

Lost Boundaries certainly highlighted various contemporary racial prejudices, including the prohibition against blacks serving as commissioned officers in the Navy, and other forms of racial

Figure 4.4. In *Lost Boundaries*, the Carters (Mel Ferrer and Beatrice Pearson) pass for white in their Keenham community until their secret is exposed. *(Film Classics, Inc./RD-DR Productions, 1949)*

discrimination in the services and in the medical profession. And it revealed the ways in which even seemingly decent people harbor race hatred: during a blood drive for the war effort, for instance, Carter's nurse Miss Richmond wants to dispose of a black chauffeur's blood rather than "mixing" it with the blood that white townspeople have donated; and Abby, a fellow parishioner at St. Paul's, after commenting on the breach of etiquette Marsha Carter has committed by inviting a "darky" to the church party, refuses to pass the desserts because she will not "be a waitress for any Negro." But, as Daniel J. Leab (152) noted, for all of its outspokenness, "the screenplay skimmed over many of the issues in the book." Some changes were minor, like altering names and telescoping the doctor's experiences into one practice in a town called Keenham. Yet other changes provided "a fascinating comment on what the filmmakers believed the American movie-going public would accept." Dr. Johnston, as White wrote, made the decision to pass in order to circumvent discrimination by whites; but in the film, much of the discrimination against the Carters is committed by blacks. For example, in an incident that is not drawn from the book, Dr. Carter accepts a position at a black hospital in Georgia, only to be dismissed on his first day by an administrator for being too light-skinned. The movie's first act of discrimination, then, is committed by a black. Moreover, since Carter's subsequent rejections from white hospitals all come in the form of letters, the sole rejection that the film dramatizes and that the audience actually sees—"*the only personified act of bigotry*," according to V. J. Jerome— is by blacks. "Thus, the onus of the guilt for [Carter's] 'passing' falls upon the Negro institution. This guilt leads logically to the assumption that one can 'hardly blame' whites for discriminating when Negroes themselves discriminate" (31). Conversely, in another scene original to the film, it is a white man, Dr. Brackett, to whom Carter confesses his racial secret and who helps Carter to establish his practice. And unlike the administrator in Georgia who discharges Carter after he and Marsha have moved from Boston and rented an apartment locally, Brackett even offers the Carters a large, comfortable, fully furnished home in which to live rent-free.

Most disturbing, however, is the ending of the film, which by its ambiguity offers no actual resolutions, just a small dose of tepid idealism. Howie, having witnessed only poverty and violence during his brief visit to Harlem, returns to Keenham and ultimately to his new responsibilities as a wartime Navy recruit—although probably not to the position of naval officer to which he had aspired before the disclosure of his racial heritage. His younger sister Shelley (Susan Douglas) reconciles with her father but continues to feel so overwhelmed by the scrutiny of the townspeople and by their cruel talk ("your folks are colored"; "they're black as coal"; "they're darkies") that she leaves church before the minister delivers his curative sermon. Shelley's departure allows her to avoid confronting her white boyfriend, Andy, who is among the parishioners; but more importantly, it allows the film to avoid having to address the issue of miscegenation that their relationship raises.[24] As for the Carters themselves, the narrator says only that Scott Carter is "still our doctor."

Yet even the pleas for tolerance that are uttered by Reverend Taylor from the pulpit at St. Paul's Church distort the message behind the film. The equal treatment of all races is not just a matter to be "tolerated" (Leab 153-54), as the minister exhorts, but rather a moral imperative. "The whites' viciousness" is therefore, according to Donald Bogle, "understated at a time when it should have been emphatic. The light-skinned Negroes appeared to have wronged the town by keeping such a secret, and the guilt was placed on their shoulders, making the blacks the tragic characters" (*TCMMB* 150). Nonetheless, the film was considered so divisive by Southern censors that they banned it for "inciting to violence or law-breaking."[25] (V. J. Jerome adds an interesting postscript: unlike the film's Dr. Carter, who—after the minister's uplifting Sunday sermon—is reinstated in the community's good graces, resumes his practice, and seems destined, along with his family, to live happily ever after, the real Dr. Johnston was less fortunate. As noted in a news item in the *New York Herald Tribune* [16 Oct. 1949]: "Dr. Albert Johnston, the Negro doctor whose story is dramatized in the motion picture *Lost Boundaries*, said last week . . . that the Elliott Community Hospital, which he has served as radiologist since 1940, this year has declined to renew his contract. . . . He would rather, Dr. Johnston said, not believe himself a victim of racial discrimination; yet he can put only this construction on the sequence of events." As Jerome concludes, "They must have been in the wrong church that Sunday morning" [30].)

Like Pinky Johnson and Scott Carter, the central character of another black-oriented problem film adapted from literature, *Home of the Brave* (Republic Pictures, 1949; dir. Mark Robson), learns to use his experience of racial discrimination to gain a better understanding of himself and of his position in postwar American society. Arthur Laurents's play *The Way Back*, on which the film is based, featured a Jewish character in the "problem" role; but the film adaptation—conveniently, at least in terms of liberal racial reasoning—turned the Jew into a black man named Moss. As Jim Pines (64) has demonstrated, similar racial-thematic substitutions occur in several later important black films and characterizations: "Notably in *Carmen Jones* (1954, from Prosper Merimée's tale via Georges Bizet's opera), *Anna Lucasta* (1958, originally a play and film about a Polish-American family), *Pressure Point* (1962, from a Jewish situation), *Up Tight!* (1968, derived from Liam O'Flaherty's Irish novel *The Informer*, which was originally filmed as such by John Ford in 1935), *Cool Breeze* (1972, a black remake of that other 'classic' *The Asphalt Jungle*), and the *Shaft* stories (derived from non-ethnic literary characters)." Novice filmmaker Stanley Kramer correctly believed that a picture reflecting the new postwar philosophy of racial tolerance would reach a wide audience and attract significant publicity, so—swearing his cast and crew to secrecy—he undertook the production of *Home of the Brave* (fig. 4.5), an independent, low-budget feature with no established stars, and managed to release it before *Pinky*, *Lost Boundaries*, and several other major studio projects that same year. Kramer's film, a critical and commercial success, was hailed as a Hollywood breakthrough in the presentation of racial discrimination as a central theme.[26]

Told in a series of flashbacks, *Home of the Brave* is the story of Peter "Mossy" Moss (James Edwards), a young black private who experiences partial amnesia and hysterical paralysis after the death of his best friend, a white man named Finch whom he has known since childhood. Both soldiers had volunteered to be part of a dangerous five-man reconnaissance mission on a Pacific island. There Moss had endured numerous racial incidents, including jibes by racist fellow platoon member T.J. (Steve Brodie), who resented having to work with "a boogie," and an ugly epithet ("yellow-bellied ni—nitwit") half-uttered by Finch in the heat of

Figure 4.5. Even the advertisements for *The Home of the Brave* suggested the racial segregation and discrimination that Mossy (James Edwards) experiences in his white platoon. *(Republic Pictures, 1949)*

an argument. As the group, which also included a sympathetic soldier named Mingo (Frank Lovejoy) and an ambitious young officer (Douglas Dick), was about to leave the island aboard a rescue boat, Finch realized that he had left behind the map case. When he returned to retrieve it, he was captured and tortured by the Japanese, after which he crawled back to the rendezvous point to ask Moss for his forgiveness and to die in his arms. Suddenly unable to move, Moss had to be carried off the beach and to the awaiting boat by T.J.

The unnamed young white psychiatrist (Jeff Corey) assigned to Moss's case knows that the psychosomatic paralysis is caused by conflicting and conflicted emotions, particularly Moss's guilt over surviving his friend, whom he heard being tortured and whom he watched die, and his repressed but recurring feeling that Finch deserved his fate for having made such a racial slur. At first unsure of how to treat the black GI, the doctor forces him to recall his experiences, beginning with his earliest memories of prejudice against him as a child. Then, in a later session, the doctor decides to provoke him by calling him a "dirty nigger." The aversion therapy is so successful that it causes Moss not only to lunge at the doctor and therefore to begin walking again but also to reveal, and then ultimately to confront, the deeper hurt of a lifetime of bigotry that culminates in the racism he suffered on the island. Moss's racial sensitivity, the doctor tells him in a platitudinous speech, is "a legacy. A hundred and fifty years of slavery, second-class citizenship, of being different. . . . You always had that guilt inside you. That's why it was so easy for you to feel guilty about Finch." The symbolic implication of the doctor's words, according to Cripps ("Death" 60), is "that Negroes can be fulfilled only on white men's terms."[27]

As the recovered but still psychologically scarred Moss prepares to leave the hospital, he bumps into Mingo and T.J., who again tries to bait him; but this time Mingo orders T.J. to leave Moss alone. It turns out that Mingo, who lost an arm in the same encounter with the Japanese during which Finch was shot and killed, has had to endure similar rude and belittling remarks from T.J. about his disability. "To that crud and all cruds like him, it's the same thing," he tells Moss. "We're easy targets for them to take potshots at." Feeling a new kinship, Mingo reminds Moss of the plans Moss and Finch had made to start a restaurant, and he suggests that he take Finch's place in the business venture. Moss indicates his assent and walks out of the hospital together with Mingo.

"I am different," Moss realizes. "Everybody's different. But so what? Because underneath we're all guys." Although such an idealistic if slightly patronizing ending may sound false today, Donald Bogle writes that at the time it was a kind of black declaration of independence. "The ending lessens the impact of much of what preceded it. . . . But there was something decent about its optimism. . . . [And] in the end, *Home of the Brave* justified itself by meeting the requirements of its age" (*TCMMB* 145).

To be sure, though, not all viewers felt uplifted by the film. Some resented the easy integrationist resolution and the inference that "a one-armed white man equals a whole Negro" (*MMB* 224).[28] Others felt that the film implied that race hatred is the "disease" of overly sensitive blacks like Moss rather than of the insensitive white racists like T.J. who perpetuate it and that it grossly downplayed the manifestations of such hatred. (T.J.'s taunting, they argued, is much softer and less physical than it would be in comparable real-life situations; and it is always rebuffed or repudiated by Mingo or the doctor.) Still others agreed with black novelist Richard Wright who, when asked about the "stimulating influence on the masses" of films like *Home of the Brave* replied: "To tell the truth, I distrust their influence. I believe that such films produce little good. They correspond rather to a search for sensation than a cause of a healthy reaction by the public" (de Vaal 158). But overall *Home of the Brave* received wide praise from blacks as well as whites, Northerners as well as Southerners; and the film itself was hailed as representative of the new Hollywood. "A commercial movie laden with racial politics in an entertaining formulaic equivalent to the war movie genre, thereby sidling toward defining the imagery and agenda of the integrationist generation to come," *Home of the Brave*, writes Cripps (*MMB* 226), had "spoken not only for the liberal center, thereby achieving the goals of its makers, but also for conservatives groping toward" their own accommodationist hope that blacks were, after all, only whites with dark skins.

Another race-themed movie that formed part of the cycle of Hollywood's black-oriented problem films of the late 1940s and early 1950s was *Intruder in the Dust* (Metro-Goldwyn-Mayer, 1949; dir. Clarence Brown). Closely and faithfully adapted from William Faulkner's 1948 novel, *Intruder in the Dust* comprised, as Donald Bogle writes, "many things—a melodrama, a detective story, a murder mystery, a condemnation of mob rule. But mainly it was a subtle study of a fearless and proud black man" (*TCMMB* 155), Lucas Beauchamp (Juano Hernandez), and of the mounting racial hostilities that surround his arrest and trial for the murder of poor-white Vinson Gowrie, with whom he had quarreled. Resentful of Lucas's defiance of white authority and of his innate sense of equality that allows him to assume many of the iconically "white" symbols of Southern society—wide-brimmed white hat, cravat, gold toothpick, revolver—the mob of rough, angry townspeople outside the jail shout that "he won't need a lawyer . . . [but] an undertaker." (Fig. 4.6.) But legal assistance is precisely what Lucas wants, and he enlists the help of Chick Mallison (Claude Jarman, Jr.), a teenage white boy who is in his debt, and Mallison's uncle, liberal lawyer John Gavin Stevens (David Brian), to ensure that he gets it. The previous summer, after saving Chick from drowning, Lucas fed him a meal and offered him the warmth of his family hearth; and although the boy had rudely tried to pay so as to avoid being indebted to a black man, Lucas had refused any compensa-

Figure 4.6. As he is taken to jail, Lucas Beauchamp (Juano Hernandez) is surrounded by an angry white mob that demands swift Southern justice in *Intruder in the Dust*. (*Metro-Goldwyn-Mayer, 1949*)

tion for his hospitality, thereby creating a sort of moral obligation that Chick now feels compelled to redeem. With the help of Miss Habersham (Elizabeth Patterson), an octogenarian spinster who also feels a spiritual link to Lucas, and a young black friend Aleck (Elzy Emmanuel), the son of the Mallisons's housekeeper, Chick sets out to exhume Gowrie's body in order to recover the lethal bullet. That bullet, it is revealed, did not come from Lucas's Colt forty-one revolver but from the gun of Gowrie's brother Crawford (Charles Kemper), who is exposed as the real killer. Apparently Lucas had known the criminal's identity all along. When Stevens asks, "Why didn't you tell me the truth that night in the jail?," Lucas counters, "Would you have believed me?" The lawyer is forced to recognize that it was never Lucas who was in trouble: "*We* were in trouble." His innocence established, the newly freed black patriarch marches into Stevens's office to pay his two dollar legal fee, awaits a receipt, and walks away across the center of town. As Stevens observes that Lucas is "the keeper of my conscience," Chick adds that Lucas is in fact "*our* conscience." Indeed, writes Thomas Cripps, "no vehicle could have done greater justice to the emerging notion of a common conscience across racial lines" (*MMB* 243).

"A superb mystery drama," according to Ralph Ellison, *Intruder in the Dust* allowed the audience to participate "in a process by which the role of Negroes in American life has been given what, for the movies, is a startling new definition" (*Shadow and Act* 274-75). From the first glimpse of Lucas from a high angle, followed by fleeting takes of his face through the mob, then in the half-light of his cell, and finally rising to full height in the square, "the whites are not free to ignore him or set him apart. He became what the war movie genre and its 'unity' propaganda had begun to assert, the center of a conscience-liberal consensus."[29]

Associated with some of MGM's most prestigious films, director Clarence Brown was a Southerner with roots in Tennessee and Georgia who remembered witnessing race riots as a child in Atlanta. After reading Faulkner's novel in galleys, he determined to bring the story of the fiercely independent and aristocratic Lucas to the screen; to Brown, it seemed "as little as I could do to make up for Atlanta," particularly with a property that was "the first of its kind" (*MMB* 240). Despite the studio's misgivings, he not only undertook the project but also decided to strive for additional authenticity by shooting it largely in Oxford, Mississippi, near Faulkner's home (with Faulkner himself around to offer occasional advice on scenes and characters). Consequently, according to Cripps (*MMB* 240), the film version effectively froze the "region in time, caught its ancient guilt over miscegenation, yet inched toward some fairmindedness toward African Americans. Still without altering the social order, [screenwriter Ben Maddow] reordered some of Faulkner's indirection, opened up the action, and cut several regional apologia and racial epithets."

The theme of racial injustice, which was handled somewhat gingerly in "passing" films like *Pinky* and *Lost Boundaries*, is unquestionably more overt in *Intruder in the Dust*, as Lucas, repeatedly derided as "nigger," is framed for murder and subjected to the lynch mentality of the white townspeople, led by the atavistic Crawford Gowrie. Blacks, fearing violence, disappear from the streets and retreat to their homes after Lucas's arrest; meanwhile, crowds of white men, women, and children, some of them arriving by car and bus to witness the spectacle of Southern justice in action, gather round eating ice cream, playing cards, and listening to the radio as if it were just another day in town. "Not only is a black man presumed guilty when charged in this environment," writes Daniel Leab, "but it is also taken for granted that 'lynch law will deny him even the most elementary forms of justice.' Unlike its predecessors, this movie did not even try to apologize for white actions and attitudes or to evade the issues" (160). (The realism of mob brutality, however, by which "all black cats look alike," is slightly undercut by the suggestion that an ancient woman with her darning in hand could block the jail's door and singlehandedly hold back a crowd of armed and angry whites or that a teenaged boy and a sympathetic Southern sheriff can ensure that justice prevails.) As Lucas Beauchamp, black actor Juano Hernandez dominated the film and made credible most of the plot twists; consequently, his portrayal of an intelligent but self-righteous man who refuses to conform to white presumptions by expecting to be treated as an equal and not as "a nigger" remains among the most powerful in cinema history.

Undoubtedly, *Intruder in the Dust* and other black-oriented postwar message or problem films exposed a variety of social concerns; but they usually explored those concerns from a white per-spective. As Ralph Ellison noted of the four films in the so-called "Negro cycle," each dealt with "some basic and unusually nega-tive asumption about Negroes" that revealed Hollywood's bias even in films that ostensibly challenged national attitudes about race. In *Home of the Brave*, the question was "Are Negroes coward-ly soldiers?" In *Intruder in the Dust*, it was "are Negroes the real polluters of the South?"; in *Lost Boundaries*, "have mulatto Negroes the right to pass as white, at the risk of having black babies, or if they have white-skinned children, of having to kill off their 'white' identities by revealing to them they are alas, Negroes?"; and in *Pinky* "should Negro girls marry white men or—wonderful non sequitur—should they help their race?" Ellison concluded that "obviously, these films are not *about* Negroes at all; they are about what whites think and feel about Negroes" (*Shadow and Act* 277).

THE NEW REALISM OF *NATIVE SON*

Blacks, although happy that Hollywood was making some progress on the racial front, wanted more. And they continued to seek out and demand increasingly realistic screen images, particu-larly images that did not depict blacks as the "problem" but rather that portrayed instead some of the real problems that blacks faced. In a letter to the *New York Times*, for instance, black actress Rose McClendon insisted that "social realism" must be used by drama-tists to "deal with Negroes, with Negro problems, with phases of Negro life, faithfully presented" (Cripps, *SFB* 350). Indeed, in lit-erature, some important new voices were doing precisely that.

Richard Wright was one of those voices. Born and raised in the South, he came of age in Chicago; but even in the North, he felt restricted and oppressed because of his race. That sense of inescapable victimization and of racial discrimination became the theme underlying all of his fiction. As the first black novelist to describe the plight of the urban masses, Wright is now considered the father of the post-Second World War black novel and one of the main precursors of the black arts movement that influenced younger writers like Ralph Ellison and James Baldwin. But Wright's importance went well beyond black literature; as Robert Felgar demonstrates in *Richard Wright*, he was "perhaps the very first writer to give the white community explanations and themes that cut through its prejudices and forced it to look at the reality of black life in America" (Clark 201).[30]

Wright's most distinguished work was *Native Son* (1940), "a good novel about a bad Negro" (*The New York Sun*, 4 Mar. 1940), which sold an extraordinary two hundred thousand copies within three weeks of its publication.[31] Wright himself described the book as being

> about the life of Negroes in the United States in their relations with whites. It is the story and the psychological portrait of a young Negro who lives in the "black ghetto" of Chicago, unemployed, with all roads closed and with the constant logical temptation to break the law. Finally, he meets a white girl who helps him, which surprises the Negro very much. In an accident, this girl dies and the Negro is accused of her death, is pursued, and after various sudden reversals in which the girl's father tries to help him, he dies in the electric chair. It is an accusation against the society of the United States and a defense of the Negro people, who still live in conditions very similar to slavery. (qtd. in Kinnamon and Fabre 32)

Based on young men that Wright had encountered in a Chicago rehabilitation school for Negro Dead End youth where he was a play instructor and on the case of Robert Nixon, an eighteen-year-old black who was sent to the electric chair for murdering a white woman with a brick, *Native Son* was both powerful and disturbing in its suggestion that black rage was a revolutionary act against a contemporary social order as degrading as slavery. The distinguished literary critic Irving Howe, in fact, remarked that on the day the novel appeared, "American culture was changed forever" (Hakutani 379).

Instead of chapters, the novel was divided into three books, "Fear," "Flight," and "Fate," which also served as recurring motifs.[32] In Book One, Bigger Thomas, the young black protagonist, describes and confronts some of his many fears, such as his fear of the huge rat that roams throughout his family's apartment and his fear of the gang violence that he perpetrates with his friends. Most of all, though, Bigger is afraid of being discovered in the bedroom of young Mary Dalton, the daughter of his white employers. As chauffeur for the Dalton family, Bigger had brought the drunken Mary home and innocently taken her up to her room. Concerned that his presence there might be misunderstood, he tried to silence Mary by putting a pillow over her face. But Mary suffocates, and Bigger—now more fearful than ever—decapitates her and burns her body in the basement furnace. In Book Two, Bigger tries to take "Flight" from his "Fear" but ultimately is unable to escape it. At first, rationalizing Mary's murder as a symbolic act against an oppressor, he directs suspicion to Mary's Communist boyfriend, Jan Erlone, and tries to capitalize on his loathsome act by collecting a ransom for the girl's return. But his plan goes tragically wrong: the lingering image of Mary's face keeps Bigger from properly disposing of the ashes, and Mary's charred remains are found. Afterwards, scared that his girlfriend Bessie might betray him, Bigger kills her too and tries to evade the police by moving from one tenement to another before being captured on a rooftop in Chicago's black ghetto. In Book Three, the only one of the books not told from Bigger's point of view, Bigger's "Fate" is revealed: tried and convicted, he is scheduled to be executed. But the focus in the final book is as much on the community as it is on Bigger himself, since—as Bigger's lawyer Boris A. Max argues—a racist society must assume some of the blame for the young man's crimes.

Thus, as J. R. Johnson (50) observed in 1940, in a profound sense Bigger Thomas is "a 'typical' Negro. His hatred of whites, his sense of his wrongs and his forcibly limited life, his passionate desire to strike at his enemies, all this is racial. He is different from other Negroes only in the fact that his nature is such that he cannot contain himself." Yet in *Native Son* Wright suggests that only through revolutionary struggle can Bigger—and the millions of blacks like him—ever achieve a clear realization of class solidarity and a sense of personal liberation.

Within a year of the book's publication, a stage adaptation of *Native Son* opened on Broadway.[33] Co-written by Wright and playwright Paul Green, directed by Orson Welles, and produced by John Houseman, the play required some reworking of the novel. The political aspect was reduced by minimizing the character of Jan, who was portrayed ironically as a militant Communist and who appeared only after Mary's death; Mary herself symbolized the rich upper-middle class. The main problem, however, was in the presentation of Bigger, played by the black actor Canada Lee. Welles wanted him to be the passive victim of the society that had conditioned him to hate and that inspired his revenge; Green envisioned him not so much the product of his milieu as a conscious agent who assumes responsibility for his actions; Wright initially thought to portray him as an expiatory victim, a sort of black Jesus, but eventually preferred a version of the hero that was closer to the novel. Ultimately, the play telescoped certain scenes, combining events such as the trial and defense into one scene (which had the unfortunate result of making the defense too brief to be convincing—one of the few weaknesses in the production); replaced the subjective viewpoint with an objective one; eliminated some of the secondary plots and themes, such as the anti-Communist prejudice of the press; used speeches by characters to explain earlier actions (Max's speech, for example, re-creates Bigger's past); and, at the end, left Bigger alone after his family's visit to ponder his destiny and to realize the meaning that the crime had given his life (Fabre 208-10). Reviewers were enthusiastic, and the play, which ran for 115 performances to sizable audiences, was considered a success.[34] Not surprisingly, talk of a film version followed.

Unlike those writers who—often disingenuously—distanced themselves and their craft from cinema, Wright loved movies. "He was an addicted moviegoer," writes Thomas Cripps in *Making Movies Black* (278); he "interrogated [Orson] Welles for inside dope, followed [John] Steinbeck and Herbert Klein to Mexico to shoot *The Forgotten Village*, offered himself to OWI, and pitched black ideas to the National Film Board of Canada, Columbia, and anyone else who listened." As Wright himself confessed, "To make the screen version of a novel [*Native Son*] into which I had put so much of myself was a dream which I had long hugged to my heart" (Delpech 143). Yet even though he believed that from the time of the book's publication in 1940, "it immediately proved itself suitable to be made the subject of a film" (Martens 148), for a while he resisted adapting the novel to film. Apparently Wright feared that studio producers would restructure his story and distort his message.[35] And indeed, early offers from American producers involved significant departures from Wright's text: MGM, for instance, wanted to change the title and turn the black characters into whites (Fabre 215). Another proposal, from a private producer named Joseph Fields, tried to recast Bigger Thomas as a member of a white ethnic minority, one of four distinct character types—a Negro, an Italian, a Jew, and a Pole—who were applying for the same position. Fields's intention, according to Wright biographer Michel Fabre, was to have the Negro and the Jew voluntarily withdraw from consideration in favor of the neediest candidate, who had a family to feed; by the film's end, all of the applicants would be aware of the benefits of solidarity, particularly among those who did not enjoy equality. The point of Fields's film would be that whenever a minority is deprived of civil rights, the quality and meaning of life suffer (Fabre 336)—an admirable sentiment, but one inconsistent with Wright's novel.

Wright apparently had greater confidence in European producers.[36] By late 1946, he met with Jacques Marceron about the prospect of producing a theatrical version of *Native Son*; and in 1948, he asked Marie-Rose Belin to adapt the work to the French stage. In the meantime, Roberto Rossellini wrote that he was interested in making the film; but Rossellini's plans, like Wright's earlier proposed collaboration with Marcel Carné and Jacques Prévert, fell through. Then Wright received a proposal from French film producer Pierre Chenal, who—during the occupation of France—had lived as a refugee in Argentina, where he had collaborated on several films with Uruguayan Jaime Prades. Impressed with a theatrical production of *Sangre Negro*, a Spanish translation of *Native Son* that he had seen in Buenos Aires, Chenal suggested a partnership with Wright. Prades would raise the money; Chenal would direct; and Wright himself would play the title role of Bigger. Significantly, unlike the offers from Hollywood, Chenal promised that his film would be faithful to the novel.

Pleased by the proposal and anticipating big profits from it, Wright discreetly bought back the film rights, assuming that even if the deal with Chenal fell through he could count on making the picture elsewhere. And he began writing the screenplay, later revising it together with Chenal. As Fabre notes, "following the novel closely, Wright cut a few episodes from the trial scene and condensed others, while Chenal added several flashbacks. Wright also decided to insert several fairly long dream sequences and to concentrate on psychological and human interest, rather than on the quasi-detective plot or ideological significance" (338). By Wright's description at the time, it was "the story of a boy born amid poverty and conditions of fear which eventually stop his will and control and make him a reluctant killer" (qtd. in Fabre 338).

A few exterior shots were filmed in Chicago, after which Wright and the cadre of actors—including Gloria Madison (Bessie Mears), Jean Wallace (Mary Dalton), Willa Pearl Curtiss (Hannah Thomas), and Nicholas Joy (Mr. Dalton)—sailed for Buenos Aires to begin production. Along the way, Wright lectured about American literature, spoke at length with reporters about racial problems, and dieted vigorously to shed enough weight to be credible in his role as Bigger. In Argentina, after the set director had designed a group of slum buildings to resemble those in Chicago and various English-speaking tourists and residents were hired to fill the secondary acting roles, filming began. Chenal expected it to be completed in sixty days, but the actual progress was slow: a month into the production, the final shooting script (which Cripps characterizes as strident and "off-the-mark," with street blacks using phrases like "hot diggity dog" and "you blokes" and voice-overs "speak[ing] in ponderous travelogue tones" [*MMB* 278]) was only half finished. The flashback and dream sequences added between the most dramatic episodes created further delays. And Wright himself became distracted by a romantic involvement with one of the cast members.

Problems developed off the set as well. Wright realized that several of his associates were engaged in dishonest dealings, and so as a way of protecting his interests he embarked on rather byzantine renegotiations, which involved the hiring of new lawyers and the use of a complicated secret code by which to communicate with them. To avoid large payments to the Argentinian government, Wright and his advisors secretly and unlawfully transferred monies out of the country. The financial concerns persisted even after the filming was completed in June, 1950; the unedited cut, with a running time of an hour and forty-five minutes, came in at more than three times the one hundred thousand dollars that Chenal had estimated. Nonetheless by October, more than a year after Wright and his company had arrived in Argentina, the film was ready for distribution.

In a daring publicity stunt devised by one of Wright's partners, the film had its world premiere aboard a Pan American strato-clipper on November 4. The complete version was shown in a Buenos Aires theater, and it was such a triumph that expectations were high for similar success at the American opening. But that was not to be. The New York State Board of Censors insisted on extensive cutting, to which the Walter Gould Agency, Wright's distributor in English-speaking countries, agreed. Consequently, some twenty-five hundred feet—about half an hour's worth—of film were excised; and the American premiere was moved back from April 15 to June 16, 1951, to accommodate the process. When the film was finally released, the New York critics were unenthusiastic. As Michel Fabre writes, "even the best reviews expressed disappointment with the amateurish acting as well as with the cuts, to which Wright attributed the failure almost entirely" (348). That August, Wright complained in a letter to his good friend Paul Reynolds:

> People everywhere know that the film was cut, that the killing of the rat was cut, that making of the homegun was cut, that the real heart of the boys' attempt at robbery was cut, that most of the dialogue between the newspaper men was cut. . . . But the cut that did the greatest damage was the cutting of the trial. As you know, the trial is shown with arms waving and mouths moving but nothing is heard. (qtd. in Fabre 348)

Wright blamed Gould for bowing to the pressure of the censors and even accused Gould, a naturalized citizen, of acting timidly out of fear that he would be labeled "un-American."[37] Nonetheless Gould endeavored to distribute the film as best he could. Local censors in Pennsylvania, Wisconsin, and Ohio refused to allow it to be shown; racial incidents in nearby Cicero and the hostile reception by the black press cast a shadow over showings in Chicago. The complications with censors had reverberations even in Europe: a disappointed Wright realized that the left-wing French press would boycott the cut version; yet the uncut version would invite suggestions of Communist intervention and criticism from American circles. Conversely, distributing the cut version would be considered concessionary by the French Left and would lead to Wright's rejection. Either way, it was clear that Wright would be unable to recoup his losses. After a partially restored print was screened at the Venice Film Festival and received good reviews, Wright's spirits revived a bit. The film began to be shown more widely—in Italy, in England, even in America (although it continued to be prohibited in several states); Wright's family was able to see it in Mississippi in the spring of 1952.

Figure 4.7. A lobby card from *Native Son* illustrates Bigger's fear. In this version, novelist Richard Wright starred as Bigger. *(Argentina Sono Film, 1950)*

The edited version of the black-and-white film released by Walter Gould (fig. 4.7) opens with some sweeping shots of Chicago—the skyscrapers, the business district, the fountains and memorials—and moves quickly to the "secret" side of the city, the "Black Belt" where residents live in a "prison without bars." In the Thomases's one-room kitchenette, Bigger sits "reading, dreaming about machines and planes. He wanted to be an explorer, a flyer," the voice-over announces, "but he's black. And when you're black, it's better to keep your dreams locked in your heart."

Dreams become a recurring motif in the film, especially as Bigger's dreams for a better life for himself and his family are consistently frustrated. Things turn even more nightmarish when he brings Mary Dalton back to her room, accidentally suffocates her, and tries unsuccessfully to cover up the crime. He is so haunted by Mary's death that he dreams the same awful dream every night until he is apprehended. In that dream, which the film depicts almost surrealistically, he is kneeling on coals trying to hide a package when his girlfriend Bessie appears, throws at him the floral corsage that Mary had worn, and points to a place where Bigger can conceal his bundle. Bigger starts running, into the cotton fields of his youth, where his father, who had been lynched twelve years earlier, waits with outstretched arms. Knowing that nothing bad can happen to him now, a tearful Bigger grabs his father's hand; but that hand becomes the hand of Policeman Britten, who laughs menacingly as he reaches for the bundle that contains Mary's head.

The film, for the most part, suffered from many of the problems that the early independent black films did. The acting is often stilted and unprofessional; Wright, in particular, substitutes broad gestures (eyes wide open to suggest terror, hand drawn across the brow to express relief) for more subtle interpretation of character. Continuity is minimal; actions seem to have no motivation or rationale; and the dialogue often has no context. (The South American accents of some of the minor players, moreover, are easily detectable; and on at least one occasion—when the custodian at the Dalton home shows Bigger how to work the furnace—the lines are actually dubbed.) There is no dialogue whatsoever during the trial scene, which in itself is absurdly brief: the camera pans away from Jan on the stand to Bigger's mother in the courtroom and then to Bigger in his jail cell. And the important, complicated relationships between the principal characters are largely or wholly undeveloped. In fact, when the reporters who help to solve the crime note that "it's the work of amateurs," it is tempting to apply their assessment to the film as a whole.

But despite its shortcomings, Wright's *Native Son* conveyed a real sense of racial politics and depicted, if not as convincingly as the novel did, the condemnation and exploitation of the black, particularly the black male, by white society. For example, when Bigger returns from the affluence of the Dalton home and sees his mother on her knees scrubbing the floor, he remarks on "how we live, how they live." And when Bigger and a friend go to a movie house, they watch a scene in which a wealthy white couple insists that the maid serve food to their dog at the table; both Bigger and his companion realize that their lives will always be worse than the dog's.

The film also makes clear the many levels of Bigger's victimization: by a society that forces him into a ghetto and defines the kind of work that he can do; by the police who treat him derisively and abusively; by the newspaper reporters who assume he is nothing more than an ignorant fool; by the citizens who congregate outside the courthouse before the trial begins to urge "lynching the nigger" and "stringing up the coon" as a way of saving the cost of a trial and expediting justice. Though Bigger tries to flee, metaphorically and literally, he cannot escape his fate, any more than the cornered rat in the Thomas home at the opening of the film can avoid his. In the climactic chase scene, Bigger dashes over tenement roofs only to be trapped atop a large neon sign ominously advertising "William's Funeral Garden, 24 Hour Service."

Interestingly, the edited version was released with two different endings. In the first, Bigger, in his cell, tells Max that he hopes "what happened to me won't happen to another black boy" and asks (incongruously, since there is no context for his request) that Max say hello to Jan on his behalf. As Max leaves, Bigger lies down on the cot inside his cell to await his execution. A song reminiscent of an old-time spiritual intones: "He's going home tonight, to meet a higher judge who can look past his sins and see into his heart. Oh, Lord, let mercy rain on him and wash his tears away." The camera then cuts to a scenic image of affluent, lakeside Chicago at dawn, as the city, unaware of—and indifferent to—Bigger's fate, awakens to a new day. In the second ending, more consistent with the tone of Wright's novel, Bigger expresses to Max his sentiment that no other "black boy" will be forced to suffer his fate and extends greetings to Jan. As Max walks down the hall away from Bigger's cell, the camera freezes on his image. In voice-over, Max says, "I left Bigger feeling that everything, including justice, was still unsettled. And today I feel even less certain of innocence and guilt, crime and punishment, of the nature of man." The first version brings the film full circle, from one image of "white" Chicago to another, just as the second version takes Bigger from Chicago's South Side, a "prison without bars," to a prison with bars—and to a conclusion that, Wright suggests, is for the most part pre-ordained.

American critical reaction to *Native Son* was generally nega-tive. Many viewers thought the film's "foreign political voice" sounded "off-key for having missed the shifting racial mentality of black and white Americans" (Cripps, *MMB* 278); and most con-curred that the acting, especially in the lesser roles, was amateur-ish, that the performance of the fifty-year-old Wright as the ado-lescent Bigger was at best awkward, and that the white characters were unconvincing. Audiences who considered the novel to be a classic were disappointed by the departures from it, including the recasting of Jan Erlone (Jim Michael) as a simple labor organizer rather than as the sympathetic leftist of the novel; the ineffective narration of Bigger's past at the beginning of the film and the equally ineffective summary that was supposed to clarify his motives for the murder;[38] and the reformulation—and reduction—of the relationship between Max and Bigger. In short, as Michel Fabre observed, those audiences expected "a passionate appeal" but instead "received a somewhat feeble replay, which, in compar-ison with the novel and the play, seemed boring and badly acted" (351). Even the NAACP pleaded "disgust" at the film's "sordid details" that might serve as "propaganda to continue race preju-dice" and "damage our cause" (*MMB* 279).[39]

Although the biggest problem with the film arose from the extreme cutting that censors required and that in turn destroyed much of the artistic integrity, Wright came to believe that *Native Son* was a complete disaster.[40] He failed to receive a penny from the receipts; what little he earned up front did not even cover his cost of buying back the film rights; and he regretted the time that he had invested in the project, time that he felt might have been bet-ter spent advancing his writing career. In the end, after the Sono-Films company went bankrupt, Wright was never able to obtain even a copy of the uncut version.

For all of its limitations, however, *Native Son* offered viewers the powerful poetry of Wright's words, albeit—according to the *New York Times* reviewer (18 June 1951)—delivered on screen "without depth and true feeling." More importantly, it afforded a portrait of a sensitive young black man rebelling against the big-otry and oppressiveness of his society—in other words, a black "problem" film, from a black perspective—and, as such, opened the door for a number of coming-of-age films produced in the 1960s and 1970s based on the literature of black writers.

Remade and released in 1986, the second film version of *Native Son*, starring newcomer Victor Love as Bigger Thomas, boasted a capable and star-studded supporting cast, including Oprah Winfrey as Bigger's mother, Elizabeth McGovern as Mary Dalton, Carroll Baker as Mrs. Dalton, Matt Dillon as Jan Erlone, Geraldine Fitzgerald as the Daltons's servant Peggy, and John Karlen as the attorney Max. (Fig. 4.8.) While it incorporated crucial images and

Figure 4.8. In the remake of *Native Son*, Bigger Thomas (Victor Love) spends a moment during his trial with his mother (Oprah Winfrey). *(Cinecom/American Playhouse, 1986)*

symbols from the book, such as blindness, whiteness, and crosses (including the crucifix Mrs. Thomas gives Bigger, since "ain't nobody but God can stop your suffering now," and the cross burned by the Klan outside Bigger's jail cell), the film downplayed or altered a number of the novel's key plots and themes. Bigger, in this version, is the victim of circumstance rather than the conscious agent of his fate: his killing of Mary is entirely accidental, and he never attempts to justify it as a retributory act or to compound it by a second murder—of Bessie. The action of the film, moreover, is collapsed, so that Mary's death (which, in this version, is not followed by decapitation) occurs within twenty-four hours of Bigger's arrival at the Dalton home; and none of the events is related from his point of view. Similarly, the courtroom scenes are deemphasized: what little trial dialogue is heard occurs largely in voice-over as Bigger sits alone in his cell awaiting his fate. Yet, despite its many shortcomings, the film captured successfully some of the trappings of ghetto life—the inadequate tenement housing, in which the entire Thomas family sleeps and lives in a single room; the neglected and abandoned buildings that once afforded blacks a sense of community; the ubiquitous "checks cashed" signs; the meat store, where sausages hang in the dark window because most residents are too poor to purchase them; the homelessness and hopelessness that reinforce the image of the black—especially the black man—as an outcast of his society.[41]

Like the film versions of *Native Son*, the movie *Knock on Any Door* (1949) offered a hard and often unflattering look at ethnic life on Chicago's South Side. Directed by Nicholas Ray, the film was based on black novelist Willard Motley's *Knock on Any Door* (1947), a realistic, naturalistic, hard-boiled novel greatly influenced by Wright's *Native Son*. Motley's work followed in the Chicago tradition of Farrell and Algren; and, as Frederick Karl writes, in *Knock on Any Door* he "repeated the environmental argument of Bigger Thomas's lawyer, to defend not a black man but an Italian, Nick Romano. But whereas Wright generated tremendous passion through his identification with Bigger and his crimes, Motley sees Nick completely from the outside, without those animating details of Italian life which would enable us to forget the schoolboy sociology" (Karl 161). And without those details, Motley was unable to establish the environment of his coming-of-age tale. His Italians are reduced to comic stereotypes, the same fate that awaited the treatment of black characters by so many white writers. Yet at times the novel achieves a power and even a poignancy, particularly in Nick's oft-repeated epitaph: "Live fast, die young and have a good-looking corpse." Unfortunately, the film was less forceful than the novel and served mainly as a showcase for the handsome young John Derek, who starred as Nick, the victim of society who turns to crime. Humphrey Bogart played Andrew Morton, his conscience-stricken attorney, who—because of his own childhood battles to rise out of the slums—champions the young man after his arrest for the wanton killing of a policeman. Morton tries to persuade the court of Nick's innocence by describing his troubled background, which is presented in a series of flashbacks: a decent, home-loving boy turned into a hoodlum after his father dies in jail; a minor delinquent sent to a brutal reformatory where he becomes hardened to life; a petty thief whose life is changed by a beautiful, supportive woman but who feels compelled to commit just one more crime; a sensitive young husband so shattered by the suicide of his wife (who kills herself out of shame over his criminal lapse) that he no longer cares about his own fate. "The device," wrote the *New York Times* reviewer (19 Feb. 1949), "is effectively used, building sympathy for the boy and prodding the civic conscience for permitting the conditions." But under cross-examination by the District Attorney, who badgers him and brings up his broken-hearted late wife, Nick cracks under the pressure and confesses. As Nick is led away to the deathhouse, Morton makes one last futile attempt to blame society for Nick's crimes (much as *Native Son* and Wright's movie version tried to contextualize Bigger's crimes).

The film, produced for Columbia by Bogart's independent production company Santana, was typical of period melodramas about juvenile delinquency but ultimately too "pretentious" (*Variety* 23 Feb. 1949) in the social statement it tried to make. Even more forgettable was the sequel, *Let No Man Write My Epitaph* (1960, Columbia), based on Motley's 1958 novel of the same name; a bizarre account of Chicago slum life, the film focused on Nellie Romano (Shelley Winters), the widow of an executed hoodlum, and her son Nick (James Darren), an aspiring concert pianist. As Nick battles a variety of tawdry neighborhood characters and the stigma of his paternity, Nellie battles an addiction to narcotics; and in the film's most urgent scene, mother and son confront each other over her drug use. Notably, Ella Fitzgerald appeared as Flora, a tired junkie. The film, however, like *Knock on Any Door*, was significant largely for its attempt to translate the so-called literary "Bigger Thomas syndrome" to the screen.

It was the major studio films in Hollywood's cycle of black-themed problem pictures of the late 1940s that helped bring racial concerns to the attention of popular audiences and pointed toward the integrationist films that dominated movie screens for the next decade or more. But it was Richard Wright's *Native Son*, in itself an imperfect film, that introduced a distinctively black and increasingly militant perspective into American cinema, a development that would find even fuller expression in films adapted from the works of Lorraine Hansberry, Chester Himes, James Baldwin, and LeRoi Jones.

NOTES TO CHAPTER 4

1. *SFB* 349, *MMB* 35. Cripps discusses in detail the difficult process of those negotiations in *Making Movies Black*, chapter 2, "Wendell and Walter Go to Hollywood," 35-63.

2. Leab 129. Leab also writes that "Willkie bluntly concluded his remarks by asserting that 'many of the people responsible for Hollywood films' belonged to 'a racial and religious group which had been the target of Hitler' and argued that 'they should be the last to be guilty of doing to another minority the things which had been done to them.'"

3. Jim Pines (57) writes that "the radical and outspoken Hazel Scott, who appears in all her films as 'herself,' especially understood what the media were about when she held up the production of *The Heat's On* (1943) until other black women in the film were given proper costumes and not depicted seeing 'their sweethearts off to war wearing dirty hoover aprons.' She was blacklisted after that. Ethel Waters was also aware of image manipulation and is known to have held up the production of *Cabin in the Sky* (1943) until the character of Petunia was properly directed." Yet while these demonstrations were significant, as Pines concludes, they "had little or no effect on the overall trend in racial depictions."

4. Even the concept of the "New Negro," as Jane Gaines observes (*FD* 127), was not new. Frederick Douglass, in his public speeches and lectures, spoke in an effort to "recreate the face of the race, its public face." The later inventors of the "New Negro" in literature also represented themselves publicly, in a kind of massive "reconstruction," which as Henry Louis Gates has noted, was not a new project but a continuation of a long struggle, beginning with African blacks arriving as slaves in America and being forced to "reconstruct" their own image in answer to what it was that whites made of them. By the end of the nineteenth century, that reconstruction had become a dialogue between positive new and pejorative old images of blacks.

5. Anderson recalled a script revision in which his studious character was expected to "revert to type" and whine for mercy from his cell. He approached Huston about the changes and argued for the integrity of the role, which Huston immediately restored. "As released, Anderson's scenes held a muted strength and a credible tension that gave Davis a chance to act with her usual authority by giving her a self-possessed character against whom to play." An earlier script also "called for Clay's jailmate to sing the stereotyped 'Nobody Knows the Trouble I've Seen' in a circle of shabby 'darkies,' one of whom squats in the pose of a gorilla." Those details, as Thomas Cripps (*MMB* 32) shows, were eliminated from the final script.

6. Similarly, Leab (125) notes that "for perhaps the first time, *In This Our Life* brought to the screen what one enthusiastic black newspaperwoman called 'the formerly taboo subject of a white girl framing a colored boy.'"

7. Shortly before becoming involved with *The Negro Soldier*, Carlton Moss had put together a highly successful revue at the Apollo, *Salute to the Negro Troops*, which had included the remarkable talents of Hazel Scott, Canada Lee, Helen Hayes, Charles MacArthur, Ben Hecht, Ethel Barrymore, Douglas Fairbanks, and others. Mounted under the auspices of Fight for Freedom, Inc., a coalition of leftists and conservatives that included Mrs. Calvin Coolidge, Richard Wright, Paul Robeson, and Jack Warner, and in conjunction with Moss's own Council on Negro Culture, *Salute* played in 1941 at the Apollo and the Mecca Temple in midtown Manhattan as a fundraiser for recreational programs for the Jim Crow Army and was revived the following spring at the Apollo, with Moss again at the center of the effort. For more information about *Salute*, Moss, and *The Negro Soldier*, see "The Making of *The Negro Soldier*," chapter 4 in Cripps, *Making Movies Black*, 102-25.

8. *The Negro Soldier* was such a success, in fact, that it spurred the production of other similar government films. As Peter Noble (108) writes, "Henry Lieven directed another [film] in the series, 'The Negro Sailor,' with Joel Fluellyn and Leigh Whipper in the leading roles, though this did not have the same wide success as 'The Negro Soldier.'"

9. *MMB* 105. Only then, according to Thomas Cripps, did the War Department "reckon that the ideology of race movies differed from the evolving racial aims of the war—that is, not until Moss's writing forced the army to think through what sort of film they wished to have speak for them to African America."

10. The film, moreover, went on to outlive the war as a voice in postwar liberal culture.

11. Lawrence Reddick concurred that the film "does not present the real problems of the Negro in the army." He added that it was "too long for a 'short' and too short for a full-length feature" and that it slid "over the Civil War period (in which some two hundred thousand Negroes fought on the Union side) in order to avoid hurt to Southern sensibilities" (20).

12. Daniel J. Leab (125-27), however, suggests that even in these films there was still much servility on display. In *Crash Dive*, for example, Carter was a "messman on a submarine—official Navy policy early in the war limiting blacks to menial roles." His character also "retained many of the movie black's less attractive characteristics." In *Bataan*, "the black soldier fires away [against the Japanese force] as stalwartly as the others; indeed, he is the workhorse of the group. Yet he is clearly in a junior, and

inferior, position at all times. He places explosive charges under instruction from his partner, who wires them and pushes the plunger. He is present during discussions about whether to continue fighting or to withdraw, but speaks out only once—to reaffirm his faith in the United States. And he spends a good part of his on-screen time humming 'St. Louis Blues.'" And in *Lifeboat*, "Joe is never really a part of the group. When the survivors vote on various decisions, Joe abstains for no discernible reason. He is made 'head of commissary,' which, as one scholar has pointed out, is a 'janitorial position.'"

13. *Lifeboat*, according to Cripps, used several angles: "the lifeboat as metaphor for the popular front, and Joe the stoker as a means of integrating blacks into the center of the action." The Allies are portrayed as being "'all in the same boat' against a common enemy" (*MMB* 78-79).

14. Cripps, *MMB* 80. Cripps writes that the two musicals went into release during nasty race riots "that simultaneously drew attention to the persistence of racism and seemed to point to race movies and other pressures for enhanced black status as *causes* of the riots. . . . [T]he musicals revived the matter of the Hollywood Negroes' place in movies in that the large casts placed them in demand again. Additionally, their release coincided with Paramount's release of a couple of biopics of oldtime minstrelmen, each wrapped in a setting of roseate Southern nostalgia at odds with the activists' plans."

15. Sterling A. Brown, in his review "*Imitation of Life*: Once a Pancake" (*Opportunity* March 1935), writes that "Delilah is straight out of Southern fiction. Less abject than in the novel, she is still more concerned with the white Jessie than with Peola. She has little faith in Peola's capacities. . . . Resignation to injustice is her creed. . . . When she refuses her twenty percent (not because it was too late) she is the old slave refusing freedom. . . . She is canny about the ways of men and women where Miss Bea is concerned; but when her daughter is yearning for music and parties, she says, 'Come on, honey I'll dance with you'" (qtd. in Everett 229).

16. Valerie Smith, for instance, in *Not Just Race, Not Just Gender*, writes that Bea—by serving as "the apologists' vision of the plantation mammy revisited"—offers "the perfect justification for black repression" (45). The image of Bea's contented, subservient domesticity is underscored by its repetition on the countless boxes of pancake flour on which that image literally appears.

17. According to Valerie Smith, Delilah swears to renounce her daughter; but ironically Delilah's death, which follows the renunciation, helps bring Bea and Jessie closer together. Bea "resolves that nothing and no one can come between her and her daughter." In the final shot of the film, Bea and Jessie embrace while Bea repeats the lines that Jessie speaks at the beginning of the film: "I want my quack quack." This circularity

"signifies a reassertion of the utopian maternal which in fact structures the entire film" (*Not Just Race* 48-49).

18. *Imitation of Life*, according to Anna Everett, broke new ground in several ways: by introducing the first interracial "buddy" relationship into film; by featuring a black actress in a central role outside the strict narrative economy of slavocracy; by casting an actual black actress in the mulatto part and then treating her character sympathetically. "In terms of locale and setting," *Imitation of Life* was also "the first mainstream film with an integral black storyline not confined spatially to a romanticized southern plantation"—although its "melodramatic plot of race, lies, and pancake fortune" is still driven by a Southern antebellum ethos (219).

19. Unlike the earlier version of *Imitation of Life*, the 1959 remake was banned in the Memphis area by the local censorship board under the direction of Lloyd T. Binford.

20. Even Pinky's name is significant. As V. J. Jerome writes, "pinky" is "a slang term for a light-complexioned Negro who can pass for white" (22).

21. Mark A. Reid demonstrates that "[in the racially dualistic world that the film valorizes] Pinky cannot celebrate her mixed racial background. She must affirm her African-American heritage and, thereby, deny her Euro-American parent." And by opening a black nursing school, "Pinky, as an agent of racial dualism, cannot contest the racially segregated education practices that forced her to enroll in a northern nursing school" (*Redefining Black Film* 45).

22. V. J. Jerome is among the critics who suggest that *Pinky* merely trades one stereotype for another. Pinky herself, he observes, "is the 'modern,' 'streamlined' version of the 'mammy' cliché. Hollywood reverses the stereotype to create the New Stereotype" (28). In "Pro-Negro Films in Atlanta," Gerald Weales discusses Southern reaction to the film, including the "stereotype" of the Mammy that "has no basis in truth" and that certain viewers found offensive.

23. "*In fact*, discrimination against light-complexioned Negro applicants," writes Jerome, "is not a practice in Negro hospitals; therefore, the very plot of *Lost Boundaries* is a structure of falsehood. *In fact*, the American Medical Association, although it has no constitutional bar to Negro membership, excludes Negro physicians in many areas. *In fact*, Negro physicians are segregated into the National Medical Association. Yet these shameful facts go unmentioned in what has been called a 'documentary' film 'indictment' of bigotry in the medical profession. Certainly, this entire sequence, in which one Negro is falsely shown to discriminate against a fellow-Negro, fits 'to order' into a film designed as a whole to divide the Negro people against itself and to divert its wrath from the legitimate target: the white ruling-class oppressors. Hollywood thus increases the load of oppression upon the Negro's shoulder's by laying there the unmentionable burden of responsibility for discrimination" (31).

24. Jerome sees a resolution—a highly artificial one. He writes, "Hollywood's slippery techniques for 'resolving' a difficult social conflict are here demonstrated in a transparently contrived scene. After the church sermon which softens the hearts of the townspeople, the young woman's white admirer smiles benignly at her brother, as he passes the pew. The implication might be that he will now resume his courtship. The Negro daughter, emotionally upset by the entire turn in the family's situation, suddenly dashes out of the church—obviously by Hollywood's design to remove any suspicions of an ending in inter-marriage" (33).

25. In "The Death of Rastus" (58), Thomas Cripps writes that "censorship has been one of the most persistent influences on the maintenance of stereotypes." He notes that both *Lost Boundaries* and *Imitation of Life* were banned by Southern censors.

26. Donald Bogle (*TCMMB* 144-45) notes that *Home of the Brave* "took the entire film industry and the country by surprise" and that "those connected with the film reaped the benefits. Producer Stanley Kramer became the high priest of the message-problem pictures of the 1950s and 1960s, spearheading with such films as *The Defiant Ones* (1958), *Pressure Point* (1962), and *Guess Who's Coming to Dinner* (1967). [Director] Mark Robson directed a series of successful melodramas. [Screenwriter] Carl Foreman emerged as a top scenarist. Black actor James Edwards went on to other starring roles."

27. "In *Pinky*, *Lost Boundaries*, and *Intruder in the Dust*," Cripps writes ("Rastus" 60), "the problems of Negroes are resolved in each case at the pleasure of upper-class white society."

28. In another of his works, Cripps cast the relationship a bit differently: "At the end of the film the audience sees a fraternal scene in which Edwards and a one-armed white man depart, suggesting Negro-white equality only as long as the whites are not complete" ("Rastus" 60).

29. *MMB* 243. Cripps adds: "Not that liberals considered this metaphor of common conscience powerful enough to solve all their problems. Its acceptance in theatres was never taken to mean that white people would break off from their racial history. Rather, except for a few who thought *Intruder in the Dust* too on-the-nose in its rhetoric, they almost unanimously read it as its makers intended: as an assertion of the thrust of liberalism in a particular time, and on a human scale that avoided the purely political and therefore offered change as a prospect rather than as a program."

30. In a story entitled "Negro Hailed as New Writer," *The New York Sun* described Wright as "a Negro who has had slightly more than eight years of schooling, who was a bad boy, who has been on relief, on WPA, a street cleaner and a ditch-digger, and who is now being compared to Dostoievski, Theodore Dreiser and John Steinbeck" (Kinnamon and Fabre 28).

31. The two hundred thousand copies of *Native Son* that sold in under three weeks broke "a twenty-year record at Harper" (Edward D. Clark 207). Moreover, according to Sterling A. Brown, "its first edition sold out within three hours, a quarter million copies called for within six weeks" ("Insight, Courage, and Craftsmanship" 53). *Native Son* was also a Book-of-the-Month Club selection.

32. These motifs also underlie other of Wright's works. In "Almos' a Man," a short story that Wright published in 1940, for instance, another black adolescent experiences turmoil in his life. In the story, which is set in the late 1930s, fifteen-year-old David is a fieldhand who feels that he has no status, even among the other farm workers. Believing that his life would be different if only he owned a gun, he talks his mother into giving him money to buy one, purportedly as a gift for his father. Once he is in possession of the weapon, David is anxious to use it; but when he fires it, he accidentally shoots and kills Jenny, a mule belonging to Mr. Hawkins, his employer. His parents, who remind him that "he ain't nothing but a boy," force him to work out an arrangement with Hawkins, by which he will work for the equivalent of two dollars a week until he pays off his debt of fifty dollars (the price of the mule). But David decides to run away instead. Firing the gun into the night and proclaiming "I'm a man!," he hops a train and leaves town. *Almos' a Man* (1976), the film adaptation of the short story, was produced as part of the American Short Story series for Public Television. Stan Lathan directed; Leslie Lee wrote the screenplay; LeVar Burton played the title character, David; and Madge Sinclair and Robert Doqui played his parents. Henry Fonda served as narrator. The excellent production focused on David's passage from boyhood to adulthood and his struggle for respect; and, as Fonda pointed out in his introduction, the battles that the young man wages at home have tremendous implications for society at large.

33. Michel Fabre writes in *The Unfinished Quest of Richard Wright* (2207) that there had been much interest in staging *Native Son*. Wright had received several offers, the first coming from Theodore Ward before the novel was even completed. Other offers, including one by Edward Lasker and Eddie Camtor to produce the play on Broadway, "had been refused by the time Paul Green suggested that he adapt the novel with the collaboration of the author himself."

34. The play was not, however, a financial success. As Michel Fabre writes, even the 115 performances "did not manage to cover expenses. Apart from the initial crowds, attracted by curiosity and admiration, the play was never able to draw those theatergoers who preferred light entertainment to a confrontation with reality. Yet Wright had never identified so completely with the black masses; it almost seemed that he was speaking from the stage on their behalf, and apparently his message was often heard" (216).

35. In an interview with Johannes Skancke Martens, which appeared as the article "A Black Writer Becomes a Movie Actor" in the Oslo *Aftenposten*, 9 Nov. 1950 (Kinnamon and Fabre 148), Wright said that some of the film producers who were interested in filming his novel wanted to make changes, such as making the hero white instead of black. "I did not want this under any circumstances, and I was hoping that one day public opinion in the United States would become liberal enough to permit seeing a film presenting in a realistic and true way the situation of blacks in American society."

36. For a full discussion of Wright's negotiations with producers and an excellent account of the process of translating the novel to film, see Michel Fabre, *The Unfinished Quest of Richard Wright*, especially chapter 15, pp. 336-53.

37. Of course, as Fabre points out, Gould rightly was afraid of such a charge "in that era of nascent McCarthyism" (348).

38. According to the reviewer in the *New York Times* (18 June 1951), "Psychologically, he [Bigger] is a man in revolt against the brutal exploitation of the white man, but that psychological basis for his subsequent actions is never made explicit by deed or nuance. It is simply told."

39. Cripps (*MMB* 279) adds that, "in a national mood in which Walter White's new book was titled *A Rising Wind*, the NAACP took credit for driving *Amos 'n' Andy* from network television, and Poitier had finished *No Way Out* and signed for Zoltan Korda's *Cry, the Beloved Country* to be shot in the heart of apartheid South Africa, *Native Son* could not help but seem an anachronistic, shoestring race movie."

40. Yet, as Michel Fabre observes, "Wright's passion for film-making continued unabated. On December 5, 1951, he submitted a screenplay to the French Association of Film Writers. 'Freedom Train,' or 'The World Between,' was the story of an engineer who detours his train to reach the American free zone in Germany. The American authorities hold the two dozen passengers in the small station for three days so that they can make the choice between East and West. . . . The allegory was clear. The situation allowed Wright to criticize East and West alike. Given the terms of his choice, is the 'world citizen' in fact capable of choosing? Or should he refuse to do so?" It was, Fabre concludes, a question that Wright continued to pose in various ways throughout his career.

41. Frederick Karl (197), for instance, suggests that the traditionally American literary theme of the outcast has special relevance for the black outcast, who as a man on the run because of some passive strain in his nature often embraces the police for his own destruction.

Chapter 5

From Eisenhower to Black Power: Radicalizing the Black Hero

> You go to the movies and, like everyone else, you fall in
> love with Joan Crawford, and you root for the Good
> Guys who are killing off the Indians. It comes as a great
> psychological collision when you realize all of these
> things are really metaphors for your oppression.
> —*James Baldwin, Interview with Studs Terkel (1961)*

Intruder in the Dust, *Home of the Brave* and the other films in
Hollywood's cycle of black problem pictures appropriately ended
the 1940s. "As well as anything else happening in the arts—on the
stage or in fiction or poetry or even politics—these movies,"
according to Donald Bogle, "indicated that racial problems could
no longer be kept in the background." Moreover, they set the tone
and the pace for the new films of the 1950s and 1960s. And
although the problem pictures "themselves were compromised
and in some ways as confused as their age, they signalled a coming of age of the racial theme in American motion pictures" and
broke ground for "intelligent statements on the black experience in
movies" (Bogle, *TCMMB* 158), especially in the handful of fine
films adapted from black literature.

POITIER: THE NEW HERO TYPE

The problem pictures also paved the way for a new black character type, best exemplified by the dignified screen persona of
Sidney Poitier, who would dominate the next two decades of
Hollywood mainstream cinema. In contrast to the degrading and
menial roles as Sambos, Toms, and Mammies[1] played by an earlier

generation of actors like Rex Ingram, Hattie McDaniel, Louise Beavers, and Canada Lee—fine black actors who, Poitier acknowledged, "died and never had a shot" but created job opportunities for the blacks who succeeded them—Poitier became the model integrationist hero in an integrationist age, an actor who, according to Thomas Cripps (*MMB* 284), "adapted his controlled persona to his craft much as Eisenhower had done to his." In his films, Poitier was educated and intelligent; he spoke proper English, dressed conservatively, and had the best of table manners. Consequently, "for the mass white audience, Sidney Poitier was a black man who met their standards. His characters were tame; never did they act impulsively, nor were they threats to the system" (Bogle, *TCMMB* 175-76).[2] And there was always a touch of decency to them that recalled the original, saintly Tom—another reason for their appeal.[3] At the same time, Poitier was important to black audiences, but for very different reasons. As Gladstone L. Yearwood demonstrates, "for blacks, on the other hand, Poitier's screen persona was one of intelligence, quick wit and control of his circumstances" (Yearwood 39). And even if blacks did not always relate to the ambitious doctors, urbane Nobel Prize aspirants, and divine messengers that he portrayed, they could at least appreciate his struggle for equality in a society that continued to resist his intrusions.

Poitier's bright, new black postwar character—like Poitier himself—debuted in *No Way Out* (Twentieth Century-Fox, 1950; dir. Joseph L. Mankiewicz), a transitional film that moved away from the black problem films of the late 1940s and toward the more integrationist message movies of the 1950s and 1960s.[4] Luther Brooks (Poitier), an over-achieving intern at a large metropolitan hospital in an unnamed Northern city tends to the Biddle brothers, two white criminals who have been wounded by police in an attempted robbery of a filling station. Suspicious that Johnny Biddle (Don Hicks) is suffering from more than just a gunshot wound to the leg, Dr. Brooks performs a spinal tap to diagnose what he believes to be brain tumor. But Johnny dies, and his psychopathic racist brother Ray Biddle (Richard Widmark), who has been watching the procedure from an adjoining bed, accuses the "nigger doctor" of murder. The accusation sets off a series of hostile encounters between the Biddles's racist cronies, who are intent on attacking "Niggertown," and the city's militant blacks, who—having learned of the racists' plan—decide to strike first. To prevent further violence, Brooks surrenders himself to authorities and is eventually vindicated by Johnny's autopsy, although not before being taken hostage and shot by Ray. After Edie Johnson (Linda Darnell), Johnny's estranged wife, intervenes, Brooks has the opportunity to turn the tables and allow Ray to die—which, of course, he opts not to do. (Fig. 5.1.) As Jim Pines observes, in a

Figure 5.1. Dr. Luther Brooks (Sidney Poitier) refuses to exact vengeance on racist Ray Biddle (Richard Widmark) in *No Way Out*. *(Twentieth Century-Fox, 1950)*

powerful sense, Biddle must be allowed to live since his character and Brooks's are interlocked in "an interminable moral cum physical struggle" for each other's destruction (74). Iconographically, the two clashing racial images are made for—even need—each other; and their relationship illustrates the conflict-motif convention of the racial genre film of the era.

Although *No Way Out* incorrectly suggested that racial hatred was a problem mostly among the uneducated lower classes, it offered an unusual cinematic look at racial violence by depicting both whites who were anti-black and blacks who were anti-white and by incorporating a broad range of social racial attitudes, from reactionary to extremely liberal to militant.[5] Unusual as well was the film's positive portrayal of the black middle class family, including Luther Brooks's attractive wife Cora (Mildred Joanne Smith), his pleasant mother (Maude Simmons), and their supportive friends. Yet most striking of all was the very character of Luther, "the clean-cut, sensitive, black loner who fights prejudice and/or evil with sharp-eyed understanding" (Marill 46), who would become the archetypal model for so many of Poitier's later screen portrayals. But the apotheosized image of Luther is more than just an archetype; as Daniel J. Leab writes, it is actually a new stereotype—that of the "ebony saint," who remains non-violent despite enormous provocation, superior in skills and ability, yet cognizant of the limitations society imposes on him. Posing no threat to the established mores, sexual or social, "he remains cool . . . like ebony itself" (163). Indeed critics, who were not overly enthusiastic about the film itself, praised Poitier's acting and commented on his "saintly" qualities, including his "quiet dignity and persuasive style" (*Hollywood Reporter*) and "his fine sensitive performance of quiet dignity" (*New York Times*).[6]

Poitier re-created the Luther Brooks character type in numerous films, including *Edge of the City* (Metro-Goldwyn-Mayer, 1957; dir. Martin Ritt), based on Robert Alan Aurthur's teleplay *A Man Is Ten Feet Tall*, in which he played Tommy Tyler, a good-natured freightcar loader who takes it upon himself to redeem Axel Nordmann (John Cassavetes), a deserter whom he has befriended. After Axel refuses to engage the gang boss Charley Malik (Jack Warden), Tommy fights in his place and is killed. Fearful that he might be exposed, Axel at first refuses to avenge his friend's murder; but ultimately he redeems himself—as Tommy knew he could—by turning the killer over to police and surrendering on the desertion charges. The well-intentioned film, which included some patronizing interracial discourse, oversimplified the race issue; yet, as the *Variety* (2 Jan. 1957) reviewer noted, it marked a "milestone in the history of the screen in its presentation of an American Negro." And while black audiences failed to identify much with Tommy, they were able to appreciate the film's implicit message:

that here, as historically, "white well-being hinges on black sacri-fice" (Cripps, *MMB* 289).

In *The Defiant Ones* (United Artists, 1958; dir./prod. Stanley Kramer), Poitier played Noah Cullen, a black Southerner jailed for attacking the white man who had insulted him. Noah finds him-self bound—literally (fig. 5.2)—to a fellow prisoner, a redneck

Figure 5.2. In *The Defiant Ones,* Noah Cullen (Poitier) finds himself chained to racist "Joker" Jackson (Tony Curtis). *(United Artists, 1958)*

bully named John "Joker" Jackson (Tony Curtis). En route to a work detail, their van crashes, and the two make a run for free-dom. Their survival depends upon their cooperation, and gradu-ally they learn to work together—to escape a clay pit, to ford a stream, to steal food from a turpentine settlement, where they nar-rowly avoid getting lynched—and even to respect each other. When they are finally separated (by a lonely woman, played by Cara Williams, who seduces Joker and deliberately sends Noah on a fatal short cut), Joker follows in order to warn Noah of the dan-ger but is shot by the woman's son. Nonetheless, the two convicts are reunited. With the posse just minutes behind, their only hope for escape is to hop a passing freight train. Noah pulls himself aboard and reaches for the wounded Joker, who falls to the ground. Knowing that he is giving up his chance for freedom, Noah then jumps off the train to attend to his friend and to await the arrival of the sheriff's men. Reviewers hailed the merits of the film; Arthur Knight, in the *Saturday Review*, noted the "dignity, power, and overwhelming conviction" with which Poitier invested his role; and Bosley Crowther in the *New York Times* wrote that "Mr. Poitier shows a deep and powerful strain of underlying compassion" (qtd. in Marill 79). Some viewers saw in the film an interesting variation on the racial interdependency theme: shackled together physically and emotionally (in their dislike for each other), Noah and Joker are equal. When their chain is broken, both realize that the ties they have developed transcend the prejudices of their separate racial identities; consequently, both men ultimately refuse selfish freedom that dooms the other (Pines 76). Still other viewers, however, faulted Poitier's subservience and suggested that Noah, like Tommy (and even Luther), was a throwback to the Toms and Mammies who gladly sacrificed all for their white masters.

In his next few films, Poitier capitalized on his growing stardom but took few risks in his choice of material. In fact, only *Porgy and Bess* (1959), based on DuBose Heyward's novel *Porgy*,[7] with its seeming ignorance of contemporary political realities and its retrogressive depictions of the good-hearted whore Bess (Dorothy Dandridge), the crippled beggar Porgy who murders to protect her (Poitier), and the evil dope-pusher Sportin' Life (Sammy Davis, Jr.), raised any controversy. Then came the wildly successful *Lilies of the Field* (1963), based on William E. Barrett's novel, in which Poitier cemented his on-screen image as ebony saint.[8] Poitier played Homer Smith, an easy-going ex-GI who meets a group of German nuns who are trying to build a chapel in the Arizona desert. After agreeing to work for them for just one day, Homer stays on, so inspired by the nuns' faith that he takes on extra jobs to help them pay for the building materials; and he musters the resources of the neighboring citizens and of a circuit-riding preacher to complete the project. The church, he realizes, is an important symbol to the community: raising it will in turn raise the hopes of the impoverished and oppressed townspeople. The day the church is to be consecrated, however, Homer takes off, knowing that he has already fulfilled both the sisters' ambitions and his own. The film, which opened to almost unanimously favorable reviews, afforded Poitier another chance to play the dependable, noble, self-sacrificing black man (or, as some viewers saw it, another unpaid servant to whites); and it earned him an Academy Award as Best Actor, the first ever Best Actor Oscar won by a black male performer (an achievement that would remain unmatched for almost four decades, until Denzel Washington's win in 2002 for *Training Day*). It also marked the start of a series of similar roles for Poitier, in films such as *The Slender Thread* (1965), based on Shana Alexander's "Decision to Die," in which Alan Newell, a University of Washington anthropology student, saves an unstable white woman (Anne Bancroft) who tries to overdose on pills by keeping her on the phone until help arrives; *A Patch of Blue* (1965), based on Elizabeth Kata's novel *Be Ready with Bells and Drums*, in which Gordon Ralfe helps to rehabilitate Selina D'Arcey (Elizabeth Hartman), a poor blind white girl abused by her sluttish mother (Shelley Winters); and *To Sir, with Love* (1967), based on the novel by E. R. Braithwaite, in which Mark Thackeray, a dedicated teacher, treats his students as equals and helps them to overcome their indifference to education and to life. (Interestingly, as Thackeray, or "Sir," Poitier is a representative of the Establishment

Figure 5.3. Southern Sheriff Bill Gillespie (Rod Steiger) meets his match in Detective Virgil Tibbs (Poitier) in *In the Heat of the Night*. *(United Artists, 1967)*

that he had so convincingly rebelled against as the menacing delinquent Gregory Miller in an earlier film, *The Blackboard Jungle*
[1955], based on Evan Hunter's novel—although even in that film,
he capitulated by taking the side of his teacher in a knife fight
against his peers.) In *In The Heat of the Night* (1967; fig. 5.3), based
on the novel by John Ball, as Virgil Tibbs, he assists the bigoted
Sheriff Bill Gillespie (Rod Steiger) in solving the murder of a
wealthy industrialist but remains—according to Hollis Alpert in
the *Saturday Review*—observant of Hollywood's rules, "a prideful,
lonely figure in the end" (Marill 154). And in *Guess Who's Coming
to Dinner* (1967), as Dr. John Prentice, a brilliant, handsome, Nobel
Prize contender who is engaged to Joey Drayton (Katharine
Houghton), a white woman, he delivers her liberal white parents
(Spencer Tracy and Katherine Hepburn) from their prejudices;
then, for good measure, he works a similar transformation with his
own parents (Beah Richards and Roy Glenn, Sr.). In true
Hollywood fashion, all of the conflicts are resolved in time for a
big family dinner that same evening. Even though *Guess Who's
Coming to Dinner* glossed over serious racial issues—and perhaps
precisely *because* the film glossed over serious racial issues—it was
a commercial success. In any event, it proved to be one of the last
explicitly integrationist message pictures (Bogle, *TCMMB* 217).

Poitier occasionally departed from his familiar character role:
in *Band of Angels* (1957), a poor adaptation of the novel by Robert
Penn Warren, for instance, he was Rau-Ru, the personal retainer
that slave trader Hamish Bond (Clark Gable) brought back from
Africa as an infant, raised as a son, and educated beyond his station; yet Rau-Ru resents his master's kindness and bides his time
awaiting the appropriate opportunity to rebel. (Fig. 5.4.) And in
Something of Value (1957), based on Robert Ruark's bestseller, Poitier
played Kimani, a Kikuyu native youth reared by colonial whites
who is torn between identification with the violent African nationalist movement and pursuit of a less violent form of biracial
appeasement. But even in those roles, which forced Poitier to revert
to an earlier black stereotype of slave/native, his character acts predictably and appropriately, at least by Hollywood's standards:
Rau-Ru, having joined the Northern forces, allows his "master" to
escape, while Kimani, unable to murder whites even though he has
joined the Mau-Maus, has enough residual trust in his white
"brother" Peter McKenzie (Rock Hudson) to surrender and make

Figure 5.4. Rau-Ru (Poitier) confronts the white master (Clark Gable) who has educated him and reared him like a son in *Band of Angels*. *(Warner Brothers, 1967)*

peace, an action that inadvertently leads to his wife's death as well as his own but ensures his infant son's survival with the McKenzie family. And even in some of Poitier's later films (e.g., *They Call Me MISTER Tibbs!* [1970]; *The Organization* [1971]), when he assumed a more militant persona, his character still projected a certain conciliatory quality or achieved some kind of racial accommodation.

As Poitier moved from just acting to acting, directing, and producing, there continued to be a sameness in the roles he played. *For Love of Ivy* (1968), based on an original story by Poitier, intended both to show a different side of the actor and to portray a cinematically atypical, passionate love affair between a black man and a black woman; but the result was simply a black version of an outdated Hollywood formula, a kind of black Rock Hudson-Doris Day light comedy. When the faithful servant Ivy Moore (Abbey Lincoln) wants to leave the employ of the Austin family, they decide to do whatever they can to keep her, even offering her a trip to Africa. The teenage hippie son Tim (Beau Bridges) then determines that what Ivy really needs is a man, so he tricks the local stud, gambler Jack Parks (Poitier), into romancing her. After some initial awkwardness, the two end up falling in love. Predictably, Jack goes straight; and the Austins's hopes of keeping Ivy are quashed. As Donald Bogle writes, while the film distinguished itself by offering "the first love scene between blacks in a popular movie" (*TCMMB* 219), the sex scene itself was surprisingly sexless and tame, wholly in keeping with what studios believed whites wanted to see and would accept. And some critics and viewers complained that despite the film's good intentions, the characters of the maid and the con man—along with the patronizing white family—"promoted the very racial stereotype [Poitier] had tried to destroy" (Marill 165).

Subsequent films, like *Brother John* (1971), the first film produced by Poitier's E & R Production Company, seemed to parody—unintentionally—the actor's almost-saintly persona; Brother John Kane was not just a superhuman figure but also literally a messenger from God. "It was the ultimate step," as Alvin H. Marill noted, "in a career of progressive role-deification, wrapped in obtuse melodrama that starts engrossingly with a mystery with sociological overtones and winds up a doomsday parable" (184). Roger Ebert, in his *Chicago Sun-Times* review, was even more direct: Poitier, he writes, "[in his two decades on film] has become so heroic and so ethical, such a figure of persecution in an intellectual liberal way, that he's been cut off from the roles he should be playing, the roles of real men with failings as big as their virtues" (qtd. in Marill 186). And Vincent Canby, commenting on the neutrality of his roles, noted that Poitier's blackness was now all but invisible.

In fact, Poitier's character roles, which had defined Hollywood's film image of blacks for so many years, were (with few exceptions) increasingly out of touch with societal developments and racial realities; moreover, it was clear that no single black image, not even one as strong as Poitier's had been, could adequately reflect the changing times. Poitier himself acknowledged the transition in his autobiography *This Life* (335-36): "[S]uddenly," he wrote, "after too many years of little more than Sidney Poitier films, came a profusion of movies with black stars, male and female; macho guys and beautiful girls. . . . the response at the box office was tumultuous. My own career went into a decline at that point."

Poitier's unique achievement is that he embodied, for white as well as black audiences (though for notably different reasons), the liberal and integrationist aspirations of the postwar era. Yet the escapist films in which he starred had overlooked much of the real turmoil of society, from the great paradoxes of the Eisenhower years (postwar prosperity, the baby boom, Joe McCarthy in the Senate, the lynching of Emmett Till in Mississippi, boycotts and bombings in Montgomery, federal troops in Arkansas, blacklisting of Hollywood talent) to the rapid upheavals of the 1960s (John F. Kennedy's hopes for a new society and Martin Luther King, Jr.'s efforts for nonviolent resolution, both of which seemed to die along with those iconic figures; other political assassinations—of Robert Kennedy, Mahatma Gandhi, Malcolm X—and scandals, which claimed even more of the nation's innocence; the explosion of race riots from Watts to Harlem). The President's National Advisory Commission had reported that America was "moving toward two societies, one black, one white, separate and unequal" (Bogle, *TCMMB* 219). But the majority of racial movies from the 1950s through the late 1960s had been expressions of social and civil rights liberalism, where—as Jim Pines noted—the black character rarely deviated from the moral determinants underlying integrationism; where the plasticized black, in achieving an image of the "Noble Negro," suffered a peculiar form of castration and thus became a stereotype of a different, but no less enslaving order; and where the cinematic black character-image finally started to congeal into its "modern" form, thus implanting the notion of the "good" image in the contemporary racial myth process (73). While Poitier had become white Hollywood's best, and at times only, representative of the contemporary black on screen, he was actually, according to Thomas Cripps, an increasingly "bland antidote to racial tension" who defined the waning years of postwar combat and message movies, each with its lone black hero, much as Eisenhower had defined the national politics of his era. The exhaustion of those movie genres and the ennui of the film audiences, "both becoming apparent as new social conditions thrust up new cinematic formulations, coincided with the exhaustion of Poitier's own genre" (*MMB* 289). Yet, as Daniel J. Leab has correctly observed, reproving Poitier for not participating in more meaningful films earlier in his career is pointless, since such films were simply not being made by the major studios; therefore, Poitier, a fine actor, cannot be faulted for the shortcomings of the industry in which he worked (231). Rather, as the Academy of Motion Picture Arts and Sciences noted in late March of 2002 in awarding him an Oscar for Lifetime Achievement, he is to be commended for the tremendous obstacles that he surmounted and celebrated for his influence on film and on society. As James Baldwin recognized in a 1968 essay for *Look* magazine, it was "the presence of Sidney, the precedent set, [that] is of tremendous importance."

Although Poitier was certainly dominant, a few other blacks also managed to achieve some screen success in the 1950s and 1960s. Most notably perhaps, the beautiful and talented actress Dorothy Dandridge, like Poitier, strove to create and cultivate a unique image on film. But, as Donald Bogle demonstrates, while that image appeared to be contemporary and daring, in fact it was essentially a reincarnation of the classic tragic mulatto of early movies. Even in her most important films—the lavish all-black musical *Carmen Jones* (1954), in which she played the sexy black factory worker; the interracial love story *Island in the Sun* (1957), in which she was the sad-eyed Margot; *Porgy and Bess* (1959), in which her sluttish but passionate Bess outshone even the memorable performances of her co-stars Sidney Poitier and Sammy Davis, Jr.—Dandridge portrayed "doomed, unfulfilled women. Nervous and vulnerable, they always battled with the duality of their personalities" and answered the demands of their times. To a dispirited nuclear age, Dandridge's characters brought "a razor sharp sense of desperation that cut through the bleak monotony of the day" (Bogle, *TCMMB* 166). Ironically, Dandridge actually lived out her tragic image, dropping involuntarily from Hollywood films by the late 1950s and drifting into depression and a pattern of self-destructive behavior that culminated in her suicide in 1965 at the age of forty-two.

Non-actors like baseball player Jackie Robinson (*The Jackie Robinson Story* [1950]); singers Nat "King" Cole (*The Blue Gardenia* [1953], *Istanbul* [1957], *China Gate* [1957], *St. Louis Blues* [1958]) and Eartha Kitt (*New Faces of 1952* [1952], *St. Louis Blues*, *Anna Lucasta* [1958]); and jazz artist Louis Armstrong (*The Strip* [1951], *Glory Alley* [1952], *High Society* [1956]) succeeded in entertaining movie audiences largely by showcasing their nondramatic talents on film, while the sassy comedienne Pearl Bailey (*Carmen Jones, That Certain Feeling* [1956], *St. Louis Blues, Porgy and Bess, All the Fine Young Cannibals* [1960]) and calypso great Harry Belafonte (*Bright Road* [1953], *Island in the Sun* [1957], *The World, the Flesh, and the Devil* [1959], *The Angel Levine* [1970], *Buck and the Preacher* [1972]) made even more successful, although relatively short-lived, transitions to the screen. And Ruby Dee continued to turn in solid, powerful performances in films like *No Way Out, The Jackie Robinson Story, Edge of the City, Up Tight,* and *Buck and the Preacher;* but the characters she typically played—loyal, understanding wives and sensitive girlfriends—afforded her little chance to break out and to enjoy a real star turn.[9]

A Raisin in the Sun: In the Tradition of Wright

In contrast both to the revived stereotypes and to Hollywood's newest stereotype of the controlled and conciliatory Poiter character was the black protagonist depicted by black writers in literature and in theater—a protagonist much like Richard Wright's disenfranchised anti-hero Bigger Thomas, who not only recognizes social inequities but reacts, often violently, in protest against them. Whereas the Poitier character was generally safe and malleable, Bigger was dangerous and unpredictable. And whereas the Poitier character touched cautiously, and usually superficially, on racial prejudice and discrimination, Bigger forced readers (and later viewers) to confront those same issues in bold ways that left no room for comfort and that often offered no resolutions at all.

Although *Native Son* was highly acclaimed both as a novel and as a Broadway play, the attempts to bring Wright's first work to the screen had been fraught with problems. The eventual film version, released overseas in 1950 and in the United States in 1951, had failed, essentially—according to Jim Pines—because a profoundly embittered, wholly violent, and extremely tragic *literary* figure such as Bigger Thomas could not be effectively reincarnated in cinematic terms. "The plastic mass-oriented medium," Pines wrote, "defined as it is historically, could not possibly accommodate what this racial anti-hero represents; nor could any Hollywood filmmaker really break from the 'sobriety' of the Hollywood liberal convention in one sweeping blow like this." Indeed, he speculates, if Bigger Thomas had worked at the cinematic level with anything near the same degree the character did in the book, "it would no doubt have undermined Hollywood's dominant 'manufactured Negro-types' completely" (Pines 84-85).

But this sort of explicitness was not feasible to any significant extent during the 1950s, a time when racial extremism was acceptable only when it was useful—that is, when it could be countermined by the dominant liberal "good" character, like the one typically played by Poitier. But, atypical as it was, Wright's effort to introduce a more radical black point of view into white liberal cinema was a remarkable step. And, although it would be almost a decade before black perspectives again found their way onto American movie screens, Wright's film of *Native Son* remains an important predecessor for the so-called "Bigger Thomas syndrome" films adapted from the novels of Chester Himes and other writers, for the black coming-of-age films that became so popular in the 1960s and 1970s, and even for the newly-empowered, liberated, and often violent heroes of the "blaxploitation" movies of the early 1970s.

Another notable black literary voice to set her work in Wright's territory of South Side Chicago and to call attention to the plight of the ghettoized black man caught in the trap set for him by a white society was playwright Lorraine Hansberry. Considerably less prolific than Richard Wright, Hansberry produced only two plays before her death from cancer in 1965, at age thirty-four; nonetheless, her contribution to the American stage and to black American culture was enormous. *A Raisin in the Sun* (1959), her first and best known play, now considered a landmark of American drama, was both the first play by a black woman to be staged on Broadway and the first work by a black American to win the New York Drama Critics Circle Award.[10] The story of a struggling black family living in a cramped and sunless Chicago apartment, *Raisin* revealed the aspirations as well as the frustrations of each of the family members, particularly of Walter Lee Younger, a despairing man who sees only a bleak future—"a big, looming blank space full of *nothing*"—for himself. A chauffeur for a wealthy white man, Walter Lee "open[s] and close[s] car doors all day long. I drive a man around in his limousine and I say, 'Yes, sir; no, sir; very good, sir; shall I take the Drive, sir?' . . . That ain't no kind of job . . . that ain't nothing at all" (61). When a friend suggests that they open a liquor store together, Walter Lee imagines himself becoming a successful businessman who can afford to buy pearls for his wife, Ruth, and to send his son, Travis, to the finest college. His realization that he will never actually have the chance to pursue his dream compounds his frustrations; after all, he cannot even raise the capital for the initial investment.

Walter Lee's mother, Lena Younger, the matriarch of the family, appreciates much of his frustration; she too wants only the best for her children, just as her devoted and hardworking late husband, Big Walter, did. When she receives ten thousand dollars in insurance from Big Walter's policy, she debates how best to honor his legacy. After making a down payment on a home in all-white Clybourne Park (since comparable homes in black neighborhoods cost twice as much), she gives the rest to Walter Lee to open a checking account for himself and a savings account for his sister Beneatha's medical school education. Lena believes that such responsibility will help to restore Walter Lee's dignity and pride. "It ain't much," she says, "but it's all I got in the world and I'm putting it in your hands. I'm telling you to be the head of this family from now on like you supposed to be" (94). (Fig. 5.5.) Mama Lena, as Steven R. Carter notes, "would like to balance all their demands, but finds that they far exceed the amount of insurance, just as the damage done to blacks in America virtually defies reparation" (126).

The sensitive Ruth shares her husband's distress, and she sees how his anguish is ruining their marriage and corroding the entire household. While she has her own dream—of moving out of the rat- and roach-infested ghetto into a real home—she alone seems to appreciate that the money is Lena's to spend as she wishes. But Ruth's discovery that she is pregnant adds to her strain and leads her briefly to contemplate abortion. Meanwhile, the intellectually inclined Beneatha provokes Walter Lee's anger by challenging the traditional roles of wife and mother, spouting popular nihilisms, flirting with African nationalism, and sporting tribal clothing.

For all of his intentions to do Lena's bidding, once Walter Lee has the insurance money in hand, he invests it in the liquor store. Unfortunately, his shady partner Willie Harris absconds with the cash. Realizing that he has squandered not only his own legacy but

Figure 5.5. In *A Raisin in the Sun*, adapted from Lorraine Hansberry's Pulitzer Prize-winning play, Walter Lee (Poitier) rants to his mother Lena (Claudia McNeil) about the indignities he has suffered. *(Columbia Pictures Corporation, 1961)*

also Beneatha's, Walter Lee feels even more bereft of hope. The only way for him to recoup the loss is to capitulate to Mark Lindner, the white man who represents a suburban "improvement association" and who had earlier offered to buy back, at an inflated price, the Youngers's recently purchased house. Swallowing what remains of his pride, Walter Lee contacts Lindner and agrees to sell; but ultimately, when Lindner appears with a contract, Walter Lee salvages his dignity—and regains his mother's trust and his family's admiration—by refusing the offer. Delving into his soul and mining the strength of his African past, of the six generations of his family in America, and especially of his father (Cheney 57), he announces to Lindner, "We have decided to move into the house because my father—my father—he earned it" (138). As the play ends, the family leaves their cramped ghetto apartment for a new home—and an uncertain future—in an all-white suburb. Yet, while the human spirit is reaffirmed, with Lena fulfilling one of her biggest ambitions, Ruth deciding to keep the baby, Beneatha learning a new tolerance, Walter Lee finally coming "into his manhood . . . kind of like a rainbow after the rain" (141), and the closeness between Walter Lee and Ruth reborn, the ending is not necessarily happy. The Youngers are aware that they will face opposition and perhaps even violence; but, as a family, they are ready to move forward in order to realize their dreams.

Interestingly, Hansberry had initially written a less ambiguous ending, in which the Youngers move to their new home and are attacked by whites, forcing Lena to prowl the house at night with a loaded shotgun—something Hansberry's own mother had done.[11] In 1938, Hansberry's father, Carl A. Hansberry, had challenged Chicago's real estate covenants by moving his family into a white neighborhood. As he risked jail and fought the racial discrimination in the courts, the family contended with neighbors who tried to force them out with verbal threats and actual violence. Despite the hostility, the family remained until a lower court ordered them to move; and even then they kept fighting. With the help of the NAACP, Carl Hansberry fought successfully all the way to the Supreme Court, which struck down the restrictive covenants in the famous *Hansberry vs. Lee* decision of 1940. (Though illegal, Chicago's discriminatory practices continued.) The original ending thus reflected Hansberry's belief that blacks were too strong to be denied forever and that all the generations of blacks in America demonstrated incredible endurance and heroism as well as a drive for change. And she agreed with the Youngers's refusal to accept social conditions not of their own making, even if the refusal could cost them their lives. Thus "like the later *Roots*," according to Steven R. Carter, "*A Raisin in the Sun* is finally less a work of protest than a multigenerational black struggle for progress" (126).

The play—whose title is taken from a line in Langston Hughes's "Harlem," which warns that a deferred dream might "dry up / like a raisin in the sun"—was initially considered to be an undesirable property because it differed so much from other Broadway productions.[12] But Hansberry's friend Philip Rose, who had never before produced a play, decided to take on the project. He sent the script to Sidney Poitier, who liked it and saw in the character of Walter Lee—a man who describes himself as "a volcano, a giant surrounded by ants" (76)—an opportunity to break from his usual film persona. Poitier also suggested his former teacher, Lloyd Richards, as director of the project, thus helping to make Richards the first black director on Broadway. With Poitier on board, Rose began assembling the rest of the cast, which included the excellent but largely unknown or underappreciated actors Claudia McNeil (Lena Younger), Ruby Dee (Ruth), Diana Sands (Beneatha), and Ossie Davis (Poitier's replacement), and writers like Lonne Elder III. After tryouts in New Haven, Philadelphia, and Hansberry's hometown of Chicago, *Raisin* opened in New York at the Ethel Barrymore Theatre on 11 March 1959. Reviews were overwhelmingly favorable, and the play enjoyed a successful run of 538 performances.

By portraying the truth of the lives of its characters, *Raisin* not only attracted white audiences; it also succeeded in drawing blacks who, as James Baldwin observed, had ignored the theater in the past because the theater had ignored them. Yet in fact Hansberry's *Raisin in the Sun* was merely the culmination of a noteworthy decade of black theater. Other important black-oriented and black-written dramas of the 1950s included Louis Peterson's *Take a Giant Step*, which opened on Broadway in 1953 and was revived off-Broadway in a critically acclaimed production in 1956. William Branch's historical dramatization of John Brown and Frederick Douglass, *In Splendid Error* (1954), was also produced off-Broadway, as were Alice Childress's satire on black stereotypes, *Trouble in Mind* (1957), and Loften Mitchell's dramatic treatment of school desegregation in *A Land Beyond the River* (1957) (Reid, *Redefining Black Film* 48).[13] But *A Raisin in the Sun* was exceptional in the way that it blended so many contrasting themes—marital and generational discord, conformity versus respect for diversity, the struggle for women's rights, idealism versus cynicism, the dangers of misdirected ambition, and religion versus atheistic humanism (Carter 126)—that were inextricably linked to a black perspective and yet were, at the same time, universal.

Movie rights were sold to Columbia Pictures in 1959, and the film itself, independently produced by David Susskind and Philip Rose, was released in 1961. The film's outstanding ensemble cast, including Claudia McNeil, Sidney Poitier, Ruby Dee, and Diana Sands, was reassembled from the play. And, although Columbia executives insisted on replacing Lloyd Richards with a more proven white director, Daniel Petri, they accepted Hansberry as scenarist, in large part because the popularity of the play *Raisin* gave her some leverage in negotiations.

There were, however, significant limits to the control she had over the final screenplay of the film. After selling the movie rights, Hansberry had written two screenplays that differed considerably from the stage version. Both added new dimensions to the characters and emphasized the ghetto environment in which they lived and worked. In one of the new scenes, for instance, Lena voices her outrage at being overcharged in a ghetto supermarket and promises the owner never to return, even though shopping elsewhere will create great hardships for her. In another of those scenes, Walter Lee seeks advice from a white liquor store owner and takes umbrage at the man's racist suggestion that he forget running a business and stay with a nine-to-five job. (In fact, the store owner is merely expressing his own financial frustrations; it is Walter Lee who misinterprets the man's motives and assumes racial bias.) Later, Walter Lee stands among a street crowd listening to a black nationalist, who denounces the American black man's disinheritance and wonders where his "lands" and "businesses" have gone—precisely the questions that Walter Lee asks himself.[14] Columbia adamantly rejected all of Hansberry's new material; as Mark A. Reid writes, they objected even to minor changes, as in the scene where Travis Younger asks his parents for money. In the play, Travis says, "This is the morning we supposed to bring the fifty cents to school" (*RBF* 8); in Hansberry's screenplay, he needs the money for special books about African-Americans. But the production executives and the story editors "'agreed that this [reference to African-American books] should be deleted" and that the addition of other similar material "'should be avoided,' because 'the introduction of further race issues may lessen the sympathy of the audience, give the effect of propagandistic writing, and so weaken the story, not only as dramatic entertainment, but as propaganda too."'[15] Ultimately, then, the film version of *A Raisin in the Sun* was a shortened version of the Broadway play and the adaptive changes were minimal. In fact, apart from the consolidation and slight reshifting of some passages of dialogue and the omission of select scenes (such as the second visit to the Younger apartment of Beneatha's boyfriend George) or sections of characters' speeches (such as the most politically charged portion of the African Asagai's dialogue, about the possibility of his "being butchered in [his] bed some night by the servants of [the] empire" [124-25]), the only other notable change was the opening up of the play to include exterior scenes—at the Arnolds's home, where Walter Lee waits to drive Mr. Arnold downtown; at the bar, where Walter Lee makes plans with Willie and Bobo and later, after a fight at home, drinks alone and where Lena eventually comes looking for him; and at the family's new home in Clybourne Park, where they tour the place that Lena has purchased for them.

Although Hansberry believed that the film was less than it could have been, the screenplay proved good enough to be nominated for Best Screenplay of the Year from the Screenwriters Guild and to receive a special award at the Cannes Film Festival in 1961. And even if it failed to convey some of Hansberry's more radical philosophical statements, it retained many of the characterizations and points of the original story—enough, in fact, to make theater owners worry about how to promote the project.[16] "I am sure you realize that the picture does present a problem from a selling standpoint due to its subject matter," one owner wrote to producer Susskind. "It is imperative that we reach a mass rather than just a class audience" (Reid, *RBF* 60).

Yet, while it was indeed a "prestige picture," *A Raisin in the Sun* succeeded in introducing audiences to the problems and concerns of working class black families. Earlier Hollywood films had already portrayed black families, for instance in the black-cast *Hallelujah!* (1929), about the tribulations of the closely knit Johnsons, and in other family-themed or family-oriented films like *The Green Pastures* (1936) and *Cabin in the Sky* (1943)—although, as Mark A. Reid suggests, many of those early studio productions were really "blackface minstrel family films," in which the characters were modernized versions of nineteenth-century racial stereo-

types, such as "the obese matriarch or mammy figure, her inartic-
ulate henpecked mate or sambo, sex-crazed black bucks, exotic
primitives, and tragic mulattoes caught in an interracial mael-
strom" (*RBF* 45). And the black-family film genre existed among
black independents more than a decade before the appearance of
Vidor's *Hallelujah!* with black-produced, black-directed, and black-
written works like the Frederick Douglass Film Company's *The
Colored American Winning His Suit* (1916) and the Lincoln Motion
Picture Company's *The Realization of a Negro's Ambition* (1916) and
The Trooper of Company K (1916). But what made *A Raisin in the Sun*
so distinctive was its portrayal of the fears, frustrations, and aspirations of the ghettoized black working class. As Donald Bogle
writes, "author Hansberry captured the tension of blacks enduring
lives of violent desperation, and she hit with unerring exactness on
a number of things never dealt with before in the movies. Her
drama took the average filmgoer into the grime and grit of the
ghetto. It exposed the matriarchal set-up in black homes and
examined the emasculation of the black male by a hostile white
society" (*TCMMB* 196).

A remake of *A Raisin in the Sun*, produced by Hansberry's widower and estate executor Robert Nemiroff and directed by black
filmmaker Bill Duke, was released in 1986 to commemorate the
film's twenty-fifth anniversary. Esther Rolle played Mama Lena;
Danny Glover (Walter Lee), Starletta DuPois (Ruth), and Kim
Yancey (Beneatha) also starred, with John Fiedler reprising his role
as Karl Lindner. But unlike the first film version, which was a star
vehicle for Poitier, the remake was even more faithful to
Hanberry's original text and afforded all of the principals an
opportunity to develop their characters. Beneatha's embrace of
anti-assimilationism, for instance, is in the remake mirrored by her
changing appearance, particularly by her rejection of "mutilated"
hair and her return to a more natural, nappy style. Glover and
DuPois speak in a more convincing and less theatrical vernacular,
a contrast to Poitier's perfect English, which was apparent even in
the colloquial lines that he uttered. And even Big Walter emerges
as a more distinctive and towering figure. His photograph is literally at the center of the Younger household: Lena touches it as she
speaks to and about her late husband, and Walter Lee personally
takes down the image just before the family leaves the Chicago
apartment for their new suburban home.

The remake also introduced a new character, Mrs. Johnson, the nosy neighbor who visits Lena with news that a Negro family has been bombed out of their home and who ominously suggests that the Youngers's house will be next.[17] The conversation between Mrs. Johnson and Lena interjects an explicitly politicized and overtly racist element into the play and hints at some of the other changes that Hansberry had hoped to incorporate into the original film version of her work. While not the landmark production that the 1961 film was, the 1986 remake of *A Raisin in the Sun* thus proved to be a worthy and satisfying successor.

Considerably less successful than *A Raisin in the Sun* but similar in its theme of struggle and accommodation was *Take a Giant Step* (1960), another black-authored, family-oriented drama adapted to film. Written by black playwright Louis Peterson and adapted by Peterson and his white colleague, Academy Award-winning white writer Julius J. Epstein,[18] *Take a Giant Step* was produced by Hecht-Hill-Lancaster, an independent film company formed in 1947 by actor Burt Lancaster and producer Harold Hecht, and distributed by United Artists. Popular rock-and-roll singer Johnny Nash starred as Spencer Scott, a black teen coming of age in a northern white community; Frederick O'Neal, a co-founder of the American Negro Theatre, played Spencer's unsympathetic father Lem; Beah Richards played Spencer's mother; and Ruby Dee was featured as the housekeeper who helped to answer some of the young man's questions about sex. (Fig. 5.6.)

In scenes that were often rather volatile for the time, the film depicted Spencer's attempt to discover and assert his identity. In one such scene, after a white teacher presumes that black slaves were simply too lazy to fight for their own emancipation, Spencer challenges the falsehood and is expelled; then he clashes with his father, who upholds the teacher's authority instead of empathizing with his son's frustration. But, even though ultimately Spencer is forced to subordinate himself, he emerges as a kind of hero figure because "his accommodation," according to Mark A. Reid, "occurs after he defies a white symbol of authority." His actions are therefore representative not merely of "an individual black adolescent [but rather of] the experiences of the African-American community" (*RBF* 51).[19]

The frank treatment of a black teenager's defiance, like the depiction of his exploration of his awakening sexual desires, raised

Figure 5.6. Troubled teen Spencer Scott (played by popular young singer Johnny Nash) comes of age in *Take a Giant Step*. *(United Artists, 1960)*

sensitive racial issues and created a host of problems for the film-makers. Spencer's use of profanity on screen, for instance, at least briefly stalled the distribution of the film and threatened to jeop-ardize its MPAA Production Code seal. Producer Hecht feared that because the "subject matter is so frankly handled—and with dia-log carrying such words as 'hell,' 'bastard,' and 'prostitute,'—that it's extremely doubtful that official sanction will be forthcoming" (Reid *RBF* 51); but he was hopeful that the Broadway version of *A Raisin in the Sun* would spark interest in his film.

Unfortunately, that interest proved to be limited, and the film's box office was poor. Theater owners complained that audiences were not interested in unknown black stars as serious actors; oth-ers suggested that racial problem pictures simply were not a draw. (Ironically, around the same time, the major studios were success-fully promoting movies about rebellious young *white* people, including James Dean, Natalie Wood, and Sal Mineo in produc-tions such as *The Wild One*, *Blackboard Jungle*, and *Rebel Without a*

Cause.) Yet, as Reid concluded, "although *Giant Step* may not have been an interesting film for a mass audience, it did give African-American youths an image of a defiant black kid who refused his ignorant white teacher's attempt to dehumanize the African-American community" and was thus "a great leap toward liberating black heroism from Hollywood's social and economic restrictions" (*RBF* 54).[20]

The lack of mass audience interest had doomed a number of earlier black-oriented films, including *Bright Road* (1953), a Metro-Goldwyn-Mayer production directed by Gerald Mayer, which was based on a short story, "See How They Run," by black writer Mary Elizabeth Vroman. In that story, a young black third-grade teacher, Jane Richards, has to learn how to fulfill her responsibilities within an imperfect school system. She discovers that educating her students means more than just teaching them to read and write: it also includes signing them up for subsidized breakfasts, tending to their medical concerns, paying for their clothes and haircuts, and—most importantly—helping them to raise their self-esteem by recognizing their unique needs and abilities (as she does with

Figure 5.7. Dorothy Dandridge stars as young teacher Jane Richards in *Bright Road*, a film based on Mary Elizabeth Vroman's short story, "See How They Run." *(Metro-Goldwyn-Mayer, 1953)*

problem student C. T. Young, for whom she designs an individualized curriculum and assignments). And, in the course of the school year, Miss Richards learns as much as she teaches, and she receives as much as she gives. The well-intentioned film (in which Harry Belafonte made his film debut in a small role as a school principal) portrayed Dorothy Dandridge (fig. 5.7) as the black teacher who struggles to reach the often troubled students in her rural school; even her most alienated student (Philip Hepburn) finds acceptance after he manages to save the class from a bee attack by identifying the queen bee and using her to lead the swarm away. But, as Thomas Cripps demonstrates, the film failed to excite either critics or paying customers. "Both blacks and Metro were at a loss, the former trapped into too loudly praising it, the latter burying it." The Urban League tried to save the film by encouraging members to promote it, by heaping awards on it, and by urging the studio to reconsider its decision not to market it in the South. Vroman concurred with the Urban League's judgment that the film might indeed appeal to Southern viewers, and she even tried to arrange an integrated premiere at Alabama's Maxwell Air Force Base. "But nothing could save it. 'We could not get anyone in to see [it],' said [studio head Dore] Schary; 'commendable' anyway, said the *Defender*" (*MMB* 262).

COMING OF AGE: *THE LEARNING TREE* AND *SOUNDER*

Fortunately, later films adapted from black literature that dealt with the coming-of-age theme met with much greater success. *The Learning Tree* (Warner Brothers-Seven Arts, 1969; dir. Gordon Parks), based on the semi-autobiographical novel *The Learning Tree* (1963) by Gordon Parks, was a nostalgic film about growing up black in the small Kansas town of Cherokee Flats during the 1920s. The hero Newton Winger (Kyle Johnson), or Newt for short, is a fifteen-year-old black boy on the verge of becoming a man. From his loving and supportive family, particularly from his devoted mother, Sarah (Estelle Evans), he learns to cultivate virtues like honesty and loyalty; from other people in the community, he learns about discrimination and violence. All of these lessons are tested when Newt witnesses the murder of Jake Kiner, a local white farmer, by Booker Savage, a black man who happens to be the father of his boyhood friend Marcus (Alex Clarke). Silas Newhall, a white fieldhand whom Kiner had recently fired because of drunkenness, is indicted and tried for the crime. Newt knows that he must come forward, but he fears that his testimony will stir up racial tensions in the town. Ultimately, with his mother's encouragement, he takes the stand and names the killer, who then steals an officer's gun, flees the courtroom, and shoots himself. Regrettably, Newt's courageous act also precipitates the death of his already sickly mother, who suffers a heart attack at the end of the trial, and evokes the wrath of Marcus, who blames Newt for his father's suicide.

Although race tensions underlay the whole film, the racial situation in rural Kansas between the two world wars was, for the most part, better than in the South. The film visually captures the essence of Cherokee Flats, which Parks had described as "wallow[ing] in the social complexities of a borderline state. Here, for the black man, freedom loosed one hand while custom restrained the other" (25). Newt, for instance, is befriended by Rodney Cavanaugh, the white town judge's younger son, and the two play together with Rodney's books, microscopes, bugs, and butterflies in the Cavanaugh home, where Newt's mother is employed as a domestic.[21] But even in Cherokee Flats, Newt experiences race hatred. He and his friends watch as Officer Kirky (Dana Elcar) breaks up a crap game and then chases down Tuck, one of the black players, whom he shoots in the back. The swimming hole, only minutes before the scene of idyllic play, suddenly turns red with blood; and after the police hire the boys to locate Tuck's drowned body, Newt becomes haunted by the memory of Tuck's face staring back at him from his underwater grave, and he begins to obsess about dying.

While the film depicts Newt's coming-of-age in a sentimentalized and moving way, it also is replete with ironies. The young black criminal, Marcus, whose mother is dead and whose father alternatively abuses or neglects him, is clearly the victim of an undeserved fate. But he reacts to his victimization by becoming a victimizer. After Newt and Marcus are caught stealing apples from Jake Kiner's trees, Marcus brutally beats the old farmer. Sentenced to serve time in a boys' reformatory, Marcus does not take responsibility for his action but blames Newt for his incarceration and determines to even the score when he is released. After being unable to best Newt publicly in a boxing match at a local carnival, he steals a gun from his employer and pursues his former friend (now his nemesis), with the intention of shooting him. But instead it is Marcus who is killed, by the same racist white officer who had killed Tuck as Marcus and Newt had watched. Shot in the back, Marcus dies just as Tuck did, his body submerged near the boys' old swimming hole.

And there are other ironies as well, almost all of which—as the *Variety* reviewer (19 June 1969) noted—are "symbolic of the racial ambiguity [novelist and director] Parks finds in America." For instance, the white judge who shows no leniency to Marcus at his sentencing pleads persuasively to the court for compassion and understanding before the start of Silas Newhall's trial; and after the death of Booker Savage, he rebukes the crowd for their mob mentality and holds them responsible for the violence that has occurred. Chauncey, the judge's white son, challenges the segregation laws by inviting Newt and his girlfriend, Arcella, for Cokes at the local drugstore where the young blacks are served their drinks "to go"; yet later, he seduces, impregnates, and abandons Arcella, leaving Newt powerless to retaliate or to relieve her shame. Mr. Hall, the school principal, sympathizes with Newt after Mrs. McClintock, a white teacher, discourages him from signing up for college preparatory courses; yet he tells the boy that he must show Mrs. McClintock "the highest respect," despite her prejudice against him.[22] And the principal compounds his hypocrisy by rationalizing that he cannot change the school's racial codes, which prohibit blacks from playing sports or attending dances with white students. Still, Mrs. Winger observes, all of these experiences are critical to Newt's character. "Some of the people are good, and some of them are bad," she tells him. "Just like the fruit on a tree. . . . Let it [Cherokee Flats] be your learning tree." (Fig. 5.8.)

But it is probably Newt's Uncle Rob, blinded twenty-five years earlier in an explosion, who offers the best assessment of racial differences. When Newt asks him if he recalls colors, Rob admits that at times he remembers them as they actually were; at other times, he has a "little fun" in his darkness. He imagines Newt with green

Figure 5.8. Protagonist Newt Winger (Kyle Johnson) learns to use his youthful experiences as his "learning tree" in *The Learning Tree*, a film adaptation of Gordon Park's semi-autobiographical novel. *(Warner Brothers/Seven Artists, Inc., 1969)*

skin and pink ears and a blue nose and purple hair. "I fill my world with all kinds of colors," he tells Newt in words taken almost directly from the novel. And he adds that "I think sometimes if all the people in the world were made up of colors instead of just black and white, it would be a happier world. A wonderful world all mixed up with wonderful colored people, nobody bein' the same as anybody else."

The film was a close adaptation of Gordon Parks's semi-auto-biographical novel, which chronicled life in a particular time and in a particular place.[23] Even more than the film version, the novel had caught the flavor of an age when boys nicknamed Beansy, Jappy, and Skunk would sit at Flynn's ballpark "awaiting the first pitch of the game between the Fort Miles Hawkeyes and the Chanute Cornhuskers" with a greasy box of popcorn disappearing rapidly among them (68). In that age, a twelve-year-old Newt loses his virginity to the amiable prostitute Big Mabel after both of them are forced to take shelter in a smokehouse during a storm; and afterward Newt is not even sure what has transpired: "all at once I had a shivery feelin' . . . and everything was like a dream . . . . It just kind'a left me feelin' good, mighty good, that's all" (32). In that age, every fumbling sexual advance in a darkened movie theater takes on almost heroic dimensions, as Newt tries to coordinate his moves with those of the on-screen characters (104): "Newt's other hand slid behind her shoulder (the villain is falling from his galloping mount) and his fingers pressed into the softness of her armpit (Hart jumps from his horse onto the villain), and Arcella pushed his hand down to her waist. (Hart and the villain are fighting at the edge of a cliff.)" In that age, families gather at the Sunday service to watch Reverend Lucius Broadnap race back and forth in the pulpit "spiking his sermon" (45) and thumping his Bible, and they spend Christmas Day by "a crackling fire" (110), unwrapping and comparing their gifts and reminiscing about years past. That age, however, is also one in which Newt's blind Uncle Rob, selling his brooms door-to-door, is called a "nigger" and is spat upon; in which black children are pushed into substandard schools without indoor toilets or other facilities in order to accommodate overcrowding in the better white schools; and in which Newt is accosted by white boys when he tries to help his light-skinned cousin Polly carry home her packages.

By necessity, the film omitted some of the peripheral events in the novel: the death of Big Mabel in a car accident with Cap'n Tuck, the razor-scarred bully who scouts under the seats at baseball games for women who are not wearing underpants and then collects "peep fees"; Newt's invitation to participate in a summer science seminar; Doc Craven's admission to Newt that Sarah had raised him after his own mother's death (which would explain why Sarah, in the film, calls the doctor by his first name, Timothy); Jappy's taking a shot in the leg from Marcus's gun.[24] But the film, for the most part, was a very literal—and a very effective—adaptation of the novel, no doubt because Gordon Parks was intimately involved in both. A renowned still photographer whose work had appeared in *Life* and other prominent publications, Parks not only produced and directed the film; he also wrote the screenplay and scored the music (the movie's only disappointing and dated element). *The Learning Tree* was thus the first film financed by a major studio to have a black director, and it opened Hollywood's doors for Parks, who went on to direct other even more commercially successful films like *Shaft* (1971), *Shaft's Big Score!* (1972), and *The Super Cops* (1974), as well as for other black directors.

The Learning Tree was just one of a number of black-oriented films released in 1969. Others—like Jules Dassin's *Up Tight*, about black revolutionaries and the separatist movement in a ghetto neighborhood of Cleveland after the death of Martin Luther King, Jr.; *Slavery*, a radicalized remake of Harriet Beecher Stowe's novel of slavery[25] that tried to make an analogy between past brutality and contemporary violence; and *Putney Swope*, the story of a token black who, after being accidentally elected the chairman of the board of an advertising agency, replaces the corruption and excesses of the white establishment with comparable corruption and excesses by his new black establishment—tended to indict the system and focus on black militancy, much as even Poitier's films of the same period attempted to do. But *The Learning Tree* succeeded not because it was progressive but rather because it was sentimental, in the best sense of that word. As the *Variety* (19 June 1969) reviewer wrote, in the film "characterizations are swift and broad, tradition and the influence of elders are emphasized, moral decisions are key plot points." *The Learning Tree*, which "often reduces a spectator to tears," is "old-fashioned, a film no young person, of any race, would make—and sometimes 'corny,' but perhaps it's to be regretted that such emotions do not come naturally to new generations as they did" to John Ford and Frank Capra. Yet *The Learning Tree* is also universal. A film about race that paradoxically almost transcends race, it presents, simply and sensitively, a boy who—according to Donald Bogle—"is black but not tortured by his blackness. He is like other boys, no matter what the color or place or time" (*TCMMB* 226), poised precariously on the brink of manhood.

Like *The Learning Tree*, *Sounder* (Paramount, 1972; dir. Martin Ritt) was a touching coming-of-age film set in the same era but in a different geographical location. Written by white author William H. Armstrong, *Sounder* was nevertheless very much a black story. Armstrong writes in the Author's Note to the book that, as a boy, he had learned to read at his kitchen table: "my teacher was a gray-haired black man who taught the one-room Negro school several miles away. . . . He worked for my father after school and in the summer. There were no radios or television sets, so when our lessons were finished he told us stories." Although he talked "little, or not at all, about his past," one night "after he had told the story of Argus, the faithful dog of Odysseus, he told the story of Sounder, a coon dog." That story, Armstrong affirms, was "the black man's story, not mine. It was not from Aesop, the Old Testament, or Homer. It was history—*his* history." And it is precisely that history that gives Armstrong's retelling such mythic resonance and enduring appeal.

The plot of the children's novel *Sounder* is simple. Close to starvation, a poor black sharecropper steals meat from a neighbor's smokehouse in order to feed his family. When the white sheriff comes to arrest him, Sounder—a coon hound named for the remarkable bark he sounds while hunting—makes a heroic effort to protect his master but is shot and seriously injured by one of the sheriff's deputies. The dog disappears into the woods, presumably to die. Meanwhile, the father is incarcerated and sentenced to hard labor at an undisclosed prison camp, and although the son searches throughout the state, he is unable to find him. Suddenly one day Sounder reappears. Maimed, starved, and seemingly incapable of barking anymore, he silently awaits the father's return. And eventually the father does return; but, like Sounder, he has suffered the vagaries of fate. Severely disabled by a dynamite explosion in the limestone quarry where he was serving his sentence, he is a broken man whose only wish is to come home to die. The loyal Sounder attends his master faithfully during his remaining days; and soon after he dies, so does the dog.

The novel, published in 1969 and illustrated with black and white sketches by James Barkley, won both the John Newbery Medal and the Lewis Carroll Shelf Award and is generally considered to be a masterpiece of juvenile fiction. But in its treatment of serious issues such as racial prejudice and discrimination, it differs significantly from other literature for children. As Leonard J. Deutsch has observed, the novel confronts the matter of racism head on and depicts numerous examples of racial discrimination, especially as perceived by the eldest boy (who, like the novel's other characters, is unnamed). "From the boy we learn that no mailman passes his house and that his family does not even own a mailbox; that he has never looked out of a window with curtains on it; and that he has smelled ham bone only twice in his life." Yet "the boy doesn't get on a soap box and denounce the injustices all around him; rather, these experiences implicitly define the inequitable caste system that invariably relegates blacks to the have-not category" (215). In fact, the very understated response of the boy makes the injustices he suffers seem all the more intense.

Like the racial issues, the often graphic episodes of violence in the novel are handled directly and explicitly. When Sounder is shot, for example, he staggers, falls, and trails blood. "There was a large spot of mingled blood, hair, and naked flesh on one shoulder. His head swung from side to side. . . . One side of his head was a mass of blood. The blast had torn off the whole side of his head and shoulder" (28). The boy searches for the wounded dog, but all he finds is a bloody severed ear, which he intends to put under his pillow so that he can wish upon it for the dog's return. When Sounder reappears, he is an utterly gruesome sight, the "living skeleton" of what had once been a mighty coon hound. "One foot dangled above the floor. The stub of an ear stuck out on one side, and there was no eye on that side, only a dark socket with a splinter of bone showing above it" (70). That is not, however, the only violence that the boy witnesses or experiences. When he tries unsuccessfully to locate his father among a group of prisoners, the boy is struck by a jagged piece of iron thrown by one of the guards. "Drops of blood from his fingers dripped down the fence," and "tears ran down over his face and mixed with the blood on his hand. Little rivulets of blood and water ran down his arm and dropped off the end of his elbow" (86). Later, when the father returns and is greeted by the maimed dog (who barks for the first time since being shot six years earlier), the boy realizes the extent of his father's injuries. The father's mutilation, in fact, parallels Sounder's: "The head of the man was pulled to the side where a limp arm dangled through the dust. What had been a shoulder was now pushed up and back to make a one-sided hump so high that the leaning head seemed to rest upon it. The mouth was askew, too, and the voice came out of the part farthest away from the withered, wrinkled, lifeless side" (107).

As realistic as the depiction of violence is the portrayal of the boy, whose thoughts and perceptions comprise much of the book.

Though told from a third person point of view, all of the events are filtered through his consciousness, so that the reader identifies with him and sees things from his perspective. When Sounder is shot and the boy assumes that he is dead, he begins to wonder:

> Maybe his mother would drag Sounder out of the road. Maybe she would drag him across the fields and bury him. Maybe if she laid him on the porch and put some soft rags under him tonight, he might rise from the dead, like Lazarus did in a meetin'-house story. Maybe his father didn't know Sounder was dead. Maybe his father was dead in the back of the sheriff's wagon now. Maybe his father had said it hurt to bounce over the rough road on his back, and the deputy had turned around on the seat and shot him.

The more of life's cruelties that the boy experiences, the keener his view of the world becomes. He learns to value those who show him kindness, like the teacher; and he grows to scorn those who hurt him, like the sadistic guard who smashes his fingers or the careless jailer who ruins the cake that was to have been his father's Christmas surprise. And the boy grows up quickly—too quickly—because he is forced to bear his sorrows like a man, even though he is still a child. By the end of the story, he has matured enough to understand that "Sounder ain't got no spirit left for living." He digs a grave under the oak tree near the fence row, so that if the ground freezes while he is away at school, his mother will be able to carry the dog there on coffee sacks and bury him. "He'll be gone before I come home again" (114), he tells her. Indeed Sounder dies shortly afterwards; and when the boy returns, he takes consolation from a passage by Montaigne in one of his schoolbooks, that only the unwise think that what has changed is dead. Now wiser than his years, the boy knows that Sounder's spirit, like his father's, will endure because he will always carry it with him in his own heart.

The film, released in 1972, transformed Armstrong's *bildungsroman* into an evocative and compelling film, due in large part to the sensitive screenplay by black playwright Lonne Elder III. But whereas the novel focused on the struggles of the boy, the film is a paean to the resilience and fortitude of the black family, whose members find spiritual sustenance in each other. In fact, as Deutsch writes (219), "the force that cements all of their relationships and ensures their survival is family love. . . . black strength is derived from a strong family (and, when the father is absent, from a supportive black community)."

The fact that the characters were unnamed and that their story was set in an unspecified locale gave the novel a sense of timelessness and universality, an impression reinforced by the indistinct, blurred brushstrokes of Barkley's illustrations.[26] The film, on the other hand, individualizes the characters—they become the Morgan family—and establishes a specific time period and place for their story: Louisiana, 1933. Nathan Lee Morgan (played by Paul Winfield, in an Oscar-nominated performance) is a proud and hardworking man; only when he is unable to feed his hungry children does he resort to stealing meat. (Fig. 5.9.) Sentenced first to jail, where he is allowed a single brief Sunday visit from his son (but never from "women folk"), and later to a prison work camp,

Figure 5.9. Nathan Lee Morgan (Paul Winfield), with his faithful dog Sounder at his side, is arrested for stealing food to feed his hungry family in *Sounder. (Twentieth Century-Fox, 1972)*

where he is isolated completely from his family, he struggles to maintain his dignity and never stops being concerned about their fate or his. In Nathan Lee's absence, his wife Rebecca (Cicely Tyson, in another Oscar-nominated performance) also worries about the future, especially after Mr. Perkins, proprietor of the general store and owner of the land that the Morgans farm, expresses doubts about her ability to bring in a crop alone. Yet she musters her reserves and assumes the arduous responsibility. With a tenacity born of great spiritual strength, she plows the dry earth, plants the crops, and harvests the sugar cane; and afterwards she refuses to accept Perkins's compliments, just as she had earlier refused the easy consolations of her minister. There is perhaps no more transcendent image of the black woman on film than that of Rebecca in a plain dress bleached of its original color and too large for her frail frame, her head wrapped in a cloth rag, sweat pouring from her as she toils under the hot Southern sun. As black critic Ellen Holly writes, her character "give[s] us, at long last, some sense of the profound beauty of millions of black women of a certain kind whose tale has almost never been told and whose praises are so wrenchingly seldom sung" (*NYT* 14 Oct. 1972). Dirt poor but infinitely proud, Rebecca is a luminous figure, at once earth mother and madonna.

But, like Sarah Winger in *The Learning Tree*, she is also a symbol of the matriarchal strength that is so integral to the well-being of the black family. Through her meticulous laundering and ironing for whites and her laborious shelling of the walnuts that she sells by the pound to Mr. Perkins, Rebecca teaches her children to seize whatever opportunities may come their way—however small they may seem—and to take pride in doing even the most menial job well. At the same time, she imparts to them her strong sense of dignity, which she demonstrates when she offers an adamant defense of Nathan Lee to the arresting officers and again when she stands up to the sheriff who will not allow her to visit her husband in jail. "You got you a low-life job, Mr. Sheriff," she tells him plainly. Above all, through the constancy of her love, the film's Rebecca sustains the whole Morgan family through the darkest of times.

It is the eldest son David Lee (Kevin Hooks) who is most directly affected by Nathan Lee's arrest and absence. An earnest and obedient boy—a boy, in fact, more virtuous than his counterpart in the novel, who imagines exacting various forms of revenge on those who hurt him—he is deeply bonded to his father.[27] The opening sequence of the film, in which the two engage in a hunt for game that takes on almost ritualistic dimensions, reveals the intimate nature of their relationship. When David Lee rationalizes their failure to catch any possum, he uses the same words—"You miss some of the time what you do go after, but you miss all of the time what you don't go after"—that he has heard his father utter so often before; and it prompts Nathan Lee to remark, "Who said I didn't put my mark on you, boy?" Nathan Lee's mark is indeed evident, particularly as David Lee assumes a number of his absent father's responsibilities—chopping wood, feeding the younger children, caring for Sounder, oiling and maintaining the hunting rifles.

In adapting *Sounder* to film, screenwriter Lonne Elder III made a number of revisions or additions to the book. Some were minor: David Lee, for instance, takes a single long journey in search of his father (who is gone less than a year), while the boy in the novel makes several such trips (since the father is serving six years of hard time). Others were more significant and often remarkably effective, such as the baseball game that occurs just before Nathan Lee returns to his cabin, where the police are waiting to arrest him. That scene, original to the film, is important because it establishes the virile and athletic Nathan Lee, whose superb pitching ensures his team's victory, as a kind of epic hero within his black community; and it counters the image of him as a common thief that is held by the white sheriff, who does not know hunger and who cannot appreciate Nathan Lee's reasons for committing the petty crime. The scene also evokes the richness of the community, even among the poorest of the blacks, as friends and neighbors, all part of an extended family, gather to watch the game, laugh, converse, and listen to the songs that family friend Ike (Taj Majal) composes about Nathan's "speedball."

Equally important is another scene original to the film, in which David Lee dreams that he sees his father in a field and goes running into his open arms. But when he approaches the spot where his father was standing, there is no one there; and, in that instant, he wakes up to nothing but the darkness of the cabin. The dream, a projection of the boy's sadness over his lost father, reinforces the notion of their special bond, as suggested not just by the opening hunting sequence but also by the special handshake that the two share during critical moments (e.g., after the unsuccessful hunt and at the end of David Lee's single visit to the jailhouse).[28] But the dream also anticipates one of the loveliest and most memorable scenes late in the film—a scene not in the book—in which Nathan Lee joins his son at the creek, takes his hand, hugs him, and speaks openly of his pride and love. "Wherever you is," he tells the boy, "I'm gonna love you." In that instant, it is as if David Lee's earlier dream about the security of his father's embrace has been fulfilled. (In the final but very brief image of the film, in fact, David Lee actually runs into his father's outstretched arms.)

Elder's greatest change in adapting Armstrong's book, however, is in its happy—but not sappy—ending. In the novel, the father, a broken man, returns home to die; in the film, Nathan Lee, an injured man, returns home to resume his life. Moreover, once reunited with his family, Nathan Lee appears to undergo a regeneration: he insists on going back to cropping, as if to prove that nothing—not even the sugar cane press, whose crossbar knocks him to the ground—will ever keep him down again. He knows that his injuries will heal, that he will hunt again with the loyal Sounder at his side, and that he will continue to enjoy the warm affections of his wife and children. Perhaps most importantly, though, he understands that, just as his experience has given him new life, he must in turn give new life to David Lee; so he encourages the boy to go away to school and get an education, despite the boy's desire to stay and help out on the farm. "That is what I want you to do," he tells his son. "I want you to beat the life they got all laid out for you in this place; cause there ain't nothing, ain't nobody here but them bastards that sent me. . . ." Like the coon hunt that opens the film and the boy's "hunt" for his missing father that constitutes much of the film's central action, the closing scene, in which Nathan Lee and David Lee (dressed in a jacket and tie) laugh and talk as they ride away to Miss Johnson's school, is appropriately enough another journey; and, like the earlier journeys, it has both cyclical and mythic resonances. (There are also other mythic overlays in the film: as Charles S. Rutherford notes, the screenwriter's use of Homeric motifs "lie[s] beneath the beautiful and moving surface of *Sounder*" [223]. The Homeric substructure, Rutherford contends, is never allowed to surface; but its timeless pattern, the motif of exile and return, plays out within a single family, particularly in the desperate need for the return of the father and the son's relentless search for him.)

Among the characters original to the film is Rita Boatwright (Carmen Matthews), a liberal white woman who employs Rebecca to do her laundry, rewards the Morgan children for delivering it, encourages David Lee to read by giving him a book about the Three Musketeers, and even intervenes with the sheriff to find out where Nathan Lee is being held. (The sheriff's office refuses to disclose the location of the prison camp to the family.) And the unnamed black male teacher in the novel, with whom the boy begins studying several years before his father's return, becomes in the film a young black female teacher, Camille Johnson. From the moment that David Lee, wounded and slightly disoriented, wanders into her schoolhouse, Miss Johnson (Janet MacLachlan) is deeply moved by his plight. After she bandages his injury, she offers him a meal and a bed; and later she provides him with intellectual nourishment as well, as she inspires him with lessons about Crispus Attucks, Harriet Tubman, and W. E. B. Du Bois. Yet Miss Johnson, like Mrs. Boatwright, never supplants but always augments the boy's family—the former by helping the boy evoke memories of his absent father, the latter by trying (in a comic scene, with her mishandling of a road map) to assist in the reunion of father and son. And neither offers easy resolutions to the boy's problems, because in fact there are none.

Ellen Holly noted in a *New York Times* review (14 Oct. 1972) that "in terms of film technique, *Sounder* offers nothing new. There are no brilliant cuts or breathtaking camera angles. Its color is merely its color and is not controlled to make a comment. It distills life into prose rather than into the denser essences of poetry. And although things occasionally achieve a powerful reality—a dry-dusty road or newly laundered wash or a bowl of gruel set down on the flaking blue paint of a wooden table—*Sounder*'s one true value lies in its living portrait gallery of people. Somehow, it is infinitely more than enough."

Lonne Elder III, whose screenplay for *Sounder* made him the first black ever to be nominated for a best adapted screenplay Oscar, concurred with Holly that the importance of the film lay not in its cinematic innovations but in the timelessness of the story, which he characterized as being about "the universality of human dignity and strength in the face of adversity" (qtd. in Rutherford 224). In fact, as a film that had no special effects and no gratuitous sex or violence, *Sounder* had been relatively inexpensive to produce. Shot on location in East Feliciana and St. Helena parishes in Louisiana, the film was directed by Martin Ritt, well known for his social consciousness; assistant director for the film was Charles Washburn, a black man whose own experiences no doubt contributed to the excellent interpretation of Elder's screenplay. Embraced by the black community for its positive depictions, *Sounder* also made money for its producers. Daniel J. Leab writes that "within nine months of its first commercial showing the film had earned over five times its production costs." Yet, although black moviegoers were a significant portion of the paying customers, black attendance was nowhere comparable to the turnout for a film like the later blockbuster *Shaft*. And "even though *Sounder* was well received, there were many blacks who criticized it as 'a white man's movie,' and as an attempt to emasculate the newly emerged image of the powerful black male" (260, 262).[29] Nonetheless it remains a glorious evocation of the ability of the black spirit to survive and triumph.[30]

GO TELL IT ON THE MOUNTAIN

Whereas *The Learning Tree* portrayed what it was like to grow up black in rural Kansas in the 1920s, *Go Tell It on the Mountain* (1984) portrayed what it was like growing up in Harlem in the 1930s.[31] The telefilm, produced as part of the *American Playhouse* series for PBS (Public Broadcasting Service) and based on James Baldwin's mostly-autobiographical first novel (1953) of the same title, told the story of John Grimes, a poor though not impoverished black boy, and his rigidly autocratic father. The novel, written when Baldwin was twenty-eight, brought him immediate acclaim as a new and authentic literary voice; yet, as Leslie Bennetts noted, by the time the novel was published, Baldwin had long since fled his origins and moved to Paris. Over the years, he continued to publish more books; and he distinguished himself in other ways as well, particularly as one of the nation's leading black spokespersons and advocates for civil rights. (He also added another dimension to his persona when he began to write about his own homosexuality in novels such as *Giovanni's Room* [Bennetts, *NYT* 10 Jan 1985: C1]). Yet *Go Tell It on the Mountain* remains the highpoint of his career as well as his best known work.

"*Mountain*," Baldwin has said, "is the book I had to write if I was ever going to write anything else. I had to deal with what hurt me most. I had to deal, above all, with my father. He was my model; I learned a lot from him. Nobody's ever frightened me since."[32] And indeed, as Frederick Karl observes, Baldwin's first novel is ironically his most mature and compelling work because "he had located himself precisely where his talent lay. So much of Baldwin's career has been based on the need to kill the father, resurrect him, and perhaps rekill him—not only his own father, of course, but [his literary father] Richard Wright and others—that he is in the constant condition of being a son." And since Baldwin's need to slay the father and assert himself as the son is so melodramatic a theme, so potentially uncontrollable for his art, his use of religious imagery and spiritualism throughout the novel is especially significant in "help[ing] him to contain it literally, giving his prose its rich burnish and yet distancing it just outside the self" (145-46).

Growing up in the intensely religious and dangerous environment of Harlem in the 1930s, Baldwin's John Grimes is trapped within a family that is held together rather tenuously by their religious faith. His domineering and messianic father Gabriel, who expects John to follow in his footsteps as a preacher, uses his Bible to warn of the sins of the world and of white people in particular. Florence, Gabriel's estranged sister, knows all too well how Gabriel's hypocrisy has already ruined many lives—their mother's, his first wife Deborah's, his mistress Esther's, his first son Royal's—and she threatens to expose his secrets. Gabriel's gentle and loving wife Elizabeth, on the other hand, tries to keep the various hatreds from imploding and destroying the family; but despite her best efforts John, a slight boy of fourteen who has learned to measure his words for fear of his father's harsh retribution, feels increasingly alienated while his rebellious younger brother Roy seems increasingly bent on self-destruction.

The powerful beauty of the novel lies in its family scenes, which reveal the tensions experienced by the family as a whole as

well as by its individual members. Although the novel begins and
ends in the Harlem storefront Pentecostal Temple of the Fire
Baptized, where John at first resists his vocation as a preacher but
ultimately finds his calling in a remarkably vivid religious experience on "the threshing floor," it is the middle section of the book
that evokes the ghosts that continue to haunt the family. The
young Gabriel had been an alcoholic, a wanton, and a womanizer;
his conversion, which occurs after his mother's death (a death that
his actions have hastened), transforms him into a self-appointed
divine messenger who, like his biblical namesake, hopes to purify
himself by punishing those around him. As part of his repentance,
he marries Florence's friend Deborah, an older, very dark-skinned
black woman who had been brutally raped by whites and who,
having "been choked so early on white man's milk . . . would
never be able, now, to find a nigger who would let her taste his
richer, sweeter substance" (107); but she proves to be as barren as
he is unfaithful. Gabriel's liaison with Esther, a younger woman of
questionable reputation, ends in her pregnancy; but his refusal to
acknowledge paternity of the baby, whom Esther names Royal,
leads first to Esther's death and then, a few years later, to his son's
murder—a loss made all the more bitter by Deborah's calm rebuke
of Gabriel's adultery and her admission that she would gladly
have raised the late Esther's child as their own, an admission that
only compounds Gabriel's guilt. After Deborah's death, as a way
of redeeming the sacrifice of his first son, Gabriel decides to
become stepfather to John, whose real father had killed himself
after being unjustly imprisoned and brutalized by the police (and
without ever having learned of Elizabeth's pregnancy). But
Gabriel has no love for the boy, and he continues for years to taunt
Elizabeth with the specter of her "sin," which John embodies;
meanwhile Roy, Gabriel's natural son with Elizabeth, who is headed for the same kind of bad end as his namesake Royal, serves as
an even greater reminder to Gabriel of his own evil.

It is Esther who recognizes that Gabriel's deeply sensual nature
is at war with his religious needs and that his talk of sinning is
merely a facade to excuse his own weakness.[33] When he speaks of
being made to fall because of a wicked woman, she responds, "You
be careful . . . how you talk to me. I ain't the first girl's been ruined
by a holy man, neither" (132). Ironically, it is Gabriel's drive for

respectability as a black man against the debilitation and degradation dealt to him by the white man that in turn deprives him of real honor and almost destroys him. As Baldwin's biographer David Leeming has observed, Gabriel's obsession with racism is understandable, both in the context of the novel and in the context of African-American history: he, Florence, and Elizabeth have all "been denied the salvation of love, not, ironically, because they were unable to say yes to love, but because the nature of racism was such as to preclude the kind of self-respect that viable relationships require." Racism drives Elizabeth's lover Richard to suicide, a rash act that ends her dream as well as his. Florence's self-denigrating hatred of her own blackness destroys her relationship with her husband Frank. And Gabriel's mistreatment of his wife and the mother of his first son has its genesis in society's racist denial of his manhood, a denial that leaves him no place to turn but "a reverse racism and self-hatred masked by his hypocritical religious vocation" (86). Yet Gabriel's actions often have unintended results: by accusing Florence of selfishness, Gabriel highlights his own irresponsibility; by demeaning the guileless Elizabeth, he diminishes his own moral authority; by attempting to crush John, he makes the boy stronger; by berating and beating Roy, he only hardens the boy's resentment of him.[34]

Unlike Roy, however, at the novel's end, John follows his father into the church, long enough at least to "go through" on the threshing floor and be saved. "Then John," Baldwin writes, "saw the Lord—for a moment only; and the darkness, for a moment only, was filled with a light he could not bear. Then, in a moment, he was set free" (204). And in that moment, as Baldwin suggests, John comes of age: he becomes the spiritual equal—even the superior—of his father and is at last able to assert his own manhood (or, in Frederick Karl's terms, symbolically to kill the father). As the family returns home together from the storefront church the next morning, John "turned to face his father—he found himself smiling, but his father did not smile." And John announces, to himself and to the world, in the last words of the book, his emancipation: "I'm coming. I'm on my way."

It is perhaps surprising that such a powerful novel about the black American experience by such an important writer would take so long to make its way to the screen. Robert Geller, the producer dedicated to the project, had proposed the adaptation as a possible television miniseries as early as 1977. But after running into both resistance and fundraising problems, he was forced to scale back the project to a two-hour movie, eventually made in 1985 through the assistance of the National Endowment for the Humanities, which covered much of the $1.3 million cost. "When multi-million dollar budgets for mediocre films have become commonplace," lamented *New York Times* critic John O'Connor, "the struggle required for a production of unusual quality and sensitivity is disheartening, to say the least."[35]

The film, considered by many to be the best American television film of the year, was a remarkably faithful rendering of Baldwin's novel and of the intricately interrelated stories that comprised it.[36] Scripted by Gus Edwards and Leslie Lee, the film simply yet skillfully conveyed the intergenerational concerns by blending enduring memories of love and searing loss with the pain of truths untold and malicious acts committed in the name of faith. The story is told largely from the perspective of fourteen-year-old John Grimes (James Bond III), a quiet boy who, unlike his more confrontational brother Roy (Rodrick Wimberly), persists in seeking the approval of his forbidding stepfather (Paul Winfield). Gabriel denies both boys the most basic of childhood pleasures, like playing in the streets with their friends; and he forces them to keep busy with household chores, Bible readings, and Pentecostal prayer meetings. Flashbacks soon reveal the reasons for Gabriel's sternness, particularly with John, whose illegitimacy he deeply resents. The past flows into the present as Gabriel's life unfolds— his early years as a hell-raiser (played by Ving Rhames) in the rural South; his finding religion (which occurs when he leaps dramatically from his lover's bed and runs into an open field, where he feels God's power and declares his conversion); his growing reputation as a fire-breathing preacher; and ultimately the tragedy arising from sins that he cannot escape. Slowly, as John O'Connor notes, Gabriel becomes "a seriously flawed but sympathetic man, a man who has survived poverty, racism and his own weaknesses but not without terrible scars" (*NYT* 14 Jan. 1985: C17). And past and present converge equally dramatically in the superb scene in which John "climbs the mountain" and feels the power of the spirit—and of his own spirit—as his "brother" Elisha (and notably not his father) prays him "over" to the other side. That climb affords John a new perspective on his father and gives him the strength to sever their old bond; and he gains an understanding that he and his father can never really be reconciled. As John says in voice-over at the end of the film, he had sought "the living word" that would conquer the great division between him and his father; but it did not come, and in the silence "something in me died, something came alive."

In the novel, John feels the desire to escape the restrictions that Gabriel imposes on him. In fact, when his mother gives him a few coins that she had saved as a gift for his birthday, he decides to travel to Manhattan, where he watches well-dressed whites strolling down Fifth Avenue near Central Park, and where he purchases a ticket on Broadway to see his first movie, which stars a white actress whose unhappiness on screen engages "all John's sympathy" (38).[37] Afterwards, his father's warning about whites rings in his head: "His father said that all white people were wicked, and that God was going to bring them low. He said that white people were never to be trusted, and that they told nothing but lies, and that not one of them had ever loved a nigger" (36).

The film dramatizes those events—and their upshot, when John, still reveling in the magic of his afternoon, comes home to find his brother injured as a result of a knife fight with white boys. But it also employs a very effective device to illustrate the conflict John feels between his two worlds: church, where his dominant father uses his Bible as a weapon to condemn those whom he fears, and school, where his white teachers recognize John's burgeoning literary talent and offer him a tool with which to surmount his poverty. In a scene original to the film, John's essay on "The History of New York Through One Native's Eyes" (a title similar to Baldwin's later collection of essays, *Notes of a Native Son*) is recognized for its excellence by the Board of Education and awarded a certificate signed by the mayor. John proudly carries the certificate home, where his mother shares his delight; but when he shows it to his father, Gabriel angrily dismisses the award as tokenism and insists that John reject it. Instead of using the occasion to praise his son's literary efforts, Gabriel reproaches him for choosing to write on a non-religious subject. But in a rare act of disobedience that foreshadows their eventual break, John takes the certificate into his room and hides it under some clothing in his drawer. The scene beautifully distills the conflict between father and son and between the secular and sacred—and the black and white—divisions that define both of their worlds.[38]

In the film version, John is not the only one to climb the mountain; both Florence and Elizabeth climb their own mountains as well. Florence, who alone knows the full extent of Gabriel's transgressions, not only threatens to make them public; in a scene original to the film, she finds religion again in his very church. In this way, on Gabriel's own turf, she lays claim to some of his moral absolutism—a bold encroachment that leaves him too stunned to conceal his displeasure. And Elizabeth, in a rare assertion of her independence, further undermines Gabriel's authority by calling him on the promises he made, but failed to keep, to her and to John. As the film of *Sounder* did, the film of *Go Tell It on the Mountain* thus acknowledges—even more than Baldwin did—the great importance and strength of the black family, and especially of the mother, in shaping moral and cultural values.

In adapting the novel, screenwriters Edwards and Lee made only minor changes: there is, for example, less exploration of Florence's failed marriage to her philandering husband, which in the novel helps to explain her disgust with Gabriel's licentious behavior and her bitterness at the way he abused the kindness of her good friend Deborah, and also little discussion of Richard, the man whom Elizabeth had loved, followed to New York, and hoped to marry. There is, however, a change in Gabriel's clerical position: he is not the minister of the Temple of the Church of the Fire Baptized, as in the novel, but rather its deacon—a small but significant diminution in his status that reflects a corresponding diminution in his character. Those changes help to tighten the story and to focus attention on the seminal relationship between John and Gabriel.

Much of the excellence of the production derived from the marvelous performances, particularly those of Paul Winfield, who brought to his role (as he did in *Sounder*) a wonderful subtlety and depth, and James Bond III, whose naturalness gave the character of John just enough innocence to be convincing. And while, as in the society about which Baldwin writes so compellingly, the men grab the most immediate attention, it is the women surrounding and supporting them—Rosalind Cash (Florence), Olivia Cole (Elizabeth), and CCH Pounder (Deborah)—who, according to Christopher Swan, "could move stones with their quiet strength." Director Stan Lathan, whose other distinctive directorial work includes the 1987 adaptation of *Uncle Tom's Cabin* for Showtime, managed to find in the details of Harlem street life and even in the Grimes's home an eloquence that often matched Baldwin's language. But it was the combination of Baldwin's story of black experience reinterpreted by a black director and black co-adaptors, along with the nuanced performance of some of America's finest black actors, that made *Go Tell It on the Mountain* rise to the peaks of black American cinema and that differentiated it from a white director's image of the black experience.

Baldwin, who was not involved in the adaptation, reportedly was "very, very happy" about the film, which he felt did not in any way "betray the book" (Bennetts C17). In fact, upon seeing the television version, he wept and said, "I have just seen my life" (Swan 27). And it is precisely this insight into black lives and experience—in full exposure, not in occasionally coded imagery (as in the black self-sacrifice for whites that is typical of the early Poitier films)—that gave *Go Tell It on the Mountain* its special cinematic voice.

BLAXPLOITATION: A NEW BLACK HERO

That voice was apparent in other adapted films of the period such as *If He Hollers, Let Him Go!* (1968), based on Chester Himes's *If He Hollers Let Him Go*, a novel similar in theme to Wright's *Native Son*. Himes, a fiercely independent novelist scorned by many black and white critics but admired by readers who compared his rough style to that of Wright and James Baldwin, incorporated into his fiction numerous elements from his own life: a hostile and loveless Southern family; arrest and incarceration at an early age; frequent unemployment and drifting from job to job; racial oppression and discrimination.[39] In *If He Hollers Let Him Go* (1945), Himes tells the story of a young black man who struggles with racism in the defense plants of Los Angeles during the Second World War.[40] Bob Jones is tormented at the Atlas Shipbuilders Corporation by Johnny Stoddart, a white co-worker, with whom he engages in a fistfight; but his real troubles come from Madge Perkins, a tough blonde Texan whose antagonism has already led to his demotion on the job from "leaderman," or supervisor of a group of mechanics, back to a regular mechanic. Madge, it appears, is a tease: although she acts hostile toward him and fearful of his sexual advances, in fact she welcomes and is excited by his attentions, which he discovers one night when he visits her apartment with the intention of humiliating her. Later, in the novel's critical scene, Jones accidentally bumps into Madge in an isolated area of the plant, where she attempts to seduce him; when they are interrupted, she accuses him of rape. Caught (as Bigger Thomas was in *Native Son*) "in the classic terror-trap of black males" (Campenni 241), Jones panics and flees but is captured.

Despite his innocence, Jones realizes that, as a black man, "I knew I couldn't beat the rap that Madge had hung on me" (175). Even after the charges are dropped, he is still treated like a criminal. Mr. Houghton, the owner of Atlas, makes an appearance in court to lecture Jones about the way "his crime of uncontrolled lust—the act of an animal" (186)—had betrayed the confidence of his superiors and disgraced his entire Negro race, and the judge orders him to join the Army. But Jones, having lost his freedom, his individuality, and his prospects of a comfortable life with his girlfriend Alice, is already a defeated man. For him, there is little distinction between "the highly regimented world of prison and the equally regimented world of the army, since both are punishments imposed upon him by a racist social system" (Butler 39).

The novel takes place over five days; each night, Jones has violent nightmares about being trapped or endangered. Those nightmares not only foreshadow coming events but also create a sense of inevitability about his fate as an oppressed minority. In the novel's opening pages, for instance, he dreams about a small black dog being led around by a piece of stiff wire that is twisted tightly around its neck; the next morning, he goes to work at a job at which he feels scrutinized, almost suffocated—and so out of his element that he imagines himself to be like "some friendly dog [that] had come in through the door and said, 'I can talk'" (9). As Frank Campenni writes, "The surrealistic quality of these nightmares underscores vividly that the doom which hangs over Jones is the product not only of his environment but of the tortured desires and twisted fears of his damaged psyche" (241). The night-mares also reflect his waking fears, which are the result of a racism that defines even the roles of the white woman and the black man and prevents the possibility of any positive relationship between them—a recurring theme in Himes's fiction.[41] Although he finds it difficult to accept restrictions that are solely racial (for example, being refused service in the fancy restaurant to which he escorts his black girlfriend Alice), Jones knows that his life is determined by others and that he is not free to be a man in the American sense of that term (Reckley 94).

The film version *If He Hollers, Let Him Go!*, the first of several movies adapted from Himes's novels, was little more than a pot-boiler; in fact, it would be largely forgotten today were it not for the fact that it was among the first films to usher in an era of "blax-ploitation." Resurrecting the early stereotype of the black brute and then essentially turning the type against itself to create a new kind of action hero, blaxploitation filmmakers (including black screenwriters and directors) showcased the new post-Poitier image of the hip, sexually charged, aggressive urban black. In the film *If He Hollers, Let Him Go!*, the Jones character, renamed James Lake, was played by the physically imposing actor Raymond St. Jacques, who—like former professional athlete Jim Brown (*Rio Conchos* [1964], *The Dirty Dozen* [1967], *100 Rifles* [1969], *El Condor* [1970])—became one of the more popular and successful black actors to emerge in the late 1960s. Like Himes's protagonist in the novel, St. Jacques's James is an intelligent black man who finds himself the victim of a false accusation. (Fig. 5.10.) But whereas in the novel, Madge Perkins's accusation of rape against him is ulti-mately withdrawn, in the film Jones is convicted of raping and murdering a white woman, Sally Blair (Susan Seaforth). He breaks out of jail only to become involved in a plot by a white man, Leslie Whitlock (Kevin McCarthy), to murder his wife Ellen (Dana Wynter), whom James ultimately saves. The story is often hard to follow: many events, particularly as they relate to the crime against Sally and to James's relationship with the sexy nightclub singer Lily (Barbara McNair), are told in incremental flashbacks; and once James is on the lam from both the police and Mr. Whitlock, the plot gets even more jumbled. The only consistent element in the film is the bigotry and physical brutality to which

Figure 5.10. James Lake (Raymond St. Jacques) is exposed to brutality and bigotry in *If He Hollers, Let Him Go!*, the first adaptation of a novel by Chester Himes. *(Forward Films/Cinerama Leasing Corporation, 1968)*

James is exposed—from the Sheriff (John Russell) and the Chief of Police (James Craig); the vengeful prosecutor (Arthur O'Connell); Sally's boyfriend, Harry (Steve Sandor); and Sally's father, Carl Blair (Royal Dano)—and against which he reacts. After a bloody shoot-out, it is revealed that Sally's killer was actually her father (although, in a crude resolution that eliminates the prospect of true incest, Carl turns out to be Sally's stepfather); and Ellen Whitlock promises to stand by James until he is fully vindicated. As Daniel J. Leab writes, "like many of the Jim Brown films, *If He Hollers, Let Him Go* relied little on logic or dramatic development and much on violence and seminude love scenes" (239), as was typical of most blaxploitation films. Even St. Jacques later declared that "artistically, it was a fake, but the 'brothers' loved it because I kicked hell out of a white man."[42]

Reviews of the film were generally unfavorable. Howard Thompson (*NYT* 10 Oct. 1968) called it "a lurid, cliché-flapping melodrama with painfully embarrassing racial trimmings" and a "contrived, unconvincing and dishonest exercise . . . [in which] a fugitive Negro convict is submitted, cliché by cliché, to layer after layer of meanness, abuse and animal brutality by a round-up of Southern caricatures, ranging from dim-witted to abominable and, for good measure, psychopathic." The *Variety* (27 Sept. 1968) reviewer was only slightly more generous, noting that the movie had potential; but its "cluttered script," frequent "plot derailments," and "hyper-concentration and heavy-handed emphasis present an artistically stacked deck, dramatically weak in credibility. . . . Those looking for more depth will regret that the good ironic premise has been smothered in script development, which drifts occasionally into talky posturing." Yet St. Jacques, in his first starring role, was usually singled out positively for his performance. Thompson, for instance, called him "the wonder and the real tragedy of this exercise," praised "the panting, articulate protagonist" that he created, and compared the "splendid actor['s]" coiled tension and honesty to "an intelligent-looking cobra."[43]

Cotton Comes to Harlem (1970), released by United Artists and based on Chester Himes's novel *Cotton Comes to Harlem* (1965/originally published as *Retour en Afrique*, 1964), soon followed. This time, St. Jacques starred as Coffin Ed Johnson; St. Jacques's co-star, comedian Godfrey Cambridge, played fellow black detective Grave Digger Jones. (Fig. 5.11.) The two become involved in breaking up a "Back-to-Africa" con (based on initiatives similar to Marcus Garvey's popular movement in the 1920s and the black power movement in the 1960s) being run by the corrupt but charismatic black preacher Reverend Deke O'Malley (Calvin Lockhart). O'Malley, however, has no intention of actually leading his followers on board a "black ark" or of returning them to their ancestral land; he simply wants to scam them out of their money—at a cost of a thousand dollars per family. When armed thugs show up at one of O'Malley's rallies and make off with the $87,000 that he has collected, Coffin and Digger are convinced that the Reverend is behind the theft. After a variety of car chases and shoot-outs, a fire at the church where O'Malley preaches, a riot at the station at which he is being held, and other violent episodes, including the death of O'Malley's assistant John Hill and the physical abuse of Iris O'Malley (Judy Pace) by Deke and by black and white police officers, Coffin and Digger fail to recover the money

Figure 5.11. One of the earliest blaxploitation films, *Cotton Comes to Harlem* featured popular detective Grave Digger Jones (Godfrey Cambridge), who—along with his partner Coffin Ed Johnson—uncovers a "Back-to-Africa" swindle and various other cons within the black community of Harlem. *(Metro-Goldwyn-Mayer/United Artists, 1970)*

from O'Malley. But the detectives pay a visit to Frank Mago (Leonardo Cimino), a white Harlem Mafia boss, from whom they extort an amount equal to that stolen by O'Malley; with those funds, they reimburse the victims of the Reverend's swindle.[44]

The stolen money, it turns out, is hidden in a large bale of cotton, which constitutes the "cotton" that "comes to Harlem." A symbol of enslavement—that is, of the romanticized past in Africa or in the South evoked by Deke's "Back-to-Africa" movement (and, in the novel, of Colonel Robert L. Calhoun's parallel "back-to-the-South" crusade, and of the modern "plantation" of Harlem created and controlled by new, more subtle forces of slavery)—the cotton bale is discovered by black junkman Booker "Uncle Budd" Washington (Redd Foxx), who "junks" it and uses the money it contains to start a new life for himself in Africa.[45]

Even though Himes describes them as "big, dangerous men" who engage in violent and criminal activities, Grave Digger and

Coffin Ed are actually, in their own way, quite moral. As Daniel J. Leab demonstrates, they are tough, aggressive nongrafters who are angry with O'Malley not so much because he is a con man but because he bilks his own people. Proud, effective, and black— "until this time an unusual combination in American movies"— the detectives are, in fact, the only really admirable characters in the film. (Lindsay Patterson calls them Harlem's "own soul version of James Bond" ["In Harlem" 101].) By contrast, the whites are depicted mainly as "thugs, junk dealers, gangsters, and morons," while the black characters apart from the detectives are more sly and more attractive than the whites but not much more principled (Leab 239-41).

If the plot of *Cotton Comes to Harlem* was fairly "standard cops-and-robbers," the film's portrait of Harlem, according to Donald Bogle, could only be considered "a picturesque merry-go-round" of "congenial coons, toms, and painted ladies . . . that not only played up to black fantasies (of a black world order) but also to white fantasies of a black world full of harmless stereotypes" (*TCMMB* 234).[46] In his autobiography *My Life of Absurdity*, in fact, Himes wrote that *"The Harlem of my books was never meant to be real; I just wanted to take it away from the white man if only in my books"* (126). But whereas a white director might have treated such material with condescension, first-time black director Ossie Davis used it, as the best race movies had, to revive the old ethnic humor. That humor was "blessed with a double consciousness": rather "than cooning or tomming it up to please whites (as Stephen Fetchit had had to do), the black comic characters joked or laughed or acted the fool with one another" (Bogle, *TCMMB* 234) and used the humor combatively to outwit the whites, as Eddie Anderson and Hattie McDaniel had done so often and so slyly on screen. The film, in fact, is replete with grotesque and often darkly comic details of Harlem life, including the Holmes Funeral Home director who, upon seeing a police chase, races back inside his establishment to don a top hat, long-tailed jacket, and other appropriate "burying" clothes for the business that he knows will be coming his way. There are also plenty of sight gags and inside jokes (many of them inversions of old stereotypes), like the reference to "a honky in the woodpile" and the image of the overturned cart of watermelons that prevents Coffin and Digger from pursuing the armed robbers after the O'Malley rally.[47] Pauline Kael noted that it was precisely the way that the film managed to turn the tables and allow the white man to be "ridiculed the way black men on screen used to be"—racial humor that "might have been considered vilely insulting from a white director" but that was actually suggestive of "the freshness that black performers could bring to movies"— that transformed the detective comedy into "a folkloric version of an early-thirties movie" ("Notes" 260).

Ossie Davis, who also co-authored the script,[48] had originally been offered a part as an actor in the production; but he declined. After becoming director, he determined to incorporate as fully as possible the spirit of Harlem, which he did by shooting on location and employing ghetto residents as extras. Consequently, as Vincent Canby observed, throughout this "film by a new black director, based on the work of a black novelist, shot in Harlem with a large and talented black cast," there is "a sense of liberation" (*NYT* 11 June 1970). But, because of concerns on the part of the producer, Davis felt unable to stress as many aspects of the black experience as he had hoped to. He recalled that "the fear was that if you didn't make a film that white folks would see and appreciate, since they constituted in Hollywood's mind the audience to whom you appeal, that you were, you know, that you were cutting your own throat." Later, he graded himself conservatively on his achievement; on a scale with one hundred as the maximum, "I give myself a score of fifty or sixty" (Leab 241). The film itself scored better: it proved to be great success, with unprecedented numbers of black viewers filling the theaters. Even Southern exhibitors were anxious to screen the film and to capitalize on its grosses.

Coffin Ed Johnson and Grave Digger Jones were featured again in *Come Back, Charleston Blue* (1972), a film based on Himes's novel *The Heat's On* (1966, originally published in France in 1961 under the title *Ne nous énervons pas!*).[49] Like *Cotton Comes to Harlem* and Himes's other Harlem detective stories, *The Heat's On* had a familiar and formulaic plot: Digger and Coffin, both legendary figures in the community, attempted in numerous ways to maintain at least a marginal kind of order in a disintegrating urban world threatened by crime, violence, and racism.[50] As Stephen F. Milliken writes, the books usually began with a bizarre "opening scene of violence" that involved "Harlem's characters in a crime that is apparently inexplicable." The detectives then employ a variety of methods ranging from subtle deduction to not-so-subtle intimidation to solve the crime, thus bringing a fragile peace to the Harlem community.[51] In *The Heat's On*, which takes place on a single hot summer day, the detectives are in search of a lost shipment of heroin worth three million dollars, and their search "heats" up as they explore the modern hell represented by Harlem, with its grotesque and surrealistic characters like Pinky, the albino giant; Jake, the humpbacked dwarf; and Sister Heavenly, the evangelist with the face of a shrunken, dried-up monkey. After Grave Digger is seriously wounded in a shoot-out with drug dealers, Coffin Ed pursues the men who nearly killed his partner and eventually overpowers them in a terrifically violent confrontation. (The violence is pervasive: at least twelve people are brutally murdered, a dog is eviscerated, and a house explodes from nitroglycerin.) Ultimately, the detectives discover that—consistent with the images of heat throughout the novel—the cretinous Pinky has thrown the heroin into an incinerator, where it has burned up. But whereas Coffin Ed and Grave Digger are able to round up the petty dope pushers such as Jake and the mid-level distributors such as Sister Heavenly, they cannot get at the syndicate, which is the real source of the cancer eating away at Harlem.[52]

Unlike the largely faithful film version of *Cotton Comes to Harlem*, *Come Back, Charleston Blue* departed radically from its source. The plot (which made no attempt to observe the novel's Aristotelian unities and which, because of poor editing, at times abandoned all sense of unity and continuity) involved Joe (Peter De Anda), a supremely self-confident and hip black fashion photographer who purports to be on a crusade to rid the community of drugs but who is actually trying to muscle, and murder, his way into control of Harlem's heroin traffic. Although Coffin Ed and Grave Digger are diverted briefly—by a series of obstacles, including the mysterious reappearance of long-dead Harlem boss "Charleston Blue," who seems to be reclaiming his old turf, and by the appointment of a new precinct commanding officer, who takes away their weapons, busts them down to traffic cops, and makes them answerable to Officer Jarema (Dick Sabol), a stooge-like white cop who was outsmarted by Iris O'Malley and left standing in her hallway, naked except for a paper bag on his head, in *Cotton*

Comes to Harlem—they eventually get their man. (Actually, it is Charleston Blue's widow, "Her Majesty" [Minnie Gentry], who gets their man: for desecrating her husband's crypt by storing heroin in his coffin, she slits Joe's throat with one of Blue's signature straight-edged razors.) Throughout, the film's violence is as excessive as it is gratuitous: a harmless junk dealer is set ablaze when an exploding football is tossed into his cart; a militant disguised as a nun shoots up the poultry plant where turkeys are being stuffed with heroin; fresh corpses are disposed of in the compactor units of garbage trucks strategically positioned throughout the community; and a so-called funeral turns into an occasion for a massive shoot-out, with the military honor guard, the presiding cleric, the grieving widow, and even the apparent corpse himself wielding high-powered weapons.

Ossie Davis, director and co-writer of the screenplay of *Cotton Comes to Harlem*, reportedly had strong reservations about the material in *Come Back, Charleston Blue* and declined any involvement in the sequel.[53] His replacement was Mark Warren, a black television director whose work included *Laugh-In*, for which he won an Emmy in 1970-71.[54] But, as Daniel J. Leab writes, "It was his [Warren's] first experience directing a feature film, and the finished movie, with its profusion of vaudeville touches, reflected his television background. The technique often seemed at odds with the story" (242). Similarly, in his review of the film (*NYT* 13 Aug. 1972), Clayton Riley criticized Warren for bringing *Laugh-In*'s "madcap sense of structure to a vehicle that needs a tighter rein, a more unified perspective." And A. H. Weiler (*NYT* 30 June 1972) wondered how a black television director making his debut on a film with "slick sleuths" and a largely black supporting cast could so completely fail to offer "a lucid, intimate view of the black man's experience, seamy or otherwise." Warren's problems were certainly reflected at the box office: not only did the film fail to break into the white market; it failed even to draw black customers, despite an extensive advertising campaign aimed specifically at them.[55]

Almost two decades passed before Chester Himes's Harlem detectives returned to the screen. *A Rage in Harlem*, originally published as *For Love of Imabelle* (1957), had been the first detective work that Himes had written as well as the first to introduce the characters of Coffin Ed Johnson and Grave Digger Jones.[56] Himes noted in *My Life of Absurdity* that when he wrote the book, he "really didn't know how to write a detective story" (111). His claim seems at least partially borne out by the fact that the detectives do not even appear until the eighth chapter and thereafter are peripheral to the plot, which revolves around a naïve young man named Jackson who needs money to marry his girlfriend Imabelle. But Jackson gets taken in by "The Blow," a swindle that promises to turn ten-dollar bills into one-hundreds through a secret chemical process; that process, however, is always interrupted by fake cops, who bust the operation and abscond with the original investment. Meanwhile, Imabelle has stolen a trunk of gold from her husband, a con artist and part of a three-member gang of crooks who have been selling fraudulent gold stock to blacks across America. (Appropriately enough, that gold turns out to be fool's gold.) To save her and himself, Jackson takes some cash from his employer, the Harlem undertaker H. Exodus Clay (a recurring character in the Harlem novels). Many violent and absurd adventures follow: for instance, Jackson's twin brother Goldy, who impersonates a nun named "Sister Gabriel" and lives with two other female impersonators known collectively as "The Three Black Widows," is killed after he gets involved in the search for the gold, and his body is stuffed in Clay's Cadillac hearse and driven through a Harlem market by none other than Jackson himself. But order is eventually restored: the villains are killed, and Jackson not only gets back his old job but also is free to marry Imabelle.

The film version of *A Rage in Harlem* (1991) was not, in any real sense, a sequel to the earlier films, even though Grave Digger Jones (George Wallace) and Coffin Ed Johnson (Stack Pierce) make brief, sporadic appearances as slightly crooked and comically bumbling cops. Shot in Cincinnati rather than Harlem, the highly stylized adaptation starred Forest Whitaker (Jackson), Gregory Hines (Goldy), Robin Givens (Imabelle), and Danny Glover (Easy Money). The story centers around Imabelle, who steals gold from her boyfriend Slim in Natchez and travels north to unload it, and the innocent but adoring Jackson, who turns his life upside down to accommodate her. When Slim and his gang follow Imabelle to Harlem, Jackson is forced to rely on Goldy, his shady estranged half-brother (not his twin brother, as in the book), for help. (Fig.

Figure 5.12. *A Rage in Harlem*, based on another of Himes's detective novels, depicted the Harlem misadventures of naïve Jackson (Forest Whitaker) and his streetwise brother Goldy (Gregory Hines). *(Miramax, 1991)*

5.12.) After the requisite bloody shoot-outs, including the killing in the street of Goldy's best friend, the transvestite bordello operator "Big Kathy," and of Slim and his friends in Easy Money's office, the brothers are reconciled; Goldy gets the money; and Jackson gets the girl, who in turn has kept some of the loot for herself.

As Vincent Canby noted in his review of the film, *A Rage in Harlem* "is a lightweight comedy caper set in 1956," but its effect is "to recall the early 1970s, the time of Ossie Davis's seminal *Cotton Comes to Harlem*, . . . when black films were discovering their own comic identity" (*NYT* 3 May 1991). Despite a rousing performance, incidental to the plot, by Screamin' Jay Hawkins at the Undertakers' Ball, and two clever running gags—about a pair of portraits that hang over Jackson's bed and about Jackson's kindly employer, an elderly undertaker who always sleeps on the job in the position of a body that has been freshly laid-out (gags, incidentally, that recall the recurring cotton bale in *Cotton Comes to*

Harlem)—the film, as Canby correctly concludes, is simply not in the same league as Davis's adaptation.

A Rage In Harlem was directed by Bill Duke, who was part of the new wave of black filmmakers to gain prominence in the late 1980s and early 1990s. Duke, who started out as an actor in series television such as *Benson, Charlie's Angels, Kojak*, and *Starsky and Hutch* and in films such as *Car Wash, Action Jackson*, and *Menace II Society*, moved to directing off-Broadway plays and episodes of television shows such as *Amen, Cagney and Lacey, Dallas, Hunter*, and *Matlock*. Among the television movies that he directed was the excellent PBS *American Playhouse* presentation of *A Raisin in the Sun*, to commemorate the twenty-fifth anniversary of the premiere of Hansberry's play; that film, like his other television movies—*The Killing Floor* (1984), about a black sharecropper who leaves the South for work in a Chicago slaughterhouse; *Johnnie Mae Gibson: F.B.I.* (1986), about the first black female FBI agent; and *The Meeting* (1989), a dramatic rendering of a fictional meeting between Martin Luther King, Jr. and Malcolm X—focused on significant black characters and themes. Some of Duke's later works, like *Sister Act II: Back in the Habit*, proved to be more commercially successful; but Duke says that in *A Rage in Harlem*, his first feature film, he tried to transcend racial stereotypes to produce a film that spoke about the nobility of the spirit since "there are so many attempts to dehumanize black people" (Moon 97). Despite Duke's noble intentions, however, the film was, at best, innocuous, occasionally funny, but ultimately incomprehensible.

Whereas *If He Hollers, Let Him Go!* and *Cotton Comes to Harlem* helped to popularize "blaxploitation" films, Melvin Van Peebles's *Sweet Sweetback's Baadasssss Song* (1971) in effect defined that particular genre. Van Peebles, who considers himself "the godfather of modern black cinema" and the "James Brown of filmmaking,"[57] had directed two earlier films: *Story of a Three Day Pass* (1967), based on an original story published in France about a brief interracial affair, as seen from a black perspective; and *Watermelon Man* (1970), a parody of the "tragic mulatto" movie, about a racist white man who wakes up one morning to find himself black and who learns to use his blackness as a form of empowerment. But it was *Sweet Sweetback's Baadasssss Song*—written, composed, produced, directed, and edited by Van Peebles—that proved that black films could indeed reach mass audiences and that offered a radical new black hero to whom black (and some white) viewers could relate, a hero diametrically opposed to the "black-as-martyr" type popularized in postwar liberal integrationist films or to the traditional accommodating but asexual black image of 1950s and 1960s popular films.

Named for his "sweet sweetback" by the prostitute who initiates him sexually, Sweetback (Van Peebles) is a black stud who performs in pornographic shows. After two policemen come to the whorehouse where he works in search of a black man whom they can exhibit as a suspect for a few days to quell public indignation over a murder, the whorehouse operator offers them Sweetback. While in their custody, he watches the officers detain and then brutalize an innocent young black militant. Unable to ignore the injustice, Sweetback assaults the officers, using his handcuffs as weapons. The young black is saved, but Sweetback, now a criminal and a fugitive, becomes the object of a massive manhunt. Forced to flee, he spends the rest of the movie evading a variety of savage, racist policemen and seeking help from pimps, whores, and ghetto residents. (Fig. 5.13.) Once, when he is recaptured,

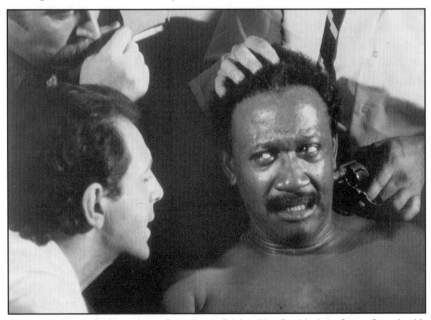

Figure 5.13. Rebellious hero Sweetback (Melvin Van Peebles), in *Sweet Sweetback's Baadasssss Song*, fights back against the white Establishment. *(Cinemation Industries, 1971)*

black youngsters set the officers' car ablaze and help Sweetback to escape; another time, he impales a policeman with a pool cue. Along the way, he engages in graphic but emotionless sexual adventures with virtually every female he encounters, from the black woman who cuts off his handcuffs to a white Hell's Angels' biker chick who saves him from the wrath of her gang. He even rapes, at knifepoint, a black woman whom he meets at a love-fest, believing that the officers pursuing him will ignore two blacks making love in the grass. As Sweetback wends his way across the desert, surviving on lizards for food and treating his wounds with his own urine, he manages to kill the dogs that have caught his scent. The film ends with the warning that "A BAADASSSSS NIGGER IS COMING BACK TO COLLECT SOME DUES."

Sweetback was, for the most part, a poorly crafted movie; yet despite—and arguably because of—its technical shortcomings, it "challenged the very foundations of the blaxploitation film to move the contemporary black image towards a more politicized point of view" (Pines 121). As a rebellious and persecuted hero, Sweetback engages in a ruthless struggle with white authority; and his personal struggle implicitly becomes a political one as well. But, as Jim Pines writes, where the black-slanted Hollywood film often depicts whites in comic-relief roles, *Sweetback* employs them as "the arch-enemy." The film thus becomes blatant propaganda that emphasizes the ugliest face of racist society and insists on portraying the black hero as someone who must violently confront that society and who must force himself to "decolonize" mentally "so that he functions regardless of society's dictates" (122-23). In Van Peebles's earlier film *Watermelon Man*, there is a suggestion of this pattern when Jeff Gerber joins the Black Power movement; in *Sweetback*, however, there is an even more significant reversal of the meaning of traditional icons. For instance, the handcuffs that the officers put on Sweetback—the shackles that traditionally suggest impotence and restraint—become the weapons that he uses so effectively and so graphically against the police. Similarly, the fugitive motif is underscored by the theme of returning to collect dues. Even black sexuality, often characterized by its violence, becomes a tool for Sweetback's (and, by implication, blacks') survival.[58] As Mark A. Reid notes, many of Sweetback's sexual encounters—for instance, with the black woman who insists that he make love to her before she cuts off his handcuffs or the white biker who challenges him to a "duel" with his choice of a "weapon"—are dispassionate: "he gives his female adversaries sexual pleasure without showing an iota of self-enjoyment. His ability to perform skillfully requires the discipline of a soldier intent upon killing the enemy; such a performance cannot be interpreted as primitive lust nor a reflection of emotional desire" (*RBF* 77).

Audiences, as Donald Bogle writes, were ready for a sexual black movie hero, especially "after decades of comic asexual black characters and an era like the 1950s when Poitier and Belafonte, while considered sexually attractive, were rarely permitted to be sexually aggressive in their films" (*TCMMB* 235). Sweetback's sexuality was overt and threatening; and it coincided with the idealizing and glamorizing of ghetto life that was occurring in some sectors of the black community in the late 1960s and early 1970s and that rejected the black bourgeoisie for colluding with white America. By glorifying Sweetback and elevating him to the "pimp/outlaw/rebel as folk hero" (Bogle, *TCMMB* 236), Van Peebles addressed this new sensibility. Moreover, he seemed to cultivate the outlaw/rebel image himself, particularly in the unusual way that he devised to produce his film outside the Hollywood system. Written by Van Peebles, the film was shot in just three weeks at a cost of approximately $500,000; that amount included $100,000 of Van Peebles's capital plus funds from friends like Bill Cosby, who contributed $50,000. Under the guise of making a pornographic film, Van Peebles managed both to circumvent union personnel and to employ blacks in virtually every aspect of the production. Once the film was completed (and, according to some film historians, after most distributors rejected it), he reached an arrangement with Cinemation Industries, which was known for its exploitation films. Van Peebles claims that he chose Cinemation over more prestigious distributors because he refused to accede to their terms. "Fuck that," he said. "I wanted bread and control. In the end I LEASED the film" to Cinemation (Leab 249). (Ironically, although Van Peebles initially strove to represent himself as a Hollywood outsider with *Sweetback*, he later tried to make the opposite claim: that he was actually the first black director in Hollywood. In an interesting revision of Hollywood's history as well as his own, he argued that Ossie Davis and Gordon Parks—

whose directorial achievements clearly preceded his—"entered the Hollywood system about that same time, but their films were shot on location, not in Hollywood" [Moon 344].)

By all measures, *Sweet Sweetback's Baadasssss Song* was a blockbuster; during its first year alone, it grossed more than ten times its cost and spawned numerous imitators.[59] It also validated Van Peebles's "quest" to prove that there was a black audience for film and to establish himself as an important force in commercial black cinema.[60] But not everyone hailed the film. White critics generally lambasted it: Vincent Canby, for example, considered it almost psychotic. James P. Murray, in *Black Creation*, was "appalled at the filth, degradation, distortion and almost total negativism of *Sweetback* . . . both as a movie and social statement to black people" (qtd. in Moon 348). Even *Ebony*'s Lerone Bennett, Jr. lamented the grim humor in the fact that the black marches and demonstrations of the 1960s reached "artistic fulfillment in the 1970s with Flip Wilson's Geraldine and Melvin Van Peebles's Sweetback, two provocative and ultimately insidious reincarnations of all the Sapphires and Studs of yesteryear." Attacking the film as trivial and tasteless, Bennett noted that "nobody ever f***ed his way to freedom" and that "if f***ing freed, black people would have celebrated the millennium 400 years ago." Yet he labeled the film a negative classic "because it is an obligatory step for anyone who wants to go further and make the first revolutionary black film" (Bogle, *TCMMB* 236; Leab 248-49). According to Mark A. Reid, the film was also criticized "both by black culture nationalists who wanted explicitly politicized black films and by other blacks who wanted films in which blacks were identified with middle-class values." Both groups argued that Van Peebles's film "exploited the tawdry underbelly of black street life," and they accused him of avoiding the dramatization of the socio-economic causes that had produced the moral decadence. And, of course, much criticism was directed at the film's portrayal of women, especially black women (*RBF* 79).[61] Nonetheless, black audiences turned out in record numbers to watch a black man strike back, with impunity, at his racist oppressors.

In the brief interview preceding the video edition of *Sweet Sweetback's Baadasssss Song*, Van Peebles recalls that he "wanted a movie where we won," and to ensure that victory he had followed four principles: (1) "No cop-outs"; (2) "I wanted to look as good as anything the man had ever done"; (3) "Entertainment-wise I wanted to be a motherfucker" and to produce "something we wouldn't be ashamed of"; and (4) "I wanted to be a living workshop . . . to be politically correct."[62] Indeed, Van Peebles's film accomplished several of those objectives. Yet, despite the film's phenomenal popular and financial success, Van Peebles was never able to capitalize on, much less equal, his early achievement. His feature film *Don't Play Us Cheap* (1972), based on his own comic play about life in Harlem, was shown in very limited release but never received distribution. More successful was *Sophisticated Gents* (1981; dir. Harry Falk), a teleplay for a miniseries that he wrote based on John A. Williams's novel *The Junior Bachelor Society*. The miniseries centered on nine longtime friends who reunite after twenty-five years to honor an old coach who guided them through their turbulent youth; each has been dealt a different hand, yet all must confront the complexity of their lives as black men in American society, a marked contrast to the innocent joy they felt as members of their boyhood club, "The Sophisticated Gents." The miniseries included among its mostly black cast such fine actors as Paul Winfield, Rosalind Cash, Beah Richards, Alfre Woodard, and Janet MacLachlan; also featured were Ron O'Neal, Raymond St. Jacques, Janet Du'Bois, Rosie Greer, and Van Peebles himself.

The very favorable box-office response to Van Peebles's new black hero in *Sweetback* ensured that similar films would follow. Among the best was *Shaft* (1971), which enlivened the white private detective created by white novelist Ernest Tidyman with a black sensibility. As played by newcomer Richard Roundtree, John Shaft was a black superhero, a renegade detective who was streetwise and savvy. Although he lives in an expensive and tastefully decorated Greenwich Village apartment and works out of a tiny office in Times Square, Shaft is never out of touch with Harlem life. When black boss Bumpy Jonas dispatches two black thugs to deliver Shaft to him, Shaft in turn dispatches them. (One is sent flying out the window to the street several stories below.) Bumpy, it seems, needs Shaft to find his daughter Marcy, who he believes has been kidnapped by black militants headed by Ben Buford, Shaft's old friend; but in fact Marcy is being held by Mafia mobsters who want to take over Bumpy's business concerns in Harlem.

Eventually, Shaft and Ben find her in an uptown hotel and rescue her. Like Sweetback, Shaft has little respect for others' authority: when a gangster calls him a "nigger," he responds by calling the gangster a "wop" and by breaking a bottle against his head. And like Sweetback, he is always ready "to get laid." (His name is, in part, a pun on his sexual prowess.) But he is able to cope with white society in ways that Sweetback could never have imagined. Shaft's appeal to contemporary audiences resulted in two sequels, *Shaft's Big Score!* (1972) and *Shaft in Africa* (1973), though neither was as popular or powerful as the original, and eventually in a remake, *Shaft* (2000), starring Samuel L. Jackson and featuring Richard Roundtree. And it led to a host of similar films, notably *Superfly* (1972), directed by Gordon Parks, Jr., and its sequels (*Superfly T.N.T.* [1973] and *The Return of Superfly* [1990]), as well as to various black female superwoman movies like *Cleopatra Jones* (1973), *Coffy* (1973), *Foxy Brown* (1974), and *Friday Foster* (1975).

BLAXPLOITATION TO BLACK MILITANCE

Blaxploitation movies reversed the Hollywood formula in which blacks were the outsiders in an alien society they were bound to accept by turning the white man into the outsider. They were not, however, the only films to explore the growing sense of black militance. A number of white independent films in the early 1960s had already begun to look at the black experience in a more daring way than most of Hollywood's major studio films had. *Shadows* (1961; dir. John Cassavetes) offered an honest and unsentimentalized portrait of a failed interracial relationship, while *One Potato, Two Potato* (1964; dir. Larry Peerce) focused on family opposition to interracial marriage; and *Nothing But a Man* (1964; dir. Michael Roemer) revealed how racist tensions almost destroy a black family.[63] Even more distinctive was *The Cool World* (1963; dir. Shirley Clarke), based on a novel by white author Warren Miller III and adapted to the screen by Miller, Shirley Clarke, and Carl Lee (son of actor Canada Lee), who also appeared as Priest. The film portrayed the brutal world of youth gang violence in Harlem, as fifteen-year-old Duke strives to gain leadership of the Pythons and defeat the rival gang, the Wolves.

Two other films, both adapted from black-authored dramas, took up these same issues of militance and of violence as metaphor; and both drew on the reactionary, revolutionary fervor that drove Sweetback and informed Shaft and Superfly and other black superheroes of the era. *The River Niger* (1976; dir. Krishna Shah) was adapted by Joseph A. Walker from his award-winning play, which was performed by the Negro Theater Ensemble off and on Broadway four years earlier. The play depicts a black family at a critical point in their lives: Jeff Williams (Glynn Turman) returns from the Air Force to his home in Los Angeles, where his house-painter father Johnny Williams (James Earl Jones), a frustrated philosopher-poet, and his mother Mattie (Cicely Tyson) have planned a celebration in honor of his successful completion of navigators' school. But in fact he has washed out, largely because he refused to act like the "supernigger" that the white officers expected him to be. Jeff is not the only one in his family with a secret: Johnny drinks too much, and Mattie has been diagnosed with terminal cancer. Further complicating Jeff's life are his old neighborhood pals Moe, Skeeter, Chips, and Al, who have formed a revolutionary army and who want his assistance, and a young woman, Ann Vanderguild (Jonelle Allen), whom Jeff hopes to marry. Although Jeff resists getting involved with Moe and his friends, the Williams family unwittingly becomes implicated in the gang's latest crime. The result is that Jeff begins to understand and appreciate Moe's cause; but it is a newly radicalized and heroic Johnny who does not simply empathize but takes action. Shot and fatally wounded protecting the young men (fig. 5.14), Johnny turns his sacrifice into a protest against a lifetime of social injustice.

Unfortunately, the adaptation of the play to film seems only to have weakened it, both as family and as protest drama. Opened up to include exterior shots, the film offers a few good images of ghetto locations. But the prosaic and unimaginative shooting style creates more problems than worthwhile effects; and the on-screen depiction of action that originally occurred offstage results in "pretty dopey" melodrama, which, according to Vincent Canby (*NYT* 15 Apr. 1976), totally lacks "cohesive style and cinematic intelligence." The camera wanders aimlessly at times, and director Krishna Shah cannot control it sufficiently to create decent successive or matching shots. Left to make stagey, pretentious pro-

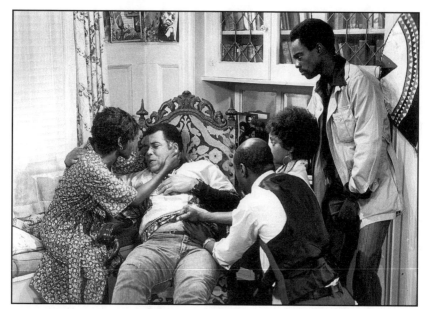

Figure 5.14. Johnny Williams (James Earl Jones) becomes increasingly radical-ized—and ultimately sacrifices himself—in *The River Niger*, based on Joseph A. Walker's award-winning play. *(CineArtists Picture Corporation, 1976)*

nouncements (or, in the case of Jones, encouraged "to chew the scenery"), the excellent cast is largely wasted (*Variety* 3 Mar. 1976). Most reviewers concurred with Canby that *The River Niger* was "an object lesson in how not to make a movie out of a theater piece" and expressed disappointment that, given the versatility of the actors and the depth of the source material, it proved to be such a failure. Yet, while the overall effect is unarguably clumsy, the film managed at least to hint at an important and recurring theme in many films of the era: that violence against white institutions may be the only way to counter the violence of white racism.

Far more effective was *Dutchman* (1966), adapted by LeRoi Jones (now Amiri Baraka) from his one-act play and expanded into a fifty-five-minute-long feature. After being approached on a New York subway train by Lula, an attractive young blonde (Shirley Knight), conservative businessman Clay (Al Freeman, Jr.) finds himself engaged in an intriguing dance of seduction. Lula, who jokingly calls herself a "hyena" and who seems to know many of the particulars of Clay's life ("I know your type"), excites Clay with her licentious behavior and her sexual promises. But

Lula turns out to be pyschotic; after throwing fruit and trash all over the car, she accosts Clay and accuses him of being an "escaped [plantation] nigger" who is "full of white man's words" and, worse yet, an Uncle Tom who is "afraid of white people." Clay responds by exploding into a rage and lashing out at her pseudo-liberalism and pseudo-intellectualism. He slaps and threatens to kill the "stupid whore" in a "simple" and righteous act of murder. Instead, it is Lula who pulls a knife from her bag and stabs Clay to death, in full view of a trainload of passive passengers, where he falls on top of her in a sexual posture before being carried away. As the play ends, Lula boards another train and approaches a new black victim. "By its conclusion," writes Donald Bogle, "*Dutchman*, better than any other piece of dramatic writing of the decade, articulated the options left open to a black man in white America: either he can survive by joining the ranks of the black bourgeousie (those apers of white manners who are doomed to lives without their manhood) or he can lash out at the dominant culture and run the risk of being chopped down. Jones's thesis was not particularly pleasant. Nor was the film. But it was dazzling" (*TCMMB* 208).

The film, directed in Britain by Anthony Harvey, was beautifully scripted and brilliantly acted. The dialogue between the two characters—the only dialogue in the film, since no other characters speak—is raw, intense, realistic. But the characters move quickly from realism to allegory. Symbolic of the historical mistreatment of blacks, the serial seductress Lula entices and then betrays Clay. The educated and civilized black who keeps himself "buttoned up" in order to contain his rage, Clay explodes at the assaults on his manhood and on his cultural history. Radicalized by the injustice which he (and, by implication, all blacks) must endure, he is transformed—virtually shaped like the clay that is an echo of his name—into a militant and ultimately persecuted for his militancy by the very white society that has forced his transformation in the first place. Like the legendary Flying Dutchman, whose ship is doomed to sail forever because of its captain's blasphemy (Cardullo 8),[64] the black—suggests Jones—is doomed to racist victimization.

Clearly, in the films adapted from the novels of Chester Himes and influenced by Richard Wright's novel and film versions of

Native Son, in the black coming-of-age films that became popular in the 1960s and 1970s, and in the newly empowered heroes of blaxploitation cinema in the 1970s, the dignified but conservative black character of the Eisenhower age symbolized by Sidney Poitier had been reinvented for an era that embraced a new and more radical kind of black power.

NOTES TO CHAPTER 5

1. Poitier described these demeaning film roles as "niggers who were lazy, shiftless, screwed around a lot" (Marill 12), and he was determined to create a different role on film, as a black hero.

2. At the same time, there was a great strength to each of Poitier's performances as well as a great symbolic importance. As Rob Edelman writes, Poitier was, historically, "the right man at the right time, the necessary and essential connection between Hattie McDaniel and Cicely Tyson, Mantan Moreland and Melvin Van Peebles, Snowflake and Spike Lee." Moreover, he "reflect[ed] the sensibilities of the younger generation of African-American filmmakers, the Spike Lees, Charles Lanes, Charles Burnetts, John Singletons, Julie Dashes, and Mattie Riches, when he observe[d], in his autobiography, *This Life*, 'We're going to have to make most of our own films. I think we should no longer expect the white filmmaker to be the champion of our dreams'" (*The Political Companion to American Film* 309).

3. In "Black Men or Good Niggers?" (186), Catherine Sugy writes of Poitier that "in his help to whites, his image again is Uncle Tom refurbished; and his films, although with some elaboration, again emphasize remoteness and victimization."

4. Bogle (*TCMMB* 154) argues that it was the first of a new cycle of problem pictures; Leab suggests that it was the last in the cycle of black problem films to come from a major studio (161).

5. Jim Pines offers an excellent illustration. He writes that the white social-racial attitudes range "from the reactionary (Biddle) to thorough liberalism (Dr. Wharton, Brooks's colleague and superior) via moderacy (characterized by the authority). Furthermore, the film sets up a similar pattern in the black sector, although the relevant part of it is in the conflict between Brooks's patent liberalism and Lefty's (Dots Johnson) outright militancy. As the second threat to Luther Brooks, then, Lefty is a decisive character because what he represents racially reciprocates the anti-black position of the Biddle character—and thus enables the film's narrative to define Brooks more concretely in liberal terms. In this way too the film's case for racial tolerance applies to both the white as well as the black point of view" (74).

6. Cited in Marill 45.

7. The novel was subsequently adapted as a play, *Porgy*, by DuBose and Dorothy Heyward.

8. "Poitier's intelligence and self-respect," noted Albert Johnson, "do not prevent him from playing a semi-educated, good-natured 'nigger': his portrayal of Homer Smith is an acutely realized interpretation of the

type of American Negro who can be thoroughly appreciated both by Negro spectators (because they will recognize the humor in his intonations, the smile *behind* the smile and the truth of Homer's reactions) and by non-Negro spectators (because Homer is not presented as a 'problem,' but as an ordinary human being)" ("The Negro in American Films: Some Recent Works" 157).

9. According to Donald Bogle, one newspaper even tagged Dee "the Negro June Allyson" (*TCMMB* 199).

10. Hansberry was not just the first black American to win the New York Drama Critics Circle Award; she was also the youngest dramatist to win the award.

11. Hansberry, in fact, dedicates *A Raisin in the Sun* to her mother: "To Mama; in gratitude for the dream."

12. Ironically, several critics later argued that the play was a guaranteed money-maker "because it resembled so many other Broadway successes with only the blackness of the characters to give it the necessary spice of the new." Others eventually criticized the play for its blackness (or alleged lack thereof). Tom F. Driver of the *New Republic* argued that the play was "old-fashioned," that it adhered to the "overworked formulas . . . of the 'domestic play,'" and that its success was due to "our sentimentality over the 'Negro question.'" He concluded that "it may have been Miss Hansberry's objective to show that the stage stereotypes will fit Negroes as well as white people." Novelist Nelson Algren claimed that "*Raisin* does not assert the hardbought values the Negro has won, but expresses only an eagerness to have a sports car in order to get to the psychoanalyst as fast as white folks do. Dramatically, *Raisin* does for the Negro people what hair straightener and skin-lightener have done for the Negro cosmetics trade" (Carter 123-35).

13. Cited henceforth as *RBF*.

14. For a further discussion of these scenes, see Clark, 127-28.

15. Reid (*RBF* 58-59) adds: "The production team also sought to eliminate Beneatha's comment that 'all Africans are revolutionaries today,' calling it an example of 'surplus in the race issue category and potentially troublesome to no purpose.' In addition, executives argued that 'Beneatha's dialogue about Africans needing salvation "from the British and French" could give the picture needless trouble abroad.'"

16. "The direction was often static and unimaginative," Steven Carter wrote. "Performances suited for the stage occasionally seemed overblown on the screen, and an uninspired musical score helped to create a sense of melodrama" (128).

17. In the remake, Mrs. Johnson appears in the equivalent of Act II, between scenes one and two.

18. With his brother Philip Epstein and Howard Koch, Julius J. Epstein had received the Academy Award for Best Screenplay in 1942 for *Casablanca*.

19. Reid also observes that, even though Spencer must subordinate himself, he is portrayed "neither as a coon nor a Tom" (*RBF* 51).

20. "Its chief virtue," Donald Bogle writes (*TCMMB* 196), "was that black playwright Louis Peterson had adapted the movie from his successful off-Broadway play. Black screenwriters were a rarity in Hollywood. One only regrets that Peterson's venture did not fare better."

21. Even though they are friends, in the novel Newt "often returned home wishing that both [boys] were either colored or white so they could spend more time exploring these wonders of Rodney's world. And Rodney was usually elated at Newt's coming, for he felt a superior satisfaction explaining the mysterious microscope and the enchanting world its thick lenses revealed" (*The Learning Tree* 83).

22. In the novel, the teacher's name is Mrs. McClinock, not Mrs. McClintock (as in the film).

23. For instance, when Jack Winger, Newt's father, "climbed the tower ladder within a few feet of the dangerously tilting spire of the African Methodist Episcopal Church" just after the big storm, Parks lyrically describes what Jack's "trained eye" noted:

> He looked back to the center of town. The stone courthouse and jail (squatting smugly, medieval-castle-like, in the square) stood out strong and unscathed in the Saturday morning sun. But the secondary business area, lying a block to the west behind it, had suffered the brunt of the storm. Talbot's harness shop was flat on the ground, its crushed sides jutting out from under the broken roof. Comstock's store front, peeping from beneath two huge maple trees, sagged, cock-eyed and windowless, against nine two-by-fours. Blake's general store, Davis' bakery, Carson's drug store, Sam Wong's laundry, Mack's hamburger shack, snuggling together when the storm struck, were now hopelessly tangled in a half-block pile of crumpled roofs and smashed walls. Sam, the village's only Chinese citizen, was dead somewhere in the rubble of broken bottles, shattered plaster, torn clothes, spoiled hamburger and baking dough, pots, pans, hardware, ladies' accessories and such. (25)

24. The film made a few small additions. For instance, in the novel, when Newt admits to taking peaches from Mr. Kiner's orchard, Sarah

Winger reprimands him for stealing, "'specially on Sunday," and goes outside to gather "switches from a small, sturdy elm tree" (57). In the film, Sarah does not whip Newt but instead makes him visit Mr. Kiner in the hospital and volunteer to work off his debt for his theft (in this case, of apples).

25. Donald Bogle (*TCMMB* 225) writes that black novelist John O. Killens was employed as one of *Slavery*'s scriptwriters, but "he seemed overwhelmed by a white director's demands. In one interesting scene, the corrupt slave master (Stephen Boyd) relates the rich history and accomplishments of African tribes to his white friends. Because the achievements are indeed real, the scene has a startling impact. Surely, Killens had something to do with writing it. But ultimately the achievements are turned against them and are used by the film as one further assertion of white power." The film, Bogle concludes, is ultimately false and hollow.

26. Deutsch (219) also cites (but does not identify) a critic who noted that the unnamed characters in the novel "are a symbol of all the poor, black or white, who face indignity with courage."

27. The boy, however, does not dominate the film in quite the same way that he did the novel. As Charles S. Rutherford demonstrates, it is not because his character has been diminished but because the other characters have been deepened. And, in fact, David Lee takes on even more of an archetypal dimension than the boy in the book as he passes the threshold from youth to early manhood in his quest, both literal and symbolic, for his father and for his own identity (226).

28. Interestingly, the last handshake depicted in the film—by the creek, in the final minutes—is initiated by the son, David Lee, and not, as the earlier ones were, by Nathan Lee. Furthermore, it comes in response to Nathan Lee's wondering aloud if the two will ever be friends. The initiation of the handshake proves that David Lee is no longer the somewhat passive boy he was before Nathan Lee's departure; he is now actively a man who follows the strong and positive example of his father.

29. Charles Michener, in "Black Movies" (246), writes: "But will *Sounder* prevail? Even here blacks are split: some, like actress [Cicely] Tyson and *Newsweek*'s Los Angeles bureau chief, John Dotson, seeing hope in the film's quiet dignity; others smelling ripoff in those same qualities. '*Sounder*,' says one black actor, 'was made for whites who want to believe that blacks are full of love and trust and patience. It avoids dealing with things like rage and bitterness and the need for some kind of release.'"

30. Michener ("Black Movies" 246) hailed the film on several counts: "its documentary feel for the historical context of American black experience; its lack of shrillness about white bigotry; its elevation of a black woman as played by Cicely Tyson into a complex, forceful human, not a

groovy sex object; and most of all, its quiet, almost mythical tale about a family of Louisiana sharecroppers in the Depression who, in Faulkner's famous words, not only endure but prevail."

31. Life in Harlem during the 1940s was also the subject of *King of the Bingo Game* (1999), a twenty-six-minute telefilm for the PBS "American Storytellers" series based on a 1944 short story by Ralph Ellison. Written and directed by Elise Robertson, the short film was set in Harlem in 1943 and focused on a character named Sonny (Colman Domingo), who attends a movie show and wins the chance to push the button that spins the bingo wheel. Realizing that "this wheel has always been here" ticking off the "unlucky numbers" of his life, he is reluctant to take his hand off the button and stop the wheel: as long as he holds the button, he is "a new man" who is in control and who has a chance at hitting the jackpot. "This is God," he says of his newfound power. But when Sonny refuses to relinquish the button, management calls the police, who disconnect the power; as the wheel lands on double zeroes (which usually means a win), the theater curtain falls and the cops begin beating Sonny.

32. Baldwin, quoted in Bennetts 17. David Leeming, in *James Baldwin*, notes that Baldwin said he "could not finish *Go Tell It on the Mountain*, or continue writing at all, until he was able to understand his stepfather's agony and therefore 'forgive' him. Of John Grimes's stepfather, Baldwin would say he was "John's first apprehension of history, and . . . history is brutal" (86).

33. Indeed, in the words of Frederick Karl, Gabriel is "a man who speaks of God and lies with the Devil" (147). Yet, as David Leeming demonstrates, John too associates sex and religion, especially in the episode during which Elisha helps him through his religious journey. John speaks in the novel of his "desire, sharp and awful" as a knife, "to usurp the body of Elisha, and lie where Elisha lay; to speak in tongues, as Elisha spoke, and, with that authority, to confound his father" (*Go Tell It on the Mountain* 194-95). Leeming writes that "here John acts out a reconciliation of sex and religion. Love, including physical love, is a sacred trust and one means by which Baldwin could be saved from the hatred represented by his stepfather." In wrestling with Elisha, in hearing his voice, and in receiving his "holy kiss," John finds some of that love (Leeming 87-88).

34. "Baldwin knew his fathers and sons," observed Frederick Karl. Specifically, Baldwin's background material "allows us to see Gabriel with some sympathy, although he is not sympathetic." And "while Gabriel cannot be excused for individual actions," his conditioning helps in part to explain his behavior (147).

35. O'Connor's review of *Go Tell It on the Mountain* appeared in the *New York Times* (14 Jan. 1985). In a later comment on this telefilm, also in

the *New York Times*, O'Connor observed that "the fact that such enormous difficulties must be surmounted to get a work of such obvious distinction onto the television screen speaks volumes about the state of the medium in this country" (*NYT* 29 Dec. 1985).

36. Although most critics felt that *Go Tell It on the Mountain* was an outstanding production, a few viewed it less favorably. Lee Margulies, for instance, wrote, "their [the Grimes family's] lives are portrayed forcefully and intriguingly, but the film doesn't pay off in the end—principally because of a fundamental difference between the print and visual media. The boy's rite of passage is a prolonged, trance-like religious experience that Baldwin explored psychologically in eloquent detail. On screen, however, because the camera cannot delve into the boy's head, the mystical journey lasts only a few minutes and, consequently, does not convey the same sense of catharsis and rebirth that the novel did" (*LA Times* 14 Jan. 1985: Calendar 10).

37. Although it is not mentioned by title in the novel, the film that John sees is the 1934 version of *Of Human Bondage*. As Cassandra M. Ellis writes in her essay "The Black Boy Looks at the Silver Screen," John clearly identifies with the lack of education and impoverishment of Davis's character, Mildred Rogers. "It is not difficult," says Ellis, "to conceive of John's connection to her disadvantaged state" (201). Ellis also argues that John, who "sees Bette Davis/Mildred Rogers through a religious lens and not, as we might expect, in terms of social class allegiance," feels an additional identification with her character. "The cinema scene . . . also often has been read to signal John's emergent homosexual identity (and an allusion to Baldwin's) in the same way that his wrestling with his Sunday school teacher, Elisha, gets coded" (203).

38. It is interesting to note, as David Leeming (47) does in his biography of James Baldwin, that the original title of *Go Tell It on the Mountain* was *In My Father's House*. "His novel," writes Leeming, "would go to the reality of life 'in my father's house,' a house that was his family's apartment on one level, Harlem on another, America on still another, and the 'deep heart's core' on another" (84).

39. Ralph Reckley (90) writes that Himes maintained that he was the product of two opposing traditions: the body-servant tradition and the field-hand tradition. His mother was almost white; her ancestors were related to a slave owner and became house servants. His father was dark, and his ancestors worked the fields. "What resulted was an intraracial family feud that disrupted Himes's early life. His mother felt that her white heritage made her superior to her husband whom she dominated and humiliated. Himes respected his father, but he maintained 'my father was born and raised in the tradition of the southern Uncle Tom: that tradition derived from an inherited slave mentality which accepts the prem-

ise that white people know best, that blacks should accept what whites offer and be thankful.'" The constant friction between a white (or near white) female and a black male becomes the subject of four of Himes's first five novels and was undoubtedly autobiographical.

40. "Los Angeles hurt me racially. The war hurt me racially. The armed services hurt me racially," recalls Chester Himes in the first volume of his autobiography, *The Quality of Hurt*. Although he never served during the Second World War ("I was too old at the beginning, and when I was finally called for a physical, in 1943, . . . my entire pelvic structure was twisted out of place"), he knew many blacks who did. "All of them told me at one time or another that racism was rampant in the armed forces dedicated to fighting against racism in other parts of the world." Himes also remembers that during the war years, he held only two skilled jobs: as an apprentice shipfitter building Liberty ships in Richmond, California, and as a shipwright's helper in the Los Angeles Shipyard in San Pedro Harbor. His wife worked as a co-director for women's activities for the Los Angeles USOs. Unlike him, she was "respected and included by her white co-workers" and rubbed "elbows with many well-to-do blacks of the Los Angeles middle class who wouldn't touch me with a ten-foot pole." Consequently, "it was from the accumulation of my racial hurts that I wrote my bitter novel of protest *If He Hollers Let Him Go*" (74-75).

41. "The very essence of any relationship between a black man and a white woman in the United States is sex, and generally sex of a nature which lends itself to pornography," Himes wrote in *The Quality of Hurt*. "Given the American background [of racism], the bare colors [of black and white] create a pornography of the mind. Just to put a black man into a woman's bed is to suggest an orgy" (285).

42. Leab (238-39) also notes that while the film was received with "contempt by the critics," St. Jacques himself received good notices. Donald Bogle, however, wrote of St. Jacques that in this, his first starring role, "he was not strong or interesting enough to carry the picture throughout. Some of his defects were quite apparent, too. His voice was still resonant but unvaried. At times his delivery was dry as a biscuit and his monosyllabic grunts and groans make him sound as if he were suffering from cinematic constipation; one hoped he would find the bathroom before the movie ended" (224-25).

43. Thompson concluded: "He [St. Jacques] has no business here, nor has anybody except those curious to see how bad a picture can be." The *Variety* review called St. Jacques's performance "excellent," but many critics and film scholars disagreed with that assessment.

44. In the novel, Calhoun is not simply a co-conspirator of O'Malley; Himes's Colonel Robert L. Calhoun is a self-styled white leader of the

parallel "back-to-the-South" crusade, which creates a "perverse [white] dialectic of deception" to balance O'Malley's black one. And together the two tricksters' movements help to create a "demonic rather than a promised land" for the people of Harlem (Muller 98), a situation that recurs in Himes's other detective novels and in the films adapted from them.

45. At first, Himes artfully uses the cotton bale to create sinister black-humor effects. As Butler writes, "it initially generates laughter because it is apparently so incongruous with a modern urban setting." And it continues to evoke laughter as various people in the film (as in the novel) try to possess it. But the bale also connotes something far more serious: it symbolizes people's enslavement (by the money that it represents, by the idealized Back-to-Africa movement, and [in the novel] by the Back-to-Southland passions it evokes). "By giving ownership of the cotton to a junkyard worker," notes Butler, "Himes suggests that everything it represents should be junked and replaced by newer, more humanizing values" (47).

46. In *My Life of Absurdity* (126), Chester Himes admitted that he "really didn't know what it was like to be a citizen of Harlem." He had "never worked there, raised children there, been hungry, sick or poor there."

47. Watermelons become part of a running joke in the films adapted from Himes's works. In the film *Come Back, Charleston Blue*, for instance, a black dealer offers a white colleague "the traditional toast of my people" and throws a watermelon boat at him.

48. Davis's co-author on the screenplay was Arnold Perl.

49. According to Gilbert H. Muller, producer Samuel Goldwyn, Jr. had "on 20 October 1966 . . . picked up an option on six detective stories containing Grave Digger and Coffin Ed" (18).

50. Himes wrote a total of nine Harlem detective novels. Only *Run Man, Run* (1966) did not feature Johnson and Jones.

51. Cited in Butler 45. "Himes's early detective novels," notes Butler, "stick rather closely to this formula, often at the expense of character development and narrative diversity, but his later crime thrillers undertake bold departures from this pattern" (45).

52. Butler (46) notes further that even though "the novel ends with mysteries solved, criminals defeated, and order restored," *The Heat's On* is "ultimately a much more disturbing book because the order achieved is so fragile and temporary. The forces of chaos are stronger and reveal themselves in more intense and widespread violence."

53. One of the projects that Davis did assume was *Black Girl* (1972), the film version of J. E. Franklin's play; Franklin wrote the screenplay for the film, and Davis directed. The story concerns Billie Jean, a high school drop-out and aspiring ballet dancer, who lives in a Southern suburb with

her mother Mama Rosie, her mother's boyfriend, her grandmother, and her two older half-sisters. The central conflict is between Netta, a neighbor's daughter who is pursuing her college degree and who encourages Billie Jean to do the same, and Billie Jean's mischievous and jealous half-sisters, who want to ruin Billie Jean by pushing her into sex and possibly early pregnancy. In adapting her play to the screen, Franklin made small changes: Earl, Mama Rosie's estranged husband, for instance, runs a shoe store, not a whorehouse, as in the play (thus making the reasons for his expulsion by Rosie less clear). But, as *New York Times* reviewer Roger Greenspun (10 Nov. 1972) noted, "the real difference between the successful play and the failed movie lies in Ossie Davis's direction, which ranges from pedestrian to downright helpless. Sloppy editing, awkward confrontations, dull and obvious camera technique—all are the director's responsibility. From time to time you can almost feel the actors asking for stage management. They don't get it—and that, in a work not without some interest, seems a pity." *Black Girl* is also discussed by Edward Mapp in "Black Women in Films: A Mixed Bag of Tricks" and Pauline Kael in "Notes on Black Movies." Mapp briefly compares *Black Girl* to other films, including *Imitation of Life* and *A Raisin in the Sun*. Kael, who finds the film "derivative" and calls its techniques "deliberately crude," concludes that the film is "too touching to be considered bad" (259).

54. In *Reel Black Talk* (355), Spencer Moon writes that Warren "worked with Samuel Goldwyn, Jr. in casting, writing, and developing *Cotton Comes to Harlem*." But that claim seems to be unsupported. There is no reference in other critical material to Warren's involvement in that project, nor does his name appear anywhere in the credits of *Cotton Comes to Harlem*.

55. Leab writes that the advertising campaign "included a radio commercial that featured a fast-talking black hustler conning a young-sounding white liberal type into paying more than the regular box-office price for a pair of tickets" (242). Leab also notes that United Artists, the studio that had released *Cotton Comes to Harlem* in 1970, decided not to undertake a second Coffin Ed and Grave Digger film because "despite its good grosses," the original film had not broken into white markets. (*Come Back, Charleston Blue* was released by Warner Brothers.)

56. The original title of *For Love of Imabelle* was "The Five-Cornered Square." Published in France as *La reine des pommes*, *For Love of Imabelle* (1957) was later retitled and republished as *A Rage in Harlem* (1965).

57. Van Peebles has repeated the statement about being the godfather of modern black cinema in numerous interviews, including the brief interview preceding the video version of *Sweet Sweetback's Baadasssss Song*. His remark about being the James Brown of filmmaking is cited in Moon 343. In an interview with Moon, Van Peebles noted that "Even to

myself it is quite obvious that I have a very pivotal role in the modern Black film industry. Sorta' the James Brown of filmmaking. I'm all for it— not for personal reasons, but it is very important that we see history. Without history we make those same mistakes over and over."

58. Jim Pines (122-23) concludes that, by reversing the traditional icons, Van Peebles creates "a viable hero-figure who has but his physical-ity and his determination to survive by, which, in societal terms, are the black's basic tools." *Sweetback* thus operates well outside "the mythic plasticity of the Hollywood racial icon" and "utilizes as its source mate-rial the potent image of the 'unsophisticated' black liberating his con-sciousness and moving in the direction of a head-on encounter with 'the enemy.'"

59. Most critics agree that the film grossed at least four million dol-lars in its first year; some suggest that the figure was actually as high as ten million.

60. Arguing that he never had the "luxury to look at [his] films as art," Van Peebles noted, "I was on a different quest. *Sweetback* . . . proved that there was a Black audience. The film possibilities without any input from the White power structure [sic]" (Moon 344).

61. Reid observes that scenes in the film were often interpreted dif-ferently by different audiences. For instance, Black Panther Huey P. Newton, who represented a street-oriented but politicized perspective, wrote of the opening scene, in which the young Sweetback is initiated into sex by a whore in the brothel where he is raised, that "this is not a sexual scene, this is a very sacred rite. For the boy, who was nourished to health, is now being baptized into manhood; and the act of love, the giv-ing of manhood, is also bestowing upon the boy the characteristics which will deliver him from very difficult situations. People who look upon this as a sex scene miss the point completely, and people who look upon the movie as a sex movie miss the entire point of the film." On the other hand, Chicago's Kuumba Workshop, a black cultural nationalist drama group, rejected Newton's male-oriented interpretation. In a pamphlet entitled "From a Black Perspective," Kuumba writes that Newton "seri-ously mistakes Van Peebles' use of sex," which is not "a spiritual force" but simply a series of nude scenes "to arouse and give his audience a vicarious thrill" (*RBF* 80-81).

62. In "A Black Odyssey: *Sweet Sweetback's Baadasssss Song*" (226-28), Van Peebles offered a comparable list of "givens" that included the fol-lowing: "1. NO COP OUT; 2. MUST LOOK AS GOOD AS ANYTHING CHUCK EVER DID; 3. ENTERTAINMENTWISE, A MOTHER FUCKER; 4. A LIVING WORKSHOP; 5. BREAD; 6. MONKEY WRENCHING; 7. UNKNOWNS AND VARIABLES." Van Peebles elaborates on each cate-gory: under "NO COP OUT," for example, he writes: "I wanted a victori-

ous film. A film where niggers could walk out standing tall instead of avoiding each other's eyes, looking once again like they'd had it" (226).

63. For a brief discussion of *Nothing But a Man*, see Albert Johnson, "The Negro in American Films: Some Recent Works," 170-72. Johnson also discusses *The Cool World* and other films of the period.

64. The title may also refer to the first slave ship that came to the colonies, a Dutch frigate that landed at Jamestown in 1619 with twenty "negars" (Cardullo 8).

Chapter 6

"Tell Them I'm a Man":
Popularizing Black History

> The artist is a revolutionary figure. The serious artist grapples with his environment, passes a judgment on it. He helps to deepen people's perceptions, quicken their thought processes. He makes them conscious of the possibility of historical change—and in that way he facilitates change.
>
> —*Richard Wright, Interview with Charles Rolo (1945)*

By the final decades of the twentieth century, black Americans had moved more fully into the system. Black superstars like Richard Pryor and Eddie Murphy reigned supreme in the entertainment industry; performers like Michael Jackson and Whitney Houston topped the music charts; and the prime-time success of "The Cosby Show" opened the door for other black-themed and black-produced programs. On the political front, Jesse Jackson made a credible run as a candidate for the nation's highest office; black Congressmen and other lawmakers were being elected in record numbers; conservative black Supreme Court Justice Clarence Thomas joined the bench; and President Bill Clinton's appointments brought a much-needed diversity to the Cabinet. Black novelists like Alex Haley and Alice Walker received Pulitzer Prizes and other awards for their fiction; and Toni Morrison became the first black woman to win the Nobel Prize for Literature. Yet, as Donald Bogle writes, "perhaps it was not surprising then that many Americans lulled themselves into the assumption that the races were at peace with one another, that inner city blight and decay as well as social tension and racial inequities had ceased to exist, that indeed America's past history of racism had vanished." Consequently, when racial incidents erupted in areas like Howard Beach, New York, in 1986 and in Los Angeles in 1992 after the

Rodney King beating, "many were jolted" into the realization that perhaps the nation had not changed so much after all (*TCMMB* 268).

As if to reinforce the notion of racial harmony throughout the land, films in the 1980s and early 1990s often featured teams of black and white buddies. Boxers Rocky Balboa (Sylvester Stallone) and Apollo Creed (Carl Weathers), fierce competitors in the ring in *Rocky* (1976) and *Rocky II* (1979), learned to respect each other and eventually became friends; by *Rocky III* (1982), Apollo even prepared Rocky to fight and defeat a new opponent, the loutish Clubber Lang (Mr T). In *The Empire Strikes Back* (1980) and *Return of the Jedi* (1983), Han Solo (Harrison Ford) and his *Star Wars* companions could always depend on trusted sidekick Lando Calrissian (Billy Dee Williams). In *Ghostbusters* (1984) and *Ghostbusters II* (1989), Winston Zeddemore (Ernie Hudson) proved to be a reliable, if underused, member of the team of paranormal investigators. Gregory Hines found himself paired with an assortment of white buddies: as American expatriate Raymond Greenwood in *White Nights* (1985), he came to the aid of prominent ballet star and Russian defector Nikolai Rodchenko (Mikhail Baryshnikov); as Ray Hughes in *Running Scared* (1986), he and his partner (Billy Crystal), a longtime street cop, went searching for one last criminal before they retired from the force; and as Albaby Perkins in *Off Limits* (1988), he and a fellow Army criminal investigator, Buck McGriff (Willem Dafoe), tracked down the murderer of Vietnamese hookers in 1968 Saigon. Eddie Murphy, as convict Reggie Hammond, helped weary cop Jack Gates (Nick Nolte) locate a disturbed criminal in *48 Hours* (1982) and later, as Detroit cop Axel Foley, hooked up with Los Angeles police officer Billy Rosewood (Judge Reinhold) to catch killers in *Beverly Hills Cop* (1984) and *Beverly Hills Cop II* (1987).[1] And in one of film's most classic pairings (fig. 6.1), Martin Riggs (Mel Gibson), an edgy borderline psychopath, was teamed with stable family man Roger Murtaugh (Danny Glover);[2] in the four *Lethal Weapon* films, they broke up drug and counterfeiting rings, busted smugglers who hid behind diplomatic immunity, and defeated a former cop turned criminal mastermind. Even in *Driving Miss Daisy* (1989), adapted from the Pulitzer Prize-winning off-Broadway play by Albert Uhry that dramatized the twenty-five-year-long relationship between a wealthy Southern Jewish woman Daisy Werthan (Jessica Tandy)

Figure 6.1. One of cinema's most classic "buddy" pairings, Martin Riggs (Mel Gibson) teamed with Roger Murtaugh (Danny Glover) in *Lethal Weapon* and its numerous sequels. *(Warner Brothers, 1987)*

and her black chauffeur Hoke Colburn (Morgan Freeman), Miss Daisy finally realized that Hoke is her "best friend."

The biracial "buddy formula," Ed Guerrero suggests, had been a Hollywood staple for many years, going back to films like *The Defiant Ones* (1958) and *In The Heat of the Night* (1967). In the late 1960s and 1970s, however, perhaps in reaction to the nascent women's movement, the emphasis shifted briefly to white male buddy movies, the most influential of which were *Easy Rider*, *Butch Cassidy and the Sundance Kid*, and *Midnight Cowboy*. But by the 1980s, biracial buddy films were back. Their return, according to Guerrero, had political implications: "In a decade most easily identified by the tenure of the Reagan Presidency, the rise of an ideologically conservative cycle of Hollywood films known as the 'cinema of recuperation' or 'Reaganite Entertainment,' and the return of big-budget films of 'blockbuster' economics, Hollywood has put what is left of the black presence on the screen in the protective custody, so to speak, of a White lead or co-star, and therefore in conformity with dominant, White sensibilities and expectations

of what Blacks should be like" ("Black Image" 239).[3] As if to confirm black filmmaker Robert Townsend's observation that
"Hollywood is afraid that if you have more than one black person
in a movie you have a black movie," the industry seemed "intent
on bringing the broadest box office possible with the installation of
crossover thematics and the recognition of a few token Black stars
[e.g., Eddie Murphy, Richard Pryor, Gregory Hines]; . . . yet dominant cinema has been reluctant to cast Black leads without a White
buddy as cultural and ideological chaperone or without a space or
point of identification structured into the diegesis for the dominant
spectator" (Guerrero, "Black Image" 239). Even in a film like *The
Green Mile* (1999), in which accused black murderer John Coffey
(Michael Clarke Duncan) possesses superhuman curative abilities,
it is his white jailer Paul Edgecomb (Tom Hanks) who must teach
him to harness his powers and who offers the audience a familiar
image to whom to relate.

A variation on this strategy was the production of films that
portrayed black social struggles as seen through white eyes. *Cry
Freedom* (1987), for instance, promised to be a provocative and
courageous attempt to dramatize apartheid; but it became another
interracial buddy movie in which the relatively petty concerns of
journalist Donald Woods (Donald Sutherland) marginalized the
historical struggles of his friend, black activist Steven Biko (Denzel
Washington). In *A Dry White Season* (1989), an adaptation of white
South African André Brink's novel, black female director and filmmaker Euzhan Palcy (who co-wrote the screenplay with Colin
Welland) tried to make the black characters pivotal to the story and
not simply backdrops for the white hero's consciousness raising.
(Unlike the novel, Palcy's film ends on a note of black resistance
when the black character Stanley shoots and kills a malevolent
white security police chief.) But clearly it is white Afrikaner schoolteacher Ben du Toit (Donald Sutherland) who emerges as the sympathetic hero, particularly after his newfound political consciousness causes him to be dismissed from his job, rejected by the community, and betrayed by the wife who leaves him and the daughter who informs on him.[4] Similarly, *Mississippi Burning* (1988)
focused more on the heroism of the two FBI agents who assume the
burden of defending and protecting the black community and the
wife (Frances McDormand) of a murdering Klansman who fur-

thers their investigation than on the black residents of Mississippi who are routinely victimized, terrorized, and violated. Told through the eyes of the agents, the story effectively reduced blacks "to passive objects of their own history."[5] Even *Glory* (1989), about the 54th Regiment composed of the first black infantrymen in the North during the Civil War, concentrated more on dramatizing the life of white officer Robert Gould Shaw (Matthew Broderick) than of black soldier and former slave Trip (Denzel Washington, who won an Academy Award as Best Supporting Actor for his performance) or other of his fellow soldiers. And in *The Long Walk Home* (1990), the plight of the domestic, Odessa Cotter (Whoopi Goldberg), who walks miles to work during the Montgomery bus boycott of 1955, is subsumed by the awakening of the social conscience of her white employer Miriam Thompson (Sissy Spacek), who defies custom by starting a carpool for protesters. Donald Bogle suggests that such focus on white characters, even in films that supposedly deal with racism, was Hollywood's way of giving "the mass white audience people it can identify with" (*TCMMB* 303) and of shifting attention from black struggles to white participation or observation.[6]

The 1980s and 1990s also saw a return to traditional black casting, even among such fine actors as Cicely Tyson, who played Sipsey, a noble servant willing to sacrifice herself for her employers in *Fried Green Tomatoes* (1991), based on white author Fannie Flagg's *Fried Green Tomatoes at the Whistle Stop Cafe*. As Geechee in *Cross Creek* (1983), a film adapted from Marjorie Kinnan Rawlings's work, Alfre Woodard portrayed another familiar faithful servant who needs a white influence in order to acquire a sense of responsibility and independence. In even more retrogressive and stereotypical roles, Mr T appeared as the coarse, black-buckish character Clubber Lang in *Rocky III*, and Richard Pryor, flying alongside Superman in *Superman III* (1983), seemed "so jittery and scared that he looks suspiciously like a replay of a terr'fied Willie Best wandering through the haunted house with Bob Hope in *The Ghost Breakers*."[7] In *The Last Boy Scout* (1991), the usually fine satirist Damon Wayans required instruction from his white sidekick Bruce Willis. And popular comedian Martin Lawrence, as FBI agent Malcolm Turner, resurrected a particularly vulgar version of the stereotype when he assumed a Mammy disguise in *Big Momma's House* (2000).

By contrast, the real sense of urban anger and discontent found brilliant expression in Spike Lee's *Do the Right Thing* (1989), an exciting, controversial film that depicted a single day in the lives of residents in Brooklyn's Bedford-Stuyvesant section and culminated in a violent racial uprising. The film not only exploded the myth of cultural harmony underlying Hollywood's interracial films of male bonding; it also, according to Bogle, "heralded the oncoming arrival of a new brand of African American commercial cinema in which the subjects of race, racism, cultural bearings, and social/political problems would move to the forefront" (*TCMMB* 323). Among that new wave of black filmmakers were the Hudlin brothers (Reginald and Warrington), whose films included the urban musical comedy *House Party* (1990) and the disappointing Eddie Murphy feature *Boomerang* (1992); the Wayans brothers (Keenen Ivory, Damon, Shawn, and Marlon), who exploded onto the national scene with the television show *In Living Color* (1990) before graduating to feature films; Robert Townsend, whose career declined rapidly after the entertaining but predictable pictures *Hollywood Shuffle* (1987) and *The Five Heartbeats* (1991); William Greaves, whose outstanding documentaries like *Ida B. Wells: A Passion for Justice* (1989) earned him the title of dean of contemporary black independent filmmakers; Ernest Dickerson, who made the transition from Spike Lee's cinematographer to director with his gritty tale of inner city violence, *Juice* (1992); and John Singleton, the first black as well as the youngest director nominated for an Academy Award for his socially realistic *Boyz N the Hood* (1991). Charles Burnett offered another strong and important cinematic voice with films that were simultaneously metaphoric and utterly real: *Killer of Sheep* (1977), his thesis film, intercut scenes of children playing in an empty lot with animals being led to the slaughter and provided an incisive commentary on the hopelessness of contemporary black life, while the family drama *To Sleep with Anger* (1990) explored the disruptions in the routines and rituals of an older couple (Mary Alice and Paul Butler) caused by their old friend Harry Mention (Danny Glover), a trickster figure who comes to visit them but never leaves. Seeking to re-create the sensation of his father Melvin's *Sweet Sweetback's Baadasssss Song* (in which he appeared as the young Sweetback), Mario Van Peebles, in *New Jack City* (1990), his film about maverick ex-cops who try to bring down a crack-dealing drug lord, inaugurated a genre that some critics have dubbed "New Jack cinema." And Julie Dash, whose stunning *Daughters of the Dust* (1990), a non-linear narrative that chronicled the experiences of a family of Gullah women who are about to leave the Sea Islands of South Carolina— and possibly lose their culture and identity—as they prepare to travel to the mainland, gave cinema a new turn by rejecting traditional portrayals of black women.[8]

Coincident with the emergence of the new generation of black filmmakers was a host of films and telefilms adapted from black literature, including important and innovative fiction by women, that challenged the depiction of black life in earlier Hollywood films. Unlike the stereotypical Toms, Mammies, servants, and side-kick roles in which blacks were traditionally cast on screen or the situation comedies and variety shows to which they were usually relegated on television, those film adaptations portrayed a wide cross section of black society, from the struggling poor to the successful professional class, and revealed new aspects of black culture, from the strong sense of community and the expanded notion of family to the significance of matriarchal structures and the tight bonds among friends and kin. Still other film adaptations brought black history to popular audiences and helped to foster an awareness of historic events of which many white viewers (and even some black viewers) were painfully ignorant. And the best of those film adaptations transformed the old cinematic formulas, often recasting blacks in relation to each other rather than in relation to whites and allowing them to speak in their own voices and to reveal their politics, sexuality, hopes, and frustrations; and they demonstrated that there was indeed a market, among black as well as white audiences, for movies featuring largely or exclusively black characters and by black filmmakers.

ERNEST J. GAINES

One of the most prominent contemporary black writers to popularize black history in his novels and stories was Ernest J. Gaines. The film versions of four of his works—*The Autobiography of Miss Jane Pittman* (1974; dir. John Korty); *The Sky is Gray* (1980; dir. Stan

Lathan); *A Gathering of Old Men* (1987; dir. Volker Schlondorff); and *A Lesson Before Dying* (1999; dir. Joseph Sargent)—were developed not for theaters but for television, a medium whose more intimate method of storytelling allowed it to reach a larger audience and to create a powerful collective experience. And the success of those films, particularly of the film version of Gaines's best known novel *The Autobiography of Miss Jane Pittman*, helped to establish a tradition of adaptation of black literature to telefilm that continued with the landmark miniseries *Roots* and other fine productions like *The Piano Lesson* and *The Wedding*. According to Mark J. Charney, it was the strong characterizations and compelling narrative lines that made Gaines's fiction so "appealing to filmmakers. Each story contains a strong protagonist or group of protagonists, a central conflict, and a variety of regional voices. Each describes a situation that not only interests readers but almost forces them to take sides. And each presents characters who are likeable and universal in their struggles—perfect subjects, especially for television drama" (124).

Like William Faulkner, one of his literary mentors, Gaines based much of his work on a small area of the South: his fictional town of Bayonne, Louisiana, was modeled after Oscar, Louisiana, and the River Lake Plantation on which he was born and on which he worked as a child. His grandparents and great-grandparents had been slaves on that plantation, and, a generation later, his parents sharecropped the same land. During the long hours that his parents spent in the fields—and especially after their divorce, when Ernest was eight years old—Gaines turned for support and instruction to his aunt Augusteen Jefferson, one of the strongest influences in his life. A paraplegic who helped to raise him as well as his brothers, she became the model for the recurring image in his fiction of the strong, determined, sacrificing older black woman who provides continuity within the family and the community.

It was Augusteen, in fact, who inspired Gaines's *The Autobiography of Miss Jane Pittman* (1971) and to whom that novel is dedicated. "My beloved aunt," Gaines called her in the dedication, a woman "who did not walk a day in her life but who taught me the importance of standing." Augusteen's fictional counterpart is Miss Jane, the 110-year-old protagonist whose life spans the period from the Civil War to the civil rights movement and who serves as an eyewitness to much of America's history.[9] Even more importantly, she provides a voice for the thousands, even millions of illiterate blacks whose experiences might otherwise be overlooked. As her *Autobiography* moves from one violent climax to another, from an act of resistance by a black hero to an act of murder by a white antagonist, Miss Jane observes and comments on what has occurred and preserves whatever has been gained, including the legend of the hero, as she prepares a new generation of rebels.[10]

The novel begins with Jane as an orphaned slave-child on a Louisiana plantation during the final months of the Civil War. After being ordered by her mistress to fetch water to the advancing Yankee soldiers, she catches the attention of Corporal Brown, who tells her that her name, Ticey, is "a slave name, and I don't like slavery. I'm go'n call you Jane" (8). After the Yankees move on, she insists on being addressed as "Jane Brown," an act of defiance that provokes her mistress and incurs a brutal beating, the scars of which Jane carries throughout her life. Once the war is over and emancipation is pronounced, she decides to head north to Ohio to find "Mr. Brown" and encourages other slaves to leave with her. A few younger blacks follow; but most of the older blacks decide to stay on the plantation and sharecrop for no pay. This tension between the more radical younger generation who seek change and are ready to risk everything, even their lives, for freedom and their more conservative elders who value security and fear confrontation, which can only exacerbate their already precarious existences, becomes one of the novel's recurring motifs.

After journeying for just a few days, Jane and her group are attacked by "Patrollers," a gang of Confederate veterans. ("Them and the soldiers from the Secesh Army," she recollects, "was the ones who made up the Ku Klux Klans later on" [21].) Only Jane and little Ned survive. But the bravery of Ned's mother, Big Laura, who slays two of her attackers before dying with her baby girl in her arms, not only inspires Jane but also becomes part of the legend of black courage that she imparts to Ned, whom she raises as if he were her own son. Together, they suffer the havoc caused by Reconstruction.

While still in his teens, Ned begins working to promote civil rights among blacks, a cause that provokes the wrath of local Klan members, who come searching for him and—as a warning—beat Jane for harboring him. After traveling to Kansas, where he completes his education, marries, and starts his own family, Ned returns to the South to teach and preach the importance of black freedom; but he is soon assassinated by Albert Cluveau, a Cajun acquaintance of Jane's. Though Jane is heartbroken by Ned's murder, she appreciates the arcane, unspoken convolutions of the Southern code that forces Cluveau to act as he does or risk being murdered himself—just as it forces Tee Bob Samson, the son of one of Jane's later employers, to take his life for love of the mulatto teacher Mary Agnes LeFabre, whom custom prohibits his marrying.

Following Ned's departure to Kansas, Jane finds happiness for a time with Joe Pittman, a kind, decent man with whom she lives but whom she never marries.[11] ("I didn't believe in the church then, and Joe never did" [78].) Through hard work, Joe buys himself out of his debt to Colonel Dye; and, with Jane, he moves to a place near the Louisiana-Texas border, where he makes his reputation as the "Chief," a renowned black cowboy and breaker of wild horses. Unlike Ned who seeks political freedom, Joe seeks economic freedom; but even though his antagonist is nature rather than racism, he too demonstrates a kind of heroism, especially in his efforts to assert his manhood and his independence and to tame the untameable (Byerman, "Gaines" 59). When he dies trying to break a horse that Jane calls a "ghost" and a "haint" (91)—a death that Jane anticipates by her recurring dreams and that she hopes to prevent with hoo-doo powder from Madame Gautier—she chooses to honor his courage by taking his last name.

After losing the two people closest to her, Jane finds solace in her religion and in her community, where she is recognized for her devotion as well as her achievement. Here too she continues to bear witness to the changes occurring in the world around her— the participation of black soldiers in Cuba; the rise of black heroes like Joe Louis ("In the Depression it was tough on everybody, but twice as hard on the colored, and He [God] sent us Joe" [201]) and Jackie Robinson; the inspirational examples of Booker T. Washington, W. E. B. Du Bois, and Reverend Martin Luther King, Jr.; and the moral authority of Rosa Parks. Community and religion, in fact, merge in the last part of the book ("The Quarters"), during which Jane—a symbolic "mother" to her people even though she herself is childless (her barrenness being another legacy of her slavery)—nurtures a young boy, Jimmy Aaron, whom most believe is "the One" to deliver them, as Ned had tried to do. After Jimmy goes away to school and returns to take up the fight, the black community is disappointed to realize that Jimmy wants to lead them not in a spiritual but a political direction—not to the Promised Land but to a land of promise through the civil rights movement. Anxious to protect what little they have gained over the years, the community members are reluctant to take up his cause.

Their fear is amplified when their landlord Robert Samson threatens to dispossess any black who marches with Jimmy or offers him any support. Even Miss Jane, who admires Jimmy's zeal as she had admired Ned's, wonders if the movement can in fact bring about real change. In the end, however, she determines that it is time for her, as the oldest black among them, to take a stand and to help Jimmy integrate the courthouse in Bayonne. As she ventures out of the quarters toward the courthouse, she is joined by a mass of people—"men, women, children"—who come towards her and stand with her. "Most of them was scared and they wasn't ashamed to show it. But they was standing there, and that's what mattered" (242). As they proceed toward the town, they are halted by Samson, who tells them that Jimmy has been shot to death and that they should disperse and return to their homes. Understanding both the inevitability of white violence towards blacks and the necessity of overcoming the black habit of accommodation to white power, Jane responds, "Just a little piece of him is dead. The rest of him is waiting for us in Bayonne." Slow but undeterred, she keeps moving. "Me and Robert," she says, "looked at each other a long time, then I went by him" (244). As Karen Carmean observes, "Jane's is not a flashy conflict resulting in Samson's acknowledgment of defeat or indeed any conscious recognition that she represents a just position." Instead, "her victory is tempered by Gaines's recognition of the limits of social progress as white society has gradually come to recognize the civil and social rights of African Americans." When Jane looks at Robert with a sense of social equality, deliberately addresses him by first name and not as "Mister," and then moves past him, she illustrates that his threats and commands no longer carry valid authority. "In the end, Robert Samson loses his strength because Jane refuses to fear him. Her courage goes beyond words, and her leadership proceeds without bluster" (Carmean 66).

The genius of *The Autobiography of Miss Jane Pittman* lies not in the actual episodes of black history that it chronicles but rather in the unique voice of Miss Jane, which articulates that history so eloquently and so powerfully. Jane's story thus becomes as much a sermon, a folk history, an oral poetry, and a traditional slave narrative as an autobiography (which, in fact, it is not—even though early readers and editors believed it to be and clamored for photos of or interviews with the fictional character).[12] Gaines observed that he originally conceived of the novel as a "folk biography" and that he wrote at least one draft with "a group of people telling of this one person's life" over a hundred years of history. But that version struck him as "untrue," so he proceeded to write from his character's point of view, with an occasional bit of help from her friends, who help her to fill in details that she has forgotten or errors that she has made.[13] Inspired by the courage of strong black women like his aunt Augusteen, Gaines re-created the language of slave narratives by reading and studying the WPA interviews collected in *Lay My Burden Down*.

In the novel, Miss Jane recounts her tale of tragedy and triumph to a young black teacher of history, who has been trying for years to get her to give an account of her life. The teacher, certain that Jane's "life's story can help me explain things to my students" (viii), observes that the "autobiography" is not only Jane's autobiography but also an autobiography of the many people who knew her and contributed to her telling.[14] "Miss Jane's story is all of their stories," writes the teacher, "and their stories are Miss Jane's" (x). As Gaines implies by this fictional construct, history is a communal experience because it is an experience of community; and often great heroism can be found in the most seemingly unheroic people and events.

The immense popularity of the book, published in 1971 on the heels of the civil rights struggle, led to its filming as a made-for-television movie in 1974; and, like the book, the film helped to explain why black Americans demanded recognition. The screenplay for the film was written by Tracy Keenan Wynn, with Ernest Gaines involved as a consultant on the project (a role he played on subsequent telefilms adapted from his works as well). Retaining the novel's basic movement from climax to climax and using Miss Jane's voice-over to provide transitions between the present and the past, Wynn trimmed the book to fit the telefilm's two-hour format by emphasizing some of its most violent episodes: the death of Big Laura (Odetta); the Klan's lynchings and destruction of the plantation school; the murders of Joe (Rod Perry), Ned (Thalmus Rasulala), and Jimmy (Arnold Wilkerson), the men closest to Jane. As Mark J. Charney writes, director John Korty builds from one act of violence to the next until he reaches the film's controversial ending. But by concentrating on the string of violent occurrences in Jane's life, Korty was forced to eliminate many of her descriptions of the shifting values, lifestyles, and perspectives of her people; and in recounting more than one hundred years of history, he lost some of "the subtle changes in vision and personality that occur during that century." For instance, instead of Jane's eloquent description of Reconstruction, which she likens to "slavery again" with "secret groups" killing even more than before (70) and carpetbaggers, black and white, moving in to "take from the South what the war didn't," the film offers a montage of burned schools, random violence, and lynched mulattos—images that Charney calls "visual clichés," reminiscent of Griffith's *Birth of a Nation*, that "elicit from audiences a textbook sense of guilt . . . without creating a method to tie it more closely to Miss Jane's voice and perspective" (Charney 131, 133).[15] Even Gaines commented on what he perceived to be the technical weaknesses of the film. "So what you have in the film now," he told an interviewer, "is peaks—a lot of peaks. But you don't have the valleys and slopes as you would have had, had the film been longer" (Rowell 49).

Korty was indeed forced to make a number of cuts; in fact, his telefilm skips the entire third book of the novel, "The Plantation," which focused on the relationship between Timmy and Tee Bob Samson, the "Two Brothers of the South," and on Tee Bob's unrequited love for the mulatto schoolteacher Mary Agnes LeFabre. The scenes that Korty depicts, however, compensate for some of the cuts by their visual power: the slaves' joyous confusion upon learning of the Emancipation Proclamation, after which they debate whether to stay and sharecrop Bryant's estate or leave, their bags packed with potatoes and apples, to seek a better life else-where; Albert Cluveau's easy familiarity with his old fishing part-ner Jane, in whom he confides his intention to kill her "son"; Ned's refusal to crawl before his white assassin, even after being shot in the knee; Jane's conversations with "Sister Oak," the noble planta-tion tree that is as old as she, under which she sits and speaks to her God.

Korty also managed to translate to film a number of Gaines's most evocative and recurring images. Horses, for instance, com-prised part of the chivalric tradition inherent to Southern mythol-ogy; possession of them denoted a certain authority.[16] Confederate officers arrived at plantations on horseback, as did the patrollers who massacred the newly freed slaves and the Klansmen who destroyed the plantation school. (Blacks, by contrast, typically drive or ride old mules.) Not surprisingly, Joe Pittman chooses to assert both his manhood and his authority by becoming a "break-er" of horses before being broken himself—and killed—by a wild stallion. Unlike the novel's black stallion, however, the film's stal-lion is white and ghostly—as white and ghostly as the apparition that haunts Jane's dreams and foreshadows her husband's death. In this way, Korty cleverly reverses color connotations: white, not black, becomes the color of evil. And indeed for Jane, as for her "sons" Ned and Jimmy, it is whites, not blacks, who cause harm and who ultimately take black lives.

Like Joe, who appropriates one of the symbols of white author-ity, Ned learns from Jane to prize the flint and the iron rocks that his mother Big Laura had used to start fires on her aborted journey north to freedom. But unlike the fires that white Klansmen and other secret groups set to terrorize blacks and burn them out of their schools and churches, the fire that Ned inherits from Big Laura creates a symbolic spark that causes him to become an edu-cator and a reformer. His mother's fire—her desire for a better life for her children—transforms Ned into the activist Ned Douglass and then into the reformer Ned Steven Douglass, just as Joe's ambition transforms him into Chief and as Ticey's determination transforms her into Jane and eventually into the matriarchal Miss Jane.

And ultimately it is the matriarchal Miss Jane who, after wit-nessing a century's worth of heroism and civil disobedience, becomes a heroine herself by engaging in a public act of defiance.

Whereas in the novel she simply stares down Samson and "moves past" him, in the film Miss Jane is driven to the courthouse, where with painfully slow steps she walks—alone—from the sidewalk to the entrance of the courthouse. At the "Whites Only" water fountain, she takes a long drink in full view of the white police officers, after which she retraces her path to the truck, where she is helped up and slowly driven away, back to the Quarters, as a group of blacks follows in solidarity with her defiance.[17] It is a dramatic ending, but it is very much a Hollywood ending; and it lacks the subtlety of the novel's conclusion. Gaines has said that ironically "most people remember the film by the ending of it, the walk to the fountain, which I did not write. . . . I don't know that my ending was the best ending. The way I had it down, I thought I was trying to prove a point" (Gaudet and Wooton 97).

In the novel, it was a young black teacher who urged Miss Jane, during nine months of taping, to record her "autobiography" as a counterpoint to the missing histories in schoolbooks; in the film, it is a white reporter, Quentin (Michael Murphy), who spends only a few days interviewing her for an assigned feature that he is preparing for his newspaper. (Fig. 6.2.) Then, as John Callahan points out, the reporter "translates her story into the page (and the

Figure 6.2. A white newspaper reporter (Michael Murphy) interviews Miss Jane (Cicely Tyson) for a feature story in *The Autobiography of Miss Jane Pittman,* an Emmy award-winning telefilm based on Ernest Gaines's novel. *(Tomorrow Entertainment, Inc., 1974)*

screen) without the communal experience so crucial to Gaines's teacher's realization of folk traditions" and of community values.[18] Critics of the film have charged that this seemingly minor change in the character of the listener, from black teacher to white reporter, undermines Miss Pittman's narrative by turning the black woman's autobiography into a biography, defined and limited by the perspective of the white male who helps to record it. Donald Bogle writes that "by using a white reporter, the film makes the familiar concession to the mass white television audience, giving the white viewers a good guy they can identify with. It also makes us believe that Miss Jane's story has been documented because a white man finds it of value" (*Encyclopedia* 316). Such appropriation of black voices, according to Ed Guerrero, although typical of Hollywood's attitude toward black-oriented narratives, deprives blacks of an active role in their own histories ("Black Image" 239).[19]

The Autobiography of Miss Jane Pittman (1974) was nonetheless a remarkable film, and it set high new standards for television. Pauline Kael believed it to be "quite possibly the finest . . . ever made for American television" (76), and Joseph Kanin of *Atlantic* called it "as moving and powerful a study of black life in this country as has yet been produced" and "unquestionably the finest film to have been made for television" (117).[20] For her performance as Miss Jane, Cicely Tyson earned an Emmy; awards also went to director John Korty, screenwriter Ann Peacock, and music composer Fred Karlin. And the film itself became a staple in libraries and classrooms nationwide.

The second of Gaines's works to be adapted as a telefilm was his widely-anthologized story, "The Sky Is Gray," first published in the collection *Bloodline* (1968). The narrator, James, is an eight-year-old with a terrible toothache; the story, reminiscent of Eudora Welty's "A Worn Path," describes the journey that he and his mother Octavia must make from their home in the quarters of a Louisiana plantation to a dentist in the small town of Bayonne. But the story is really about the relationship between James and his mother and about their struggle for self-respect in a racist society.

Despite his youth, James has little chance to be a child. His father, an Army draftee, is gone, and James—the eldest of four small children—must assume the role of "the man" of the house and a "sample" (example) to his siblings. To prepare him for that responsibility and for the inevitably hard life ahead of him, his mother tries to teach him to be unafraid. James, however, sometimes responds to her good intentions with disappointment, confusion, even fear. For instance, when Octavia forces him to kill the redbirds that he and his brother have caught in their traps "'cause we needed the food," he cries because he wants to set them free. But Octavia slaps him, grabs a fork, and sticks it through the neck of one of the birds; then she beats James with a switch until he stabs the second bird. Afterwards, she cooks the redbirds for dinner. "Ain't had but a little bitty piece each," he recalls, "but we all had a little bitty piece, and everybody just looked at me 'cause they was so proud" (89-90). Only later does James realize that his mother wants him to be able to survive and to support the family should something happen to her. (Karen Carmean suggests that Octavia never explains to James her reasons for forcing him to act because there is no reasonable way to "explain the kinds of unspoken rules, restrictions and insults James will encounter on a daily basis because of his race" [142-43].) Because he loves his mother, James does not want her to worry, so even after he develops a toothache "he never said nothing" and tries not to "act like a crybaby" (84). But after a month, the pain becomes too intense for him to ignore.

In order to see the dentist, James must wake up early and wait in the cold with his mother for the bus that will take them to Bayonne. Since there are no seats left in the rear—and since James knows better than to sit in the "white" section—he stands the whole way. In town, the chill wind blows in their faces, and James wishes that he could warm himself in the café where white people gather and eat. At the dentist's, Olivia and James wait—and wait—their turn in a segregated area, but the office closes for lunch and they are told to return in the afternoon, even though there is no place for them to go in the meantime. Hungry and cold, James feels his feet turn numb; he tries "to work his toes" but no longer has any sensation. "Look like I'm go'n die," he thinks. "Look like I'm go'n stand right here and freeze to death" (106). Octavia leads him to a hardware store; pretending to be examining some ax handles, she positions him near a stove to warm up. When she sees that he is better, they leave without buying anything. In this way, his mother teaches James another lesson in survival: "she provides him an example of how to get the necessities of life without giving whites the satisfaction of seeing her beg" (Byerman, "Gaines" 57).

After Helena and Alnest, two kindly white shopkeepers, offer them lunch, Octavia accepts; but she insists that James work for their meal by performing chores for the couple. Before leaving, Octavia wants to buy some salt pork. When Helena gives her more than she paid for, Octavia returns the extra portion and takes only what is fair—although she tells Helena that her "kindness will never be forgotten."[21] Again, his mother's actions teach James the importance of maintaining dignity even in poverty. That lesson is reinforced in the story's final line, when she reminds him to turn down the coat collar he has raised to protect himself from the heavy sleet: "'You not a bum,' she says. 'You a man'" (117).

Directed by black director Stan Lathan (whose work includes the acclaimed made-for-television movie of *Go Tell It on the Mountain* and the Showtime production of *Uncle Tom's Cabin*) from a screenplay by black playwright Charles Fuller, *The Sky Is Gray* (1980) was produced as part of the "American Short Story" series for public television. In the forty-six-minute-long telefilm, Lathan stunningly re-created the beginnings of James's odyssey to manhood by depicting the critical details of segregated life in the South in the 1940s, from the ramshackle nature of the quarters in which James (James Bond III) lives with his mother Octavia (Olivia Cole), his "Auntie" (Margaret Avery), and the rest of his family, to the shabby gentility of Helena (Susan French) and Alnest's half-empty shop in Bayonne.[22] But more than just the details of the locations, Lathan captured many of the nuances of black life: the automatic walk to the rear of the bus, the stepping aside for whites to pass on the sidewalks, the blacks' averting of their eyes when white people approach them, and the numerous other customs, both spoken and unspoken, that assume white superiority.

What defined Gaines's story, however, was the boy's internal narrative voice. For instance, in the story, James soon realizes why he had to kill the redbirds in the cage: "Suppose she [his mother Octavia] had to go away? That's why I had to do it. Suppose she had to go away like Daddy went away?" (90). But in the film, when Octavia orders James to impale the birds and then starts beating him because he wants to keep them as pets, her actions seem cruel and almost incomprehensible. As Mark J. Charney writes, "the audience senses only James's fear and Octavia's violence, not the son's efforts to understand the actions of his mother. As the screenplay for the adaptation suggests, rather than acting out of a sense of responsibility, James kills the birds to escape the wrath of his mother." Ironically, therefore, in the film Octavia comes to represent the very violence from which she tries to protect her son. Without James's tempering perspective, her actions seem pointless, particularly since the film makes no connection between the killing of the birds, which Octavia regards as a form of a survival that the boy must learn, and the disappearance of James's father, which necessitates such knowledge. "Without the benefit of his internal voice," as Charney concludes, "the viewer cannot achieve a complete understanding of Octavia's purpose," an inability that ultimately "reduces the thematic thrust of the story adaptation" (128).

The father's absence in James's life, as suggested in the episode with the trapped birds, was of critical importance in Gaines's story: James, in fact, defines events by the role his father played in them. At one point, he recalls how happy the family used to be before his father was taken away by the Army; at another, he expresses his desire to "make all this up" to his mother by serving as a kind of substitute for his father and buying her a new coat. In the film, James's aunt makes reference to the unfairness of Octavia's situation—that is, being left both without a husband and without any government compensation for his service to the Army. But the film's minimizing of the father as a character—albeit an absent one—also minimizes the underlying irony of the story: that while the father is risking his life in defense of his country overseas, his family's lives are at risk at home. In their own town, they cannot even find a safe place to eat or to take shelter from the inclement weather. That is precisely the point that the militant young black student in the dentist's office tries to make to the minister about the restrictions on the liberties and freedoms of the black man in America. "What," he asks, "do words like Freedom, Liberty, God, White, Colored mean?"

Gaines was generally pleased with the film version, even though he noted that Lathan had changed some of the particulars—the field depicted in the adaptation was a cornfield instead of a canefield; the boy's trap held large birds instead of scrawny redbirds; and the sky was pale blue, never gray. More significant to Gaines, however, was the casting: "In 'The Sky Is Gray,'" he noted, "the main character is a little boy about eight years old, and they [the filmmakers] could not find a little boy eight years old to carry the story. So they had to get a larger boy about thirteen years old—and that makes a difference on the effect of the story. It makes a big difference" (Gaudet and Wooton 88). Despite Gaines's reservations, audiences were deeply affected by the fine performances and profoundly moved by the telefilm, especially by the close bond it portrayed between James and his mother as she teaches him how to be a man and how to survive in a hostile society.

The third telefilm adapted from a work by Gaines, *A Gathering of Old Men* (1987/released on video under the title *Murder on the Bayou*), based on his fifth novel, *A Gathering of Old Men* (1983), was also a study of dignity and manhood. Set on the former Marshall plantation in 1979, the novel opens with part-owner Candy Marshall sending word to a group of old men that they are to bring their twelve-gauge shotguns and spent shells to the home of Mathu, an elderly black sharecropper who helped to raise her. Convinced that Mathu is responsible for the murder of Beau Boutan, a racist Cajun farmer and work boss who leases some of the Marshalls's land, Candy plans to protect her old friend by confessing to the crime.[23] Her hope is that the other men will also offer their confessions and thereby obfuscate Mathu's guilt, since Mathu's antipathy toward Boutan is both longstanding and widely known. The men who gather in response to Candy's call, most of them in their seventies, see an opportunity to respond to some of the injustices they have experienced over the years. As Mat says, God "works in mysterious ways. Give a old nigger like me one more chance to do something with his life. He gived me that chance, and I'm taking it" (38). And each man—for different reasons—confesses responsibility for Boutan's murder. Meanwhile Sheriff Mapes, confronted with an excess of suspects and the possibility of racial violence, feels compelled to sort through all of their stories.

The novel, which takes place during a single eight-hour day, has the feel of a classical tragedy. Divided into twenty chapters spoken by fifteen different narrators (three of whom speak more than once), it blends white, black, and Cajun voices to create—

even more than in *The Autobiography of Miss Jane Pittman*—a kind of communal story. Significantly, however, the three central characters—Candy, Mathu, and Mathu's godson Charlie—never speak directly; their words and actions are reported by others.

As the old men—including Chimley, Mat, Cherry, Clatoo, Rufe, Rooster, Coot, Sharp, and Dirty Red—recall aloud Mathu and Beau Boutan, they also reveal much about themselves, particularly about the inhumane treatment they have suffered over the years from the Boutan family and from other bigoted whites. And it becomes clear why they "want the credit" (16) for the shooting. Eighty-year-old Uncle Billy, the first of the old men to be interrogated and beaten by the sheriff, says that he shot Beau because of "what they [Fix Boutan and his family] did to my boy . . . years back, when he come home from that war . . . with Hitler and them Japs . . . . The way they beat him. They beat him till they beat him crazy . . . he didn't even know me and his mama no more" (80). Mat recalls his own son Oliver and "how they [whites] let him die in the hospital just 'cause he was black. No doctor to serve him, let him bleed to death, 'cause he was black" (38). Johnny Paul says that he killed Beau to protect the black cemetery that the whites want to plow over and, by implication, the black heritage that they want to eradicate. Tucker tells Mapes that he acted in memory of his brother Silas, "the last black man round here to sharecrop on this place" before the good land was given to the Cajuns and before the blacks, "who had been working this land a hundred years for the Marshall plantation" (93-94), were left with the useless bottomland near the swamp. Yank, once a renowned breaker of horses, has no more horses left to break since the tractors and cane cutters took over the farm work: "Maybe that's why I shot the man who took the horse from me" (99). Gable remembers how his sixteen-year-old son, who was "half out of his mind," was put "in the 'lectric chair on the word of a poor white trash," how the chair malfunctioned on the first try, and how he and the undertaker had to wait outside the prison until a repairman arrived from Baton Rouge. "Some went so far to say my boy shoulda been glad he died in the 'lectric chair 'stead at the end of a rope. . . . And it was best we just forget all about it and him. I never forgot. It's been over forty years now, but every day of my life, every night of my life, I go through that rainy day again" (102-03). Coot makes his confession wearing his First World War Army uniform with military decorations because "the first white man I met" after returning to Louisiana "told me I better not ever wear that uniform or that medal again no matter how long I lived. He told me I was back home now, and they didn't cotton to no nigger wearing medals for killing white folks" (104).

The experience of discrimination and abuse that the old men share gives them a sense of solidarity, a singular purpose, and an extraordinary dignity. That solidarity is reinforced when they assemble in the black cemetery where their ancestors are buried; it is there that each man searches among the unmarked graves overgrown with weeds for his own kin, as if to draw strength and resurrect past suffering. As Mary T. Harper writes, "this unkept burial ground, covered with weeds and grass like the landscape of the Quarters, also parallels the fear which stifles their lives. But among the weed-covered graves is life . . . [and the mens' spirits are] nourished, even as they realize that their actions may result in their deaths" (Harper 302). From the cemetery they head to Mathu's place, prepared to stand up to Sheriff Mapes and to become a virtual wall of resistance against white injustice: "not a wall of brick, stone or wood, but a wall of old black men with shotguns" (59). And, for perhaps the first time in their lives, they are "all heroes" (61), unafraid of the consequences of their actions.

As important as the voices of the old men are the outside narrative voices. Lou Dimes, a white reporter from Baton Rouge who is also Candy's fiancé, is by profession an acute observer of events; and in the novel he becomes perhaps the best commentator on the racial politics. Candy sends for him immediately upon Beau's murder, and his presence on the scene offers the reader an objective perspective on the situation at the same time that his ironic observations lend comic relief. Reportedly Gaines had experimented with Dimes as the narrator of the whole novel, but he realized that a white journalist from outside the community could never have had access to all of the necessary information.[24] Instead, Gaines limited Dimes's voice to four chapters—although with four separate narratives, Dimes still has a larger speaking role in the volume than any other character.

Interesting as well are the narratives of such disparate characters as Sully and Snookum. Sully, the white friend of Beau's younger brother, Gil ("Salt"), is a renowned halfback at Louisiana State University, where he plays the backfield with black fullback, Cal ("Pepper") Harrison; together they make a remarkable winning team in a state where football is as revered as religion. After Beau's death, however, Gil is forced to reassess his relationship with Cal, a situation that creates concerns for Sully, too, since he is also Cal's friend and teammate. As an outsider unfamiliar with the Boutans's heritage of racial reprisals, Sully offers a different, and largely impartial, slant on race issues in the South. Snookum, on the other hand, is a black child from the plantation; among the first to see Beau's body, Snookum is dispatched by Candy to gather the old men. According to Karen Carmean (101), although he is an innocent and honest observer, Snookum complicates the story "by providing a generational measure between the elderly, who have been subjugated through insults and beatings, and the young, who fail to show the deference demanded by custom"; yet by witnessing the actions of the adults around him as events unfolds, he "absorbs the lessons of manly behavior" and carries on the cultural message of defiance, particularly in his emboldened conduct with Sheriff Mapes.

Contrary to everyone's suspicions, however, Mathu is not the killer; rather, it is Big Charlie, long considered the most acquiescent of the local men, whom Mathu, his parrain (godfather), tries to protect. A giant of a man—Lou Dimes describes him as "the quintessence of what you would picture as the super, big buck nigger" (186)—Charlie characteristically avoids confrontation; when he finally strikes back at Beau, it is simply in self-defense and not out of hatred (although there is certainly enough cause for hate). Even then, he runs away and begs Mathu to take the blame for him. Only after experiencing a kind of spiritual conversion in the swamps where he goes to hide and where he hears the voices of his ancestors ("a voice calling my name. . . that voice was calling me back here" [192-93]) is Charlie able to stop running and return to face the consequences of his actions.

As Charlie explains to the sheriff, his problem with Beau "didn't start back there in the field." It started "forty-five years ago. 'Cause that was about the first time I run from somebody." But after so many years, "I said to myself I been 'bused enough. No matter if I did the work any other man could do, he 'bused me anyhow. . . Cussed me for no cause at all. Just to 'buse me. And long as I was Big Charlie, nigger boy, I took it. . . . But they comes a day! They comes a day when a man must be a man! (189). Even Mapes seems to sympathize, and "after a respectful moment of silence" he addresses Charlie as "Mr. Biggs." But just as Chimley had recognized earlier that there is no way that a black in the parish can assault a white, even accidentally, and escape with his life, Boutan's friend Luke Will fires upon Charlie; and, after a brief exchange of shots, both Charlie and Luke Will are killed. In the trial that follows, all of the black men are exonerated but—along with the white defendants—are put on probation "for five years, or until their deaths—whichever came first" and prohibited from firing a weapon or being in the company of anyone who is armed (which as Lou Dimes wryly observes, is "like telling a Louisianian never to say Mardi Gras or Huey Long" [213].)

The telefilm of *A Gathering of Old Men*, which first aired on 10 May 1987, was based on a screenplay written by playwright Charles Fuller and directed by Volker Schlondorff. Lou Gossett, Jr. starred as Mathu and Richard Widmark as Sheriff Mapes; Holly Hunter was Candy; Will Patton was Lou Dimes; and the old men included Joe Seneca, Woody Strode, Tiger Haynes, Sandman Sims, and Julius Harris. A number of real Louisiana residents were cast in minor roles, and—as Mark Charney writes—that casting, like the rustic use of the camera (often resembling a home movie), proved to be an effective device. With exquisite landscape shots of the bayous draped in Spanish moss, the sugar cane fields smoldering with harvest-time fires, and the small cemetery overtaken by tall weeds and grasses, director Schlondorff captured the sense of Louisiana's backwoods atmosphere that is so integral to the theme of the book. He also succeeded in visually emphasizing the struggle and power of the group of men. (Fig. 6.3.) But he lost "the delicate balance between the individual and the community that creates much of the thematic strength and humor in the novel" (Charney 134). The sense of community that grows in the novel is surprising and somewhat ironic, particularly since each man has different reasons for joining the group; but the screenplay glosses over the individual motivations and "implies that the community is formed as quickly as the men gather." It is not clear that Chimley goes to Marshall to support his friend Mat as much as to support Mathu, or that Cherry comes because he recognizes the newly

Figure 6.3. Based on a screenplay by playwright Charles Fuller, the film version of *A Gathering of Old Men* depicted the suffering and the dignity of a community of elderly blacks in Louisiana. *(Orion, 1987)*

found pride within the community and wants to share a part of it. According to Charney, the distinctive personal histories of the men are lost to the audience and consequently the film's momentum "is driven by the questions what will happen next and who will pay. The novel, on the other hand, is driven more by the transformation of the individual consciousness into a communal perspective" (134-35).

In rendering such a complex narrative design to film, it is not surprising that Schlondorff felt the need to consolidate some of the voices and merge the stories. Yet his choices were often puzzling: Yank and Dirty Red, for instance, become one character in the film. The two, however, are actually very different personalities; and, as Gaines said, combining them is "like trying to mix oil and water" (Gaudet and Wooton 99). Similarly, in highlighting the heroism of the other old men, Schlondorff diminished rather than enhanced the role of Mathu, who, in the book, affords his fellow blacks a model for their brave behavior. Most surprising, however, was the change in the ending of the film: after Mapes peaceably removes Charlie, a number of drunken whites and Cajuns arrive at Mathu's place to avenge the death of Beau; but seeing and sensing the solidarity of the blacks who have gathered, the whites flee in fear. As Mathu announces "We done did it," the blacks shoot their guns off in celebration. The film seems to suggest that the strong sense of community among the old men has obviated the need for violence. But, as the novel demonstrated, violence is necessary: it stirs a sense of accomplishment among the blacks, reminds them of the glories of victory, and symbolizes a final stand, a risk that is worth the potential danger (Charney 136). Violence, moreover, is a metaphor: the victims of white man's violence, blacks must answer in kind in order to redress their injuries. Even Gaines, who told an interviewer that "I never argue with what they do in Hollywood," was taken aback by the ending. "I think what I was trying to do in that entire book," he said, "was show a group of old men standing. They brought guns, and I still believe in the old Chekhovian idea that if the gun is over the mantel at the beginning of the play, the gun must go off by the time the curtain comes down. And I thought that the only way the gun could go off in my book was Charlie and Luke Will out on the street shooting at each other. They [the director and producers] felt they didn't have to stick too close to Chekhov." Perhaps, Gaines suggests, the film-makers "just didn't want a black and white shootout, killing each other off" (Gaudet and Wooton 97). But many viewers agreed with Gaines and were disappointed by the final scenes.

The telefilm, Gaines later reported, "did a pretty good job," especially in re-creating authentically the scenery of the story. In at least one interview, though, he commented extensively on other aspects of the film—the names of certain characters, the number of the old men who speak, the combining of dialogue from several characters to one, the change in the clothing and accents, even the size of the characters (e.g., the "big" Mapes becomes the "thin" Widmark)—that he observed were certainly "different" from his own telling.[25] He also remarked on the loss of some of the novel's comic subtleties, many of which were dependent upon the idiomatic sense of the language. The use of a German director who was wholly unfamiliar with the idiocyncracies of the American South no doubt exacerbated the problem. As Gaines noted, "You can bring anybody [in to direct] and make it dramatic, but you can't come in and make it funny. He must know the subtleties in order to bring this off and bring the humor out of that story. It just didn't come off" (Gaudet and Wooton 91). Instead, the film often replaced the delicious humor of the dialogue with broader comedy, such as the car backing into the hearse, that Gaines felt smacked of "cheap Hollywood."

Yet, while the telefilm missed many of the nuances of Gaines's rich text, it brought much of its emotion to the screen. As *Washington Post* reviewer (9 May 1987: G1) David Richards noted, the film version of *A Gathering of Old Men* "is more than a dramatization of late-blooming black solidarity. It's also a lament for a vanished way of rural life; an elegy to the land before it was despoiled by the tractors; and (for TV) a fairly understanding exploration of the complex social contact that knits whites, blacks and Cajuns together, not necessarily in animosity."

In his most recent novel, *A Lesson Before Dying*, published in 1993, Gaines again focused on the themes of manhood and of community. In a Louisiana parish in the late 1940s, a young black man known only as Jefferson is convicted and sentenced to death for the murder of a white storekeeper, Mr. Alcee Gropé. Jefferson had been caught in the store, with money from the register in his pocket, an opened bottle of whiskey in his hand, and the bloody bodies of his black friends, Bear and Brother, and of Mr. Gropé nearby. The defense argues that Jefferson is innocent of all charges except for being in the wrong place at the wrong time; that he had accepted a ride from his friends and unwittingly accompanied them to the store, where they tried to get liquor on credit and where the frightened owner first grabbed for his gun; that he had taken whiskey from the shelf only to calm his nerves after the shootings; that he had reached into the register out of hunger and stupidity. "Unaware of right and wrong," he was admittedly "a boy and a fool"; but clearly he lacked the intelligence to plan such a robbery. There would be no justice in putting such a creature, such a "cornered animal," to death. In fact, concludes the defense, "I would just as soon put a hog in the electric chair as this" (7-8).

After the sentencing, Jefferson's nannan (godmother) Miss Emma asks Grant Wiggins, the "Professor," to meet with her godson and make him understand that he is not a hog; she wants Jefferson to be able to go to his death like a man. At first, Grant is reluctant to intervene and does so only at the insistence of his Tante Lou, Emma's dear friend, and of his girlfriend Vivian.

Though well-educated and articulate himself, Grant appreciates Jefferson's hopelessness; most of his own friends, men and women as young and disenfranchised as Jefferson, have already gone—"to southern cities, to northern cities, others to the grave," victims of violence or of the unjust justice of the South that presumes a man's guilt solely on the basis of his color. Grant recalls the pessimistic prediction of his own teacher, Mr. Antoine, who counseled him "to run" or to have the white man "make you the nigger you were born to be" (65). Determined to prove Mr. Antoine wrong, Grant had not run; although he left the quarters long enough to attend the university, he returned to Bayonne to teach in the plantation school. But after six years of teaching, he has lost faith—in the possibility of bringing about real change, in the richness of the community of which he was once a part, in the religious values of his youth, even in himself. And he wonders whether he ought not to escape again, as he did years before to California, before he becomes utterly compromised by his circumstances.

Jefferson, on the other hand, is full of cynicism and self-loathing, the result of a lifetime of being treated as a no-account. Bereft of hope, he refuses to acknowledge any of the visitors, even his nannan Emma, who come to his cell; does not touch any of the food that Emma prepares, even though she cooks all of his favorites; and takes no consolation from Reverend Ambrose, who wants him to find religion before he dies. "It don't matter," Jefferson tells himself. "Nothing don't matter" (73). Only through his conversations with Grant, which help to reconnect him to the community, and through the personal thoughts he records in his journal (a means of self-expression that Grant proposes) does Jefferson begin to reclaim his silenced voice. (Even at his trial, he was denied the chance to present his side of the story.)

As the two men learn more about each other, they develop a bond of friendship; and ultimately both undergo a remarkable metamorphosis that affords them a better understanding of the value of their lives. The alienation Grant observes in Jefferson causes him to confront his own alienation and to appreciate more fully his own marginalization. As Karen Carmean writes, Grant is a member of a small, intimate community and has knowledge of that community's unspoken rules of behavior and expectation. At the same time, he is also one of the few college-educated characters in the novel, "and this makes him an anomaly not only because his grammar marks him as different from most characters—white or black—but because his experience has been broadened outside this confining system. Thus, Grant feels like an outsider, existing on the margins of his society, even while he is an insider" (120). To his surprise, Grant discovers that he still has much to offer—to the community, as a teacher and a moral example; to Vivian, as a husband and stepfather to her children; to his Tante Lou, in repayment for the lifelong sacrifices she has made for him. Escaping to another state, as he earlier considered, would be just that: escape, not resolution. And escape would only ensure that nothing would ever change, that "too many more would end up as [Jefferson] did" (249), without anyone even to shed a tear over them.

For his part, Jefferson comes to realize that, despite its brevity, his existence also has meaning, not only for himself but for Emma and Tante Lou, whose faith he must redeem; for Grant and Vivian, who touch him, literally and figuratively, with true affection and empathy for his plight; for the "chiren," who bring him pecans and peanuts and who visit him in the jailhouse; for "my litle cosin estel . . . [who] come up an kiss me on the jaw an i coudn hol it back no mo" (230). His journal entries demonstrate, eloquently if ungrammatically, that in his last days he has indeed come into his manhood: "Man walks on two foots; hogs on four hoofs" (220). That recognition gives him a dignity that allows him not just to endure but, in his own small way, to prevail. Before he dies, he thanks his jailers for their courtesy toward him, assures his nannan that he will be waiting for her in heaven, generously disperses his few belongings, and directs the deputy to give Grant the journal he has kept, in which he acknowledges his debt to his teacher and bids him farewell: "good by mr. wigin tell them im strong tell them im a man" (234). And, although Grant cannot bear to watch the actual execution, he knows Jefferson will be brave. Still uncertain of God and of the laws in which others trust but needing to believe in something good and true, Grant concedes that "My faith is in you, Jefferson" (249). In the beginning of the novel, Grant had wondered how he was supposed to teach a man how to die when he himself was still trying to figure out how a man should live; in the end, Jefferson's purposeful death gives Grant a new purpose in his life.

Gaines's novel, which won a National Book Critics Circle Award and was hailed by the *Chicago Tribune*, among other publications, as an instant classic, could easily have engendered a film adaptation that was respectful but singularly uninspired. Instead, the film version of *A Lesson Before Dying* (HBO Original Films, 1999; dir. Joseph Sargent) was as compelling and as profound as the text on which it was closely based. Ken Ringle spoke for a multitude of viewers and reviewers when he wrote in the *Washington Post* (22 May 1999: C1) that "you're unlikely ever to see a more intelligent, compelling and beautifully crafted film anywhere."

Filmed in the canefields of the Louisiana bayou country where Gaines was born and where he set all of his novels, *A Lesson Before Dying* richly evoked the enduring legacy of the Old South, from the nineteenth-century courthouse and the declining but still magnificent plantations to the small former slave cabins that became homes to freed blacks. Significantly, though, the film managed to avoid a common pitfall of modern "period" films, particularly telefilms, about the nation's segregated past—that is, the tendency, usually to the detriment of the story, to caricature Southern whites of the bygone era as simplistically as Hollywood studio films had once stereotyped blacks. But, as Ringle notes, *A Lesson Before Dying* respects both its audience and its subject too much to do that. Just as in Gaines's book, "the whites in the film are not so much evil as flawed humans cast by fate into positions of economic and social power—people stalked by guilt and brittle self-deception and a need to believe they behave humanely within their racially stratified society" (1). And the blacks in the film are just as distinctly drawn and even more complex, thus allowing the film to touch on potentially explosive issues of religion and skin color within the black community without ever stooping to sensationalism or exploitation.

As Grant Wiggins, Don Cheadle captures perfectly the dilemma of a man who is blinded by racial injustice and who lacks ready answers as he tries to help another man shape his remaining days and give meaning to his life.[26] Similarly, Mekhi Phifer's Jefferson is as stunning in his despair as in his transformation. Both men, writes Greg Braxton (*LA Times* 16 May 1999: Calendar 5), "are trapped by the torturous and inhumane legacy of slavery, even though they have learned to survive and adapt in the aftermath."

Yet both continue to be imprisoned in spirit by "the chains of their own self-inflicted fears and limitations." On screen, their opposition—Grant's articulate speech and proud bearing, Jefferson's inarticulateness and shame—is, at least initially, even more dramatic than in the book. But as the two men acknowledge their common roots and their connections to the larger community, their differences quickly dissolve: in Jefferson's cell, they sit alongside each other discussing mutual acquaintances, even sharing an occasional laugh. Together, they give a special resonance to their characters, of whom Gaines said: "I was trying to show two men who had not really lived their lives. Jefferson had not lived because of the environment he was in, and now he was going to die. Grant Wiggins had wanted to escape his environment. He is very limited because of being a black man in the South. Grant can't become a lawyer or a businessman or a doctor. He winds up almost choking to death. One's a condemned man and the other is just running in place" (Braxton 5).

The performances of the women who provide the story's moral center are just as impressive. Cicely Tyson, unforgettable in her earlier role as Miss Jane Pittman, plays Grant's Tante Lou with a marked subtlety and restraint. Her moral authority is absolute; when she tells Grant to visit Jefferson, he can offer no adequate refusal. Lou's utterances usually consist of just a few simple words: "Go round back," she tells her nephew, who wants them to enter the Pichots's home from the front, as white visitors do. Grant finds her request humiliating but complies, because he knows that she is right: to maintain her position of moral superiority to the whites, she must observe the coded symbols of black inferiority, such as entrance from the rear. Even Lou's looks and glances carry great import, particularly since Grant is aware of the expectations that she silently conveys.

As Miss Emma, Irma P. Hall is superb. A bow-legged, slow-moving, sickly old woman, she is undoubtedly the strongest character in the film, as she was in the novel. Like Lou, she has sacrificed all of her life; although childless herself, she has raised someone else's child, caring for Jefferson as if he were her own flesh and blood. Her heart breaks when he is sentenced to death—her sorrow, in fact, is palpable—yet she refuses to give up hope. It is she who goes with Lou and Grant to the home of "Mr. Henri" (Pichot), for whom she was cook and nanny, to ask that Jefferson be allowed unlimited visits from the teacher. When Henri tells her that he will consider her request, she reiterates it politely, making clear that she is aware of his family's debt to her for her years of tireless service. Knowing that she will not be denied, Henri accedes—just as Miss Guidry (Dana Ivey) agrees to intercede with her husband, the sheriff, regarding Emma's subsequent request that Jefferson be permitted to meet guests in the dayroom of the jail rather than in his cell. Emma, like Lou (and like Miss Jane and Octavia before her), is a transcendent symbol of the unselfish black matriarch whose strength and determination kept—and continue to keep—the black family and the black community vital, even in times of greatest adversity. Vivian Babtiste (Lisa Arrindell Anderson), the woman whom Grant loves, shares a similar "kwaly" (quality). It is she who encourages him not simply to go through the motions with Jefferson, as Grant initially intends to do, but to make the best effort he can (a fact that Jefferson recognizes when he writes about Vivian in his diary). With wisdom and quiet grace, she supports Grant and helps him to rediscover what it means to be a man and to impart that same knowledge to Jefferson. But whereas Tante Lou and Miss Emma are Grant's links to his past, Vivian is his link to the future and his means for reconnection to and reconciliation with his community.

Director Joseph Sargent admits that he was concerned about the film's tone: he wanted to tell Gaines's story with emotion but also restraint, to convey the message but not dilute it in sentimentality. He worried especially about the key scenes, such as the one in which Miss Emma visits Jefferson for the first time and brings him food, which he refuses to eat. Since home cooking is the only way she has left to reach out to him, Emma is shattered by his rejection. Yet she persists in sending food with Grant whenever he travels to the jail so that Jefferson is aware that she will not give up on him. When Jefferson is brought to the day room for his final visit with her, Emma again offers him food that she has prepared, and again he refuses. But ultimately he eats, and Emma beams with pride—not because Jefferson has accepted her gesture but because he has understood at last what the food connotes: an unbreakable bond of love. And through his understanding of her gesture, he demonstrates to her that he has changed, that he no longer sees himself as an unfeeling hog but as a deep-feeling man; and she is reassured that he will be able to face death with dignity.

The novel (apart from chapter 29, "Jefferson's Diary," and chapter 30, which relies on the narrative perspectives of several of the townspeople as they describe the impact of Jefferson's execution) is told from Grant's point of view. By contrast, the film portrays events both objectively and chronologically; and it offers, for the most part, a very literal adaptation of the novel. One of the few episodes that director Sargent and screenwriter Ann Peacock excised, however, is the annual visit to Grant's classroom by the white school superintendent, Dr. Joseph Morgan. As Gaines makes clear in the novel, black children must work from mid-April through late October, the period during which plantings and harvests occur on the plantation; consequently, the black school year runs only six months, allowing Morgan to visit only once (in contrast to his twice-yearly inspections of white schools, which run nine months). In the novel, that distinction is subtle but at the same time terribly important: it proves that Southern black education (like the Southern treatment of blacks in general) is separate but *un*equal, a fact reinforced by other details of black life, such as the separate toilet area for blacks in the basement of the courthouse. Moreover, Morgan's inspection is limited largely to an examination of the children's hygiene—clean hands and nails, brushed teeth—and of their ability to recite Bible passages and the Pledge of Allegiance; he seems little concerned with their actual learning. At one point, as Grant watches Morgan peering into his students' mouths, he recalls reading about "slave masters who had done the same when buying new slaves, and I had read of cattlemen doing it when purchasing horses and cattle" [56]. The visit, which concludes with Morgan's turning a deaf ear to Grant's request for better books and more materials and his compliment to Grant on his "excellent crop," not only suggests the racism of white authority but also underscores Grant's doubts about the integrity of his profession.

In the film, Peacock uses a different but very effective means by which to highlight Grant's frustration: the character of Clarence, a small black boy who serves as a kind of foil for both Grant and Jefferson. Clarence, Grant assumes, is unmotivated and tardy; but in fact the boy, although hindered by his circumstances, has great intellectual curiosity. Like Jefferson, who was sent to the fields at the age of six, Clarence works the water wagon, distributing water to the thirsty fieldhands. That responsibility often makes him late (even though he runs to school to avoid punishment for tardiness); and it necessitates that he return to the fields as soon as school is over. Yet more than any of Grant's other students, Clarence wants to learn: fascinated by geography and especially by the globe in the schoolhouse, he imagines the wonderful places like Yugoslavia (which he pronounces "Yugo-slave-ia") to which he might travel if he did not have to labor on the plantation. By recognizing the hope that Clarence finds in his dream of travel and of escape from his difficult and at times abusive situation, Grant begins to understand the possibilities of his role as a teacher who can broaden his students' horizons and inspire their imaginations to take flight. From Clarence, Grant also learns the importance of creating hope for another of his students, Jefferson, who might have achieved his dreams had his circumstances been less limiting and had his fate not been pre-ordained.

Part of that hope comes in the form of the radio that Grant buys for Jefferson. The radio, which is one of the few new things that Jefferson has ever owned, becomes more than just a prized possession or a symbol of friendship; it serves as a crucial link to the world outside his cell, outside the jail, outside Bayonne. Grant creates further connections by bringing his schoolchildren for visits; in this way, Grant makes Jefferson realize that he is part of a community, and he forces the community to acknowledge its connection to Jefferson as well. (In the novel, Gaines establishes an additional connection by Grant's insistence that the community contribute to the actual purchase of the radio.) And indeed, as Karen Carmean notes, "as the community, including Grant, comes to recognize itself in Jefferson, it also begins to respect his value" (130).

Ultimately, Grant gains as much hope as he imparts. In a scene original to the film, Vivian and Grant drink together at Claiborne's Rainbow Club on the night before Jefferson's execution. When Vivian offers a toast "to flight," Grant—whose earlier desire was to flee the plantation as soon as possible—counters with a toast "to life." And in the final scene of the film, as he sits on the schoolhouse steps at the very hour that Jefferson is being executed, he takes consolation in the students around him. He is their best hope, and they in turn are his. (By contrast, in the novel, Grant instructs his students to get on their knees at noon—the hour that the execution is to occur—and to pray until he tells them otherwise; after being informed by the deputy that Jefferson is dead, Grant returns to his desk in tears. It is the first sign of vulnerability that the otherwise disciplined teacher reveals to the children,[27] but it too is a kind of necessary instruction about the value of human life and about his own humanity.) Like the adaptations of *The Autobiography of Miss Jane Pittman*, *The Sky is Gray*, and *A Gathering of Old Men*, the film version of *A Lesson Before Dying* is thus a lesson not so much about dying but about living with dignity and honor, about loving, and about survival and endurance.

Alex Haley

If the film version of Gaines's *Autobiography of Miss Jane Pittman* was hailed as a television landmark, then the television miniseries *Roots: The Triumph of an American Family* was nothing short of a cultural phenomenon. Based on Alex Haley's *Roots: The Saga of an American Family*, a novel that was still unpublished at the time the miniseries went into production, it became the surprise hit of the 1977 television season. In fact, according to Les Brown in his *Encyclopedia of Television*, when the miniseries first aired, it "emptied theaters, filled bars, caused social events to be cancelled and was the talk of the nation" (467).

Blacks, as Leslie Fishbein writes, had gained visibility on television, but their presence (with the notable exception of the CBS telefilm of *The Autobiography of Miss Jane Pittman*) had been confined largely to situation comedies and variety shows rather than drama. "*Roots'* makers," therefore, "had serious reservations about whether the public would accept a historical drama about slavery as seen from the vantage point of the slave" (271). ABC network head and program executive Fred Silverman, however, had tremendous confidence in the quality and the viability of the twelve-hour production; and he scheduled it to be shown in one- and two-hour segments over eight consecutive nights (January 23-30), not over twelve weeks, as originally planned. That decision, which Fishbein says "derived from an odd blend of courage and caution," contributed to the amazing success of *Roots*; and Silverman's innovative use of consecutive programming made television history.[28] Audience response to *Roots* was also unprecedented: Nielsen ratings indicated that a record 130 million Americans—that is, eighty-five percent of all homes with televisions—had seen at least part of the miniseries; and over eighty million viewers watched the final episode. Critics were as enthusiastic as viewers: *Roots* received an astonishing thirty-seven Emmy nominations and ultimately won nine, including the Emmy for outstanding limited series; it was also named program of the year by the Television Critics' Circle Awards.

The book, released in October of 1976 with a hardcover first printing of two hundred thousand copies, was a similar success. An instant hit, it remained on the best-seller list for months, was widely translated, and sold more than a million copies in 1977 alone. That same year, it garnered numerous honors, including a National Book Award and a special Pulitzer Prize.[29] And Alex Haley found himself vaulted to literary celebrity.

A chronicle of Haley's family history, the novel *Roots* had truly been an epic undertaking. Haley recalled that, when he wandered into the National Archives Building in Washington, D.C., to begin investigating his genealogy, he never imagined that the project would consume twelve years of his life and lead him to "50 or more archives, libraries and research repositories on three continents" (Kern-Foxworth 117).[30] Kunta Kinte, a Mandinkan from the small village of Juffure in the Gambia, West Africa, who was captured into slavery (fig. 6.4) but who refused to accept the culture or customs of his white masters, was "the African" about whom Haley's grandmother and his other relatives had so proudly and so often spoken. In *Roots*, Haley tried to re-create the circumstances of Kunta's enslavement and his experiences in the new world, where he persisted in asserting some measure of freedom (even losing part of his foot in punishment for one of his later attempts to escape). After marrying Bell, a cook in the big house of the plantation, Kunta has a child, Kizzy, whom he regales with stories of his rich African heritage.

Kizzy gives birth to a son George, fathered by her master; and, as Kunta had taught her, she passes down to George the sounds and traditions of Africa. "Chicken George" grows up to be a

Figure 6.4. As "the African" Kunta Kinte in the miniseries *Roots*, LeVar Burton painted a vivid portrait of black slavery for American television audiences. *(BBC, 1966)*

renowned gamecock trainer; after marrying Mathilda, he fathers eight children, one of whom, Tom, is eventually sold to a tobacco farmer in North Carolina. Tom marries a half-Indian girl Irene, who in turn bears eight children. One of those children— Cynthia—is taken on a wagon of freed slaves to Henning, Tennessee, where she meets and marries Will Palmer. Their daughter Bertha marries Simon Haley; and the two become parents of *Roots*'s author Alex Haley, who reworks their history and his family's longstanding oral tradition into his own remarkable retelling, a retelling that "penetrated domestic, foreign, societal, cultural, geographical, racial, gender, age, and socioeconomic barriers with a laser effect" and that Paul Zimmerman called "bold in concept and ardent in execution."

Adapting such a mammoth work to film, even over the twelve hours of a television miniseries and at a cost of six million dollars, was no easy task. In *The Inside Story of TV's "Roots,"* producer David Wolper described the process, beginning with the difficulty of finding a way to make the story of a black slave, enacted with a predominantly black cast, acceptable to network executives, to conservative advertisers, and to an overwhelmingly white audience. "Now, if people, most people that is, perceived *Roots* as a black history show, then the ratings for the show would go down, *way* down," recalls Wolper. "If we did the show just for blacks and every black person in America watched it, the ratings would still be disastrous, and more importantly we would not have reached white America, whom we wanted to see this story" (56-57).

It was precisely the concern for the sensitivities of white audiences that led to many of the changes in the adaptation. In order to give white viewers figures with whom they could identify, the filmmakers altered a number of Haley's white characters: some were developed more fully to give them more complex personalities and important positions within the narrative; others were modified or softened. Still others were simply invented, apparently with the full consent of Haley. Captain Davies, the guilt-ridden slaveship officer portrayed by popular actor Ed Asner, for instance, never appeared in the book; in the film, however, he is depicted as a deeply religious man who begins his voyage on the Sabbath because it seems the Christian thing to do. Although Davies is an intelligent and capable sailor, he is relatively unfamiliar with the transportation of slaves as cargo and therefore defers to his more experienced first mate, the inhumane Slater; in this way, he avoids responsibility for the abusive treatment that occurs on his watch. Head writer for the miniseries William Blinn acknowledged that Davies was "certainly not a sympathetic man," and it would have been absurd to depict him as likable. But "it was equally unwise, we thought, to do four hours of television without showing a white person with whom we could identify" (Wolper 48). (Unlike the essentially decent Davies, in the book the various nameless and faceless white men ["toubobs"] that Kunta Kinte encounters on the slave ship *Lord Ligonier* are pale and "horrible, their faces pitted with the holes of disease, . . . some had ugly scars from knives, or a hand, eye, or limb missing" [162]; they shout at their terrified captives, beat them mercilessly with "whips [that] lashed down amid screams of pain" [161], and force them to submit to tortures like kicking, chaining, and branding.)[31]

Television critic Sally Bedell confirms that a major consideration at the network was the injection of white characters into the story. "Our concern," Bedell quotes an ABC executive as saying, "was to put a lot of white people in the promos. Otherwise we felt that the program would be a turnoff." Bedell also cites another network executive, Lou Rudolph, who remarked, "I think we fooled the audience. Because the white stories in most cases were irrelevant. It was a matter of having some white faces, particularly in the opening episodes."[32] The accommodations to white viewers also included a star-studded cast of white actors, many of whom were familiar television personalities: Lorne Greene (*Bonanza*), Chuck Connors (*The Rifleman*), Ralph Waite (*The Waltons*), and Robert Reed (*The Brady Bunch*).[33] ABC's Brandon Stoddard noted: "We made certain to use whites viewers had seen a hundred times so that they would feel comfortable" (Bogle, *Encyclopedia* 340). And indeed "the audience's strong identification of these stars with their positive television personas," according to Lauren R. Tucker and Hemant Shah, "became a cushion between the audience members and the characters portrayed by these stars." White audiences could thus distance themselves psychologically from the negative connotations of the white characters' involvement "in the cruel business of the slave trade" (332). A similar distancing was achieved by the casting of prominent black actors like Cicely Tyson, Leslie Uggams, Ben Vereen, John Amos, and Lou Gossett, Jr. in the major black roles; their star status prevented them from being absorbed by the abused and demeaned characters that they played. Just their familiar presence "reassured the viewers that while something most interesting was to be televised, nothing too serious would happen on either side of the set" and reinforced "titillating cultural innocuousness" (Adams 134). Wolper himself admitted that he deliberately set out to get black actors "who were acceptable and recognizable" to white audiences. "We had to have black actors with whom whites felt comfortable. That was the criterion" (56-57). In an interview with Quincy Troupe, Wolper noted that the reason he was trying to "reach and manipulate" whites was because they "make up 90% of the audience." So a little "mind manipulation" was essential to reduce "white guilt" (173).

The production also resorted to other familiar devices, such as the emphasis on violence, greed, and sex that ensured a wider audience share. For instance, Fanta (Ren Woods), the slave who is Kunta Kinte's first love and whom he first glimpsed in a neighboring village during his manhood training, never appears in the book; she is purely an invention of the filmmakers, who use her to sensationalize his attempt to escape. In episode three of the mini-series, Kunta (LeVar Burton) expends valuable time and energy by running to the next plantation to find her; but Fanta, the companion of his middle passage, has made the adjustment to the white world and become a docile slave who accepts a bed, food, and a roof without asking for anything more. Not only does she loudly rebuff his plea to join him in his flight; her cries alert the slave catchers to Kunta's presence and lead eventually to his anguishing return to slavery. When Kunta's foot is amputated as punishment,[34] she hears his cries of pain yet demonstrates no sorrow or compassion for his plight, which she has exacerbated. Thus Fanta's behavior is both illogical in itself and inconsistent with the slave culture that Haley describes,[35] but her presence adds a note of sexual tension and drama that the filmmakers believed was necessary to enhance the scene.

"There was a lot of nitpicking about the way we changed Alex's book to make the film," Wolper later reflected. "Some say we ruined the book, but Alex thought we translated his book correctly and that the show was terrific." Since "a film is an emotional experience, seen in a moment," Wolper explained, "you don't go back to it to look up details." Film, he concluded, is "not for reference, but for emotional impact" (Wolper 150). Yet, contrary to Wolper's assertion, the loss of some of Haley's "details" correspondingly reduced the emotional impact of the film. In the first episode, for example, the filmmakers narrowed the role of Kunta's parents, who helped him to develop his identity and his heritage in Juffure. Binta, Kunta's mother, was a singularly important character in the book: a woman in a male-oriented society, she was able to maintain a strong presence in her son's life without disrupting the patriarchal order. On the screen, however, she has less depth and serves largely to suggest the tension that arises when Kunta wants to leave home.[36] That home life is also notably altered: in the book, Kunta and his fellow students rose to the rigorous challenges posed by his schoolmaster, who—along with the elders and other villagers—helped to define Kunta's role as a leader. The televised version, however, highlights a more primitive and stereotypical vision of African life, in which the children are at best noble savages seen running or herding goats, never being educated or taught enduring African traditions.[37]

Yet some reworking of Haley's narrative was necessary in order to preserve the novel's essence while containing its excesses. In keeping with Wolper's belief that in drama "you must have characters that last throughout the story" so that an audience gets a chance "to know" and "to spend time" with them and thus to develop an "emotional response to them" (58), the film expanded the roles of characters like the Wrestler. In Haley's version, the Wrestler never left the village; but the film brings him forward and enlarges his role. Accompanying Kunta on the ship, he serves as a kind of side-kick and confidant: Kunta Kinte shares with him thoughts that could not otherwise be easily or credibly expressed on the screen. Wolper also developed the popular Fiddler "to meet certain requirements of the visual story-telling." A combination of three of Haley's characters, the film's Fiddler became a single "continuing character" who meets Kunta at the dock, assists him in his early training, and remains with him through much of his life. "Kunta Kinte," explained Wolper, "had to have somebody to talk to—Kunta Kinte kept saying 'I want to escape, I want to escape'—it had to be some character that you understood. He couldn't say it to himself, and he can't keep blurting it out to ten different characters" (178).[38]

Despite the filmmakers' intention to present the story of a black slave from a black perspective, only one of *Roots*'s episodes—the second hour of episode six, in which Chicken George is sent to England as payment for his owner's debt—was directed by a black director. Gilbert Moses, whose background was in black theater, was brought in only after other more established black directors like Gordon Parks, Sr., Gordon Parks, Jr., and Michael Schultz proved unavailable. Unfortunately, Moses's limited film experience at the time prevented him from putting a personal stamp on his segment of the production. Moses later admitted, "Sure, I had problems. It was the first television show in my life, so I would be lying if I said I didn't have problems. . . . but the fault lay in my own insecurity and hesitancy in attacking the medium as though I owned it" (Wolper 122). More successful was Joe Wilcots, who served as one of the two "DPs" on *Roots* and who had earlier distinguished himself by becoming Hollywood's first black director of photography; Wilcots shot eight of the miniseries' twelve hours. Producer Stan Margulies recalls that Wilcots's presence on the set "mean[t] a lot to the black actors" (Wolper 56).

While some critics called the miniseries "crude mass culture"[39] and charged that it destroyed the ideological perspective of Haley's story by recasting the unique and tragic socio-historical experience of slavery into a classic, almost generic immigrant story that ignored the distinctiveness of Kunta Kinte's struggle, others found much to praise. Russell L. Adams singled out, among many other achievements, the telefilm's success in re-creating the awesome middle passage, outlining in graphic terms the collision of blacks and whites via the institution of chattel slavery during the seedtime of the nation, reopening and vastly popularizing issues concerning African survival, and contrasting the black family's use of ancestral memory as a vehicle of community and identity with white impulses toward acclimation and acculturation.[40] Michael Steward Blayney observed that the miniseries, which captured the era's "growing disillusionment with the efficacy of politics," capitalized on "the emotional letdown of the sixties" by looking backward for its inspiration: "Its sentimental treatment of the family shifted attention away from political concerns toward heroic feats of individual characters" (13-14). And Vernon Jordan, then Executive Director of the National Urban League, called Roots "the single most spectacular educational experience in race relations in America" (qtd. in Wolper 251).

Although Roots succeeded in reversing the story of slavery as told from a Southern perspective in popular films like The Birth of a Nation and Gone With the Wind, the phenomenon of Roots was eventually tainted by the revelation that Haley had been careless with some of his dates and with evidence of his genealogical connection to "the African" and that he had plagiarized many passages from other works. As Linda Williams writes, "many influential readers who enthusiastically embraced Haley reacted subsequently with silence" (Race 236). But the popularity of the miniseries seemed largely undiminished and led to a sequel in 1979.

Roots: The Next Generation (known familiarly as Roots II) offered viewers the rest of the story of Haley's Roots and featured a large and distinguished cast that included James Earl Jones as Haley and Marlon Brando as George Lincoln Rockwell, the leader of the American Nazi party, whom Haley had interviewed years earlier for *Playboy*. Spanning an eighty-five year period, *Roots II* focused on black middle-class life against the backdrop of events like the rise of the Ku Klux Klan, the World Wars, the Great Depression, and race riots. For the shooting, the production re-created an exact life-size replica of the author's childhood home in Henning as well as other sites associated with the Palmer family. But less to Haley's liking "were some of the liberties that the director and writers took with the facts and events that it had taken him so long to get right. In one particularly glaring scene, Haley's grandfather, Will Palmer, held the infant Alex to the starlit sky in the same mysterious ritual with which Kunta Kinte named his daughter Kizzy several generations earlier, giving viewers the mistaken impression that it was grandfather Will, and not his wife Cynthia, who was heir to the Kinte legend" (Shirley 93). Again, though, viewers responded enthusiastically. By the time *Roots II* aired, more than half the people in America had seen a part of the *Roots* saga portrayed on television.

A Christmas special, *Roots: The Gift* (dir. Kevin Hooks), loosely derived from the book, followed in 1988. (Fig. 6.5.) Lou Gossett, Jr. and LeVar Burton reprised their roles as Fiddler and Kunta Kinte in this story of a secret plot to lead fellow slaves to freedom one Christmas Eve via the Underground Railroad; yet, as Leonard Maltin noted, after two epic *Roots* miniseries, the telefilm seemed like an afterthought and a pointless contrivance.

After the publication of *Roots* in 1976, Haley continued to explore and document his family history. A novel *Queen*, based on the life of his paternal grandmother, was scheduled to be released in 1993 to coincide with its three-part, six-hour NBC network television adaptation. Queen's grandfather, Haley had discovered, was a white slave holder and Civil War colonel of Irish descent; the novel and the miniseries, then, were supposed to be Haley's attempt to deal with his white ancestors and to chronicle their lives before immigrating and becoming slave holders in colonial America. The miniseries was already in production—although the novel was still incomplete—when Haley died suddenly of a heart attack in February, 1992. (The novel was later completed by Australian screenwriter David Stevens, who had been working with Haley on the script for the television production.)

In some ways—particularly in its romantic presentation of the love story between Queen's parents, slave owner Colonel James

Figure 6.5. LeVar Burton and Lou Gossett, Jr. reprised their roles as Kunta Kinte and Fiddler in *Roots: The Gift*, one of several sequels to *Roots*. *(1988)*

Jackson, Jr. (Tim Daly) and the black slave girl Easter (Jasmine Guy) to whom he is devoted—*Queen* proved to be just as controversial as *Roots*. But as *New York Times* reviewer Melinda Henneberger (14 Feb. 1993: 2.1) noted, "*Queen* is not *Roots*; its scrappy heroine, black dialect and dialogue owe more to *Gone With the Wind*." Queen (Halle Berry), who calls herself Little Miss In-Between, does indeed find herself caught between two worlds.

Abused by blacks as well as whites, she is raped, abandoned, and run out of town for attempting to pass; yet after finding love with a black ferryman, she amazingly concludes that racial distinctions do not matter—an upbeat, love-conquers-all ending to an over-simplified story of miscegenation.

Although Haley alleged that the defining relationship, between James and Easter, was true, others were skeptical. As Henneberger writes, producer Mark Wolper (whose father David L. Wolper had produced *Roots*) said that the master-slave sexual relationship is one "we've seen a million times, but not as love; it's always shown as rape. It certainly would have been controversial to me if Alex Haley hadn't told me it was true." Scholars like Henry Louis Gates, Jr., reluctant to contradict Haley's account directly, suggested only that consensual, lifelong relationships between slaves and owners were exceedingly rare. Curtis Flowers, a white descendant of Colonel Jackson, noted, "I find it hard to imagine the scenes I read in the script, with the family-like por-trayal of James and Easter and their child." And even Haley's son William admitted that he did not accept his father's version and wondered if viewers would reject it as well (Henneberger 1). Yet despite its glib treatment of interracial relationships and of "high yellow" (light-skinned) blacks, *Queen* contained some powerful moments, such as the one in which a house servant (Ossie Davis) listens as nearby Yankee cannons cause his master's china to shat-ter. With an almost indescribable joy, he picks up several dishes and smashes them himself. But such scenes were lost within the overall falsity of the plot and overshadowed by the unconvincing performances of Berry and Guy in the major roles.

Another of Haley's stories about the continuity and the com-plexity of black life found its way to the screen in *Mama Flora's Family* (1998; dir. Peter Werner), a two-part CBS telefilm written by David Stevens and Carol Schreder and based on a novel begun by Haley and completed by Stevens. Drawn less directly from Haley's own history than *Roots* or *Queen, Mama Flora's Family* was inspired by his maternal relatives; but, like Gaines's novel *The Autobiography of Miss Jane Pittman*, it centered on a fictional hero-ine whose experiences are representative of the struggles of black Americans throughout the course of the twentieth century. Flora, beautifully played by Cicely Tyson (who had starred as the indomitable Miss Jane—and who, by now, was the indisputable first choice of casting directors for strong black matriarchal roles), is born to impoverished sharecropper parents in Mississippi just before the turn of the century; is seduced and exploited by Lincoln Fleming (Shemar F. Moore), the handsome son of the "high-yellow" black family who owns the land that her family farms; gives birth to a son, who is taken from her by the Flemings to raise; marries Booker T. Palmer, a black man who is killed after he steals cotton to provide for his family; and finds herself alone to care for their son Willie (Blair Underwood) and a niece, whom she raises as her daughter. Eventually, Flora is reunited with her son by Fleming. A successful lawyer who is bitter about racist society, Luke (Mario Van Peebles) feels jealous of Willie for always having had the love and support of their mother. In turn, Willie, a decent but frustrated man who is unable to get the respect he covets and who sometimes misdirects his anger toward his own family (especially after the untimely death of his wife Ernestine),[41] resents Luke for having had the advantages of education and fortune that were denied to him. Their mutual resentment is increased after Flora calls upon Luke to defend Willie against a false accusation of robbery and again when Willie needs Luke's help in representing his son Don.

Like Gaines's Miss Jane, Mama Flora eventually engages in an act of quiet defiance: Flora takes a seat at the counter of a segregated diner in Tennessee and requests a cup of coffee, which she ultimately receives. But of greater consequence is her role as the guardian of the family's identity and traditions. Like Miss Jane, who inspires and teaches each succeeding generation of rebels, Flora must restore hope and purpose to her dissolute granddaughter Diana (Queen Latifah), the disheartened mother of a toddler son. By taking Diana back to her home in Stockton, Tennessee, Flora manages to make Diana see her hardships in the larger context of Flora's own stories and experiences. And, in a marvelous reunion scene that serves as the film's climax, Mama Flora gets the miracle that she has prayed for, when her kin reconcile and gather together to celebrate her eightieth birthday. While the film depicts a variety of unsettling and often violent events (many of them told in flashback), such as a retributory mob attack on a black church, it is ultimately—as Thomas Shales notes—"a story of black

Americans who are defined by far more than their relationship to whites. There are, in fact, relatively few white speaking parts in the enormous cast, and though many black characters suffer the outrageous indignities of bigotry, they have many other human problems to deal with as well." Although the film, which simplifies some of the novel's plotlines and offers a neater overall resolution, did not have the impact on the national psyche that either *The Autobiography of Miss Jane Pittman* or Haley's *Roots* had, *Mama Flora's Family* is ultimately a very satisfying adaptation that is full of drama, social resonance, and fine acting (*Washington Post* 8 Nov. 1998: G1).

Before embarking on the researching and the writing of *Roots* and the related projects that focused on his own family's history, Haley had collaborated on an "autobiography" with black leader Malcolm X, whom he had earlier interviewed for *Playboy*. From the beginning of their relationship, Haley had been fascinated by the Black Muslim minister's keen awareness of the powerful role that race played throughout society and particularly in the life of his people. As David Shirley noted, for Malcolm X, "being black was not an obstacle to be overcome but a source of identity and pride" (70).[42] In *The Autobiography of Malcolm X*, Haley attempted to document the ways in which Malcolm Little—born into poverty, victimized by social service agencies after his father was killed and his mother was institutionalized for mental illness, imprisoned for crimes arising from the wild street life he led in Detroit—was able to reclaim his black identity as he transformed himself into Malcolm X (whose full Muslim name was El-Hajj Malik El-Shabazz), a respected figure in the black community before he broke faith with Elijah Muhammad, head of the Black Muslims. The autobiography ends with Malcolm's trip to Mecca, during which he begins to redefine his conception of whites as "devils." As Marilyn Kern-Foxworth notes, the book was well received and became required reading for many college courses. But it also had tremendous popular appeal: "[I]t was not uncommon to find young black men on street corners, in subways, or walking along the streets with copies of the book in their hands" (116). And Malcolm X's assassination in 1965 only enhanced its popularity, since the volume was among the most significant of the materials that he left behind.

It was innovative black filmmaker Spike Lee who assumed the challenge of adapting Malcolm X's story to the screen. Lee's film, which invited controversy even before release, was based largely on Haley's *The Autobiography of Malcolm X* and on a screenplay written almost twenty years earlier by Arnold Perl. (Vincent Canby suggests that a variety of other distinguished names had also worked on the project before Lee came to it: there were adaptations by James Baldwin, David Mamet, Calder Willinghan, David Bradley, and Charles Fuller.) In retelling the vivid testament that Malcolm X had written with Haley and that consolidated his position as a great American folk hero, Lee—according to Canby— "attempted the impossible and almost brought it off." His *Malcolm X*, if "not exactly the equal, or the equivalent, of the book," was nonetheless "an ambitious, tough, seriously considered biographical film that, with honor, eludes easy characterization" (*NYT* 18 Nov. 1992: C19).[43]

But, like *Roots*, not every word of the autobiography was necessarily true. As both producer Marvin Worth (who owned the rights to the book since 1967 and who made his own documentary about Malcolm's life in 1972) and Malcolm's family acknowledged, Malcolm may have embellished or glamorized parts of his life, such as his criminal past (although the film portrays him as rather inept at crime). And scholars like political scientist and Malcolm biographer Bruce Perry suggested evidence of other inaccuracies, some of which Malcolm's family vehemently denied. According to Perry, the fire in the family's Nebraska home, which Malcolm reported had been set by white men, was in fact set by Malcolm's own father after he had been unjustly evicted on racial grounds. (Malcolm's mother and sister-in-law also told Perry that an earlier fire blamed on the Ku Klux Klan and depicted that way in the film never occurred.[44]) Still other errors crept into the book because Malcolm died before it was completed: Haley, for instance, misstated that Malcolm's oldest daughter, Attallah, was named after Attilah the Hun; but Attallah insisted, more plausibly, that her name means "gift of God" in Arabic (Pristin, *LA Times* 15 Nov. 1992: Calendar 6).

In adapting the book to film, Lee took his own small liberties with the invention of characters like Malcolm's friend Shorty (played by Lee), who served to move the plot along and who—like

Baines (Albert Hall), the prison inmate who introduced Malcolm to Islam and later turned against him—was a composite of several real people. Yet Lee remained faithful (perhaps at times a little too reverently so) to the book's spirit, especially to its movement from the exuberance of Malcolm's youth to the austerity of his conversion and the somberness of his assumption of power within the Nation of Islam.[45] (Fig. 6.6.)

Figure 6.6. Denzel Washington stars in *Malcolm X*, Spike Lee's film based on *The Autobiography of Malcolm X*, an "autobiography" collaboratively written by Malcolm X and Alex Haley. *(40 Acres and a Mule Filmworks, 1992)*

Denzel Washington proved to be an actor able to integrate the stridency of Malcolm's militant rhetoric against whites, and especially Jews, with the quiet intellectualism of his growing awareness of the importance of language in his struggle to raise black consciousness. Accordingly, Lee did not insert into the film any ponderous or didactic speeches designed to guide audience response; rather, he allowed Malcolm's own words and actions to stand as the statement of his beliefs. Moreover, the making of the film was in itself a statement for Lee, who subsidized a third of the thirty million dollar production costs with contributions from prominent members of the black community, including Bill Cosby,

Tracy Chapman, Prince, Michael Jordan, Janet Jackson, and Oprah Winfrey (all of whom he photographed wearing *Malcolm X* caps over the final credits). As Lee noted in *By Any Means Necessary: The Trials and Tribulations of the Making of Malcolm X*, "Definitely a historic event, it was a precedent, this had never been done before, and the world needed to be told. We can do for ourselves . . . I don't and I'm not waiting on white folks. If you know only one thing about Malcolm, that should be it" (166).

The film intensified the debate over Malcolm's life and evoked strong and often conflicting emotions about his legacy. Poet and playwright Amiri Baraka (formerly LeRoi Jones) attacked the production, arguing that it dwelt too much on the early Malcolm, then known as Detroit Red, who exploited women sexually, straightened his hair, and ran numbers. Baraka also feared that Lee's movie allowed the man and his message to be trivialized by an indiscriminate popular culture. "Malcolm X has long been popular among black people," he observed. "What we have now is white people exploiting the image for their own gain. Seeing young people wearing the X-baseball caps is one thing, but seeing Malcolm X in Bloomingdale's boutique is another matter" (Felicia R. Lee, *NYT* 1 Nov. 1992: 4.6). By contrast, Haley (to whom the film was dedicated), after seeing some of the roughs, was favorably impressed. "It was pure power. What I saw was heavy, heavy stuff" (Jacqueline Trescott, *Washington Post* 11 Feb. 1992: E1).

Haley once remarked to an interviewer that he had been told his own history so often because "storytelling was our family's television" (Shirley 68). With *Roots* and his other works, he turned the story of his family into everyone's television; and he helped to usher in a new era of black film, especially film adapted from black literature, for both television and theatrical release.

BEYOND *ROOTS*: WILSON, FULLER, AND MOSLEY

Like Haley's family sagas, playwright August Wilson's *The Piano Lesson* (1990) examined one family's slave heritage and the tumultuous battle over how best to honor it. As actor Charles Dutton, who played the lead character in the stage and film versions of the production and for whom the Pulitzer Prize-winning play was originally written, recognized, "August encompassed the entire African American experience and managed to dramatize the same universal legacy that 'Roots' did." Created at the Yale Repertory Theater by Wilson and longtime collaborator Lloyd Richards (who was the first black director on Broadway, with *A Raisin in the Sun*), *The Piano Lesson* went on to Broadway, where it received great acclaim. Adapted to film by Wilson and directed by Richards, it was first telecast in 1995 on CBS as a "Hallmark Hall of Fame" presentation.

A deceptively simple story, *The Piano Lesson* begins in 1936, as Boy Willie (Dutton), accompanied by his friend Lymon (Courtney B. Vance), arrives in Pittsburgh to sell a truckload of watermelons. With that money, and with the profits from the sale of an old family piano, he intends to buy a piece of property in Mississippi that his family had worked as slaves. Wilson suggests that the piano is a sensible and worthwhile trade-off for the self-independence that land-owning would give Boy Willie, who carries his family's history "in every heartbeat" and therefore needs no other reminders of it.

The piano, however, is half-owned by Boy Willie's sister Berniece (Alfre Woodard), a frustrated widow who lives with her young daughter Maretha (Zelda Harris) and her kindly uncle Doaker (Carl Gordon). Although she no longer plays it, Berniece refuses to part with the instrument because of the memories it evokes for her. Berniece, writes Sandra G. Shannon, "carries the weight of several generations of her family on her shoulders, as symbolized by her attempts to preserve and idolize" the old piano that she believes has been anointed by the spirits of her ancestors (160). Preacher Avery, who hopes to marry Berniece, would also like to get possession of the piano and move it into his new church.

In the course of the film, the piano itself becomes a character. Intricately carved with scenes from the lives of the Charles family, the piano had been bought for the wife of a plantation owner named Sutter in exchange for "one and a half slaves" (a slave woman and her young son) and bears their blood. The piano also bears the blood of Berniece and Boy Willie's father, Boy Charles, who stole the piano from the Sutters and was killed on a boxcar as he tried to escape, and of Berniece's husband Crawley, whose violent death Berniece blames on her brother. (Crawley was shot and killed in a wood-hauling venture with Boy Willie and Lymon, which, Berniece contends, was actually a poorly executed robbery. While it was Crawley who fired first in the shoot-out with the sheriff, Berniece convinces herself that Boy Willie was responsible for his death; and for years afterwards she refuses any attempt at reconciliation.) Haunted by these family ghosts, the piano seems to take on a life of its own and starts playing suddenly without anyone touching its keys.[46]

There is also another ghost in the Charles's house: the ghost of the piano's former white owner, Robert Sutter, a direct descendant of the slave-owning James Sutter, who acquired it from a poor white farmer in a barter for Berniece and Boy Willie's great-grandparents. Sutter, who still lays claim to the piano, terrorizes Berniece and Maretha by his intrusions into their home to tinkle the keys from time to time. Exasperated by Sutter's presence, Boy Willie confronts the ghost and banishes him in a climactic exorcism, as Berniece plays and sings a song of appeal to their ancestors (not, as in the original play, a prayer to God—"Oh Lord, I want you to help me"—repeated fourteen times in succession). The shared experience reminds Berniece and Boy Willie of their strong kinship, which transcends all their petty animosities; and afterwards, Boy Willie relinquishes his claim to the piano. He does, however, make Berniece and Maretha promise to keep playing—that is, to keep reconnecting to their shared past. Otherwise, "ain't no telling. Me and Sutter both liable to be back."

The telefilm was, in many ways, a fairly straightforward adaptation of Wilson's play; yet, since the film was an hour shorter than the stage version, Wilson had to make selective cuts. Richard Welsh, the show's executive producer, recalls that "it pained August to shorten scenes and edit long speeches," but he ultimately cut by half the prison work song sequence where the men sit and sing around the kitchen table and lost other "bits of dialogue from the play" (Loynd, *LA Times* 5 Feb. 1995: 5). Writing the screenplay, however, offered Wilson a new creative opportunity: to visualize "as only he could things that are only described on the stage." Such visualization was, for him, a crucial difference between stage and film that had to be respected: on stage, the story is told "with the ear; the other way [film] is telling the story with the eye" (Loynd 5). Accordingly, several scenes of the telefilm were recast with a focus on "the eye." Some of the opening scenes, for instance, were taken outside of the Doaker house, a move that *New York Times* reviewer John J. O'Connor praised as a judicious way of "open[ing] up the play" (*NYT* 3 Feb. 1995: D26).

The acting by the ensemble cast was consistently superb. Best of all was Charles Dutton, the former star of the television show *Roc*, who demonstrated his inventive orchestration of a one-note character. Critics remarked on Dutton's skill in creating a performance of symphonic proportions, full of "growling and thundering, wheedling and threatening, seducing and repelling" (O'Connor 26). And they praised the poignant way in which Wilson collided the historical past with the living present by imbuing a conflict between siblings over a single family heirloom with the haunted music and haunted voices of their own ancestors that is their shared and inescapable heritage.

Whereas *The Piano Lesson* explored family tensions, *A Soldier's Story* (1984) dramatized internal frictions among another group of blacks, GIs stationed in the South during World War II, and revealed "the conflicts which hide behind race, the color bar, and class distinctions, and that impede social and economic progress, as well as the attainment of aspirations" (Githii 108). Based on Charles Fuller's Pulitzer Prize-winning drama *A Soldier's Play* (1981) with a screenplay by Fuller, the film centered on the murder of a black army sergeant, Vernon Waters, on a Louisiana military base in 1944. Suspicion falls immediately on the Klan and then on two white officers who admit seeing Sarge and even beating him shortly before he was killed; but Captain Davenport (Howard E. Rollins, Jr.), a black lawyer from Washington, refuses to accept the obvious solution and keeps investigating the crime. What he discovers is that Waters (Academy Award-nominated supporting actor Adolph Caesar) was the victim of a different kind of racial hatred. Flashbacks reveal that the dead sergeant had been intensely despised by the soldiers in his all-black unit. Mean, contemptuous, and seething with self-loathing, Waters had brutalized his men for reminding him of a racial condition he could not escape (Taylor, "Ironies" 186). Opposed to any expression of black culture, which he perceived as weakness, among his soldiers, Waters had persecuted to death the young and much-liked Private C. J. Riley, a gentle, innocent country boy who enjoyed singing the blues on his guitar and telling folktales.

Like the play, the film portrayed the complex dynamic that exists between the late Waters, whose identity becomes as important as the identity of his killer, and Davenport, a fellow officer who also encounters racial discrimination within the U.S. Army. Although Waters at times seems almost a metaphor for black neoconservatism, he is actually quite a complicated character: militant in his own assimilationism, he criticizes other black troops for acting like Uncle Toms; yet he has a grudging respect for one of his own black soldiers, Melvin Peterson, who stands up to him and fights back. ("The crucial origin of Peterson's characterization," writes Clyde Taylor, "lies in the historical personality of Malcolm X. This affinity was furthered by casting Denzel Washington who, as Peterson, physically resembles Malcolm" and who played Malcolm X in *The Conversation*—and again later in Spike Lee's film—and whose rhetoric at times recalls specific, well-known speeches of Malcolm ["Ironies" 188].) Davenport, on the other hand, is depicted as the conflicted beneficiary of the affirmative action of his day: he is among the first blacks to be given real opportunity for promotion as the Army tentatively moves towards desegregation. White officers find his presence disturbing, and they question whether he can succeed. And indeed, to succeed, he must find a way of accommodating without compromising. Ultimately Davenport discovers that Sarge's murderer was not a white man but one of the black soldiers under his command—Peterson—who blamed Waters for Riley's death and who hated everything that the sergeant represented. As Taylor writes, "by honoring rather than short-circuiting the institutional rules of the game," Davenport shows that "he upholds the institutional rules even against errant members of his own tribe." Such willing adherence to military principles makes Davenport a character who is acceptable to white audiences and with whom they can relate, while Davenport's "heroic endurance of heavy pressures while contesting small gains within racist U.S. institutions" allows black spectators a point of identification as well ("Ironies" 199).[47]

Fuller had written *A Soldier's Play* as an homage to his childhood friend and fellow playwright Larry Neal, who died suddenly in 1981.[48] The play, first introduced off-Broadway by the Negro Ensemble Theater and later adapted as an acclaimed film directed by Norman Jewison, proved to be an overwhelming success. It also, according to Clyde Taylor, offered "the critical advantage of exhibiting an adaption from minority to majority expression" ("Ironies" 185). As Taylor demonstrates, some of the changes made by the movie are entirely predictable: "illusory representation, diversified locales, and the infusion of harmonica/banjo music to signify 'Negro environment.'" Other changes "are more ideological but no less formulaic, like the enlarged roles of Whites, all officers, in the movie. [And] as predictable as a law of physics is the mediation of the original text toward the truisms of the master narrative." In the play, for instance, Peterson's flight and capture are narrated as off-stage action; but the film creates a confrontation in which Davenport slyly forces Peterson to admit his guilt, after which the officer pronounces a kind of righteous judgment: "Who gave you the right to judge? To decide who is *fit* to be a Negro and who is not?" Taylor suggests that this pronouncement is little more than "a put-down of Black militance . . . [and] echoes an obligatory representation" in Hollywood movies ("Ironies" 191).

Another ideological alteration is evident at the conclusion of the film. The play, almost an absurdist parable, had offered a kind of postscript in which Davenport recounts events—including the extermination of Waters's unit in the Ruhr Valley; the military mix-up that listed Waters as killed in action and led to his posthumous decoration as a black war hero; and the "madness of racism" that left "two colored men dead," two other colored men on their way to prison—and comments to Captain Taylor, his white colleague, on the futility of the struggle with military racism. The postscript, however, is eliminated from the film, which ends with the black troops, having earned the privilege of overseas combat, marching through camp on their way to fight on the European front. (Fig. 6.7.) And Davenport, on his way back to Washington, waves down Captain Taylor's jeep to get a lift. Agreeing that they were wrong about each other, Taylor admits he will "have to get used to Negroes with bars on their shoulders"; and Davenport replies, "you can bet your ass on that." As they pass the reviewing stand, both salute. The suggestion is that their shared experience has made them equals—grudging equals, perhaps, but equals nonetheless. Yet such a conclusion is not only too pat; it also is the converse of the play's, in which Davenport confirms that blacks are still very much unequal.

Figure 6.7. Like young Private Riley, whose death he has been sent to investigate, Captain Davenport (Howard E. Rollins, Jr.) is a victim of racial discrimination by the Army in A *Soldier's Story*. *(Columbia Pictures, 1984)*

Vincent Canby wrote of the film that it was an "efficient, solid screen version of the play," a "tightly constructed, socially conscious, entertaining melodrama, unusually well acted and shot with a kind of no-nonsense, self-effacing approach to the material." But, while Davenport's role was well written and Rollins's acting fine, "the character is almost unspeakably noble, so perfect that he appears to be the kind of role-model that Mr. Poitier was more or less compelled to play" in movies like *In the Heat of the Night*, another Jewison film, as well as in *To Sir, with Love* and *Guess Who's Coming to Dinner*. Thus, concludes Canby, "It's a measure of how little real progress there has been in the attitude of American movies toward black culture that *A Soldier's Story*, which could as easily have been made in 1964 as in 1984, seems newsworthy today for its broad popular success" (*NYT* 16 Dec. 1984: 2.21).

A mystery of a different kind—but set in the same era as *A Soldier's Story*—was *Devil in a Blue Dress* (1995), a superb adaptation of the first of Walter Mosley's popular detective novels. Newly unemployed mechanic Ezekiel (Easy) Rawlins, played by

Denzel Washington, needs money to make his house payment. When DeWitt Albright (Tom Sizemore) offers him a quick hundred dollars to locate Daphne Monet (Jennifer Beals), the girlfriend of a local politican who frequents the black areas of Los Angeles ("She likes jazz and pig's feet and dark meat; you know what I mean?"), he accepts. But Rawlins is no detective; in fact, he is a rather ordinary fellow from Houston who, having completed a stint in the Army during the Second World War, has moved to California in search of the American Dream.

Naturally, the job is not as simple as it seems: although Easy locates Daphne, he soon finds himself on the bad side of Albright, the police, and a mayoral candidate named Terell (Maury Chaykin). After being seduced, misled, and beaten up, he also discovers that he has been implicated in two murders, of Daphne's black friend Coretta and of the white photographer who was somehow involved with her. Realizing that, with a white man dead, the police will be "playing for keeps," Easy sends to Houston for his childhood pal, Mouse (Don Cheadle), a gold-toothed psychopath who helps him to unravel the various mysteries. (Fig. 6.8.)

The film, written and directed by Carl Franklin,[49] not only re-created all of the conventions of the hard-boiled detective novel of

Figure 6.8. In *Devil in a Blue Dress*, Easy Rawlins (Denzel Washington) relies on help from his childhood friend, Mouse (Don Cheadle). *(TriStar Pictures, 1995)*

the 1940s—"the pithy, poetic narrator who gets recruited to find a lost siren in big trouble and big shoulder pads; the search that takes him to the mansions of the rich, the low-rent apartments of the working class and the beach; the gangsters who ambush him in his home or office"—it also brilliantly depicted an era when veterans like Rawlins used the GI Bill to move from the South in search of a job at a shipyard or aircraft factory. "It was a time when cars looked like lima beans, everyone wore hats, and a loaf of bread cost 15 cents" (Lynn Smith, *LA Times* 5 Oct. 1995: Calendar 13). But it was also a time when segregation and prejudice were facts of life, and people were understandably afraid of crossing racial boundaries. When Easy goes to meet Daphne at the whites-only Ambassador Hotel, a bellman must sneak him up the back to her room. And when he drives Daphne through a white neighborhood at night, he says in voice-over: "Nervous? Here I was in the middle of a white neighborhood with a white woman next to me. I wasn't nervous. I was stupid."

But, as reviewer Desson Howe (*Washington Post* 29 Sept. 1995: N44) noted, writer-director Carl Franklin refrained from "period-movie attention getting. Although he painstakingly re-created the Central Avenue storefront-nightclub world, he doesn't push it in your face." The characters are also "lightly stylized, rather than loud, flashy and up-tempo; their feet are firmly anchored in realism. And although the racial undertones are an integral part of the story, they're hardly intended to be shocking revelations."

In adapting the novel to film, Franklin tried to retain Easy's Everyman qualities, particularly his integrity and his skin color, which enables him to go where few other detectives could, into the homes and clubs and storefronts of black Los Angeles. At the same time, Franklin streamlined the rather complicated plot. He began by eliminating Easy's World War II history and his early life in Houston, which is alluded to in a brief flashback as well as in Easy's association with his psychopathic buddy. A character killed offstage was also eliminated; and in at least one instance, the identity of a murderer was changed for clarity. Mouse, a key character in the novel, had been excised from an earlier draft of the screenplay; in the final version, his role was not only restored but also enhanced for comedic effect. But the most fundamental changes, as John Clark (*LA Times* 24 Sept. 1995: Book Review 14) suggests, involved character motivations. "Always in film," Clark quotes Franklin as saying, "we're trying to heighten the stakes." The novel's Daphne, for example, is the young mistress of a powerful banker, from whom she steals thirty thousand dollars. But the film's Daphne, the fiancée of millionaire politician Todd Carter (Terry Kinney), is older and more sincere; her actions are prompted not by revenge or greed but by love. When rival candidate Terell threatens to expose her mixed-race heritage and ruin her lover's mayoral ambitions, Carter's family pays her to leave town. Daphne, however, does not leave; instead she tries to help Carter by destroying Terell, in the hope that by preventing Terell from revealing her secret, she can marry Carter and live happily ever after. And, although she succeeds in undermining Terell, she fails to win back Carter, who still loves her but who now can never marry her.

Franklin also managed to dramatize Easy's love of his home and his commitment to his neighborhood, without belaboring them, by fabricating a character (the only wholly fabricated character in the adaptation): a crazy neighbor who wanders up and down Easy's street trying to chop down trees. "Even though he's a nuisance, he's someone who everyone in the neighborhood relates to," said Franklin. "In the end, he's one more loving image of the neighborhood, all building to what Easy was striving for, which was to save his house and his piece of the American Dream" (Clark 14).

For Franklin, in fact, the whole film was about just that—about a black man coming of age, trying to claim his share of the American experience. "Easy has to make a pact with the devil to save his house, which to him represents everything about the opportunities he was fighting for during World War II," said Franklin. "By the end of the story, Easy has learned the world is a very complicated place, where you can't wait for things to come to you. You have to go out and get them" (Goldstein, *LA Times* 24 Sept. 1995: Calendar 3).

Although a number of other black actors, including Danny Glover, Wesley Snipes, and Tim Reid, had expressed interest in the role soon after the novel's publication in 1991, Franklin found the ideal Easy in Denzel Washington (a remarkable actor whose versatility has earned him a record two Academy Awards by a black performer[50]—in 1990, as Best Supporting Actor for *Glory* [1989], and in 2002, as Best Actor for *Training Day* [2001]). To help Washington get a better feel for the role of Easy, Franklin shared period photographs with him; and reportedly he had Washington read various works by Chester Himes, including *Cotton Comes to Harlem* and his bitter autobiography, *The Quality of Hurt*. The two even began calling each other by mordant nicknames (Pain, Slice, and Hurt) that derived from Himes.[51] Washington appreciated the directorial honesty and power that Franklin had demonstrated in his debut film, *One False Move* (1992), and in the splendid HBO miniseries *Laurel Avenue* (1993); and he recognized that much of the success of *Devil* was due to Franklin's personal experiences. "I think," said Washington, "that being black, Carl definitely brings something to the movie that a white director couldn't" (Goldstein 3). Indeed, the film's black voice combined with the strong acting and directing, excellent writing, and vivid re-creation of black life in Los Angeles in the late 1940s to make *Devil in a Blue Dress* not just a stellar movie but also one of the finest film adaptations of black fiction.

NOTES TO CHAPTER 6

1. Murphy's buddy films were tremendous box-office hits that propelled the comedian/actor to the position of top entertainer in America by the mid-1980s. But "notably, his comedy-adventure *The Golden Child* (1986), and his Black-focused comedies *Coming to America* (1987) and *Harlem Nights* (1989), all of which situated Murphy in Third World or Black environments and supported him with non-White or Black casts," according to Ed Guerrero, "came nowhere near the box office earnings of his buddy movies." ("The Black Image in Protective Custody" 241).

2. At least by making Glover the stable family man, the *Lethal Weapon* films gave the biracial buddy formula a slight twist: for a change, it was the black family that represented the American ideal to be preserved.

3. That custody was literal in a film like *48 Hours*, which launched Murphy's film career. He is temporarily paroled to assist a white officer in solving a string of crimes but remains in white custody.

4. Donald Bogle, *TCMMB* 309. Bogle observes that "once again, sympathies are to be extended to the violated good white man. Still, with *A Dry White Season*, Palcy emerged as possibly the first black woman to direct a major studio production and also the first black director to shoot a mainstream production dramatizing the violence of South Africa's apartheid system."

5. Guerrero ("Black Image" 239) notes that this reduction to passivity occurs "when a key event in the insurgence of a sixties, activist, Black, political consciousness is told through the experiences and emotions of two White FBI agents." Similarly, Bogle (*TCMMB* 303) writes that, in *Mississippi Burning*, "Director Parker's decision to focus on the white characters . . . reveals Hollywood's cynicism about black subjects." He concludes that even when a film supposedly focuses on racism, "it was believed best to explore that racism through white eyes."

6. According to Chris Vognar ([Rochester] *Democrat & Chronicle* 31 Jan. 2000: C6), "Hollywood's historical problem has been that it loves these guardian angels [whites instrumental in civil rights causes] so much that it buries harsher elements of such stories beneath layers of self-congratulating platitude."

7. Bogle, *TCMMB* 280. "No two ways about it," Bogle writes, "the part's old-style coon."

8. Among Julie Dash's earlier work was a 1977 short thirteen-minute film shot in black and white in 16 mm., *Diary of an African Nun*, based on an Alice Walker short story. In that film, according to Spencer Moon (83), a young African novice is consumed with a religious and cultural conflict expressed through an interior monologue.

9. Whereas in *The Autobiography of Miss Jane Pittman*, the fictional character Miss Jane recalls over a century of the history she has witnessed, in *Having Our Say* (1999), one of the most unusual and interesting adaptations of contemporary black literature, two real-life centenarian sisters do the same. The telefilm (directed by Lynne Littman and co-produced by Camille Cosby) was based on the Delany sisters' memoir, the best-selling *Having Our Say: The Delany Sisters' First 100 Years* (1991), which was originally adapted to the stage as the hit Broadway play of the same name, and in which Sarah L. "Sadie" Delany (1889-1999) and A. Elizabeth "Bessie" Delany (1891-1995) recounted in alternating chapters the socio-historical events that they have observed over the last century. Like the telefilm of *The Autobiography of Miss Jane Pittman*, *Having Our Say* incorporated the occasionally distracting character of a white newspaper reporter who appears in search of a feature story. In this case, the reporter is Amy Hill Hearth (Amy Madigan), the *New York Times* journalist who first persuaded the Delanys to publish their story. Bessie, the funnier and feistier "baby" sister, balks at sharing their past with an unfamiliar, occasionally forward white woman; but Sadie, the more genteel and disciplined, takes a liking to Hearth and persuades her sister to consent to an interview, which evolves into their biography and an informal history of race in America.

10. Keith E. Byerman, "Afro-American Folklore and the Shape of Contemporary Black Fiction: The Example of Ernest Gaines's *The Autobiography of Miss Jane Pittman*" 50. Karen Carmean, in *Ernest J. Gaines: A Critical Companion*, suggests another way of analyzing the novel's structure: by way of the men in Jane's life. Each of the four parts of the novel ("The War Years," "Reconstruction," "The Plantation," "The Quarters") centers around a man: Ned, Joe, Tee Bob, and Jimmy.

11. In the novel, Jane lives with Joe but never marries him. In the film, they are husband and wife. When the Pittmans decide to leave the Dye plantation, the Colonel insists that Joe reimburse him for money he paid out to the Klan on his behalf. Joe does so by selling all of his belongings. But then Dye demands interest of five dollars. At that point, Jane takes off her gold wedding band and gives it to him as a way of resolving the debt.

12. In *A Gathering of Gaines: The Man and the Writer* (247), Anne K. Simpson writes that "in 1970, when the manuscript of *Miss Jane* was finished, Gaines sent it to *Cosmopolitan* hoping that this magazine would choose to serialize it. Favorably excited, *Cosmopolitan* agreed. But through ensuing correspondence the editors discovered that the book was a novel, not an authentic autobiography, and they reneged. Many other readers of *Miss Jane*, including a representative of *Newsweek* who wanted a photo of Miss Jane, were also reluctant to accept her as a fictitious char-

acter. Gaines recalls an elderly woman's answer when asked who she thought Ernest Gaines was: 'Well, I guess he edited the book for Miss Pittman.'"

13. John Lowe, ed., *Conversations with Ernest Gaines* 101 and Karen Carmean, *Ernest J. Gaines: A Critical Companion* 59.

14. As a "fictional" autobiography, *The Autobiography of Miss Jane Pittman* recalls another novel that also purported to be an autobiography, James Weldon Johnson's *Autobiography of an Ex-Colored Man* (1910).

15. Mark J. Charney, in *Critical Reflections on the Fiction of Ernest J. Gaines* (131), goes so far as to suggest that Korty "indicates none of the subtle changes" in vision and personality. Charney, moreover, is not the only critic to make the analogy to *Birth of a Nation*. John Callahan, in "Image-Making: Tradition and the Two Versions of *The Autobiography of Miss Jane Pittman*" (57), writes that "Despite Gaines's complex, concrete account [of Reconstruction], the screenwriter slips into Jane Pittman's mouth a vision of Reconstruction right out of D. W. Griffith's *Birth of a Nation*."

16. Carmean notes that the man on the horse was "an emblem of the old South" and demonstrates that mounted figures in art and literature usually suggested authority. "The horse helps to distinguish social position," she writes, "and in many instances indicates attainment of some sort of leadership position. Often, the type of horse suggests something essential about the mounted figure, stallions having particularly emblematic significance" (63).

17. In *Blacks in American Films and Television: An Encyclopedia* (316), Bogle writes that "it is her first taste of freedom and the beginning of a movement for a new generation."

18. John Callahan (59) also points out that the black history teacher is "a figure for Gaines himself."

19. Manthia Diawara, in "Black Spectatorship: Problems of Identification and Resistance," published in *Black American Cinema*, argues that "the dominant cinema situates Black characters primarily for the pleasure of White spectators." Even in contemporary Hollywood, he contends, blacks are made less threatening "either by White domestication of Black customs and culture—a process of deracination and isolation—or by stories in which Blacks are depicted playing by the rules of White society and losing" (215). In "The Black Image in Protective Custody: Hollywood's Biracial Buddy Films of the Eighties" (239), an essay in the same volume, Ed Guerrero demonstrates that many popular films such as *Mississippi Burning* appropriate black voices.

20. Although she considered *The Autobiography of Miss Jane Pittman* to be possibly the finest movie ever made for television, Kael ("Cicely Tyson

Goes to the Fountain," *New Yorker* 28 Jan. 1974: 73-75) wrote that she believed it "isn't a great movie, though with more directorial freedom and a better script it might have been." Both Kael and Kanin ("Peripheral Vision," *Atlantic* April 1974: 117-18) are cited on p. 129 by Charney.

21. Olivia truly appreciates Helena's generosity. But Karen Carmean suggests that Olivia's comment to Helena that her kindness will never be forgotten is a statement of fact, "not an expression of gratitude but rather a recognition of action" (144).

22. Gaines noted in an interview that he could not be bothered by the accuracy of every detail. "By the time you make a film of a book, the writer—unless he's a one-book writer—has just about forgotten about the book, and he's gone on to something else. And it's a different medium altogether. You just feel like, OK, let them do what they want to do. You know, take the money and do something well with the money. Buy something, invest the money if it's enough, and if not, just pay off the bills. And you just hope that they'll make a decent film and the people will watch it and those people will go out and buy the book. It's the book that you're much more interested in selling than you are the film" (Gaudet and Wooton 87).

23. To be sure, Candy feels a great affection for her old friend Mathu. At the same time, however, there is a certain paternalism in her actions. As Mary T. Harper notes in "From Sons to Fathers: Ernest Gaines's *A Gathering of Old Men*," "Candy sees these blacks as extensions of the plantation's property and has difficulty understanding that she no longer owns them." Moreover, "she fails to understand the changes that are continually occurring. For example, she becomes irate when the men exclude her from their conference inside Mathu's house, not understanding that their excluding her, their refusal of her paternalistic protection, is another meaningful step towards their manhood" (306).

24. Anne K. Simpson quotes Gaines (in an interview in *The Southwestern Review*) as saying of his book, then in progress: "The narrator of the story is a Cajun. He's going to be the hero of the book. Now you know I'm saying something now that maybe I shouldn't say, because I don't know how the book is going to turn out. I've written now about 20-30 pages of it. But he's the narrator. I'm going to have him say somewhere that he's a Cajun. He is the most *decent* person in the entire book, as of right now. . . . He is going to be the one to tell the story exactly as he saw it . . . a newspaper man from Baton Rouge. He is going to visit both black and white and try to see just what the problem is" (310).

25. "These are changes that are done" in adaptation, Gaines philosophically observed (Gaudet and Wooton 90).

26. "What Don really contributed to in this part was the inner side of the character, the hidden values," said director Joseph Sargent. "He did

not shy away at all from playing the character with all his warts, and it was that much more effective because of it" (James Sterngold, *NYT* 16 May 1999: Arts 21).

27. Grant, in many senses, is a man of measure. That image is reinforced by the Wescott ruler that he always carries in his hand.

28. Leslie Fishbein (272) writes that it was actually producer Stan Margulies who first suggested the concept of a *Roots* week. An ABC executive, however, was fearful of the consequences of a low audience share the first night, so the idea was dropped. A year later, when the production was completed, scheduling decisions arose again. At that time, recalls Margulies, "to his credit Freddie Silverman, who was then head of the network, said, 'We've done something in making this that no one has done before. Let's show it in a way that no one has ever shown television before!" Brandon Stoddard, then executive in charge of ABC's novels for television, viewed Silverman's decision as simultaneously bold and circumspect: "It's certain that Fred's idea of scheduling it in one week was at the time very daring and innovative and theatrical and, I think, added a tremendous amount to the success of *Roots*—there's no question about it." Yet Stoddard noted that, significantly, the network chose to air the show in January rather than the more significant February sweeps week in the event that it did not draw a mass audience (qtd. in Fishbein 272).

29. The Pulitzer Committee, writes David Shirley (97-98), "acknowledged their own problems with some of the historical content of Haley's story by awarding him a 'special' prize, rather than an award in the category of history. Haley's work, the committee insisted at the time, 'did not accommodate itself to the category of history but transcended it.'" Later, in defending the award, the committee stood by its original decision but stated that "regardless of error, the historical essence of [Haley's] book was truthful."

30. According to Shirley (67), Haley first came up with the idea for an article about the history of his maternal grandmother's family while he was still working as a messboy on the USS *Murzin*. His grandmother had been regaling him with stories of the tales of her ancestors since Haley was a child.

31. Wanting to experience in some small part the agonies that Kunta Kinte and other slaves endured in their passage to the new world, Haley reportedly flew to Africa, where he located a freighter called the *African Star* whose route was similar to that of the *Lord Ligonier* two centuries earlier. "Securing a place on board, he made special arrangements with the ship's captain to simulate the conditions he learned were involved in an actual slave crossing. 'After each late evening's dinner,' Haley later described, 'I climbed down successive metal ladders into [the ship's] deep, dark, cold cargo hold. Stripping to my underwear, I lay on my back on a wide rough bare dunnage plank and forced myself to stay there

through all ten nights of the crossing, trying to imagine what did he see, hear, feel, smell, taste—and above all, in knowing Kunta, what things did he think'" (Shirley 85).

32. Bedell et al. are quoted by Donald Bogle in *"Roots," Blacks in American Films and Television: An Encyclopedia* 339-40.

33. Wolper writes, "You have got to remember that the audience, the TV audience, is mostly white, middle-class whites. That's why we picked Ed Asner, Sandy Duncan, Lloyd Bridges, Chuck Connors, Lorne Greene, Cicely Tyson, Ben Vereen, and Leslie Uggams, all known TV actors. This was planned like this, because again here, we were trying to reach the maximum white audience" (148).

34. Kunta is given a choice of punishments: castration (loss of his sexual organs) or amputation of his foot (loss of his organs of flight). As Linda Williams (*Race* 225) writes, "the choice to retain virility . . . makes the *Roots* story of generation possible."

35. "Thus," conclude Tucker and Shah, "in one of the rare instances in which the makers of *TV Roots* added a black character to the story line, they did so in a way that revealed a lack of understanding of and sensitivity for the black culture Haley described" (330-31).

36. While the role of Kunta's mother is deemphasized, the role of his grandmother, Nyo Boto, is highlighted. The producers transformed her character (played by popular writer and personality Maya Angelou) in such a way as to create a "patriarchal gender politics of a West African Moslem village reminiscent of a down-home African-American matriarchy." In the book, Kunta visits Nyo Boto after his manhood training in the hope of reestablishing his close relation to her; but he discovers that he must give up demonstrations of affection for the more distanced respect he commands as a man. In the miniseries, however, as Linda Williams writes (*Race* 244), "Maya Angelou is a commanding presence, towering over Kunta Kinte in a blue turban and sheath." When he rejoices that he has now acquired his own hut, she gives him a tongue-lashing and warns him that "You can grow as tall as a tree and I will *still* be your grandmother!" "Reminding him that Allah is still considered greater than he," concludes Williams, "she insists that he make himself useful to his mother and brother. Women still rule, Angelou's performance seems to say, so don't take all this patriarchal Africanism too seriously."

37. For a fuller discussion of the image of the noble savage and of the "Garden-of-Eden effect in which Africans lived innocently in harmony with nature" that David Wolper tried to create in the scenes that take place in the African village, see Michael Steward Blayney's essay on *"Roots* and the Noble Savage."

38. Lou Gossett, Jr., who played Fiddler, recalled that "when he first accepted the role, everyone felt that Fiddler was a 'Step-n-fetchit' character." But Gossett changed him by "showing the humanity of the man." Fiddler,

he contends, "has a mask for every situation. Nobody ever knows what he is thinking." As Gossett started making subtle changes in the character, "some got scared" and some "weren't sure, altogether, what I was doing with Fiddler. All they knew is that I was playing him differently from what they first imagined him to be. But then they finally trusted what I was doing. . . . Then I realized I had a chance to show somebody who had never been on the screen before" (Wolper 87-88).

39. Attributed by David L. Wolper (253) to William Styron, *The* (Toledo, Ohio) *Blade* (1 March 1977).

40. Russell L. Adams argues that "as television, *Roots* was more powerful than the book for it dealt with images which have floated about the national consciousness for hundreds of years." It evoked "a period which hitherto had to be fully imagined by the reader or animated by the pictorial observer." Of special importance was the way that the miniseries reversed the portrayal of blacks in television's situation comedies, in which black characters "were presented as caricatures of masculinity or snippets of femininity" (132-33).

41. By contrast, in the novel, Ernestine does not die.

42. Leslie Fiedler commented on the connection: "Even as the living Haley ghostwrote the *Autobiography*, Malcolm X, from beyond the grave, ghostwrote what is most authentic and moving in *Roots*—the story of Kunta Kinte" (cited in Williams, *Race* 235).

43. "One of the most gratifying effects of Spike Lee's film 'Malcolm X' is that its success has prompted the restoration of Malcolm's autobiography to the best-seller lists," wrote Henry Louis Gates, Jr. (*NYT* 21 Feb. 1993: 7.11). "The country is *reading* the 1965 book once again, as avidly, it seems, as it is seeing Mr. Lee's movie."

44. As Terry Pristin (*LA Times* 15 Nov. 1992: Calendar 6) points out, "convinced that Perry was bent on demolishing Malcolm's reputation, his widow, Betty, and daughters declined to cooperate with him. Attallah Shabazz, in a telephone interview, characterized the book as 'slanderous.'" And producer Marvin Worth, who had not read the book, pronounced the findings to be "utter nonsense."

45. The film, as Vincent Canby (*NYT* 18 Nov. 1992: C19) writes, effectively portrays this progression. "It is full of color and exuberance as it tells of life on the streets in Boston and New York, but it grows increasingly austere when Malcolm is arrested for theft and sent to prison." By the time Malcolm is a Muslim minister, the movie becomes "well-mannered and somber, like Malcolm's dark suits and narrow ties."

46. According to Michael Morales (106), by functioning as a mnemonic device for the transmission of oral history and as a sacred ancestral altar, the piano also serves to elucidate "Wilson's framing of black American history as an active relation (kinship bond) between the living and the dead."

47. Manthia Diawara (217) offers a different argument with respect to the gratification (or, more specifically, the lack of gratification) of the black spectator. Diawara writes that "the surprise twist at the end of the narrative, which sacrifices one more Black man in order to show that justice exists, fails to satisfy the expectation, on the part of the Black spectator, to find the Klan or a White soldier responsible for the crime. The plot of *Soldier's Story*, with its predominantly Black cast, suggests a liberal reading of race in the American South; but by implicitly transferring villainy from the Klan to the Blacks, it denies the pleasure of resolution to the Afro-American spectator."

48. *A Soldier's Story* was also, as Clyde Taylor demonstrates in "The Ironies of Palace-Subaltern Discourse," a contemporary recasting of Melville's "Billy Budd," another classic political drama enacted in a military setting and in a time of war. In Fuller's version, Waters corresponds to the morally depraved Claggart, master-at-arms of the man-of-war *Bellipotent*, who badgers Billy mercilessly; Davenport is the humane Captain Vere, who must arbitrate the two extremes; and the childlike C. J. and his protector Peterson are merged in the single character of Billy Budd.

49. Mosley had written an early draft of the script when the movie was in development at another studio, but the screenplay for the film starring Denzel Washington was written by Carl Franklin. According to Sean Mitchell (*LA Times* 26 June 1994: Calendar 6), "This suits the author just fine. 'I'm not a cinematic thinker,' Mosley confides. Nevertheless, TriStar has retained him as an associate producer. 'Basically Carl calls me up and asks questions. He had to change the name of a character the other day and called me up and we talked about it.'"

50. Sidney Poitier, the first male black actor to win any Academy Award and the first black to win the Best Actor Academy Award, received his first Oscar for his performance in *Lilies of the Field* (1963). At the 2002 Academy Awards ceremony (during which Denzel Washington was recognized as Best Actor for his performance in *Training Day* [2001], an award that distinguished him as only the second black performer to win a Best Actor Oscar), Poitier received his second Oscar, an honorary award for lifetime achievement. Since Poitier's most recent Oscar is an honorary award, to date Washington remains the only black actor to win two Oscars for specific performances.

51. Patrick Goldstein (*LA Times* 24 Sept. 1995: Calendar 3) writes that Himes's accounts of his troubles gave the director and the actor a black-comic bond—in both senses of the word. "We had this ongoing Chester Himes thing where we'd try to find new ways to hurt each other's feelings," recalls Washington. "I'd say to Carl, 'Brother, I saw some of your work yesterday and it was terrible!' And then he'd say to me, 'That's just what I was thinking about your work, brother!'"

Chapter 7

History to Herstory:
New Voices for a New Century

> The onliest time I be happy seem like was when I was in
> the picture show. Everytime I got, I went. I'd go early,
> before the show started. They'd cut off the lights, and
> everything be black. Then the screen would light up, and
> I'd move right on in them pictures. White men taking
> such good care of they women, and they all dressed up
> in big clean houses with the bathtubs right in the same
> room with the toilet. Them pictures give me lots of pleas-
> ure, but it made coming home hard.
> —*Toni Morrison, The Bluest Eye*

It was not only literature by black male writers that more richly
portrayed the black cultural experience, helped popularize black
American history, and served as the basis for important adapted
films. Fiction by black women offered some innovative perspectives and strong new voices as well.

VOICES OF CHILDHOOD: CHILDRESS, ANGELOU, AND TAYLOR

Alice Childress's *A Hero Ain't Nothin' But A Sandwich*, first published in 1973, was a revolutionary novel for young adults. In language that was familiar and colloquial, it told the story of a young
boy's addiction to heroin without offering easy solutions or glamorizing his plight. Thirteen-year-old Benjie Johnson lives in
Harlem, in a neighborhood that "ain't no place to be a chile in
peace," a place where "somebody gonna cop your money and
might knock you down cause you walkin with short bread and
didn't even make their while to stop and frisk you over. Ain't no
lectit lightbulb in my hallway for two three floors and we livin up

next to the top floor. You best get over bein seven or eight, right soon, cause seven and eight is too big for relatives to be holdin your hand like when you was three, four, and five. No, Jack, you on your own" (9). And Benjie certainly feels that he is on his own, especially since his father walked out on the family four years earlier. His mother Rose, nicknamed "Sweets," is busy with a new man in her life, the decent and hardworking Butler Craig, who tries to act as a surrogate father. But Benjie's feelings about Butler are ambivalent: he admires Butler's "cool" self-assurance but resents his intrusiveness, particularly Butler's suggestion that Benjie is an addict. Benjie's household also includes his widowed grandmother, Mrs. Ransom Bell, a deeply religious woman whose recent mugging makes her reluctant to leave the apartment.

Benjie's addiction begins with a simple act of bravado, when he shoots up on a dare from a young man named Tiger. Soon he is "skin-poppin" regularly, stealing cash from his grandmother to support his habit, and isolating himself from his old friends like Jimmy-Lee Powell, who are not part of his new drug culture. After two of his teachers, the black nationalist Nigeria Greene and the conservative white Bernard Cohen, report him to the principal, Benjie is forced into a hospital detoxification program. But once home, he returns to his old ways and brings new sorrows to the family: his grandmother, fearful of his temper, begins hiding herself behind the locked door of her bedroom; Butler, exasperated that Benjie has stolen his best suit and overcoat to buy more drugs, leaves the apartment and takes a room with Miss Emma, who lives a few floors below; and his mother visits a fortuneteller to solicit remedies like "Indigo Blue" with which to "wash off my hard luck" (96). Only after he comes close to dying on the roof of their building—a death he seems to invite ("Let me be dead!" [110]) but from which he is rescued by Butler—does Benjie start reaching out, literally as well as figuratively, for help, and reporting to his social worker. Yet while Butler dedicates himself to helping his "son" recover, Benjie's resolve is less certain. The novel ends with his promise to reform—a promise that he has made and broken many times over. Nevertheless, the reader cannot help but share the optimism of Butler, who stands on the street corner waiting for Benjie to show up for rehab and saying to himself, "Come on, Benjie, I believe in you."

The novel, told in a series of first-person narratives, including several by Benjie and others by members of his family, his friends, and his teachers, conveyed the hopelessness of the young boy's life in Harlem and the inadequacy of his real-life role models. Disappointed by everyone in whom he has placed his trust, Benjie declares that "a hero ain't nothin' but a sandwich." Yet Rose, despite her criticisms of her son, has an unshakeable love for him; and Butler, who loves Rose and wants to do right by Benjie, determines to become the hero and the father that the boy has been seeking. Unlike the social worker, who suggests that Benjie needs to identify with "'colored' movie stars and great sports figures," Butler knows that the real heroes are not celebrities but people like himself, who "gotta get up to face the world every damn mornin with a clear head and a heavy heart" and who "support three adults, one chile, and the United States government on my salary . . . and can't claim any of em for tax exemptions" (126).

The film version of *A Hero Ain't Nothin' But A Sandwich* (New World Pictures/distributed by Paramount, 1977; dir. Ralph Nelson), starring Cicely Tyson as Rose, Paul Winfield as Butler, and Larry B. Scott as Benjie, was based on a screenplay by Alice Childress; but it lacked some of the gritty realism of the novel. Instead of a cramped tenement in New York's Harlem, the Johnsons live in a comfortable house in Los Angeles, with lawn chairs and an arbor in the backyard and a peach tree and a picnic table in the front. Although the empty lot adjacent to the house is supposed to suggest urban blight, the ocean is within walking distance. As Elbert R. Hill notes, "the effect of moving Benjie from what is clearly an ugly, threatening environment, as portrayed in the novel, to the movie's world of beautifully landscaped parks, palm trees, and beachfront, is to mute the dreariness that characterizes Benjie's environment in the book" (238). Similarly, Benjie's mother is described by Childress as a "plump lady," not really "fat" or "tall or short" and "not so pretty as to make you feel shame" (103); in the film, however, she is beautiful, slim, stylish, well-coiffed and impeccably made-up—Hollywood's version of the hip young black single parent. (In fact, after bathing Benjie in the "Indigo Blue" prescribed by fortuneteller Mme. Snowson, Rose realizes the foolishness of her actions and falls, laughing, into the tub with him.) And while the facility to which Benjie is sent in the novel is the spartan Harlem Hospital, in the film he is admitted for detoxification to the suburban Queen of Angels, where after going through withdrawal (effectively depicted in a series of still black-and-white images), he engages in a lengthy outdoor California-style encounter group with a panel of former addicts.

For expediency, the screenplay combined some of the characters in the novel (the two pushers Tiger and Walter merge into a single drug dealer played by Kevin Hooks, and Carwell [Erin Blunt] becomes the composite of the novel's Kevin and Cantwell) and eliminated other characters (Miss Emma Dudley, from whom Butler leases a room after he leaves Rose's apartment, and the school principal, who must confront Benjie and his parents about his drug use). And some episodes were enhanced for dramatic effect: for instance, when Benjie steals from Butler in order to raise money for drugs, he does not take his clothing but instead his carat-and-a-half heirloom diamond and sapphire cufflinks; and before Benjie is rescued by Butler on the rooftop, he dangles not from the edge of an air shaft but from a fire escape ladder that has snapped off the side of the building above a busy highway.

Of greater consequence, though, was the film's shift in point of view. In the novel, the characters spoke in the first person as they described events related to Benjie's situation. That device allowed them to reveal as much about themselves—about their own hopes, fears, and frustrations—as about Benjie. Nigeria Greene, for instance, the teacher whom Benjie idolizes, expresses disappointment that his students fail to heed his lessons about black nationalism and that they allow themselves to become "slave bodies" (100) to acid and other drugs. Bernard Cohen, another teacher, enumerates the reasons for his tense relationship with Nigeria, who tries to make him out to be "whitey, . . . the goat" (34), and who refuses to see that Cohen is looking out for his students' welfare—albeit in a different and less radical way than Nigeria. Benjie's one-time friend Jimmy-Lee, who used to smoke marijuana before discovering that there was "somethin else for a dollar to do" (23), wishes there was "someplace to go without bein in trouble" (85), someplace other than a hospital or drug center to help Benjie get straight. But the film, which is unable to convey the interior narratives of these characters, correspondingly reduces their roles. Nigeria (Glynn Turman) and Bernard (David Groh) have difficulty finding common ground, while Jimmy-Lee (transformed into Nigeria's son) seems entirely disconnected from Benjie's reality.

Yet while it neglects to explain as fully as Childress did in the novel the sense of abandonment and loneliness that causes Benjie to turn to drugs in the first place, the film sensitively develops the characters of Benjie and Butler and evokes the crucial bond between them. (Fig. 7.1.) Butler, whose on-screen role is in every way equal to Benjie's, becomes the absent father that the boy desperately seeks; and it is Butler's confidence that helps Benjie to

Figure 7.1. Surrogate father Butler Craig (Paul Winfield), with Benjie's mother Rose (Cicely Tyson), tries to teach Benjie (Larry B. Scott) the true meaning of the word "hero" in *A Hero Ain't Nothin' But a Sandwich. (New World Pictures, 1977)*

rehabilitate himself (as demonstrated in the ending of the film, in which Butler waits at the Rehab Center and Benjie actually appears). In fact, as Elbert R. Hill writes, "from the very beginning of the film Butler seems so clearly concerned about Benjie that it is difficult for the viewer to understand why the boy holds him at arm's length for so long" (240). Despite its compromises and its understandable cinematic simplifications, the film version of *A Hero Ain't Nothin' But A Sandwich* tells a compelling story of black adolescent turmoil and of a boy's coming-of-age in a modern society that is hostile to him.

Childhood is also the subject of *I Know Why the Caged Bird Sings* (1970), the first of four autobiographical volumes in which Maya Angelou described the heart-wrenching spiritual and literary odyssey that began when she was quite young. "If growing up is painful for the Southern Black girl," she recalls, "being aware of her displacement is the rust on the razor that threatens the throat" (3). When she was three and her beloved brother Bailey was four, their parents divorced and the children were sent to live with their maternal grandmother, "Momma" Annie Henderson, and their disabled Uncle Willie, who kept a country store in Stamps, Arkansas. The town was much like any other small town in the deep South, the same, Angelou writes, as "Chitlin' Switch, Georgia; Hang 'Em High, Alabama; Don't Let the Sun Set on You Here, Nigger, Mississippi" (40). By night, when Klan members patrolled the area, the family would hide Uncle Willie in the store's fruit and vegetable bins, where he remained entombed until morning; by day, Momma would force herself to smile and pray aloud as the children of her poor white trash tenants mocked her to her face.

Maya deplores the mistreatment and resents her own blackness; she even imagines waking up white and blonde-haired from her "black ugly dream." The spirit of the black community around her, however, instills a certain pride in her; and Momma's strong example shows her how to triumph over circumstance. For instance, when many local families, black and white, are forced to seek relief during the Depression, Momma keeps the store going by clever management: she begins accepting government provisions in trade. And when the local dentist refuses to treat Maya's toothache, saying that he would rather stick his hand "in a dog's mouth than in a nigger's," Momma calls in the interest on his old debt to her; and with the cash from him in hand, they head to another dentist in Texarkana. (The interest payment is a point of honor. Momma insists on it only because the dentist, by not treating Maya, seems to have forgotten his moral debt.)

When Maya is eight, her father Bailey Sr. comes to Stamps for a visit, after which he takes the children away with him. Maya assumes they are heading to California, where Bailey Sr. lives; instead, he delivers them to St. Louis, to their beautiful but irresponsible mother, Vivian Baxter, and to her politically-connected family. The visit proves utterly traumatic: Maya is raped by her mother's boyfriend, Mr. Freeman, who is tried, released, but soon found kicked to death by Vivian's brothers. Assuming responsibility for Freeman's death because she did not know how to discourage his advances, Maya responds to the experience by not talking. Her mutism and her "grim presence" become too difficult for Vivian to handle, and the children are sent back to Stamps. It is years before Maya's voice returns, restored by the sounds of the great literature to which she has been introduced by Miss Flowers, one of the town's few black gentlewomen.

After Maya graduates from eighth grade, her mother moves the children again, this time to San Francisco, where she has remarried and is working as a gambler and the owner of a boarding house. Maya continues both her formal education by concurrently attending high school and taking dance and drama lessons at the California Labor School and her informal education by observing her sophisticated mother, her high-rolling stepfather, and the parade of black underworld characters who pass through their boarding house. Her innocence is further violated during a visit one summer with her father in southern California, where—after an argument with his girlfriend—Maya ends up living among homeless children in a junkyard. Upon her return to San Francisco, Maya, though still in school, decides to get a job; and, with her usual persistence, she manages to become San Francisco's first black streetcar conductor. As anxious to assert her womanhood as she was her maturity, Maya soon becomes pregnant and delivers her son just a month after her high school graduation. The volume ends with Maya's fears and hopes for her own child and her mother's assurances that "if you're for the right thing, then you do it without thinking" (246).

The film, released in 1979 by Tomorrow Entertainment, was directed by Fielder Cook from a teleplay by Leonora Thuna and Maya Angelou. Rather than depicting the many small stories that comprised the rich fabric of Angelou's memoir, it focused on certain representative events, which were highlighted for visual and dramatic effect. In one scene, for example, after the Sheriff drives up to the general store to warn Momma that she should expect a visit from the "boys" that night in retaliation for the fact that some "crazy nigger messed with a white lady," not only does the family hide Willie in the traditional place; Momma then sits at the window, waiting and watching, as the Klansmen ride up in their automobiles, fire some rifle shots, and set aflame a large cross on a hill adjacent to their property. The cross is still smoldering when Willie walks out onto the porch the following morning. (By contrast, in the book the children empty out the bin and, with a "tedious and fearful slowness," lay their uncle out flat and cover him "with potatoes and onions, layer upon layer, like a casserole. Grandmother knelt praying in the darkened Store." And although "the 'boys' didn't ride into our yard that evening and insist that Momma open the Store," Maya writes that "even after the slow drag of years, I remember the sense of fear which filled my mouth with hot, dry air and made my body light" [14-15].) Similarly, during the graduation ceremony in the film, local white politician Mr. Donleavy articulates his proposal to improve black education by helping students to become better "cooks and housekeepers" (or, in the case of the very fortunate few, better basketball players or athletes). In her valedictory address, Maya rebuts his racism by thanking Mr. Donleavy for the chance he offers blacks: "but I don't think I'm going to take it." Instead, she announces that she intends to emulate her own heroes, including her teachers and her grandmother, who taught her to sing. "In order to lift your voice," says Maya, "you have to lift your head; when you lift your head, you are looking at heaven." Maya then leads the audience in a spirited rendition of the Negro National Anthem, a song that the school board had specifically banned at assemblies. Her defiant assertion of black pride is a rousing conclusion—to the ceremony and to the film—and confirms that Maya, having found her voice, will use it to speak out in the cause of civil rights. (In the book, however, it is her friend Henry Reed, not Maya, who is the class valedictorian; he recites not an extemporaneous rebuttal to Donleavy but a memorized address, "To Be or Not To Be." And the Negro National Anthem is part of the scheduled program.) By ending with Maya leading the audience in song as scenes from her earlier life flash on screen, the film eliminates chapters 25 through 36 of the book—the portions in which Maya returns with Bailey to live with their mother in California, visits her father and his new girlfriend, continues her education in San Francisco, and ultimately gives birth to a son—but creates a fine symmetry. A silent and silenced child, the film's Maya emerges as a young adult who has found her voice.

Roll of Thunder, Hear My Cry, a 1978 telefilm directed by Jack Smight from a teleplay by Arthur Heinemann and based on the award-winning novels *Roll of Thunder, Hear My Cry* (1977) and *Song of the Trees* (1975) by Mildred D. Taylor,[1] tells a similar though less compelling story of black family kinship. Cassie Logan (Lark Ruffin) is an eleven-year-old black girl growing up in Mississippi during the Depression. Her parents are hardworking decent people: mother Mary (Janet MacLachlan) is a teacher in the Negro school that Cassie and her brothers attend; father David (Robert Christian) works on the railroad to earn the money to pay the mortgage on their land, which was originally part of the Granger plantation. But Mr. Granger (Ray Poole), the head of the local bank and owner of most of the businesses in the area, is pressuring the Logans to sell their land back to him. They appreciate the consequences of not complying with Granger's demands: the Berrys, a neighboring black family, have already been burned out of their home and Mr. Berry killed; and David himself has been visited by a group of white nightriders, who shot him and ran a mule-driven wagon across his leg to incapacitate him and teach him a lasting lesson. When Granger calls in the note for the balance of the mortgage, the Logans worry that they will be forced to lose not only their land but also the money they have invested in it. But David's brother, Uncle Hammer (Morgan Freeman), sells his new car and other belongings (the particulars are unclear) to raise the cash; and—to Granger's surprise—the Logans are able to claim clear title to their property.

Cassie experiences difficulties of her own. After accidentally bumping into white Lillian Jean Wallace on the sidewalk, she is pushed into the street by the girl's racist father Kaleb Wallace, who forces Cassie to apologize properly to his daughter. Grandmother "Big Ma" empathizes and tries to ameliorate Cassie's sense of humiliation; but seeing the growing crowd and knowing the trouble that could arise, Big Ma forces her to accede to Kaleb's request. (In the novel, Cassie, who had already apologized once, recalls "a painful tear" sliding down her cheek and her trembling lips: "'I'm sorry. . . M-Miz. . . Lillian Jean.' When the words had been spoken, I turned and fled crying into the back of the wagon. No day in all my life had ever been as cruel as this one" [*Roll of Thunder* 87].) The incident makes Cassie even more conscious of the discrimination that Southern blacks face.

Yet, while the film captures the closeness of the Logan family, it is predictable in virtually all other aspects. Most characters are depicted as extremes, either wholly evil or good: Kaleb Wallace is an irredeemable bigot whose constant scowl suggests his villainy. By contrast, the kindly attorney Mr. Jamison is ubiquitous: a veritable white *deus ex machina*, he appears at the first sign of trouble to defend the Logans and other blacks; he even uses his own money to establish credit in their names.

The portrait of racial relations is equally naïve. Perhaps as an accommodation to younger viewers who comprised its target audience, the film portrays little of the violence that surely would have been perpetrated against those blacks like the Logans who defied Southern custom by organizing a boycott of white-owned stores. Even the depiction of Depression hardships is surprisingly mild: nothing seems in short supply; the Logan family is relatively well dressed; and Hammer has enough cash to afford a fancy car—fancier, even, than Mr. Granger's. Both as cinema and as popular history, therefore, *Roll of Thunder, Hear My Cry* is little more than a footnote to other more artistic and authentic telefilms with racial themes and is notable largely for its enthusiastic celebration of black family spirit.

THE COLOR PURPLE

Far more significant and far more controversial was Steven Spielberg's adaptation of Alice Walker's Pulitzer Prize-winning novel *The Color Purple* (1982).[2] Protests mounted even as the film was in production; and pickets and demonstrations in many major cities greeted the film's release in December, 1985. The adaptation itself was roundly criticized for its oversimplifications, particularly the racial clichés and Hollywood stereotypes that it perpetuated, and denounced for its unrealistic representation of the black experience. John Simon, who called the film an "infantile abomination from a perpetually young filmmaker," noted that it evidenced a bitter hostility toward black males; all of the black characters, he observed, were constructed to resemble animals (*National Review* 14 Feb. 1986: 56). Spike Lee agreed that the men in the film were depicted as "one-dimensional animals" and implied that nothing less could be expected from a writer like Walker who had problems with black men. After all, noted Lee, "the quickest way for a Black playwright, novelist or poet to get published is to say that Black men are shit."[3] Manthia Diawara concurred that the black male characterized on screen in *The Color Purple* was quintessentially evil while the black female was quintessentially good and suggested that such a simplistic portrayal "prevent[ed] the film from dealing with such complex issues as Black female and Black male relationships, White racism, sex and religion that Alice Walker's original text addressed."[4] David Ansen merely dubbed *The Color Purple* "the first Disney film about incest" (*Newsweek* 30 Dec. 1985: 59).

Oprah Winfrey, making her screen debut, explained that the movie was "not trying to represent the history of black people in this country any more than *The Godfather* was trying to represent the history of Italian-Americans. In this case, it's one woman's story." And indeed many of the black women in the audience identified with that story; according to Cheryl B. Butler, "black female spectators" recognized themselves "in the sympathetic black female upon the screen" and consequently accepted both that self and "the film's discourse" (64-65). Yet even some of the feminists who had hailed Walker's "womanist" portrait of a black woman's journey to empowerment remarked on the film's melodramatic reduction of the novel and on "Spielberg's elimination of Walker's formal innovations" (Shattuc 149).

Alice Walker's novel was certainly a complex and sophisticated work. As the novel opens, the heroine Celie is a frightened girl of fourteen, whose father is using her as a sexual surrogate for her ailing mother. "You better not tell anybody but God," Pa warns her. "It'd kill your mammy" (11). And so Celie begins writing letters to God in which she confides the secrets of her abuse and her other sorrows. "Written as she would have spoken," notes Joan Digby, "the letters tell her life-story with an ingenuous simplicity that the reader responds to as the poetic voice of betrayed innocence." (158). Twice impregnated by her father (and left sterile after the second birth), Celie is helpless to prevent him from selling her children or marrying her off to a local farmer, a widower who had wanted to wed her younger and more attractive sister Nettie but who settles for the ugly, "spoiled" Celie instead—after Pa throws in a cow as part of the bargain. Celie's new life, however, is no improvement over the old: her husband, whom she calls "Mr. ___," demeans and abuses her as much as her father had; and Mr. ___'s cruel, undisciplined children treat her with a similar contempt. "I spend my wedding day running from the oldest boy," Celie writes to God. "He pick up a rock and laid my head open" (21).

When Pa begins making sexual advances towards her, Nettie runs to Celie for protection; and, for a while, Celie is able to shield her from harm. But when Mr. ___ demonstrates that "he still like her" (25) best and Nettie rejects him, Celie is powerless to keep her husband from ordering her sister out of his home. "Write," Celie makes Nettie promise; and Nettie replies, "Nothing but death can keep me from it." But "she never write" (26)—or so Celie thinks. In fact, Nettie writes, and keeps writing, for almost thirty years. (Her letters comprise much of the second half of the book.) The bitter and vengeful Mr. ___ hides the letters, and a solitary Celie is left to ponder her beloved sister's fate.

Written in a more formal, tutored English that contrasts with Celie's simple dialect, Nettie's correspondence offers a vivid portrait of her life in Africa, where she begins to discover her racial past. But, ironically, part of Nettie's role as a Western missionary is to bring Christianity to the Olinka natives—that is, to alienate them from their own heritage. At the same time, as Wendy Steiner writes, capitalist road-builders cutting through the jungle literally destroy the Olinka villages. The roofleaf plant that was the basis of the Olinkas's economic and religious life no longer grows, and "the builders mow down Nettie's round hut, the symbol of her wholeness, femininity, and identity" (511). In what some critics have called the weakest part of the novel, Walker thus attempts to parallel the greed of the patriarchal colonialists with the oppression that Celie experiences at the hands of the men in her life, from Pa and Mr. ___ to God himself.[5]

Nettie's letters also contain several of the novel's important subplots. They reveal how, thanks to Celie, Nettie comes to live with Corinne and Samuel, the childless missionary couple who take her with them to Africa; how Corinne and Samuel adopt Celie's children Olivia and Adam as their own; how Adam grows up alongside and eventually weds Olivia's African friend Tashi; and how Samuel and Nettie, after Corinne's death, fall in love and marry. Although reconciled to Nettie before she dies, Corinne had harbored a great jealousy of Nettie; noting the resemblance to

Adam and Olivia, she suspected Nettie of being Samuel's lover and the children's real mother. After Corinne's death, Samuel confesses a secret of his own to Nettie: that "Pa," the man she and Celie had assumed was their father, was in fact their stepfather. (Their real father had been lynched. And, as Celie later discovers, he had willed to his daughters the property that Mr. ___ used as his own, along with a small dry-goods store in town—both of

Figure 7.2. In *The Color Purple*, Shug Avery (Margaret Avery) befriends Celie (Whoopi Goldberg) and helps her recover the letters that Nettie has been writing—but that Mr.___ has kept hidden—for years. *(Warner Brothers, 1985)*

which Celie eventually reclaims as their inheritance.) Meanwhile, Olivia and Adam, having learned the identity of their birthmother, look forward to returning to America and being reunited with her.

Nettie's letters come to light through the intercession of Shug Avery, who finds them locked away in Mr. ___'s trunk. (Fig. 7.2.) A flamboyant blues singer, Shug is Mr. ___'s longtime mistress and the mother of three of his children; but she also becomes Celie's friend and lover. More importantly, Shug, whose feminine charm rivals her masculine tenacity, empowers Celie: after intervening with Mr. ___ to stop his physical abuse, she convinces Celie to leave him and to come live with her in Memphis. There, she helps

Celie reclaim her sexuality as well as her identity. She nurtures her creativity by encouraging her to pursue her interest in sewing; and when Celie starts turning out a remarkable variety of unisex pants, Shug subsidizes what becomes a rather lucrative business, Folkspants.[6] Literally and symbolically, then, Shug teaches Celie not only how to wear the pants—that is, to challenge the male hierarchy that has oppressed her—but also how to manufacture them and thus to find the economic freedom that precludes further oppression.

The discovery of Nettie's letters, however, causes Celie to suffer a new crisis of faith. By allowing Mr. ___ to keep her separated from her beloved sister, God—she reasons—is no different from any of the other men in her life in whom she mistakenly placed her faith; and she can no longer sustain her old religious belief. In fact, her letters to God stop and are replaced instead by her letters to Nettie. Shug, who has become a kind of sister to Celie in her real sister's absence, again offers good counsel: she urges Celie to redefine her notion of God, from one who is as "trifling, forgitful and lowdown" as any man to one who is human enough to share Celie's need for love and compassionate enough to rejoice with his people when they find it, even in its most blatantly sexual forms (Winchell 288). Shug's image of God, which Celie comes to share, is genderless: "God is inside you and inside everybody else," Shug tells her. "You come into the world with God. But only them that search for it inside find it. . . . God ain't a he or a she, but a It" (177). And indeed, when Celie is ultimately reunited with Nettie and the rest of her family at the end of the novel, it is this new pantheistic God that she hails: "Dear God. Dear stars, dear trees, dear sky, dear peoples. Dear Everything. Dear God" (249).

Although Celie's new image of God is neither male nor female, it is through traditionally female conventions—sewing together and reading Nettie's letters—that Celie and Shug solidify their developing friendship. As Joan Digby writes, like the stock character of the confidante in the epistolary novel, Shug teaches Celie by "didactic example." But Shug's lessons are specifically about "the rewards of feminine strength and the cultural bonding that makes women powerful allies in subverting male control. Shug's examples validate Walker's 'Womanist' philosophy and coax Celie to find her voice. She teaches Celie that washing her body feels like praying, that blues is 'something you help scratch out of my head,' and that sewing is a form of thought." Those particular examples of woman's work demonstrate "how Walker appropriated the epistolary novel invented by European men to educate women and grafted it to an oral, Afro-American folk expression of women who were otherwise denied a voice" (159-60).

Shug, however, is not the only woman to help Celie find her voice. Unlike the passive Celie, Sofia, her proud, outspoken daughter-in-law, is a fighter. "All my life I had to fight," she confesses; "I had to fight my daddy. I had to fight my brothers. I had to fight my cousins and my uncles. A girl child ain't safe in a family of men." But even she is not prepared to have to fight in her own home. When her husband Harpo complains (albeit with some pride) to his father that she refuses to mind, Mr. ___ urges him to beat her, which Harpo does. But Sofia fights back so hard that she blackens Harpo's eye, cuts his lip, and leaves his face "a mess of bruises" (43). Afterwards, when she learns that Celie had concurred with Mr. ___'s advice, she not only confronts Celie, forcing her to justify having sided with an abuser; she also angrily returns the curtains that Celie had given her, along with thread and a dollar in rent for their use. Celie, already keenly aware that she had "sin[ned] against Sofia spirit" (45), can only apologize for her own foolishness and her lack of courage. Sofia—"she mad before, sad now" (46)—is moved by Celie's inability to "stand up," and the two begin to talk earnestly for the first time. Afterwards, Celie runs for her pattern book to "make quilt pieces out of these messed up curtains" (47). Significantly, the quilt they make is called "Sister's Choice"; and, as a token of their new sisterhood, Celie later gives the quilt to Sofia.

Sofia also teaches Celie about the importance of fighting back when she defies the wife of the white mayor who wants to engage her services as a maid. Although Sofia is beaten, jailed, separated from her children, and ultimately forced—as a condition of her parole—to accept the very job she had so vehemently and violently resisted, her defiance makes her a model, along with Shug, of women who can hold their own. Moreover, Sofia's marriage is much tempered by her suffering, "and in the end Harpo becomes a doting husband who bows to her authority" (Digby 160). Yet Sofia's marriage, like Celie's, is tested first, by the presence of her husband's jazz-singing mistress Squeak, whom Harpo finds after Sofia walks out on him and after he turns their house into a juke joint. At one point, Sofia and Squeak get into a barroom brawl, during which the Amazonian Sofia clearly gets the better of her rival. But when Sofia is jailed for attacking the mayor's wife, it is Squeak who comes to her aid, raising Sofia's children in her absence and even submitting to rape by her white uncle, the jail warden, in order to secure Sofia's release. And Sofia returns the favor when she agrees to raise Squeak's child after Squeak decides to pursue her singing career and later to follow Grady, Shug Avery's husband, to Panama.

Just as Sofia and Harpo find their way back to each other after years of difficulty and estrangement, so, in many ways, do Celie and Mr. ___. But, as Donna Haisty Winchell writes, their reconciliation is possible only after a reexamination of their culturally defined sex roles. "They grow toward wholeness by becoming more like each other, achieving wholeness and finding peace only when they achieve an androgynous blend of traditionally male and female characteristics. By the end of the novel, Celie is wearing pants, running her own business that makes unisex pants, and smoking a pipe. Albert [Mr. ___] is keeping house for himself, even cooking, and late in the novel is shown sewing on the porch with Celie, designing shirts to go with her pants" (289). Both have lost Shug, the woman they love, to a younger man, but that mutual loss serves only to bond them more closely to each other. Near the end of the book, Celie is even able to say of Mr. ___ that while "he ain't Shug, he begin to be someone I can talk to" (241). And although she turns down his proposal to remarry, this time in spirit as well as in flesh, she makes clear her hope that "let's us be friends" (247). Like Sofia, who goes to work in the store that Celie inherited from her father, and Harpo, who no longer needs to assert his manhood by violence and is content to stay at home, Celie and Mr. ___ learn to forge a new and more enduring relationship.

To be sure, shaping Walker's story into a film was, as *Los Angeles Times* critic Sheila Benson put it, "a heroic notion" (*LA Times* 18 Dec. 1985: Calendar 1). The most immediate challenge for Spielberg was deciding how to translate the epistolary novel to film. Sustained voice-over to indicate the reading or writing of letters would quickly have proven grating and tiresome; and Nettie's letters were dangerously close to polemic (Digby 162). Spielberg's solution was to reshape the letters dramatically to show their impact on the pivotal character of Celie (played by Whoopi Goldberg as an adult and by Desreta Jackson as a girl). Screenwriter Menno Meyjes cut out most of the African subplot and Spielberg converted Nettie's descriptions of Africa into tableaux that intersect Celie's landscape physically as she reads them: an elephant appears over the railing of Celie's porch; her footpath becomes the African road under construction; the bulldozer that razes the African mission seems to crash through the church where Celie sits reading in the pew.[7] And the African scarification ritual that both Tashi and Adam undergo flashes in her mind as she shaves Mr. ___. But while the connections that Celie makes in her imagination between Nettie's experiences—the elephant, the footpath, the bulldozer—and her own are at best attenuated, the film's association of shaving/throat-slitting with scarification is simply wrong. By decontextualizing the tradition of scarification, through which native peoples affirm their solidarity and tribal identity, Spielberg reduces it to a mere act of primitive violence, like Celie's passing desire to slit her husband's throat. But face-scarring is not a negative act of punishment or revenge, as Celie's throat-cutting would have been; it is a positive, historically significant gesture, as Adam realizes when he scars his own face in solidarity with Tashi. By misconstruing ritual scarification, then, Spielberg reveals his unfamiliarity with some of the African-American folkways that underlie Walker's work.[8]

The epistolary nature of the novel also forced Spielberg to focus on the power and importance of language. Walker's Celie begins to find her voice not through verbal interaction but through letters, first to God and then to Nettie. Spielberg's Celie has to make a similar odyssey from silence to self-assertion; and in two scenes original to the film, Spielberg suggests her progress. In the first, Celie, who has been forced by her father to drop out of school because of her pregnancies, is taught to read by Nettie, who pins words to her dress; Nettie's lessons thus give Celie the tools for her empowerment. In the second scene, Celie—now unhappily married to Mr. ___—starts to put those tools to use, as she sits alone reading *Oliver Twist*, whose sad story of abuse parallels her own.[9]

Initially in the film Celie observes in silence everything that goes on around her: when she speaks, she uses the hushed nervous tones of a frightened child; even as a woman, she covers her mouth and bows her head, as if to imply that she has no right to be heard. Correspondingly, early in the film, Spielberg uses voice-over to convey the thoughts that Celie is unable to express. For instance, when her father-in-law (Adolph Caesar) visits Mr. ___'s home to criticize Shug, Celie attends to him in silence; but the audience is told—in Celie's voice-over—that she has spit in his water and that next time she intends to flavor his drink with a little of Shug's urine. But as Sofia (Oprah Winfrey) and especially Shug (Margaret Avery) help Celie to appreciate her self-worth, she learns to articulate her thoughts. By the time that the extended family gathers around the table for Easter dinner, a symbolic family occasion invented by Spielberg for the film, Celie erupts into a dramatic monologue in which she talks down Old Mr. and announces her intention to leave young Mr. ___. "Any more letters from Nettie come?" she asks Mr. ___. Then she curses him—"Until you do right by me, everything you touch will crumble"—and concludes with a triumphant declaration: "I'm pore, I'm black, I may be ugly . . . but I'm here." For as long as she accepts her abuse, writes Digby, "her sententious perceptions are presented as voice-over." But "when she takes control of her life she delivers her one-liners out loud" and forces most of the principal characters involved in her oppression to "witness the awesome power of Celie's spoken truth" (163).

Spielberg, in his film adaptation, altered Walker's novel in several other significant ways: by simplifying or eliminating altogether some of the plots; by adding a major subplot of his own; by recasting the male characters; and by changing the ending. In addition to reducing the African episodes, Spielberg simplified some of the sexual involvements: instead of two husbands, as in the novel, Shug has just one, Grady; and he never becomes involved with Harpo's mistress Squeak (who in the novel runs away with him to grow marijuana on a farm in Panama). More importantly, Spielberg minimized—and virtually eliminated—the pivotal sexual relationship between Celie and Shug. It is through this lesbian relationship that Celie learns to embrace her own sexuality and to love herself in other crucial ways as well; the unleashing of Celie's sensuality coincides with the outpouring of her creativity. And it is through the complicated triangle of interrelationships—of Celie, Mr. ___, and Shug—that the three major characters are developed and linked throughout their lives, despite the changes that they undergo and the difficulties that they endure. But in the film, the physical relationship between Celie and Shug is reduced to a single almost sisterly kiss. (Their bond is also alluded to in the song that Shug sings: "Miss Celie's Blues," also known as "Sister.") Spielberg apparently felt that a more overt display of sexuality would diminish the popular appeal of his film; but, in fact, it was the timidity of the depiction that diluted the essence of his story.

A similar timidity was evident in the elimination of the rape scene involving Squeak and the jailer. Squeak's self-sacrifice contributes significantly to the reinforcing of the novel's other notable triangle—Sofia, Harpo, Squeak. In that second triangle, Sofia's tribulations parallel Celie's and enhance the notion of sisterhood, which Squeak fosters by raising Sofia's children as her own and which Sofia reciprocates by raising Squeak's child. (It is essential to recall that Shug and Mr. ___ had had three children together, that Celie becomes foster mother to his children, and that Shug ultimately helps to reunite Celie with her own natural children.) As Harpo's jazz-singing mistress, Squeak also serves as a double for Shug, while Harpo's evolution from abuser to caring husband parallels Mr. ___'s growth in the novel. These rich interconnections, which interwove the various characters into Walker's literary quilt, are largely absent in the film.

In simplifying the film's plot, Spielberg also neglected or eliminated entirely some of the plot points that moved the novel's storyline and that made it comprehensible: missing from the film, for example, is Samuel's disclosure of Nettie's parentage. So is the lucrative business that Celie starts and that Shug encourages and subsidizes: Celie's ultimate "success" in the film is therefore not the product of her own labors as much as it is an inheritance from her real father (and thus a link to the very patriarchy from which Walker's Celie breaks). And Sofia and Harpo, whom Spielberg transforms into more comic and occasionally buffoonish characters, never achieve the accommodation that they do in the novel, in which they are able to accept their differences and reverse their old roles (with Sofia going to work in Celie's store while Harpo stays home and cooks). In the film, after they are reconciled, Sofia, instead of asserting the strong-willed independence of her character, is content to assist Harpo in the running of his juke joint.

Yet, while Spielberg reduced existing plots, he felt compelled to add an original and rather time-consuming subplot involving Shug Avery and her disapproving father, Preacher. In the novel, Walker alludes to the fact that Shug, because of her free-wheeling lifestyle, is estranged from her parents as well as her children. In the film, however, Shug reveals her overwhelming need to be reconciled with—and forgiven by—her father (John Patton, Jr.), a stern man who is shown riding past her with disdain and shutting his church doors against her. Even when she visits him to tell him how sick she has been and, later, to show him her wedding band, a symbol of her newfound respectability, he continues to scorn her. Their differences, supposedly as wide as the divide between his gospel music and her jazz singing, are breached only when, in a moment of pure and rather pointless Hollywood spectacle, she leads her audience out of the juke joint and into his church, where the two congregations join in singing "Lord is trying to tell you something" and where he at last absolves her sins and embraces her. Having rediscovered her father's love, Shug no longer needs to seek affection from other men: the flashy, free-thinking, free-loving mistress is transformed into a dependent, desexualized, approval-seeking daughter. Spielberg's subplot signals a tremendous shift away from Walker's vision of the character, whose great strength empowers Celie to defy Mr. ___ and to assert her own identity. But in the film, while Celie breaks from her traditional role, the very nontraditional Shug runs to the bosom of her father (though, interestingly, not to her mother or her children), thus solidifying the notion of male authority and undercutting the novel's feminist premise.[10] Perhaps Spielberg intended the episodes with Preacher, particularly the church interludes that emphasize his old-time religion, to counterbalance the controversial passages in Walker's novel in which Celie engages in religious heterodoxy by denying God, whom she rejects for acting "like all the mens I know" (175). But even on that level, they work against the overall story.

Whereas Spielberg undermined Shug's character by forcing her to seek patriarchal validation, he enlarged the role of Old Mr.

and suggested that his castrating bitterness helped turn his son Mr. ___ into the unfulfilled and brutal man he is. In the novel, Old Mr. appears only once, when he visits Mr. ___'s home to disparage Shug Avery, the singular passion of his son's life. "She black as tar, she nappy headed. She got legs like baseball bats," he tells Mr. ___. "She ain't even clean. . . . And her mammy take in white people dirty laundry" (58-59). In the film, however, he has a greater presence; he is among the family members in the Easter dinner scene original to the film in which Celie finally tells off her husband for his years of abuse. Mr. ___'s father tries to stop her outburst: "You can't talk to my boy that way!" Celie responds, "Your boy? Seem like if he hadn't been your boy he might of made somebody a halfway decent man." As Carol A. Dole notes, "The film's vilification of Mister's father thus removes part of Mister's responsibility for his mistreatment of his wife" (13). And, indeed, in Celie's absence, as Mr. ___ literally and symbolically starts getting his house in order, one of the first things he does is to kick his father out.

The character of Mr. ___ is also enhanced in the film. When Celie leaves him in the novel, she goes to Memphis, where she develops her relationship with Shug and embarks on her lucrative pantsmaking business; only when she returns home does she learn of Mr. ___'s breakdown following her departure. In the film, however, the focus remains on Mr. ___ during Celie's absence, and his dissolution is depicted in great detail; by contrast, her transformation is indicated only by her new clothing and her opening of a shop upon her return. "Spielberg's attention to Mister was such," writes Dole, "that Alice Walker, who was closely involved with the making of the film, worried that, since Danny Glover was in almost every scene, 'it was going to become his story—Mister's story, not Celie's'" (13).

Although Mr. ___ changes for the better in the course of the film—in fact, it is he, not Shug (as in the novel), who locates Nettie through the Office of Immigration and helps to reunite the sisters—he and Celie are never reconciled. In the novel, they eventually become friends after breaking from their old culturally defined roles: empathizing with each other over their mutual loss of Shug, they sit together, sewing and smoking, on the porch of Celie's house. But in the film Spielberg excises all references to Mr. ___'s interest in sewing or other traditionally feminine activities. Thus, he affords Mr. ___ no means by which to overcome his alienation from Celie. Whereas Walker, according to Gerald Early, turns Mr. ___ into "a feminized man by the end" (271) of her novel, "Spielberg's conclusion allows both for audience gratification, in seeing the heroine's tormentor mend his sorry ways, and simultaneously for Mister's retention of his male dignity. Spielberg's Mister repents of the horrible wrong he did in depriving Celie of her sister, but, unlike Walker's, does not yield himself to a new, female-centered order" (Dole 14).

By changing the character of Mr. ___ and the nature of his relationship with Celie, Spielberg also created an ending that, while happy, is considerably different from Walker's. In the novel, surrounded by Shug and Mr. ___ when Nettie arrives with Olivia and Adam, Celie tearfully introduces them as "my peoples" (250). And with her whole extended family—"me and Nettie and Shug and Albert [Mr.___] and Samuel and Harpo and Sofia and Jack and Odessa" (251)—Celie celebrates a literal and symbolic Independence Day. In the film, however, Celie is with Shug and Sofia when Nettie's car comes down the road; Mr. ___, a marginalized, receding, silent figure standing in a distant field, is barred from sharing in Celie's joy. The film ends with a shot of the reunited sisters clapping hands in a field of purple flowers, an image that brings the film full circle. But just as the whole of his film substitutes "exquisitely sunny photography for a story full of emotional darkness, a big thumping background score when simplicity was necessary" (Benson 1), Spielberg neglects the elements of reconciliation and redemption that are critical to Celie's—and to Walker's—story. Mr. ___ is redeemed by his entry into a female-ordered world, whose "emblems are domestic and nurturing activities coded as feminine" (Dole 14); and, like Sofia, who is reconciled to Harpo after she finds him sleeping with his ailing father in his arms, Celie is reconciled to Mr. ___ through her similiar longing for Shug and through the traditionally feminine bonds—sewing and talking together—that they share.

Critics noted the importance of the film but nonetheless found much to fault. For Sheila Benson, it was the "antic disposition" that Spielberg attached to the film, prettifying or coarsening the events, making comic scenes broadly slapstick and tiptoeing over the story's crucial relationship—in short, "purpling" the film (1). For Janet Maslin, it was "the film's peculiar unevenness"—that is, its way of combining wild extremes, some rapturous and stirring, others hugely improbable, with unpredictable movement from one mode to another (*NYT* 18 Dec. 1985: C18). For Charles Champlin, it was Spielberg's inability to make the necessary shift away from a mass-audience film and his need to cater to "populist intentions" with slapstick car scenes and "goin' to glory" production numbers (*LA Times* 28 Dec. 1985: Calendar 5). And for Vincent Canby, it was the lavender quality of the film, in particular the lavender-colored glasses that transformed the events of the novel "into fiction of an entirely different order . . . the kind of fiction that would have been enthusiastically endorsed by an old-time Hollywood mogul like Louis B. Mayer, who didn't believe it was Hollywood's job to depress its customers by reflecting life's bleaker truths" (*NYT* 5 Jan. 1986: 2.1).

But the critics were almost unanimous in their praise for the excellent cast, especially the women. Remarking on her slow, incandescent smile, Sheila Benson called Whoopi Goldberg "compelling" as Celie: "her growth comes with the sweet inevitability of stop-motion flower photography, from a clenched bud to a full-blown, heavy-laden flower" (1). (In the press kit for the film, Goldberg recalls that after hearing Alice Walker reading from her novel, she sat down and wrote her a letter "telling her I would go *anywhere* to audition if this was made into a movie." She felt a particular kinship to Celie because she too had "talk[ed] about God a lot," the way Celie and Shug do.[11]) As Shug Avery, Margaret Avery was magnetic in her movement from the tenderness of friendship to the flamboyance of juke-joint jazz. And as the indomitable Sofia, recast as a more comic character than in the novel, Oprah Winfrey was in every sense larger-than-life. Only Adolph Caesar (Old Mr.) and Dana Ivey (Miss Millie, the mayor's wife), perhaps reacting to the extreme nature of their roles, came off more as caricatures than as well-developed characters.

Despite its artistic shortcomings, the film was a commercial success. By fall of 1986, within nine months of its release, it had made over $100 million; and, as one of "the top hundred all-time best-selling videos" (Peacock 127), its video sales and rentals grossed many millions more. Its popularity proved the strength of the market for black stories, even stories of black feminism, among both white and black audiences—although re-creating that popularity would be neither easy nor immediate for other filmmakers.

THE WOMEN OF BREWSTER PLACE

Almost as controversial as Spielberg's film version of *The Color Purple* was the television miniseries *The Women of Brewster Place* (1989). Gloria Naylor's American Book Award-winning first novel had been praised for its rich prose and its lyrical portrayals of the black female characters, most of whom—according to Vashti Crutcher Lewis—were "based on black women Naylor had observed and been fascinated by all her life" (171). The novel also revealed Naylor's keen understanding of black experience and vernacular as well as her familiarity with black literary tradition, no doubt derived from her undergraduate study of African-American literature at Brooklyn College and her graduate work in Afro-American Studies at Yale, where she served as a teaching assistant in a course entitled "Black Women and Their Fictions."[12] In fact, according to Henry Louis Gates, Jr., "perhaps no author has been more immersed in the formal study of that tradition" than Naylor; and, "while she is a citizen of the republic of literature in the broadest and most cosmopolitan sense" (ix), her work suggests linkages to the fiction of other important writers like James Baldwin and Toni Morrison.

Subtitled "a novel in seven stories" and set largely in the 1960s with occasional flashbacks to earlier times, *The Women of Brewster Place* (1983) depicted the lives of seven women who reside in a decaying tenement on a dead-end street in an unnamed Northern city. A brick wall at the end of the street, erected as a result of political and economic machinations, separates them from the rest of the world. The wall, write Jacqueline Bobo and Ellen Seiter, "comes to stand for racism, and its effects are felt daily in the women's lives" (145). Brewster Place is truly "the end of the line": "They came because they had no choice and would remain for the same reason" (4).

The novel's pivotal character is matriarch Mattie Michael, who serves as the voice—and the heart—of the Brewster Place community. As a young girl in Tennessee, Mattie suffered emotional and physical abuse at the hands of her beloved father, who had responded with violence to the news of her pregnancy and her refusal to reveal the paternity of her baby. After moving to Detroit with her son Basil, Mattie is befriended by the kindly Miss Eva, with whom she lives for many years and who bequeaths her house to Mattie upon her death. For the first time, Mattie has a place to call her own; and she maintains it with great care and pride. But after putting the house up as collateral for Basil, who jumps bail on a murder charge and disappears, Mattie loses the property and is forced to move to a small rented apartment on Brewster Place.

There she is joined by her longtime friend, Etta Mae Johnson, an aging femme fatale who survives by attaching herself to successful men. What Etta Mae really wants, however, is a husband who will lift her out of poverty and offer her social respectability. But Etta Mae's choices in men are unfortunate; even the preacher whom she pursues treats her no better than he would a whore. Mattie is also reunited with Lucielia ("Ciel") Louise Turner, Miss Eva's granddaughter, who grew up in the same house with Basil. Ceil is unhappily married to Eugene, an abusive man who blames her for his failures and who repeatedly leaves her, ostensibly to seek better opportunities for himself. After each of his departures, Ceil waits helplessly for his return. During one of their bitter arguments, which occurs just as Eugene is ready to walk out again, their daughter suffers a fatal accident. Ceil is so grief-stricken that she wills herself to die; and it falls to Mattie, who knows all too well what it is like to lose a child, to "rock" the young woman out of her sorrow and back to life:

> Mattie rocked her out of that bed, out of that room, into a blue vastness just underneath the sun and above time. She rocked her over Aegean seas so clean they shone like crystal, so clear the fresh blood of sacrificed babies torn from their mothers' arms and given to Neptune could be seen like pink froth on the water. She rocked her on and on, past Dachau, where soul-gutted Jewish mothers swept their children's entrails off laboratory floors. They flew past the spilled brains of Senegalese infants whose mothers had dashed them on the wooden sides of slave

ships. And she rocked on. She rocked her into her childhood and let her see murdered dreams. (103)

Also residing at Brewster Place is Kiswana (formerly Melanie)
Browne, a young woman who has repudiated her affluent parents'
values and embraced the ideals of black nationalism of the late
1960s. Kiswana hopes to form a tenants' association and to introduce some elements of high culture to the disenfranchised folk
whom she calls "my people." Neighbor Cora Lee, a welfare mother, loves babies so much that she keeps having more and more; but
once her babies grow up, she is no longer able to cope with them.
Cora Lee's sloppy apartment and her undisciplined children incite
Miss Sophie, the resident busybody. Lesbians Lorraine and
Theresa also provoke gossip; they have arrived at Brewster Place
from other, better neighborhoods because there is no place left for
them to go. Theresa, who refuses to move again, is seemingly
oblivious to their poor treatment; but Lorraine, especially after
being ostracized by her family and fired from her teaching position
due to her sexuality, longs to become part of her new community.
One night, after being rebuffed in her attempt to participate in the
newly formed block organization, she ventures out alone and is
raped in an alley by several local thugs.

Although each of the women is a distinctive character with a
separate identity, all blend fluidly. "They were hard-edged, soft-
centered, brutally demanding, and easily pleased," writes Naylor.
"They came, they went, grew up, and grew old beyond their years.
Like an ebony phoenix, each in her own time and with her own
season had a story" (5). Their personal histories, as Dorothy
Wickenden demonstrates, share a common denominator: violence
and abuse at the hands of men. Adoring fathers beat their daughters senseless and turn them out of the house when they become
pregnant; lovers fracture their jaws when they burn dinner; sons
are transformed into juvenile delinquents who steal their love and
money. "But these women are amazingly resilient" (Wickenden 5),
and they learn to adapt when their aspirations for better lives are
repeatedly met with ridicule and random brutality. When
Lorraine, for instance, regains consciousness after being gang-
raped in the alleyway, she mistakes the kindly superintendent Ben
for one of her attackers; in her traumatized and agitated state, she
beats to death the man who has come to help her. The violence of
the episode shocks and saddens the other women; but it also

unites them in their suffering. Ultimately, in a pattern common to Naylor's fiction, destruction leads to healing and rebirth. The final chapter, "The Block Party," reveals the new order that arises from the chaos surrounding the brutal rape and murder. It is, as Gates suggests, an order based on the female protagonists' comprehension of their interconnectedness (Gates 61), which is the central theme of the novel.

Naylor's novel was adapted as a 1989 telefilm scripted by Karen Hall and co-produced by Oprah Winfrey, who also starred as Mattie Michael.[13] Donna Deitch, an independent filmaker best known for her lesbian love story *Desert Hearts* (1985), directed. Jacqueline Bobo and Ellen Seiter suggest that Deitch was probably selected "because of her past focus on the relationships between women and her handling of the lesbian romance using the techniques of commercial mainstream cinema." They note that her selection was also noteworthy since it marked the first time that a woman directed a media adaptation of the work of a black woman author, a result that proved "vastly more promising than Steven Spielberg's self-selection as director of Alice Walker's *The Color Purple*" (147). Naylor had originally hoped that her novel would be adapted by the noncommercial Public Broadcasting System, which might have allowed the hiring of a black woman director; but Naylor had lost control of the screen rights for her book in her publishing contract and thus had no say in the eventual ABC television miniseries.[14]

At first glance, the telefilm seemed to be a rather typical melodrama that chronicled the changing fortunes of decent, hardworking people like Mattie. But, in fact, a number of critical elements distinguished the production from other Hollywood film narratives. Paramount among them was the strong cultural sense of community that the production portrayed. At Brewster Place, the women rediscover the essential solidarity—the sisterhood—that is lacking in their lives, and they experience a kind of redemption that gives them a chance to heal and to grow. This is not to suggest, however, that the film's image of community is utopian: "poverty, violence, and bigotry are permanent features, and these are shown to deform personal relationships and threaten women." Yet the film "contains striking instances of deeply held values that are starkly opposed to the values of the mainstream white culture and economy" (Bobo and Seiter 148). Mattie, for example, is taken in off the street by Miss Eva, an absolute stranger, who helps to raise Basil as if he were her own child. And Mattie's loving care of the grieving Ceil restores her to life; they become almost mother and child, virtually re-creating Mattie's earlier bond to Eva. The film's notion of family, consistent with the black female literary tradition, thus encompasses far more than mere blood ties. (White family melodrama, by contrast, is preoccupied with blood kinship—e.g., the determination of paternity, a staple in women's films and soap operas, or the conflict within the family between mothers and daughters.[15])

The unusual relationships between Eva and Mattie and Mattie and Ceil are typical of the bonds that are forged among the women in the film. The single, affluent, educated Kiswana befriends the poor, uneducated Cora Lee and prompts her to aspire to new and higher goals for herself and her children. The heterosexual but celibate Mattie helps libertine Etta Mae understand the affection between Lorraine and Theresa by admitting that she too has loved women (although in a non-sexual way) all of her life; in fact, Mattie says, she has loved some women, Etta Mae among them, more deeply than she ever loved any man. Like Mattie, Ceil, and Etta Mae, the women have all known violence, discrimination, racism, and poverty; and they survive precisely because they have learned to identify with each other.

In depicting the closeness of the women, however, the telefilm tended to exclude or, more significantly, to vilify the men. Indeed, with the exception of the alcoholic superintendent Ben, the black male characters are all despicable: unemployed louses, spouse beaters, child abusers, hypocritical preachers, angry rapists. Black critic Dorothy Gilliam observed that, through such extreme portrayals, *The Women of Brewster Place* "serves as one of the most stereotype-ridden polemics against black men ever seen on television." And because "there are so few black dramas on television"—and therefore such a limited context for the wider society to understand blacks in their complexity and diversity—"such shows convey to a susceptible world that this is the way blacks are" (*Washington Post* 23 March 1989: C3).[16] Tom Shales, who called the film a "talky and man-hating downer," went even further: he wrote that "if a bunch of men got together and were silly enough to make a correspondingly antifemale film, they would be run out of town as misogynistic louts" (*Washington Post* 18 March 1989: C1).

The telefilm is not only unusually harsh in its depiction of black men; it loses much of the subtle richness of Naylor's novel in other ways as well. Cora Lee, for instance, is portrayed more as a caricature than as a character; her conversion to model mother after a single exposure to a performance of Shakespeare produced by Kiswana's boyfriend is correspondingly incredible. In the novel, Cora Lee, a more psychologically complex character, is suspicious and understandably resentful of the intrusions of Kiswana, the self-appointed rebel who lives at Brewster Place by choice and who at any time can return to the upper-middle-class comforts of her parents' home in Linden Hills. As Barbara Christian notes, Kiswana "does not risk survival, as the others would if they rebelled; nor has she yet been worn down by the unceasing cycle of displacement that the others have experienced" (121). And the glamorous presentation of Lorraine precludes a more realistic exploration of the dangers of both homophobia and petty jealousy that contribute to her brutalizing.

Most striking, however, is the film's upbeat ending, which radically alters the vision of the novel. In Naylor's version, after Lorraine is gang-raped and killed, the women are haunted for a week by their inability to prevent the violence; Mattie, in particular, dreams of tearing down the wall in a symbolic protest against the forces that led to Lorraine's death. The block party that follows gives them a way of coming together to reaffirm their solidarity and to expiate their guilts and fears over their failure to prevent the earlier tragedy. The telefilm, however, compresses events, including the block party and the rape of Lorraine (who is assaulted by a single rapist and who survives the attack), into one evening, after which Mattie spontaneously starts chipping away at the wall. The other women join her; and, in a collective effort that harks back to the opening narrative (in which Mattie says that "we learned that when we women came together, there was a power inside us we never felt before"), they break through to the other side. There is, however, no indication that this act is imagined, not real, or that it follows much introspection about the nature of violence by—and against—the women in the community.

Yet, as Bobo and Seiter have demonstrated, while the telefilm falls well short of the novel, it nonetheless makes a significant contribution to the canon of black and women's films. "As a popular work written by a black woman author, adapted for the screen by a white [woman] director and screenwriter, it opens up questions about the nature of women's experience and of differences stemming from work and class," and it violates the expectations about representations of black women long familiar from movies and television series—that is, of the black woman as defined by her sexuality, by her relationship to white people as a domestic servant, and by her role in the nuclear family as a domineering or restraining force. It also violates expectations of the characters' sexuality. "One of the most lascivious characters is Miss Eva, a woman in her seventies; one of the most glamorous is Lorraine, a lesbian. The scarlet woman, Etta Mae, is perfectly happy to settle down with Mattie, her best friend," while Mattie, who is involved in the film's only extended love scene, "remains celibate after her teenage pregnancy" (154).

Reviewers were not kind to *The Women of Brewster Place*. They criticized its self-pitying and formulaic melodrama, its situation-comedy look, its black-soap-opera plot, and its fitful and uninspired direction. But audience response was strong, and the tele-film became the highest-rated miniseries of the television season (John J. O'Connor, *NYT* 1 May 1990: C13). Its success led to a short-lived television series, *Brewster Place*, directed by black director Bill Duke, scripted by Donald Sipes and Earl Hamner (who created *The Waltons*), and co-produced by Oprah Winfrey, who reprised her role as Mattie Michael. In response to the criticism that in the original film males were invisible, despicable, or hopeless, the series offered new and positive male images, including a single-parent household headed by a father, Ralph Thomas (John Cochran, Jr.), Mattie's widower cousin who arrives from the South with his three young children and proves to be a stern but loving figure in their lives. Even the series' women were newly empowered: a younger and less long-suffering Mattie, for example, is devoid of the bitter hatred she felt toward men. Fired from her beauty parlor position for refusing to use lye on a customer's hair, she decides to go into business with Etta Mae; they become co-owners of a local restaurant formerly operated by whites who, having recognized the realities of the changing neighborhood, sell the property and move to Florida. "You're dreaming," Mattie tells Etta Mae when they discuss starting their new business. "Damn right," replies Etta Mae; "and you look to me like you could use a good dream." The changes among the characters are mirrored by the larger social changes around them: a radio reports that a new heavyweight champion named Cassius Clay has been stripped of his crown for refusing to fight in Vietnam; street signs urge voter registration; and a photograph of Martin Luther King, Jr. hangs in Mattie's new restaurant. In brief, like the television milestone *The Cosby Show*, *Brewster Place* attempted to show positive black characters in a dramatic setting. Unfortunately, the series lasted only two months, from May 1 to July 11, 1990. But, like the telefilm on which it was based, *Brewster Place* heralded a shift in the way television portrayed black characters and suggested the clout wielded by prominent blacks in the industry, like Oprah Winfrey, in bringing their projects to fruition.

TERRY MCMILLAN: GOING POP

Like *The Women of Brewster Place* and *The Color Purple*, Terry McMillan's *Waiting to Exhale* portrayed the healing strength of the bonds that exist between black women. And, like *The Women of Brewster Place* and *The Color Purple*, *Waiting to Exhale*, which was based on McMillan's third novel (1992) and released in 1995, confirmed that black life stories—in this case, of middle class, professional blacks—offered lucrative possibilities for filmmakers (something early race filmmakers had recognized). Two subsequent adaptations, *How Stella Got Her Groove Back* (1998) and *Disappearing Acts* (2000), based on McMillan's second and fourth novels (respectively published in 1989 and 1996), introduced her vivid, independent, and largely autobiographical female characters to an even broader mainstream audience.

Despite her tremendous popularity (particularly among black women, whose grassroots support vaulted her to literary celebrity), McMillan is rarely grouped with more prominent and respected black women writers like Alice Walker and Toni Morrison. Critics generally perceive McMillan's novels not as serious art but as popular romance that skillfully manipulates many of the formulas of women's genre fiction by adapting conventional forms and themes to reflect an African American world view. Other critics are even more dismissive, attacking the plots of her fiction as superficial, her characters as shallow, and her male-bashing as offensive and tedious. Consequently, as Paulette Richards writes, even though she has made important contributions through her teaching, scholarship, and mentoring of younger writers, "the question of McMillan's ultimate critical reception remains open" (1).

Whatever its literary merit, McMillan's work clearly lends itself to adaptation as film, a genre that McMillan studied in graduate school at Columbia. Disappointed in Columbia's film program and believing that she and the only other black student in the program were being treated unfairly, McMillan left well short of a degree. But the experience no doubt helped to hone the writing skills she had already begun developing and increased the cinematic scope of her literary vision. It also gave her material to incorporate in her fiction, which she did by making Savannah Jackson, the central character of her best known popular novel, *Waiting to Exhale*, a television producer.

Like McMillan, who moved to Phoenix to accept a creative writing position at the University of Arizona, the novel's Savannah moves to Phoenix in the hope of improving both her professional and her social prospects. She soon forms a tight circle with her old college roommate Bernadine Harris and with two other friends, Gloria Johnson and Robin Stokes, each of whom has significant personal issues with which she must deal. Savannah, the strongest character in the novel, has been helping to support her mother since her father's desertion; already in her late thirties, she feels pressure to get married, despite the dismal marriages she has witnessed within her immediate family and despite the reluctance of her married boyfriend Kenneth to leave his wife. Bernadine, by contrast, until recently has enjoyed a charmed life: a large house, expensive automobiles, private schools for her two children, a thriving software business that she co-founded with her husband John. But when John decides to divorce her for a white woman, Bernadine feels utterly betrayed. She sees his defection not only as a personal affront but as an assault on the honor of black women; and her "winning a just settlement, therefore, comes to symbolize all black women's desire for just treatment in the society at large" (Richards 103). Yet such justice seems increasingly difficult to achieve, especially after Bernadine discovers that John has closed their accounts, left her with no money to make mortgage or other payments, and manipulated the value of his assets so that she will receive only a fraction of the community property and child support to which she is entitled. Gloria, a single mother who lavishes too much of her attention on her teenaged son, has equally pressing concerns. Even though she is the operator of a successful beauty salon, she neglects her own health and ignores the very real problems of obesity and high blood pressure that have resulted from overeating, her compensation for the emptiness she feels. And Robin, a highly competent underwriter who manages her professional life with great skill, seems unable to control her personal life: drawn to men only by their good looks, she ends up in a series of bad relationships. For several years, she financially supports one man, Russell, in the hope that he will marry her. But he leaves her for another woman with whom he starts a family; even then, in the belief that he will divorce his wife, Robin naïvely takes him back.

With the support of her "sistah friends," each woman finds some resolution. Savannah, realizing that she does not need a man to define her, ends her on-again/off-again relationship with Kenneth and redirects her nurturing instincts toward herself and her friends. Bernadine receives a million dollar settlement from John and discovers new love with a black man who restores her racial honor. (In a rather hokey twist, his first wife—a white woman—has died of breast cancer. By falling in love with Bernadine, he reverses John's betrayal of her.) Gloria, after suffering a heart attack but being nursed back to health by family and friends, finds the possibility of new romance with a widowed neighbor. And Robin winds up pregnant by Russell and disillusioned—but still warmly embraced by her friends, who disapprove of her choices but who continue to support her through every crisis.

Alternating between first-person (Savannah, Robin) and third-person narratives (Bernadine, Gloria), the novel juggles multiple characters and story lines. Yet, to McMillan's credit, each character emerges as a distinct personality, with her own style and eccentricities. At the same time, the similarities that the women share—ages, interests, family responsibilities, college educations, professional positions in a white corporate world—allow them to form a fast and rich friendship that is ultimately the most genuine and credible relationship in the book (in large part because there is insufficient development of the male characters for a convincing heterosexual relationship).

The novel, which McMillan has said arose out of a telephone conversation with a friend about the dearth of romantic prospects for professional women like themselves, hit a responsive note with millions of women; and it quickly became a best seller. Capitalizing upon her success, McMillan began negotiating a film contract with Twentieth Century-Fox that gave her an unprece-

Figure 7.3. Their lives intertwined, the four women in *Waiting to Exhale*—Gloria (Loretta Devine), Savannah (Whitney Houston), Bernadine (Angela Bassett), and Robin (Lela Rochon)—form their own special sisterhood. *(Twentieth Century-Fox, 1995)*

dented degree of artistic control over the film adaptation. On the recommendation of her friend Amy Tan, McMillan (who also served as executive producer) chose Ron Bass, who had sensitively adapted *The Joy Luck Club*, one of the few Hollywood films to focus on the Asian American experience, to collaborate with her on the screenplay. Moreover, she handpicked black actor/director Forest Whitaker to direct the project and ensured that many of the other technical and managerial positions were filled by blacks as well. In this way, suggests Paulette Richards, "McMillan used her clout to empower her own community" (9).

Released in December, 1995, the film version of *Waiting to Exhale* had "gorgeous stars, drop-dead clothes, glamorous settings"—all the trappings, according to Kenneth Turan (*LA Times* 22 Dec. 1995: Calendar 1), "of a lush, old fashioned melodrama," the kind of classic women's picture that was popular in the 1940s and 1950s (although with much looser standards of sexual frankness). More importantly, however, the film evinced a smart black sensibility that allowed Hollywood to do something it had never done before: build a glossy piece of commercial filmmaking around a quartet of African American actresses playing accomplished professional women. (Fig. 7.3.) In the book, Savannah, newly arrived in Phoenix, was the anchor character; yet in the film Savannah (Whitney Houston) is overshadowed by the glamorous Bernadine (Angela Bassett), who moves convincingly from fragility after her husband announces his decision to leave her for a white woman, to rage over his betrayal, and finally to self-confidence, which proves to be the sweetest revenge. Robin (Lela Rochon), the bad girl of the group, demonstrates a spunky charm as she keeps being drawn to the very men who hurt her. Yet it is Gloria (Loretta Devine), fretting over her weight, her bisexual ex-husband, and her teenaged son, who is the most touching because she is the most realistic. Unfortunately, in adapting the novel to the screen, McMillan and Bass not only avoided reference to Gloria's heart attack but also skipped all discussion of the serious cultural health issues involving her character; she was simply a beautiful "big woman," a portrayal more consistent with the pleasant and undemanding nature of the film.

Using their friendship as the bond, director Forest Whitaker deftly interwove the stories of the four women over the course of a year. But perhaps Whitaker's greatest skill was in establishing the right balance between drama and laughter, particularly in the comic bedroom scenes[17] between Robin and the oafish Michael (Wendell Pierce) and Savannah and the self-absorbed Lionel (Jeffrey D. Sams); in the opulent look he achieved with his richly colored interior shots, which mirror the spectacular desert landscape shots; and in his use of a pop musical score that served as a kind of choric commentary on the women's romantic adventures and misadventures. Thus, according to Stephen Holden (*NYT* 22 Dec. 1995: C3), even though "as storytelling, the movie [was] little more than a collection of vignettes strung around candy-sweet soundtrack," *Waiting to Exhale* offered "a series of star turns by four appealing divas conjuring dramatic fireworks for a director who clearly loves them."

The fault in this otherwise entertaining comic melodrama lay largely in its depiction of the male characters, all of whom (with the exception of the sympathetic widower Marvin [Gregory Hines], who befriends Gloria and her son Tarik [Donald Adeosun Faison]) come across as shallow monomaniacs, buffoons, freeloaders, or lying cads. The women respond to their egotism, double-dealing, and sexual ineptitude with varying degrees of tolerance and amusement, until "in time-honored soap opera fashion, they tell off the men who have mistreated them in speeches that have a flouncy dramatic flourish" (Holden, *NYT* 22 Dec. 1995: C3). Yet despite the turbulence of their love lives, all four women continue to seek the romantic fantasy of Mr. Right. According to Jay Carr, it was precisely "the inexhaustible spirit of the well-matched quartet and the[ir] surprising emotional subtleties" that raised the story above the usual cinematic soap opera (*Boston Globe* 22 Dec. 1995: Living 57), just as the film's rich texture and funkiness ensured its commercial—and crossover—success and established *Waiting to Exhale* as one of Hollywood's all-time most popular black-cast and black-directed films.

If the problem in *Waiting to Exhale* was how to find a good man, Terry McMillan resolves that problem in *How Stella Got Her Groove Back*. Stella Payne is a forty-two-year-old woman who has everything that money can buy (a spectacular house, an expensive car and truck, financial security) as well as a few things that it cannot (a taut and well-toned body, a perfectly-behaved young son, a supportive relationship with her sisters, a congenial ex-husband). After shipping her son Quincy off for a two-week visit with his father, she looks forward to some vacation time away from her job. But the recent loss of her best friend to cancer and the lack of a man in her life leave Stella feeling unsettled. When she sees a television commercial for Jamaica, she buys a ticket and impulsively hops a plane for a ten-day first-class stay. Soon after her arrival, Stella attracts the attention of Winston Shakespeare, a handsome medical school drop-out who is half her age, with whom she begins a passionate affair. Back home in San Francisco, Stella cannot seem to forget her young admirer; and when Quincy mentions that he would love to visit Jamaica, Stella books a trip for the two of them. Stella and Winston rekindle their passion, and Winston and Quincy bond as well.

Back home again, Stella realizes that her feelings have grown serious. When her employer fires her, Stella determines to leave the corporate world and return to more artistic pursuits, such as the furniture designing and building that she enjoyed years earlier. She also decides to take another risk and sends Winston a first-class ticket to California. In the weeks before he comes, she worries about how she will adapt to a new man sharing her space as well as her life. Once together, however, they are able to share their fears and concerns; and by the time Winston proposes, Stella happily accepts.

Figure 7.4. Stella (Angela Bassett) and Winston (Taye Diggs) reveal their best assets to each other in *How Stella Got Her Groove Back*, based on Terry McMillan's popular novel about friendship and romance. *(Twentieth Century-Fox, 1998)*

Based on McMillan's experiences, including the death of her best friend and her own successful older woman-younger man live-in relationship that began on holiday in Jamaica, the novel draws on most of the conventions of popular romance. The only departure from those conventions is the first-person narrative that limits the perspective and occasionally raises the possibility that Stella is not a reliable commentator on events. But there is so little going on in terms of plot that Stella's potential unreliability is of small consequence. In fact, because the action is so limited, Stella is left to wax deeply on topics as trite as how much feminine hygiene deoderant she should use to maintain her clean smell, particularly if she does not wear underwear. Moreover, as if to underscore the fact that Stella's narration is supposed to be stream-of-consciousness, McMillan at times forgoes internal punctuation and shifts tense structures within the text. While some critics have praised these technical devices as a way of allowing readers inside Stella's head and permitting them to see, along with Stella, in real time, others have faulted McMillan for such self-conscious artificiality.

Film rights to *How Stella Got Her Groove Back* were purchased for two million dollars by Twentieth Century-Fox, the same studio that had released *Waiting to Exhale*; and McMillan again co-produced and co-wrote the script with Ron Bass. Angela Bassett, who had played Bernadine in the earlier film, starred as Stella; newcomer Taye Diggs, recently of Broadway's *Rent*, was cast as Winston. (Fig. 7.4.) But apart from their toned bodies and the lush Jamaican scenery, there was little to recommend the film. Perhaps *Chicago Sun-Times* reviewer Roger Ebert summed it up best when he wrote, "*How Stella Got Her Groove Back* tries to turn a paperback romance into a relationship worth making a movie about, but fails" (14 Aug. 1998: Weekend 27).

Rita Kempley concurred that the movie was not good; but, in her opinion, it was nonetheless "the chick flick to end all chick flicks. I dare say, it is the *Saving Private Ryan* of the much maligned and misunderstood girls-night-out-movie. It isn't realistic, it isn't graphic and only one person dies. But she dies only so that we can have a good cry—tears, along with great sex and an even greater wardrobe, are the imperatives of film peignoir" (*Washington Post* 14 Aug. 1998: D1), The death in question is that of Stella's best buddy, Delilah (Whoopi Goldberg). But whereas in the novel Stella flies to Jamaica in part to relieve her grief over the loss of her friend, in the film Delilah is still very much alive, at least at this point; in fact, it is she who—at Stella's initial suggestion—books the trip, boogies the tropical nights away with two aging football players, and urges Stella to give young Winston a chance. Even after Delilah is diagnosed with liver cancer back in New York City, with her dying breath she helps to move Stella and Winston's relationship along. And her funeral, at which Stella delivers the eulogy, affords Winston the perfect opportunity to show up unannounced and to stand silhouetted in the church doorway offering Stella the support he knows that she needs. Afterwards, Stella decides to take him home with her to San Francisco. The whole love-death scenario is nothing short of Hollywood spectacle.

Kevin Rodney Sullivan, directing his first feature film, tries hard to string together a series of such scenarios, most of them handsomely framed and shot; but the film's haphazard rhythm ultimately defeats his attempts. As Michael O'Sullivan observes, in the film's "surprisingly clumsy screenplay, . . . funny, raunchy, maudlin and angry episodes slam into one another with a herky-jerky lack of grace as the film trudges toward its predictable and unpersuasive conclusion" (*Washington Post* 14 Aug. 1998: N39). What makes the screenplay so herky-jerky is the introduction of additional and awkward impediments to Stella and Winston's relationship, which clutter the plot instead of enhancing the drama of the novel's relatively straighforward romance. Even the film's ending is jerky and illogical: after Stella rejects Winston's proposal, he decides to return to Jamaica to begin medical school. The cab he calls to take him to the airport gets caught in traffic; when he arrives, he finds Stella waiting for him, suddenly anxious to accept his proposal. (How she, departing later, avoids the traffic and beats him to the airport is never explained; nor is her change of heart.) Equally difficult to accept is the attraction between the two. Beyond sex, they appear to have little in common; in fact, Winston seems to be more compatible with Stella's son Quincy, to whom he is closer in age, than with Stella. Perhaps, in this thoroughly undemanding film, the sex alone is enough to give Stella back her groove; but the film—a love story with a preposterously fairy-tale-type happy ending that tries to serve as an allegory for the creative process—too often finds itself stuck in a rut.

Disappearing Acts (1989), McMillan's second novel, was able to do what her later novels could not: offer insight into male as well as female characters. In alternating sections told in the first person, McMillan portrayed the relationship between Zora Banks, a twenty-nine-year-old music teacher, and Franklin Swift, the handsome man who is renovating the apartment to which she is moving. Unlike the college-educated Zora, Franklin is a high school dropout who works the occasional construction job because he is unable to find a better position. Beyond their physical attraction, however, they share an artistic vision: he (like the empowered Stella in *How Stella Got Her Groove Back*) wants to custom design furniture; she wants to write and sing songs.

At first, the two seem to bring out the best in each other. With Zora's encouragement, Franklin is able to land a good position in construction; with his first check, he helps her to get her piano out of storage so that she can begin playing and singing again. But the romance soon starts to sour, especially after Franklin withholds from Zora the truth about his job and about the wife whom he has never divorced. Zora too is hiding something: epilepsy. Her illness manifests itself after an unpleasant Thanksgiving dinner with Franklin's family.

Although they persevere, their lives together are not easy: Franklin loses job after job; Zora spends her savings, borrows from her father, and keeps deferring her songwriting dreams. Then, after terminating her first pregnancy by Franklin, she becomes pregnant again. Franklin, upset by her earlier abortion and intent on providing properly for this child, grows increasingly frustrated by his failure to get ahead; at one point, he even strikes Zora in anger. She in turn remains committed to Franklin but begins to develop other friends and resources. By the time her baby Jeremiah is born, she has completed a number of songs and realizes that she can reach an audience through writing, even if she never performs. But Zora's contentment only exacerbates Franklin's unhappiness. Drinking heavily, he threatens her; she goes to the police for a restraining order. Furious that she has used white authority to undermine him, he destroys all the furniture he has created in their apartment and leaves. Months later, when he returns to assume his responsibilities, Zora is not sure whether to take him back. Although she loves him, she decides to go home to Toledo and to a new teaching job. "Our lives need to keep going," she tells him. "That's been a big part of our problem. I think we both kind of disappeared somewhere along the way and just stopped moving altogether." She does, however, hold out the possibility of reconciliation by telling him "[when] you feel like you're ready, come get us" (382).

Unlike *How Stella Got Her Groove Back*, there is no happy ending; unlike *Waiting to Exhale*, there is not even any real resolution to the situation. There is only the hope that these two earnest young people will eventually learn to trust themselves—and each other—and find fulfillment together. But, as Paulette Richards demonstrates, as long as Franklin fails to take responsibility for his own life, he "disappears" as a human being; and as long as Zora tries to assume responsibility for him, her own power wanes. "*Disappearing Acts* therefore calls for a new paradigm of black male/female relationships in addition to indicting the political and economic oppression under which African Americans live" (99). By depicting two equally complex characters, McMillan not only overturns "some of the pernicious stereotypes about black love and black sexuality" but also offers a more interesting and realistic examination of the relationships between men and women than in her later formulaic popular romance novels.

Soon after publication in 1989, *Disappearing Acts* was optioned by Metro-Goldwyn-Mayer; McMillan wrote the screenplay.[18] But when that version never materialized, HBO (Home Box Office) Films picked up the option, produced the picture based on a different screenplay (by black screenwriter Lisa Jones), and premiered it in December, 2000. Gina Prince-Bythewood directed; McMillan and Wesley Snipes were co-producers; and Snipes also starred as Franklin Swift, with Sanaa Lathan (daughter of director Stan Lathan) cast as Zora. The film, for the most part, followed the book. But by focusing almost exclusively on the relationship between Zora and Franklin, it reduced or eliminated the roles of many of the supporting characters like Franklin's parents and Zora's friends Portia and Claudette, who gave the novel some of its quirky appeal and whose own stories comprised its various subplots. In the novel, for example, Franklin comes from a severely dysfunctional family. His "Pops," according to Franklin, is a "chump," and his "Moms" is a "bitch." When Franklin brings Zora to their home and she suggests over Thanksgiving dinner that the reason many blacks fail "goes back to our parents" (179), Moms becomes so agitated that she throws potatoes in Zora's face. (Significantly, later that night, Zora has an epileptic seizure, brought on by the stress of the evening with Franklin's family.) Later, after Franklin's sister Darlene, using one of her father's guns, tries to commit suicide in the family home, Pops finally leaves Moms and moves in with his troubled child. Upon hearing the news, Franklin says, "I felt myself smiling. So finally you [Pops] decided to be a man, huh?" (283). But in the film, the whole dysfunctional family dynamic, which is repeated in Franklin's relationship with his first wife and which anticipates his relationship with Zora, is reduced to Franklin's offhand remark that he hates his mother and to a single brief segment in which he introduces Zora to his parents (CCH Pounder and John Amos). Consequently, the important parallel—between Pops leaving home to assume responsibility for the care of his daughter and Franklin returning home to assume responsibility for his son by Zora—is lost.

Like his fictional counterpart, the film's Franklin is a passionate and essentially decent fellow; he is, however, considerably less vulgar in his speech and less violent in his actions. In the novel, as Zora recounts, Franklin "hauled off and slapped me so hard my head hit the headboard on the bed. I don't know what I saw, but something silver was swirling around in front of my eyes, and I felt the right side of my face stinging" (291). Later, after Jeremiah's birth, as their relationship continues to devolve, he stumbles drunkenly into their bedroom and rapes her; afterwards, he refuses to let her get up to wash herself. "I want you to sleep in it, so you'll know you slept with a real man all night" (350). Later still, having threatened Zora with more violence and told her he is leaving her, he gets drunk and destroys much of the apartment. "I wanted to make sure Zora gon' know I was gone," he says. "I was breaking up things so fast I couldn't even slow down long enough to realize what was mine and what wasn't. By the time I finished, it was so much sawdust in here that I couldn't breathe" (370). But in the film, although Franklin gets upset with Zora, he never slaps, physically abuses, or rapes her. And even when he turns destructive in his anger over their break-up, he destroys only those items that have a symbolic association—the bookcase, mirror, and coat rack that he built; the mantelpiece that he renovated; the mattress on which they slept. Significantly, he does not touch Zora's piano.

In the screen version, the character of Zora is also somewhat modified and, in contrast to the character of Franklin, enhanced.

Her two pregnancies by Franklin (the first terminated by an abortion) are collapsed into a single one, which she determines to see to term, with or without his support. The epilepsy from which she suffers in the novel and which serves as a physical manifestation of her emotional weakness becomes almost incidental. Her only seizure occurs one night while she is sleeping, not after the stressful first meeting with Franklin's parents; and it is never referred to again. And whereas in the novel Franklin threatens to leave their apartment, never really believing that Zora will let him go, in the film it is a newly empowered Zora who tells him, bluntly, to get out. Similarly, in the end, although Franklin is making a serious attempt to straighten himself out personally as well as professionally, it is Zora who succeeds in combining the challenges of parenthood and career; and it is she who seems to define the new terms of their relationship. That is why, as Leona Thompson writes, *Disappearing Acts* is a movie "designed for women" (*Boston Herald* 9 Dec. 2000: Arts and Life 28)—although there is enough in it, including some erotic interludes, for men to enjoy as well.

As reviewer Daryl H. Miller observed (*LA Times* 9 Dec. 2000: Calendar 2), *Disappearing Acts* is generally an honest and sensitive portrayal of a couple struggling to stay together; but the adaptation clearly softens the novel. Ron Wertheimer suggests that the softening results from the homogenization of the point of view, which—unlike the novel's alternating focus and alternating narrators—denies "Franklin the depth and rage that might explain some of his less-than-noble behavior while chipping away at Ms. McMillan's secondary characters and subplots" (*NYT* 8 Dec. 2000: E1). Although the film sizzles during the "lovely love scenes" between Zora and Franklin, according to Wertheimer, once "the hot stuff stops, the film cools down" considerably.[19] Yet, unlike the other adaptations of McMillan's works, the film version of *Disappearing Acts* at least attempts to show the complexities of a real relationship by depicting, if not always equally, female and male concerns.

THE WEDDING

A relationship between a mismatched couple is also the subject of Dorothy West's *The Wedding* (1995), another important black novel recently adapted to film. Shelby Coles, a light-skinned black woman who comes from a wealthy, upper-class black family, is engaged to be married to Meade Howell, a poor white jazz musician with limited financial prospects. Shelby's parents, Corinne and Clark, are understandably concerned about Meade's suitability as a husband—not because of his color, but because of his class. "The right color," Corinne says, is always preferable, "but not as mandatory as the right class" (90).

Clark wonders aloud why Shelby is marrying Meade. "I've never seen you give your trust to a colored man, and I can't help but think that maybe that's because you saw in the one you know best [himself] a man who can't be trusted," he tells her. "And I've never seen you give your respect to a colored man, and I can't help but think that maybe that's some warped extension of this family's social snobbery" (201). Clark appreciates that he has set a bad example for his daughters with his own opportunistic choices. As a young graduate from Harvard Medical School, at his parents' urging, he had rejected Sabina, the girl he truly loved, to marry Corinne, the light-skinned, well-connected daughter of a college president who could help him get ahead professionally. And for almost two decades, to compensate for the emptiness of his marriage, Clark has carried on a relationship with Rachel, his nurse, whom he hopes eventually to marry. But only days before Shelby's wedding, fearing that Clark will change his mind about getting a divorce, Rachel shocks him with the news that she has wed another man. The middle-aged Clark is left to face the terrible cost of the burden of his parents' expectations and the consequences of his own self-hatred: "Advanced social position did not come without an abnegation, an obliteration of the personal, the intimate, the hidden, the passionate" (196).

Corinne, a singularly undemonstrative woman, had married Clark for the same reason he had married her: because it was the socially appropriate choice. A generation earlier, out of loneliness and poverty, Corinne's white mother Josephine had wed the dark-skinned Hannibal; and, although Hannibal became a professor and eventually a college president, Josephine always regretted her choice. Moreover, she grew to despise Corinne, the baby who reminded her of her husband's blackness and of her own fall from Southern grace. Determined not to repeat her mother's mistake,

Corinne, a "product of her conditioning—no more, no less" (216), had married within her class, in a union of mutual convenience. For years, however, she has had discreet affairs with men as dark-skinned as the father who loved her and who Gram, her white grandmother, had disdained. "Her lust for dark black men under cover of night mirrored her repulsion [of them] during the day" (216). When Corinne and Clark's light-skinned daughter Liz decides to marry a dark-skinned doctor, Corinne refuses to invite his working-class family to the wedding, forcing Liz and Lincoln to elope—an act that neither the couple nor Corinne is able to forgive, even three years later. And although Corinne "actually didn't mind Meade" (215), she realizes grimly that perhaps her own bitterness over Liz's husband caused her younger daughter Shelby to choose "a white man as the lesser of two evils." Ironically, just as Corinne had snubbed Lincoln's parents, Meade's parents snub her by refusing to attend their son's wedding.

Gram (Great Grandmother Caroline Shelby, daughter of Southern Colonel Lance Shelby) has come a long way towards overcoming her old prejudices since Josephine ran away from home to marry Hannibal. The family matriarch, Gram had moved north to care for her ailing daughter, raised Corinne after Josephine's early death, and orchestrated a good marriage for Corinne to the up-and-coming Clark. Yet she delights in the prospect that Shelby's children, unlike Liz's young daughter, will likely be light-skinned and straight-haired—in other words, more white.

Complicating Shelby's life even more than the reservations of her family is the presence of Lute McNeil, who is renting a neighboring house for the summer. The father of three girls by three wives, Lute is handsome and wealthy; but he is not from the same social circle as the Coles. Nonetheless, his attraction to Shelby (who he boldly promises his girls will be their next mother) creates tension with Meade and conflict for Shelby, who finds herself strangely drawn to him. On the morning of her wedding, however, Shelby finally realizes just how selfish and duplicitous Lute really is: in the course of a violent argument with his third wife Della, from whom he is not yet divorced (despite his earlier attestation that he is already unattached), he accidentally runs over and kills one of his own children. "The scales," writes West, "had fallen from her [Shelby's] eyes. All of Lute's words about remaining true to one's race, all his subtle slurs, all were lies, pretexts. All of his deception and envy had led to this . . . Shelby could only thank God that it was not too late for her and Meade" (240).

The novel adroitly interweaves these various stories—of Shelby and Meade; of Lute and his wives; of Clark and Corinne Coles; of Hannibal, Josephine, and Gram; and of Clark's ancestors—and imbues all of the characters with an "abundance of psychological and historic richness." As *Washington Post* reviewer Elizabeth Benedict noted in 1995, West can be "wickedly eloquent about the costs of living in a world where the shadings in the color of one's skin are more important than the bonds between blood relatives" (qtd. in Andrew L. Yarrow, *NYT* 19 Aug. 1998: A29).

Unfortunately, the telefilm of *The Wedding* (1998), an ABC production released by Oprah Winfrey's Harpo Studios as *Oprah Winfrey Presents: The Wedding*, failed to convey the nuances of the interrelationships that undergird the narrative. Directed by director and accomplished playwright Charles Burnett from a screenplay by Lisa Jones, the film faithfully re-created the era that West so elegantly described: the grand houses and the vast expanses of beach in the exclusive "Oval" section of Martha's Vineyard; the carefully tended country clubs, parks, and gardens; the old-monied casualness of expensive furnishings that had remained within families for generations. But, unlike the novel, which creates a complex, multilayered story of love, identity, and family, the film focuses largely on the relationship between Shelby (Halle Berry) and Meade (Eric Thal) in the week prior to their wedding. They quarrel; they experience discrimination (in a scene original to the film) at a local restaurant, after which they rather belatedly begin contemplating the potential difficulties of their life together as an interracial couple; they break up; and they quickly reconcile—all with nary a hitch in the elaborate wedding plans.

By focusing on Shelby and Meade, however, the telefilm deemphasizes the complex canvas of events over four generations that made the novel so compelling. For instance, Clark's grandfather Preacher appears briefly in a flashback segment that suggests he was an eccentric character who made his livelihood by farming. (Preacher's wife, Butternut Woman, is never depicted.) By contrast, in the novel Preacher's savvy is described at great length, especially the way that he contracts with Mr. White Trash for a mule, a cow, and a pig as well as the manner in which he convinces the Bank President to give him wood to build his farm and a horse with which to transport the materials. Preacher does all of this because he is "determined to free the Coleses now and forever from the animal terms of 'struggle or die,' so that his son and those who came after him would eat without wolfish hunger and learn to reach for more than meat and bread" (130). And indeed Preacher's son Isaac becomes a Harvard-educated physician and the first in the family to spend his summers on Martha's Vineyard—although "the central irony of Isaac's life might have been that all of the material comfort he would obtain had less to do with his own (unimpeachable) toil than it did with the emotional emptiness of his marriage" (152), a pattern repeated in the unhappy marriage of Isaac's son, Clark. But in the film, the vital connection between Preacher and Isaac, not to mention between Preacher and Clark, is obscured.

In adapting West's novel to film, screenwriter Jones and director Burnett made a number of changes, some of which were significant. The film, for instance, offers virtually no hint of the psychological complexity of Lute (Carl Lumbly); he is portrayed as an infatuated and ultimately selfish man who hopes to become part of the black Cape community. West, however, gives a different, fuller portrait of the man. She writes that because he was abandoned by his mother, Lute tends to treat women with great disrespect and to engage in affair after affair—so much so, in fact, that even he lost count of the "women from the street on whom he practiced a savage carnality as if each wore the face of his mother, that face of which he did not know one line" (22). His three children are by three different white women, each of whom he threatens and abuses until she consents to divorce him so he can move on to a new victim. He lies to Shelby, telling her he is a free man when he is still secretly married to the wealthy Bostonian Della; attempts to undermine Shelby's relationship by saying that all Meade really wants is a taste of her exotic black lovemaking; and opportunistically hopes to position himself and his children in the "Oval" society. (Sharing "upper-class life" through marriage to Shelby: that was what "he had worked for all summer, for himself and his family" [234-35].) Even on the evening before her marriage, he extracts from Shelby a promise to meet him the following morning, in the hope of persuading her to abandon Meade.

While the film ends joyously with Shelby and Meade's wedding, at which the family is, for the most part, reconciled (Lincoln with the Coles, and the Coles—Corinne [Lynn Whitfield] and Clark [Michael Warren]—with each other), the novel ends well in advance of the wedding, with the death of Lute's daughter Tina. In that tragic instant, Shelby realizes the extent of Lute's duplicity, while Gram,[20] thinking "of Josephine, whom she had held the same way so many years before," reaches instinctively and protectively for her dark great-grandchild Laurie. "She could not turn the clock back. She could not change the past or do much about the present. But she could spend the little time she had left on earth making things a bit better for the future" (240). It is an ending full of subtle hopes and promises, but it is clearly not the Hollywood-style ending of the film version, in which everyone lives happily ever after, as indicated by the new family photo of the wedding party that is added to the mantle.

Novelist Dorothy West was keenly familiar with the world of *The Wedding*. Although her father was born a slave, his success in the fruit and produce business propelled the family into the black upper middle class of Boston and the Oak Bluffs section of Martha's Vineyard. West, who had begun writing stories at the age of seven in her family's elegant four-story townhouse in Boston, was barely twenty when one of her stories won a prize from the Urban League's *Opportunity* magazine. Encouraged, she moved to Harlem to join the poets, novelists, musicians, and artists who were forging a cultural rebirth there; in fact, she became the youngest (and the last surviving) member of the Harlem Renaissance. "We were all young and we fell in love with each other," she told an interviewer in 1995. "We all had the same ambitions: writers and painters and so forth. We were free. . . . We had an innocence that nobody can have now" (Yarrow A29). In 1932, West travelled to the Soviet Union with Langston Hughes (who nicknamed her "The Kid") and twenty other black Americans to work on a movie about racism that ultimately was never made. Back in the United States, she shared an apartment with Zora Neale Hurston; received a proposal of marriage from Countee Cullen; was scolded by Claude McKay for not writing more; and

founded several magazines to showcase the talents of black writers. Her own first novel, *The Living Is Easy*, a semi-autobiographical tale based on her mother, was not published until 1948, long
after the Harlem Renaissance had faded; and it was not until her
second novel *The Wedding*, begun in the 1940s, was published in
1995 and became a best seller that she was rediscovered. It is, however, a testament to her skill and prescience that the themes of *The
Wedding*—interracial and intraracial bigotry—seem as relevant
today as they were more than a half century ago.

Director Charles Burnett, who appreciated the distinctiveness
of West's novel, attempted to translate it accordingly to film. For
him, there were no villains in the piece. "I never looked at it in
terms of good and bad guys. I looked at it in terms of people with
their own dilemmas and problems they are trying to work out. We
were trying to make these people as human as possible and as
well-rounded and fully dimensional." Burnett added, "I tried to
alter people's awareness of a black family. This is a family and they
are not on drugs or committing crimes. It's a different type of tension and drama" (Susan King, *LA Times* 22 Feb. 1998: TV Times 4).
And indeed, by exploring the Coles family in terms of class rather
than race, Burnett—as West had done—brought black life from the
margins and into the mainstream of American life and culture.

Beloved

A different type of tension and drama was apparent in Toni
Morrison's Pulitzer Prize-winning novel *Beloved*, which portrayed
the endurance of a black woman who attempts to reconcile the
past and ensure a future for herself and those whom she loves. But
Beloved was remarkable in the way that it combined the elements
of a slave narrative with those of a ghost story. As Denise Heinze
writes, in *Beloved* "Morrison embraces the supernatural as perhaps
the ideal vehicle for the investigation of slavery, an institution so
incomprehensible that Morrison suggests that most Americans
would like to bury it, since it is the most historical reminder of a
national disgrace" (182). Morrison herself was reluctant to resurrect, much less to personalize, the Civil War slave era. The basis of
her novel was the true story of a slave named Margaret Garner,

who murdered her own child rather than return her to slavery; Garner was then tried, not for the crime of murder but for running away, and was given back to her master, who sold her down the river to an uncertain fate. But Morrison admitted that while she was fascinated by the murder itself, she was not so much interested in the particulars of Garner's life. Her intention was to invent the details and to use Garner as a metaphor for the whole black slave experience. But she knew that, as an author, she would have "to enter that life," and initially that realization frightened her: "It was an unwillingness and a terror of going into an area for which you have no preparation. It's a commitment of three or four years to living inside [a character and an era]."[21]

Yet Morrison's use of the supernatural to explore the historical was, according to Margo Jefferson, a brilliant choice. "Ghosts embody what is almost past enduring: murder, imprisonment, guilt and shame over deeds that cannot be undone. The nineteenth century produced some of our greatest ghost stories . . . [not only novels but also black folklore,] all of those slavery-shaped tales in which bloody bones rise up to utter curses and devils stroll into backyards to make small talk before the deadly bargain is struck. Richard Wright wrote that if Edgar Allan Poe had been black, he would not have invented horror, horror would have invented him. In *Beloved*, the inventor and the invention are as one" (*NYT* 19 Oct. 1998: E1).

That oneness is evident throughout the screen adaptation of *Beloved*, in which mother and child, living and dead, past and present, good and evil, dreams and nightmares become at times interchangeable. Directed by Jonathan Demme from a script by actress-screenwriter Akosua Busia (who played Nettie in the film of *The Color Purple*), Richard LaGravenese, and Adam Brooks, the film version of *Beloved* opens with the stark image of a headstone, on which is inscribed the single word "Beloved." From the silence of the cemetery, the camera moves to the explosive scene inside a home that is obviously haunted: objects inexplicably fly around the kitchen, tiny handprints appear mysteriously on the top of a cake, a mirror shatters as soon as someone looks into it, and a dog is flung so hard against a wall that his eye is left hanging outside of its socket. As Sethe, the house's owner, tries to calm her daughter Denver and tend to the suffering pet, her two sons, Buglar and

Howard, grab some food from the table and flee for their lives.

Eight years later, it is 1873: with Sethe's boys long gone and with her mother-in-law Baby Suggs (Beah Richards) dead soon after their leave-taking, only Sethe (Oprah Winfrey) and Denver (Kimberly Elise) are left in the house. Only Sethe and Denver—and "baby ghost," that is, the spirit of the beloved infant that Sethe, a former slave, lost eighteen years earlier, soon after she had escaped from Sweet Home, the Kentucky plantation where she had worked for much of her early life. Having arranged to send her three young children ahead to Baby Suggs, a freed slave living in Ohio, Sethe had followed alone. In a boat on the banks of the Ohio River, she had gone into labor; with the assistance of a strange white girl, she had given birth; and through the kindness of Stamp Paid (Albert Hall), a black ferryman, she had made her way to Baby's house, where she enjoyed twenty-eight days of freedom before the slave catchers caught up with her to bring her back to the plantation.

When Paul D (Danny Glover), a slave who had worked alongside Sethe and her husband Halle at Sweet Home, seeks her out after almost two decades, his presence seems to awaken the house's spirit: a pulsing scarlet light tries to push him back the instant that he crosses the threshhold. But Sethe's reassurance that the spirit is not evil, just "sad," and the silent memories of his own travails combined with his great desire to find a place to call home keep Paul D from retreating. Within days, the two old friends settle into a comfortable familial accord. But as soon as Sethe shares with Paul D some of the secret sorrow she has endured—the "tree" on her back (evoked in a brief and aesthetically problematical flashback) that she received in punishment at the plantation, the "haint" in her house, and the daughter that she holds so tightly in her arms because she is the only thing that stands in between—the haunting resumes. It is clear that the spirit wants Paul D out; but, having established himself in the household and in Sethe's life, he refuses to move. In fact, his refusal is so insistent that he appears to succeed is displacing the spirit. Denver, however, knows differently: "I think the baby ain't gone," she says; "I think the baby got plans."

To introduce a little happiness and normalcy into their lives, Paul D invites Sethe and Denver to a local carnival. Upon returning home, they are startled to discover in their front yard a strange, beautiful, but almost catatonic figure who has apparently emerged clothed and wet from a nearby stream. When asked her name, she replies in a croaking voice that she is "Beloved." Despite having the physical appearance of a young woman in her late teens, Beloved possesses the smooth perfect skin of a baby and the manner of an infant: she walks unsteadily, giggles, rages, stuffs food into her mouth without chewing it, feels uncontrollable cravings for sweet things, snores, slobbers, drools, vomits, and soils herself.

Unable or unwilling to say where she came from, she arouses Paul D's suspicions. Yet Denver, who is so psychically scarred by the traumatic events she has suffered over the years that she never ventures beyond the yard, is delighted by her company: Denver wants simply to care for and love her. But Beloved is interested only in Sethe. And with her eerie, insinuating questions and her irresistible requests to "tell me, tell me," she draws from Sethe stories of her past that Sethe has never before been willing to tell, stories of the horrors she experienced at Sweet Home, when her milk was taken from her breasts and when her back was split with cowhide, and of the comfort she received from Baby Suggs, the preacher whose words helped to bind and restore the struggling

Figure 7.5. In *Beloved*, after Beloved (Thandie Newton) mysteriously appears in their lives, Sethe (Oprah Winfrey) and Denver (Kimberly Elise) must struggle to reconcile the past. *(Touchstone Pictures, 1998)*

black community. Yet Beloved already knows things about Sethe that no one else does, like the gift of crystal earrings that she received on her wedding day and carried with her to Ohio to "light" the way for her husband Halle to follow.

Convinced that Beloved is her baby girl who has come back to her from the dead—and who is beginning life anew at the very point at which she died—Sethe gives her everything that her heart can offer and her money can buy: cakes and candies, ribbons, new dresses, a cloth doll. But Beloved wants more: she wants Sethe's soul. After seducing Paul D, Beloved drives him out of the house, the same way he tried to drive her spirit out soon after his arrival, so that she can have Sethe all to herself. As Margo Jefferson writes, the film offers a full-blown Freudian black family romance: "children witness the primal scene (their mother having sex with a man who is not even their father); daughters punish the male intruder with rejection or attempts at seduction; sisters compete for their mother's love. And over it all is a past that has laid siege to every sanctioned notion of what a family can or should be" (1).

In his effort to resist Beloved's advances, Paul D tries to reaffirm his relationship with Sethe by suggesting that they start their own family. ("A way to hold on to her, document his manhood and break out of the girl's spell—all in one" [128], writes Morrison in the novel.) His seemingly loving sentiment forces Sethe's deepest secret: that, when the slave catchers had come searching for her after her escape eighteen years earlier, she had murdered her infant daughter and tried to kill her other children so that they would not have to live out their days as slaves at Sweet Home. A shocked Paul D calls Sethe a four-legged animal and walks out the door, pushing Sethe further into the arms of Beloved.

Caring about little else besides the daughter who has returned to her, Sethe shows up late for work and loses her job; afterwards she rarely leaves home again. Denver realizes that it is up to her to deliver her mother from the madness into which she is sinking. First by seeking assistance from the black community from which Sethe had isolated herself over the years and then by finding employment in town with the Bodwins, Denver reverses roles with Sethe and assumes responsibility for the household. (Fig. 7.5.) But one afternoon, as Denver waits outside for Mr. Bodwin to pick her up for work and a group of women arrives to pray over the house, a naked, pregnant Beloved appears on the porch; mistaking Bodwin for the white slave catcher from Sweet Home, a crazed Sethe tries to attack him with an ice pick. In that instant, Beloved disappears and Sethe is left even more bereft, at least until Denver locates Paul D and urges him to return. His reunion with Sethe raises the redemptive possibility of their becoming a family once again, a family that loves "thick" and honors the "rememory" of all who are beloved.

To be sure, among the most distinguished features of the film were its fine performances: as Paul D, a slave who has suffered much, including the madness of his friend Halle after he witnessed the assault on Sethe at Sweet Home (a fact of which Sethe is long unaware), Danny Glover is at times almost heartbreaking. Afraid of revealing the secrets and emotions that he has hidden deep within his "red heart," he seeks the solace of Sethe, who can understand what he cannot express because she too has lived through unspeakable horror. Yet, when she finally utters her own long-held secret, the intimacy that had once consoled him now repels him. Effortlessly, flawlessly, Glover conveys the requisite emotional shifts.

As Denver, Kimberly Elise is full of repressed emotion and silent yearning for another life. To get free of the ghosts that haunt her family, she must break from the house that contains them. A vivid, watchful presence, she does not say much; but it is clear that she has inherited her mother's strength and that she sees and understands everything around her. But, as Jay Carr notes, whereas her mother embodies the past, Elise's Denver "represents the future," especially as "she emerges into the bustling post-Civil War city of Cincinnati, filled with expansionist energies" (*Boston Globe* 16 Oct. 1998: C1). Elise's performance, as she moves from sullen silence and jealousy of Paul D—and later of Beloved—to surprising self-assertion, is subtle and nuanced. Paul Ansen, in fact, writes that "her transformation from outcast to independent woman gives the movie its defining arc" (*Newsweek* 19 Oct. 1998: 76).

Equally strong is Thandie Newton's bold and sensual rendering of Beloved, a haunted and haunting spirit made flesh. Margo Jefferson notes that Newton "rolls her eyes constantly, the way slightly brain-damaged children do, but also the way those repellent caricatures of pickaninnies used to. She is terrifying to watch"

(1), largely because she manages to maintain the mystery and otherworldliness of her character. And Oprah Winfrey, while the least intuitive actress in the film, conveys the secrecy and the vulnerability that is appropriate to Sethe. With a stubborn strength born of conviction, she fights for her children; and even in the aftermath of her tragic choice, she exhibits an enormous dignity. Most touching, however, is the way that Winfrey's Sethe responds to what little affection she is offered: she knows how to deal with hardship, because it is so familiar to her, but is ill-prepared to accept or acknowledge tenderness. (The younger Sethe, who is featured in the harrowing flashback scenes shot by longtime Demme cinematographer Tak Fujimoto on special, deliberately grainy film stock, is beautifully realized by Lisa Gay Hamilton.)

While the screenplay was largely faithful to Morrison's mythic novel, effectively capturing its central and specific tragedy, it did not "evoke the sweeping, multilayered lyricism of a great work of fiction."[22] Nor did it incorporate the novel's most brutal or heartbreaking details, such as the story behind the gravestone, which taught Beloved her name and for which Sethe paid with blood and soul. More importantly, it eliminated much of the background of Sethe's loved ones, particularly the extended look at life at Sweet Home, the ironically named plantation, where Sethe's horror began. Kenneth Turan was correct in observing that the screenplay took "the sane way out, paring the book down to its essential events." But he agreed that the background information was critical to the film's impact; and the exclusion or abbreviation of it into "short, often frenzied bursts" contributed to the difficulty of following the plot. ("To read Morrison's novel after seeing the film," he writes, "is frequently to say, 'So that's what that was all about.'"[23]) Similarly, David Ansen noted that one of the difficulties in translating the book to screen is "that most of the story's crucial events take place in the past"; and while Demme is understandably reluctant to linger on the abuses of slavery, "it's a dramaturgical mistake. The quick, shocking flashbacks of Sethe's brutalization by her white masters don't do the job—they're horrific, but with a B-movie luridness" (76).[24]

Lost in the film's paring down of events[25] is the full extent of the laceration and degradation of the characters' lives—of Paul D's misery, which often parallels Sethe's: his brutal treatment on the prison chain gang, where he lived in a barred, subterranean box, and on the plantation, where he was beaten and subjected to tortures like an iron collar and a bit; where he was worked like an ass and treated worse than a dog; where he watched his fellow slaves driven mad or burned alive as punishment; where he suffered the indignity of seeing the once-puny rooster he raised being addressed as Mister when he knew "wasn't no way I'd ever be"; where he learned to bury his red heart "in that tobacco tin buried in his chest" and felt its lid rust shut (72-73). Baby Suggs also suffers the indignities of slavery: never having been allowed to get to know her children before they were stolen from her (all she remembers about one of her girls is that she liked the crusty bottom of bread), Baby is unable to celebrate her freedom because her son Halle buys it at the cost of his own. Even as a freed black, she continues to suffer, forced to witness the slavers try to take from Sethe what they already took from her. Believing "*they* had won" (184), she stops preaching at the Clearing, gives up on everything but her fascination with colors, and takes to her bed to die.

Like Baby Suggs's children, Sethe never had the chance to know her mother. Young Sethe, in fact, had been forced to watch her mother hang for crimes that she could never comprehend. And afterward she learns to repress her pain and stifle her tongue, the same way the slave owners had stifled her mother's mouth with a bit (which, in the film version, is glimpsed but never explained). The bit, Morrison has said, was a "signal instrument of silence . . . [used] to shut you up, so that you could not say, you could not talk back, you could not articulate a contrary position or do any violence with your tongue or your words. And that was a complete erasure of language that the victim or the oppressed had" (qtd. in Silverblatt 3). The silence that Sethe imposes on herself thus mirrors the silence imposed upon her mother.

Even for Denver, the only one of Sethe's children not born into slavery, the past is never just the past. She fears that Sethe will cut her throat, the way she did her sister's: "All the time, I'm afraid the thing that made it all right for my mother to kill my sister could happen again. I don't know what it is, I don't know who it is, but maybe there is something else terrible enough to make her do it again. . . . Whatever it is, it comes from outside this house, outside the yard, and it can come right on in the yard if it wants to. So I never leave this house and I watch over the yard, so it can't happen again and my mother won't have to kill me too" (205). When Beloved suddenly appears, Denver recognizes her and remembers swallowing her blood along with milk from her mother's breast. Believing that "Beloved was *hers*" (104), she tries to shield her from Sethe; but she soon realizes that it is Sethe whom she must shield from Beloved. "The job she started out with, protecting Beloved from Sethe, changed to protecting her from Beloved. Now it was obvious that her mother could die. . ." (243). From her early traumatic deafness to her paralyzing fear of leaving the property, Denver shares fully in the legacy of her mother's slavery.

If the past is never quite the past in Morrison's *Beloved*, it is always inextricably linked to the present, even if the film at times fails to depict that link. And people and events are similarly interconnected. The Garners, who own Sweet Home, for example, bring the newly freed Baby Suggs to the Bodwin residence in Cincinnati. The Bodwins give Baby work and offer her a home outside of town in which to live (the home later occupied by Sethe and Denver); it is to that home that Stamp Paid delivers Sethe's children after ferrying them across the same river, and over the river that he transports Sethe, too, with her newborn Denver. After Sethe serves her jail term—a sentence not even alluded to in the film—the Bodwins intercede to get her a position as a cook at Sawyer's; and the Bodwins help Denver when she approaches them for help after her mother is fired. Mr. Bodwin is also the man whom Sethe mistakes for the slave catcher and whom she attacks (an action that, in the book, leads to her eviction from the home that is still owned by the Bodwins). All of the characters thus become like threads in a single tapestry; and when one begins to unravel, the texture of the whole is affected.

Many critics responded enthusiastically to the film. Jay Carr called it "a strong, dark, tangled powerhouse of a film that comes to grips with the scars of slavery as no previous American film has" and that is difficult to sit through, not because of its length but because of the slow, heavy, sad journey it takes (*Boston Globe* 16 Oct. 1998: C1). Margo Jefferson found *Beloved* to be so deep and rich that it was actually several movies in one. As a women's picture, it was a fierce melodrama about a woman cast out by her community for a deed as noble as it was monstrous. As a plantation saga, it offered a vision radically different from other big Hollywood films like *Gone With the Wind* (though, as Jefferson demonstrates, "Sethe has managed to improve her lot simply by acquiring what Scarlett O'Hara deemed the mark of her degradation: a piece of property no one else cared for and a subsistence living"). As a multilayered ghost story, it brought the unquiet dead back to claim the souls of the living. And, even if the film occasionally staggered under so much weight, it was nonetheless "truthful" and "compelling" (1). Kenneth Turan thought *Beloved* to be full of confounding contradictions but also full of power; once the film gets its bearing, he wrote, "the unsentimental fierceness of its vision brushes obstacles and quibbles from its path" to create a large and poetic story (*LA Times* 16 Oct. 1998: F1).[26]

But, despite Oprah Winfrey's aggressive promotion on her talk show and in numerous newspaper, magazine, and television interviews of the film she called "my *Schindler's List*" (Jefferson 1)—that is, a story as uniquely about black survival as Spielberg's epic was about the survival of Jews—audiences failed to embrace it. Joe Roth, Chairman of Disney Studios, which produced *Beloved* at a cost estimated to have been between $75 and $80 million, could speak only of the "pain" of the film's poor box office. (In the month after its release, *Beloved* had grossed around $20 million; by contrast, the sophomoric Adam Sandler comedy *The Water Boy*, another Disney release, grossed almost twice that amount in its first weekend.) Serious, artistic movies, Roth admitted, rarely attract the moviegoing public anymore: "It's like barking in the wind" (Weinraub, *NYT* 9 Nov. 1998: E4). *Beloved*'s low box office came as a shock not only at Disney but also at rival studios. After all, according to Bernard Weinraub, *Beloved* "had been seen almost as a test case of whether an expensive and serious film that dealt with the black experience would appeal to mainstream audiences." And given the film's disappointing grosses, many movie executives agreed that it would "almost certainly make it even more difficult for filmmakers to find studio support for large-budget movies involving racial themes."[27]

Gene Seymour (*Los Angeles Times* 5 Dec. 1998: Calendar 20), however, suggests that industry eyes may have been too swift in transforming "Sure Thing to Cautionary Tale" and "aficionados of celebrity crash-and-burn" too ready to revel "in watching Oprah's

Oscar Triumph morph into Oprah's Box-Office Waterloo. Worse, industry mavens have attached a toe tag to this movie even as it continues to play at a theater near you." Seymour writes that *Beloved* did not deserve such negative treatment any more than it deserved the hosannas that garlanded its arrival at the multiplexes. Nonetheless, some lessons could be derived from its tribulations, among them that slavery and other serious topics related to blacks have not yet become easy or profitable subjects for feature movies. *Beloved*'s dismal financial showing followed similar poor grosses for *Amistad* and *Rosewood*, released a year earlier—all of which offered "a cold slap in the face to black filmmakers who entered the decade believing that they could finally tell 'their stories' on the big screen to 'their audiences.'" Seymour concludes that, while the success or failure of any single film should not be allowed "to set the table for what comes afterward," black filmmakers' best hope for artistic and financial fulfillment within the commercial marketplace is "to infiltrate established formulas," like romances and soap operas, a suggestion borne out by the success of black films like *Waiting to Exhale* and *Eve's Bayou* (20).

Writer-producer Tina Andrews, on the other hand, was convinced that the problem with *Beloved*'s appeal had to do with its medium. "I really believe," she writes, "that *Beloved* would have done well if it had premiered on television. Audiences don't want to sit around with a bunch of strangers, spend all this money for popcorn, baby sitters and parking, to be browbeaten for three hours. . . . I really think that the acceptance of these projects has to do with the medium" (qtd. in Greg Braxton, *LA Times* 26 Feb. 2000: A1). Los Angeles television and film critic Greg Braxton similarly observed that while people seem unwilling to pay to sit in a theater and visit the horrors of slavery or desegregation, "they will gather around their television set at home to watch visceral, often painful depictions of racial conflict" (Braxton 1). Even as serious films like *Beloved* floundered at the box office, growing numbers of telepictures that focused on turbulent racial events—like the CBS miniseries *Sally Hemings: An American Scandal*, about Thomas Jefferson's longtime black slave mistress; *Freedom Song* (TNN), about forced integration in Mississippi; and *Parting the Waters* (ABC), based on Taylor Branch's Pulitzer Prize-winning book about civil rights—attracted the interest of filmmakers and audiences alike.

Morrison had found much to praise in Winfrey and Demme's film adaptation of her novel *Beloved*. But in an interview with Michael Silverblatt, she remarked on the "powerful difference" between the two mediums, which goes well beyond mere reduction: "You have a major void in a movie, which is: You don't have a reader, you have a viewer, and that is such a different experience. As subtle as a movie can be, as careful and artful as it can be, in the final analysis it's blatant because you see it. You can translate certain things, make certain interpretations, create wonder, certainly there can be mystery, but the encounter with language is a private exploration."[28] Yet among the most notable achievements of the film *Beloved* was the way that it created not only wonder and mystery but also its own cinematic language—an achievement that harked back to the best of the black filmmakers and the white producers of black-oriented and black-themed films over the years.

CONCLUSION

At the beginning of the twentieth century, black representation in film consisted largely of stereotypes that distorted the black experience and were shaped by the sentimental racism of American culture as well as the more overt racism of society reflected by prominent early directors and filmmakers like D. W. Griffith, who turned Thomas Dixon's *The Clansman* into a masterpiece of bigotry. For years, especially after the rise of the oligopolistic Hollywood studio system, blacks on screen were limited to minor and often demeaning roles as servants and clowns, brutal bucks and tragic mulattoes, amusing "pickaninnies" and lazy "darkies," roles that derived from popular literature by whites and from nineteenth-century minstrel shows and popular theater productions; and blacks were largely precluded from making significant contributions off screen.

The early black independent filmmakers, particularly Noble Johnson and Oscar Micheaux, were determined to counter the old stereotypes and negative portrayals with more realistic images of black Americans, often drawn from literary works by black writers. In their black-produced and black-cast movies, these race filmmakers created an alternate set of cultural referents and established new character types and situations that challenged conventional racist representations of blackness. In Micheaux's films alone, black protagonists ran the gamut from teachers and farmers to men of fortune and millionaires; women played key roles; and racially charged depictions of contemporary events included Klan lynchings and enactments of restrictive real estate covenants. But these noteworthy advances were arrested and the burgeoning black film industry halted by a number of unfortunate events, including underfinancing, high production costs, poor distribution, increased competition from big studios, and the Depression.

Hollywood's early sound films of the 1930s and of the 1940s rehashed many of the standard and stereotypical elements of earlier silent productions. In the plantation sagas, the greatest of which was *Gone With the Wind* (based on Margaret Mitchell's bestselling novel of the Old South), blacks worked in the fields as contented slaves or in the homes as devoted Toms and Mammies; in the jungle and African-themed films like *King Kong* and *Tarzan* (based on Edgar Rice Burroughs's literary hero), they appeared as bestial primitives who were clearly inferior to their white colonizers; and in the black-cast Jim Crow musicals like *The Green Pastures* (based on Marc Connelly's play), they were caricatured as crapshooters, gun toters, policy players, loose women, and trickers who were unable to fend for themselves. Virtually all of these films reinforced racial myths by betraying a nostalgia for the happy old days (Mitchell called it the "lavender-and-old-lace-moonlight-on-the-magnolia" tradition) and by promoting racial segregation that suggested blacks belonged among their own kind—but always, of course, under the guiding hand of whites.

The Second World War helped to heighten racial consciousness as pressure developed within American society to rectify racial inequalities. The government and the movie industry collaborated on *The Negro Soldier* (scripted by black playwright Carlton Moss), an important tribute to black participation in the war effort, and other similar initiatives; the "New Negro" began making his way to the screen in studio films like the movie adaptation of Ellen Glasgow's *In This Our Life*; and postwar agreements between the major studios and the NAACP, prompted by protests against dishonest and demeaning racial representations, forced Hollywood to reconsider some of its more blatant stereotyping, which persisted as late as the much-maligned *Song of the South* (1946), Disney's regressive version of the Uncle Remus tales, and beyond. The racial and social message films of the postwar period, particularly the crucial 1949 cycle of films that included *Pinky*, *Lost Boundaries*, *Home of the Brave*, and *Intruder in the Dust* (all adapted from literature), helped to modify and liberalize black racial imagery; and Richard Wright's film of his novel *Native Son* introduced a black perspective that would signal an exciting direction for later Hollywood films.

The "problem pictures" of the late 1940s and early 1950s, which broke ground for more intelligent explorations of the black experience in movies, also paved the way for another new black character type, the integrationist hero played by Sidney Poitier, who for almost two decades would dominate Hollywood mainstream cinema in films like *Edge of the City*, *Porgy and Bess*, *A Patch of Blue*, and *To Sir, with Love* (many of which were also adapted from literature). But as the Eisenhower era gave rise to the age of black power, other new black character types appeared: the emerging militant in Lorraine Hansberry's *A Raisin in the Sun* and LeRoi Jones's *Dutchman*; the young protagonist coming of age in *The Learning Tree*, *Sounder*, and *Go Tell It on the Mountain*; the tough, self-confident action hero in *Cotton Comes to Harlem* and the other films based on the fiction of Chester Himes and in *Shaft* (which lent a black sensibility to Ernest Tidyman's novel), among the earliest anti-Establishment "blaxploitation" movies.

By the final decades of the twentieth century, as blacks had started to move more fully into politics, entertainment, and society at large, Hollywood, too, tried to promote the notion of black assimilation, often by projecting images of racial harmony through its biracial buddy movies, essentially unequal pairings in which whites continued to be dominant, or by portraying the struggles for civil rights, although usually from a white rather than a black perspective. By contrast, the films of the new wave of black directors, including Spike Lee, John Singleton, and Mario Van Peebles, and the host of important films and telefilms adapted from the works of contemporary black writers challenged conventional Hollywood depictions of black life. (In his recent film *Bamboozled* [2000], in fact, Lee decried the familiar stereotypes that Americans—white and black—continue to endure and perpetuate:

he condemned whites for manufacturing "the old image of the shiftless, larcenous Negro" and for still seeing blacks through that warped prism, and he chastized blacks for inhabiting new and polar-opposite categories—and new stereotypes—like "the gangsta and the Buppie."[29]) Those black-produced or black-oriented films broke cinematic formulas, offered realistic visions of the black experience (from politics to sexuality, from professional aspirations to female bonding), and demonstrated the existence of a growing market—among black as well as white audiences—for movies that featured black characters.

Over the course of the century, some of the most interesting and sympathetic representations of ethnic life derived from literature by authors like Paul Laurence Dunbar in the 1910s and 1920s; Langston Hughes and James Weldon Johnson in the 1930s and 1940s; Richard Wright in the 1950s; Lorraine Hansberry, Chester Himes, Ernest Gaines, and Gordon Parks, Sr. in the 1960s and 70s; Alice Walker and Gloria Naylor in the 1980s; and Terry McMillan and Toni Morrison in the 1990s. Today, filmmakers are beginning to turn more frequently to black literature for the subjects of their films; and those adaptations—most good, some bad—are becoming what adaptations of literature by white authors have been since the beginning of cinema: an essential part of the commercial and artistic process. Theatrically released feature films—and, increasingly in recent years, high-quality made-for-cable movies and network telefilms—based on black works have indeed, to borrow Oscar Micheaux's words, presented "the race . . . in the light and background of [its] true state" and "raised [black] people to greater heights." And not only black film but the whole of American cinema is that much richer for the efforts of filmmakers and writers from Micheaux to Morrison.

NOTES TO CHAPTER 7

1. *Roll of Thunder, Hear My Cry* was the winner of the 1977 Newbery Medal for the Most Distinguished Contribution to Literature for Children. *Song of the Trees*, also about the Logan family, won the Council on Interracial Books Award in the African American category and was named an Outstanding Book of the Year in 1975 by the *New York Times*.

2. In "Sifting Through the Controversy: Reading *The Color Purple*," Jacqueline Bobo wrote that "The film *The Color Purple* has been constructed as controversial by the media coverage of the protests against it, as have the novel, and, by extension, Alice Walker. In a sort of revolving door operation each subject involved in the controversy has taken on a controversial aspect: the novel, the author, the film, the director. At times even the defenders of the works have come under fire. Armond White of the New York *City-Sun*; Vernon Jarrett of the Chicago *Sun-Times*; and Kwasi Geiggar, head of a Los Angeles group, the Coalition Against Black Exploitation, appeared as part of a panel on *Tony Brown's Journal* to debate the effect of the film. When White declared that there was something worthwhile that could come from the film, Jarrett replied that if White liked the film he may as well be white. In another instance, a clip of Whoopi Goldberg was shown on *The Phil Donahue Show* while Tony Brown was a panelist. Goldberg said that those who criticize *The Color Purple* for showing negative images of black men should also criticize Prince for the disturbing images he showed of black women being dumped in garbage cans in *Purple Rain*. Brown replied in response to her statement that there were those who practiced the art of saying what white people wanted them to say" (333).

3. Marlaine Glicksman, "Lee Way," *Film Comment* October 1986: 48.

4. Manthia Diawara, "Black Spectatorship: Problems of Identification and Resistance," in *Black American Cinema* 218.

5. Walker also draws the parallel between the oppression of black women in the American South and the oppression of black women in Africa in various of her other works, including *Possessing the Secret of Joy*.

6. Celie's making of pants with Shug is, according to Mary Jane Lupton (414), the equivalent of her quilting with Sofia. Pantsmaking is also a way by which Celie takes control of her life; it allows her creativity in a male sphere.

7. Joan Digby (162) also notes that while it was Meyjes who adapted the novel, Walker herself "stayed close to the project, assisting in the revisions of dialogue necessitated by Spielberg's direction of the piece as an evolving drama."

8. Scarification is not the only African American folkway that Spielberg misconstrues; the practice of "signifying" is another. For a discussion of signifying in *The Color Purple* (film and novel), see John Peacock's essay on "Adapting *The Color Purple*: When Folk Goes Pop," in Barbara Tepa Lupack's *Take Two: Adapting the Contemporary American Novel to Film*, 112-30.

9. Jacqueline Bobo, in *Black Women as Cultural Readers* (80-84), observes that, in the film, Spielberg incorporates *Oliver Twist* at several important points: when Nettie uses it to teach the young Celie how to read; when Mr. ___, on horseback, chases and assaults Nettie, and her books (including a copy of *Oliver Twist*) fall to the ground; and when the older Celie, alone in the house after Mr. ___'s departure, picks up the novel and begins to read from it. Bobo concludes: "Spielberg's sense of the novel *The Color Purple* that the life of a young black girl growing up in a world in which she has no access to power until she empowers herself is equivalent to the life of Oliver as chronicled by Dickens (or translated in film versions of his novels), reveals much about the overall mood of the film. It is one of 'sweetness and light' rather than of horror and evil; it is stylized and stagy, as was much of Dickens; and it played too much to the comic elements of life instead of dealing substantially with emotional issues" (84).

10. Bobo notes that "in the novel, Shug has a carefully thought-out system of values. She lives her life according to her standards and is free to do so because she is not dependent on anyone emotionally or economically. In the film she is controlled by all the men connected to her: Mister, her father, Grady. She is not the self-possessed woman of the novel but someone who is pulled by the strings of her sexuality and her insecurity about the way she lives her life. The film casts a moral judgment on Shug" (*Black Women* 71-72).

11. Whoopi Goldberg originally wrote a letter to Alice Walker in the hope of being allowed to play Sofia. "But Spielberg, after seeing her perform, wanted her for Celie. The flexibility of her body-language and facial gestures enabled her to assume every archetypal mask of black portraiture" (Digby 170).

12. Nonetheless, as shrewd and lyrical as Naylor's portrayals are, *The Women of Brewster Place*, according to Annie Gottlieb, is not realistic but mythic fiction. "Nothing supernatural happens in it, yet its vivid, earthy characters (especially Mattie) seem constantly on the verge of breaking out into magical powers." This is particularly true of the book's two climaxes—one of healing and rebirth, as Mattie wrestles Ciel back to life; the other of destruction, as Lorraine, rejected by the others, is gang-raped, "a blood sacrifice proving the sisterhood of all women" (4).

13. Tom Shales notes that Oprah "generously gave herself star billing, above the title, while far more accomplished actresses . . . are relegated to

supporting status down below." Her Mattie, supposed to be "the Mother Catalyst of the piece," is more of "a passive blob, at least until the last five minutes, when she attacks the oh-so-symbolic wall separating Brewster Place from the rest of the world." Shales also observes that the script by Karen Hall lacks dramatic momentum and is so full of long dangling conversations "that it often turns into a talk show—appropriately, perhaps," since Oprah plays the lead character (*Washington Post* 18 March 1989: C1).

14. Bobo and Seiter write that (as of the time of the production of *The Women of Brewster Place*) "with the exception of Euzhan Palcy (*A Dry White Season*, 1989), no black women directors have succeeded in making commercial films in the United States, although independent filmmakers such as Julie Dash, Debra Robinson, and Zeinabu Irene Davis, or television directors such as Caroll Parrott Blue, M. Neema Barnette, and Debbie Allen certainly had the qualifications to take on such a project" (147).

15. Bobo and Seiter examine the ways that the telefilm reorders the conventions of the television melodrama by exploring the range of relationships between women: "as friends, roommates, lovers, mothers, and daughters" (150-51).

16. "Television," as Gilliam rightly observes, "is the way the white world gets much of its information on blacks and other people of color." But for Gilliam, it is not just the men who are poorly portrayed. *The Women of Brewster Place*, she writes, also revives every stereotype of the black woman that "ever festered in the mind of the most feverish racist. . . . They're sexy, sultry, lazy, wildly religious, carefree, aggressive and destined to be alone. They achieve identity only through children."

17. Kenneth Turan (*LA Times* 22 Dec. 1995: Calendar 1) writes: "The best and funniest stuff in *Waiting to Exhale* is the women's acerbic outlook on the sexual predilections of the men they become entangled with." He adds that "the only thing wrong with *Exhale's* sexual humor is that there isn't nearly enough of it. . . . the film's serious moments are stiff, standard, and not nearly as affecting as what's accomplished with comedy." But Terry McMillan felt that the film at times sacrificed emotional depth for sexual comedy. According to Edward Guthmann (*San Francisco Chronicle*, 8 Feb. 1998: Datebook 38), McMillan noted that a "brilliant scene" in which Lela Rochon interacts with her father, who has Alzheimer's, "got thrown out because it was a minute and a half too long. But then they'll put in gratuitous sex scenes which get a laugh—and that's somehow more important."

18. After writing the screenplays for *Waiting to Exhale* and *How Stella Got Her Groove Back* and a screenplay (never used) for *Disappearing Acts*, McMillan announced, "I learned that I'm not doing it again. Without sounding ungrateful, what it really boils down to is that screenwriting, where you sort of write by committee, is a lot different than writing a novel." She concludes that "I don't have the temperament for it [writing

adapted screenplays]. I have a lot of respect for the medium and the power of it, and I'm not saying I wouldn't write an original screenplay. But no more adaptations" (Guthmann 38).

19. If the movie, writes Ron Wertheimer (*NYT* 8 Dec. 2000: E1) "could sustain some of those therms when its sultry stars are not in the clinch, it would be remarkable. But it can't, and it isn't. When the hot stuff stops, the film cools down faster than this attenuated metaphor. Brrrrr."

20. Tom Shales calls Gram, as played by Shirley Knight, "seemingly the whitest white woman in the world, next to Queen Elizabeth, of course" (*Washington Post* 21 Feb. 1998: C1).

21. Toni Morrison interview with Elizabeth Kastor, as cited in Heinze 182.

22. "Dense with allusion and shifting time and narrators," according to Gail Caldwell, "Morrison's *Beloved* is wed to a sonorous, Faulknerian prose, and it suggests that the pure act of telling a story can supersede its evil: If a dead child can reappear to love a mother out of her mind, so, too, can a cri de coeur from an old woman take on the magical force of a eulogy recited in starlight. No visual medium can fully encompass that, any more than a poem can deliver the colors of the canvas it seeks to describe" (*Boston Globe* 1 Nov. 1998: M1).

23. Turan concurs that at times the film's story "seems to be too large and too poetic to fit comfortably into a film of any length." But the "work that has resulted, strange, troubling, and powerfully imagined, is rough going at first, but the more time you spend with it the more the strength of the underlying material exerts its will" (*LA Times*: Calendar F1).

24. David Denby also remarked on the "trap for adaptors" posed by the book, a trap into which—he claims—the screenwriters fell. "Most of the emotionally significant events take place in the past; the present is a shuddering remnant, struggling to exist. We are in the Ohio farmhouse, a gray and featureless place, and when we are shown a past event—say, an ex-slave's memory of being whipped or shackled—the image flares luridly on the screen for an instant and disappears. Many of these flashbacks will mean nothing to the uninitiated, while those who have read the book may be shocked by the blunt stupidity of mere illustration—shocked by stupidity of movies" (249-50).

25. While the screenplay reduces a number of Morrison's scenes and characters, Demme occasionally heightens the novel's pulse by adding original elements. As Janet Maslin writes, "those insects and butterflies [that herald Beloved's appearance] are his visual inventions, as eerily tuned to Ms. Morrison's story as the drumbeats and a cappella voices that enhance Rachel Portman's stirring score" (*NYT* 16 Oct. 1998: E1).

26. David Ansen called it "a bold and frustratingly uneven movie" (76), while Will Joyner noted that *Beloved* does not simplify Morrison's "difficult esthetic to attract a wider audience and become a blockbuster in

the process." Rather, "it takes the opposite tack: It stubbornly reinforces a literary way of looking at things, whereby allusion counts for more than action or illusion" (*NYT* 18 Oct. 1998: Arts 13).

27. Weinraub quoted a number of industry insiders to explain the film's poor gross. Martin Grove, a box office analyst on CNN and a columnist at *The Hollywood Reporter*, said that there was no crossover audience: "Disney brought in the core audience initially. But after that it was up to the movie. And the problem seems to be that when a movie is three hours long, and word of mouth says that it is depressing and brutal, most people would rather do something else." Paul Dergarabedian, president of Exhibitor Relations, which monitors box office receipts, concurred that Disney's marketing was good but that poor word of mouth doomed the film: "There's no amount of marketing that can overcome word of mouth. And the word of mouth was that it was grim and hard to follow." Even the director of *Beloved*, Jonathan Demme, conceded that "the odds are stacked against" the film, because "it's a difficult picture. The material is demanding. You have the length of the picture, too." But Demme added that "the big surprise for me is how prematurely the death of the movie has been foretold."

28. "First of all," stated Morrison in the same interview, "it was important to me at least on the paperback jacket not to see Beloved's face. That she must be someone the reader invents. Well already when you're in the movie, you have a face that fixes it. And it moves from there to other kinds of scenes, gestures, voices, some of which enhance the dialogue. You hear amazing things with very good actors—and they're very good in this movie. On the other hand, there are whole areas that not only are not there, but they're not even gestured toward. The mechanics of cinema doesn't work that way" (Silverblatt, *LA Times* 1 Nov. 1998: Book Review 3).

29. Richard Corliss (*Time* 9 Oct. 2000: 108). "Satire," Corliss observes, "typically proceeds from two impulses: rage at the powerful and contempt for the masses." By condemning blacks as well as whites for perpetuating the stereotypes, Lee "is an equal opportunity annoyer."

WORKS CITED

Note: Film reviews are listed by date in the text and are generally not repeated in the Works Cited. Frequently cited materials may be abbreviated in the text (e.g., Thomas Cripps's *Slow Fade to Black* and *Making Movies Black* appear in embedded notes as *SFB* and *MMB*; Donald Bogle's *Toms, Coons, Mulattoes, Mammies, & Bucks* appears in embedded notes as *TCMMB*). Citations in the text to authors of multiple works are usually indicated by author's last name and an identifying word/words from the title (e.g., Thomas Cripps's "The Making of *The Birth of a Race*: The Emerging Politics of Identity in Silent Movies" appears in embedded notes as "Making").

Adams, Russell L. "An Analysis of The *Roots* Phenomenon in the Context of American Racial Conservatism." *Présence Africaine* 116.4 (1980): 125-40.

Anadolu-Okur, Nilgun. *Contemporary African American Theater: Afrocentricity in the Works of Larry Neal, Amiri Baraka, and Charles Fuller*. New York: Garland, 1997.

Anderson, Lisa M. *Mammies No More: The Changing Image of Black Women on Stage and Screen*. Lanham, MD: Rowman and Littlefield, 1997.

Andrews, Hannah Page Wheeler. "Theme and Variations: 'Uncle Tom's Cabin' as Book, Play, and Film." Diss. U of North Carolina at Chapel Hill, 1979.

Angelou, Maya. *I Know Why the Caged Bird Sings*. New York: Bantam, 1971.

Armstrong, William H. *Sounder*. Illustrated by James Barkley. New York: Harper & Row, 1969.

Arthur, Timothy Shay. *Ten Nights in a Bar-Room, and What I Saw There*. Ed. Donald A. Koch. Cambridge: Belknap P of Harvard UP, 1964.

Babb, Valerie Melissa. *Ernest Gaines*. Boston: Twayne, 1991.

Baldwin, James. "*Carmen Jones*: The Dark is Light Enough." In *Black Films and Film-Makers*. Ed. Lindsay Patterson. 88-94.

———. *Go Tell It on the Mountain*. 1952. New York: Dell, 1974.

———. *Notes of a Native Son*. 1955. New York: Bantam, 1968.

———. *One Day, When I Was Lost: A Scenario Based on Alex Haley's The Autobiography of Malcolm X*. New York: Laurel, 1972.

Ball, Jane. "Gordon Parks." In *Afro-American Writers After 1955*. Ed. Thadious M. Davis and Trudier Harris. *Dictionary of Literary Biography*. Vol. 33. Detroit: Gale, 1984. 203-08.

Bathrick, Serafina Kent. "Independent Woman, Doomed Sister." In *The Modern American Novel and the Movies*. Ed. Gerald Peary and Roger Shatzkin. New York: Ungar, 1978. 143-55.

Benchley, Robert. "*Hearts in Dixie* (The First Real Talking Picture)." In *Black Films and Film-Makers*. Ed. Lindsay Patterson. 84-87.

Bergman, Andrew. *We're in the Money: Depression America and Its Films*. New York: New York UP, 1971.

Bernardi, Daniel. "The Voice of Whiteness: D. W. Griffith's Biograph Films." In *The Birth of Whiteness*. Ed. Daniel Bernardi.

Bernardi, Daniel, ed. *The Birth of Whiteness: Race and Emergence of U. S. Cinema*. New Brunswick: Rutgers UP, 1996.

Birdoff, Harry. *The World's Greatest Hit: Uncle Tom's Cabin*. New York: S. F. Vanni, 1947.

Blayney, Michael Steward. "*Roots* and the Noble Savage." *North Dakota Quarterly* 54.1 (Winter 1986): 1-17.

Bloom, Lynn Z. "Maya Angelou." In *Afro-American Writers After 1955: Dramatists and Prose Writers*. Ed. Thadious M. Davis and Trudier Harris. *Dictionary of Literary Biography*. Vol. 38. Detroit: Gale, 1985. 3-12.

Bobo, Jacqueline. *Black Women as Cultural Readers*. New York: Columbia UP, 1995.

———. "The Color Purple: Black Women as Cultural Readers." In *Female Spectators*. Ed. E. Deidre Pribram. 90-109.

———. "Reading Through the Text: The Black Woman as Audience." In *Black American Cinema*. Ed. Manthia Diawara. 272-87.

———. "Sifting Through the Controversy: Reading *The Color Purple*." *Callaloo* 12.2 (Spring 1989): 332-42.

Bobo, Jacqueline and Ellen Seiter. "Black Feminism and Media Criticism: *The Women of Brewster Place*." In *Vision/Re-Vision: Adapting Contemporary American Fiction by Women to Film*. Ed. Barbara Tepa Lupack. 145-57.

Bogle, Donald. "Black Beginnings: From *Uncle Tom's Cabin* to *The Birth of a Nation*." In *Representing Blackness*. Ed. Valerie Smith. 13-24.

———. *Blacks in American Film and Television: An Encyclopedia*. New York: Garland, 1988.

———. *Toms, Coons, Mulattoes, Mammies, & Bucks: An Interpretive History of Blacks in American Films*. New 3rd ed. New York: Continuum, 1994.

Bowser, Pearl and Charles Musser. "Richard D. Maurice and the Maurice Film Company." In *Oscar Micheaux and His Circle*. Ed. Pearl Bowser, Jane Gaines, and Charles Musser. 190-94.

Bowser, Pearl and Louise Spence. "Identity and Betrayal: *The Symbol of the Unconquered* and Oscar Micheaux's 'Biographical Legend.'" In *The Birth of Whiteness*. Ed. Daniel Bernardi. 56-80.

———. "Oscar Micheaux's *The Symbol of the Unconquered*: Text and Context." In *Oscar Micheaux and His Circle*. Ed. Pearl Bowser, Jane Gaines, and Charles Musser. 81-96.

———. *Writing Himself into History: Oscar Micheaux, His Silent Films, and His Audiences*. Foreword by Thulani Davis. New Brunswick: Rutgers UP, 2001.

Bradford, Roark. *Ol' Man Adam an' His Chillun: Being the Tales They Tell about the Time When the Lord Walked the Earth Like a Natural Man*. New York: Harper and Brothers, 1928.

Bridges, Herb and Terryl C. Boodman. *Gone With the Wind: The Definitive Illustrated History of the Book, the Movie, and the Legend*. New York: Simon & Schuster/Fireside Books, 1989.

Braxton, Joanne M., ed. *Maya Angelou's I Know Why the Caged Bird Sings: A Casebook*. New York: Oxford UP, 1999.

Brown, Jayna. "Black Patriarch on the Prairie: National Identity and Black Manhood in the Early Novels of Oscar Micheaux." In *Oscar Micheaux and His Circle*. Ed. Pearl Bowser, Jane Gaines, and Charles Musser. 132-46.

Brown, Les, ed. *Encyclopedia of Television*. 3rd ed. Detroit: Gale, 1992.

Brown, Sterling A. "Insight, Courage, and Craftsmanship." *Opportunity* 18 (1940): 185-86. Rpt. in *Critical Essays on Richard Wright's Native Son*. Ed. Keneth Kinnamon. 53-55.

Bruck, Peter, ed. *The Black American Short Story in the 20th Century*. Amsterdam: Gruner, 1977.

Butler, Cheryl B. "*The Color Purple* Controversy: Black Woman Spectatorship." *Wide Angle* 13.3-4 (1991): 62-69.

Butler, Robert J. "Chester Himes." In *American Novelists Since World War II*. Third Series. Ed. James R. Giles and Wanda H. Giles. *Dictionary of Literary Biography*. Vol. 143. Detroit: Gale, 1994. 33-50.

Byerman, Keith E. "Afro-American Folklore and the Shape of Contemporary Black Fiction: The Example of Ernest Gaines's *The Autobiography of Miss Jane Pittman*." In *Designs, Patterns, Style: Hallmarks of a Developing American Culture*. Ed. Dan Harkness. New York: American Studies P, 1983. 49-50.

———. "Ernest Gaines." *American Novelists Since World War II*. Fourth Series. Ed. James R. Giles and Wanda H. Giles. *Dictionary of Literary Biography*. Vol. 152. Detroit: Gale, 1995.51-64.

Callahan, John. "Image-Making: Tradition and the Two Versions of *The Autobiography of Miss Jane Pittman*." *Chicago Review* 29.2 (1977): 45-62.

Campbell, Edward D. C., Jr. *The Celluloid South: Hollywood and the Southern Myth*. Knoxville: U of Tennessee P, 1981.

————. "Film as Politics/Film as Business: The Blaxploitation of the Plantation." In *Hollywood as Mirror: Changing Views of "Outsiders" and "Enemies" in American Movies*. Ed. Robert Brent Toplin. 1-18.

————. "The Old South as National Epic." In *Gone With the Wind as Book and Film*. Ed. Richard Harwell. Columbia: U of South Carolina P, 1983. 175-83.

Campenni, Frank. "Chester Himes." In *American Novelists Since World War II*. Ed. Jeffrey Helterman and Richard Layman. *Dictionary of Literary Biography*. Vol. 2. Detroit: Gale, 1978. 240-44.

Carby, Hazel V. *Race Men: The Body and Soul of Race, Nation and Manhood*. Cambridge: Harvard UP, 1998.

————. *Reconstructing Womanhood: The Emergence of the Afro-American Woman Novelist*. New York: Oxford UP, 1987.

Cardullo, Bert. "Lula and the *Dutchman*." *Notes on Contemporary Literature* 18.5 (1988): 8-9.

Carmean, Karen. *Ernest J. Gaines: A Critical Companion*. Westport, CT: Greenwood P, 1998.

Carter, Steven R. "Lorraine Hansberry." In *Afro-American Writers After 1955: Dramatists and Prose Writers*. Ed. Thadious M. Davis and Trudier Harris. *Dictionary of Literary Biography*. Vol. 38. Detroit: Gale, 1985. 120-34.

Charney, Mark J. In *Critical Reflections on the Fiction of Ernest J. Gaines*. Ed. David C. Estes. 124-38.

Cheney, Anne. *Lorraine Hansberry*. Boston: Twayne, 1984.

Chesnutt, Charles W. *The Conjure Woman and Other Conjure Tales*. Ed. and intro. by Richard H. Brodhead. Durham: Duke UP, 1993.

————. *The House Behind the Cedars*. 1900. Intro. by Donald B. Gibson. New York: Penguin, 1993.

Childress, Alice. *A Hero Ain't Nothin' But A Sandwich*. New York: Avon, 1973.

Chopin, Kate. *The Awakening*. Chicago: H. S. Stone & Co., 1899.

Clark, Edward D. "Richard Wright." In *Afro-American Writers, 1940-1955*. Ed. Trudier Harris and Thadious M. Davis. *Dictionary of Literary Biography*. Vol. 76. Detroit: Gale, 1988. 199-221.

"A Conversation with Richard Wright, Author of *Native Son*." *Romance* 1 (15 June 1940). Rpt. in *Conversations with Richard Wright*. Ed. Keneth Kinnamon and Michel Fabre. 31-33.

Creekmur, Corey K. "Telling White Lies: Oscar Micheaux and Charles W. Chesnutt." In *Oscar Micheaux and His Circle*. Ed. Pearl Bowser, Jane Gaines, and Charles Musser. 147-58.

Cripps, Thomas. *Black Film as Genre*. Bloomington: Indiana UP, 1978.

————. "The Death of Rastus: Negroes in American Films Since 1945." In *Black Films and Film-Makers*. Ed. Lindsay Patterson. 53-64.

————. *Making Movies Black: The Hollywood Message Movie from World War II to the Civil Rights Era*. New York: Oxford UP, 1993.

————. "The Making of *The Birth of a Race*: The Emerging Politics of Identity in Silent Movies." In *The Birth of Whiteness*. Ed. Daniel Bernardi. 38-55.

————. "Oscar Micheaux: The Story Continues." In *Black American Cinema*. Ed. Manthia Diawara. 71-79.

————. "'Race Movies' as Voices of the Black Bourgeoisie: *The Scar of Shame*." In *Representing Blackness*. Ed. Valerie Smith. 47-59.

————. *Slow Fade to Black: The Negro in American Film, 1900-1942*. New York: Oxford UP, 1977.

————. "Winds of Change: *Gone With the Wind* and Racism as a National Issue." In *Recasting: Gone With the Wind in American Culture*. Ed. Darden Asbury Pyron. 137-52.

Crowdus, Gary, ed. *The Political Companion to American Film*. Foreword by Edward Asner. N.p.: Lakeview P, 1994.

Crowther, Bosley. "The Birth of *Birth of a Nation*." In *Black Films and Film-Makers*. Ed. Lindsay Patterson. 75-83.

Cummings, E[dward] E[stlin]. *Tom*. New York: Arrow Editions, 1935.

Delany, Sarah and A. Elizabeth, with Amy Hill Hearth. *Having Our Say: The Delany Sisters' First 100 Years*. New York: Kodansha International, 1993.

Delpech, Jeanine. "An Interview with Native Son." *The Crisis* 57 (1950): 625-26, 678. Rpt. in *Conversations with Richard Wright*. Ed. Keneth Kinnamon and Michel Fabre. 143-45.

Deutsch, Leonard J. "The Named and the Unnamed." In *Children's Novels and the Movies*. Ed. Douglas Street. New York: Frederick Ungar, 1983. 214-26.

de Vaal, Hans. "An Interview with Richard Wright." *Litterair Paspoort* 8 (1953), 161-63. Rpt. in *Conversations with Richard Wright*. Ed. Keneth Kinnamon and Michel Fabre. 154-59.

Diawara, Manthia. "Black Spectatorship: Problems of Identification and Resistance." In *Black American Cinema*. Ed. Manthia Diawara. 211-20.

————, ed. *Black American Cinema*. New York: Routledge, 1993.

Digby, Joan. "From Walker to Spielberg: Transformations of *The Color Purple*." In *Novel Images*. Ed. Peter Reynolds. 157-74.

Dismond, Geraldyn. "The Negro Actor and the American Movies." In *Black Films and Film-Makers*. Ed. Lindsay Patterson. 117-21.

Dole, Carol M. "The Return of the Father in Spielberg's *The Color Purple*." *Literature/Film Quarterly* 24.1 (1996): 12-15.

Downing, Henry Francis. *The American Cavalryman: A Liberian Romance*. 1917. New York: AMS P, 1973.

Draper, Arthur. "Uncle Tom Will Never Die!" In *Black Films and Film-Makers*. Ed. Lindsay Patterson. 30-35.

Dunbar, Paul Laurence. "The Scapegoat." In *The Heart of Happy Hollow*. New York: Dodd, Mead and Co., 1904. 3-31.

——. *The Sport of the Gods*. In *The Paul Laurence Dunbar Reader*. Ed. Jay Martin and Gossie H. Hudson. New York: Dodd, Mead and Co., 1975. 339-404.

Dyer, Richard. "Into the Light: The Whiteness of the South in *The Birth of a Nation*." In *Dixie Debates*. Ed. Richard H. King and Helen Taylor. 165-76.

Early, Gerald. "*The Color Purple* as Everybody's Protest Art." *The Antioch Review* 44.3 (1986): 261-75.

Elder, Arlene. "Oscar Micheaux: The Melting Pot on the Plains." *The Old Northwest* 2 (1976): 299-307.

Ellis, Cassandra M. "The Black Boy Looks at the Silver Screen: Baldwin as Moviegoer." *Re-Viewing James Baldwin: Things Not Seen*. Ed. D. Quentin Miller. Philadelphia: Temple UP, 2000. 190-214.

Estes, David C., ed. *Critical Reflections on the Fiction of Ernest J. Gaines*. Athens: U of Georgia P, 1994.

Everett, Anna. *Returning the Gaze: A Genealogy of Black Film Criticism, 1909-1949*. Durham: Duke UP, 2001.

Fabre, Michel. *The Unfinished Quest of Richard Wright*. 2nd ed. Urbana: U of Illinois P, 1993.

Faulkner, Virginia, ed. With Frederick C. Luebke. *Vision and Refuge: Essays on the Literature of the Great Plains*. Lincoln: U of Nebraska P, 1982.

Fauset, Jessie. *Plum Bun*. New York: Frederick A. Stokes, 1929.

Fishbein, Leslie. "*Roots*: Docudrama and the Interpretation of History." In *Why Docudrama?* Ed. Alan Rosenthal. 271-95.

Fleming, Robert E. "Willard Motley." In *American Novelists Since World War II*. Third Series. Ed. James R. Giles and Wanda H. Giles. *Dictionary of Literary Biography*. Vol. 143. Detroit: Gale, 1994. 188-95.

Fontenot, Chester J., Jr. "Oscar Micheaux, Black Novelist and Film Maker." In *Vision and Refuge*. Ed. Virginia Faulkner and Frederick C. Luebke. 109-125.

Fuller, Charles. *A Soldier's Play*. Garden City, NY: Nelson Doubleday, 1982.

Furnas, Joseph Chamberlain. *Goodbye to Uncle Tom*. New York: William Sloan Associates, 1956.

Gaines, Ernest J. *The Autobiography of Miss Jane Pittman*. New York: Dial Press, 1971.

——. *A Gathering of Old Men*. New York: Knopf, 1983.

——. *A Lesson Before Dying*. 1993. New York: Vintage Books, 1994.

——. "The Sky Is Gray." In Ernest J. Gaines. *Bloodline*. New York: Dial Press, 1968. 83-117.

Gaines, Jane. "*The Birth of a Nation* and *Within Our Gates*: Two Tales of the American South." In *Dixie Debates*. Ed. Richard H. King and Helen Taylor. 177-192.

———. *Fire and Desire: Mixed-Race Movies in the Silent Era*. Chicago: U of Chicago P, 2001.

———. "Fire and Desire: Race, Melodrama, and Oscar Micheaux." In *Black American Cinema*. Ed. Manthia Diawara. 49-70.

———. "*The Scar of Shame*: Skin Color and Caste in Black Silent Melodrama." In *Representing Blackness*. Ed. Valerie Smith. 61-81.

———. "*Within Our Gates*: From Race Melodrama to Opportunity Narrative." In *Oscar Micheaux and His Circle*. Ed. Pearl Bowser, Jane Gaines, and Charles Musser. 67-80.

Gates, Henry Louis, Jr. and K. A. Appiah, eds. *Alice Walker: Critical Perspectives, Past and Present*. New York: Amistad, 1993.

———, eds. *Gloria Naylor: Critical Perspectives, Past and Present*. New York: Amistad, 1993.

———, eds. *Richard Wright: Critical Perspectives, Past and Present*. New York: Amistad, 1993.

Gaudet, Marcia and Carl Wooton. *Porch Talk with Ernest Gaines: Conversations on the Writer's Craft*. Baton Rouge: Louisiana State UP, 1990.

Gehr, Richard. "One-Man Show." *American Film* May 1991: 34-39.

George, Nelson. *Blackface: Reflections on African-Americans and the Movies*. New York: HarperCollins, 1994.

Gibson, Gloria J. "Cinematic Foremothers: Zora Neale Hurston and Eloyce King Patrick Gist." In *Oscar Micheaux and His Circle*. Ed. Pearl Bowser, Jane Gaines, and Charles Musser. 195-209.

Githii, Ethel W. "Charles H. Fuller, Jr." In *Afro-American Writers After 1955: Dramatists and Prose Writers*. Ed. Thadious M. Davis and Trudier Harris. *Dictionary of Literary Biography*. Vol. 38. Detroit: Gale, 1985. 104-09.

Gossett, Thomas F. *Uncle Tom's Cabin and American Culture*. Dallas: Southern Methodist UP, 1985.

Green, J. Ronald. "Micheaux contro Griffith/Micheaux v. Griffith." *Griffithiana* 20.60-61 (1997): 32-49.

———. "Oscar Micheaux's Interrogation of Caricature as Entertainment." *Film Quarterly* 51.3 (1998): 16-31.

———. "The Reemergence of Oscar Micheaux: A Timeline and Bibliographic Essay." In *Oscar Micheaux and His Circle*. Ed. Pearl Bowser, Jane Gaines, and Charles Musser. 211-27.

———. *Straight Lick: The Cinema of Oscar Micheaux*. Bloomington: Indiana UP, 2000.

———. "'Twoness'" in the Style of Oscar Micheaux." In *Black American Cinema*. Ed. Manthia Diawara. 26-48.

Griggs, Sutton E. *The Hindered Hand, or, The Reign of the Repressionist.* Nashville, TN: Orion Publishing, 1905.

Gruppenhoff, Richard. *The Black Valentino: The Stage and Screen Career of Lorenzo Tucker.* Metuchen, NJ: Scarecrow P, 1988.

Guerrero, Ed. "The Black Image in Protective Custody: Hollywood's Biracial Buddy Films of the Eighties." In *Black American Cinema*. Ed. Manthia Diawara. 237-46.

———. *Framing Blackness: The African American Image in Film.* Philadelphia: Temple UP, 1993.

Hakutani, Yoshinobu. "Richard Wright." In *American Short-Story Writers, 1910-1945.* Second Series. Ed. Bobby Ellen Kimbel. *Dictionary of Literary Biography.* Vol. 102. Detroit: Gale, 1991. 378-86.

Haley, Alex. *Roots: The Saga of an American Family.* New York: Doubleday, 1976.

Haley, Alex and David Stevens. *Mama Flora's Family.* New York: Scribner, 1998.

———. *Queen: The Story of an American Family.* New York: Morrow, 1993.

Hansberry, Lorraine. *A Raisin in the Sun.* New York: Random House, 1959.

Hansen, Miriam. *Babel and Babylon: Spectatorship in American Silent Film.* Cambridge: Harvard UP, 1991.

Harper, Frances E. W. *Iola Leroy, or, Shadows Uplifted.* Philadelphia: Garrigues, 1892.

Harper, Mary T. "From Sons to Fathers: Ernest Gaines' *A Gathering of Old Men.*" *College Language Association Journal* 31.3 (1988): 299-308.

Harris, Tina M. "Interrogating the Representation of African American Female Identity in the Films *Waiting to Exhale* and *Set It Off.*" *Popular Culture Review* 10.2 (1999): 43-53.

Harris, Tina M. and Patricia S. Hill. "'Waiting to Exhale' or 'Breath(ing) Again': A Search for Identity, Empowerment, and Love in the 1990's." *Women & Language* 21.2 (1998): 9-20.

Harris, Trudier. "Alice Childress." In *Afro-American Writers After 1955: Dramatists and Prose Writers.* Ed. Thadious M. Davis and Trudier Harris. *Dictionary of Literary Biography.* Vol. 38. Detroit: Gale, 1985. 66-79.

Harrison, William. "The Negro and the Cinema." In *Black Films and Film-Makers.* Ed. Lindsay Patterson. 129-33.

Harwell, Richard, ed. *Gone With the Wind as Book and Film.* Columbia: U of South Carolina P, 1983.

Hebert, Janis. "Oscar Micheaux: A Black Pioneer." *South Dakota Review* 11.4 (1973): 62-69.

Heinze, Denise. "Toni Morrison." In *American Novelists Since World War II.* Third Series. Ed. James R. Giles and Wanda H. Giles. In *Dictionary of Literary Biography.* Vol. 143. Detroit: Gale, 1994. 171-87.

Hildreth, Margaret Holbrook. *Harriet Beecher Stowe: A Bibliography*. Hamden, CT: Archon Books, 1976.

Hill, Elbert R. "*A Hero* for the Movies." In *Children's Novels and the Movies*. Ed. Douglas Street. New York: Ungar, 1983. 236-43.

Hill, George H. *Ebony Images: Black Americans and Television*. Carson, CA: Daystar, 1986.

Hill, George, Lorraine Raglin, and Chas Floyd Johnson. *Black Women in Television: An Illustrated History and Bibliography*. New York: Garland, 1990.

Hill, George H., Lorraine Raglin, and Robert Davenport. *African American Television Experience*. Los Angeles: Daystar, 1987.

Himes, Chester. *Cotton Comes to Harlem*. 1965. New York: Dell, 1970.

———. *The Heat's On*. New York: Putnam's, 1966.

———. *If He Hollers Let Him Go*. 1945. London: Sphere Books, 1967.

———. *My Life of Absurdity: The Autobiography of Chester Himes*. Vol. 2. Garden City, NY: Doubleday and Co., 1976.

———. *The Quality of Hurt: The Autobiography of Chester Himes*. Vol. 1. Garden City, NY: Doubleday and Co., 1972.

———. *A Rage in Harlem*. New York: Avon, 1965.

hooks, bell. *Black Looks: Race and Representation*. Boston: South End P, 1992.

———. *Reel to Real: Race, Sex, and Class at the Movies*. New York: Routledge, 1996.

Hoyt, George H. *Ebony Images: Black Americans and Television*. Preface by Marla Gibbs. Carson, CA: Daystar, 1986.

Hughes, Glenn. *A History of the American Theatre: 1700-1950*. New York: Samuel French, 1951.

Jafa, Arthur. "The Notion of Treatment: Black Aesthetics and Film, based on an interview with Peter Hessli and additional discussions with Pearl Bowser." In *Oscar Micheaux and His Circle*. Ed. Pearl Bowser, Jane Gaines, and Charles Musser. 11-18.

Jerome, V. J. *The Negro in Hollywood Films*. New York: Masses and Mainstream, 1952.

Johnson, Albert. "Beige, Brown, or Black." In *Black Films and Film-Makers*. Ed. Lindsay Patterson. 36-43.

———. "The Negro in American Films: Some Recent Works." In *Black Films and Film-Makers*. Ed. Lindsay Patterson. 153-81.

Johnson, James Weldon. *The Autobiography of an Ex-Colored Man*. 1912. Grand Rapids, MI: Candace, 1996.

———. *Lift Every Voice and Sing: Selected Poems by James Weldon Johnson*. Preface by Sondra Kathryn Wilson. New York: Penguin, 1993.

Johnson, M. K. "'Stranger in a Strange Land': An African American Response to the Frontier Tradition in Oscar Micheaux's *The Conquest: The Story of a Negro Pioneer*." *Western American Literature* 33.3 (1998): 228-52.

Jones, G. William. *Black Cinema Treasures: Lost and Found.* Foreword by Ossie Davis. Denton: U of North Texas P, 1991.

Kael, Pauline. "Notes on Black Movies." In *Black Films and Film-Makers.* Ed. Lindsay Patterson. 258-67.

Kaplan, E. Ann. *Looking for the Other: Feminism, Film, and the Imperial Gaze.* New York: Routledge, 1997.

Kendall, Steven D. *New Jack Cinema: Hollywood's African American Filmmakers.* Silver Spring, MD: Denser, 1994.

Kern-Foxworth, Marilyn. "Alex Haley." In *Afro-American Writers After 1955: Dramatists and Prose Writers.* Ed. Thadious M. Davis and Trudier Harris. *Dictionary of Literary Biography.* Vol. 38. Detroit: Gale, 1985. 115-19.

Kinnamon, Keneth, ed. *Critical Essays on Richard Wright's Native Son.* New York: Twayne, 1997.

Kinnamon, Keneth and Michel Fabre, eds. *Conversations with Richard Wright.* Jackson: U of Mississippi P, 1993.

King, Richard H. and Helen Taylor, eds. *Dixie Debates: Perspectives on Southern Cultures.* New York: New York UP, 1996.

Klotman, Phyllis R. *Frame by Frame: A Black Filmography.* Bloomington: Indiana UP, 1979.

———. "Planes, Trains, and Automobiles: *The Flying Ace,* the Norman Company, and the Micheaux Connection." In *Oscar Micheaux and His Circle.* Ed. Pearl Bowser, Jane Gaines, and Charles Musser. 161-177.

———, comp. "Norman Film Manufacturing Company: Production and Theatrical Release Dates for All-Black-Cast Films." In *Oscar Micheaux and His Circle.* Ed. Pearl Bowser, Jane Gaines, and Charles Musser. 286-88.

Klotman, Phyllis R. and Gloria J. Gibson. *Frame by Frame II: A Filmography of the African American Image, 1978-1994.* Bloomington: Indiana UP, 1997.

Larsen, Nella. *Passing.* 1929. Salem, NH: Ayer, 1993.

Lauritzen, Einar and Gunnar Lundquist. *American Film Index, 1916-1920.* Stockholm, Sweden: Film-Index, 1984.

Leab, Daniel J. *From Sambo to Superspade: The Black Experience in Motion Pictures.* Boston: Houghton Mifflin, 1975.

Lee, Spike. *By Any Means Necessary: The Trials and Tribulations of the Making of Malcolm X...* With Ralph Wiley. Intro. by Terry McMillan. New York: Hyperion, 1992.

Leeming, David. *James Baldwin: A Biography.* New York: Knopf, 1994.

Lewis, David Levering, ed. *The Portable Harlem Renaissance Reader.* New York: Viking, 1994.

Lewis, Nell Battle. "Scarlett Materializes." In *Gone With the Wind as Book and Film.* Ed. Richard Harwell. 170-74.

Lewis, Vashti Crutcher. "Gloria Naylor." In *American Novelists Since World War II*. Fifth Series. Ed. James R. Giles and Wanda H. Giles. *Dictionary of Literary Biography*. Vol. 143. Detroit: Gale, 1996. 277-93.

Locke, Alain and Sterling A. Brown. "Folk Values in a New Medium." In *Black Films and Film-Makers*. Ed. Lindsay Patterson. 25-29.

Lowe, John, ed. *Conversations with Ernest Gaines*. Jackson: U of Mississippi P, 1995.

Lupack, Barbara Tepa, ed. *Nineteenth-Century Women at the Movies: Adapting Classic Women's Fiction to Film*. Bowling Green, OH: Bowling Green State U Popular P, 1999.

———, ed. *Take Two: Adapting the Contemporary American Novel to Film*. Bowling Green, OH: Bowling Green State U Popular P, 1994.

Lupton, Mary Jane. "Clothes and Closure in Three Novels by Black Women." *Black American Literature Forum* 20.4. Women's Writers Issue (1986): 409-21.

Mapp, Edward. "Black Women in Films: A Mixed Bag of Tricks." In *Black Films and Film-Makers*. Ed. Lindsay Patterson. 196-205.

Marill, Alvin H. *The Films of Sidney Poitier*. Secaucus, NJ: Citadel P, 1978.

Marten, Johannes Skancke. "A Black Writer Becomes a Movie Actor." Oslo *Aftenposten* 9 Nov. 1950. Rpt. in *Conversations with Richard Wright*. Ed. Keneth Kinnamon and Michel Fabre. 148-50.

Martin, Jay and Gossie H. Hudson, eds. *The Paul Laurence Dunbar Reader*. New York: Dodd, Mead, 1975.

Marsden, Michael T., John G. Nachbar, and Sam L. Grogg, Jr., eds. *Movies as Artifacts: Cultural Criticism of Popular Film*. Chicago: Nelson-Hall, 1982.

Mattox, Michael. "The Day Black Movie Stars Got Militant." In *Black Films and Film-Makers*. Ed. Lindsay Patterson. 190-95.

Mayne, Judith. *Cinema and Spectatorship*. London: Routledge, 1993.

McMillan, Terry. *Disappearing Acts*. New York: Viking, 1989.

———. *How Stella Got Her Groove Back*. New York: Viking, 1996.

———. *Waiting to Exhale*. New York: Pocket Books, 1992.

McNeil, Alex. *Total Television: A Comprehensive Guide to Programming from 1948 to the Present*. 3rd ed. New York: Penguin, 1991.

Merritt, Russell and J. B. Kaufman. *Disney in Wonderland: The Silent Films of Walt Disney*. La Giornate Del Cinema Muto. Distrib. by Johns Hopkins UP, 1993.

Micheaux, Oscar. *The Case of Mrs. Wingate*. New York: Book Supply Company, 1945.

———. *The Conquest: The Story of a Negro Pioneer*. 1913. Rpt. Lincoln: U Nebraska P, 1994.

———. *The Forged Note: A Romance of the Darker Races*. Lincoln: Western Book Supply Company, 1915.

————. *The Homesteader: A Novel.* 1917. Rpt. College Park: McGrath Publishing, 1969.

————. *The Masquerade: An Historical Novel.* New York: Book Supply Company, 1947.

————. *The Story of Dorothy Stanfield.* New York: Book Supply Company, 1946.

————. *The Wind From Nowhere.* New York: Book Supply Company, 1944.

Michener, Charles. "Black Movies." In *Black Films and Film-Makers.* Ed. Lindsay Patterson. 235-46.

Midnight Ramble: The Story of the Black Film Industry. Northern Lights Production/The American Experience. Dir. Bestor Cram and Pearl Bowser. 1994.

Miller, D. Quentin, ed. *Re-Viewing James Baldwin: Things Not Seen.* Philadelphia: Temple UP, 2000.

Miller, Warren. *The Cool World.* New York: Fawcett, 1969.

Mitchell, Margaret. *Gone With the Wind.* New York: Macmillan, 1939.

Moon, Spencer. *Reel Black Talk: A Sourcebook of 50 American Filmmakers.* Westport, CT: Greenwood P, 1997.

Morales, Michael. "Ghosts on the Piano: August Wilson and the Representation of Black American History." In *May All Your Fences Have Gates.* Ed. Alan Nadel. 105-15.

Morrison, Toni. *Beloved.* New York: Penguin/Plume, 1987.

————. *The Bluest Eye.* New York: Penguin/Plume, 1994.

Moss, Carlton. "An Open Letter to Mr. Selznick." In *Gone With the Wind as Book and Film.* Ed. Richard Harwell. 156-59.

Muller, Gilbert H. *Chester Himes.* Boston: Twayne, 1989.

Murray, James P. "The Subject Is Money." In *Black Films and Film-Makers.* Ed. Lindsay Patterson. 247-57.

————. *To Find An Image: Black Films from Uncle Tom to Super Fly.* Indianapolis: Bobbs-Merrill, 1973.

Musser, Charles. "Colored Players Film Corporation: An Alternative to Micheaux." In *Oscar Micheaux and His Circle.* Ed. Pearl Bowser, Jane Gaines, and Charles Musser. 178-87.

————. *The Emergence of Cinema: American Screen to 1907.* Scribner's Sons, 1990.

————. "To Redream the Dreams of White Playwrights: Reappropriation and Resistance in Oscar Micheaux's *Body and Soul.*" In *Oscar Micheaux and His Circle.* Ed. Pearl Bowser, Jane Gaines, and Charles Musser. 97-131.

Musser, Charles, Corey K. Creekmur, Pearl Bowser, J. Ronald Green, Charlene Regester, and Louise Spence, comps. "An Oscar Micheaux Filmography: From the Silents through His Transition to Sound, 1919-1931." In *Oscar Micheaux and His Circle.* Ed. Pearl Bowser, Jane Gaines, and Charles Musser. 228-77.

Nadel, Alan, ed. *May All Your Fences Have Gates: Essays on the Drama of August Wilson.* Iowa City: U of Iowa P, 1994.

Naylor, Gloria. *The Women of Brewster Place.* New York: Penguin, 1983.

"Negro Hailed as New Writer." *New York Sun* 4 March 1940. Rpt. in *Conversations with Richard Wright.* Ed. Keneth Kinnamon and Michel Fabre. 28-30.

Nesteby, James R. *Black Images in American Films, 1896-1954: The Interplay Between Civil Rights and Film Culture.* Lanham, MD: UP of America, 1982.

Neupert, Richard. "Trouble in Watermelon Land: George Pal and the Little Jasper Cartoons." *Film Quarterly* 55.1 (Fall 2001): 14-26.

Niver, Kemp R. *The First Twenty Years: A Segment of Film History.* Los Angeles: Locare Research Group, 1968.

Noble, Peter. *The Negro in Films.* New York: Arno Press and the New York Times, 1970.

Null, Gary. *Black Hollywood: The Negro in Motion Pictures.* New York: The Citadel P, 1975.

Ogle, Patrick. *Facets African-American Video Guide.* Chicago: Facets Multimedia, 1994.

Parker, Jeffrey D. "Frank Yerby." In *Afro-American Writers, 1940-1955.* Ed. Trudier Harris and Thadious M. Davis. *Dictionary of Literary Biography.* Vol. 76. Detroit: Gale, 1988. 222-32.

Parks, Gordon. *The Learning Tree.* New York: Harper and Row, 1963.

Patterson, Lindsay, ed. *Black Films and Film-Makers: A Comprehensive Anthology from Stereotype to Superhero.* New York: Dodd, Mead & Co., 1975.

———. "In Harlem, a James Bond with Soul?" In *Black Films and Film-Makers.* Ed. Lindsay Patterson. 101-105.

———. "*Sounder*—A Hollywood Fantasy?" In *Black Films and Film-Makers.* Ed. Lindsay Patterson. 106-108.

Peacock, John. "Adapting *The Color Purple*: When Folk Goes Pop." In *Take Two: Adapting the Contemporary American Novel to Film.* Ed. Barbara Tepa Lupack. 112-30.

Pines, Jim. *Blacks in Films: A Survey of Racial Themes and Images in the American Film.* London: Studio Vista/Cassell & Collier Macmillan, 1975.

Poitier, Sidney. *This Life.* New York: Ballantine Books, 1980.

Powers, Anne, ed. *Blacks in American Movies: A Selected Bibliography.* Metuchen, NJ: Scarecrow P, 1974.

Pribram, E. Deidre, ed. *Female Spectators: Looking at Film and Television.* London: Verso, 1988.

Pyron, Darden Asbury. "The Inner War of Southern History." In *Recasting: Gone With the Wind in American Culture.* Ed. Darden Asbury Pyron. 185-201.

————, ed. *Recasting: Gone With the Wind in American Culture*. Miami: UP of Florida, 1983.

Quarles, Chester L. *The Ku Klux Klan and Related American Racialist and Antisemitic Organizations: A History and Analysis*. Jefferson, NC: McFarland, 1999.

Reckley, Ralph. "Chester Himes." In *Afro-American Writers, 1940-1955*. Ed. Trudier Harris and Thadious M. Davis. *Dictionary of Literary Biography*. Vol. 76. Detroit: Gale, 1988. 89-103.

Reddick, Lawrence. "Of Motion Pictures." In *Black Films and Film-Makers*. Ed. Lindsay Patterson. 3-24.

Regester, Charlene. "The African-American Press and Race Movies, 1909-1929." In *Oscar Micheaux and His Circle*. Ed. Pearl Bowser, Jane Gaines, and Charles Musser. 34-49.

————. "Headline to Headlights: Oscar Micheaux's Exploitation of the Rhinelander Case." *The Western Journal of Black Studies* 22.3 (1998): 195-204.

————. "The Misreading and Rereading of African American Filmmaker Oscar Micheaux: A Critical Review of Micheaux Scholarship." *Film History: An International Journal* 7.4 (1995): 426-49.

————. "Oscar Micheaux on the Cutting Edge: Films Rejected by the New York State Motion Picture Commission." *Studies in Popular Culture* 17.2 (1995): 61-72.

————. "Oscar Micheaux the Entrepreneur: Financing *The House Behind the Cedars*." *Journal of Film and Video* 49.1-2 (1997): 17-27.

Reid, Mark A. "African-American Filmmakers." In *A Political Companion to American Film*. Ed. Gary Crowdus. N.p.: Lakeview P, 1994. 3-9.

————. *Redefining Black Film*. Berkeley: U of California P, 1993.

Rexroth, Kenneth. *"Uncle Tom's Cabin," The Elastic Retort: Essays in Literature and Ideas*. New York: Seabury P, 1973.

Reynolds, Peter, ed. *Novel Images: Literature in Performance*. London: Routledge, 1993.

Richards, Larry. *African American Films Through 1959: A Comprehensive Illustrated Filmography*. Jefferson, NC: McFarland, 1998.

Richards, Paulette. *Terry McMillan: A Critical Companion*. Westport, CT: Greenwood P, 1999.

Rolo, Charles J. "This, Too, Is America." *Tomorrow* (4 May 1945). Rpt. in *Conversations with Richard Wright*. Ed. Keneth Kinnamon and Michel Fabre. 67-71.

Rosenthal, Alan, ed. *Why Docudrama? Fact-Fiction on Film and TV*. Carbondale: Southern Illinois UP, 1999.

Rowell, Charles. "'This Louisiana Thing That Drives Me': An Interview with Ernest Gaines." *Callaloo* 1.3 (1978): 39-51.

Rugoff, Milton. *The Beechers: An American Family in the Nineteenth Century.* New York: Harper and Row, 1981.

Rutherford, Charles S. "A New Dog with an Old Trick: Archetypal Patterns in *Sounder.*" In *Movies as Artifacts: Cultural Criticism of Popular Film.* Ed. Michael T. Marsden, John G. Nachbar, and Sam L. Grogg, Jr. Chicago: Nelson-Hall, 1982. 223-29.

Sampson, Henry T. *Blacks in Black and White: A Source Book on Black Films.* 2nd ed. Metuchen, NJ: Scarecrow P, 1995.

Schneiderman, Elizabeth Kline, ed. *By and About Women: An Anthology of Short Fiction.* New York: Harcourt Brace Jovanovich, 1973.

Shannon, Sandra G. "The Ground on Which I Stand: August Wilson's Perspective on African American Women." In Alan Nadel, ed. *May All Your Fences Have Gates.* 150-64.

Shattuc, Jane. "Having a Good Cry Over *The Color Purple*: The Problem of Affect and Imperialism in Feminist Theory." In *Melodrama: Stage, Picture, Screen.* Ed. Jacky Bratton, Jim Cook, and Christine Gledhill. London: British Film Institute, 1994. 147-56.

Shirley, David. *Alex Haley.* New York: Chelsea House, 1994.

Slout, William L. "*Uncle Tom's Cabin* in American Film History." *Journal of Popular Film* 2.2 (1973): 137-51.

Simpson, Anne K. *A Gathering of Gaines: The Man and the Writer.* Lafayette: Center for Louisiana Studies, 1991.

Smith, Lillian. *Strange Fruit.* New York: Reynal and Hitchcock, 1944.

Smith, Valerie. *Not Just Race, Not Just Gender: Black Feminist Readings.* New York: Routledge, 1998.

Smith, Valerie, ed. *Representing Blackness: Issues in Film and Video.* New Brunswick: Rutgers UP, 1997.

Snead, James. *White Screens, Black Images: Hollywood from the Dark Side.* New York: Routledge, 1994.

Steiner, Wendy. "Women's Fiction: The Rewriting of History." In *The Cambridge History of American Literature.* Vol. 7: *Prose Writing, 1940-1990.* Ed. Sacvan Bercovitch. Cambridge: Cambridge UP, 1999. 499-527.

Stowe, Harriet Beecher. *Uncle Tom's Cabin.* With an Afterword by John William Ward. New York: Penguin/Signet Classic, 1981.

Stribling, T. S. *Birthright: A Novel.* New York: The Century Co., 1922.

Styron, William. *Tidewater Tales: Three Tales from Youth.* New York: Random House, 1993.

Sugy, Catherine. "Black Men or Good Niggers?" In *Black Films and Film-Makers.* Ed. Lindsay Patterson. 182-89.

Taylor, Clyde R. "Black Silence and the Politics of Representation." In *Oscar Micheaux and His Circle.* Ed. Pearl Bowser, Jane Gaines, and Charles Musser. 3-10.

————. "The Ironies of Palace-Subaltern Discourse." In *Black American Cinema*. Ed. Manthia Diawara. 177-99.

————. *The Mask of Art: Breaking the Aesthetic Contract—Film and Literature*. Bloomington: Indiana UP, 1998.

————. "The Re-Birth of the Aesthetic in Cinema." In *The Birth of Whiteness*. Ed. Daniel Bernardi. 15-37.

Taylor, Mildred D. *Roll of Thunder, Hear My Cry*. New York: Bantam, 1984.

Thompson, Sister Francesca. "From Shadows 'n Shufflin' to Spotlights and Cinema: The Lafayette Players, 1915-1932." In *Oscar Micheaux and His Circle*. Ed. Pearl Bowser, Jane Gaines, and Charles Musser. 19-33.

Tibbetts, John C. and James M. Welsh. *The Encyclopedia of Novels Into Films*. New York: Facts on File, 1998.

Toplin, Robert Brent, ed. *Hollywood as Mirror: Changing Views of "Outsiders" and "Enemies" in American Movies*. Westport, CT: Greenwood P, 1993.

Tourgee, Albion W. *A Fool's Errand, by One of the Fools: The Famous Romance of American History*. New York: Fords, Howard, and Hulbert, 1880.

Tucker, Lauren R. and Hemant Shah. "Race and Transformation of Culture: The Making of the Television Miniseries *Roots*." *Critical Studies in Mass Communication* 9.4 (1992): 325-36.

VanEpps-Taylor, Betti Carol. *Oscar Micheaux: A Biography. Dakota Homesteader, Author, Pioneer Film Maker*. Rapid City, SD: Dakota West Books, 1999.

Van Peebles, Melvin. "A Black Odyssey: *Sweet Sweetback's Baadasssss Song*." In *Black Films and Film-Makers*. Ed. Lindsay Patterson. 220-31.

Vroman, Mary Elizabeth. "See How They Run." In *By and About Women: An Anthology of Short Fiction*. Ed. Elizabeth Kline Schneiderman. 159-79.

Wade, Wyn Craig. *The Fiery Cross: The Ku Klux Klan in America*. New York: Simon and Schuster, 1987.

Walker, Alice. *The Color Purple*. New York: Washington Square P, 1982.

Walker, Joseph A. *The River Niger*. New York: Hill and Wang, 1973.

Wallace, Michele. "Oscar Micheaux's *Within Our Gates*: The Possibilities for Alternative Visions." In *Oscar Micheaux and His Circle*. Ed. Pearl Bowser, Jane Gaines, and Charles Musser. 53-66.

————. "Race, Gender, and Psychoanalysis in Forties Film: *Lost Boundaries, Home of the Brave*, and *The Quiet One*." In *Black American Cinema*. Ed. Manthia Diawara. 257-71.

Weales, Gerald. "Pro-Negro Films in Atlanta." In *Black Films and Film-Makers*. Ed. Lindsay Patterson. 44-52.

West, Cornel. *Race Matters*. New York: Vintage, 1994.

West, Dorothy. *The Wedding*. New York: Doubleday, 1995.

White, Walter. *Flight*. New York: A. A. Knopf, 1926.

Williams, Linda. *Playing the Race Card: Melodramas of Black and White from Uncle Tom to O. J. Simpson*. Princeton: Princeton UP, 2001.

Willis, Sharon. *High Contrast: Race and Gender in Contemporary Hollywood Film*. Durham: Duke UP, 1997.

Wilson, Sondra Kathryn, ed. *The Selected Writings of James Weldon Johnson*. 2 vols. New York: Oxford UP, 1995.

Winchell, Donna Haisty. "Alice Walker." In *American Novelists Since World War II*. Third Series. Ed. James R. Giles and Wanda H. Giles. *Dictionary of Literary Biography*. Vol. 143. Detroit: Gale, 1994. 277-93.

Woll, Allen L. and Randall M. Miller. *Ethnic and Racial Images in American Film and Television: Historical Essays and Bibliography*. New York: Garland, 1987.

Wolper, David L., with Quincy Troupe. *The Inside Story of TV's "Roots."* New York: Warner Books, 1978.

Wood, Gerard. "From *The Clansman* and *The Birth of a Nation* to *Gone With the Wind*: The Loss of American Innocence." In *Recasting: Gone With the Wind in American Culture*. Ed. Darden Asbury Pyron. 123-36.

Woodland, J. Randal. "Oscar Micheaux." In *Afro-American Writers Before the Harlem Renaissance*. Ed. Trudier Harris and Thadious M. Davis. *Dictionary of Literary Biography*. Vol. 50. Detroit: Gale, 1986. 218-25.

Wright, Richard. *Native Son*. New York: Harper and Brothers, 1940.

Yearwood, Gladstone L. *Black Film as a Signifying Practice: Cinema, Narration and the African-American Aesthetic Tradition*. Trenton, NJ: Africa World P, 2000.

Yerby, Frank. *The Foxes of Harrow*. New York: Dial, 1946.

Young, Joseph A. *Black Novelist as White Racist: The Myth of Inferiority in the Novels of Oscar Micheaux*. Westport, CT: Greenwood P, 1989.

Index

A

Abrams, Edward 128
"Abyssinia" (musical show) 69
Addams, Jane 30
Advance Motion Picture Company 73
Africa-Based Films 33, 216-23,
    229-30, 507
Afro-American Film Company 70
Aiken, George L. 9
Alice, Mary 384
Alexander, Shana 305
Alger, Horatio 72, 76
Algren, Nelson 288
"Alias Jefferson Lee" (story) 142
Allen, Jonelle 363
The American Cavalryman 143
American Film Institute Norman
    Collection xviii
Amos, John 417, 488
Amos 'n' Andy 223
Andra, Fern 10
Anderson, Eddie ("Rochester") 41,
    45, 199, 350
Anderson, Ernest 248
Anderson, Lisa Arrindell 410
Andrews, Lisa 505
Angelou, Maya 444n36, 452-54
Anna Lucasta 159
Apfel, Oscar 88
Applegate, Roy 10
Armstrong, Louis 47, 310
Armstrong, Robert 221, 223
Armstrong, William H. 328-29, 331
Arthur, Timothy Shay 88
Askins, Ida 80
Attucks, Crispus 336
Aurthur, Robert Alan 302
Avery, Margaret 396, 459, 466, 469

B

Babb, Kroger 18
Bailey, Pearl 311
Baker, Carroll 287
Baker, Edna Mae 145
Baker, Sam 221
Baldwin, James 21, 276, 290, 299,
    310, 316, 337-44, 426, 470
Ball, John 306
Bancroft, Ann 305
Baraka, Amiri (see LeRoi Jones)
Barkley, James 329, 332
Barnum, Phineas T. (P. T.) 2, 243
Barr, Edna 226
Barrett, William E. 304
Barrymore, Ethel 38, 260
Barrymore, Lionel 24
Baryshnikov, Mikhail 380
Baskett, James 49-50, 211, 213
Bass, Ron 480, 484
Bassett, Angela 480, 481, 483-84
Be Ready with Bells and Drums
    (novel) 305
Beals, Jennifer 435
Beavers, Louise 37, 42, 43, 201, 230,
    254, 256, 265, 300
Bedell, Sally 416-17
Belafonte, Harry 39, 311, 323, 359
Belin, Marie-Rose 280
Bennett, Bruce 252
Bennett, Joan 205
Bergen, Edgar 221
Berry, Halle 422, 423, 492
Best, Willie ("Sleep 'n' Eat") 47,
    225, 230, 383
"Bigger Thomas" Syndrome 290,
    312
Billbrew, A. C. 189

Billbrew Chorus 188
Bizet, Georges 269
Blackface as theatrical/film practice
    6-7, 10, 19, 29, 41, 48, 50, 52n6,
    87, 88, 125, 190, 217, 219, 231n1-
    2, 318
  as employed by Jolson 186-87,
    188
  as part of Duncan Sisters' act
    15, 16, 48
Black Boy (novel) 153
Black Boy (play) 245
Black Power 358
Blackton, J. Stuart 9
Blaxploitation 312, 344-62, 366, 508
Blinn, William 415-16
Blunt, Erin 450
Bogart, Humphrey 289
Boles, Lottie 76
Bond, James, III 341, 343, 396
Book Supply Company of New York
    148
Booker T. Film Company 85-86
Boucicault, Dion 36
Bowman, Laura 134, 144, 224, 225, 226
Bowser, Aubrey 83
Boyer, Elizabeth 82
Bradford, Roark 197
Bradley, David 426
Braithwaite, E. R. 305
Branch, William 316
Brando, Marlon 420
Breen, Bobby 201, 202, 203
Brent, George 247
Brian, David 273
Bridges, Beau 307
Brinks, André 382
Broderick, Matthew 383
Brodie, Steve 269
Brooks, Adam 496
Brooks, Avery 20, 21
Brooks, Clarence 76, 78, 79, 86,
    129, 246

Brooks, Dudley 76
Brooks, Eunice 123
Brown, Clarence 272, 274-75
Brown, Everett 206, 246
Brown, George 83
Brown, G. Edward 82
Brown, J. C. 84
Brown, James 356
Brown, Jim 346, 347
Brown, John 6, 52, 157, 316
Brown, Karl 27
Brown, Lucille 82
Brown, Sterling A. 189
Brown vs. Topeka 261
"Buck" as film stereotype xiv, 25,
    31-33, 50, 219, 319, 346, 360, 383,
    401, 506
  in *Birth of a Nation* 31-33
  in jungle films 219-21
Buck and Bubbles (song, dance,
    and comedy team) 71
"Buddy" Films 380-83, 508
Bufford, Daisy 225
Burnett, Charles 384, 492, 493, 495
Burroughs, Edgar Rice 218, 220,
    507
Burton, LeVar 415, 418, 421, 422
Busia, Akosua 496

C

Caesar, Adolph 431, 464, 469
Calloway, Star 140
Cambridge, Godfrey 348, 349
Capra, Frank 249, 328
Carrizal, Battle of 77, 184
Carter, Benny 252
Carver, George Washington 251
Cash, Rosalind 344, 361
Cassavetes, John 25, 39, 362
Chapman, Tracy 428
Chaykin, Maury 435
Cheadle, Don 408, 435
Chenal, Pierre 280-81

Chenault, Lawrence 79, 83, 88, 97, 100, 128, 136, 144
Chesnutt, Charles W(addell) 34, 35, 135, 137-39, 156-58, 213
Chester, Alfred ("Slick") 97
"Chicago After Midnight" (story) 145
Childress, Alice 316, 447-51
Chloe, Aunt (in *Uncle Tom's Cabin*) 4, 9, 22
Chopin, Kate 34
Christian, Robert 455
Christie, Al 88, 223
Cimino, Leonardo 349
The Clansman (novel and play) 26-27, 506
Clark, Marguerite 11
Clarke, Alex 324
Clarke, Shirley 362
Clay, Cassius 477
Clements, Stebeno 78
Clemmons, Hal 10
Clinton, Bill 379
Cochran, John, Jr. 476
Cohen, Octavus Roy 88, 223
Colbert, Claudette 43, 254, 256
Cole, Nat "King" 310
Cole, Olivia 344, 396
Cole and Johnson's "A Trip to Coontown" Company 69
Collins, Leroy 159
Colonel Heeza Liar 18
Colored Feature Photoplay, Inc. 86
Colored Players Film Corporation xviii, 88-92, 195
Coming-of-Age Films 287, 288, 312, 323-44, 366, 437, 447-56, 508
Communist Party 102, 105, 155, 238n42, 263, 278, 279, 282
The Competitor (magazine) 79
Connelly, Marc 197, 198, 200, 507
Connors, Chuck 417
Cook, Fielder 453

Cook, Jota 126
"Coon" as film stereotype xiv, 44-50, 71, 86-88, 125, 130, 201, 350
   as reversal of stereotype by Micheaux 125, 130-31
Corey, Jeff 271
Cosby, Bill xv, 359, 379, 427, 477
Cosby, Camille xv
Cowan, Verlie 159
Crabbe, Buster 221
Craig, James 347
Crain, Jeanne 38, 260, 261, 263
Crane, Frank 9
Criner, Lawrence 184
The Crisis 30, 72, 139, 210
Crosby, Bing 47
Crystal, Billy 380
Cullen, Countee 494-95
Cumby, William 199
Cummings, Irving 10
Curley, James 30
Curtis, Tony 25, 39, 303
Curtiss, Willa Pearl 281

D

DaFoe, Willem 380
Daley, William Robert 10-11
Daly, Tim 422
Dandridge, Dorothy 39, 194, 227, 245, 304, 310, 322-23
Daniels, Bebe 205
Dano, Royal 347
"Darky" as film stereotype xiv, 44, 267, 506
Darnell, Linda 301
Darren, James 289
Dash, Julie 385
Dassin, Jules 328
Daugherty, Romeo L. 79, 185
Davis, Bette 40, 205, 247-48
Davis, Elmer 249
Davis, Ossie 316, 350, 351, 353, 355, 359, 423

Davis, Sammy, Jr. 194, 304, 310
Dawley, J. Searle 11
Day, Doris 307
"The Day of Atonement" (story) 185
Dazey, Frank 245
Dean, James 321
De Anda, Peter 352
De Carlo, Yvonne 39
De Havilland, Olivia 247
De Rochemont, Louis 265
Dee, Ruby 311, 316, 317, 320
Dee, Sandra 258
Deitch, Donna xv, 473
DeKnight, Belle 191
Demme, Jonathan 496, 501, 506
Derek, John 289
Dern, Bruce 20
Devine, Loretta 480, 481
Diaz, Hazel 147
Dick, Douglas 270
Dickerson, Ernest 384
Dickson, Harrison 87-88
Diggs, Taye 483-84
Dillon, Matt 287
Dinky Doodle 18
Disney, Walt 18, 49, 50, 211, 213, 457, 504, 508
Dixie Jubilee Choir 192
Dixon, Thomas 26-28, 31, 221, 506
Donahue, Troy 37, 259
Dones, Sidney P. 86
"Double Mammoth" (Tom Shows) 2
Douglas, Susan 268
Douglass, Frederick 316
Douglass Film Company (see Frederick Douglass Film Company)
Downing, Henry Francis 143
Driscoll, Bobby 49, 211
Du Bois, W. E. B. 30, 41, 72, 152, 336, 388

Du'Bois, Janet 361
Duke, Bill 319, 356, 476
Dunbar, Paul Laurence xvi, 80, 82-83, 509
Duncan, Michael Clarke 382
Duncan, Rosetta and Vivian (Duncan Sisters) 15-16, 48
Duncan, Vernon S. 121
Dunham, Katherine 245
Dunne, Philip 264
DuPois, Starletta 319
Dutton, Charles 428-31

E

Ebony Film Corporation 86-88
Edison (Film Company) 4, 47, 71
Edwards, Gus 341
Edwards, James 269, 270
Edwards, John 218
Edwards, Mattie 140, 218
Eisenhower, Dwight D. 259, 299, 300, 309, 366, 508
Elcar, Dana 324
Elder, Lonnie, III 316, 331, 334, 335, 336, 337
Eline, Marie ("The Thanhouser Kid") 9, 10
Elise, Kimberly 497, 498, 500
Eliza (in *Uncle Tom's Cabin*) 2, 4-5, 10, 13, 14, 17, 19-22
Ellington, Duke 126, 245
Ellison, Ralph 274, 276, 371n31
Emmanuel, Elzy 274
Emmeline (in *Uncle Tom's Cabin*) 6, 11, 21
The Emperor Jones 13, 200, 228
Epstein, Julius J. 320
Europe, Jim 252
Eva (in *Uncle Tom's Cabin*) (see Little Eva)
Evans, Estelle 323
Everett, Estelle 78

F

Faison, Donald Adeosun 482
"The Faker" (story) 144
Falk, Harry 361
Fanchon Steppers 188
Farrell, James 288
Faulkner, William 272, 274-75, 386
Fauset, Jessie 34
Female Spectatorship xvii
Ferber, Edna 38
Ferrer, Mel 38, 265, 266
Fetchit, Stepin (Lincoln Theodore Monroe Andrew Perry) 45-47, 71, 189, 190, 196, 203, 230, 350
Fields, Joseph 280
Fischer, Margarita (Mrs. Harry A. Pollard) 12, 14
Fitzgerald, Ella 18, 290
Fitzgerald, Geraldine 287
Flying Dutchman 365
A Fool's Errand 129
Ford, Glenn 25
Ford, Harrison 380
Ford, John 246, 269, 328
Foster, William xvi, 50, 67, 68-71, 185
Foster Photoplay Company 69, 71, 72
Fountaine, William 191, 194
The Foxes of Harrow (novel) 214-16
Foxx, Redd 349
Frank, Leo M. 104, 127, 152
Franklin, Carl 435-38
Frederick Douglass Film Company 80, 81, 86, 319
  aims of company 80
Freeman, Al, Jr. 364
Freeman, Bea 97, 129
Freeman, Morgan 381, 455
French, Susan 396
Frohman, Daniel 73-74
Fujimoto, Tak 501

Fuller, Charles 396, 402, 403, 426, 431-32

G

Gable, Clark 39, 205, 306, 307
Gaines, Ernest 385-413, 423, 424, 509
Gaines, Harris 159
Gandhi, Mahatma 309
Gardner, Ava 38
Garner, Margaret 496
Garrison, Harold 195-96
Garvey, Marcus 348
Gates, Henry Louis, Jr. 423, 291n4, 470, 445n43
Gaumont Film Company 219
Gavin, John 259
Gay, John 20
Geller, Robert 340
Gentry, Minnie 353
"The Ghost of Tolston Manor" (story) 139-40
Gibson, Mel 380-381
Gilbert, Mercedes 83
Gillingwater, Claude 205
Gilpin, Charles 13-14, 88
Giovanni's Room (novel) 338
Gish, Lillian 27, 29
Givens, Robin 354
Glasgow, Ellen 247, 507
Glenn, Roy, Sr. 306
Glover, Danny 319, 354, 380-81, 384, 437, 467, 497, 500
Goldberg, Jack 99, 250
Goldberg, Whoopi 383, 459, 463, 469, 484
Goldwyn, Sam 244
Gordon, Carl 429
Gorman, Grant 141
Gossett, Lou, Jr. 402, 417, 421, 422
Gould, Walter 282, 283
Grady, Lottie 69
Grant, Ulysses 6

Gray, Harry 191
Greaves, William 384
Greeley, Horace 157
Green, Cora 147
Green, Paul 79, 245, 278
Greene, Ward 230
Greer, Rosie 361
Griffin, Douglass 136
Griffith, D. W. xiv, 1, 11, 16, 23-24, 25-33, 35, 41, 67, 72, 73, 95, 205, 217, 391, 506
  as film innovator 28
Griffith, "Roaring Jake" 27
Griggs, Sutton E. 34
Groh, David 450
Guy, Jasmine 422, 423

H

Haggard, H. Rider 229
Halberstam, David 506
Haley, Alex 379, 413-28
Hall, Albert 427, 497
Hall, Beulah 76, 77
Hall, Iris 107, 121
Hall, Irma P. 409-10
Hall, Karen 473
Hall, Lindsay J. 82
Hall Johnson Choir 199, 201, 203
Hamilton, Lisa Gay 501
Hammerstein, Oscar 223
Hamner, Earl 476
Hanks, Tom 382
Hansberry, Lorraine 290, 312-19, 320, 356, 508, 509
  as award-winning playwright 312, 318
Hansberry vs. Lee 315
Harlem Renaissance 101, 189, 201, 494-95
Harlemwood Studios 226-27
Harper, Frances E. W. 34
Harris, Eliza (see Eliza)

Harris, George (in *Uncle Tom's Cabin*) 19, 20, 21-22, 211-12
Harris, Joel Chandler 49
Harris, Julius 402
Harris, Zelda 429
Harrison Dickson Film Company 87
Harrison, Rex 214
Harpo Studios 492
Hart, Albert Bushnell 72
Hartman, Elizabeth 305
Harvey, Anthony 365
Hastie, William 249
Hawkins, Screamin' Jay 355
Haynes, Daniel L. 191, 192, 227
Haynes, Hunter C. 70
Haynes, Tiger 402
Hays Office 220, 244
Hays, Will 244
Hecht, Harold 320, 321
Heinemann, Arthur 454
Hellbound Train 193, 233n12
Hemmings, Myra 227
Henderson, Harry 90
Henry, William 102
Henson, Josiah 21
Hepburn, Katherine 306
Hepburn, Philip 323
Hernandez, Juano 95, 97, 140, 273, 275
Heyward, DuBose 304
Heywood, Donald 126
Hicks, Don 300
Himes, Chester 290, 312, 344-56, 365, 438, 508, 509
Hines, Gregory 354, 355, 380, 382, 482
Historical Feature Films 87
Hitchcock, Alfred 253
Hitler, Adolf 250, 399
Holder, Roland 126
Homer 329, 335

Hooks, Kevin 333, 421, 450
Hoover, Herbert 184
Hope, Bob 47, 225, 383
Horne, Lena 17, 39, 194, 244, 245, 263
Houghton, Katherine 306
"House of Horror" (story) 223
"House of Mystery" (story) 141
Houseman, John 249, 278
Houston, Whitney 379, 480, 481
Howard Beach 379
Howard, Shingzie 95, 136
Howard, Trevor 205
Howe, Irving 277
Hudlin Brothers (Reginald and
    Warrington) 384
Hudson, Ernie 380
Hudson, Rochelle 255
Hudson, Rock 306, 307
Hughes, Langston xiii, xvi, 40, 201,
    202-04, 245, 316, 494, 509
Hull, Edith M. 219
Hunter, Evan 306
Hunter, Holly 402
Hunter, Ross 257
Hurst, Fannie 37
Hurston, Zora Neale 200, 494
Huston, John 247
Hylton, Richard 266

I

"In Dahomey" (musical show) 69
In Splendid Error (play) 316
Ince, Thomas 33
Ingram, Rex 198, 199, 227, 252, 300
Intruder in the Dust (novel) 272-73
Isaacs, Edith 1, 15
Ivey, Dana 410, 469

J

Jackson, Andrew 251
Jackson, Desreta 463
Jackson, Eugene 189
Jackson, J. A. 134

Jackson, Janet 428
Jackson, Jesse 370
Jackson, Michael 379
Jackson, Samuel L. 20, 22, 362
Jarman, Claude, Jr. 273
Jasper "Puppetoon" series 45
Jefferson, Augustine 386-87, 390
Jeffries, Herb 245
Jewison, Norman 432, 434
Jim Crow 18, 184, 210, 229, 252,
    264, 507
Johnson, James Weldon 30, 103,
    185, 196, 204, 227, 509
Johnson, George P(erry) 75, 78,
    79-80
  as head of Lincoln Motion
    Picture Company 79
  as screenplay author 79
  negotiations with Micheaux
    120-21
Johnson, Hall (see also Hall
    Johnson Choir) 245
Johnson, Kyle 323, 326
Johnson, Noble M. xvi, 75-79, 183,
    506-07
  as actor 17, 75, 77, 78, 79, 227
  resignation from Lincoln 78
Johnson, Ralph 140
Johnston, Albert H. 265, 267-68
Johnston, Annie Fellows 24
Johnstone, Norman 90
Jolson, Al 40, 185, 186, 188
Jones, Brutus 13
Jones, James Earl 363, 364, 420
Jones, Juli (pseudonym of William
    Foster) 69
Jones, LeRoi (former/given name
    of Amiri Baraka) 290, 364, 428,
    508
Jones, Lisa 487, 492, 493
Jones, Peter P. 85
Jonson, Tefft 44
Jordan, Michael 428

Jordan, Vernon 420
Joy, Nicholas 281
Jump for Joy (stage satire) 245-46

K

Kael, Pauline 351, 394
Kahn, Richard 223, 224
Kalem (Film Company) 9, 70, 219
Karlen, John 287
Karlin, Fred 394
Kata, Elizabeth 305
Kazan, Elia 260
Keighley, William 197
Kelly, Howard 69
Kemp, Mae 83
Kemper, Charles 274
Kennedy, John F. 309
Kennedy, Robert 309
Keystone Kops 48, 71
"The Killer" (story) 144
Kinney, Terry 437
King, Edward E. 100
King, F. 80
King, Reverend Martin Luther, Jr.
    309, 328, 356, 388, 477
King, Rodney 380
Kinte, Kunta 414-21
Kitt, Eartha 18, 310
Kitzmiller, John 19
Klein, Herbert 279
Knight, Shirley 364
Kohner, Susan 37
Korty, John 385, 391, 392, 394
Kramer, Stanley 269, 303
Ku Klux Klan 26, 29-30, 100, 118,
    206, 263, 288, 382, 387-88, 391,
    392, 421, 426, 431, 446n47, 452-53,
    455, 507
Kurtz, Wilbur 206-207

L

L. C. Borden Productions 203
Laemmle, Carl 12, 72, 95

Lafayette Players 81, 96, 97, 121,
    143, 201
LaGravenese, Richard 496
Lancaster, Burt 320
A Land Beyond the River (play) 316
Langford, Sam 97
Langston, Tony 79, 87
Lantz, Walter 18
Larsen, Nella 34
Lathan, Sanaa 487
Lathan, Stan 20, 21, 23, 344, 386,
    396-97
Laurents, Arthur 269
Lawrence, Martin 51, 383
Lay My Burden Down 390
Lee, Canada 253, 279, 300, 362
Lee, Carl 362
Lee, Leslie 341
Lee, Robert E. 6
    as name of boat in Porter's *Uncle
        Tom's Cabin* 5
Lee, Spike 96, 384, 426-28, 456-57,
    508, 509
Legree, Simon 2, 8, 10, 11, 13, 14,
    17, 18, 20-22, 202
    as Lagree in *Onkle Tom's Hütte*
        18-19 19
    in Porter's film 6
    in Stowe's novel 1
Leigh, Vivien 205, 208
Leighton, Fred 80
LeRoy, Mervyn 230, 246
Lesser, Sol 201, 202, 244
Levette, Harry 197
Levy, Robert 81, 85
Lewis, Lucille 136
Lewis, Theophilus 102
Library of Congress xviii-xix,
Lichtman, Al 244
Lincoln, Abbey 307
Lincoln, Abraham 6, 14, 25, 31,
    72-73, 74, 157

Lincoln Motion Picture Film
    Company xviii, 75-80, 120,
    183, 319
Lincoln Players 201
Little Eva
    in film versions of *Uncle Tom's
    Cabin* 4, 5, 7, 9, 10, 11, 15-17,
    18, 19, 22
    in Stowe's novel 1
    in Tom show productions 2
    in *Topsy and Eva* 17
Little Rascals 48-49
Locke, Alain 189
Lockhart, Calvin 348
Lockridge, Ross, Jr. 39
Long, Huey 402
Long, Walter 29
Lord, Del 15
Lord Ligonier (slave ship) 416
Losee, Frank 11
Louis, Joe 250, 388
Louisiana (play) 226
Love, Victor 287
Lovejoy, Alec 134
Lovejoy, Frank 270
Lowe, James B. 12, 13, 15
Lubin, Sigmund 8
Lubin (Film Company) 70, 71
Lucas, Charles 121
Lucas, Sam 10
Lumbly, Carl 493
Lynch, Silas 28-29, 31-32, 35
Lynching xiv, 19, 29, 59n41, 100,
        103, 104, 127, 130, 131, 141, 210,
        238n42, 244, 275, 284, 285, 390,
        391, 399, 459, 507
Lysistrata 41

M
Machen, Yvonne 159
MacLachlan, Janet 336, 361, 455
Madam X (play) 111
Maddow, Ben 275
Madison, Gloria 281

Magnolia (novel) 205
Mahon, Carl 124, 136, 140
Majal, Taj 334
Malcolm X 309, 356, 425-428, 432
Mamet, David 426
Mammy as type and stereotype
        xiv, 1, 41-44, 47, 49, 50, 147, 189,
        194, 201, 203, 209, 219, 251, 299,
        304, 319, 383, 385, 507
    in *Jasper* series 45
    in *Gone With the Wind* 42-43, 206,
        208-09, 507
    in non-plantation films 43-44, 51,
        255-57, 264-65, 383
"The Man Who Would Be White"
    (story) 83
"Mandy" (story) 147
Mankiewicz, Joseph L. 300
Marceron, Jacques 280
Margulies, Stan 420
Marks, Lawyer (in *Uncle Tom's
    Cabin*) 2, 4, 6
Marsh, Mae 29
Massey, Raymond 15
Matthews, Carmen 336
Maurice, Richard 86
Maurice Film Company 86
Mayer, Gerald 322
McAvoy, May 186
McCarthy, Joseph (Joe), Senator
    309
McCarthy, Kevin 346
McClendon, Rose 276
McCracken, Reverend N. J. 109,
    117
    as basis for hypocritical preach-
    ers in Micheaux's fiction and
    films 117-20
McCracken, Orlean (Mrs. Oscar
    Micheaux) 109-10
McDaniel, Hattie xiv, 41, 42-43,
    49, 208-09, 210, 230, 245, 247,
    265, 300, 350
McDonald, Jack 69

McDormand, Frances 382
McGarrity, Everett 191
McGovern, Elizabeth 287
McKay, Claude 495
McKinney, Morris 226
McKinney, Nina Mae 191, 192, 194, 262
McMillan, Terry 477-89, 509
McNair, Barbara 346
McNeil, Claudia 314, 316, 317
McQueen, Butterfly 230
McWade, Edward 10
Méliès, Georges 4
Merimée, Prosper 269
Meyjes, Menno 463
Michael, Jim 286
Michaux, Elder Solomon Lightfoot 250
Micheaux, Bell Willingham 108
Micheaux, Calvin S. 108
Micheaux, Oscar xv, xvi, xvii, 50, 68, 83, 93-160, 183, 184, 193, 200, 225, 247, 249, 250, 506-07, 509
    adaptation of black literature 101, 135-39, 143-46
    adaptation of his own fiction 101, 121-22, 139-43
    adaptation of literature by white authors 132-35
    anti-Semitic motifs 152-53, 156
    as self-promoter 97-99, 114, 121, 122
    bankruptcy of his film corporation 98-99
    The Betrayal xviii, 94, 158, 159, 230
    breadth of genres in his films 100, 184, 507
    The Case of Mrs. Wingate 151-53, 156
    The Conquest 108, 110-13, 114, 116, 117, 149, 151
    contempt for corrupt preachers 115, 117-20, 123
    contrast between city and frontier 110, 111-13, 114, 124-25, 146, 151
    correspondence with Charles Chesnutt 138-39
    cost of his filmmaking 95-96
    emphasis on middle and professional class 102-03
    The Exile 123-25, 126, 127, 128, 137, 144-45, 146, 149, 15
    The Forged Note 113-14, 115, 117, 127, 128, 151
    gender issues in his films xvii, 143-144
    The Homesteader as film 94, 97, 121, 122, 128, 149, 158
    The Homesteader as novel 114-17, 119-20, 139, 151
    incorporation of aspects of popular culture 101, 125-26, 193
    incorporation of his biography 108-10
    issues of black skin color in his films 92, 101-03, 105, 146, 157-58
    issues of urban blacks and northern migrations 89, 106, 125, 195
    Jean Baptiste as fictional alter-ego 114
    The Masquerade 139, 148, 156-58
    mulatto theme 34-35, 123, 135-136, 137
    negotiations with George Johnson 120-21
    Oscar Deveraux as fictional counterpart 110-13
    positive portrayals of women 106-07, 156, 507
    problems with censors 102-06, 121-22, 127, 134, 136
    racial identity in his films xvii, 100, 105, 114-15, 123, 129-30, 135-37, 143-44, 145, 146, 150, 155, 157
    racial slant in his films 96, 100-101

reversal of racial stereotypes 123, 125, 129-30, 137, 141, 143-44, 145

role in film history 94, 153, 509

Sidney Wyeth as cinematic counterpart 128, 131

Sidney Wyeth as fictional alterego 113-14, 128, 155, 153

The Story of Dorothy Stanfield 117, 148, 153-56

technical limitations of his filmmaking 94-97

transition to sound films 94, 125-26, 127

treatment of caste xvii, 92, 102-03, 135, 157

treatment of class xvii, 131, 135-37

use of cabaret scenes 125-26

The Wind From Nowhere 149-151, 158

Micheaux, Swan, Jr. 98, 142-143

Micheaux Film and Book Company (later the Micheaux Film Corporation) 93, 97, 121-22, 125, 142

Michelina, Theresa 10

Midnight Rambles 92

Milestone, Lewis 246

Miller, Dorie 252

Miller, Warren, III 362

Mineo, Sal 321

Minstrel Tradition xiii, 15, 16, 48, 87, 148, 186, 187, 188, 204, 245, 318, 506

"Miss Celie's Blues" (song) 465

Mitchell, Loften 316

Mitchell, Margaret 205-209, 507

Moore, Charles 123

Moore, Juanita 37, 257, 258

Moore, Shemar F. 424

Moreland, Mantan 47, 230

Morrell, Stanley 123, 124

Morris, Earl 225

Morrison, Frederick Ernest ("Sunshine Sammy") 49

Morrison, Toni xv, 379, 447, 470, 477, 495-506, 509

Morton, Edna 79, 81, 83

Moses, Ethel 134, 146

Moses, Gilbert 419

Moses, Lucia Lynn 90, 91

Mosley, Thomas M. 80

Mosley, Walter 434

Moss, Carlton 209, 249-50, 507

Motley, Willard 288-89

Mott, Robert (see also Pekin Theatre) 69

Mr T 380, 383

Muhammad, Elijah 425

Mulatto 33-39, 216, 265, 388, 391, 506

as played by white actresses 38, 263, 265

as tragic stereotype in film xiv 33-39, 255, 260, 310, 319, 356

as treated by other black filmmakers 34-35, 137

as treated by Micheaux 34-35, 61n52, 117, 134-37, 143-44, 158

as treated by white filmmakers 33-34, 35, 255, 310

in *Birth of a Nation* 28-29, 35, 276

in *Imitation of Life* 37, 255-56, 258-60, 294n18

in literature 34, 61n54

Muni, Paul 246

Murphy, Eddie 379, 380, 382, 384

Murphy, Michael 393

Muse, Clarence 25, 33, 71, 88, 189, 190, 195, 201, 202-04, 227, 230

Myrick, Susan 206-07

N

NAACP xv, 21, 30, 50, 72, 196, 209, 212, 220, 243, 244, 248, 250, 253, 261, 286, 315, 507

"Naomi, Negress" (story) 146

Nash, Johnny 320, 321

National News Service 80
Native Son (novel) 153, 230, 277-79, 285, 288, 290, 311-12, 366
Native Son (play) 278, 280
Naylor, Gloria 470-77, 509
Neal, Larry 432
Negro Ensemble Theater 432
Negro Minutemen 250
Negro National Anthem 454
Nelson, Ralph 449
Nelson, Thomas 205
Nemiroff, Robert 319
"New Jack Cinema" 385
"New Negro" 27, 246-48, 249-65, 254, 255, 291n4, 507
Newbery Medal 329
Newsome, Carmen 134, 146, 147
Newsome, Nora 123, 124
Newton, Thandie 498, 500-501
Nichols, Dudley 264
Nilsson, Anna Q. 10
Nixon, Robert 277
Noisette, Katherine 143
Nolte, Nick 380
Norman Film Manufacturing Company xviii, 88, 89, 183, 184

O

Octoroon stereotype (see Mulatto)
O'Brien, Margaret 17
O'Connell, Arthur 347
O'Flaherty, Liam 269
O'Hara, Maureen 214
O'Hara, Scarlett 42, 97, 205-10, 504
O'Neal, Frederick 320
O'Neal, Ron 361
O'Neil, Frederick 262
O'Neill, Eugene 13, 228
Odetta 391
Office of War Information (OWI) 158, 248-49, 253, 279
Ol' Man Adam an' His Chillun (sketches) 197

Olcott, Sidney 219
Olinkas 457-58, 463
Ophelia
in other film versions 47
in Porter's *Uncle Tom's Cabin* 5, 9
in Vitagraph's *Uncle Tom's Cabin* 9
Ottley, Roi 200
"Our Gang" 48-49
Ovington, Mary White 72

P

Pace, Judy 348
Palcy, Euzhan 382
Paragon Pictures Corporation 86
Parks, Gordon, Jr. 362, 419
Parks, Gordon, Sr. 323-28, 359, 419, 509
Parks, Rosa 388
"Passing"
as film theme 34-36, 37-38, 61n52, 83, 84, 100, 105, 135-36, 137, 143, 157, 255, 258, 260-61, 263, 265-66, 267, 276
as literary theme 34, 83, 265
Pathé (Film Company) 70, 71
Patterson, Elizabeth 274
Patton, John, Jr. 466
Patton, Will 402
Peacock, Ann 394, 411-12
Pearson, Beatrice 265, 266
Peerce, Larry 362
Pekin Theatre (see also Mott, Robert) 69
Perry, Lincoln Theodore Monroe Andrew (see Fetchit, Stepin)
Perry, Rod 391
Peter P. Jones Photoplay Company (see Jones, Peter P.)
Peterson, Louis 316, 320
Petrie, Daniel 317
Pettus, William E. 90
Phenias (in Porter's *Uncle Tom's Cabin*) 4

Phifer, Mekhi 408
"Pickaninny"
  as film stereotype xiv, 9, 47-49,
    188, 189, 501, 506
Pickens, Albertine 78
Pickford, Mary 82, 92
Pierce, Stack 354
Pierce, Wendell 481
Pilot, Bernice 189
Plantation Tradition xiv, 7-9, 10,
    19, 24, 32, 42-43, 47, 49, 87, 243,
    294n18, 188-89, 194, 197, 202-03,
    204-17, 229, 232n10, 235n27, 349,
    387, 408, 504, 507
Poe, Edgar Allan 496
Poitier, Sidney 25, 39, 300-10, 311,
    314, 317, 319, 328, 344, 346, 359,
    366, 508
  as ebony saint 302, 304, 305, 308
  as producer and director 307-08
  as Oscar-winning actor 305, 310
  as reminiscent of saintly Tom 25,
    300, 304, 306
"The Policy Players" (story) 140
Polk, Oscar 97, 199
Pollard, Harry A. 12-15, 95
Poole, Ray 455
Porgy (novel) 304
Porter, Edwin S. xiv, 1, 4-8, 67
Pounder, CCH 344, 488
Powell, William 96
Prades, Jaime 280
Pratt, William W. 88
Preer, Evelyn 97, 121, 127, 133, 137,
    140
Press, Black xvi, 30, 68, 71, 104, 189,
    245, 249, 253
  criticism of racist caricature 87,
    200, 210
  criticism of shortcomings of race
    films 93
  importance of 30, 92-93, 184
Press, Gloria 146

Prince 428
Prince-Bythewood, Gina 487
Pryor, Richard 379, 382, 383
Puciato, Carroll 15

Q
Quakers 5, 21, 54n14
Quality (novel) 38, 260
Queen Latifah 424

R
Race Movies 67-68, 75, 89, 94, 98,
    200, 203-04, 227, 230, 250, 284,
    290n39
  as adapted from literature by
    black authors 79, 80, 81, 82,
    83, 84, 185
  as stories of racial achievement
    77, 79, 85, 111, 126, 133, 136,
    147-48, 159
  competition from white producers
    86-93, 143
  creation of black world in 68, 204,
    350
  criticism of by Micheaux 99-100
  depictions of class strife in 90-92
  effect of new sound technology on
    93, 184, 185
  financial problems of 79, 92, 183
  hopes for financial success through
    69-71
  reception of 77, 78, 80
  return as recurring narrative device
    77
  problems of distribution with
    70, 71, 79, 81-82, 92, 94, 183
  proliferation of race filmmakers
    in 1920s 85-93, 92
Racial Covenants 100, 132-133,
    231n4, 254, 315, 507
"The Racial Tangle" (play) 143
Radványi, Géza van 18-19

A Raisin in the Sun (play) 312-17, 318
Raphaelson, Samson 185
Rashad, Phylicia 20, 22
Rastus xiv, 44-45, 71, 217-18, 219
Rasulala, Thalmus 391
Rawlings, Marjorie Kinnan 383
Ray, Arthur 225
Ray, Nicholas 288
Razaf, Andy 183, 210
Reagan, Ronald 381
Reed, George 197
Reed, Robert 417
Reid, Tim 437
Reinhold, Judge 380
Reol Productions 81-85, 89, 90, 183
Remus (see Uncle Remus)
Revere, Paul 74
Rhames, Ving 341
Richards, Beah 306, 320, 361, 497
Richards, Lloyd 316, 317, 429
Richardson, Jack 33
Richardson, Sallie 78
Ritt, Martin 337
Roach, Hal 48
Robeson, Paul 97, 118, 195, 204, 227-29, 246, 249
Robinson, Bill "Bojangles" 24-25, 40, 41, 126, 196, 253
Robinson, Jackie 310
Robson, Mark 269
Rochon, Lela 480, 481
Rockwell, George Lincoln 420
Roemer, Michael 362
Rogers, Buddy 205
Rogers, Will 45
Rolle, Esther 319
Rollins, Howard E., Jr. 431, 434
Roosevelt, Franklin Delano 249
Roosevelt, Theodore 218
Rosamund, Clinton 246
Rose, Philip 316, 317
Rosebud Film Corporation 86

Rossellini, Roberto 280
Roth, Joe 504
Rothacker Film Manufacturing Company 74
Roundtree, Richard 361, 362
Ruark, Robert 306
Ruffin, Lark 455
Russell, Alice B. (Mrs. Oscar Micheaux) 95, 143, 146
Russell, John 347
Russell, Julia Theresa 95

S

Sabol, Dick 352
Sack, Alfred 249
Salem, Peter 250
"Sambo" Stereotype 44, 71, 153, 299, 319
Sams, Jeffrey D. 481
Sandor, Steve 347
Sands, Diana 316, 317
Santana (production company) 289
Sargent, Joseph 386, 408-11
Saunders, Elsworth 78
"The Scapegoat" (story) 80-81
Scardon, Paul 10
Scarification as ritual xv, 463, 511n8
Scherick, Edgar J. 20-21
Schlondorff, Volker 386, 402-05
Schmeling, Max 250
Scott, Dred 157
Scott, Emmett J. xvi, 50, 72-75
Scott, Hazel 245
Scott, Larry B. 449
Scott, Randolph 204
Schiffman, Frank 99
Schreder, Carol 423
Schultz, Michael 419
Seaforth, Susan 346
"See How They Run" (short story) 322
Seigmann, George 29
Selig Polyscope Company 4

Selig, William 73, 74

Selznick, David O. 17, 42, 205-06, 208, 209, 210

Seminole Film Company 85

Seneca, Joe 402

Sennett, Mack 15

Servant Stereotype 39-40, 198, 201-02, 207-09, 217, 228, 230, 254, 259, 305, 324, 476

Sexuality 41, 141, 154, 302, 307-08, 309, 320-21, 326-27, 339-41, 345, 346, 362, 358-59, 385, 476, 481, 484-85, 487, 493, 499

  as racist fear 31-36, 39, 359

Seymore, Larry 147

Shah, Krishna 363

Sheldon, Edward 36

Sherick, Edgar J. 20, 21

Sherman, William 14

Shipp, Jessie 85

Signifying as practice xv, 147

Silverman, Fred 413-14

Simmons, Joseph ("Doc") 30

Simmons, Maude 302

Simon, John 456

Sims, Sandman 402

Sinatra, Frank 39

Singleton, John 384, 508

Sipes, Donald 476

Sirk, Douglas 259

Sleep 'n' Eat (see Best, Willie)

Smight, Jack 454

Smith, Dr. A. W. 86

Smith, Inez 121

Smith, J. Augustus 226

Smith, Jimmy 77

Smith, Lillian 153

Smith, Mildred Joanne 302

Smith, Reverend Dr. W. S. 80

Snipes, Wesley 437, 487

"Sonny Jim" 44-45

Spacek, Sissy 383

Spencer, Kenneth 252

Spielberg, Steven xv, 456-57, 462-69, 473

St. Clair, Augustine (in *Uncle Tom's Cabin*) 5-6

  in film versions 5-6, 10, 13, 17, 19, 20, 21

  in Stowe's novel 1

St. Jacques, Raymond 346, 347, 348, 361

Stahl, John 214

Stallings, Vernon 18

Stallone, Sylvester 380

Starks, William 140

Steiger, Rod 305

Steinbeck, John 279

Stereotyping of Blacks 15, 28, 32, 51, 67, 75, 86-88, 194, 199, 200, 207, 209, 213, 217, 221, 243, 245, 254, 257, 259, 262, 276, 308-09, 316, 318-19, 356, 360, 385, 408, 456, 507, 508, 509

  as afraid of ghosts 45, 48, 218, 226

  as chicken thieves xiii, 44-45, 160

  as dice/craps shooters xiii, 6, 17, 86, 193, 243, 324, 507

  as gin tipplers or drunks xiii, 87

  as ignorant 87, 88, 154, 285

  as shiftless 44, 45, 87, 190, 248, 507

  as watermelon lovers xiii, 44, 45, 86, 160

  of black religion 191, 193, 194-95, 197-99, 200, 226, 243

Sterne, Elaine 72, 73

Stevens, David 421, 423

Stevens, James 83

Storey, Moorfield 30

Stowe, Harriet Beecher 1, 2, 4, 5, 7, 8, 12, 14, 17, 18, 19, 20, 21, 22, 23, 26, 47, 132, 328

Strange Fruit (novel) 153

Strayhorn, Billy 245

Stribling, T. S. 132, 134

Strode, Woody 402

Sullavan, Margaret 33, 197, 205
Sullivan, Kevin Rodney 485
Sumner, Cid Ricketts 38, 260
"Sunshine Sammy" (see Morrison, Frederick Ernest)
Susskind, David 317, 318
Sutherland, Donald 382

T

Tableaux vivant 4
Take a Giant Step (play) 316
Tan, Amy 480
Tandy, Jessica 380
Tara (plantation) 207
Tarkington, Booth 205
Tarzan 230
  in films 218, 220-21, 245
  in literature 218, 220
  on television 220
Tatum, E. G. 104, 140
Taylor, Elizabeth 39
Taylor, Mildred D. 455
The Tempest 113
Temple, Shirley 24-25, 40, 41, 47, 196, 202, 205, 220
Temptress as stereotype 41-42, 191-92, 194, 304, 310
Ten Nights in a Bar-Room, and What I Saw There (novel) 88
Ten Nights in the Bar Room (play) 88
Thal, Eric 492
Thanhouser Film Company 8-9
Thomas, Clarence 379
Thomas, D. Ireland 92
Thompson, Anita 79
Thompson, Edward 140
Thompson, Walker 100, 107
Thuna, Leonora 453
Tidyman, Ernest 361, 508
Till, Emmett 309
Toddy Pictures 249
Toddy, Ted 249
Tom Jubilees 2

Tom Operas 2
Tom Shows and Parades 2, 4, 11, 16, 26, 27, 58n33, 187, 204
Tomming Troupes (see Uncle Tom's Cabin Companies)
Toones, Fred ("Snowflake") 40
Topsy
  in Daly's *Uncle Tom's Cabin* 10
  in Porter's *Uncle Tom's Cabin* 5, 8
  in Tom shows 3
  in *Topsy and Eva* 15-17, 48
  in Turner's *Uncle Tom's Cabin* 10
  in Vitagraph's *Uncle Tom's Cabin* 9
Townsend, Robert 382, 384
Tracy, Spencer 306
  in other film versions 11, 47-48
Trouble in Mind (play) 316
"Trucking" (dance motion) 193
Trumbo, Dalton 209, 243
Tubman, Harriet 336
Tuchock, Wanda 196, 214
Tucker, Lorenzo 96, 98, 103, 136, 143
Tully, Jim 245
Turman, Glynn 363, 450
Turner, Lana 37, 257, 258
Turner, Otis 10
Tuskegee Institute 72, 73, 76, 77, 183
Tutt, J. Homer 100, 133
Tyson, Cicely 333, 363, 383, 393-94, 409, 423, 449, 451

U

Uggams, Leslie 417
Uhry, Albert 380
Uncle Remus Stereotype xiv, 49-50, 211-13, 508
  in literature 49, 211
Uncle Sam 50
Uncle Tom 1-23, 47-48, 50, 202, 229, 245-46, 299-300, 304, 350, 385, 432, 507
  as a character in Stowe's novel 1-2

as a character in cartoons 18
as anti-stereotypic depiction 15, 20
as film character in Porter's film 4-6
as first black major movie character 6
as Uncle Tom stereotype xiv, 2-4, 7, 13, 19, 23-25, 33, 135, 188, 189, 190, 203, 219, 243, 256, 365
Uncle Tom's Cabin Companies 2, 3, 4
Underground Railroad 11, 421
Underwood, Blair 424
Unique Film Company 85
Universal-Imp (Imperial) Company 10
Up From Slavery 73-74
Urban League 323, 420, 494

V

Valentino, Rudolph 96
Vance, Courtney B. 429
Van Engle, Dorothy 129
Van Peebles, Mario 384, 424, 509
Van Peebles, Melvin 33, 356-62, 361, 384
Vann, Robert L. 79
Vaudeville xiii, 15, 68-69, 70, 87, 92, 193, 353
Vereen, Ben 417
Verwayen, Percy 83, 137
Vessey, George 134
Vidor, King 191-197, 201
Vitagraph Film Company 8-9, 49
Voodoo 189, 217, 225-26
Vorhaus, Bernard 201
Vroman, Mary Elizabeth 322

W

Waite, Ralph 417
Walker, Alice 379, 456-70, 473, 477, 509

Walker, Joseph A. 363, 364
Wall, Boots 10
Wallace, Edgar 228
Wallace, George 354
Wallace, Jean 281
Walthall, Henry B. 27
Walton, Lester 30, 68, 88
Wanger, Walter 211
Warner, Jack 244
Warren, Mark 353
Warren, Michael 494
Warren, Robert Penn 39, 306
Washington, Booker T. 72, 73, 111-12, 160, 251, 388
Washington, Denzel 305, 382, 383, 427, 432, 435, 437-38
  as Academy Award-winning actor 437-438
Washington, Fredi 37, 255
Washington, William 204
Waters, Ethel 38, 43, 126, 230, 245, 260, 261, 264-65
The Way Back (play) 269
Wayans Brothers (Keenen Ivory, Damon, Shawn, and Marlon) 384
Wayans, Damon (see also Wayans Brothers) 383
Weathers, Carl 380
Weber, Lois 15
Webb, Mrs. Miles M. 85
Weems, Walter 188
Weill, Jules B. 15
Welles, Orson 278, 279
Wellman, William 246
Welty, Eudora 394
Werker, Alfred L. 265
West, Dorothy 490-95
West, Mae 41, 97
Westward Journey
  as motif in race films 78
  as used by Micheaux 124-25, 146, 151

Whipper, Leigh
  as actor 117, 246
  as filmmaker 85
Whipple, Prince 250
Whitaker, Forest
  as actor 354
  as director 480
White, Frank 78
White, Walter 34, 209, 213, 244
White, William L. 265
Whitfield, Lynn 494
Whitman, Ernest 199, 227
Whitney, Salem Tutt 133
Widmark, Richard 300, 301, 402, 404
Wilcots, Joe 419-20
Wilkerson, Arnold 391
William, Warren 255
Williams, Billy Dee 380
Williams, Cara 303
Williams, John A. 361
Williams, Leon 82
Williams, Spencer, Jr. 223-25, 226-27,
  250
Williams, Zack 224
Williams (Bert) and Walker (George)
  Musical Comedy Team 69, 85,
  223
Willinghan, Calder 426
Willis, Bruce 383
Willkie, Wendell 244
Wilson, August 428-31
Wilson, Flip 360

Wilson, Woodrow 28, 184
Wimberly, Rodrick 341
Winfield, Paul 332, 341, 343, 361,
  449, 451
Winfrey, Oprah xv, 287, 428, 457,
  469, 473, 476, 492, 497, 498, 501,
  505, 506
Winters, Shelley 289, 305
Wolper, David 415-19, 423
Wolper, Mark 423
Wood, Natalie 39, 321
Wood, Trevy 121
Woodard, Alfre 361, 383
Woods, Frank 27
Woodward, Edward 20, 429
Worth, Marvin 426
Wright, Richard 96, 153, 230, 272,
  276-86, 288, 289, 290, 311-12, 338,
  344, 365, 379, 496, 507, 509
Wynn, Tracy Keenan 390
Wynter, Dana 346

Y
Yancey, Kim 319
Yerby, Frank 213-16
Young, Stark 33, 197

Z
Zanuck, Darryl 244
Zombies 225-26
Zulus on film 217-18

Index of Films

A

Absent 86
The Adventures of Robinson Crusoe 163n15
The Adventures of Tarzan 218
Africa Speaks English 221
The African Queen 221
Aladdin Jones 87
Alice Adams 42
Alice Gets Stage Struck 18
All the Fine Young Cannibals 311
Almos' a Man 296n32
Amistad 505
L'Amitié noire 204
The Angel Levine 311
Anna Lucasta 269, 310
Arrowsmith 246
The Asphalt Jungle 269
Aunt Huldah, Matchmaker 41
The Autobiography of Miss Jane Pittman 385, 390-94, 399, 413, 423, 425

B

Bamboozled 508
Band of Angels 38-39, 306, 307
The Bar Sinister 36
The Barber 70, 71
The Barnstormers xix, 186
A Barnyard Mix-Up 63n62
Bataan 252-53
The Battle 27
Belle of the Nineties 41
Beloved 495-506
The Betrayal xviii, 94, 158-59, 230
Beverly Hills Cop 380
Beverly Hills Cop II 380

Big Boy 187
Big Momma's House 50,51,383
The Birth of a Nation 1, 23, 25, 28-32, 33, 35, 36, 41, 50, 72, 73, 74, 95, 100, 104, 195, 205, 209, 210, 212, 218, 219, 391, 420
The Birth of a Race xviii, 72, 73-75
Birthright 94, 100, 104, 130, 132-35
The Biscuit Eater 40
Black and Tan 176n82
Black Girl 364n53
Black Gold 88
Black Magic 45
Black Moon 225
The Black Network 177n82
A Black Sherlock Holmes xix, 87
The Blackboard Jungle 25, 306
Blood of Jesus 341n59
The Blue Gardenia 310
Body and Soul xviii, 94, 97, 105, 117, 118
Boomerang 384
Boyz N the Hood 384
The Brand of Cain (see Murder in Harlem)
Bright Road 311, 322-23
Broken Chains xv, 32
Broken Strings 203-04, 230
The Broken Violin 141-42
Bronze Buckaroo 224
Brother John 308
Brown Grary 88
The Brute 97
Buck and the Preacher 311
The Bull's Eye 163n15
The Bully 86
The Burden of Race 84
The Bushman 221

The Busted Romance 86
Bustin' Loose 50
Butch Cassidy and the Sundance Kid 381
The *Butler* 70
By Right of Birth xviii, 79

C

C-H-I-C-K-E-N Spells Chicken 45
Cabin in the Sky 42, 97, 194, 245, 253, 318
The Call of His People 83-84
Can This be Dixie? 56n21
Carmen Jones 42, 194, 269, 310, 311
Cause for Thanksgiving 44
Chased by Bloodhounds 45
Chicken Thief (ca. 1910-11) 44
The Chicken Thief (1904) 45
China Gate 310
Christmas Turkey 45
The Chocolate Soldier 204
The Clansman (see *The Birth of a Nation*)
Clara's Heart 50
Claudine xv, 50
Cleopatra Jones 362
Coffy 50, 362
A College Chicken 45
Colonel Heeza Liar in Uncle Tom's Cabin 18
The Color Purple xv, 21, 456-70, 473, 477, 496
The Colored American Winning His Suit 80, 319
Colored Troops Disembarking xix
Come Back, Charleston Blue 351-53
The Comeback of Barnacle Bill xviii-xix, 87
Coming to America 439n1
The Confederate Spy xiv, 7
The Conjure Woman 137-39
Cool Breeze 269
The Cool World 362
Coon Town Suffragettes 41

Cora Unashamed 236n31
Cotton Comes to Harlem xix, 348-51, 352-53, 355-56, 508
Crash Dive 252
Cry Freedom 382
Cry, the Beloved Country 297n39
The Custard Nine 87-88

D

Dark Princess 178n93
Dark Rapture 220
Darktown Duel 63n62
The Darktown Revue xix, 125
Darktown Wooing 63n61, 64n62
A Daughter of the Congo 96, 143-44
Daughters of the Dust 385
David Harum 196
The Dawn of Truth 162n9
A Day with the Tenth Cavalry at Fort Huachuca 163n13
The Death of Simon La Gree 186
The Debt xiv, 36
Deceit 105, 118
Deep South 235n24
The Defiant Ones 25, 303-04, 381
Desert Hearts 473
Devil in a Blue Dress 434-38
Diary of an African Nun 439n8
Dimples 186
Dinky Doodle in Uncle Tom's Cabin 18
The Dirty Dozen 346
Disappearing Acts 477, 485-89
Dixiana 205, 213
Dixie Duo Down South 45
Do the Right Thing 384
The Dolly Sisters 56n21
Don't Play Us Cheap 361
Driving Miss Daisy 380
A Dry White Season 382
Drums O'Voodoo (also released as *Voodoo Drums* and *Louisiana* and re-released as *She Devil*) 226

The Dungeon 104, 106
Dutchman 364-65, 508

E

Easy Rider 381
Easy Street 181n107
Easy to Get 250, 266
Edge of the City 25, 302-03, 311, 508
El Condor 346
The Elite Ball 63n62
The Emperor Jones 200, 228, 246
The Empire Strikes Back 50, 380
Everybody Sing 186
Eve's Bayou 505
The Exile xix, 94, 123-127, 137, 144, 145, 146, 149, 158

F

The Fall Guy 70
The Fighting Coward 237n32
The Five Heartbeats 384
The Flying Ace xix, 88, 184
Follow Your Heart 201
A Fool's Errand 129
For Love of Ivy 307-08
The Forgotten Village 279
For Massa' Sake xiv, 7
48 Hours 380
The Foxes of Harrow 213-16
Foxy Brown 50, 362
The Framing of the Shrew 88
Free and Equal xv, 33
Freedom Song 505
Friday Foster 362
Fried Green Tomatoes 383

G

A Gathering of Old Men 386, 398, 402-05, 413
Ghost 45
The Ghost Breakers 47, 225, 383
Ghostbusters 380

Ghostbusters II 380
The Girl From Chicago xix, 140, 141, 145, 154, 156
The Girls and Daddy 58n37
Glory 383, 437
Glory Alley 310
Go Down, Death! 226-27
Go Tell It on the Mountain 20, 337-34, 508
The Godfather 457
Go Into Your Dance 40
God's Step Children 94, 102, 105, 146
The Golden Child 439n1
The Golden West 41
Gone With the Wind xiv, 17, 42-43, 97, 205-11, 213, 420, 422, 504, 507
Gorilla Hunt 221
The Grafter and the Maid (also released as *The Grafter and the Girl*) 70
The Green-Eyed Monster 163n19
The Green Mile 383
The Green Pastures xiv, 49, 97, 197-200, 202, 253, 318, 507
Guess Who's Coming to Dinner 39, 306, 434
The Gunsaulus Mystery 104, 127-28, 131, 151-52

H

Hallelujah! 42, 93, 191-97, 200, 214, 257, 318, 319
Harlem Nights 439n1
Harlem on the Prairie 224
Harlem Rides the Range 224
The Haunted Bachelor 63n60
Having Our Say 440n9
The Heart of a Negro 79
Hearts and Flags 24
Hearts in Dixie 25, 93, 188-91, 195, 197, 200, 201, 257
Hell Bound Train 233n12
A Hen House Hero 45

A Hero Ain't Nothin' But a
     Sandwich 449-51
Heroic Negro Soldiers of the World
     War 81
High Society 310
His Trust xix, 23-24, 27
His Trust Fulfilled xix, 23-24, 27
Hollywood Shuffle 384
Home of the Brave 39, 269-72, 276,
     299, 508
The Homesteader 34, 94, 97, 105,
     121-22, 127, 144, 149, 158
A Hot Time in Punkville 63n62
The House Behind the Cedars 35,
     102, 135-36, 137, 139
House Party 384
How a British Bulldog Saved the Union
     Jack 217
How Rastus Got His Pork Chops 44
How Rastus Got His Turkey 44
How Stella Got Her Groove Back 477,
     482-85, 486, 487
Huckleberry Finn 25, 201

I

I Am a Fugitive from a Chain Gang
     246
I Know Why the Caged Bird Sings
     452-54
I Walked with a Zombie 225
Ida B. Wells: A Passion for Justice 384
If He Hollers, Let Him Go! 344-48, 356
I'm No Angel 41
Imitation of Life (1934) 37, 38, 43-44,
     200, 214, 254-57, 263, 264
Imitation of Life (1959) 37, 254, 257-
     60
In Humanity's Cause xiv, 36
In Old Kentucky 27, 45
In Slavery Days xiv, 35
In the Heat of the Night 306, 381, 434
In This Our Life 247-48, 507

In Zululand 218
The Informer 24, 269
Ingagi 221
Injustice (also released as *Loyal Hearts*)
     162n9
Intruder in the Dust 97, 272-76, 299,
     508
Island in the Sun 310, 311
Istanbul 310

J

The Jackie Robinson Story 310, 311
Jasper and the Haunted House 45
Jasper and the Watermelons 45
The Jazz Hounds 84
The Jazz Singer 185-87
Jericho 229
Jezebel 205, 212, 213
Johnnie Mae Gibson: F.B.I. 356
The Joy Luck Club 480
Judge Priest 45, 196
Juice 384
The Jungle Outcasts 219
The Jungle Trail 218

K

The Kaffir's Gratitude 58n29
Kid 'n Africa 220
Killer of Sheep 384
The Killing Floor 356
King Kong 221-23, 507
King Kong (sequels and remakes)
     240n55
King of Cannibal Island 219
King of the Bingo Game 371n31
King of the Jungle 221
King of the Zombies 225
King Solomon's Mines 229
Kings Go Forth 39
A Kiss in the Dark xix
Knock on Any Door 288-89, 290
Know for Sure 250

L

The Lad and the Lion 218
Lady by Choice 40
The Lady Fare 88
Lady for a Night 235n26
The Last Boy Scout 383
The Law of Nature 77-78
The Learning Tree 193, 323-28, 333, 337, 508
Lem Hawkins' Confession (see *Murder in Harlem*)
A Lesson Before Dying 386, 408-13
Let No Man Write My Epitaph 289-90
Lethal Weapon 380, 381
Lethal Weapon (sequels) 380
Life in Senegal 218
Lifeboat 253
The Light of Western Stars 57n23
Lilies of the Field 304-05
Lincoln's Dream 72, 73
The Little Colonel 24, 196
Little Eva Ascends 186
The Littlest Rebel 24-25, 47, 196
The Long Walk Home 383
Lost Boundaries 38, 265-69, 275, 276, 508
Lost Horizon 235n26
The Lure of the Circus 163n15
Lying Lips xix, 95, 97

M

Malcolm X 426-28
Mama Flora's Family 423-25
Mammy 186
Mammy's Ghost or Between the Lines of Battle 24, 43
Mammy's Rose 43
A Man's Duty 79
Marching On 250
The Marrow of Tradition 85
Marse Covington 24

Melinda 33
The Melancholy Dame 88
The Meeting Place 356
Midnight Cowboy 381
Mighty Joe Young 223
The Millionaire 105, 125
The Missionary and the Maid 219
Missionaries in Darkest Africa 218
Mississippi 205, 212, 213
Mississippi Belle 211
Mississippi Burning 382
Money Talks in Darktown 87
Murder in Harlem (also released as *Lem Hawkins' Confession* and *The Brand of Cain*) 106, 128-32, 247
Music Hath Charms 88

N

Native Son (1950) 230, 279-87, 288, 290, 311-12, 366, 508
Native Son (1986) 287-88
The Naughty Nineties 186
The Negro Soldier 249-52, 507
The Negro Speaks of Rivers 204
The New Governor (originally titled *The Nigger*) 36
New Jack City 384
The Nigger (retitled *The New Governor*) 36
A Nigger in the Woodpile xix, 45
A Night in the Jungle 218
No Way Out 300-02, 311
None Can Do More 24
Nothing But a Man 362
The Notorious Elinor Lee 97, 106

O

The Octoroon xiv, 36
Of Mice and Men 246
Off Limits 380
Oft in the Silly Night 88

Old Mammy's Charge 43
Old Mammy's Secret Code 43
The Old Oak's Secret 24
One False Move 438
100 Rifles 346
One Potato, Two Potato 39, 362
Onkle Tom's Hütte 18-19
The Open Road 186
The Organization 307
The Ox-Bow Incident 246

P

Parting the Waters 505
A Patch of Blue 39, 305, 508
Pennies From Heaven 47
The Piano Lesson 386, 428-31
Pickaninnies and Watermelon 44
The Pickaninnies Doing a Dance 47
Pickaninny Blues (alternatively titled
    Uncle Tom and Little Eva) 18
Pinky 38, 260-65, 269, 275, 276, 508
Porgy and Bess 194, 245, 304, 310,
    311, 508
Pressure Point 269
The Proud Valley 246
The Pullman Porter (see *The Railroad
    Porter*)
Purple Rain 510n2
Putney Swope 328

Q

Queen 421-23

R

A Rage in Harlem 353-56
Raiders of the Lost Ark 221
The Railroad Porter (also released
    as *The Pullman Porter*) 69, 71
Rainbow on the River 42, 201
Raintree County 38
A Raisin in the Sun (1961) xix, 314,
    317-19, 508

A Raisin in the Sun (1986) 319-20,
    356
The Ranch Chicken 64n63
Rastus and Chicken 44
Rastus in Zululand 44, 217, 219
Rastus Knew It Wasn't 63n62
Rastus' Rabid Rabbit Hunt 63n62
Rastus' Riotous Ride 63n62
The Realization of A Negro's Ambition
    75-77, 183, 319
Rebecca of Sunnybrook Farm 197
The Return of Superfly 362
Return of the Jedi 380
Revenge of the Zombies 225
Rhodes of Africa 219
Rio Conchos 346
The River Niger 363-64
River of Romance 205
Rocky 380
Rocky II 380
Rocky III 380, 383
Roll of Thunder, Hear My Cry 454-56
The Romance of Happy Valley 179n100
The Romance of Tarzan 218
Roots 386, 413-20, 422, 423, 425,
    426, 428, 429
Roots: The Gift 421, 422
Roots: The Next Generation (*Roots II*)
    420-21
Rosewood 505
A Royal Romance 201
Rufus Jones for President 177n82
Running Scared 380

S

Sahara 252
Sally Hemings: An American Scandal
    505
Sanders of the River 228
Saratoga 41
Saratoga Trunk 62n58
Saving Private Ryan 484
The Scapegoat 80-81

The Scar of Shame xviii, 90-92, 145, 195
Schindler's List 504
A Scrap in Black and White xix
The Secret Sorrow 84, 90, 145
Selling Old Master 62n60
Simba 221
Shadowed by the Devil 85
Shadows 39, 362
Shadows and Sunshine 85
Shadrach 239n45
Shaft (1971) xv, 33, 269, 328, 361-62
Shaft (2000) 362, 508
Shaft in Africa 362
Shaft's Big Score! 328, 362
She Devil (see *Drums O'Voodoo*)
She Done Him Wrong 41
Show Boat (1929) 186
Show Boat (1936) 186, 201, 246
Show Boat (1951) 38, 186
The Singing Fool 187
Sister Act II: Back in the Habit 356
The Sky is Gray 385-85, 394, 396-98, 413
Slaughter 33
Slavery 328
A Slave's Devotion 24
The Slender Thread 305
So Red the Rose 33, 197, 201, 205, 212
A Soldier's Story 431-34
Something of Value 306
Son of Ingagi 223-25
Son of Kong 223
A Son of Satan 105
The Son of Tarzan 218
Song of Freedom 229
Song of the South xiv, 49-50, 211-13, 508
Sophisticated Gents 361
Sounder 193, 328-37, 343, 508
A Special Messenger 24
The Spider's Web 105, 140, 141, 154
Spirit of Youth 201
The Sport of the Gods 82
Spying the Spy xix, 87

St. Louis Blues 310, 311
Stand Up and Cheer 45, 196
Steamboat 'Round the Bend 45, 196
Stormy Weather 253
Story of a Three Day Pass 356
The Story of Temple Drake 41
The Strip 310
The Super Cops 328
Superfly xv, 33, 362
Superfly T.N.T. 362
Superman III 383
Swanee River 187
Sweet Sweetback's Baadasssss Song 33, 356-62, 384
Swing! 147-48
The Symbol of the Unconquered xviii, 94, 100, 107, 118, 130, 137, 139, 144

T

Take A Gaint Step 320-22
Tales of Manhattan 235n26
Tarzan and the Golden Lion 218
Tarzan and the Tiger 218
Tarzan of the Apes 218, 220
Tarzan, the Ape Man 220, 507
Tarzan the Mighty 218
Tarzan (other film sequels and remakes) 239n52, 245, 507
Ten Minutes to Live xix, 144-45, 195
Ten Nights in a Barroom xviii, 88-89
Ten Pickaninnies xiv, 47, 71
The $10,000 Trail 86
That Certain Feeling 311
They Call Me MISTER Tibbs! 307
They Won't Forget 230, 246
Thirty Years Later (also titled *Thirty Years After*) 34, 143-44
Through Darkest Africa: In Search of the White Rhinoceros 221
To Sir, with Love 305, 434, 508
To Sleep with Anger 384
Topper Returns 45
Topsy and Eva 15-17, 48

Topsy Turvey 18
Toussaint L'Ouverture 201
Trader Horn 219, 220
Trading Places 50
Training Day 305, 438
Trooper of Troop K (also released as
    Trooper of Company K) 77, 183, 319
Tuaregs in Their Country 218
Twentieth Century 40

U

Uncle Pete's Ruse 24
Uncle Remus' First Visit to New York
    49
Uncle Tom and Little Eva (alterna-
    tively titled *Pickaninny Blues*) 18
Uncle Tom Wins 52n2
Uncle Tom's Bungalow 18
Uncle Tom's Cabaña 18
Uncle Tom's Cabin (*Uncle Tom's Cabin
    or Slavery Days*) (1903/Edison)
    xiv, xix, 1, 4-8, 25, 52n5
Uncle Tom's Cabin (1903/Lubin) 8
Uncle Tom's Cabin (1910/Thanhouser)
    8-9
Uncle Tom's Cabin (1910/Vitagraph)
    8-9
Uncle Tom's Cabin (1913/Kalem)
    9-10
Uncle Tom's Cabin (1913/Universal-
    Imp [Imperial]) 10
Uncle Tom's Cabin (1914) 10-11
Uncle Tom's Cabin (1918) 11
Uncle Tom's Cabin (1927/Universal)
    12-15, 95
Uncle Tom's Cabin (1958 reissue of
    1927/Universal) 15
Uncle Tom's Cabin (1965) 18
Uncle Tom's Cabin (1987) 19-22, 344
Uncle Tom's Cabin's Parade 4
Uncle Tom's Caboose 18
Uncle Tom's Crabbin' 18
Uncle Tom's Gal 186

Underworld xix, 96, 97, 145-46
Up Tight 269, 311, 328

V

The Vanishing Virginian 211
Veiled Aristocrats 34, 103, 136-37
Verdict Not Guilty 233n12
The Virgin of the Seminole 105
Virginia 211
The Voice of Conscience 225
Voodoo Vengeance 218

W

The Wages of Sin 105, 142-43
Waiting to Exhale 477-82, 484, 487,
    505
The Water Boy 504
A Watermelon Contest xix
Watermelon Man 47, 356, 358
Way Down South 201-03
The Wedding 386, 490-95
We've Come a Long, Long Way 250
When True Love Wins 163n19
The White and Black Snowball 45
White Nights 380
Who Said Chicken? xix
Why We Fight 249
Within Our Gates xviii, 94, 103, 104,
    106, 117, 130, 140
The Women of Brewster Place xv,
    470-76, 477
Wonder Bar 187
The Wooing and Wedding of a Coon
    71
The World, the Flesh, and the Devil
    311
Wrong All Around 164n24
Wurra Wurra 219

Z

Zulu 239n48
The Zulu King 218
The Zulu's Heart xix, 217